RAYMOND KASPAR
6418 W 27TH PL
BERWYN ILL

GU 4 0628

Preface to the Second Edition

It is the object of this book to set forth the essentials of the auditing art. It deals with the performance of the public accountant in the conduct of the annual examination of a business of moderate size: his objectives, the scope of his work, his methods, and his endproducts. Although it presumes a knowledge of the fundamentals of accounting and business practices, accounting principles are reexamined in relation to their importance to the auditor, and many of the administrative and management conventions associated with the conduct of a business enterprise are restated in terms familiarly employed by the professional accountant.

Emphasis in present-day auditing practice continues to be placed on internal controls and the extent to which the auditor may rely on them rather than on a detailed examination of transactions. In this book a chapter (The Procedural Review) has been devoted to the over-all aspects of the subject, and in each succeeding chapter the principal features of internal control to which the auditor now directs his attention have been set forth. The term "internal controls" is no longer confined to the safeguards surrounding cash and bookkeeping operations generally but has been extended to the authority exercised by all levels of management in the conduct of business. In the light of this concept, transactions—the one and only component of accounts —are interpreted as consequences of top-management policies and of the procedures and controls growing out of policy applications; hence authority, responsibility, and accountability for transactions are not the functions of the bookkeeper or controller but are of the essence of management. It is highly important, therefore, to recognize that a primary task of today's auditor is to point out weaknesses in policy and delegated authority that may adversely affect transactions and to suggest ways and means for their removal.

An annual observer of the operations of many enterprises, the public accountant has come to be regarded by his clients as well fitted to give sage counsel on almost any business matter. His techniques must therefore be broad-gaged so that they may yield the greatest practicable amount of operating information: for his own protection, to be sure, and as insurance against an unqualified report, but also to serve as a factual background so that for others he may analyze correctly and advise wisely. From this it may justly be inferred that the primary responsibility of the public acocuntant of the future may be on *interpretation* rather than *verification*. The practical implications of this growing function, considered at greater length in Chapter IV, have in no small degree influenced the subject matter of this book.

Continued emphasis also attaches to the examination of profit-and-loss details. Despite frequent references to the increased importance that the auditor ought to attribute to the income statement, little of significance has emerged in the way of suggestions for modifications of audit procedures. In this respect, the comments on operations in Chapter V may be regarded as a departure from the usual treatment of the subject. The author's experience points to the need for examining the causes behind the profit-and-loss accounts: an inquiry pursued for the most part by directing questions at management and by scanning. Through a comprehensive carrying out of such processes, the author has found that a sharper meaning is imparted to individual and collective income and expense accounts, and to many real accounts as well; and that their fluctuations as between years are more likely to be accurately understood and intelligently described.

In the preface to the first (1947) edition the author expressed the hope that besides serving as a text the book might aid in promoting accepted minimum-practice standards in public-accounting offices where it is used as a staff manual or supplement to such a manual. The book has indeed served these purposes and has further been consulted by persons outside the public-accounting profession—bankers, business executives, controllers, and government officials—who for varied reasons have wished to acquaint themselves with professional methods and standards.

As compared with the first edition, the text has been expanded at various points, the illustrative audit originally appearing in a separate volume has been brought up to date and combined with the text, new problem-and-question material has been added, and practices recently codified by the Committee on Auditing Procedure of the American Institute of Accountants have been incorporated to the extent they had not already been expressed in the earlier edition.

When employed as a textbook the problems and questions at the end of each chapter may be supplemented at the option of the instructor by a separately published practice problem that requires the student to make up the working papers of an audit engagement and draft reports based thereon. This supplementary problem, continuing the audit illustrated in the text, covers the next following year's transactions of a manufacturing concern. It acquaints the student with characteristic situations faced by the public accountant in his field work. The instructions furnished the student are the rough equivalents of those supplied the junior accountant in an actual engagement. The student's work in this connection may be made a part of his homework assignments or it may be regarded as "laboratory" material in those schools that provide student-workroom facilities.

Of the sixteen chapters, Chapters V to XII inclusive follow the arrangement generally established for these chapters in the first edition: the subject terms are defined and audit objectives are outlined; then follows a brief statement of governing accounting principles; accounting practices the auditor frequently encounters in the field; management devices commonly regarded as constituting elements of internal control; standards of statement presentation; a representative audit program; audit procedures; illustrative working papers with comments; and finally problems and questions for assignment.

A manual for instructors is available; it contains solutions and answers to problems and questions, along with suggestions as to the use of the illustrative working papers in the text. A solution to the supplementary audit problem is also available to instructors in a separate volume.

The author wishes to acknowledge the valuable aid given him on various sections of the book by his brother, Frank E. Kohler, CPA, by Ambrose M. Reiter, CPA, and by numerous other accountants who have used the book as a text or as a professional guide.

E. L. KOHLER

Contents

List of Working Papers

List of Working Papers *(Continued)*

CHAPTER I

The Meaning of Auditing

The work of the public accountant is firmly established as an indispensable service to the world of business. He is a member of a dignified and respected profession. A notable aspect of his profession is that he is responsible not only to the persons by whom he is employed but, in an ever-increasing degree, to investors, the government, and the general public. His knowledge of organizational practices and relationships is extensive, because accounting now permeates almost every human activity and is becoming a more and more essential ingredient of operating controls, whatever the organizational form. And, in his reviews of the accounting and financial policies of an individual enterprise, the public accountant often finds himself squarely in the midst of problems popularly associated with the fields of management and business ethics. His function is of first importance to society at large, for he is the only outsider who periodically appraises and reports on the over-all results of business operations. Moreover, his findings, in the case of larger and even many smaller business enterprises, are required by custom, law, and regulation to be made public in reports the scope and language of which are of his own choosing.

Scope of Professional Services

Public accountants have wide and varied activities. The most frequent use of their services is in examinations that precede the issuance of periodic corporate financial statements to stockholders, regulatory bodies, and the public: examinations commonly referred to as balance-sheet audits—or simply audits—the outline and discussion of which are the objects of this book. The preparation of income-tax returns and the review and assistance

1

given in connection with income-tax problems also occupy an important place in the work of every public-accounting firm. Other activities consist of advice and constructive work on financial and management policies and procedures, accounting and cost systems, budgetary practices, and internal controls. Many business managements defer embarking on new ventures until they have reviewed with their public-accounting advisers the feasibility of the proposals and the practical consequences that are likely to grow out of their adoption.

Very little is done by the public accountant today that may not affect persons other than the client immediately served. In his certificate or report, following an audit, the accountant nominally addresses the directors or stockholders; but he knows that once the financial statements and his report have been made public, his responsibility reaches out to third parties. This point is illustrated whenever the financial statements, accompanied by the auditor's report, are used for credit purposes.

Auditing, an indispensable function of accounting, supplies the professional review and resultant correctives that insure an output of dependable financial data from business and other organizations.

Professional Qualifications

Like a member of any other profession who offers his services to the public, an individual is licensed to practice as a public accountant by one or more of the forty-eight states after he has qualified for and successfully passed a written examination. Thereafter he is permitted to use the title Certified Public Accountant (CPA) and to practice in his own name or in partnership with others similarly qualified. State laws take numerous forms, but most of them have at least three prerequisites for the examination: a minimum age, a minimum education, and a minimum number of years of experience in the field of accounting. Twenty-one is the usual age minimum, graduation from high school a frequent educational standard, and three years in the office of an already established certified public accountant a typical experience requirement. In recent years there has been a growing tendency to increase the educational standard, several state laws now calling for a minimum number of hours of accounting instruction at the college level, and even college graduation. In some states a deduction may be made from the experience requirement for academic work.

In May and November all the states present a uniform examination prepared by and often graded under the direction of a committee of the American Institute of Accountants known as the Board of Examiners. The subjects covered are accounting theory, accounting practice (two sessions), auditing, and commercial law. Some state laws require an examination in such other subjects as governmental accounting and economics. Every person who aspires to a career in accounting should qualify himself as a certified public accountant.

Preparation for the profession may be pursued by full-time attendance at any of the numerous institutions of higher learning, by evening-school work in larger communities, by the in-service training provided by numerous accounting firms, by correspondence, or by a combination of these methods. Courses of instruction having immediate importance to accountants are accounting principles and practice, auditing, accounting problems, income-tax procedure, business management, corporation finance, statistics, and business law. Equally important is the pursuit of subjects designed to make the individual an intelligent, responsible member of society: the social, physical, and biological sciences, history, literature, English composition, and public speaking. Minor accomplishments, quite essential, however, to entrance into the public-accounting field. include an ability to perform arithmetic operations quickly and accurately and a fair facility in the use of the several types of adding and calculating machines. The accountant's handwriting must be neat and legible, and his figures clearly and firmly made.

These accomplishments may be acquired by an intelligent individual through training. But there are a number of personal attributes that experience has shown to be equally fundamental: a well-developed imagination tempered by a good stock of commonsense, a liking for detail and analysis that has been well disciplined by an ability to generalize and to draw realistic and convincing conclusions, and a lasting supply of idealism that continues uninterrupted, notwithstanding the mundaneness of daily labors and the growth of earning capacity. Implied in this last quality is intellectual honesty: the public accountant must live up to the performance demanded by professional standards and the instructions of his superiors, and he must also have a courageous conscience. He must not permit himself to be persuaded to do or not to do a certain thing in violation of his convictions.

Once the prospective accountant enters the employ of a member of the public-accounting profession, he acquires the lessons that only practical experience can give him: how to adapt himself to his surroundings, how to rate the accounting processes he encounters, how to judge the relative importance of the events and conditions revealed by books of account, how to be tactful in his dealings with others, how to secure information and decisions from superiors or from members of a client's staff without upsetting their daily routines, and how to be self-possessed and tactful under trying circumstances.

Meaning of "Profession"

Broadly, the profession[1] of accounting includes public accountants, controllers and other "private" accountants in the full-time employ of a single business or other organization, internal auditors, teachers of accounting, and government (Federal, state, and local) accountants. The last-named group is made up of controllers (comptrollers) or chief accountants of individual agencies, internal auditors, experts attached to commissions and other bodies as consultants on accounting, financial, pricing, and rate problems, and staff members and supervisors in the Federal General Accounting Office and corresponding state agencies. Professional status is commonly regarded as having been reached by an individual once he has secured his CPA certificate, regardless of the individual's occupation at the time or thereafter, and possession of the certificate may be required as an essential qualification for employment in any of the above groups. In this book the term "auditor" is used to designate a public accountant or staff member of professional rank in charge of the field work involved in the examination of business, government, and other enterprises.

In a narrower sense the terms "accounting profession" and "professional accountant" may refer only to the work of the public accountant. Today, however, the coverage of these terms has been extended to those who assume a leading responsibility in any of the various areas of accounting activity.

---

[1] A profession is "a vocation (a) generally recognized by universities and colleges as requiring special training leading to a degree distinct from the usual degrees in arts and sciences, (b) requiring principally mental rather than manual or artistic labor and skill for its successful prosecution, (c) recognizing the duty of public service, and (d) having a code of ethics generally accepted as binding upon its members." Kohler, *A Dictionary for Accountants* (New York: Prentice-Hall, Inc., 1952), p. 338.

Professional Ethics

The American Institute of Accountants, with its predecessor, the American Association of Public Accountants, has been in existence as a national professional body since 1887. In 1936, by merging with the American Society of Certified Public Accountants (which had been established in 1921), it became the one national organization of professional public accountants. The Institute's bylaws state that its objects are:

> . . . to unite the accountancy profession[2] in the United States as constituted by the certified public accountants of the several states, territories, possessions, and the District of Columbia; to promote and maintain high professional and moral standards within the accountancy profession; to assist in the maintenance of high standards for the certified public accountant certificate in the several states, territories, possessions, and the District of Columbia; to develop and maintain standards for the examination of candidates for admission; to safeguard the interests of certified public accountants; to advance accounting research; to develop and improve accountancy education; and to encourage cordial relations among certified public accountants practicing in the United States of America and accountants of similar status in the other countries of the world.

In addition to the American Institute of Accountants, there are societies of certified public accountants in each of the forty-eight states, the District of Columbia, the three territories, and the Virgin Islands. Most of them are loosely affiliated with the national organization.

Many of these professional organizations have codes of ethics that apply to the practice of public accounting. Resembling professional codes in other fields, they are designed to keep the work of the public accountant on a dignified basis, protect the society's members in their relations with each other, and provide assurance that the profession in its service to the public will maintain high levels of responsibility and performance. The code of the American Institute of Accountants, officially designated *Rules of Professional Conduct,* consists of sixteen articles; an infringement of any of them may lead to suspension or expulsion from the Institute. A summary follows:

1. Accounting firms [individuals or partnerships] may employ the phrase "Member(s) of the American Institute of Accountants" in their reports.

---

[2] Not defined in the bylaws but generally interpreted in its broadest sense.

2. A member may not permit another person not a partner or employee to practice in his name.

3. A member must not accept a fee or commission on work secured by another person upon the member's recommendation, or pay a fee or commission to another upon obtaining professional work.

4. A member engaged in public accounting may not carry on a collateral activity "incompatible or inconsistent" with the profession.

5. In or attached to financial statements audited by a member, there must be a disclosure of every material fact which if omitted might mislead the reader, of any material misstatement, or of a material departure from any generally accepted, applicable accounting principle or audit procedure; and the opinion of a member as to financial statements may not be given on the basis of inadequate information or where his exceptions have the effect of making his opinion meaningless.

6. A member's signature on an audit report is prohibited where the audit has not been made by the member, an employee, or a licensed accountant.

7. Solicitation of business by circulars and advertisements, or by means of contact not the outgrowth of existing personal relations, is prohibited; and the practice of another member is not to be encroached upon.

8. Employment may not be offered to an employee of another public accountant without first informing the employer, unless the employee seeks a change on his own initiative or in response to an advertisement.

9. Contingent fees are permitted in tax cases or in situations where their amounts are fixed by courts or other public authorities, but are forbidden elsewhere.

10. Advertising is prohibited, and professional announcements (of personnel of firm, or of change of address) are restricted in size and content. A paid directory listing may not appear in display type or be otherwise distinctive.

11. Members are not permitted to be connected with a corporation engaging in public-accounting practice.

12. A member may not subscribe to the accuracy of an estimate of future earnings or permit any inference to that effect.

13. A member may not certify to the financial statements of an enterprise—financed by a public distribution of any of its securities—in which he or one of his family has an interest "substantial either in relation to its [the enterprise's] capital or to the

individual's personal fortune." A similar prohibition attaches to the certification of financial statements to be used for credit purposes unless such interest is disclosed in the member's report.

14. Competitive bids are not forbidden unless they violate rules laid down by state or other local accounting boards or societies.

15. A member performing services similar to those rendered by public accountants is expected to observe the Institute's rules of professional conduct.

16. There must be no violation of the confidential relationship between a member and his client.

Professional Responsibilities

Rule 5, setting forth very generally the framework within which the public accountant performs his services to the public, has been commented on at length by various writers and by the U. S. Securities and Exchange Commission and other government agencies. The following elements of the public accountant's professional responsibilities appear to be well established:

1. Since he holds himself out to the public as an expert, the public accountant must perform his work in a manner comparable with that displayed by any conscientious member of the profession.

2. Ignorance of any usual audit standard or procedure does not excuse its omission in the conduct of a professional engagement. The public has the right to expect performance of a high order and reasonable care in everything the public accountant does.

3. A mistake that conceivably might be made by any public accountant under similar conditions may be condoned but only if it is an honest one and in no way related to the known attitude or expressed wish of a client or to any other unprofessional motivation.

4. The public accountant is responsible for the work of his staff members.

5. Essential facts require disclosure. Professional custom rather than individual judgment is the best determinant of what "essential" means.

6. Where during the course of an audit the public accountant suspects an irregularity, he should thereupon institute a sufficiently thorough investigation to lay bare the details and satisfy himself that a material irregularity does or does not exist. Denial

of access to records, agreement as to audit scope, or limitation of fee does not lessen his responsibility in such instances.

7. In his report equivocal language must not be employed.

8. The public accountant must assume a broad responsibility for statements made by him in a professional capacity, regardless of the person to whom they are addressed. He prepares his report as though it were to be presented to unknown third persons, notwithstanding assurance that it will not be so employed.

9. The existence and possible effect of any material limitation on the character or extent of the audit or of any important divergence from an accounting principle or canon of professional practice should be clearly expressed in the audit report.

Because the professional fee is paid by the organization on which he is reporting and because of the potential within the profession, no matter how slight, of competition between its members, the findings of the public accountant are sometimes thought to be biased in favor of the management of the organization that employs him. However, the profession is well aware of this ever-present danger, and has made earnest efforts to forestall it by devising and publicizing accounting and auditing standards, promoting improvements in state laws that prescribe professional qualifications and govern the issuance of licenses to practice, and cooperating with such public and quasi-public bodies as the U. S. Securities and Exchange Commission and the New York Stock Exchange in their endeavors to raise the sights of American business. By so doing the accountant's responsibilities have been more accurately defined and the positions he takes on the problems facing him have been better respected by others. In recent years, particularly during and since World War II, public accountants have been employed by regulatory bodies and the defense agencies of government in securing and evaluating needed information on business enterprise, thereby obviating other forms of governmental investigation and fact-finding. Reliance by public officials on information thus secured has had a marked effect in further strengthening the objectivity of the accountant's relations with business and in giving form and direction to his responsibility to the world at large.

Professional Liabilities

Legal actions against accountants have for the most part been confined to suits brought by persons who have allegedly suffered losses because of their reliance on financial statements bearing the accountant's certificate or report. In a few instances judgments have been entered against the accountant or cases have been settled out of court where fraud or extreme negligence has been involved. In most of these cases the evidence of such irregularities has been clear and in none does it appear that the accountant's judgments rather than facts have been the issue.

In general, courts have held that the relation between the accountant and his client, similar to other professional relations, requires not only honesty and due care from the accountant but also the special skills common to those who practice the profession. If any of these factors is missing, a liability on the part of the accountant to his employer may arise. As to third persons: those who rely on the public accountant's report may suffer damages—damages that may be recoverable from him where it can be established that he knows the report to be false, where he has certified to the truth of the report when he had no knowledge of its truth or falsity, or where the report has been prepared with such gross negligence as to amount to constructive fraud.

Nature of Auditing

In its most general application, "audit" means any inspection, professional or lay, of accounting records or reports. When used by the public accountant, the word applies, in a more restricted and professional sense, to his activities in performing a periodic or "balance-sheet" examination.

Some years ago a great deal of attention was given to the classification of the work of the public accountant. Elaborately defined audit types were proposed and attempts were made to distinguish between the purpose, scope, and form of various sorts of reports. Fortunately these proposals have now been forgotten; had they prevailed, it would have been necessary to lead the nonaccountant reader of financial statements through a maze of technical auditing practices in order to give him the background essential to an understanding of what the auditor had done. Today it is recognized that a certain minimum standard of performance by the public accountant must underlie every group of financial statements to which he attaches his name; otherwise, grades of dependability for financial statements would have to be developed—a situation that would confuse everybody: most of all, public accountants themselves. Early regulations and opinions of the U. S. Securities and Exchange Commission had the salutary effect of leading accountants back to the single audit standard, which means that if a certain audit objective has been reached, the accountant may express an opinion, amplified or qualified where necessary. If the accountant cannot attain that objective, he may indicate that because of his inability to satisfy himself as to certain items or because of the limited scope of his examination he is unable to express an opinion.

Before attempting a definition of the audit objective, it is necessary further to explore the meaning of a periodic or "balance-sheet" audit. Originally the term referred to the work of the accountant in his "verification" of a balance sheet only. When it became the practice to present in annual reports to stockholders an income statement along with the balance sheet and the auditor's "certificate," public accountants began to include in the latter references to the income statement also; but for many years auditing techniques underwent little change. Thus, as late as 1936, in the pamphlet *Examination of Financial Statements by Independent Public Accountants,* an official publication of the American Institute of Accountants, the income statement and its elements were accorded only passing mention. But the recognition of the need for extending audit techniques beyond their traditional boundaries has steadily increased. Not only has an examination, even though limited, of various profit-and-loss aspects become standard practice, but the auditing process is pushing on still further to embrace management policies affecting various aspects of business operations.

The professional examination of business has thus proceeded far beyond its original bounds, though "balance-sheet audit" is an expression still in common use. There is some tendency at present to accept the simpler term "audit" as designating the public accountant's work preceding the issuance of his report. "Examination" is preferred by some in that it appears to give a somewhat better indication of the broad scope of what the public accountant does.

As employed in this book an audit is *an exploratory, critical review by a public accountant of the underlying internal controls and accounting records of a business enterprise or other economic unit, precedent to the expression by him of an opinion of the propriety of its financial statements.* The purpose of the opinion is to assure others that current, objective standards of information and presentation have been observed: standards to which both professional and public bodies have contributed for many years, standards designed to provide readers of financial statements with useful information. Because financial statements are at best conventional summaries of thousands of transactions new varieties of which are always in the making, it is not difficult to imagine that the standards for determining what is "useful" will continue to change in the future as they have in the past. A part of the auditor's function therefore is to keep his clients abreast of the times in this respect and himself sensitive to public opinion as well as to advances in the art.

The words of the above definition require no special technical interpretation; they have fairly specific and commonly understood meanings among persons familiar with business operations. A public accountant not only looks at the books of account; he must know what the policies controlling the internal affairs of the business have been, how well under the existing management these policies have been carried out, and to what extent the accounts reflect them. That is to say, he regards the accounts—and the financial statements prepared from the accounts—as the practical expression of the basic business and accounting principles that have been accepted by management and under which management has operated. A lack of strength in devising and establishing policies or in giving effect to them is of concern to him, for it may extend the scope of his inquiries beyond the original plan and lead to the discovery of irregularities of various sorts. All this is necessary before he can give his opinion of the financial statements—his opinion of their ability to convey clearly the meaning of what they purport to stand for.

Auditing Conventions

A number of practical conventions have come to be associated with the ordinary audit. They help further to define the character of the work of the auditor. Among them are the following:

1. *Timing.* The bulk of the public accountant's work may be performed either before or after the close of the period covered. In many cases, "preliminary work" during the audit period eases the seemingly inevitable "busy season" with which the public-accounting profession must contend; at the same time the auditor may be able to correct practices that would be more difficult to alter after the books are closed. In larger organizations, where the standards of internal control are high, it is possible to complete most required tests before the end of the period, for if the auditor can satisfy himself during the period that transactions are being

and will continue to be competently compiled, his work at the end of the period can be reduced almost to a formality. In such cases, however, the audit objective remains unchanged. The audit methods described in Chapters V to XIII are followed with varying degrees of emphasis and detail, according to the requirements of the particular case.

2. *Relation to internal controls.* Not only do internal controls competently instituted and maintained by management lighten the work of the auditor: they make possible a better audit. Every public accountant is familiar with what has now become a truism: that the detail involved in an audit varies inversely with the excellence of the internal controls. Not all public accountants have actually modified their procedures in accordance with this belief, however. Many a conscientious auditor becomes immersed in detail that might in a large measure be eliminated by a better appraisal and understanding of the workings of internal controls. Where the controls are inadequate, the auditor's examination must be extended in accordance with such procedures as those discussed in Chapter XIV; at the same time the auditor will doubtless endeavor to persuade his client to strengthen the internal controls of the business so that the dependability of the records of succeeding years may be improved. Internal controls and their relation to the auditor are discussed at length in Chapter IV.

3. *Sampling.* Examinations of accounts are, for the most part, dependent for their effectiveness on sampling or testing. From the meaning and accuracy of a number of entries in an account or by examining a number of supporting documents the meaning and accuracy of the whole account or a series of accounts are judged. When serious errors and other irregularities are discovered, the examination must be extended. The quality of the examination has depended largely on the skill, experience, and subjective judgments of the individual auditor.

In recent years the profession has given increased attention to the adequacy of typical examinations by auditors. Experimental use has been made of probability-sampling methods in the audit of receivables and other items, the purpose being to (a) evaluate typical sampling methods currently in use, (b) simplify or otherwise improve these methods, (c) determine the areas in which statistical devices may be employed, and (d) formulate a number of audit standards having a quantitative basis. Some progress has been made and more may be expected. However it should be recognized that there can be no mechanical substitute for the auditor's value judgments leading to applications of statistical methods and to conclusions and inferences deriving from the results of such applications.

4. *Fraud.* Except as they may be revealed by following ordinary procedures, fraud and other irregularities are not disclosed by an annual audit; even a detailed audit may not uncover certain types of fraud. It is now generally recognized by accountants and by business management that the most practicable safeguards against fraud and other possible losses are well-designed internal controls, and that audits extensive enough to cover even the more common varieties are both costly and unnecessary. This does not mean that the auditor is no longer on his guard against the possibility of irregularities; in fact, he would be negligent in his work if he failed to pursue certain well-established audit procedures, noted in subsequent chapters, that are specifically aimed at uncovering certain types of fraudulent practices. But the discovery of fraud is no longer a major object of the annual audit.

Auditing Standards

Professional attempts to codify standards upon which the auditing process might be based began in 1917 with the pamphlet *Uniform Accounting: A Tentative Proposal Submitted by the Federal Reserve Board.* With slight modification it was put out again in the following year as *Approved Methods for the Preparation of Balance-Sheet Statements.* Viewed from the vantage ground of the present day, a leading purpose of the pamphlet was to provide an outline of the possible inclusions under each of the principal headings of the balance sheet. The methods to be followed by the auditor were subordinated in an effort to make sure that the various balance-sheet items were given their proper classification and description.

Both pamphlets had been prepared by committees of the American Institute of Accountants; in 1929 a revision, *Verification of Financial Statements,* not only repeated the ideas of its predecessors as to classification but described at some length recomended audit procedures. A further and final version, *Examination of Financial Statements by Independent Public Accountants,* appeared in 1936. Audit procedures were elaborated, the word *verification* was omitted from the title, financial statements were recognized as management's, and the public accountant's function was limited to a review of the statements and the institution of specified *tests* whereby statement propriety or "fairness" might be established. The use of the descriptive term *independent,* a practice suggested by the Federal Security Act of 1933, has continued until the present day in the regulations of the U. S. Securities and Exchange Commission and elsewhere, although it is now held that *independence* is but one of the several essential attributes that should characterize the work of the public accountant.

In May 1939, a few months after details of the McKesson & Robbins case—involving the certification by a firm of public accountants of erroneous financial statements—had come to light, the council of the American Institute of Accountants approved a report of a Special Committee on Auditing Procedure. The report laid a foundation for a more rigorous examination of receivables and inventories—the two items so seriously overstated on the McKesson & Robbins balance sheet. Attention was also given to the form of the auditor's certificate or report. Later in the same year, the committee's findings were embodied in the first of a series of bulletins called *Statements on Auditing Procedure,* and a permanent Committee on Auditing Procedure was established. During the ten years following a total of twenty-four bulletins was issued, most of them concerned with the same subject matter or with problems growing out of wartime audits. However, it was soon recognized that the peculiarities inherent in the great variety of transactions encountered by the auditor in any one business enterprise made even any very general specification of audit procedures a virtual impossibility, and the further dissemination of the twenty-four bulletins and the earlier *Examination of Financial Statements* was thereupon discontinued. In its 1948 report the committee stated:

> While it is not practicable because of the wide variance of conditions encountered to issue anything like an "all-purpose" program of auditing procedures it is possible to formulate a pronouncement with regard to the auditing standards requiring observance by the accountant in [the exercise of] his judgment . . . as to procedures selected and the extent of the application of such procedures through selective testing.

The Committee then proceeded to differentiate between auditing standards and auditing procedures, the latter covering "acts to be performed," the former meaning "the quality of the performance of those acts, and the objectives to be obtained in the employment of the procedures undertaken."

In October 1947 the Committee had published a preliminary report entitled *Tentative Statement of Auditing Standards—*

Their Generally Accepted Significance and Scope.[3] It was in this report that the Committee exemplified its ideas on "standards." It proposed nine standards which were formally approved by the membership of the Institute at its annual meeting in September 1948. In condensed form these are:

General standards: (1) The audit must be conducted by a person of adequate technical training and experience. (2) The auditor must maintain an independent mental attitude. (3) "Due professional care" must be reflected in the conduct of the audit and in the audit report. *Field-work standards:* (4) The audit must be adequately planned, and assistants, if any, competently supervised. (5) Internal controls must be studied and evaluated as a basis for reliance and for the determination of the scope of testing procedures. (6) Adequate evidence, obtained through inspection, observation, inquiries, and confirmations, is a necessary prerequisite to the auditor's opinion expressed in his report. *Reporting standards:* (7) The report must indicate whether the financial statements conform to "generally accepted principles of accounting." (8) The report must state whether these principles have been consistently followed and whether they deviate from those of the preceding period. (9) Disclosures in the financial statements, including footnotes, will be regarded as adequate unless exception is taken in the auditor's report.

By this action the Institute for the first time gave formal approval and meaning to the term "generally accepted auditing standards"—a term that, as will be observed in Chapter XVI, constitutes an important feature of the auditor's report.

In 1951 the Institute published *Codification of Statements on Auditing Procedure,*[4] containing a digest of the audit standards that had appeared to survive from the twenty-four bulletins and containing also the nine general standards. In subsequent chapters references will be made to portions of the *Codification* that continue to be of importance.

In 1953 the American Institute of Accountants published *CPA Handbook,* which deals with various aspects of the work of the professional public accountant. Of particular interest to the student of auditing are Chapters 13-16; these cover standards, planning and controlling of audit procedures, audit working papers,

---

[3] Republished in 1953 as Appendix A, Chapter 13, *CPA Handbook,* by the American Institute of Accountants.

[4] Republished in 1953 as Appendix B, Chapter 13, *CPA Handbook,* by the American Institute of Accountants. The principal recommendations in this codification will be discussed in subsequent pages of this book.

and internal controls—the subject matter of the first four chapters of this book.

Permanence of Financial Reports

When an auditor appends his name to a financial statement, a period of time may have elapsed since the close of the period or the point of time that appears on the statement. Weeks or months may pass before the statement will have been reviewed by persons whose decisions and actions will be influenced by the information it reveals. Years later, the statement may again be examined, this time by persons whose critical faculties have been sharpened by hindsight. It is important, therefore, that the auditor should impart to the product of his art those objective qualities that will give it the greatest degree of intelligibility and continuing worth. This end is commonly regarded as attainable by:

1. *Following carefully devised audit procedures.* Audit procedures are discussed in very general terms in textbooks on auditing and accounting, pronouncements issued from time to time by such regulatory bodies as the U. S. Securities and Exchange Commission, the *CPA Handbook* of the American Institute of Accountants, audit cases published at intervals by the Institute's Committee on Auditing Procedure, articles in current journals, and court decisions dealing with derelictions of members of the profession. Specific procedures, however, are almost certain to reflect practices followed in individual situations: practices that do not necessarily have application elsewhere. At best their value lies in serving as illustrations of the infinite variety of audit methods. The public accountant profits from learning of the experiences and ideas of others and is likely to observe closely the nine standards above refererd to; but the character and scope of his field work are the product of his own special skills and foresight applied to particular cases, and they reflect directly his professional attainments. To each engagement program, therefore, he must give individual, careful attention.

2. *Subscribing to a highly objective basis of reporting.* Reporting expedients, designed to serve purely temporary purposes, are sometimes suggested to the auditor by management. Many of them, when given effect, have been found to contribute to clarity and various other virtues the auditor hopes to see reflected in financial statements. They always deserve the auditor's

careful consideration. When they obviously violate the accepted canons of the profession by giving wrong, distorted, or too little information to readers of financial statements, the auditor must insist on the observance of the more traditional standards of reporting. When these standards collide, as they occasionally do, the auditor's position is not an easy one.

An example may be found in the conflicting standards on net-worth accounts. The auditor may be asked to recognize direct surplus charges or charges to contingency reserves so that in years of moderate or low profits the income statement may show a larger return on the investment than would otherwise be the case. In prosperous years, provisions for such reserves in the income statement have the effect of lowering profits to an allegedly "normal" level. By being persuaded to adopt such an elastic standard for a contingency reserve the public accountant unwittingly becomes a party to the creation and maintenance of what most accountants would designate as an equalization reserve and to the acceptance of other practices that may tend to misinform investors and others who rely on financial statements. The reason often cited as justifying such practices is that the annual income statement should reflect "earning power"—that is, more uniform profits—but the experience of most accountants has been that the concept of "earning power" cannot be made sufficiently objective in character to eliminate the possibility of manipulatory practices. Furthermore, a marked absence of regularity in the flow of the profits of many enterprises is an important factor in appraising the strength or weakness of management, the risk inherent in the business or industry, and other conditions that may be of prime importance to investors and interpreters of financial statements. A far more objective and long-range criterion for the annual income statement is that it should reflect all revenues, gains, expenses, and losses recognized during the year, as has been repeatedly urged by the American Accounting Association and strongly advocated from time to time by the U. S. Securities and Exchange Commission. Professional opinion is not united on this point, however, and may not be for many years to come.[5]

3. *Encouraging the adoption of improved accounting standards.* In recent years the public accountant has had as an integral part of his annual-audit procedures the review of his clients' ac-

---

[5] Thus the AIA's committee on accounting procedure, although disapproving provisions for *general* contingency reserves as expense, remains silent on provisions for other forms of contingency reserves (Bulletin 28 [1947]).

counting practices and internal controls and the consistency of their application from one period to another. Through persuasion and occasionally through his insistence on disclosure of less desirable practices, he has often been able materially to raise the level of accounting performance, and he will continue to do so as his own standards become more firmly rooted. The result has been a more secure base for his audit and a much greater probability of maintaining a secure base in the future.

4. *Acquiring an intimate knowledge of business controls.* A natural consequence of the emphasis on internal controls has been the realization by both professional accountants and business executives that these controls are the outgrowth of top-management policies, extend throughout the organization, and involve many matters heretofore regarded as outside the accountant's purview. It is now recognized that both accounting and the internal controls associated with accounting should reflect management policies and that the auditor's familiarity with this field must be substantially greater than it has been in the past. A careful weighing of these policies may affect the style and content of the presentation of its financial statements, and may give to the final product an authentic and lasting quality it would not otherwise possess. These points are further developed in Chapters IV and V.

Illustrative Audit

In the pages following and at the end of the succeeding chapters in this book are groups of "working papers" that together constitute an "illustrative audit": the complete record of an audit by a firm of professional accountants. In the final chapter are drafts of the auditor's two reports. The audit is one of a series of annual examinations that began with the organization of the Martin Manufacturing Company in 1941. Working papers covering a previous examination were published in a separate volume accompanying the first edition of this book.[6]

The purpose of the Illustrative Audit is to acquaint the reader with typical conditions under which an audit is conducted and with the practices the auditor follows and the records he prepares during his engagement. In this case the auditor's working papers

---

[6] *Illustrative Audit* (New York: Prentice-Hall, Inc., 1947). Copies of the audit for the year ended December 31, 1945, are available from the publisher.

reflect in varying degrees the general audit standards described in this book, the standards of the accounting firm by whom he is employed, the instructions from his superior relating to the immediate engagement, and last but by no means least the individual professional skill that he exercises and is expected to exercise at almost every point in his work. Chapter II, dealing with the "mechanics" of auditing, will be concerned with the form, content, and general objectives of working papers. As an introduction, however, something may be gained by a quick glance at the list of the working papers of the audit on pages x and xi. It will be observed that there are two sections of working papers, the first covering an audit for the year ended December 31, 1952; the second (PF-O) a "permanent file" of papers containing matters of general information, such as the nature of the organization, personnel, methods of internal control, and transcripts of continuing accounts showing little or no change over the years. The position of each worksheet in the auditor's file of working papers is indicated by its serial letter and number, and its location in this book by the chapter number. The reader may have no occasion to refer to the index after leaving this chapter; its reproduction here serves merely to give him some idea of the scope of the auditor's work.

Pages PF 2-5 are presented at this point as an introduction to the business concern under audit: a medium-size manufacturer of machines and appliances. They constitute a section of the accounting firm's permanent file on its client: a compendium of particular value to staff members on their first assignment to the job. Pages PF 2-5 are filled-out forms; the same forms are likely to be found in the permanent files of each of the firm's clients.

Field work completed 3-11-53
Audit report dated   3-11-53
Report delivered   3-13-53

MARTIN MANUFACTURING COMPANY

Working Papers

covering

Audit For Year Ended December 31, 1952

Frank La Crosse F. L.
Henry Rice   H R
Basil Bentley   B.B.

Hyatt, Paterson & Company
960 Hudson Bldg.
Chicago 4

P E R M A N E N T   F I L E   C O V E R

Client _____ *Martin Manufacturing Company* _____

1688 S. Federal Street _____ *Chicago 16, Illinois*

I N D E X

PF - 0

F.L.

CONTRIBUTORS TO AND REVIEWERS OF FILE		
Name	Changes were made on pp.	Date
W. S. Chapin	original schedule	march 2, 1943
Glenn Lundquist	none	April 2, 1944
Charles R. Sand	3, 5, 14, 22, 28, 29, 51, 52, 93	Feb. 28, 1945
Charles R. Sand	14, 22, 28, 29, 31, 51, 52, 61, 71, 83,	
	88, 89, 93	
Frank La Crosse	71, 72, 73	march 10, 1950
Frank La Crosse	rewrite of whole file	march 20, 1953
Basil Bentley	rewrite of "books of account" PF 36-7	March 21, 1953
Basil Bentley	restatement of PF 38-9-40	March 21, 1953

PF-1

GENERAL INFORMATION F.2.

1. Exact corporate name _Martin Manufacturing Company_
2. Address _1688 S. Federal St., Chicago 16, Illinois_
3. Incorporation date _Aug. 1, 1941_ State of Incorporation _New York_
4. Other states in which authorized to do business:

State	Date
Ohio	June 30, 1941
Illinois	July 18, 1941

5. Subsidiaries and branches:

Name	Location	Books kept
Burton-Makun Co.	2580 Cedar St., Cleveland	Full set of books

6. Securities listed _Common_ Exchange _Midwest_
7. Capital-stock transfer agent: _First National Bank, Chicago_.
   Capital-stock registrar: _Harris Trust & Savings Bank, Chicago_
8. Fiscal year ends _December 31_
9. Persons responsible for records:

Name	Title	Location
Arthur P. Collins	controller	1688 S. Federal St.
Sidney S. Shell	asst. ˮ	ˮ ˮ ˮ
Myra Lyons	G/L bkpr.	ˮ ˮ ˮ
Andrew R. Fisher	cashier	ˮ ˮ ˮ
Sarah Jopplin	petty cashier	ˮ ˮ ˮ

PF-2

10. Copies of reports were distributed to:

1950	1951	1952	1953
Edw. Stebbins (4)	same (4)		

11. Names of directors and principal officers and executives

Names of directors and principal officers and executives	Title	Salary Amount	Approved by	Year
Edw. Stebbins	Pres. + Dir.	48,000	Board	1947
Bascal G. Hanson	V-P + Dir.	20,000	✓	1949
Earle C. Peyton	Secy. + Dir.	12,500	✓	1948
Ernest Holdover	Chr. + Dir.	1,000	✓	1940
Bayford Kronk	Dir.	80	✓	1940
J. B. Huddle	Treas.	8,250	✓	1950
Arthur P. Collins	Controller	15,000	✓	1948
Sidney Shell	Asst. Cont.	6,500	Pres.	1949
B. B. Sorry	Sales mgr.	15,000	Board	1948
George Shuffle	Plant mgr.	15,000	Pres.	1948
Carl Hibbs	Int. auditor	6,200	Controller	1951
Laurence Calsp	Personnel Dir.	6,500	Pres.	1952
Henry T. Flood	Personnel Relations	6,500	✓	1952

PF-3

12. Depositaries

Name of depositary	Nature of account	Signature required Name of individual	Title	Key below
Jackson Natl. Bank	General	Andrew R. Fisher	Cashier	A
		or Frank Markham	Asst. Cashier	A
Howard Natl. Bank	Payroll	Sidney Shell	Asst. Cont.	B
		or Jack Johnson	Cost Clerk	B

Countersignatures required

Name of individual	Title	Key above	Remarks
J. B. Huddle	Treas.	A	
or John Sutherland	Asst. Tr.	A or B	
or Andrew R. Fisher	Cashier	B	

13. Owners of 10% or more of each class of capital stock (to be filled in where practicable)

Class of stock	Number of shares	Owner
Common	1,100	Ernest Holdover

PF-4

14.

General class of assets mortgaged or pledged	Nature of obligation	Year
all "fixed assets"	First·mortgage Bonds	1942

15. Leases of tangible assets of substantial amount

Lessor or lessee (indicate which)	Class of asset	Year

16. Federal income-tax status

Date last examination	Year	Principal Adjustments	Closed
Dec. 1950	1948	none	may 1951
may 1951	1949	none	may 1951

17. Bonus plans in effect for--

Officers: _____ none

Other employees: _____ none

Problems and Questions

1. The following statement is a copy of the only information received from a prospective customer by the credit department of a wholesale house in response to questions concerning financial standing. A representative of the department, about to call on the prospect (in a nearby city) comes to you for suggestions as to what to look for in attempting to form an opinion of the prospect's financial situation.

Relying on the data given below, you are asked (a) to prepare rough drafts of an income statement and balance sheet, and (b) to suggest ten or more questions that you would raise with the prospect and his bookkeeper.

Henry Brander Corporation
Statement of Condition, per books April 30, 19–3

Debits		*Credits*	
Store fixtures (3 monthly installments)	$ 20,130	Investment	$ 50,000 *C.S.*
Life-insurance policy on Mr. Brander	10,000	One-half of note remaining unpaid on purchase of store fixtures	19,800
Line of credit at bank	15,000		
Total credit sales to 16 customers at 150% of cost since beginning business on February 1, 19–3	38,496	Merchandise purchased (12 invoices)— Paid for	20,773
		Unpaid	24,792 *N.P.*
Running expenses paid	13,521	Checks 1 to 23	54,424
Cash put in bank— Original deposit	40,000	Excess of debits— Profit for 1st 3 months (3.2% return on capital stock)	1,604 *N.P.*
Collected on credit sales	13,473		
Merchandise paid for	20,773		
Total resources	$171,393	Total credits	$171,393

2. Outline the requirements for the CPA degree in the state in which you live.

3. What do you understand by "independence" as applied to accountants? What rules of professional conduct prohibit actions that might result in the impairment of an accountant's independence?

4. What is the general meaning (that is, outside the field of auditing) of "sampling" and "testing"?

5. Wherein do the functions of the auditor and the accountant differ?

6. Why is advertising on the part of the members of the professions of law, medicine, and accounting regarded as unethical?

7. Rule 5 of the AIA rules of professional conduct forbids a member from expressing an opinion on financial statements where his "exceptions" have the effect of negativing his opinion. List a number of imaginary situations that, as you understand it, might give rise to this type of exception.

8. In rule 9 of the AIA rules of professional conduct, a prohibition appears against contingent fees except in tax cases. Why do you suppose the prohibition was not extended to all professional compensation?

9. What justification lies in the prohibition against the certification of estimated future earnings?

10. What difference in the degree of legal liability arises from an auditor's "mistake" growing out of (a) ignorance of ordinary audit procedures, (b) an error that even the best of auditors occasionally makes, and (c) a client's influence on the auditor to do a certain thing that most auditors would characterize as "bad accounting"?

11. What is meant by the term "third persons" when referring to the accountant's liability in performing audit services, and who is likely to be included under such a head?

12. Why may professional custom rather than individual judgment be a guide in determining the meaning of evidence regarded as essential from the legal point of view? Does this mean that in unusual cases, where precedent is lacking, individual judgment is also to be disregarded?

13. Discuss the possible connection between the budget of a business enterprise and the annual audit of the enterprise by the professional accountant.

14. In the definition of "audit," reference is made to the "propriety" of financial statements. Indicate several characteristics of financial statements that this word suggests to you.

15. Name six items you believe to be essential to every income statement intended for stockholders, and six items that you would suggest merging with other items on the income statement.

16. Outline briefly your present understanding of the importance of internal controls to the auditor.

17. During preliminary conversations with the management of a new client, a small manufacturing company, you learn that the accounts are in poor condition. You quickly acquire substantial evidence of careless vouchering, books out of balance, inaccuracies in taking and pricing physical inventories, failure to carry through on discovered errors, and internal reports six months or more in arrears. The management disclaims responsibility for the situation, and lays the blame on the previous auditors who appear never to have submitted any complaint, written or oral, dealing with these matters. Aside from the appointment of a new controller, what responsibility should attach to the top management with respect to the specific conditions you have encountered?

18. Would you classify the absence of a good cost system in a manufacturing establishment as the consequence of a poor management policy or of a poor accounting policy?

19. A client has sent a public accountant the journal, general ledger, and all paid vouchers (about 50) relating to a joint venture now closed, and has requested that an audit be made of these records. What additional information do you suppose the public accountant would be likely to ask for before completing his examination and preparing a report?

20. You have before you the comparative profit-and-loss statements for the past two fiscal years of a manufacturing enterprise. Discuss

briefly the truth or falsity of each of the following propositions relating to these statements:

(a) Each item of income and expense of the later year differs by not more than 5% from the corresponding item of the earlier year and the net profit comes within 2%; hence, since the accountant, a year ago, made a thorough examination of the income and expense accounts of the earlier year, he does not need to examine the later year's income and expense accounts.

(b) The management was unusually efficient in maintaining operations at so nearly the same level.

(c) No new policies affected operations during the later year.

(d) Although a new product line was introduced during the later year it had no effect on earnings.

(e) A difference of only 5% in gross volume indicates that the business has reached a stable level of production.

CHAPTER II

The Mechanics of Auditing

Before proceeding with a discussion of how audit engagements
are arranged, planned, and controlled it will be helpful to consider briefly some of the features of the auditor's work in the
field: the persons and the materials he deals with, the types of
investigations he makes, and the varieties of schedules, abstracts,
and notes that constitute his "working papers."

Contacts with Client's Personnel

In larger engagements the auditor deals with the controller or
chief financial officer whose functions and relationships are considered in Chapter IV. The controller provides workspace for
the auditor and his assistants and possibly a filing case or other
temporary repository for the auditor's papers. He supplies records, vouchers, and other documents as the auditor may require,
and makes himself and his subordinates available for questioning
and often for work assignments. As the audit progresses, various
points may be discussed with the controller and his staff and
disposed of or referred elsewhere by the controller for consideration and action. The controller may arrange conferences between
the auditor and persons within the organization. At the conclusion of the audit, adjustments proposed by the auditor may be
discussed with the controller, often in the presence of the auditor's principal[1] and other officers of the client.

In many instances the auditor may contact none of the client's
officers or other personnel outside the controller's office: a situa-

---

[1] As employed here, "principal" means "a partner or other person in a professional firm authorized to deal and agree with clients on major problems."
Kohler, *A Dictionary for Accountants*, p. 335.

tion arising from any of several causes. Sometimes the audit is regarded as involving little other than routine work, thus not warranting other contacts. Elsewhere it may be customary for the auditor's principal to make these contacts, since his acquaintance with the client's affairs is very likely to have extended over a longer period than the auditor's, and since such contacts often involve policy matters that may demand high-level decisions. Occasionally the client's officers refuse to be concerned with accounting matters or do not wish to discuss business problems with outsiders. Finally the youth or inexperience of the auditor may not, in the eyes of his principal, qualify him to deal with seasoned businessmen. Without the presence of the principal there may be fear of an agreement on some accounting matter that would be in conflict with firm policy. On larger assignments, however, the auditor in charge may virtually have the status of a principal. As preliminary and in-service training of accountants progresses, a steady increase in the auditor's responsibility in this respect may be anticipated.

In smaller business concerns the auditor deals directly with the principals of the business as well as the office staff. As a rule no restrictions are placed on whatever contacts he may wish to make within the organization.

What the Auditor Examines

During an audit all the client's records are expected to be made available for examination. If for some reason any records are withheld, the auditor must be satisfied that the information they contain is in no way related to the accounts; in addition he will likely ask for a written representation from the management to that effect. Most business concerns make it a point to conceal nothing from the public accountant, although some are still found who believe that the auditor should not be exposed to information that could by any chance be of value to a competitor. Today, however, business management is less apprehensive of losing competitive advantage, recognizing that the practice of exchanging trade information through technical journals, trade associations, and engineering and management consultants is almost invariably beneficial, since a much wider source of technological improvements and other benefits is thereby made available—the condition, of course, being that such exchanges involve giving as well as receiving. Moreover, auditors are no longer regarded with the suspicion they once were. The continued growth of their professional status has gained for them a constantly increasing respect and confidence on the part of business management.

, Among the records, files, and other data the auditor will in most instances examine—in more or less detail—are the following:

General Records	*Supporting Data*
General ledger	Paid vouchers
Subsidiary ledgers for—	Unpaid vouchers
Investments	Notes receivable
Receivables	Canceled notes payable
Inventories	Income-tax returns and reports of
Fixed assets	revenue agents
Payables	Credit files
General expenses	Claims files
Factory operations	Purchasing files
Books of original entry—	Receiving records
Cash receipts	Shipping records
Check register	Insurance policies
Voucher register	Leases
Insurance register	Contract files
Payrolls	Stock-certificate books
Other journals	Correspondence with customers, suppliers, attorneys, banks, branches, government agencies
	Minutes of directors and of executive, budget, equipment, and other committees
	Office manuals, directives, and memorandums covering organization, accounting, etc.
	Valuation or appraisal reports
	Management surveys

What the Auditor Does

It would be difficult to imagine two audit engagements in which the field-work performance had been the same. Organizations differ as do natural persons. Moreover, the work of one public-accounting firm differs from that of other firms, and the approach of one auditor will differ from that of another even where both are employed by the same firm. The result is an individual build-up of procedures and data, although the endproduct (for example, the same uniformly worded, unqualified report) may be identical. Yet, in the final analysis the differences of methods are in the details rather than in principle. As narrated in this book the principles behind what the auditor is expected to do and the general range within which he operates receive first emphasis. This is accompanied in each case by illustrative procedures of what may be expected of the typical auditor in a typical engagement.

As in all practical situations, various conditions contribute to the character of the auditor's work. Perhaps the most important is time. Fee limitations may set a tight working schedule; in recent years the pressure on public-accounting firms has often made it necessary to divide the working hours of top-staff men between several engagements simultaneously in progress, especially during the January-April "busy season." Again, the method of accounting may affect the auditor's activities. The system of vouching may be weak, with transactions inadequately supported. In some cases punched-card accounting makes account analyses difficult and sources hard to trace down. Internal controls may be faulty, permitting the recording of transactions without crosscheck or internal audit. Perhaps the office personnel has been insufficiently trained, and much more work than originally planned must be spent on running down errors—to the detriment, for example, of the study and appraisal of top-management policies. Not infrequently the auditor finds working conditions difficult: noise, dirt, constant interruptions, or poor lighting may lower his efficiency. It may be that restrictive burdens are likely so materially to affect the quality of his work or the meaning ordinarily associated with financial statements that with the help of his principal he will have to determine quickly whether it is going to be practicable to continue with the engagement. In the great majority of cases, however, the limitations the auditor encounters are surmounted. A skilled auditor prides himself on his ability to overcome major difficulties without allowing the quality of his work to be in any way impaired.

Materiality

One of the characteristics of an experienced auditor is a well-developed sense of materiality. What may appear significant or unimportant to one of less experience may be viewed by him in a much different light. Thus an error or departure from principle —of no seeming consequence in itself—may point to the possibility of a series of irregularities seriously affecting financial position, in which case an extensive followup would be called for.

On the other hand a random error not capable of being repeated may give rise to no action other than its rectification, and that only if its importance warrants. Most auditors and their principals come to conclusions concerning materiality not by applying rules of thumb—although in attempting to convince others such rules may have to be invoked—but by *value judgments*. By a value judgment is meant a "practical" determination: one reached after considering the interplay of a series of relevant factors: accounting principles, conservative financial policy, statistical probability, possible effect on investors, custom of the trade, condition of internal controls, and so on. The relative value of the auditor to his firm is not infrequently measured by observing the character of his value judgments. A seasoned auditor is one whose value judgments on matters of materiality command the respect of his principal.

Questions of materiality arise in every audit engagement. Examples of material items appear in subsequent chapters. Some are judged to be so serious as to warrant the auditor's refusal to approve the financial statements. Others, of less importance, may justify a qualification in his report, perhaps accompanied by a disclosure of their quantitative effect. Still others call for discussions with the controller or other representative of management looking to the elimination of the difficulty, at least for the future; or if minor they may be called to the attention of the employee responsible, noted for reexamination on the next following audit, or possibly ignored altogether.

Determination of Audit Procedures

Early in his experience the auditor learns that notwithstanding striking differences in purposes, forms, and ways of doing business human institutions have a surprising number of characteristics in common. Invariably present wherever people work together, no matter how small the group, are the familiar problems of policy-making, top-management structure, and "down-the-line" fixing of points of authority, responsibility, and accountability. Internal controls instituted by management may be exercised in different ways but their purpose is always to keep the organization "in order": carrying out management policies, minimizing costs, meeting production and delivery schedules, assuring uniformity and quality of output, keeping employees occupied and honest. In turn the accounting system, simple or complex, is always found to be built around the routinizing, safeguarding, classifying, reviewing, and reporting of transactions. Whether the organization be large or small, a business enterprise or a co-operative, publicly or privately owned, organized for profit or not for profit, the subject matter as well as the objectives of management and accounting are largely the same.

From this it might be inferred that auditing procedures can be reduced to uniform rules. If the effectiveness of management and internal controls were everywhere alike, auditing could, indeed, be carried on by a comparatively few simple, statistical procedures. Yet it has already been observed that attempts by the profession to devise uniform rules that reach down into procedural details, once believed to be possible, have now been abandoned. Thus a satisfactory plan for the examination of the receivables of one organization may for many reasons be unsuitable elsewhere. The problems of management and the subject matter of accounting may well be regarded as unchanging; but their application and effectiveness vary from group to group, not infrequently as between the divisions of a single organization. Rules or procedures must therefore be devised for each engagement: a practice now almost universally followed.

In planning procedures the auditor performs a series of operations that fall into several classes of activities. These will be discussed in subsequent pages.

The Nature of Audit Procedures

In Chapters V-XIII are outlines of a "representative audit program," designed to illustrate advance preparation for the character and scope of the auditor's work in the field. They are worded as instructions from principal to auditor and for all but larger engagements are not elaborated on unless staff members are to work on assignments, as at branches of the client, where they will not be under the daily supervision of the auditor in charge. In that event the auditor may prepare an elaborating narrative defining more precisely the steps (and the time) to be taken on each item, an outline of the worksheets to be prepared, the persons to contact, and what to do in case unusual situations arise.

Many accountants, the author included, would regard these representative programs or their equivalent (depending on the character of the business) as minimum standards for the balance-sheet audit of a medium-size business corporation. The time and detail work devoted to each item would depend on the character and quality of internal controls. Weaknesses or informalities in internal controls at any one point might require a more extensive investigation.

Each of the representative audit programs appearing in Chapters V-XIII begins with a verb of instruction. Each verb has a generally accepted meaning as described in the paragraphs immediately following, but it must not be supposed that any of them has an exact and inflexible definition. To some extent these verbs are interchangeable. Their more precise applications are determined from the context.

Analyzing Accounts

To analyze an account is to set forth its contents, item by item, or in subtotals by classes of items, with explanations obtained from or verified by examination of source documents. Major amounts are reconciled with and cross-referenced to related accounts. Numerous examples of account analyses are given in the working papers of the Illustrative Audit.

An account analysis usually includes the following elements:

Balance at beginning of audit period. This relates, of course, to balance-sheet acounts. In a repeating engagement the balance found in the books is always compared with that appearing in the previous working papers.

Transactions during the year. For most purposes, only a summary need appear on the worksheet in the form of totals by classes of debits and credits, each accompanied by a full explanation of its source and meaning. Where trends are to be studied or attention is to be given to variations as between months or quarters, each class may be broken down by periods within the year, some form of spread sheet then being required.

Adjustments prepared by the auditor. These may be included in each summary-of-transactions figure or may be appended at the end of the analysis.

Balance at the end of the audit period, before and after adjustment. The closing balance is compared with the corresponding item on the working trial balance before and after adjustment.

This type of analysis may be observed in the summary of fixed assets and reserves for depreciation appearing in the Illustrative Audit. The procedure on the summary of asset costs (H 1, p. 377) was as follows: columns 1 and 6 were filled in from the books and the amounts or totals were compared with the working trial balance; analyses were made of additions and retirements (schedules H 2 and H 3), which incorporated the adjustments determined by the auditor to be necessary, thus leading to the amounts transferred to columns 5, 4, 2, and 3, in the order given. The comments on the lower half of Schedule H 1 were filled in by the auditor when his analysis had been completed and schedules H 2 and H 3 had been prepared.

Another type of analysis is that which sets forth on the working paper some sort of detail of the balance making up an account on the audit date. This procedure is illustrated in such schedules as N 1 and O 1. The latter schedule consists primarily of an adding-machine tape prepared by the auditor from the open items in the vouchers-payable register. An analysis of the accounts-payable account covering the period of the audit is rarely necessary. The summary at the bottom of the schedule shows the unadjusted, adjusted, and reclassified totals, respectively, following the determination of the adjusting and reclassifying entries. The explanation for each of these entries could have been shown in the accounts-payable schedule, but in most cases an adequate explanation attaching to the entries themselves is sufficient for the auditor's record.

Testing

To *test* means to determine accuracy by selecting and studying representative items or samples from a given collection or class of transactions or other data. In choosing samples, the auditor seeks not only quantitative information (for example, dollars, numbers of units) but qualitative information as well (for example, correctness of classifications, conformity to prescribed procedures). Conclusions as to accuracy are nearly always dependent on both types of information. Transactions having the same description may constitute the bulk of the dollar amount of an account, and an examination of a small portion of these transactions may give assurance on all of the same type, though it will prove nothing with respect to transactions making up the remainder of the account. Qualitative tests must be applied to this lesser fraction, as it not infrequently happens that where numerous small components make up a comparatively unimportant total, employees, as well as the procedures under which they operate, devote little attention to safeguards, and errors are therefore common. A fair sampling of each class of smaller transactions is essential to every testing operation.

Samples with which the auditor deals are of four principal varieties: *arithmetic*—accuracy of extensions and footings, agreement of entries with postings, or of postings with entries, of checks with vouchers; *classificational*—whether transactions have been carried to the proper accounts in accordance with the classificational design and whether any material changes therein have taken place during the year as compared with the previous year; *procedural*—whether the handling of the client's everyday business has followed predetermined outlines or, if not, whether required approvals have been secured, and whether the procedures reflect generally accepted accounting principles; and *internal-control*—whether accounting and management methods actually employed provide adequate safeguards against frauds and other irregularities and against poor business standards, or, on the other hand, whether they are so elaborate and cumbersome that the accounting and reporting process has been unnecessarily slowed down at any point.

Part of the testing process may consist of a complete coverage of all transactions for a limited period. This procedure is of value in situations with which the auditor is relatively unfamiliar or in which new procedures or a new type of business is involved. By going through a brief, detailed examination, the auditor is often in a better position to do a more intelligent job for the balance of the period selected for testing.

Occasionally, testing will disclose that the same type of error has been made repeatedly by the client's staff or that some other deep-seated fault will require a material revision of the records. This condition may call for a suggestion to the controller that he or some person designated by him make a detailed review of the difficulty in order to establish a proper basis for the accounts. To conform to professional standards, the auditor, even though the client is willing to extend the scope of his services, must not perform bookkeeping work except under conditions approved by his principal.

Scanning

To *scan* means to look over rapidly but skillfully in order to discover the more general, qualitative aspects of a procedure, account classification, or account content. Scanning accounts calls for the auditor's best value judgments. It is something that cannot be delegated to junior staff members because a good job of scanning can be done only by a person who possesses a background accumulated over many years of experience in auditing the accounts of a variety of business enterprises. It means looking at individual ledger acounts briefly and expertly, understanding their meaning, observing the nature of postings and testing their sources, but making no working-paper notations or investigations of details except for unusual items. The skill of the auditor is well tested by his ability to recognize unusual items and, further, by what he does following their discovery. Where internal controls are good, his investigation of such items will be less rigorous than where controls have not been well maintained. But he will always be on the lookout and satisfy himself as to causes for:

Errors of classification

Changes of classification

Variations, between months *and* between years, in totals, the number of transactions, and the size of individual transactions

Entries from uncommon sources

Material adjustments

Debit entries in income accounts and credit entries in expense accounts

Faulty explanations accompanying postings

Scanning is usually an adequate substitute for what would otherwise be detailed and pointless analyses of the ordinary run of income and expense accounts.

Other Procedural Terms

Among other terms and their meanings employed in the representative audit programs of Chapters V-XIII are the following:

Review: to study critically a procedure or series of transactions.

Compare: to establish the correspondence or similarity of differently located items.

Trace: to ascertain whether an item has been disposed of in accordance with source indications.

Investigate: to search for and relate underlying causes.

Account for: to obtain an accurate breakdown and explanation of an amount expended.

Examine: to probe into records, under predetermined standards and procedures, for the purpose of arriving at opinions of accuracy, propriety, sufficiency, and the like.

Verify: to confirm ("check") the accuracy of, by competent examination. Use of the unqualified verb "check" should be avoided because of its varied, always uncertain meanings.

The above ten terms have been described in language meant to be nontechnical. The audit activities that they suggest are not mutually exclusive, for as already indicated the meanings of these words overlap. Thus, when an account is "examined"—by observing a prescribed procedure—the visible result at the end of the examination may be an account analysis or a series of scanning notes, as nearly all auditing work involves some sort of analysis or scanning. The choice of method is frequently left to the judgment of the auditor after he arrives in the field. Again, when a posting is "verified" by "tracing" it back to the journal or voucher from which it originated, the auditor's act may be a part of the procedure he establishes for himself in "analyzing" an account.

How Audit Instructions Are Followed Out

Inherent in each audit instruction is the implication of a professional intelligence on the part of the auditor that will give the product of his work the stamp of competence. In following out an instruction the auditor is always expected to:

1. Have well in hand the features of the client's internal controls relating to each item examined.

2. Be able to detect and deal with the client's employees when departures from established internal controls have been noted.

3. Determine what additional audit steps, such as those contemplated in a detailed audit, are necessary to offset flaws in internal controls.

4. Be alert for irregularities, inconsistencies, irrelevancies, bad arithmetic, insufficient explanations, and alterations.

5. Depend as infrequently as possible on the client's written procedures and on oral statements made by the client's staff; rely rather on first-hand investigation.

6. Regard formal audit procedures and any specific programs or instructions as general guides, subject to supplementary extensions, within such time or other limits as may have been imposed, wherever the following of any prescribed procedure has not yielded or will not yield an adequate answer.

7. Sense what is important and distinguish between major items that require a working-paper record, the preparation of an

adjusting journal entry, or other action, and minor items that may be safely ignored or referred to the client's staff without further action. (The determination of items as minor may be left to the auditor's judgment or may come within a predetermined percentage or amount.)

8. Dispose of items well within his field of knowledge and his jurisdiction and refer to his principal, with suggestions for action, matters with which he may be less familiar or that may require negotiation by his principal with the client.

9. Conduct himself professionally; follow and persuade others to observe the best accounting and auditing standards; and sense the practical effect of deviations from such standards.

10. Detect and weigh carefully any change during the period in accounting procedures that might alter present or future operating results or financial position, determine its current effect on the accounts, and, where its importance warrants, discuss with his principal its possible disclosure in the report.

11. Set forth in his current working papers a concise narrative of the work he has done on each item in the audit program, and, where an adjustment or disclosure has been waived or where a disclosure in the report is deemed necessary, include full reasons therefor in the narrative.

12. Keep in mind the elements of the final report to be given the client so that as the audit progresses the data required for the report is being accumulated. Thus if a breakdown of accounts payable by classes of creditors is to be supplied in the report, the grouping should be made at the time the accounts are under examination. Should the work be performed at a later date, some needless "backtracking" would almost inevitably be required.

In the audit instructions, the clue does not appear for disposing of differences, oddities, or irregularities that may be revealed as the result of following out the instructions. A cataloguing of the variables that the auditor may discover would be impossible. The experienced auditor will be able to come to practical conclusions on most of them; some of them he will dismiss as having no importance; others he will discuss with the management, as the result of which no action is taken, future procedures are changed, or an adjusting journal entry is made; still others he will refer to his principal. The primary purpose of any audit procedure is to lead the auditor to opinions of correctness or incorrectness of the accounts as he finds them. Corrections, if important enough to warrant an adjusting entry, are made in the light of what the auditor conceives good accounting to be.

Meaning of Working Papers

Frequent reference has been made to "working papers." As used by the public accountant this term designates the file of analyses, summaries, comments, and correspondence built up by him during the course of the field work of an audit engagement. A new file is prepared with each succeeding audit, and when completed is carefully indexed and preserved for many years. Working papers are the public accountant's property and their contents may not be revealed to others without the consent or direction of the client.[2]

Working papers serve a number of purposes: they constitute the record of what the auditor has accomplished in the field, provide the basis of a "field" or "office" review by the auditor's principal or other designated person, support the opinion expressed in the audit report, supply information on points that may come up during the ensuing period, and establish a background for succeeding audits.

Individual working papers take many forms. They range from elaborate account summaries to brief narratives. In recurrent audit engagements, the form and content of working papers may closely resemble the previous year's: a custom that auditors readily acquire and that is unobjectionable if the preceding papers are of high quality. However, many working papers can be improved upon, and the events of each new year may demand a different emphasis. Experienced auditors find it wise to vary their approach to the same problem from year to year; they often recast, condense, add to, or omit altogether what was done during previous audits. Material variations, however, must usually be assented to by the auditor's principal before they are put into effect, so that matters of firm policy are not overlooked.

Working-Paper Standards

Public-accounting firms adopt working-paper standards in order to secure uniformity (for ease in current and future reviews) and to insure that the firm's audit procedures have been followed. Necessarily, field work must be assigned to professional employees whose backgrounds of experience and personal preferences may differ widely. Yet a fair degree of similarity is found

---

[2] A decision, often cited, supporting this point of view may be found in *Ipswich Mills v. Dillon*, 260 Mass. Rep. 453 (1927). A number of states have enacted this protection of the auditor's working papers into law.

in the audit working papers of all public-accounting firms, and little difficulty is ordinarily encountered by a newly employed auditor whose professional habits have been acquired elsewhere.

An auditor is often judged—and quite properly so—by the character of the working papers prepared by him or under his direction.

Among working-paper standards in common use among public-accounting firms are the following:

1. Everything appearing in the working papers should have a purpose related to the assignment, and the purpose should be clear not only to the auditor but to others who may have occasion to review the papers when the auditor is not present.

2. No questions, question marks, open points, incomplete notes, or other indications of unfinished work should remain on a working paper. Reasons should appear for "passed" items.

3. An "agenda" worksheet (also called "point list") may be employed for noting items of work to be done that cannot be completed at the moment by following the usual sequence of procedures. This list, serving simply as a reminder, is added to as points arise, and is cross-referenced to related working papers. When the item of work is completed, a note is made of the work done or reference is made to the worksheet on which the information appears. Before the report is released to the client, the agenda worksheet is finally reviewed to make sure that each item has been disposed of.

4. Adjustments and reclassifications made by the auditor should be spread on the working papers so that working-paper references and totals will be in agreement with the adjusted trial balance.

5. At the time the audit program is being drafted, it is usually determined by the auditor and his principal what working papers, if any, the client's staff will be asked to prepare. These papers may include such items as trial balances and various account analyses and supporting detail. The practice of asking for the assistance of the client's clerical staff on such matters reduces audit expense and enables the auditor to concentrate on other problems. But the auditor must not rely upon any figures or other information contained in such papers until they have been carefully tested.

6. Sources of figures and other information appearing in working papers should always be indicated. In the Illustrative Audit the general source of information is given in the upper left-hand corner.

7. Each worksheet, or in larger engagements the top worksheet for a group of worksheets, should contain a narrative of what the auditor or his assistant actually did. The audit program, described in the next chapter, indicates the work as *planned;* the working-paper narrative, the work *done.* Often appearing at the bottom of the worksheet, the narrative should not repeat, in fact should avoid, the language of the audit program or other instruction, even where the program or instruction has been fully carried out. The narrative need follow no particular pattern; it should be worded informally; it should be brief but factual, understandable by and convincing to others; and it should be prepared after the work to which it refers has been completed—but before the details have been forgotten.

8. The title space at the top of each working paper should show the name of the client, the period covered by the audit, and a clear indication of what follows. In the upper right-hand corner of each worksheet of the Illustrative Audit appear the initials of the person who has prepared the worksheet together with the date of its completion.

9. Cross-referencing on the same worksheet or to other worksheets should be as complete as possible, with a distinctive checkmark or key for each type of reference.

Indexing Working Papers

As a rule, annual-audit working papers are uniformly indexed within each public-accounting firm. Many different schemes are in use, but the following is characteristic:

Cover—containing name of client, period covered, names of auditor and assistants, and date of audit report

Analyses and comments on accounts:

1	Working trial balance	P	Accrued liabilities
2	Adjusting journal entries	Q	Federal income tax
3	Reclassification entries	R	Contingent liabilities
4	Agenda	S	Long-term debt
A	Cash	T	Reserves
B	Marketable securities	U	Capital stock
C	Receivables	V	Surplus
D	Inventories	AA	Sales
F	Long-term investments	BB	Cost of sales
H	Fixed assets	CC	Manufacturing expense
J	Depreciation reserves	DD	Selling expense
K	Intangibles	EE	General and administrative expense
L	Deferred charges		
N	Notes payable	FF	Other income
O	Accounts payable	GG	Other expense

Minutes
Notes on conferences
Engagement memorandum
Audit program

The numbers and letters may be followed by a separate number series for individual worksheets. Thus, in the Illustrative Audit, C 1 is a cash summary, C 2 and C 3 are bank accounts, and so on. Working-paper references on the working trial balance make the latter an index for most of the working papers.

Working Trial Balance

The working trial balance serves as the auditor's top control. It is prepared preferably in financial-statement order, regardless of the ledger sequence. Trial-balance schedules may be made up on the auditor's working paper by the client's clerical staff. The principal features incorporated in a working trial balance like the one accompanying the Illustrative Audit are these:

1. Spaces may be provided on the left margin for (a) working-paper reference and (b) ledger-account number.

2. Balances of the accounts at the beginning of the year, taken from the books, serve as a basis of comparison for current-year accounts. They are compared with last year's papers to make sure that the books were conformed to the auditor's report. They may also have the effect of calling attention to important changes in classification or content during the year.

3. Separate sheets may be provided for assets, liabilities, income, and expense, thus eliminating the need for extra debit or credit columns.

4. Adjusting journal entries are usually numbered serially, made up in conventional form as soon as decisions to make them are reached, and posted both to the related worksheet and to the working trial balance. Care must be taken that the accounts adjusted are correctly named and numbered in the journal entry and that explanations are full and complete, so that at the conclusion of the audit a typed copy of the adjustments (omitting references to working papers) may be presented to the client without further editing for formal entry on the records.

5. The "after adjustment" column should reflect the correct amounts of the ledger accounts as they are ultimately to appear on the books.

6. A "reclassifications" column and a "report" column usually

prove to be time-savers for most auditors. Formal reclassification entries are prepared at the conclusion of the audit in order to conform this year's statements with the financial-statement sequence as now determined or as followed last year. Each year, however, the propriety of such entries should be re-examined. When separation lines are drawn between account groups that are to be combined for report purposes, the sources of each report figure are apparent. If, for some reason, the account cannot be arranged in financial-statement sequence of the working trial balance, the auditor may have to employ a supplementary "grouping sheet" in which the balances of individual acounts, as adjusted, are added together.

7. A "remarks" column may be provided for comments that relate to the accounts or to their position in the financial statements. Where the balance of an account has remained unchanged during the year, the letters "NC," followed by the page number of the permanent file (see below), may be put in the remarks column, and no analysis need appear in the current year's working papers.

A working trial balance should be provided for a private ledger, expense ledger, or any other separately maintained collection of accounts, and adjusting entries affecting these control accounts should be so designed as to preserve any self-balancing features maintained in these ledgers.

Permanent File

For every repeating audit engagement, a permanent (or carry-over) file should be carefully built up and maintained. The purpose of the permanent file is threefold: from it can be obtained, by persons unfamiliar with the peculiarities of the client's affairs, a quick picture of the financial background and operating performance of the business; it provides a ready reference for and a brief summary of recurring or continuing items, thus eliminating repeated reviews of lengthy documents and searches among old working papers; and it serves to eliminate the preparation, year after year, of new working papers covering items that are likely to show few or no changes. If carefully bound, the permanent file may be carried into the field along with the working papers of the period immediately preceding. To it will be added whatever recent changes have occurred in the items it contains and, when the audit has been completed, it will be reviewed by the auditor's principal, along with the current working papers, as a part of the record of work done. Even where the "quick picture" afforded by the permanent file is of advantage principally to succeeding years' auditors, it serves a most useful purpose for them; it refreshes their memories or, for auditors newly assigned, it gives them a readily assimilable introduction to the client's operations. Every conscientious auditor takes professional pride in adding accuracy and useful information to the permanent file for the benefit of next year's field staff. In the event of a reorganization or the public offering of a security issue, the permanent file plays an important part in building up the history of the business and in supplying analyses of its assets and earnings.

Summaries of analyses, or where practicable the analyses themselves, are provided for the more important accounts, particularly for such accounts as:

Long-term investments	Long-term liabilities
Land	Reserves
Buildings	Capital stock
Machinery	Paid-in surplus
Furniture and fixtures	Earned surplus, including dividend record
Reserves for depreciation	
Intangibles	Sales by products
Long-term deferred charges, such as a bond-discount-amortization schedule	Cost of sales by products
	Cost of sales or production by objects

Where the current audit work required on any of the above items is minor, the detail added to the record in the permanent file need not again appear in the current working papers. Reference on the working trial balance to the page number of the permanent file serves as an index to the detail of changes.

Once an account summary has been filled in, it serves as a basis for each succeeding year's review. Changes are recorded on the summary until space for further amendment has been exhausted. At that time a new page is prepared on which matters of continuing interest are carefully transcribed. The superseded page may then be placed in a "transfer" file or filed with the current year's papers. As a rule, statement and account summaries should never be removed from the permanent file, otherwise their value as bases of comparison will be lost. To reduce the bulk of account summaries, the space devoted to changes should be confined to the minimum permitted by the need for clarity.

Other information and documents or briefs thereof that will increase the usefulness of the permanent file include:

History of business, added to with each expansion, financing, change in product, or reorganization	Bonus and profit-sharing plans
	Pension plans
	Labor agreements
	Stock and bond samples or photostats
Organization chart	
Plant and office layouts	Minutes of stockholders
Articles of incorporation	Minutes of directors
Bylaws	Minutes of executive and other committees
Notes on internal controls	
Accounting policies	Patent-litigation details
Manual of accounts	Leases
Office memoranda relating to accounting	Long-term contracts
	Guarantee agreements
Inventory procedures	Principal forms employed

Bulky long-term documents, such as trust indentures or contracts, should be placed in a "Permanent-File Appendix." If briefs are prepared for the permanent file proper, the appendix need not accompany the auditor to the field.

Abstracts of Minutes

During an early stage in the audit, often as part of the preliminary examination, the auditor reads the corporate minutes: that is, the minutes of stockholders, directors, the executive committee and other committees subordinate to the directors. Many kinds of decisions, affecting any part or all of the organization, will be found in resolutions or in less formal actions of these groups. Time will be saved if arrangements can be made with the company's secretary whereby an extra copy of each set of minutes is earmarked for the auditor. The extra copy will be a carbon copy in the case of smaller organizations where it is not the custom to supply copies of minutes to members of the groups named above, and dittoed or mimeographed copies where the reverse is true. When copies are given to the auditor, a statement over the secretary's signature, similar to the form shown below, should indicate their completeness. If copies cannot be given to the auditor, he must read the minute books themselves and make such abstracts as are necessary. In addition, he must procure from the company's secretary some such statement as the following, indicating that the minute books examined are complete and up to date.

Messrs. Hyatt, Paterson & Co.
960 Hudson Building
Chicago 4, Ill.

Dear Sirs:

I have furnished you with copies of the minutes of the meetings of the stockholders, board of directors, and executive committee. These copies are the complete, official minutes for the period from _____ to _____ [the dates should preferably be the final field-work dates of last year's and this year's audit], as follows:

Meeting of   *Date of meeting*

Very truly yours,

_____
(name of company)

_____
(signature of secretary)

In some cases the auditor finds that summaries of actions taken at board and committee meetings have been distributed to officers and directors. Copies of these distributions may serve the auditor's purpose, but he should in addition scan the minute books for other matters of interest—perhaps pending items of importance on which formal action has not yet been taken.

The minutes or abstracts from the minutes may be placed in the permanent file in their entirety, or, better, brief abstracts of items having effect beyond the current year may be placed in the permanent file, the minutes or longer abstracts remaining with the current working papers.

Among points of importance that the auditor should look for in the minutes are the following:

Officers elected

Compensation of officers and executives

Profit-sharing bonus, and pension plans

Dividends declared

Authorizations of changes in capital stock and funded debt

Designation of depositories

Contracts with employees

Settlements of litigation and disputes

Purchase and sale of securities

Authorization of construction contracts

Approvals of plant additions and disposals

Surety bonds required

Illustrative Audit

Worksheet requirements and techniques deserve careful study. Although the general standards have been laid down in this chapter, the preparation of worksheet forms has been left to the illustrations in this and following chapters. Throughout, the student will find his attention called to numerous points relating to worksheet construction and content; in addition, many other features have been built into the worksheets that will be revealed by close scrutiny. To bring them out and to become familiar with worksheet preparation, the student should copy a number of the worksheets, item for item, on regular 7- and 14-column forms obtainable from any stationer. The result will be a better understanding of the meaning behind the worksheets and an improved facility in reading other worksheets more completely and understandingly, with less preoccupation with the mechanics of their preparation.

Worksheets. The worksheets of the 1952 audit were bound together at the conclusion of the audit by inserting a removable staple in the upper left-hand corner; they could also have been bound at the top or side by using an Ecco or similar fastener, with or without manila or pressboard covers, front and back. The top worksheet—which may be the cover—identifies the job and contains the names and identifying initials of the staff members who prepared the worksheets. The small group of permanent-file worksheets is bound together in a similar manner.

The original worksheets, of which the following pages are photographic reproductions, are 8½″ × 13″ (single sheets) or 17″ × 13″ (double sheets) in size. The paper stock is a 28-pound buff ledger paper with light-green rulings. Specifications for the vertical rulings are: each money column 1.19″ wide, with right and left margins .085″ each. Within each money column, there are three faint rulings, spaced .255,″ .34,″ .34,″ and .255,″ respectively, or as near to that spacing as printers' ruling machines will permit. The horizontal rulings are .25″ apart, each third line being somewhat heavier, with 2.625″ at the top for headings, and a margin of .375″ at the bottom. In this book, the worksheets have been reproduced at approximately ⅔ of their original size.

Worksheets are prepared in pencil as a rule, although a few accounting firms still require that pen and ink be used. With improved techniques in the performance of an audit, the advantages of inked working papers have disappeared. At one time, erasures on working papers were not considered good form—a rule corresponding to that which still applies to books of account; but today a good pencil eraser is an essential part of the auditor's basic equipment. Without it, or with one that smears, the auditor will emerge from his engagement with exceedingly messy papers.

Auditors are required to be careful with their handwriting, and their figures must be exceptionally clear. The need arises not only from the review to which the working papers will be subjected before the report is released but also from the fact that the working papers constitute a long-time record of work done, and must stand up under frequent handling.

Dollar signs are not used on working papers, although they often appear on report drafts as a guide to typists, or in narratives on working paper where the money columns are disregarded.

Each worksheet is headed with the name of the client (a rubber stamp may be employed), the worksheet subject-matter, and the audit date or period. To the left of the heading is the first source of the data appearing on the worksheet, and, to the right, the initials of the person who prepared the worksheet and the date on which he *completed* it. Sometimes the initials of the person reviewing the worksheet are inserted there also. Correspondence of the worksheet total with a trial-balance item as corrected is indicated by the symbol "TB." The number of the worksheet is at the bottom. Practices among accountants with respect to the position of these identifying symbols are quite varied.

Trial balances. There are five trial-balance sheets, TB 1-5, three of them on 14-column paper and, for reproduction purposes, occupying facing pages. On TB 1, the first of these sheets, notice the headings of the nine columns of figures, and the account names on the left. Only assets appear on this sheet, and space has been left between certain items to denote natural groupings or to allow for additional space where past experience has indicated that there may be a number of adjusting journal entries (AJE's). The five trial-balance sheets serve as an index (and cross reference) to supporting working papers and to the general ledger or other source of the figures, and they are thus the top worksheets in the file.

The first money column contains the balances of the accounts at the beginning of the year, unconsolidated. These are customarily transcribed from the papers of the preceding audit and may be inserted before the auditor commences his post-year-end work. The ledger-account numbers and even the worksheet-page numbers may also be inserted in advance, although, if the same worksheet-index scheme is followed as is employed in these papers, it is better to insert both worksheet letters and numbers after the worksheets or various sections of them have been completed. Last year's figures serve as a general guide in identifying this year's accounts, and as this year's account balances are being obtained from the general ledger reference may be made to the opening ledger balances for correspondence with working-paper figures. The latter operation may occasion some difficulty, especially where last year's AJE's were posted after, say, a month's entries of the current year had been spread on the records. Sometimes the comparison will provide a quick survey of important changes, particularly where no preliminary work has been done by the auditor. In the present case, the auditor has put checkmarks after some of the asset amounts at the beginning of the year; this was his own device for indicating that, where an analysis of a general-ledger account appears in the current-year's papers, the opening balance in the analysis agrees with this trial-balance amount.

On this sheet (TB 1) and on subsequent sheets, a minus sign precedes certain figures. This sign (an asterisk or "ring" may also be employed) always means "subtract" when totals are being obtained. An auditor in performing his field work may use the same device; a more frequent practice is to write a negative figure in red. Here the printer's reproduction in black and white requires the use of the less common method.

In the second money column of worksheet TB 1, the figures have been taken directly from general-ledger accounts. Notice that the items of the trial balance here and on TB 2 and 3 are in "financial-statement order" rather than in general-ledger or working-paper sequence, thus obviating as many reclassification entries as possible.

Columns 3 and 4 contain the AJE's, numbered as on AJE 1–6. Each AJE number is followed by a bracket to avoid confusing it with the money amount. Notice that the footings of these two columns on TB 1 are not the same as the footings of columns 3 and 4 on TB 2, although their differences are identical. The footings of the other columns agree with those of corresponding columns on TB 2.

Column 5 is the parent-company's adjusted figures as they should appear in the general ledger after the AJE's have been posted. The checkmarks after the figures in this instance are explained by the auditor as meaning that he has made the comparison with the general ledger.

The reclassification entries in column 6 are breakdowns made necessary by the fact that several general-ledger accounts contain combinations of items that require regrouping; these postings are not made in the general ledger. Horizontal lines were inserted by the auditor at certain points in columns 5, 6, and 7 as aids in pointing to group totals in column 7.

Column 7 has as one of its purposes the presentation of sub-totals showing at various points in the working papers. The checkmarks were made by the auditor as an indication of support-ing worksheets bearing the same totals. On individual worksheets "TB" opposite an adjusted total means that the auditor has made sure that the total is in agreement with its counterpart on the trial balance.

Column 8 contains the asset totals of the Burton-Makun Com-pany, the Cleveland subsidiary, taken from worksheet D 4.

Column 9 subtotals are the amounts appearing on the financial statements prepared at the conclusion of the audit (RS 2).

TB 2 resembles TB 1 in appearance and treatment. Notice references to the permanent-file section of the working papers. No information on these items appears in the current section of the working papers aside from the trial-balance amounts.

TB 3 follows a slightly different form. The accounts, arranged in income-statement sequence, are necessarily a mixture of debits and credits, coming out to zero at the bottom when the residual figure, net income, is added in with the debits. An alternative could have been two columns each in place of money columns 1, 2, 5, 6, and 7, but the result would have been a much wider work-sheet difficult to follow across. Compact worksheets are preferred; they are always more easily read even though red figures are plentiful. Notice that since no reclassification entries were made on TB 3 that column has been eliminated. Notice also the use by the auditor of the margin of TB 3 in summarizing certain figures needed in his report. Observe the tie-in of TB 3 with the net-income line of TB 2.

Worksheets TB 4 and 5 illustrate a further simplification in presentation. Notes appear at the bottom of each of the two worksheets, containing information not warranting a separate and full-scale analysis.

Only one side of working paper is customarily ruled and used. In this Illustrative Audit the printer makes use of both sides to conserve space.

Adjustments and reclassifications. In this audit there have been twenty-seven adjustments of the ledger accounts and five reclassifications, the latter, as already explained, being necessary breakdowns of individual accounts. The entries are prepared in customary journal-entry form, preferably at the time the need for the adjustment is determined and the information is fresh. Explanations following entries should be prepared in such a manner that they will serve both as an integral part of the auditor's working papers and also as suitable attachments to entries to be made by or under the direction of the client's accounting officer. Reference to the worksheets on which they have been given effect should always accompany each entry, but the worksheet reference is of course omitted when the entry is copied into the client's records. Sometimes the entries are typed in the auditor's office and formally presented for discussion with the client's representatives; or they may be presented and agreed to informally while the field work is in progress, in which case a transcript may be prepared immediately by an employee of the client (perhaps directly on a journal voucher), no formal copying or other notification being required. In any case, the auditor must make sure before the report is released that the adjusting entries have actually been incorporated into the general-ledger accounts affected by them.

Reclassification entries are usually put in a separate column (or columns) of a working trial balance in order that the adjusted ledger accounts may first be shown. If it were not for this need, they could be combined with the adjusting entries.

Permanent file. A permanent file warrants considerable attention each year. It should be capable of furnishing to an auditor having no previous contact with the engagement a brief but accurate history of the company, its internal controls, its principal personnel and method of operation, and the constituent elements of net-worth and other long-lived accounts. Sometimes, as in the present case, the public-accounting firm adopts a series of printed forms in which specific data are inscribed. This procedure is illustrated by pages PF 2–5, containing general information, and pages PF 21–32 describing internal controls. It is intended that a line be added to PF 1 whenever pages in the permanent file are changed; the form provides for the signature of the auditor as an indication of his responsibility for (a) reviewing the whole file for his own information and (b) having brought the file up to date. In the present instance, it is apparent that the permanent-file forms were first filled out in 1943 and, because of what appear to have been numerous changes, completely rewritten during the 1952 audit.

Statements of subsidiary. The financial statements of the subsidiary, the Burton-Makun Company, appear in D 4 and PF 52–3. They have been abstracted from reports of the Cleveland accountants who audited the Burton-Makun books. Worksheet D 4 affords a more familiar comparison between years than does the summary on PF 52–3.

Summary of parent company's statements. Worksheets PF 41–2 are useful summaries employed in various ways. They supply ready information on certain accounts and trends without the necessity of going over the reports or working papers of prior years.

Minutes. Minutes of the stockholders' annual meeting and of the several meetings of the Board of Directors during the year are summarized in worksheets X 2–3. Some auditors make it a point to transcribe original excerpts but in most cases the action of interest to the auditor can be reduced to fewer words.

W/P	A/c	ASSETS	12-31-51 (our papers)	Books unadjusted	December Adjustm DR
C-2	01-1	Jackson National Bank	35781293	28520967	
C-3	01-2	Howard National Bank	1597832	1618557	
C-4	01-9	Petty Cash	50000	50000	
D-2	11-1	U.S. Treasury securities	30361846	40278246	
E-3	27-1	Notes receivable - customers	18576080	25993489	
E-2	27-0	Accounts receivable - customers	13130628 7	10702389 2	13) 197128
E-7	29-0	Reserve for bad debts	-1587500	-3126888	2) 2022126
E-4	27-2	Officers accounts	1360000	1310000	
E-2	27-0	Travel advances	220000		
E-2	27-3	Employees accounts	346810		
D-2	27-4	Accrued interest - investments	224364	224364	20) 331708
E-3	27-5	Accrued interest - customers notes	180117	180117	3) 35502
P-1	115-0	Creditors debit balances			
F-1	31-3	Finished goods	50586873	51728196	18) 313058
F-1	31-2	Work in process	18120976	28426132	18) 926569
F-1	31-1	Raw materials & parts	49620859	43563902	18) 1671373
F-1	31-4	Supplies	30253982	12513215	
D-3	28-1	Reserve for intercompany profit	-1106890	-2089723	23) 780927
G-1	27-7	Unexpired insurance	2685772	4114474	
Q-2	132-2	Prepaid taxes	280500		1) 225000
E-3	27-1	Customers notes due after 1953	6100000		
D-2	11-3	Investments in stocks	7390000 0	37415210	
D-2	11-2	Burton-Matun investment	10000000	10000000	
D-3	27-9	Burton-Matun advances	1981649	3771295	
H-1	91-0	Fixed assets	163383734	218969564	x) 468725
J-1	92-0	Reserves for depreciation	-9011244	-83349630	
		TB-1	534112440	537135379	6972116

-56-

31, 1952 ents CR	Books adjusted	Reclassi-fications	M-M totals	B.M totals	Consoli-dated
15) 1971 28	383238 39*				
	16185 57*				
27) 269 61	230 39*		399654 35	34281 04	433935 39
24) 513 89	402268 57*		402268 57		402 268 57
	259934 89*	D) -158167 00	101767 89		
3) 6545 25 2022126	1045443 69*	2) 15 00006 B) 44 14672	110459047	1623752	122259588
5) 1460496	-2565258*		-2565258	- 100000	-2665258
	13100 00*				
		C) 200000			
		C) 528954	20389 54		20389 54
25) 224364	33170 8*				
	215619*				
		E) 196625	7439 52		7439 52
	5204125 4*				
	2935270 1*				
	4523527 5*				
18) 271580	1224163 5*		138870865		
	-130879 6*		-1308796	1439675 1	151958820
19) 294642	3819832*				
	225000*		404483 2		404483 2
		D) 158167 00	158167 00		158167 00
	37415210*		37415210		37415210
	10000000*		10000000	-10000000	
25) 212975	3558320*		3558320	- 3558320	
	219438289*		219438289	926874	22036516 3
X) 196845	-8354647 5*		-8354647 5	- 540504	-84086979
5613031*	53849446 4*	684025 7*	545334721*	6176657*	551511378*

General Ledger

Martin Manufac
Working Tr
December

W/P	A/c	LIABILITIES	12-31-51 (our papers)	Books unadjusted	December Adjust Dr
N-1	110-0	Bank loan	300000 00	550000 00	
N-1	111-0	Trade notes		15000 00	
P-1	115-0	Accounts payable	107220 16^	177393 81	
P-5	115-1	Employees bond payments	5100 00	6300 00	
E-2	27-0	Due to employees	34 50		
E-2	121-1	Advances on contracts	33800 00		
E-2	27-0	Customers credit balances	15848 97		
PF-85	137-1	Accrued income tax	151045 51^	341 63	
Q-1	131-1	Accrued payroll	24761 05^	39239 86	
P-2	131-2	Accrued commissions	4500 00		
Q-5	131-3	Accrued royalties	655 08	1480 68	
Q-2	132-1	Accrued property taxes	4210 75	5400 00	
Q-2	132-3	Accrued unemployment insurance	27681 96^	27265 40	
Q-2	132-4	Accrued FICA taxes	19236 22^	21130 96	
Q-2	132-5	Accrued withholding tax	22367 15^	72169 77	
Q-4	27-8	Deposits on withholding & FICA taxes		-60848 46	
N-1	135-1	Accrued interest, notes payable	958 33	1593 75	
S-1	135-2	Accrued interest, bonds	14900 00	14500 00	(15) 8200 00
PF-83	161-1	Reserve for pension plan	293135 00^	336820 00	
S-1	151-1	First-mortgage bonds	745000 00	725000 00	11) 410000 00
S-1	151-4	Sinking fund	-213158 6	-214790 2	
S-2	151-5	Bonds repurchased		-450593 25	
PF-91	190-0	Preferred stock	500000 00	500000 00	
PF-91	190-1	Common stock	500000 00	500000 00	
PF-92	195-0	Paid-in surplus	102542 10	102542 10	
PF-93	199-0	Earned surplus	2453866 68^	2489443 48	
TB-3	199-1	Net income	160576 80^	443653 08	TB-3 284073 04
X-2	199-2	Dividends paid	-125000 00^	-125000 00	
	TB-2		5341124 40^	5371353 79^	702273 04^

31, 1952 ments CR	Books adjusted	Reclassi- fications	M.M. totals	B.M. totals	Consoli- dated
	55000000		55000000		55000000
	1500000				
2e) 297683					
1c) 238501	18275565 E)	− 196625	19972190	499175	20471365 ×
	630000				
		3) − 412729	1042729 ✓		1042729 ✓
		8) − 4414672			
		3) − 1816231	6230903 ✓		6230903 ✓
2c) 20500000	20534163		20534163	352117	20886280
	3923986				
4) 611743	611743				
	148068				
	540000				
	272654				
	2113096				
	7216977				
	− 6084846				
	159375				
	630000		11984939 ✓		11984939 ✓
	3368200 00		336820 00		336820 00
	315000 00		315000 00		315000 00
	− 2147902		− 2147902		− 2147902
11) 45059325					
	500000 00		500000 00		500000 00
	500000 00		500000 00		500000 00
	1025421 0		1025421 0		1025421 0
	248944348		248944348	5503758	254448106
7-8 3) 4879137	20837141		20837141	− 1000000 821607	20658748
	− 125000 00		− 125000 00		− 125000 00
715863 89	53849444 64	− 684025 7	545334721	6176657	5515113 78

W/P	A/c	INCOME & EXPENSE	1951 (our papers)	Year ending Dec Books unadjusted	Adjust Dr
A-1-3	201	Sales	-79856 5320	-78849 8158	17) 6545 25
A-3	211	Returns & Allowances	11584011	2716320	
A-3	212	Freight out	1489251	1262281	20) 212625
Q-5	213	Royalties on sales	2500835	2004347	
A-3	214	Discounts on sales	6668643	5559228	
A-5	221	Purchases	30972935	31226711 15	16) 238501
A-5	222	Freight in	5282813	3352894	
A-5	224	Discounts on purchases	- 1880350	- 1496137	
A-6	231	Direct labor	25409009 3	26862678 8	
TB-4	241	Factory expense	9704845	9549224 64	x) 362521
A-4	251	Inventory variation	- 3255024	- 5389522	
D-3	261	Cost of shipments to branch	- 8142638	- 9828328	
D-3	266	Intercompany profit realized	- 1102560		
A-7	264	Installation & service	10015474	11102934 x	212975
TB-5	271	Selling	3284520	32110633 x	628908
TB-5	276	General & administrative	47071265	46969044 x	1262171
D-2	281	Interest on investments	- 538125	- 566598 25	25) 224364
E-3	282	Other interest earned	- 626348	- 862495 24	24) 51389
D-2	283	Dividends received	- 1750000	- 8376250	
D-2	298	Gain on sales of securities		- 17515210	
N-1	291	Interest on notes payable	412200	443542	
S-1	292	Interest on bonds	3020000	2940000	17) 315850
S-2a	295	Bond-repurchase expense			17) 3743475
PF-83	294	Provision for pensions	2950000	3320000	
PF-86	299	Income taxes	15100000		26) 20500000
PF-93	199-1	Net income	16057680	44365308	- 28407304
				0	0

TB-3

-60-

ember 31, 195r nents CR	Books adjusted	BM totals	Consoli- dated			
	-7760888 32*	148 117 49	-7909005 81			
	3143623 73					
	r68626788			Change in inventories	
	958547 85			FG	+ 14543 81
18) 29 110 00	- 83005 22*			WP	+ 112 317 r5
	- 98283 28*			RM	- 43855 84
					+ 83005 22*
				S	- 180 1r3 47
23) 7809 27	- 7809 27*	8590196			- 97 118 r5*
	1131 59 09	2590849	6824311 23		
	3273954 1*	245690	351965 21	% Disposition of depreciation	
				24 41	71r2088
	4823 12 15*		4823 12 15	27r4	1287 50
				2784	379r 08
25) 3317 08	- 6rr5 53				76300 46
3) 355 02	- 8979 97		- 1520550		
	- 8376 50	1000000	- 7376 50		
	-17515210*		-17515210		
	443542				
4) 8r00 00	24 358 50		28793 92	x-4	
	37 434 75*		37 434 75		
	33r00 00		33r00 00		
	r0500000	3521 17	208 521 17		
- 48r91 37*	208371 41*	- 1000000	206587 48*		
		8216 07			
o	o	o	o		

-61-

Martin Manufacturing Company
Manufacturing Expenses
Year ended December 31, 1952

F.L.
3-6-53

W/P	A/c		December 31, 1952 Books unadjusted	Adjustments		Books adjusted	1951

Fixed costs –

W/P	A/c		Books unadjusted	Adjustments		Books adjusted	1951
A-6	2411	Supervision (½)	4342066			4342066	407223x
Q-2	2421	Real-estate tax	309161			309161	339050
G-1	2431	Insurance	3360000	19) 257812		3617812^	3295209
				15) 1887			
J-1	2441	Depreciation	6905292	13) 213909		7120088^	6884323
A-6	2443	Shop expense (½)	13845685	18) 135790		13981475^	13083418
A-6	2451	Repairs	7414794	6) –195856			7408869
				7) –195856			
				6) –68453			
				8) –162436			
				9) –62280			
				10) 20300			
						6944069^	
		Total fixed	36176998^	141673^		36318671^	35083101^

Variable (direct) costs –

W/P	A/c		Books unadjusted	Adjustments		Books adjusted	1951
A-6	2411	Supervision (½)	4342066			4342066	407223x
	2412	Power, purchased	15323198			15323198	15540240
	2413	Fuel	11618848	2) 850 58		12469 06^	11512 68
	2414	Water	55004			55004	56317
Q-2	2422	Social-security taxes	11185038			11185038	11298040
A-6	2443	Shop expense (½)	13845684	18) 135790		13981474^	13083418
A-7	2452	Pattern expense	2481517			2481517	1786348
A-7	2481	Equipment rental	4636915			4636915	4645075
A-7	2484	Changes in design	1984594			1984594	3394256
A-7	2485	Product development	3040980			3040980	6361084
A-7	2491	Scrap & spoilage	1535068			1535068	827266
A-7	2492	Sales of scrap	– 276646			– 276646	– 250001
		Total variable	59315266^	220848^		59536114^	61965544^
		Total factory cost	95492264^	362521^		95854785^	97048645^

Recap of principal components of operating costs (after our adjustments) –

A/c	Direct labor (from payroll) 1952	1951	Raw materials & supplies (from A/cs 221 and 31-4) 1952	1951
2411	82351 43	74664 08	1861 0x	1551 89
2443	128133 22	120513 23	14142098	132531 46
2451	30342 30	47413 33	18202 03	6785 2x
2452	1x008 34	8274 50	632x 77	6094 03
2484	8811 x1	2x769 45	224928	1859 68
2485	156833 1	316345 1	1x270 46	242x5 65
2491	6x47 61	2893 55	7581 01	458010
264	54x49 x4	50634 05	27829 01	4x89x78
2741	6x50 05	5785 69	1x871 2x	1302 6xx
2749	235 98	3346 71	6634 15	671340
2784	xx403 88	20958 17	(a) 2859053	1552689

(a) Includes writedown of old supplies during the year; see worksheet F-8.

TB-4

Martin Manufacturing Company
Selling and Administrative Expenses
Year ended December 31, 1952

F.L.

3-6-53

W/P no.	a/c no.	Selling expense	December 31, 1952 Before adjustment	Adjustment	after adjustment	12-31-51 (final, our papers)
	2711	Salary of sales manager	28 275 00		28 275 00	28 250 00
	2712	Salesmen's salaries	75 809 26		75 809 26	15 154 78
X-3	2713	Salesmen's commissions	28 473 01	(4) 6 117 43	34 590 44	34 516 47
	2714	Travel and entertainment	51 261 49		51 261 49	50 167 54
	2721	Rent – sales office	10 950 00		10 950 00	10 600 00
J-1	2724	Automobile expense	17 409 57	(14) – 12 50 (a)	17 397 07 (a)	17 509 28
A-7	2731	Advertising	70 572 45		70 572 45	69 784 55
	2741	Office expenses	25 119 87		25 119 87	25 539 87
	2749	Miscellaneous	13 235 68	(19) 184 15	13 419 83	16 892 71
		Totals	321 106 33	6 289 08	327 395 41	328 415 20
		Administrative expense				
A-8	2761	Officers' salaries	104 750 00		104 750 00	104 550 00
	2762	Office salaries	171 697 63		171 697 63	170 625 49
Q-2	2771	Personal-property taxes	18 730 29		18 730 29	22 396 28
Q-2	2772	General taxes	25 826 90	(1) – 2 250 00	23 576 90	26 017 59
E-7	2781	Provision for bad debts	24 000 00	(5) 14 604 96	38 604 96	25 449 95
A-8	2784	Office expense	55 784 28	(19) 184 15 / (19) – 187 01 / (27) 269 61	(b) 56 051 03	49 326 27
A-8	2785	Legal and accounting	26 175 00		26 175 00	37 448 75
A-8	2788	Recreation	15 296 45		15 296 45	10 892 59
A-8	2791	Donations	12 950 00		12 950 00	9 575 00
	2792	Collection	8 627 14		8 627 14	8 821 23
	2794	Dues + subscriptions	5 852 75		5 852 75	5 609 50
		Totals	469 690 44	12 621 71	482 312 15	470 712 65

(a) Includes depreciation on automobiles, $1,287.50 (1952) and $1,478.75 (1951)
(b) " " " office building, $2,229.09 (1951 and 1952), and furniture and fixtures, $1,562.99 (1952) and $1,363.36 (1951).

Note: Above accounts for 1952 were also adjusted for (a) gain on sale of auto, $250, and (b) loss on disposal of furniture + fixtures, $84.11. (H-3a)

TB-5

Martin Manufacturing Company
Adjusting Journal Entries
December 31, 1952

F.L.

(1)

Prepaid taxes	132-2	2250 00	
General taxes	217-2		2250 00
Prepayment of franchise tax	Q-3		

(2)

Reserve for bad debts	29-0	2022 126	
Accounts receivable – customers	27-0		2022 126
Uncollectible accounts –	E-7		
Employees –			
H. Andrews	285 –		
T.C. Birchwood	78 27		
Bruce Effingham	526 14		
Raymond Richardson	109 21		
Customers –			
Aluminum Products Co	210 28		
Bieber & Bieber	3609 75		
Falcon Products Co	1296 53		
Jarord & Sons	95 42		
Majestic Mfg (1951)	2548 02		
Saltonberg & Sons (1951)	5927 56		
Starr Mfg Co	2608 18		
Wrigley Mfg Co	139 34		
Yates Tool Mfg Co.	1804 56		

(3)

Accrued interest, notes receivable	27-5	355 02	
Interest on notes receivable	28-2		355 02
Increase in accrued interest over			
Jan. 1 balance	E-3		

(4)

Salesmen's commissions	271-3	6117 43	
Accrued commissions	131-2		6117 43
Additional commissions approved by			
Board of Directors 12-15-52	R-2		

AJE 1

(continued)

(5)			
Provision for bad debts	278-1	1460496	
Reserve for bad debts	29-0		1460496
Additional provision to bring total			
to 25,652.58	E-7		
(6)			
Factory building	91-122	68453	
Repairs – buildings & equipment	2451		68453
Items charged against (maintenance)			
work order-5 should have been			
charged to W/O 1-1; amount relates to			
electrical cable installed in floor			
for motor outlets; req. AF6646	H-2		
(7)			
Foundry machinery	91-131	95723	
Factory machinery	91-132	100133	
Repairs – buildings & equipment	2451		195856
Labor costs by repair-service unit			
applied to machinery foundations and			
other installation operations W/O 8-1138	H-2 & 2a		
(8)			
Factory machinery	91-132	162436	
Repairs – buildings & equipment	2451		162436
Four motors added to Birmingham			
hydraulic press and rewiring on			
repair work order 4-53	H-2		
(9)			
Factory machinery	91-132	62280	
Repairs – buildings & equipment	2451		62280
Purchased parts charged on repair			
W/O 2-58 to maintenance but applicable			
to new planers purchased during			
year	H-2a		

AJE 2

(continued)

(10)

Repairs – buildings & equipment	2451	20300	
Patterns & Flasks	91-134	6773	
Construction in process	91-19		88034
Items completed; see also R/G A	4-2a		

(11)

First – mortgage bonds	151-1	410 000 00	
Premium and expense on repurchases	295	37434 75	
Interest on bonds	292	3158 50	
First-mortgage bonds reacquired	151-5		45059325
Disposal of repurchase account;			
expenses consisted of premium, $33,825,			
and expenses of security – dealer agent,			
$3,609.75	S-2a		

(12)

Accounts receivable – customers	27-0	1971 28	
Cash in Jackson National Bank	01-1		1971 28
NSF check from Gates Mfg Co. This			
check redeposited 1-21-53 and cleared	C-2		

(13)

Depreciation expense	2441	21390 9	
Reserves for depreciation	92		21390 9
Depreciation computed during year on			
1-1-51 balances; should have been 1-1-52:			

Account	Books	Corrected	Adjustment			
Foundry bldg	14107 96	14676 73	568 77	92-121		
Factory	3168 02	3293 99	125 97	92-122		
Foundry mchny	5541 86	5859 82	317 96	92-131		
Factory	18882 01	19261 77	379 76	92-132		
Patterns	25153 07	25899 70	746 63	92-134		
Totals	66852 92	68991 01	2139 09	J-1		

Martin Manufacturing Company
Adjusting Journal Entries
December 31, 195x

(Continued)

(14)

Depreciation expense					2441	28 87	
Reserves for depreciation					9x	170 64	
Automobile expense					272-4		12 50
Office expense					278-4		187 01
Corrections of annual provisions —							

Account	Books	Corrected	Adjustment			
J & J	1750 00	1562 99	–	187 01	92-16	
Trucks	2200 00	2228 87	+	28 87	92-17	
Autos	1300 00	1287 50	–	12 50	92-17	
Totals	5250 00	5079 36	–	170 64	J-1	

(15)

Accrued interest on bonds		135-1	8200 00	
Interest on bonds		29x		8200 00

Reduction of accrual on principal of
410 M acquired bonds now in hands
of Jackson National bank

S-1

(16)

Purchases	22-1	2385 01	
Accounts payable	115-0		2385 01

Three items received or held for delivery,
not yet recorded as purchases but
included in inventory:

R22601 Anderson Bros Co (raw material) 347 80	P-2	
R22608 M.S. Parks Co (parts) 254 67	P-2	
Robertson Foundry Co. (parts) 1782 54	F-11 b	

(17)

Sales	20 1	6545 25	
Accounts receivable — customers	27-0		6545 25

Elimination of invoice C-12581 from
sales; shipment not made and order not
filled until 1-6-53. The item is included
in inventory.

F-7

AJE 4

(continued)

		(18)			
Finished goods	31-3	3130 58✓	
Work in Process	31-2	9265 69✓	
Raw materials & parts	31-1	16713 73✓	
Shop expense	2443	2715 80✓	
Supplies	31-4		2715 80✓
Inventory variation	251		29110 00✓
Listing, pricing, and extension errors			
corrected and credited to inventory			
variation	F-1		

		(19)		
Insurance - factory	2431	2578 12✓	
Misc. selling expenses	274-9	184 15✓	
Office expense	278-4	184 15✓	
Unexpired insurance	27-7		2946 42✓
Adjustment of account balance	G-1		

		(20)		
Fuel	2413	850 58✓	
Freight out	2-12	2126 25✓	
Accounts payable	115-0		2976 83✓
Unrecorded liabilities	T-2		

(21) [canceled]

		(22)		
Installation & service	264	2129 75✓	
Advances to Button-Maker Co.	27-9		2129 75✓
Additional service charges billed	D-3		

		(23)		
Reserve for intercompany profit	28-1	7809 27✓	
Intercompany profit realized	266		7809 27✓
Portion of intercompany profit realized			
by sales to outsiders (1/11 of $85,901.96)	D-3		

AJE 5

(Continued)

(24)

Interest on investments	281	513 89	
U.S. Treasury bonds & notes	11-1		513 89
Amortization of discount and premium	D-2; PF-51		

(25)

Accrued interest on Treasury securities	27-4	3317 08	2243 64
Interest on investments	281	2243 64	3317 08
Opening and closing balances of interest receivable	D-2		

(26)

Income and profits taxes	299	205000 00	
Federal income tax payable	137-1		205000 00
Federal income-tax provision for 1952	PF-85		

(27)

Office expense	278-4	269 61	
Petty cash	01-9		269 61
Vouchers paid in December 1952 and reimbursed in January 1953:	P-2 O-4		
Repair of office roof	233 86		
Christmas gifts to postman and truckers	35 75		

AJE 6

(A)

Patterns & flasks	91-134	3 088 91	
Construction in process	91-19		3 088 91
Items uncompleted in part on w/o 1-253;			
w/o closed out in February 1953	H-1		

(B)

Accounts receivable – customers	27-0	44 146 72	
Advances received on contracts	121-1		44 146 72
Advance payments on sales contracts			
on which no deliveries have been made			
as of 12-31-52	E-2		

(C)

Accounts receivable – customers	27-0	15 000 06	
Employees accounts receivable	27-0	5 289 54	
Travel advances	27-0	2 000 00	
Due to employees	27-0		4 127 29
Customers credit balances	27-0		18 162 31
Items not representing amounts			
due from customers	E-2		

(D)

Customers notes receivable due after 12-31-53	27-1	158 167 00	
Customers notes receivable	27-1		158 167 00
Notes due after 12-31-53	E-3		

(E)

Creditors debit balances	115-0	1 966 25	
Accounts payable	115-0		1 966 25
Amount owing from Jasper Mfg. Co.			
for defective parts returned	P-1		

RE

Martin Manufacturing Company
Financial statements of Buxton-Makin Company
1950 - 1952

BB.
3-5-53

Income & Expense	Years ended December 31			
	1950	1951	1952	1953
Sales of appliances, net	-1393436 1*	-1907483 7*	-148117 49*	
Cost of sales	900 07 32	12 12 81 59	85 90 196	
Service Costs (labor)	21 598 19	38 665 76	25 908 49	
Sales manager	66 00 00	72 000 00	72 000 00	
Office rent	48 000 0	48 000 0	48 000 0	
Other office expense	10 587 00	11 875 90	12 569 80	
Federal income tax	13 22 75	19 90 97	35 21 17	
Net income	44 28 35	49 34 15	82 16 07	

Balance Sheets
Assets

	1950	1951	1952
Cash	35 880 40	43 898 38	34 281 04
Customers	11 725 08	13 089 75	16 237 52
Reserve for bad debts	-9000 00	-1 000 00	-1 000 00
Inventories at cost	15 347 0 43	12 175 786	14 396 751
Fixtures at cost	83 62 95	92 68 74	92 68 74
Reserve for depreciation	-3 97 687	-4 47 8 17	-5 40 504
Total assets	20 4561 99*	18 253 456*	197 349 77*

Liabilities

	1950	1951	1952	1953
Federal income tax	13 22 75	19 90 97	35 21 17	
Other current liabilities	39 06 72	56 89 52	49 91 75	
Due Martin Manufacturing Co.	44 229 09	19 81 6 49	35 583 20	
Capital stock, authorized & issued	100 000 00	100 000 00	100 000 00	
Earned surplus January 1	50 675 08	55 103 43*	55 037 58*	53 253 65*
Net income for year	44 28 35	49 34 15	82 16 07	
Dividends paid		-5 000 00	-10 000 00	
Total liabilities	20 4561 99*	18 253 456*	197 349 77*	

The above statements have been abstracted from reports of Burns, Sutton, & Co., Cleveland, CPA's. Reports are kept in controller's files.

Depreciation expense is included in "other office expense" and is 10% of the opening balance at the beginning of the year.

Inventories are priced at parent company's cost, plus 10%; they consist of appliances.

D-4

Stockholders' annual meeting   April 29, 1952:

Stockholders present:

Class of stock	Shares	
	In person	By proxy
Preferred	350	4,127
Common	2,128	2,308

The proxies present were solicited by a management group consisting of Messrs. Stebbins, Huddle and Collins.

Directors elected: the five incumbents (see PF-3).

Accepted audit report; approved appointment of HPK Co. as auditors for calendar year 1952.

Ratified all acts in 1951 of directors and officers.

√ Approved plans to repurchase outstanding bonds, details of which are to be worked out by the Board of Directors.

Board of Directors - meetings held quarterly on the third Monday of March, June, September and December. Special meetings are called in accordance with provisions in the by-laws.

Dividends declared:

Date of			Rate of dividend	
Declaration	Record	Payment	Preferred	Common
3-17-52	3-20-52	3-31-52	1¼%	5%
6-16-52	6-20-52	6-30-52	1¼%	5%
9-15-52	9-20-52	9-30-52	1¼%	5%
12-15-52	12-20-52	12-31-52	1¼%	5%

√ } PF 93

March 17:

Approved exchange of $50,000 of Treasury C/D - Series A-1952 - maturing on 4-1-52, for $50,000 of 1⅞% Treasury C/D Series A-1953, dated 3-1-52, due 2-15-53.

√ Authorized purchase at market of 2,000 shares of no-par common stock of McGrew Mfg. Co. a supplier of parts, to establish better business relations.

√ Authorized contribution of $2,000 to Associated Colleges of Illinois, Inc. (see CK 2791 on A-8).

Approved 1951 audit report.

May 21 - special meeting:

√ Voted to repurchase as many of the outstanding 4% first-mortgage bonds as possible. Authorized president to advertise the following offer:

"To buy outstanding 4% first-mortgage bonds at par plus accrued interest plus a premium equal to:

.5% on 1953 maturities,

1.0% on 1954 maturities,

1.5% on 1955 maturities, and ½% additional for each succeeding maturity until the premium reaches 10% on 1972 maturities."

The president was further authorized to "negotiate with the trustee, Liberty National Bank, and with Porter Houseman & Co., security dealers, to solicit repurchases" in return for which the bank and the dealer were to be "paid not more than a ¾% fee plus out-of-pocket costs." Advertising was to begin in June and repurchases were to be made "at any time between July 1 and October 31, 1952." Jackson National Bank was appointed paying agent. See S-2.

June 16: Authorized purchase at not more than $20 per share, 750
√ shares of Liberty Products Co. no par value common stock.

√ Received final report of Mr. Stebbins on cost of new assembly plant; approved total cost of $325,127.89 (original appropriation of $300,000 was approved in 1951). See H-2c.

√ September 15: Messrs. Stebbins and Huddle were authorized to negotiate sale at the best price obtainable (with no time limit) 8,000 shares of Barkley Corp. common stock.

√ Authorized sale at market of 1,700 sh. of Vault Importers, Inc. common stock (D-2)

December 15: Approved purchase on 11-26-52 of $100,000 treasury
√ bills: 201-day-tax anticipation series. (D-2)

√ Authorized bonus to each salesman of 5% on his 1952 sales over $400,000 - see P-2.

√ Approved budget for 1953 (summary on X-4).

√ All officers were reelected for the year 1953 and are to receive the same compensation as in 1952; see A-8.

√ Gave retroactive approval to assessment by Ridgway Recreational Assn. of $6,000 toward construction of clubhouse and to donations of $10,950 for welfare payments to employees. (A-8)

X-3

-73-

Assets	8-1-41	12-31-41	12-31-42	12-31-43
Current assets:				
Cash	39 275 80	25 156 64	10 104 93	320 492 38
United States securities	-	-	539 191 32	5 225 955 21
Receivables, net	64 635 07	76 195 28	156 291 87	283 481 29
Inventories	72 349 18	235 661 15	134 940 98	532 116 86
Prepaid expenses	-	-		
Total current assets	176 260 05	337 013 07	840 529 10	6 362 045 74
Investments in stocks	-	58 000 00	127 000 00	203 500 00
Investment in and advances				
to subsidiary	104 727 68	102 185 43	105 369 48	112 735 00
Reserve for unrealized intercompany				
profit	- 9 691 80	- 9 978 28	- 11 911 53	- 13 136 78
Other assets	-	10 106 58	21 963 58	42 780 88
Fixed assets	672 464 77	809 765 70	1 074 193 30	1 132 060 27
Reserve for depreciation	- 534 585 25	- 549 839 05	- 560 655 53	- 599 488 25
Total assets	409 175 45	757 253 45	1 596 488 40	7 240 496 86
Liabilities				
Current liabilities:				
Bank loans	30 000 00	50 000 00	-	
Federal income taxes	-	8 614 79	62 318 25	3 305 491 64
Other	126 633 35	322 988 76	136 849 89	299 852 33
Total current liabilities	156 633 35	381 603 55	199 168 14	3 605 343 97
Accrued pension obligations	-	-		61 750 00
First mortgage bonds (net)	-		990 000 00	954 850 00
Preferred stock	50 000 00	50 000 00	50 000 00	500 000 00
Common stock	100 000 00	100 000 00	100 000 00	500 000 00
Paid-in surplus	102 542 10	102 542 10	102 542 10	102 542 10
Earned surplus:				
Balance at beginning of year	-	-	123 107 80	154 778 16
Net income	-	123 107 80	41 212 04	1 384 982 63
Dividends paid	-	-	- 9 541 68	- 23 750 00
	409 175 45	757 253 45	1 596 488 40	7 240 496 86

(a) = Prepaid expenses from 1951 are shown as current assets

(b) = Inventories of finished goods and work in process produced in 1952 include only variable factory overhead.

PF - 41

	12-31-44	12-31-45	12-31-46	12-31-47	12-31-48	12-31-49	12-31-50
	72700 86	57820 67	85168 16	125482 23	140923 32	164537 53	.153 677 74
	1837785 71	2523214 44	1752271 95	1884675 12	1622618 56	1460903 91	1651568 82
	918059 82	1017369 62	759328 41	802191 63	724309 51	852635 42	939460 27
	879780 32	1412402 38	1211691 34	1147585 66	1419975 42	1436094 77	1523760 57
	-	-	-	-	-	-	
	3708326 71	5010807 11	3808459 86	3959033 64	3907826 81	3914171 63	4268467 40
	360000 00	339000 00	339000 00	339000 00	339000 00	339000 00	339000 00
	112967 66	128965 53	128062 41	131180 05	136506 89	129673 37	144229 09
	- 13360 38	- 13947 97	- 13484 42	- 1306556	- 14648 92	- 14579 66	- 13951 86
	73874 82	60272 10	63158 22	46358 12	53806 34	40702 58	51263 05 (a)
	1098444 38	1365025 20	1433407 58	1522568 28	1527449 77	1568954 99	1581042 87
	- 615008 37	- 623345 87	- 644687 39	- 675288 49	- 732618 55	- 792049 91	- 860353 79
	4725244 82	6266776 10	5113916 26	5310692 04	5217322 34	5185873 00	5509696 76
	100000 00	500000 00	300000 00	100000 00	150000 00	150000 00	300000 00
	540000 00	1158000 00	159699 12	177473 19	110040 41	131567 23	121647 43
	344173 13	414347 62	388434 39	643530 21	517624 14	381108 51	527334 87
	984173 13	2072347 62	848133 51	921003 40	777664 55	662675 74	948982 30
	81300 00	100000 00	128100 00	163110 00	200710 00	229510 00	260460 00
	884598 50	854607 62	834403 70	804197 74	783989 72	764005 62	743845 68
	500000 00	500000 00	500000 00	500000 00	500000 00	500000 00	500000 00
	500000 00	500000 00	500000 00	500000 00	500000 00	500000 00	500000 00
	102542 10	102542 10	102542 10	102542 10	102542 10	102542 10	102542 10
	1516010 79	1672631 09	2137278 76	2200736 95	2319838 80	2352415 97	2427139 54
	281620 30	514647 67	263458 19	269101 85	157577 17	199723 57	151727 14
	- 125000 00	- 50000 00	- 200000 00	- 150000 00	- 125000 00	- 125000 00	- 125000 00
	4725244 82	6266776 10	5113916 26	5310692 04	5217322 34	5185873 00	5509696 76

PF-41a

	12-31-51	12-31-52
	374 291 25	399 654 35
	303 618 46	402 268 57
	1,506 261 58	1 208 534 84
	1 485 826 90	1 388 708 65 (L)
	29 662 72	40 448 32
	3 699 660 91	3 439 614 73
	739 000 00	374 152 10
	119 816 49	135 583 20
−	11 068 90	− 13 087 96
	61 000 00	158 167 00
	1 633 837 34	2 194 382 89
−	901 121 44	− 835 464 75
	5 341 124 40	5 453 347 21
	300 000 00	550 000 00
	151 045 51	205 341 63
	281 274 17	392 307 61
	732 319 68	1 147 649 24
	293 135 00	336 820 00
	723 684 14	293 520 98
	500 000 00	500 000 60
	500 000 00	500 000 00
	102 542 10	102 542 10
	2 453 866 68	2 489 443 48
	160 576 80	208 371 41
−	125 000 00	− 125 000 00
	5 341 124 40	5 453 347 21

	Five months ended December 31 1941	Year ended December 31 1942	1943
Gross sales	-6518 28 59	-17085 26 33	-99761 58 54
Sales deductions	5902 67	26582 92	36148 28
Purchases (net)	223645 32	498566 89	2351724 86
Direct labor	257122 53	452965 41	1696086 65
Factory expense (a)	131409 38	319641 73	1087026 34
Installation and service	6287 92	28675 47	35598 46
Inventory variation (b)	-16359 45	98786 92	-302 47
Cost of shipments to subsidiary	-9257 69	-53911 01	-426526 1
Realized intercompany profit	6392 9	-3457 85	-30400 1
Selling expenses	25029 57	58263 09	101596 28
General and administrative expenses	43613 94	166095 35	273814 56
Interest and dividends received	-3408 19	-11593 46	-19201 35
Interest expense	3601 75	25890 05	49397 67
Provision for pensions	-	-	504500 0
Profit (-) or loss on sale of securities	396 54	-1509 47	-962 39
Provision for income taxes	8614 79	62318 25	2975491 64
Net income	123107 80	41212 04	1384982 63

	Year ended December 31 1951	1952	1953
Gross sales	-7985653 20	-7878436 33	
Sales deductions	222427 40	117548 01	
Purchases (net)	3131303 98	3143623 73	
Direct labor	2540900 93	2686267 88	
Factory expense (a)	970488 45	958547 85	
Installation and service	100154 74	113159 09	
Inventory variation (b)	-32550 24	-83005 22	
Cost of shipments to subsidiary	-81426 38	-98283 28	
Realized intercompany profit	-11025 60	-7809 27	
Selling expenses	328415 20	327395 41	
General and administrative expenses	470712 65	482312 15	
Interest and dividends received	-29144 73	-98968 00	
Interest expense	34322 00	66228 67	
Provision for pensions	29500 00	33200 00	
Profit (-) or loss on sale of securities	-	-175152 10	
Provision for income taxes	151000 00	205000 00	
Net income	160576 80	208371 41	

a = Includes variation in inventory of factory supplies
b = Excludes variation in inventory of factory supplies

PF-42

1944	1945	1946	1947	1948	1949	1950
-5 789 606 20	-6 499 210 96	-6 858 058 46	-7 268 734 70	-6 549 897 17	-8 262 829 67	-8 548 382 23
49 045 10	53 081 15	62 264 89	66 156 28	61 995 41	72 043 58	75 772 48
1 689 542 95	1 798 153 53	1 981 409 64	2 177 792 62	2 298 758 49	2 635 472 77	2 609 508 26
2 168 646 05	2 107 550 35	2 259 317 51	2 380 153 81	2 202 039 29	2 842 354 68	3 177 702 81
1 188 765 33	1 046 556 37	1 158 754 81	1 259 087 56	1 017 562 91	1 309 806 53	1 286 035 42
54 317 27	105 169 12	136 051 86	171 395 82	147 329 68	203 463 75	218 523 46
- 347 887 06	- 533 209 65	201 174 59	36 824 85	- 172 963 84	- 89 359 68	- 112 248 52
- 30 192 98	- 46 082 95	- 51 327 54	- 59 178 62	- 93 598 17	- 71 182 47	- 75 546 81
- 2 795 70	- 4 020 70	- 5 596 30	- 6 336 72	- 7 776 46	- 7 187 51	- 8 182 48
134 778 52	140 823 78	260 598 23	315 238 47	338 516 22	489 263 75	510 623 48
350 987 00	394 718 52	420 723 54	458 197 53	461 208 73	512 506 38	563 952 97
- 28 735 93	- 41 041 51	- 37 518 27	- 39 263 09	- 35 962 54	- 29 436 21	- 31 506 81
52 655 81	46 540 28	42 962 75	39 542 90	39 256 09	36 018 67	34 150 41
17 100 00	17 700 00	21 600 00	24 000 00	25 600 00	27 100 00	28 100 00
1 759 54	9 0625 00	184 56	- 978 56	354 19	1 241 86	- 1 229 58
21 000 00	808 000 00	144 000 00	177 000 00	110 000 00	131 000 00	121 000 00
281 620 30	514 647 67	263 458 19	269 101 85	157 577 17	199 723 57	151 727 14

PF-42a

Problems and Questions

1. From the following information prepare a working trial balance similar in form to that appearing in the Illustrative Audit:

a/c no.	Account	December 31, 19–0 Debit	December 31, 19–0 Credit	December 31, 19–1 Debit	December 31, 19–1 Credit
1	Accounts payable		$ 35,916.46		$ 105,649.27
2	Accrued expenses		8,691.79		12,064.05
3	Accounts receivable	$ 235,150.11		$ 277,965.63	
6	Allowance for depreciation		311,816.47		367,809.30
8	Assembly-department expense	205,003.31		215,720.31	
14	Building expense	100,870.80		101,023.19	
15	Burden absorbed in production		823,527.59		774,782.56
21	Cabinet-shop expense	214,470.78		235,573.75	
22	Capital stock		1,150,000.00		1,150,000.00
23	Cash	186,104.80		237,247.51	
28	Cost of production			2,850,076.92	
41	Earned surplus		398,427.57		431,413.24
51	Finished parts	2,386.45		2,386.45	
52	Finished product	235,252.22		261,625.70	
71	Land, buildings, & equipment	1,152,020.11		1,236,584.81	
81	Machine-shop expense	215,297.62		232,495.06	
86	National Parts Associates, Inc.	100,000.00		125,308.29	
87	Note receivable	6,743.88		1,000.00	
91	Raw materials	80,265.40		80,265.40	
93	Receiving expense	27,087.41		28,914.45	
95	Reserve for taxes		71,732.85		68,822.01
101	Sales		3,287,625.90		3,543,166.35
111	Selling & administrative expense	321,223.68		398,807.84	
122	Warehouse & shipping expense	60,797.67		62,078.99	
123	Work in process	106,632.48		106.632.48	
	Receivable—National Parts	20,015.36			
	Dividend paid	115,000.00			
	Opening inventory	431,362.07			
	Materials consumed	1,290,209.69			
	Direct labor	586,995.70			
	Factory overhead	683,912.91			
	Closing inventory		424,536.55		
	Depreciation expense	60,907.00			
	Federal income tax	74,565.73			
		$6,512,275.18	$6,512,275.18	$6,453,706.78	$6,453,706.78

Adjustments or reclassifications:

(a) The costs appearing in the income statement are to consist of opening inventory, components of production expense (materials, labor, factory overhead, and depreciation), closing inventory, selling and administrative expense, and Federal income tax.

(b) The amount added to the opening inventory of finished product, $26,373.48, represents returned sales and should be transferred to sales.

(c) Inventories at the end of the year were raw materials $119,-372.63, finished parts $3,258.67, work in process $86,275.83, and finished stock $223,638.07; these amounts are to appear on the balance sheet and in total on the income statement.

(d) The National Parts Associates, Inc. is a distributor of the company's products. The account represents a permanent investment in stock, $100,000, a minority interest, and a current account of $25,-308.29 collectible in the ordinary course of business which is to be classified as an account receivable.

(e) These accounts are to be combined or offset for statement purposes: 3, 87, and 86 (in part) ; 2, 95; 8, 14, 15, 21, 81, 93, 122.

(f) Cost of production is made up of expenditures during the year for direct labor $583,246.80, direct materials $1,431,000.33, and burden $774,782.56; included also is depreciation of $61,047.23; these four items are to appear separately on the income statement.

(g) Ninety per cent of the building expense and its components (material $24,582.60 and labor $76,440.59) is to be added to production costs, the remaining 10% to be included in selling and administration expense.

(h) Selling and administration contains the provision for Federal income tax shown as an accrual. This expense is to appear as a separate item in the income statement.

2. Examine a number of the worksheets of the Illustrative Audit and describe the practice followed with respect to title, date, source of information, and cross reference to other sheets.

3. What safeguards should surround the acceptance by the auditor of worksheets prepared by the client's staff at his request?

4. An auditor's working trial balance is sometimes referred to as a "key" to his audit. Examine the working trial balance appearing in the Illustrative Audit and describe its relationship to (a) the books of account, (b) the working papers, and (c) the financial statements.

5. What do you conceive to be the elements that should go into every carefully prepared adjusting journal entry appearing in the auditor's working papers?

6. Distinguish between adjustments and reclassifications. Should they both be expressed in the books of account?

7. Describe a process whereby the auditor may eliminate most formal reclassifications.

8. Prepare a summary of the index letters and numbers used in the Illustrative Audit.

9. What types of items would you expect to find on an "agenda" sheet?

10. What are the various purposes served by a permanent file?

11. Under what conditions might it be desirable to maintain a permanent-file section on cash?

12. Describe briefly the methods by which an account may be "analyzed."

13. Outline the general process followed by the auditor when he "scans" an account.

14. The following is summarized from an auditor's analysis of the sales account of a client for a recent fiscal year (the phraseology and figures are the auditor's):

Sales this year to customers	$3,047,695.80
Prior-year sales not accounted for in last year's receivables as an addition or in last year's inventory as a reduction	26,125.43
Scrap sales	4,244.26
Total credits in sales account	$3,078,065.49
Returns of last year's sales	$ 80,427.60
Returns of this year's sales	62,781.11
Bad-debt writeoffs on—	
Prior-year sales	3,268.08
This year's sales	1,530.00
Cost of operating credit office	30,135.63
Small items (under $1,000 each), too numerous to look for; but ran a tape which gave a total of	101,687.97
Total debits in sales account	$ 279,830.39
Balance—OK per trial balance	$2,798,235.10

Comment on the analysis, the need of adjustments and reclassifications, and the desirability of securing additional information.

15. What disposition should be made by an auditor of each of the following situations discovered by him during the course of a calendar-year audit:

The general-ledger debits exceed the general-ledger credits by $110.00

The customers'-ledger bookkeeper has "plugged" his trial balance by 20 cents in order to secure an agreement with the general-ledger control.

Factory-overhead allocation during the year was changed from a labor-hours to a labor-cost basis.

The office payrolls were not tested by the internal auditor this year although he made thorough tests of such payrolls last year.

Bank-service charges of $1.78 for December were recorded as an expense of the month following.

16. A petty-cash reimbursement voucher, dated in January of a calendar year under audit, and another such voucher, dated in December of the same year, have been carefully examined by an auditor and have been found to be in good order. May the auditor then conclude that any testing of such vouchers for the balance of the year would be superfluous?

17. In scanning an account, an auditor pays attention to the possibility of "faulty explanations accompanying postings." What importance would you attach to inaccurate explanations?

18. During an audit it is discovered that numerous changes have been made in the classification of expense accounts. What attention would you give to such changes, and what result might they have on the financial statements you prepare?

19. Discuss briefly the meaning of the instruction: "Depend as infrequently as possible on the client's written procedures and on oral statements made by the client's staff."

20. A recurring problem in audit field work is the disposal of small items. On a certain engagement during the past year an auditor reported to his principal that he discovered the following items but regarded them as unimportant and hence took no steps to correct them:

(a) Folio references frequently missing in general ledger.

(b) Erasures of postings, claimed by bookkeeper to be clerical corrections.

(c) Adjustments made directly by debiting and crediting general-ledger accounts, not supported by journal entries.

Do you agree?

CHAPTER III

Planning the Audit

In a public-accounting firm the personnel consists of various employee classes that may be designated as follows:

Titles	Simplified titles
Senior partners Junior partners Managers or supervisors	Principals
Accountants-in-charge Seniors	Auditors
Semiseniors Juniors	Assistants
Office assistants and proofreaders Clerks and stenographers	Office staff

The simpler classification, followed in this book, indicates the levels at which audit work is planned and carried out. It is in use among a number of accounting firms for the same reason.

In addition to the above classifications larger firms employ accountants and occasionally attorneys whose time is devoted to some specialized field such as income taxes, cost accounting, systems, management, contract renegotiation, and SEC applications and reports. They function usually in a staff capacity, reviewing tax returns prepared in the field; working with auditors on system and organization problems; reviewing reports to governmental agencies; and, when requested by clients, arranging, preparing for, and attending conferences with representatives of such agencies. Their work supplements that of the auditor who has little opportunity for the high degree of specialization required in these fields.

The policies and procedures of a firm of public accountants are determined by the partners and are made known to employees through manuals, memorandums, conferences, training courses, and individual instruction. Responsibility for each engagement rests on a specific partner. However, except in smaller firms, the partner can devote only a minor amount of time to any one audit, and he must depend on a manager or other subordinate for the supervision of and contact with the auditor in the field. A partner ordinarily does not examine working papers in detail; he depends on the manager for a thorough review of the engagement and for assurance that the auditor's working papers provide adequate backing for the report.

How Public Accountants Are Chosen

Public accountants are, as a rule, chosen by management. The decision may take the form of a direct appointment by the executive head of a business or of an appointment emanating from the board of directors following a recommendation from the executive head. However, the method of selection generally preferred by public accountants themselves is that they be nominated by a committee of nonofficer board members and appointed by the stockholders at their annual meeting. In recent years this method has gained considerable ground and has been supported by the U. S. Securities and Exchange Commission and the stock exchanges. It does not insure that the stockholders are acting independently in choosing their auditors. As is so often the case in American business, the great majority of stockholders (and boards of directors) follow the recommendations of management. But once the selection of the public accountant has been made by the stockholders, his independence of whatever factions may exist within the business tends to be complete, especially in larger enterprises having listed securities; for if a change of accountants is proposed to the stockholders, reasons for the change will probably be made public. Should by any chance the management object to the accountant because of his assertion of independence, the stockholders, even though complaisant on most matters, would undoubtedly align themselves on the side of the accountant.

Regardless of how he is appointed, the public accountant may be asked to confer from time to time with the board or its audit committee, and to address his report to the stockholders. The continued development of these relationships has increased the accountant's feeling of independence as well as his independence in fact and has enhanced the value of his findings to management and investor alike. Where accountants have been chosen by the stockholders, they customarily attend stockholders' meetings in order to answer questions put to them on matters pertaining to their reports or coming within the field of general financial policies and problems.

Arrangements with Client

Before concluding an agreement to perform an audit, the public accountant and his client come to a common understanding on the nature of the audit and the audit report, the time of performance, the date the report is to be delivered, and the accountant's compensation. A proposal may be submitted at the client's request, addressed to the president or other officer, or to the board of directors or stockholders, embodying these details. If the proposal is approved, one copy bearing the client's endorsement and returned to the accountant has the force of a contract. In some cases the auditor prepares a letter for the client's signature confirming the arrangement; or he may prepare a resolution for adoption by the board of directors or by the stockholders. No particular form of letter or resolution has become standardized but it will be likely to contain references to the work of the auditor as including:

A review of and report on the company's internal controls. This has the effect of calling attention directly to management's responsibility for such controls and of suggesting that protection against and discovery of fraud and other irregularities is a function of the controls system.

An examination or testing of the records and supporting data following generally accepted and applicable auditing standards and other procedures judged necessary by the auditor, without making a detailed audit. Here the effort is to emphasize the modern practice of sampling as contrasted with an examination of every transaction.

An opinion of the ability of the financial statements of the business to portray fairly its condition on a given date and operating results for a stated period ending on that date, of the conformance of the statements to accepted accounting principles, and of the consistency of the statements with those of the preceding period. This brings out the three standard elements—fairness, conformity, and consistency—of the auditor's formally prepared opinion; see "opinion" paragraphs illustrated on page 583.

Some accountants, desiring to keep their relations with clients on a "personal" basis, do not send or ask for confirming letters. The more formal procedure is, however, to be preferred, and should be regarded as essential in arranging major engagements.

The usual type of audit is often referred to in arrangement memoranda as an "annual audit," "balance-sheet audit," or "examination of the balance sheet [at a given date] and the income statement [for a specified period]." Reference may also be made to a detailed audit for a limited portion of the period, or to any special work, such as the preparation of an income-tax return, that is to be carried on at the same time.

Audit reports, described in Chapter XVI, may be in any form. A frequently recurring type, at least in the case of larger corporations, is the brief one- or two-paragraph "certificate" illustrated on page 582. Supplementing the certificate in many instances is the less formal report or commentary on internal controls, which usually takes the form of a letter to the management pointing out weaknesses and possible remedies. For smaller or closely held corporations, or for partnerships, trusts, private investment concerns, proprietorships, and the like, a more extended form, often containing no "certificate," may be followed. Such a report, in draft form, appears in the Illustrative Audit. It may contain the auditor's comments on internal controls, but usually the auditor's report on internal controls is a separate document.

Despite agitation for the adoption of a "natural business year," as much as two-thirds of the average public accountant's regular annual-audit reports must be issued during the first few months of each calendar year. Even where an audit is made promptly after the fiscal period has ended, a month may elapse before the audit report can make its appearance. In the interest of prompt reporting public accountants are constantly extending the coverage and techniques of their "preliminary examination" (see below), thereby cutting down on the time required for the post-year-end work and the release of their reports.

Compensation of public accountants may be on a flat-fee basis; a per-diem basis plus traveling expenses, if any; or a per-diem basis plus expenses with a maximum total fee. Naturally, the accountant prefers a per-diem arrangement in order that unforeseen situations, which may arise in the midst of any audit engagement, may be adequately explored. With a top limit on his fee, he may seek to have it raised when confronted with unexpected problems, or run the risk of incurring a loss. Average per-diem rates for principals range from $50 to $150; for auditors from $25 to $75; for assistants from $20 to $30; for office staff from $10 to $20. In each case, the per-diem rate contemplates a seven- or eight-hour day with overtime at the same rate.

Audit Manual

Many public-accounting firms have prepared manuals for the guidance of their staffs in audit planning and performance. These manuals establish the background for the annual audit and for the conduct of the auditor in the field. They outline various standards of accounting and internal controls, give particulars of the preparation of working papers, discuss valuation problems, and provide guides for audit procedures and for the construction of reports.

Opinions differ on the value of applying minimum standards or ready-made procedures to every annual-audit engagement. Such a program has been adopted by a number of public-accounting firms and works well when carefully controlled. But there is always the danger that minimum procedures may become maximum procedures and that the auditor's initiative may be cramped by too much uniformity. Besides, books of account and internal controls differ so widely that no single set of procedures can be regarded as the precise minimum required by good auditing practice for any one engagement. Nevertheless, in the opinion of the author, minimum *standards,* as distinct from procedures, deserve an important place in every public-accounting organization as well as in the general concept of auditing itself. In fact, minimum standards of procedure may be looked upon as an enlargement of the auditing definition: a practical application of what would otherwise remain an abstraction. It is true that a given set of standards, no matter how carefully devised, invariably refers to an *average* situation—a situation that no one actually encounters. But if the accountant keeps that fact in mind, he will have little difficulty in adapting accepted standards to his immediate needs. For each engagement he must determine a set of procedures for which the ideal standards will serve as a point of departure.

Audit Memorandum

Before auditors commence their field work, it is customary to prepare a memorandum containing useful information regarding the business of the client and details of the agreement as to when the work will start and other conditions relating to the audit. This memorandum should be the work of a principal and should be put together at about the time the audit is arranged. It will be fairly extensive if the audit is being made for the first time, and possibly quite brief if a similar audit has been made before. The purpose is to record preliminary observations and understandings, particularly for the benefit of the auditor who will be responsible for the field work. It provides him with an introduction to the organization and its personnel and may disclose a number of specific problems that will be encountered.

In most cases, the audit memorandum tends to be little more than a record of conversations with the client's officers. Among the points it may profitably contain, in the event of a first audit, are these:

Ownership and control; reorganizations in recent years
A brief history of the net-worth accounts
Principal kinds of products
Nature of the market in which the products are sold
Price conditions and trend of sales
Advertising methods
Location of plants and offices
Character and adequacy of manufacturing facilities
Sources of raw materials and trends in prices
Names and interrelation of principal officers
Responsibility of controller
Books of account, nature of and where kept
Who gets controller's monthly reports and how they are used
How this year differed from last year: new products, new equipment, changes in cost, financial problems
How next year will differ from this year: changes in production, plan, costs, management
Purpose of investments
Purpose of contingency and similar reserves
Subsidiary companies and how they are operated and controlled
Special problems raised by management: opinions of internal controls, accounting policies, costing methods, promptness and accuracy of internal reporting
Tax returns: preparation or review
Preparation of government reports

Documents like the following, which the principal may bring back from his preliminary survey, will help materially in building up the audit program:

Manual of organization
Functional and organizational charts (an informal diagram of relationships may prove to be even more informative)

Recent annual reports to stockholders, notices of annual meetings, and proxy solicitations

Recent monthly financial statements and reports issued by controller

Once information of the type described above has been put into an audit memorandum, there is no need for repeating the process in succeeding years. Subsequent annual-audit memoranda may be limited to changes and new problems.

An audit memorandum should be regarded as primarily informative in character. As it may be a report of conversations, it may contain factual inaccuracies and is never intended as a substitute for original investigation by the auditor.

Often the annual-audit memorandum is supplemented by a "memorandum of engagement," a single-page printed form, a copy of which is furnished to the auditor by his principal and is included in his working papers. An example follows:

HYATT, PATERSON & COMPANY
Certified Public Accountants

	PREPARED BY____AHP_____ DATE__8-1--3__
MEMORANDUM OF ENGAGEMENT	ASSIGNED TO J.S.Burke_____ DATE__8-6--3__

CLIENT_____F. L. Barnes & Co._____

ADDRESS_____1490 Edison Building, Chicago_____

TELEPHONE_____CEntral 6-5846_____

CONFERENCE_____

LETTER_____July 12, 19-3_____

REPORT TO BE ADDRESSED TO_Board of Directors_____

REPORT DUE_____March 5, 19-4_____

ACCOUNT TO BE CHARGED____F. L. Barnes & Co._____

FEE BASIS_____$100, $50, $25, $20, with top of $1,800_____

LOCATION OF BOOKS_____as above_____

NATURE OF BUSINESS_____manufacturer wood specialties_____

AUDIT COVERAGE_____annual audit, 19-3; income-tax return_____

PRELIMINARY WORK_____October_____

PERSONNEL____1-1_____ FOR_____3 weeks_____

SPECIAL INSTRUCTIONS_____Comments on internal controls to be addressed to

_____president and dispatched not later than February 1.

Audit Program

An audit program bears the same relation to a forthcoming audit as a budget to future operations. It is the plan of work to be done and a connecting link between principal and auditor. It is made up in the public acountant's office before the field work commences. In the field it serves as a directive and guide against which actual performance is ultimately compared. Like any other type of planning well conceived, a carefully drawn and executed audit program gives order, point, and coherence to the audit undertaking.

Attention has already been called to the representative audit programs in Chapters V to XIII. In the form of instructions they are abbreviated or amplified at the discretion of the principal, depending on a number of factors. Occasionally, an auditor whose professional attainments have been well tested is given an assignment by his principal with virtually no instructions. This might occur in a first audit where the principal has been unable to make a preliminary survey. Some accounting firms prepare an audit program only for their larger assignments. In other instances, audit instructions such as those contained in this book might be too brief and would require considerable amplification in order to make them workable in the hands, for example, of assistants who cannot be under the daily supervision of the auditor—a situation that arises when an assistant is sent to a branch office or another plant. Detailed instructions may also be required where weaknesses in internal controls are discovered or are known to exist, where the records are unusually complicated, or where for other reasons the principal desires to have out-of-the-ordinary tests applied.

It has been the author's consistent experience that some form of written audit program is essential to every engagement. The program should indicate in broad strokes the work to be done, the time allotted to each section of the audit, and, as the various stages of the work are completed, the time actually consumed. The time estimate for a first audit will necessarily be tentative, but it can be based on the firm's experience in other engagements, often with a fair degree of accuracy. When supplemented by a weekly report from the field on work done, the principal is able to follow the progress of the audit, watch for overruns, give assistance to the auditor on any revision of his program, determine when his (the principal's) presence is needed on particular problems or to wind up the engagement, estimate the time at which the auditor and his assistants will be available for other work, and have at hand a good guide for the program of the following audit.

The time at which next year's audit program should be prepared is at the conclusion of this year's audit. Deficiencies in this year's audit performance, weaknesses disclosed in principles and procedures followed by the client, needed followups on transactions not yet completed—all these are matters that are fresh in the minds of both principal and auditor when the current year's work is ended; too often these matters are of necessity imperfectly recorded in the working papers. Some of them may require action early in the new fiscal year. Much time is lost and important points may be overlooked when principal and auditor leave the drafting of the program to a later month.

One method of making up an audit program is to prepare a list of the items of work to be done and the estimated time required, with blank spaces for the name or initials of the staff member to whom the work was assigned in the field and for the hours actually spent. If the cash program is to be the "minimum" procedure suggested in Chapter VI, the list of work items might appear thus:

HYATT, PATERSON & CO.
Certified Public Accountants

CLIENT F. L. Barnes & Co.

AUDIT PROGRAM DETAIL   PERIOD Year ended Dec. 31, 19-3

STANDARD PROGRAM	DETAIL OF WORK	ASSIGNED TO	ESTIMATE OF HOURS	ACTUAL HOURS
	Cash--			
1	Bank letters (Jan. 9 cutoff)	-	-	
2	Cutoff reconciliation (2)	1	10	
3	Year-end items	-	1	
4	Year-end reconciliation (2)	1	10	
5	Checks on hand, recorded as issued	-	1	
6	Receipts and deposits, -5 and +5 days from 12/31	2	-	
7	Transfers, -5 and +5 days from 12/31	1	1	
8	Petty-cash review	-	1	
9	Restrictions on balances	-	-	
	Marketable securities-- etc.			

The totals of each section of the work list may be assembled on a summary sheet having the form appearing on the next page.

In both forms illustrated, it is assumed that two grades of hours are to be billed to the client, thus requiring separate accumulations for each. The first half of each hour-column contains the auditor's (senior's) time, and the second half that of his assistants. No estimated or actual time need be shown, as a rule, for fractional hours. For example, the work detail entitled "Bank letters" is estimated here as requiring less than an hour. Space is provided on the summary sheet for "unallocated field time"— time spent on conferences and on other work that may not be worth while classifying. Allowance must be made, of course, for "office" time—that is, the job of putting working papers together, bringing up the permanent file, and reviewing the papers and report with the principal.

HYATT, PATERSON & CO.

Certified Public Accountants

CLIENT F. L. Barnes & Co.

AUDIT PROGRAM DETAIL

PERIOD Year ended Dec. 31, 19-3

INDEX	NATURE OF WORK	ESTIMATE OF HOURS		ACTUAL HOURS		COMMENTS
1	Working trial balance	4	4	6	5	
A	Cash	5	24	2	35	
B	Marketable securities	1	10	1	9	
C	Receivables	22	48	18	40	
FF	Other income	1	6	2	4	
GG	Other expense	8	-	2	5	
	Minutes	8	-	10	-	
	Financial statements	16	8	12	7	
	Report	16	16	22	14	
	Unallocated field time	16	8	15	3	
	Office time	8	8	5	-	
	Total	168	224	152	231	

The work titles on the "Audit Program Detail" illustrated above are abbreviated as much as possible. Where instructions must be elaborated by the principal, they may be included as a part of the audit memorandum.

When the auditor assigns any item of the program to an assistant, he will explain in detail the character of the work to be done and the nature of the working papers that will constitute the endproduct. The instruction will be given orally or in writing as the occasion may demand, this being left to the auditor. Time estimates shown on the program detail should not, as a rule, be communicated to the auditor's assistants, but he should make clear to them the details of what they are to do and how they are to do it and he should provide adequate supervision while their work is in progress. When the assignment is completed, the working papers are reviewed by the auditor and put into final form. Both the auditor and his assistants will probably keep in diaries or on worksheets a record of their time, program items running one way and dates the other.

Schedules Prepared by Client

Mentioned in Chapter II was the common practice of asking the client to prepare, in advance of the auditor's arrival, various schedules that will become a part of the working papers. The principal may make general arrangements for such work at the time the audit is agreed to, and somewhat later the principal, with the assistance of the auditor, will prepare a list of the schedules desired. This list will be given to the client's controller along with worksheets (some of them will probably have been headed by the auditor), and the request will be made that they be ready by a certain date.

Preliminary Work

By "preliminary examination" is meant time spent on an audit assignment by principal, auditor, and assistants before the close of the period under review. Comment has already been made on the growing practice of increasing the time spent on preliminary work, thereby decreasing the time required after the audit period has ended.

Tests applied by the auditor during a preliminary examination are similar to those applied in the more conventional audit, the one difference being that dates within the period rather than at the year end are selected as those at which balance-sheet accounts are tested. In succeeding chapters the features of these tests are discussed. For the present it may be observed that the newer procedure relies more heavily on a knowledge of how the business and the business records have been operating—a knowledge gained in part by observations at the time transactions are taking place. Some danger exists if auditors permit themselves to be drawn into discussions of operating problems before transactions are concluded; they may thus become preauditors rather than postauditors and adopt an operating point of view rather than that associated with the typical audit. The auditor's program and the supervision given him by his principal must be such as to insure that he is not in effect absorbed by the client's organization. Rotation during the year of auditors assigned to such work may aid in maintaining audit independence.

Problems of the First Audit

Where a firm of public accountants is making its first examination of a going concern that has been audited previously by other accountants, the auditor faces the necessity of assuring himself of the character of the assets and liabilities at the beginning of the period he is to review and of the operating accounts for a number of years preceding the current year.

The auditor's first step, after acquainting himself with the audit memorandum prepared by his principal, might be to take a quick look at available audit reports and stockholders reports covering, say, a five-year period. This may better enable him to determine the accounts and data to be analyzed for his permanent file, and, once he has familiarized himself with the books of account, the period to be covered therein. For example, as a minimum he may conclude that he should have information on receivables and payables for a two-year period; on current investments back to their acquisition; on permanent investments, intangibles, long-term investments, and net-worth accounts covering the life of the enterprise; on inventories, fixed assets, and depreciation reserves for the ten years preceding; and on such other items as are listed in Chapter II. The extent and character of these probings into the past and the time required to complete them will in great measure be dependent on the effectiveness of internal controls and the care with which the records and supporting documents have been maintained. Often available are independent details of the accounts from which the auditor can derive summaries, provided by a liberal testing he can be assured of their sufficiency and accuracy. Such analyses may appear, in part at least, in audit reports, schedules of income-tax examiners, appraisal reports, security applications, reports and working papers of internal auditors, reports to stockholders, and running analyses that the controller himself may keep for his own information and guidance. Where staff members of the client's organization including internal auditors can be made available for such tasks, considerable time and cost will be saved in view of their familiarity with the records and past transactions appearing therein.

Having laid his plans for securing basic information for his permanent file the auditor may proceed to obtain further particulars of the nature of the business and how it is being conducted. His study of comparative income statements over a five-year period might supply him with some clues as to profit trends; these he would supplement by obtaining sales and cost-of-sales breakdowns by product quantities and amounts, and in his preliminary talks with executives by ascertaining their views on the causes and significance of changes revealed by revenue-and-cost comparisons over a period of several years. An escorted trip through the plant would give the auditor a more realistic notion of such operating problems as product quality and quantity controls, changes in output and production methods, obsolescent processes and equipment, new building and equipment programs, current problems of the cost accountants, accidents and losses, shutdown periods, cutoff problems, cost-conscious characteristics of plant operators and the types and uses of cost reports that they receive and on which they are expected to act.

In evaluating accounting policies, the auditor normally learns from the controller how and by whom policies have been established, recent policy changes, how budgets are prepared, the degree of control secured by budgetary devices, what persons in the organization are charged with the over-all administration of the budget and those charged with carrying out its provisions for programs and projects, how equipment purchases are held within prescribed monetary limits and who passes on the need therefor, the points in the organization where spending authority has been fixed, locations of books and of subsidiary, departmental, and branch records, and the degree of management control over accounting practices and personnel of subsidiaries and other subdivisions of the organization.

If an accounting manual has been instituted by the controller and kept up to date, a study of its general provisions and recent changes therein may provide the auditor with a clear picture not

only of accounting policies but also of practical operating details
by which the accounts are kept, and a working knowledge of the
various devices by which the internal controls of the organization
are maintained.

Illustrative Audit

As stated in preceding paragraphs the audit instructions in
Chapters V-XIII in this book may be regarded as the principal
sections of an audit program. They are useful as general guides
in new engagements or as guides to auditors upon their first assignment to repeating engagements. Worksheets X 6–8 follow
this model and serve also as a staff-assignment and check list.
Prepared in outline form at the close of the 1951 audit by the
auditor's principal, the program sets the pace for the succeeding
examination, being based on the conclusions, impressions, and
lessons derived from the preparation and review of the 1951
papers—before they were forgotten. Work to be performed if
possible before the end of the year to be audited has been designated by "x's." The language employed, although at times cryp-
tic, can be readily interpreted by any auditor of experience,
particularly with last year's papers at hand. The directive words
scan, review, analyze, and other terms employed have the meaning ascribed to them in the preceding chapter. In a few instances,
no word of direction or scope appears, the nature and extent of
the task being left to the determination of the auditor after he has
reached the client's office. The columns "assigned to" and "completed" are filled out as work on the audit progresses.

Most audit programs do not indicate the sequence in which
the work is to be performed. The order in which the program is
carried on depends on such factors as the character of the work,
who is available to do it, what records are ready, and the convenience of the client's staff. A study of the weekly time summary (X 9) shows that the work was well scattered over various
parts of eight weeks. The auditor in charge of the field work ordinarily determines the time at which any one section of the program is to begin and when it is to be completed. The "estimated
hours" of "senior" and "junior" time are filled in when the program is prepared, and the completed time summary is available
to the principal upon his final review of the papers. Where the
auditor finds his time running in excess of that allotted on the

program, he is expected to keep his principal informed of the reasons. This is of particular importance in fixed-fee audits.

Worksheets PF 11–14 provide a brief history of the business dating from 1941 when the company was established by the transfer of the net assets of a predecessor corporation to a newly established enterprise. These worksheets are again referred to in Chapter XIII.

Prepared by -
N. A. Cord
March 25, 1952

MARTIN MANUFACTURING COMPANY
Audit Program
Year ending December 31, 1952

To be done	Do be- fore year end	As- signed to	Com- ple- ted
Revenue & expense			
Break down sales and cost of sales by product lines and compare with same items for last year, noting trends		ƎL	✓
Break down sales of product lines A, F, & H by principal products, noting price and volume trends, and ascertain reasons for principal differences from preceding year		ƎL	✓
Survey sales-order procedures, following through sample orders from origin to collection; purposes: possible system improvement; possible collection irregularity	x	ƎL	✓
Break down cost of sales by material, labor, and overhead; ratio of raw material to direct labor should have decreased during year because of MM pay boost and but few materials price increases		BB	✓
Determine reduction in earnings arising from company's adoption of direct costing for product sold and for product remaining in inventory		BB	✓
Reconcile monthly income statements with books and ultimately with our figures as adjusted		BB	✓
Analyze officers' salaries account, legal fees, taxes, major items if any in miscellaneous income	x	ƎL	✓
Review 1952 budget: note method of preparation, use as a control device, study of variations; compare with 1953 budget and ascertain reasons for any expected differences of a material character	x	ƎL	✓
Scan all income and expense accounts not analyzed and make note of unusual items, sources of transactions, monthly volume, transfers to and from other accounts, and trend over the year as well as variation from preceding year	x	ƎL	✓
Cash			
Prepare bank letters (cutoff date 1-10-53)	x	ƎL	—
Review cutoff of receipts and disbursements at 12-31-52		HR	—
Scan recorded receipts and disbursements for entire year for unusual items		HR'	—
Review client's reconciliations at 5-31 and 10-31; foot cash records for these months and trace postings to general ledger	x	HR	✓
Count petty cash; scan first reimbursement in 1953	x	FL	✓
Review client's reconciliation at 12-31-52		HR	—
Compare recorded receipts with deposits, 12-26-52 to 1-10-53		HR	—
Trace interbank transfers for same period		HR	—
Prepare cutoff reconciliations as at 1-10-53		HR	—

X - 6

Securities

Prepare confirmation letter to Howard National Bank   x   FL ✓
Count stock certificates in safe-deposit box   FL-HR ✓
Ask for letter on last vault opening   x   HR ✓
Verify changes during year; ascertain reasons   x   FL ✓
Verify interest and dividends, including discount and
    accrual; review tax status of interest   x   HR ✓
Secure market quotations   HR ✓
Add to PF-52-3 (summary statements of subsidiary)   BB ✓
Prepare comparative 3-year statements of Burton-Makun
    Company   BB ✓

Receivables

Have client list and age accounts receivable; testcheck   FL ✓
Prepare notes receivable schedule   HR ✓
Scan control accounts   x   HR ✓
Review cutoffs on sales; look for predating, postdating   HR ✓
Circularize officers' receivables and payables; cus-
    tomers' receivables exceeding $20,000, positive form;
    65 other accounts, chosen at random, negative form   HR ✓
Compile confirmation results   HR ✓
Examine January 1953 allowance register for 1952 items   BB ✓
Review reserve; discuss requirements with credit man-
    ager and treasurer; review chargeoffs and authority
    therefor   x   HR ✓
Review discount transactions for year; test in detail
    for July   x   HR ✓
Scan transactions in control accounts for unusual
    transactions   HR ✓

Inventories

Review company plan for physical inventory   x   FL ✓
Watch count; test actual operation of plan; obtain
    and watch test recounts   FL-HR ✓
Test material price records against late invoices and
    quotations in trade journals   FL ✓
Review listing procedure on in-process items and
    method of valuation   FL ✓
Reclassify expense orders in process   FL ✓
Review pricing bases   x   FL ✓
Test clerical accuracy and scan other items in in-
    ventory   FL –
Study cutoff controls on purchases   FL ✓
Observe, and secure comments from others, on obsolete
    and slow-moving items   x   CR –
Review commitments for size, and for price changes   x   HR –

Fixed assets

Analyze additions and deductions in assets and in re-
    serve accounts; review source documents   x   HR ✓
Examine authorizations of Equipment Committee and com-
    pare with requisitions   x   HR ✓
Review pricing of equipment and repair orders and
    overhead spread; discuss with Mr. Shuffle   x   HR ✓
Compute depreciation and determine reason for rate
    changes   x   FL ✓
Study company's review of physical existence and con-
    dition   x   HR ✓
Review test, during year, of reserve adequacy   x   HR ✓
Bring PF-71, 72, 73 up to date   HR ✓

X - 7

<u>Other assets</u>
Analyze insurance prepayments & expense   *BB* ✓
Ask for letter from Chicago Mutual   x   *BB* ✓

<u>Liabilities</u>
Verify items on notes-payable schedule, including in-
    terest paid & accrued   *FL* ✓
Letters to holders of trade notes payable   x   *FL* ✓
Compare notes canceled against schedule   x   *FL* —
Review changes in notes since year end   *FL* —
Tape open items in voucher record and reclassify ac-
    crued and other items   *FL* —
Test payment in 1953 of open items   *FL* ✓
Look for 1952 items in Jan-Feb voucher record   *FL* —
Look for receiving tickets unmatched at 12-31-52   *FL* —
Examine cutoff control in receiving room   x   *HR* ✓
Find reason for continuing old payables   x   *FL* ✓
Note any major open purchase orders & commitments
    at 12-31   *FL* ✓
List advances on contracts; discuss with Mr. Collins   x   *HR* ✓
Analyze accrued royalties, and prepaid and accrued
    property and miscellaneous taxes   *HR* ✓
Summarize income-tax computation, and amounts payable
    this year and balance from prior years   *BB* —
Bring in, for office review, current income-tax com-
    putation, and any recent BIR report   *BB* —
Compare this year's and last year's accrued expenses,
    for completeness and changes in method   *FL* ✓
Bring up to date in permanent file: bond, bond-in-
    terest, S/F-trustee, pension-plan, capital-stock,
    and surplus accounts; verify changes in balances   x   *FL* ✓

<u>General</u>
Reminder: get from Mr. Collins security analysis for
    year; 12-31 bank reconciliations; tape of cash
    collections during Jan and Feb on 12-31-52 balances   *FL* ✓
    of accounts receivable; fixed-asset-and-reserve
    analysis for year; notes-payable analysis for year
Review internal-control data in permanent file, and
    test for continued existence of controls; rewrite
    PF-21-30   x   *FL* ✓
Revise cost comments on PF-31   x   *FL* ✓
Get representation letter similar to last year's   *FL* ✓
Bring other PF data up to date   x   *FL* ✓
Secure approval of Mr. Collins on AJE's and finan-
    cial statements   *FL* ✓
Make final review of financial statements and foot-
    notes for data that should be supported in working   *FL* ✓
    papers
Review financial statements prepared by Mr. Collins
    for Jan & Feb; note changes in classification and
    variations in income-and-expense rates; scan sup-   *BB* ✓
    porting papers and AJE's for unusual items
Scan books for period from Jan 1 to date of report
    for items affecting year-end statements   *FL* ✓

X - 8

HYATT, PATERSON & COMPANY
Time Summary

F. L.

Client *Martin Manufacturing Company* Audit *Year ending* 12/31/52

Program item	Estimated hours S	J	Actual hours S	J	Dec 20 S	J	Jan 3 S	J	Feb 7 S	J	Feb 14 S	J	Feb 21 S	J	Feb 28 S	J	Mar 7 S	J	Mar 14 S	J
Working trial balances	8	20	6	32					1	8	3	2	2			10	10	2		
Sales & cost of sales	60	24	44	33			13				21	28		10	5					
Expenses	40	40	52	48	3		12						26	19	14	26				
Internal controls	28	8	24	18	4	10	8	20												
Cash	12	32	10	30	5	5	2		2	6	1	10	3		6					
Securities	4	16	4	12					4	6	6									
Receivables	4	60	13	62	8	6			2		3	5	24		25		2			
Inventory count	24	64	24	70	6		18	62	8											
Inventory – other	36	60	26	71				10	4	26	12	28	6	5	4	2				
Fixed assets & reserves	16	24	6	26			2		2	12		6	8	2						
Other assets	8	8	3	12										8	3	4				
Current liabilities	24	16	21	27		1				6		5	12	10	8	6				
Pension fund	2	2	4	1									4	1						
Bonds payable	8	4	8	6	8	4			2											
Capital stock & surplus	1	0	1		1															
Statements and reports	32	8	43														33	10		
Permanent file	3	20	7	6			4											5	2	2
Scanning 1-1 to 3-14	8	8	30																30	
Conferences with client	24	16	40	2	2	8									16		12		4	
Conferences at own office	16		8												5				3	
Totals	358	430	374	456	32	30	31	84	60	74	40	90	48	80	62	84	50	12	51	2

X-9

Incorporated: Aug. 1, 1941 (New York) — Certif. of Inc. # 35-047-1

Incorporators:	Title	Qualifying Shares Preferred	Common
Ernest Holdover	Pres.	5	1
Edward Stebbins	V-P	5	1
J. B. Huddle	Treas.	5	1

Authorized capital stock, all of $100 par value—

$5 preferred, cumulative as to
  dividends and assets   10,000 shares
Common   10,000 shares

Opening entry, Aug. 1, 1941 (General Journal, p. 1):

	Pfd.	Comm.		
Cash			500 00	see (a)
Subscriptions receivable —				on next
E. Holdover	—	100 00		page.
E. Stebbins	500 00	100 00		
J. B. Huddle	500 00	100 00		
Souse, Maus & Co.	48 500 00	99 700 00	149 500 00	(b) & (c), next page
To — Preferred stock — 500 shares, $100 par				50 000 00
Common stock — 1000 shares, $100 par				100 000 00

Payment of subscriptions:

E. Holdover — cash, Aug. 1, 1941	100 00	see (a), next page
E. Stebbins — cash - - -	600 00	
J. B. Huddle — cash - - -	600 00	

Souse, Maus & Co. (brokers) negotiated a
purchase of Holdover Radiator Company by
effecting an exchange of 3,680 shares Holdover Common
($50 par) for Martin preferred and common, as follows:

Class	Shares
Preferred	460
Common	920

Holdover was dissolved on Aug. 1, 1941, and its net
assets were transferred to Martin at a net value
of   245 742 10 (see (b), next page)

Souse, Maus then purchased the remaining
25 preferred shares and 77 common shares,
for cash, at   5 000 00 (see (c), next page)

The difference in par value and cash price in the
latter deal, $5,200, was charged against paid-in
surplus on Aug. 1, 1941

PF-11

-103-

Opening balance sheet, Aug. 1, 1941:
   Following our audit as at July 31, 1941 of the Holdover Company, we prepared the following balance sheet (here condensed) of the new company (see our report date Sept. 6, 1941):

AUGUST 1, 1941

	Holdover Radiator Company	Initial transactions of new company	Martin Manufacturing Company
Assets			
Cash	32 475 80	(a) 1 800 00	39 275 80
		(c) 5 000 00	
Receivables, less reserve of $10,260.44	69 362 75		69 362 75
Inventories "at cost which was less than market"	72 349 18		72 349 18
Burton-Makun Company, cost in 1933	100 000 00		100 000 00
Fixed assets, at cost	672 464 77		672 464 77
Reserves for depreciation (straight-line)	-534 585 25		-534 585 25
Total assets	412 067 25		418 867 25
Liabilities & Capital			
Current liabilities	166 325 15		166 325 15
Preferred stock, 500 shares		(a) -1 500 00	
		(c) -2 500 00	
		(b) -46 000 00	50 000 00
Common stock, 1000 shares		(a) - 300 00	
		(c) - 7 700 00	
		(b) -92 000 00	100 000 00
Paid-in surplus		(c) 5 200 00	
		(b) -107 742 10	102 542 10
Common stock, less 320 treasury shares	184 000 00	(b) 184 000 00	
Earned surplus	61 742 10	(b) 61 742 10	
Total liabilities + capital	412 067 25	—	418 867 25

Additional financing and listing:
   First Mtge. Bonds, Series A: par value, $1,000,000 (see PF 88 for other details), sold through E. Holdover and syndicate formed by him (see WP HH 1942) at par. Printing, filing fee, taxes, and other expenses of issue, $2,022.87, were charged to expense in 1942. Date of sale, July 1, 1942.

   Preferred stock: 4500 shares sold 7-1-43 at par } through Borchard, Bankup + Co., in-
   Common stock: 4000 shares sold 7-1-43 at par } vestment bankers and the common shares were immediately offered for listing on the Chicago (now Midwest) Stock Exchange, and have been so listed since Sept. 10, 1943.

Management:

Ernest Holdover, president and general manager of Holdover Radiator Company (predecessor company) established the predecessor in 1924 by incorporating a partnership which had previously been doing a machine-shop, general-repair business at 1502 Lakewood Ave., Chicago. Born in 1871, he virtually retired in 1941 and, following the reorganization, he turned the active management over to Mr. Stebbins and has since acted in an advisory capacity. He is a C. E. (MIT).

Edward Stebbins, president, was Mr. Holdover's choice as a successor. He is an M. E. (Cornell, '22) and was the shop manager of the Holdover company from '33 to '41. He spends one-half his time (his own estimate) in the research laboratory of the factory and has worked for some years in an attempt to perfect a series of thermostatic-control switches which the company has been manufacturing experimentally since 1934.

Bascal G. Hanson, vice-president, acts as a general manager; the plant manager and sales manager report to him. He reviews production schedules and during the war period has been in constant touch with Army munitions people who have kept the plant supplied with contracts for the manufacture of devices which circulate glycol as a coolant in certain types of artillery. Formerly controller (to 2-15-43).

George Shuffle, plant manager, prepares production schedules, plans the factory operations, expedites orders, supervises the 15 factory "service departments" and 11 production centers. His employment dates from July 31, 1943; prior to that time he was a colonel in the Signal Corps on active duty in the S. W. Pacific and was retired because of injuries (1 arm). He is 52, a W.P. graduate, and also studied E.E. at Univ. of Mich.

B. B. Sorry, sales manager, has been with Holdover interests for 25 years, starting as factory helper at 16. He was loaned to the WPB for the duration and headed up the priority group in the Chicago office until Aug. 1945, his specialty being nonferrous metals. His salary continued during this service.

Arthur P. Collins became controller in 1949; he was a former staff member of H.P.+Co. He is a CPA (Iowa 1946); AIA (1948), and CI (1952).

Earle C. Peyton, secretary, was formerly asst. cashier of the Howard National Bank (until 1935) and has been with Holdover interests since. He is now 87 and not too active.

PF-13

Organizational Relationships –

No organization chart has ever been prepared, but the relationships may be represented thus:

GENERAL COUNSEL (Beggs, Baggs, & Boggs)	BOARD OF DIRECTORS	PUBLIC ACCOUNTANTS (Hyatt, Paterson & Co.)
	E. HOLDOVER Chairman	BUDGET COMMITTEE (Chr., Pres., Plant Mgr. and Cont.)
SHOP COMMITTEE (employee griev-ances. Treas., Pres., Dir. & Shop Representatives)	E. STEBBINS President	EQUIPMENT COM-MITTEE (Pres., Plant Mgr. & Cont.)

E. C. PEYTON Sec'y	B. G. HANSON Vice-Pres.

B. B. SORRY sales manager	GEO. SHUFFLE Plant Mgr.	A.P. COLLINS Controller	J. B. HUDDLE Treas.	L. CALSP Pers. Dir.
2 salesmen in 1943; nor-mally (i.e., in 1941) 5 sales engi-neers and 5 salesmen	Factory man-agement (1); 347 employees in 1941 & 565 on July 13, 1943 Service (2) Depts.	Books & Reports (1) SEC, OPA, and (2) other Govern-ment relation ships Office man-(3) agement Credits and (4) collections Internal audit (5)	Banks and (1) brokers Cash receipts (2) and deposits General labor (3) policies Suggestions (4) plan	Classification (1) Hiring (2) CIO relations (3) Work standards (4) Employee (5) relations
5 & 7 at 12-31-52	695 at 12-26-52			

Bylaws

A standard set of bylaws, put out by the Corporation Service Co., was adopted in 1941. Blanks filled in: date of stockholders' annual meeting: last Tuesday in April; date of directors meeting: second Tuesday of each month.* Some 16 other blanks were never filled in, and no changes have been made since. *Changed in 1950 to quarterly meetings.

PF – 14

Problems and Questions

1. In 1943 Martin Manufacturing Company undertook and completed a war contract for the manufacture of certain mechanical controls and at the end of the year found itself in the possession of a large stock of factory supplies. These were carried for several years and largely disposed of in 1952.

Prepare a schedule showing the balances of supplies included in year-end inventories since the beginning of the company in 1941. These may be derived from a study of the comparative financial statements appearing in TB 1, PF 41, and PF 42. Your schedule should include all the figures on which the determination of your balances is dependent.

2. What are the principal objects for which an auditor's working papers are made and preserved?

3. What position would you take if a client demanded your working papers after you had completed your audit?

4. Give reasons why most auditors regard it as important that an adjusting journal entry be prepared promptly when an error is discovered. *correct books, not forget. correct so mistake not made again*

5. In auditing the accounts of a corporation for the first year of its existence, what records and documents would you expect to examine in addition to the books of account and vouchers? *min, audit papers, stockholder reports Acct manual.*

6. The president of a company who has recently completed arrangements with you to audit for the first time the company's books for the fiscal year just beginning tells you that you are at liberty to attend the forthcoming annual meeting of stockholders. Should you attend? Why? If you decide to go to the meeting what might you expect to learn from the proceedings?

7. When an auditor, employed to examine the accounts of a manufacturing enterprise, finds that the current work is far behind and that no trial balance has been taken of the general ledger in more than a year, what course should he follow?

8. What responsibility should an auditor assume for the opening balance sheet in a first engagement—where previous audits have been made by other firms of public accountants having a high professional standing? *to extent know well audit covered satisfy himself.*

9. Does a trial balance furnish conclusive evidence of the absence of clerical errors in the accounts? *No*

10. Many accountants observe a formal procedure in making their annual arrangements with clients. One accountant, for example, prepares a letter for his client's signature, in which appear such details as audit scope, provisions for advance billings (relating to fees), nature of the audit report, and date of delivery. Another accountant maintains the necessary personal contacts with his clients, and he and his fellow principals often enter into audit arrangements over the telephone without any interchange of correspondence. Discuss these two extremes.

11. Do you believe that a professional accountant should accept an audit engagement under any of the following limitations?

(a) Access will be given to journals and ledgers but not to original documents, such as paid vouchers.

(b) Access will be given to all bookkeeping records and supporting-papers, but the auditor will not be permitted to question or consult with any employee.

(c) The only limitation placed on the auditor's activities is that he will not be allowed to talk to employees outside the controller's office.

(d) The auditor will not be permitted to modify in any way the financial statements presented to him by the management, although no impediments will be put in his way in the conduct of his audit, and there will be no objection to any qualifications he may wish to include in his certificate or report.

(e) The only restrictions imposed are that there must be neither an examination of the cashbook nor a reconciliation or verification of a certain two out of five bank balances.

Give reasons in each case.

12. During the course of an examination of a corporation you ask the secretary for permission to inspect the minute books. He is reluctant to grant your request but offers to give you a certified copy of all resolutions relating to accounting matters. What position would you take, and how would you explain that position to your client?

13. A statement often repeated is that "the accountant is not a valuer." Explain.

14. In what specific ways do you imagine the work of a public-accounting principal is aided by a carefully worked-out audit program?

15. A retail store is changing hands and the parties involved have agreed among themselves that a public accountant will be called in in order that the exchange price will be equal to the "net worth of the business, determined in accordance with prevailing accounting practices, without allowance for goodwill or other intangible asset." Because of varying accounting standards, what specific points would you suggest that the parties agree on so that the accountant may proceed with the net-worth computation?

16. A controller in speaking of his general ledger described it as containing only controlling accounts. If you were auditing his accounts what subordinate records would you expect to find in support of these items: cash, notes receivable, fixed assets, capital stock, earned surplus?

17. What types of entries would you look for in a controlling account for accounts receivable? Give an example of the contents of an imaginary accounts-receivable controlling account for one month and describe briefly what you might expect in the way of records from which postings to the account were made during the month.

18. Outline briefly the principal functions served by a budget.

19. Where an auditor is chosen by the management for the regular annual examination and report on the books and records, would his primary responsibility be different if he were chosen by a committee of the directors or by vote of the stockholders?

20. A professional accountant, following the delivery of his audit report to a client, is asked by the chairman of the board of directors to

attend a board meeting and there to explain in simple language the meaning of the following terms that they have found in the report:

    (a)   Depreciation

    (b)   Earned surplus

    (c)   Commitment (involving a contingent liability)

    (d)   Working capital

    (e)   Internal controls

    (f)   Lifo

You are called upon to suggest a paragraph of explanation for each of these items in accordance with the board's request.

CHAPTER IV

The Procedural Review

A feature of present-day audits by public accountants is a procedural review—a study of the structural and operating characteristics of the organization under examination.[1] There are two purposes:

(1) To acquire a useful working knowledge of how the affairs of the organization are carried on. In planning an audit and assigning field work to staff members information on the nature of the business, its management, and the way it operates is obviously essential. The quick survey that usually precedes the preparation of an audit memorandum covering a first engagement is merely a "starter"; it is left to the auditor to develop the inquiry in accordance with the practices established by his office. For repeating engagements the planning and assignments can be carried out with assurance as to the range of conditions that will be encountered.

(2) To develop an opinion of the adequacy and reliability of the internal controls by means of which management policies and decisions are given expression. Such an opinion is required, as noted in Chapter I, as "a basis for reliance and for determining the scope of the auditor's testing procedures."

On a first audit the auditor's review is necessarily detailed and comprehensive. It is preferably undertaken by the auditor during, rather than after, the period to be audited, for the conditions it reveals may have an important influence on the scope and di-

---

[1] Elsewhere the author has defined "procedural review" as a "critical examination [by a public accountant] of internal controls and other procedures employed by an organization, (a) looking to recommendations for their improvement whether by simplification, elaboration, or adaptation, or (b) as a regular feature of a periodic examination . . . "; and "internal control" as "the general methodology by which management is carried on within an organization; also, any of numerous devices for supervising and directing an operation or operations gener-ally." Kohler, *A Dictionary for Accountants*, pp. 337, 232.

110

rection of the remainder of his work. In succeeding audits the review may again be a general one or it may be limited to a segment of the business; it is often put on a rotating basis whereby within, say, a three- or four-year period all segments will again be covered.

Many firms of public accountants have devised a series of printed forms that make possible a uniform inquiry concerning various details of each client's organization. The forms are filled out in the first instance by the auditor, or by the controller, with a subsequent review by the auditor and his principal. There are many varieties of these forms; some contain a list of questions demanding merely "yes" or "no" answers; others require narrative statements of procedures. Strong support may be found for any of these methods; but all agree in that the one adopted must be faithfully carried out and that the questionnaire must be short and the answers brief if perfunctory treatment is to be avoided.

Early in his experience the auditor learns that each organization has individual operating characteristics not encountered elsewhere, many of them—reflecting the particular genius of past or present management—having become traditional within the business. Some of these may account for the success with which the business has been conducted; others, leading perhaps to inefficiencies, are of a minor character and do not warrant suggestions that they be modified; nevertheless they must be understood if transactions, accounts, and financial statements are to be viewed in their proper setting. In recent years legal requirements, the exchange of information among business executives, the development of management literature, tax laws, and the regulations of government agencies have tended to eliminate various areas of difference in the conduct of business—a situation fortunate, perhaps, for the auditor, whatever its effect may be on the future of individual enterprise. An example may be observed in the corporate pattern of American business, which is now much the same regardless of location or the state of incorporation. Yet the auditor must always anticipate in the transactions he is about to examine a reflection of organizational uniqueness that will call for his most discerning study and critical appraisal.

Internal Controls

In the definition of *audit* on page 10 the periodic examination of the public accountant was described as including in part "an exploratory, critical review . . . of the underlying internal controls . . . ." It is now necessary to examine more closely what is meant by "internal controls" and what the auditor does when he "reviews" them.

Broadly, internal control is the "general methodology by which management is carried on within an organization." [2] "Internal controls" are the particular means whereby management policies are given effect. It would be natural to infer from this that a system of strong internal controls is synonymous with good management and a poor system of internal controls with weak management. But it should not also be inferred that strong controls emanate from the application of autocratic, harsh, or highly personal methods of operation. The modern business enterprise today, large or small, is a cooperative undertaking to the success of which employees of all ranks contribute through the operation of more or less carefully developed internal controls.

There are many types of internal controls. Most of them may be described as devices instituted at the top-management level and operating at some other level of the enterprise. Among such devices are:

Clear definition and separation of custodial, operational, and accounting functions
Clear definition and matching assignments of responsibility, authority, and accountability
Employee training
Standard costs
Budgets
Internal auditing
Internal reporting

An examination of internal controls is now recognized as a necessary accompaniment of every annual or balance-sheet audit. Formerly mentioned as a feature of the uniform audit report ("We . . . have reviewed the system of internal control . . ." [see page 582], the attention given to internal controls in everyday audit procedures is now understood to be of such general acceptance as no longer to require mention.

How far the auditor should go in his review and re-reviews of internal controls varies with the instructions given to him and with his own good sense of what is fitting in individual cases. No standards of reliance on internal controls have as yet been set by the profession itself or by any regulatory body, and the practices of individual accounting firms vary widely. The one ac-

---

[2] Kohler, *A Dictionary for Accountants*, p. 232.

cepted rule today is that the review of internal controls is an audit necessity. The term covers more ground than the older term, "system of internal check," which usually has reference only to types of crossrelations essential to the establishing of safeguards over cash and receivables; but in the brief time allotted to the annual examination of an individual business enterprise the auditor can hardly be expected to familiarize himself with every internal control projected or in force during the audit period. Many of them will be found to be related to the purpose of his survey only remotely, if at all. On the other hand, members of the profession now realize that ledger accounts are the consequence of many operating controls to which in the past they have paid but slight attention. A better understanding of these controls invariably gives color and meaning to accounts, individually and collectively, that they would not otherwise possess. An account can have but little significance to the auditor if he searches only for irregularities in its component transactions. Interpreted in the light of business policy, the account takes on a new importance. It becomes a means of appraising financial statements: the endproduct of management.

In each of the nine chapters immediately following, the reader will find a section devoted to internal controls. These sections contain the principal features of the controls an auditor would expect to observe in a well-run establishment of medium size. If they or equally effective devices are not present the auditor would very likely recommend their adoption.

How An Organization May Be Viewed

The carrying on of human activities within institutional forms, business or governmental, may be regarded by the auditor as involving the division of labor among four more or less distinct levels of effort. These levels are the principal "horizontal" divisions of the business, roughly comparable to those that may be observed in an organizational chart:

First, the entrepreneurial or conceptual level: this is the point of view of the economist. To him the individual organization is a factor of society, contributing to the total welfare; it is operated by a composite individual (entrepreneur) who promotes the enterprise in the first instance and maintains it after it has been established. This is the vantage point also of stockholders and other investors who contribute capital, employ management, and as a group constitute the ultimate repository of all controls.

Second, the top-management level, where concepts of organization and general purpose are translated into policy. It embraces the positions of both the board of directors and board-approved officers of a corporation; it involves a continuous flow of decisions dealing with the determination of the general character of operations, goods and services dealt in, types of customers served, locations of plants and offices, price system observed, accounting and budgetary principles followed, and so on.

Third, the control level. Only occasionally is this a clearly marked point in any organization. It may be a management staff charged with the translation of policy into procedures. More often it is a secondary function of top management; and it may also be found in areas normally associated with operations. For example, a large degree of autonomy with respect to both procedures and operations may attach to the vice-president in charge of a limited portion of the business such as maintenance, a plant, a product line, and so forth. At this level there is also a constant flow of decisions: but decisions more directly relating to the governance of the various sectors of operations. It is here that activities, organizational subdivisions, operating schedules, and internal controls are authorized, modified, consolidated, or abandoned; budgets are prepared and, after adoption, enforced; in general, it is that sector of management in which top-management policies are converted into working realities.

Fourth, the operating level. At this level are the units of activity of both factory and office where the everyday work of the organization takes place: goods are ordered, received, stored, fabricated, and finally marketed; services are employed and applied to the objects of the enterprise; assembly lines are kept moving. It is to activate and regulate this sector that the other levels of the business exist.

The division of labor that gives rise to the orderly coexistence of these levels is made possible by delegations of authority, responsibility, and accountability to individuals stationed at various key points throughout the organization. Functional charts, organization or office manuals, and specific directives formalize these delegations. In all but larger enterprises, however, many delegations are informal, and not always adequate. Thus an individual may be assigned the responsibility for the purchasing activity of a business but is without authority to restrain department heads from placing orders directly with suppliers of their choice. Failure to provide authority arises from uncertainty as to what or how much is required or can be assumed; from the fear that another person may be "upset," the hope being that somehow "the two will adjust themselves to the new situation" or that the individual "will work out his own salvation"; from the mistaken idea that an assignment of responsibility carries with it the "necessary" authority: the causes are many and varied. In a smoothly running establishment the lines of authority are invariably clear-cut, and responsibilities can readily be identified with particular individuals.

The reverse is also of frequent occurrence: the assignment of authority with no attendant responsibility for action taken. Perhaps the most striking example of this may be found in the Federal government. Until the Budget and Accounting Procedures Act of 1950 was adopted by the Congress, authority for the expenditures of a governmental agency rested on clerical employees known as certifying and disbursing officers. No real responsibility for expenditures existed. Attempts to fix responsibility on these officers for improper expenditures where no question of personal dishonesty on their part was involved resulted in passage by the Congress of an incredible volume of "relief" bills that extended over a century of the nation's history. The simple expedient in the 1950 legislation of recognizing the agency head as the source of both authority and responsibility for the agency's expenditures was a tardy acknowledgment by the Congress of the applicability to governmental affairs of management practices of long standing. From this it should not be inferred that the auditor will never encounter the same fault in business enterprise. "Buck passing" on expenditures can be found in almost every human endeavor, and where the basic responsibility for a transaction can be shifted or cannot be readily traced—notwithstanding an approved voucher with orderly, duly authenticated attachments—the auditor has cause for calling to the attention of top management a serious gap in internal controls.

A cohesive force that serves as a vertical support for the four horizontal sectors of an organization, a support without which their separate identities might not be easily sustained, may be designated by a term borrowed from the engineers: _feedback_. Applied to a factory, feedback suggests a control board where electronic devices keep a process at a predetermined standard of excellence, rate of output, or both; or a statistical-quality-control chart—exposed to public view—to which the outcome of hourly tests of samples are posted by an inspector, thus proclaiming to all who pass the ability of an operator and his machine to stay within established tolerances. Applied to the sales staff, feedback suggests a report from the sales manager to the president explaining the obstacles encountered in reaching a planned sales goal. Applied to an office operation feedback suggests a comparison of actual expenditures with budgeted allowances and an explanation of the reasons behind each major divergence. Always involved are a forward plan, an assessment of results, and corrective action or revised forward planning. In typical situations feedback may be found within—or connecting—any of the levels from which an organization may be viewed. In the form of internal and external auditing and reporting—the work of the controller, the internal auditor, and the public accountant—it may be observed extending from one level to another or through all levels of the organization, even as far as the general public that views the public accountant's report or reacts to the company's products.

Organizational Structure

A first step in the auditor's study of an enterprise is to learn how top management operates. Organizational and functional charts are of aid, but if they are not available the auditor can prepare his own versions as he becomes acquainted with the personnel and with the departments and functions into which the business is divided. An organization manual is helpful provided it is kept up to date and is respected by the management. The auditor's interest at this point lies in ascertaining where responsibilities reside and the persons with whom policies and controls may be discussed.

An outline such as the following may be of assistance in preparing a record for the permanent file of organizational structure and relationships:

Stockholders
    Nature of annual meeting
    Control by management through:
        Stock ownership
        Bylaws
        Proxies
    Matters referred to and acted on by stockholders during past five
        years

Directors
    Character of membership:
        Management representation
        Outsiders, how and why selected
    Frequency of meetings
    Delegation of responsibilities to management by:

Directors (Cont.)
General directives ⎫
Specific directives ⎬ written or oral
Review of proposed actions
Approval of reported actions
Activities of board committees
Types of actions at periodic meetings

General management
Scope of activities of president or chief executive
How organizational plan is set and maintained
Selection and maintenance of effective personnel
Setting of plans or objectives
Controls over capital expenditures
Operating budget: how established and enforced
Coordination of top-executive activities
Testing departmental performance

General-management delegations
Staff vice-presidents or managers
Management committees
Departmental authority
Plant and branch autonomy
Service units
Responsibility and authority of foremen
Types of conflicts and their disposal

Stockholder Policy

Stockholders of larger corporations have virtually nothing to do with the conduct of the business enterprise they own. As owners, under the corporation laws of every state, they are the undisputed source of both policies and powers within the organization; as a group, they rarely take concerted action independently of management. In practice, independent action is rare, either because its potentiality exercises a sufficiently restraining influence on those who would overlook stockholders' interests or because stockholders have no readily available means for acting as a unit. Management, on the other hand, has devices in its favor, supported by law and custom, that tend to perpetuate it: an annual meeting with stockholders that it usually dominates with ease, stock control secured by direct ownership, voting trusts, or proxies, and bylaws that give management technical advantages in meetings and elections. Individual stockholders representing only a minority interest are in most states given the right to examine the books of account and to procure other information, and the courts have often aided them in preventing undesirable management actions. But for the most part stockholders who are not numbered among the management play no role whatever either in policymaking or in administration; in the average case, it is safe to say, the "outside" stockholder regards his everyday interests as being too far removed from management affairs to justify active participation. The moral influence of "outside" stockholders, however, may be potent.

A review of the bylaws and of the minutes of stockholders for a period of several years will give the auditor an accurate picture of the character of that body, if he will but bear in mind the voting controls management may have secured by soliciting and obtaining proxies. The result of the proxy count appears in stockholders' minutes.

An active, intelligent, nonmanagement minority group occasionally goes far in influencing management policies. The auditor should pay particular attention to the inquiries and criticisms of minority stockholders, for if he is asked to be present at a stockholders' meeting he must be prepared when called upon to answer their questions and those of any stockholder's representative.

In smaller corporations, especially those whose stock is closely held, the minutes as well as the meetings of stockholders are likely to be wholly nominal in character, their primary and often sole function being to provide a record of the annual re-election of directors and of blanket approval to the activities of directors and officers after the close of each year.

Board Policy

A typical board of directors has from five to ten members consisting of management representatives and outsiders, the latter chosen for their connections or for their general knowledge of business operations. Under the laws of some states not all directors are required to be stockholders. Typically, the board meets once a month at the office of the company and its agenda are prepared in advance by the management. Directors are chosen by the stockholders to give general supervision to the operating management. If management representatives make up the board or dominate it, the board's activities may be obscured in a conflict of interests. As directors, however, they have the obligation of taking the point of view of the stockholder.

A basic function of directors is to establish the broad operating program administered and reported on by management. It takes the form of making decisions on financial problems, choosing cash depositories, appointing officers and fixing their compensation, adopting pension, stock-option, and other benefit plans for officers and employees (which stockholders are frequently asked to approve), declaring dividends, and reviewing the work of management and the results of operations. Meetings of directors are often attended by principal officers of the company who are not board members in order that they may report on the operating sectors for which they are responsible.

In most corporate enterprise the demarcation between board and management functions, aside from those already mentioned, is not clearly drawn. The chief executive who heads the top-management group may have implicit authority to act on such matters as he may choose and refer others to the board for decision. This is often the case where management dominates the board; board approval under such circumstances, especially where secured after the fact, serves merely to give added authority to action taken or to relieve management of legal or other ultimate responsibility. A rubber-stamp board, however, serves no real function and is something to be avoided in corporate enterprise; its character is not always indicated by the appearance of the minutes, since opposing views and arguments preceding the adoption of resolutions more often than not are omitted. The auditor's information on board functions will depend on his conversations with the management and with members of the board with whom he is thrown into contact.

In larger corporations there may be several committees of the board, such as an executive committee, finance committee, and committees dealing with the compensation of top management. The executive committee is customarily given the full authority of the board between board meetings and may be limited to members active in the management. The finance committee reviews budgets and proposed financial changes before they are presented to the full board. In his review of minutes the auditor should recognize that the minutes of board committees may be fully as important as those of the board itself.

The auditor visualizes as best he can the delegations of authority that the board has made to the management, since they are formalized in writing only in rare instances. Very general descriptions of the duties of the board and of the principal officers will appear in the bylaws; these will be supplemented by the board in some cases by more specific general delegations or by delegations to take action on specific matters.

General Management Controls

Administration, as compared with policy-making, is a full-time job. In smaller companies the burden of administration usually rests on the chief executive—the president, executive vice-president, or general manager. But in a company with a large sales volume, several branches, or a number of product lines, the administrative task requires a division of labor among assistants— general assistants having a company-wide point of view similar to the chief executive; staff assistants each charged with a separate function such as sales, manufacturing, or distribution; departmental assistants who, for example, control different product lines; and regional assistants who operate in distinctly separate districts. These four types of assistants or any combination of them may coexist in the same organization.

The top executive's job in almost any situation will consist at least of the following primary responsibilities: establishing and maintaining the plan of organization and settling promptly jurisdictional problems as they arise; following up on responsibilities delegated to assistants and frequently testing their abilities; setting goals of performance for the organization as a whole and its principal divisions and seeing to it that these goals are reached; and making the budget work. *General* assistants may share these responsibilities with him, acting as he would act when he is absent or otherwise engaged, or acting on specific assignments in accordance with a preconceived plan. *Staff* assistants must be given adequate authority to establish policies and procedures within such limits as may be defined. In a single-product or single-plant organization they may be operating heads; in larger enterprises they may act in a functional capacity only, with departmental chiefs responsible for operations reporting directly to the top executive.

The success or failure of any plan of organization may often be observed by the auditor in the administration of the budget. If the responsibility for expenditures is divided along organizational lines, as it usually must be, and the organizational heads not only recognize their individual responsibilities but demonstrate that they have complied with the expenditure pattern set for them, the auditor may be justified in assuming that at least prima-facie evidence exists that the organizational plan outlined to him is, indeed, a reality.

There are several other tests for good management that the

auditor may find revealing. The first, which is an inquiry as to the existence of an ever active top-management followup on assignments of staff and line duties, can be made where the chief executive maintains staff assistants and at the same time has departmental or regional heads reporting to him. For example, assume a staff vice-president such as a general sales manager, and a regional branch-office vice-president to whom a local sales manager reports. Does the general sales manager go over the head of the branch-office vice-president and deal directly with the local sales manager in setting regional policies? If so, a good deal of irritation with a consequent failure of controls is likely to be the result; good management calls for full knowledge and consent on the part of the branch-office head in dealing with the local sales manager, and it calls also for participation by the branch-office head in any problem relating to local policy or operating tactics.

A second test, sometimes closely related to the first, lies in observing whether adequate authority accompanies delegations of responsibility to operating heads. "Responsibility without authority" is a common complaint at various management levels. An operator, charged with a function that he may be fully competent and willing to perform, is unable to proceed because decisions having a vital effect on his function continue to be made by others; elsewhere, the needed authority may have been given, but it has not been exercised because of the lack of administrative capacity on the part of the operator. In either case, the effect may be that the job to be done has not been done, or it has been done at a high cost.

A third test may be made of the relations existing among service units in a manufacturing plant, the supervisor of the units, and the factory divisions served. A service unit, carelessly supervised, may expand its activities and costs by engaging in work that is being done or could be better done elsewhere in the plant or on the outside. Thus, a research group may be conducting experiments already made and fully reported upon by others. In a successfully managed service unit, there should be ample evidence of careful planning, periodic reviews of the unit's plans by higher authority, and agreement on the propriety of its charges to other factory units by the recipients of its services.

A fourth test is whether the accountability that must follow the assignment of authority and responsibility has been given full expression. Accountability originates with the person or group charged with a responsibility; in its best form it requires the application to itself of some yardstick of performance and a periodic reporting on the findings that may serve as the basis of acceptance or other action on the part of those to whom the reporting is directed. Thus in a factory service unit the unit head should report periodically on the conditions under which his operation has been carried on, the unit costs of the services he produces, the trend of such costs, and the relative efficiency of his operation as compared to similar operations in other branches of the organization or outside the organization.

The Treasurer

Many professional accountants advocate the separation of the cash-receipts-and-disbursements and cash-custodianship function from the office of the controller, where it often resides. This is in line with the general notion that physical controls over assets and the accounting for them do not go well together. Where the "treasury" function has been so separated, the treasurer usually receives and deposits cash, makes disbursements, controls cashiers and disbursing agents, and maintains financial relationships with other organizations.

Whether the offices of treasurer and controller are combined or separated may in actual practice be a matter of no great importance. There are some advantages gained, in both large and small organizations, by combining these responsibilities under a single officer. The treasurer and controller must always work closely together on both policies and administration, and the ideal line of authority between the two is always difficult to draw. With carefully operated internal controls surrounding the treasury function—and these should exist anyway—a combination of the two offices is unobjectionable and may improve top-management relationships.

The Controller

From the point of view of the auditor, the key to the most important group of internal controls is the controller. His position calls not only for accounting skills, but also independence, integrity, and a general knowledge of business and business organization and management. He must be a good administrator, able to win and keep the loyalty of his subordinates, cooperate with the top-management staff, and constantly seek improvements in management methods to the end that internal controls may be strengthened and remain strong. He should be able to train his assistants in such a way that a portion of his time will be available for following developments within the fields of accounting and administration and, where practicable, applying them intelligently to his own organization. He should constantly strive to improve internal and external reporting methods, a task never completed, and be always responsive to management and stockholder demands for information. He should not be afraid to discontinue reports no longer useful, nor to combine, add to, condense, or rearrange others to make them more useful. He should minimize the lapse of time between the occurrence and reporting of events. He should be a member of the Controllers Institute of America, the American Institute of Accountants, the National Association of Cost Accountants, and the American Accounting Association and participate as time and opportunity permit in the constructive affairs of these organizations: all of this in order that he may give a high degree of professional objectivity to his daily work. In short, he must be second to no other member of the top-management staff in his knowledge of management methods and ability to apply them; and he must view his work as being linked strongly to external standards and social controls in the interests of which he should endeavor to serve as the agent—subject, obviously, to whatever limitations of authority have been imposed on him.

The controller is always one of the top-management staff. He is preferably appointed by the board, and he may report to the board rather than the top executive: a practice advocated for many years by the New York Stock Exchange. This privilege gives him a degree of independence, which many think the chief accounting and reporting officer should have.

The Internal Auditor

An important linkage between management and operations is the method by which internal audit is maintained. In larger organizations the position of internal auditor has been created during the past two decades. The internal auditor reports in most instances to the controller. Occasionally he reports directly to the treasurer, president, or chairman, and his responsibilities cover elements of industrial engineering as well as accounting. The Institute of Internal Auditors, an organization established in

1941, has done much to improve the professional standards and standing of its members.

The program of the internal auditor may be left to his own planning, or he may follow that outlined for him by his superior. In either case he is usually permitted to act with a great deal of independence within the organization and he is rarely restricted in his inquiries to the accounting records and the controller's staff. He should be free to discuss the questions raised by his assignments with any person, including members of top management who have or should have any connection with the subject matter of his investigations. His knowledge of administrative methods should be extensive, for even though it be the general intention to confine his efforts to accounting records and procedures he will not get far without recognizing and dealing with both the possibilities and the limitations inherent in the varying combinations of human effort required to run a business. He should, for example, spend enough time with plant technicians to become familiar with the major processes being followed, and with the sales staff to learn the principal problems of distribution.

Cooperation between the internal auditor and the external auditor has the effect of increasing the independence of the former and decreasing the quantity of detail testing performed by the latter. The public accountant may, in fact, be called upon to assist in planning the investigative program of the internal auditor and thus be able to direct attention to weak links at the operating level that he has discovered as the result of his most recent examination. During the period of the audit engagement, the internal auditor may assist in many ways, and between audit engagements he may supply copies of his reports to the external auditor and discuss various matters with him, in this way disclosing new problems the auditor may expect to encounter.

In smaller organizations a part-time internal-audit function may be carried on by the controller or an assistant. However, the effectiveness of this arrangement may in most cases be questioned, since the "third-person" attitude so necessary to audit work is absent in individuals who have administrative as well as audit responsibilities.

Types of Policies

As the auditor studies the management and observes the interplay of relationships between organizational units, he notes the business policies emerging at the different levels: how they originate; how they are given expression; who is responsible for their operation; who follows up, enforces, and reports on them; and, finally, how they are periodically reviewed and coordinated at the top-management level. In most cases he will find obvious gaps—controls presumably established but not enforced and hence not in operation, policies misinterpreted, impracticable policies, policies originating at too low a level and not reviewed at a higher level, policies or controls needed where none exist, policies conflicting and needing restatement, and so on.

An organizational policy whether or not expressed in writing may be regarded as falling under one of three classes: (1) those established by custom, law, rule of a regulatory body, or other outside source, and followed as a matter of course; (2) those established within a single enterprise at the top-management level and usually affecting the enterprise as a whole; and (3) those established at lower levels and limited in application to organizational units within the business. Typical examples of these three types of policies appear below; they have been selected from among those observed in a certain manufacturing enterprise:

1. *General policies*

A classification of accounts following standards long in use in the trade.

Purchasing standards patterned after those recommended by the National Association of Purchasing Agents.

Sales prices conforming to principles of the Robinson-Patman Act.

Credit terms of 1% 15 days, net 30, agreeing with industry practices.

2. *Over-all company policies*

Product specifications originally established and thereafter altered when necessary by a committee consisting of the president, chief design engineer, and the plant superintendent.

No changes in product styles during a period of 18 months commencing October 1.

No guarantees against defective materials and workmanship for periods longer than 90 days from the date of sale.

No further sales on approval.

Refresher courses for stenographic employees, conducted once annually in each office.

3. Local policies

Office hours in the Kirkville branch: 9:00 A.M. to 5:00 P.M., Monday through Friday.

Because of restricted supplies no more than one dozen of product X will be sold to a single customer during any 30-day period.

Journal entries containing month-end adjustments must be cleared with the assistant controller by the 3rd.

Nature of Accounting Principles, Policies, and Procedures

Accounting has always been looked upon as a process for recording costs and income. Out of this process, in the course of many centuries, principles and procedures have emerged that contribute uniformity and a wider comparability, understanding, and integrity to the results. Moreover, controls have always been associated with accounting: for example, safeguards against internal frauds and manipulations, and methods that would insure regularity and dispatch in the handling of transactions. Protective devices have broadened in character and number with the passing of the years and the growth of industry; at the turn of the century they were few in number and enforcement devices were lacking. As a matter of fact, the principal function of a public accountant at that time was to look for irregularities and determine losses attributable to badly conceived internal controls. It may even be said that the causes which have led to the present professionalization of accountants and accounting are to be found in the basic drives for intelligibility and common honesty. These motivations lie behind many accounting principles and practices and have served to tinge them with moral and social implications. The nearly universal adherence to cost as a standard of value may be explained in terms of the need for a common basis of interpretation and the desire to prevent manipulation harmful to investors and consumers.

Accountants have often been inhibited in their thinking, like groups in other fields, by overlooking the definitions of terms they use. The term "accounting principle" has given much trouble; to refer to "cost" as a "principle" has been criticized, and "convention," "postulate," "standard," and other terms have been suggested as substitutes. For present purposes it may be assumed that a "principle" is simply a basic proposition that is generally agreed to and one on which various practices can be built. A "standard" is the adaptation of a principle to a limited area for the purpose of achieving a desired end result. A "policy," still more restricted in its application, usually means the attempt by the management of an enterprise to give effect to a given principle or standard in a particular field of activity; it may take any one of several forms. When a policy is adopted, it is put into being by the institution and enforcement of a "procedure," thereby creating an internal control.

The public accountant's uniform report contains the clause ". . . in conformity with generally accepted accounting principles applied on a basis consistent with that of the previous year." Two things are implied: that the auditor has satisfied himself that the internal controls which assure that these principles have been followed by the client conform to common standards, and that they have not changed during the year (except as disclosed in the report).

No exhaustive statement of accounting principles has ever been prepared. The nearest approach, one particularly directed to annual audits by public accountants, was issued in 1936 and reissued in 1941 and 1948 (with subsequent supplements) by the executive committee of the American Accounting Association. This statement undertook to establish a series of coordinated principles relating to the financial statements of corporate enterprise, and may be paraphrased as follows:

1. Accounting is the language of everyday economics and has as its purpose the supplying of orderly aid in the conduct of business affairs and of information for all who have occasion to view the financial position and operating results of individual enterprise.

2. The subject matter of accounting is the classification, recording, summarization, and reporting of the transactions of individual entities in terms of revenues, transfers, and costs, including the conversion of costs into cash and other assets, and their dissipation as expense or loss.

3. Because management has the ever-present obligation of striving for and maintaining lowest possible costs, much of the accounting process is constructed with the view of aiding in the attainment of that obligation.

4. The basis of asset-and-expense valuation is price: the amount of money or objectively established money's worth paid in an exchange between independent parties. Arm's-length price is the only objective basis of value; being the consequence of actual transactions it is comprehensible to and serves the interests of management, investor, and consumer. Moreover, it is an oper-

able medium for the application of a wide variety of internal and external controls and for portraying the degree of responsibility attained in the discharge of management accountability.

5. A lump-sum purchase of a group of assets is spread over the assets or asset classes on the basis of their current values or depreciated costs. In public utilities, and often in competitive enterprise, the excess over depreciated original cost of the price paid for an asset or asset group is regarded as the purchase of excess earning power, separable from depreciated cost and amortizable over the years to which the continuance of the excess earning power has been imputed.

6. Where buyer and seller are under common control, transactions between them are not sales in the ordinary sense and the seller's depreciated cost continues on the records of the transferee.

7. Replacement cost, index-number valuation, or other hypothetical worth exceeding cost varies in amount with underlying assumptions and as they neither have objective existence nor reflect management accountability, none of these substitutions for cost is suited as a basis for accounting records and reports. As supplemental data they may have some significance, as yet not fully developed, to management, investors, and others. The accounting recognition of appreciation, discovery values, and various forms of accretion comes about only through arm's-length sales and purchases.

8. Accounting often involves the spread of costs over present and future operating periods. For fixed assets the process is known as depreciation accounting, the asset costs being assigned to operating periods as nearly as possible in proportion to the useful services the assets are expected to yield for these periods.

9. A portion of the cost of an item of inventory may be expensed before the item is sold in order that the remaining cost may be not greater than (a) the probable future outlay for a similar item; or, (b) if a similar item is not necessarily to be acquired, the expected future disposal price less any estimated, identifiable increment in cost to be incurred in completing, carrying, or selling. The identification of cost with particular items sold has been generally regarded as dependent on whether the practice within the business has been to put into production or sell earliest-purchased items (fifo), latest-purchased items (lifo), or any item of the same kind without regard to the time of its purchase (average cost). The adoption of a lifo-valuation method to reduce income taxes does not of itself establish its validity for general accounting purposes.

10. Discount and expense on long-term obligations is, in effect, interest not yet accrued, payable at maturity, and is an offset to the face value of the indebtedness; in practice, however, the item appears as a deferred charge on the balance sheet. Unamortized discount and expense remaining from an obligation that has been refunded is an expense of the year in which the refunding takes place.

11. Income from construction contracts or installment sales, involving periods greater than a year, may be recognized in proportionate amounts as billings are made or collections received.

12. A breakdown of sales and costs of sales by products or departments is a necessary addition to an income statement wherever the disclosure is of importance to the interpretation of the statement. A major trend in any of these items calls for comparisons with preceding periods.

13. The income statement reflects revenue and expense recognized during the period covered by it, notwithstanding that certain of its components may be associated with operations of prior years; but recognition does not include anticipated revenue or expense relating to transactions of future periods, which if they ever occur will be dependent on events or conditions that have not yet taken place.

14. The provision for taxes in an income statement should be the best available estimate of taxes to be paid because of events and conditions that have already occurred. It is a period cost, and no part of it should be allocated to a past or future period or to surplus.

15. A final section of the income statement may be employed for material items of nonrecurring income and expense, extraordinary losses, "prior-year" charges, capital gains and losses, gain or loss from the discharge of an obligation at less or more than its recorded amount, and other items worth distinguishing from those comparable with preceding periods. *Net* income (or loss) is what remains after all these items have been taken into account. Under this concept no income, expense, or loss may be credited or charged direct to earned surplus or to a contingency reserve.

16. Provisions for contingencies, general or specific, and other possible future losses are not items belonging to an income statement; on a balance sheet they are reservations of earned surplus classifiable as subdivisions of earned surplus. Related expenses and losses are not chargeable to contingency reserves but are income-statement items of the period in which they are recognized. Reserves of this character serve no useful purpose, and

they often confuse readers of financial statements. The same result can be accomplished by a simple buildup of earned surplus and an explanatory statement describing the need for retaining earnings.

17. "Reserves" should be eliminated as a separate section of the balance sheet and should be classified according to their nature—as subdivisions of earned surplus, as asset or liability valuation accounts, or as liabilities.

18. Corporate net worth (invested capital) consists of paid-in capital (stockholders' contributions) and earned surplus (retained income).

19. A reacquisition of shares of capital stock is chargeable against contributed capital in an amount not exceeding the average paid in for that class of stock, any excess of reacquisition cost being, in effect, a distribution of retained earnings. Resales are recorded in the same manner as original sales.

20. A reduction of the par or stated value of capital stock for the purpose of absorbing a deficit is a "quasi reorganization" subject to the approval of the stockholders; thereafter, earned surplus is so labeled as to indicate that it dates from the time the deficit was eliminated.

Supplemental statement 1 (1951) affirmed the previous stand on reserves, urging that the term "reserve" be abandoned.

Supplementary statement 2 (1951) affirmed the principle of historical costs as the valuation basis to be followed in financial statements. If changes were ever to be made in the future, preference for a general price index was expressed.

Supplementary statement 3 (1952) endorsed the practice of including as current assets or liabilities items likely to be liquidated or paid within the normal cycle of the business, which might extend beyond the usual determinant of one year.

Supplementary statement 4 (1952) urged amendments in the income-tax law that would eliminate or at least reduce the differences that have steadily increased in number and complexity over the years between net income for accounting purposes and taxable net income.

It is believed that these principles are now recognized as a standard by the profession. It is not the usual practice, however, to take exception to a conflicting principle where the effect is minor or the reader of the financial statement is not likely to be "misled." Thus, varied practices persist for the disposal of treasury stock, for the reason that some accountants are not yet firm enough in their belief in the universality of principle 19, above, to insist on its application to every situation. They rely, rather, upon a full disclosure of the item wherever it appears—a much less logical solution, but one that has little or no consequence on financial-statement interpretation.

There have been numerous pronouncements on accounting principles by other accounting bodies and by individual accountants. Thus the Committee on Accounting Procedure of the American Institute of Accountants over the past two decades has issued a series of statements dealing with a wide variety of practices requiring attention at the time, and many of these have had lasting effect. Originally made public in 42 separate bulletins they have been compiled in a single volume and deserve careful study.[3] They conflict with the statement of the American Accounting Association on two major issues: (a) net income is held to consist only of items pertaining to the period covered by the income statement and is conceived as a reflection of earning power; hence if "significant" the following items are to be excluded: charges or credits pertaining to preceding periods, capital gains and losses, nonrecurrent, uninsured losses, writeoffs of intangibles, writeoffs of bond discount upon refunding (bulletins 8, 32, 35, and 41); and (b) recommendation is made (bulletin 23) that the current provision for income tax be allocated to items of income (as a debit) or expense (as a credit) where such items for ordinary accounting and reporting purposes have been excluded from the income statement.

A permanent-file section may be reserved for a general statement of the client's accounting policies. In this section the auditor may set forth a summary of all principal policies, or simply:

(a) Those for which no well-established general standards exist. A characteristic example under this head are policies pertaining to fixed assets. Numerous capitalization methods are in use that in the long run do not materially affect the financial statements, particularly the income statement, for any one period, provided they have been followed consistently from year to year. Often variations in method as between different enterprises are occasioned by the lack of any generally adopted standards either because of the absence of accounting development in that direction or because the device followed simplifies the accounting process.

(b) Those that are departures from accepted standards. There are many possibilities here. For example, a coal-mining company

---

[3] *Accounting Research Bulletin No. 43*, (1953).

records depletion at the rate of five per cent of its gross business, in conformity with permissive income-tax regulations. Such a provision is a distinct departure from the usual cost basis and, in reporting that fact, the auditor should include any data that will throw light on the actual depletion that is being, or has been, sustained, thereby giving some notion of the importance of the departure.

Where approved, commonly found practices have been adopted and the records have been carefully conformed to them, the auditor's memorandum on accounting policies may be silent. Thus, the fact that the accrual basis is being followed requires no mention because the accrual basis is all but universal; any important deviation from that method, however, should be described, and a computation or other indication should be given of the practical effect on the financial statements.

Consistency in policies may continue to exist despite minor changes in method. Each year the permanent-file section on accounting policies should be corrected where necessary by a narrative added to the memorandum and a cross reference made to the matter changed.

Internal-Control Analysis

In the Illustrative Audit appears a simple form of internal-control analysis or questionnaire (PF 21-32). Its purpose is to make the client's practices with respect to the "standard" controls a matter of record. Once it is filled out, it becomes an important section of the permanent file and is modified and added to each year as may be necessary.

It will be observed that the analysis incorporates, wherever possible, usually accepted internal-control standards; if the auditor finds such standards present, he indicates a simple affirmation to that effect. Sometimes a number of standards exist any one of which may meet the demand for good controls; in such cases, the standard may be briefly described but in language that will clearly reveal its propriety or impropriety.

If at any point no commonly accepted standard is being followed, the auditor must be satisfied that the procedures in force supply controls adequate for the business; or he must seek the advice of his principal in so extending the scope of his examination as to explore the possibility of irregularities of a material character to which the existing methods may give rise. A minor weakness in internal-control methods may often be corrected at once by a suggestion from the auditor; other weaknesses may necessitate conferences with officers, followed by a memorandum to the company, particularly where serious irregularities have occurred or may occur in the future. In many instances a special letter or report, separate from the audit report, commenting on the methods of internal control, will be prepared and sent to the client. As already mentioned, this is a regular feature of the service rendered by many auditors.

A primary requirement of internal controls is that no employee having physical custody of assets should be permitted access to the books of account, and that bookkeeping controls for each principal class of assets not only should be in existence but also should in some effective manner be compared periodically with the physical existence and condition of the assets themselves. In small organizations where the division of duties necessary for internal controls cannot be made, a brief narrative covering general operating procedures may be substituted for the more formal analysis; in such cases it may be necessary that correspondence with the client confirming the audit, and the audit report as well, point out the absence of such controls and the necessarily qualified nature of the examination.

Some auditors assume that in a small enterprise (a three- or four-man office, for example) insistence on internal controls might as well be forgotten. This is a mistake. Not only does the auditor find in small offices many of the features of internal control common to larger organizations—as a consequence of the applied intelligence of a few people who are required to work closely together, but with little effort he will very likely be able to suggest other devices borrowed from larger concerns that can be employed with equal effectiveness.[4]

In his review of internal controls, the auditor's findings must result from his personal, firsthand observations. Statements made to him by the client's employees, especially supervisors and executives, will have to be put to practical test if facts, rather than allegations, are to be truly recorded. The experienced auditor not infrequently finds an accounting or other procedural manual out of date, unenforceable, or not understood by those very persons to whom it was designed to apply. He knows also that nearly all well-designed and carefully installed procedures change over

---

[4] See, for example, comments on this point in Chapter 16, "Reliance on Internal Control," *CPA Handbook* (New York: American Institute of Accountants, 1953), p. 17.

the course of time and that an annual procedural review may bring to light modifications of importance concerning which the accounting principals of the organization have no knowledge.

Standards referred to in the illustrative internal-control analysis are intended to be typical minimum requirements for the business of average size; frequently, especially in larger enterprises, these standards may have to be altered or increased, or there may be activities for which further standards may have to be devised and enforced. This means that the auditor must not regard these standards as a maximum of desirable procedures; he should supplement them with an active imagination that is alive to the best modern business methods, the needs of good management within a particular organization, and the ways and means of bringing the two together.

Illustrative Audit

The internal-control forms (PF 21-32) are reviewed by the auditor at the outset of the engagement. He bears in mind the internal-control highspots as he comes into contact with the company's personnel and records. His review of internal controls for the current year may take place at one time, preferably before the year end, or it may be scattered through the audit as the different items are examined, before or after the year end. In a first audit, as stated on a previous page, the former method is always preferable. Where a similar examination has been made the year before by the same auditor, the relation of internal controls to audit scope will have been well established, and any major change in internal controls will in most cases be known in advance of the audit, thus permitting changes in the audit plan where that seems desirable. In such event, the determination of whether established internal controls have been maintained during the year is likely to be spread over successive audit steps.

It is the practice of a number of public-accounting firms to require that an internal-control "questionnaire" be filled out for each client. The author has found that where the questionnaire is elaborate or is to be made out each year, the answers tend to be weak. The kind of internal control referred to in the auditor's standard form of certificate is generally understood to be of the broadest variety, extending to many aspects of the business and closely related to top-management policies; hence, an internal-control outline or "questionnaire" should be—and, if it is to be given a conscientious annual going-over, *must* be—very brief and phrased in very general, yet pointed, terms. An attempt along this line has been made in the character of the information furnished on worksheet pages PF 21-32. However, as already noted, the form of analysis used here is effective for the enterprise of average size and complexity. Larger enterprises, or very small ones, might require other types of writeups.

INTERNAL CONTROLS

I. GENERAL

1. General nature of internal-audit system in use *An internal auditor, Carl Hibbs, spends the bulk of his time on reviews of cash receipts and disbursements, bank reconciliations, factory accounts, receivables, and payables.*

2.
Employees handling cash or securities or signing checks or notes	Operation	Amount of bond
Andrew R. Fisher	cashier	$25,000
Frank Markham	asst. ✓	25,000

3. Access to securities may be had only by two or more employees acting jointly ☒ Yes   No ☐

Location of securities	Employees who have access
Howard National Bank	J. B. Huddle
Jackson National Bank	John Sutherland
	Arthur P. Collins
	B. G. Hanson
	any two acting jointly

PF-21

4. Exceptions to standard that employees having responsibilities relating to cash, receivables, and payrolls are rotated or take annual vacations:

Name of employee	Position	Year
none		

II. CASH RECEIPTS

1. List of incoming receipts is prepared and such list is thereafter independently compared with cashbook entries ☐ Yes No ☒ ; *all
receipts from customers by check; checks are sent by mail
clerk to cashier who keeps cash-receipts book and makes
deposits*

2. One employee makes cashbook entries; another makes up deposit slip; a
third posts to ledgers ☐ Yes No ☒ ; *deposit slip made by
cashier; cash receipts posted to ledgers from cash-receipts
book by bookkeeper*

3. Receipts are deposited intact daily ☒ Yes No ☐ ; _____

4. Collectors are rotated ☐ Yes No ☐ ; further safeguards:_____
        no collectors

5. Proceeds of cash sales are_____
        no cash sales except for scrap

PF-22

6. Income from rents, sales of scrap, and miscellaneous sources is scheduled by *no schedule prepared* and receipts are safeguarded by *receipts (in check form only) recorded and deposited, like other receipts, by cashier*

III. CASH DISBURSEMENTS

1. Petty cash is maintained on an imprest basis ☒ Yes No ☐ ; _____

2. Disbursements, except from petty cash, are made by check ☒ Yes No ☐ ;

3. Personal checks of employees or others, if cashed as accommodation, have cleared promptly ☒ Yes No ☐ ; _____

4. Payroll and other advances to employees are authorized by_____
    H. J. Flood, personnel-relations officer, or John Burt, asst. plant manager

5. Reimbursements to salesmen and other employees for expenses are approved by *J. B. Huddle, treasurer*

6. Checks are prenumbered and fully accounted for ☐ Yes No ☒ ; *they are numbered as used (general account); and prenumbered (payroll account)*

7. Checks are signed or countersigned at the time of payment; never in advance ☒ Yes No ☐ ; *Checks on general account prepared by voucher clerk*

8. Nature of document inspection by those who sign and countersign checks:
    ordinary vouchers examined for propriety and completeness by treasurer or asst. treasurer following their approval by Stanley Rohr, voucher clerk; in the case of payroll checks following approval of payrolls by controller or asst. controller

PF-23

_F.L._

9. Vouchers are audited by _voucher clerk_ who has neither purchasing nor disbursing functions ☒ Yes No ☐ ; _____

10. Safeguards against payments of same or duplicate invoices: _(1) creditor index which supplements voucher record   (2) receipt - and - inspection forms attached to voucher and canceled along with voucher by a perforating machine._

11. Bank balances are reconciled by employees having no other duties con-
nected with cash ☐ Yes No ☒ ; _reconciled by cashier; reviewed by internal auditor and by controller at year end; internal - audit program calls for monthly review_

12. Verification of canceled checks consists of _examination (by person other than cashier designated by controller) of signatures and comparison with check record, with checkmark of different color for each month of year_

IV. PAYROLLS

1. An individual record is maintained under careful control showing original and subsequent wage rates for each employee ☒ Yes No ☐

2. Wage rates are approved by _plant manager under personnel-classi-fication plan approved by board of directors_

3. Time is recorded on clock cards ☒ Yes No ☐ , job tickets ☒ Yes No ☐ ;
clock cards are checked against job tickets ☒ Yes No ☐ ; _____

4. Review of payroll after its preparation and before payment takes place
consists of _comparison by asst. controller against addresso-graph authorizations and factory labor-cost summary prepared by cost clerk. Office salary roll prepared on pre-determined-total basis, changes being authorized only by cont. or asst._

5. Employees' compensation is paid by ☐ cash or check ☒ , and distribution is made by persons other than those who prepare payroll or write
checks ☒ Yes No ☐ ; _____

PF-24

6. Payroll is signed by employees ☐ Yes No ☒ ; receipts are taken ☐ Yes No ☒ ; *signature on check deemed sufficient*

7. Unclaimed wages are *turned over to asst. controller for disposal*

8. Procedure followed in purchasing and delivering ~~war~~ savings bonds: *savings-bond clerk keeps subsidiary ledger on Burroughs machine, posted from payroll detail; she also purchases and distributes bonds*

9. Safeguards surrounding other payroll deductions: *other deductions reviewed monthly by personnel director who makes detailed audit of one payroll each quarter except for extensions and footings.*

V. RECEIVABLES

1. Controlling accounts are maintained ☒ Yes No ☐

2. They are balanced monthly with detail ledgers ☒ Yes No ☐

3. Bookkeepers on receivable ledgers are rotated ☐ Yes No ☒
   2 bookkeepers work interchangeably

4. Routine for sales orders:

   Price *approved and initialed by sales department*

   Credit ✓ ✓ ✓ ✓ *credit manager*

   Stock *checked by clerk in stockroom 4*

   Production order *initiated by John Burt, asst. plant mgr.*

5. Verification of and control over sales invoices:

   Price *compared by invoice clerk with original approved sales order*

   Terms *compared by invoice clerk with original approved sales order*

   Quantities *evidenced by packing slips, shipping tickets, receipt of customer, or other outgoing receipt*

PF-25

Clerical accuracy _initials of invoice clerk's supervisor appear on each invoice, indicating clerical accuracy_

Issue of invoice numbers _controlled by controller's office; a new block of numbers is issued each month; completeness of sequence of numbers used tested by internal auditor_

6. Statements are prepared monthly ☐ Yes No ☒ ; _reliance is had on invoices only_

7. Employees other than ledger bookkeepers compare statements with ledger balances and mail them ☐ Yes No ☐ ; _no statements_

8. Complaints or other communications from customers are sent from mail room to _sales manager_

9. At intervals of _30 days_ reports of past-due balances are given to _treasurer and credit manager_

10. Bad-debt chargeoffs are approved by _Treasurer_ upon recommendation of _assistant controller_

11. Charged-off bad debts are under the control of _treasurer_

12. Notes receivable and related collateral are in the custody of _treasurer_

13. Partial payments are endorsed on notes ☒ Yes No ☐ ; _____

14. Controls over returns and discounts and other credits to customers: _any special allowances not covered by original sales agreement are approved by sales manager and reviewed each month by controller_

VI. INVENTORIES

1. A purchase order is prepared in advance for each purchase ☒ Yes No ☐ ;

it is approved by _purchasing agent and department head_

2. Purchase-order copy sent to receiving clerk omits quantities ☐ Yes No ☒ ; _frequent tests are made by asst. controller to make sure positive counts are made_

3. Receiving tickets are prepared for all classes of materials ☒ Yes No ☐

PF-26

-141-

4. Inspections for quality and quantity are made by _H. A. Conway, materials inspector_

5. Copies of purchase order and receiving ticket are compared with and attached to invoice by _voucher clerk_ before voucher is paid
☒ Yes No ☐ ; _____

6. Prices, terms, discount, and quantities shown on invoice are verified by _voucher clerk_

7. Extensions and footings are verified by _voucher clerk_

8. Invoices are approved for record by _asst. controller_ and for payment by _treasurer_

9. Method by which assurance is given that liability for or payment of items included in inventory, in materials used, or in cost of goods sold has been recorded, is: _receiving report prepared for all materials received – Receiving reports are prenumbered and all accounted for. At end of period liability is set up for receiving reports not matched with invoices._

10. Freight and ———————————, representing additional costs of materials are included in unit costs of inventory items ☒ Yes No ☐ ;
_____

11. Controls over materials returned to and credits received from suppliers: _materials returned are billed to suppliers at cost and credited to purchases and accounts payable debited._

12. Procedure for establishing and revising minima and maxima controls: _Set by asst. factory superintendent — changed when bills of material are revised._

13. Perpetual-inventory records showing quantities ☐ or quantities and costs ☒ , are maintained for _supplies only; annual physical inventory taken of other inventory items_

_____

_____

_____

_____

PF-27

14. Perpetual inventories are compared with actual counts by *storekeeper and internal auditor* at least once during *each year* ; differences are disposed of by *charge to cost of sales*

15. Materials are issued from stores only on requisition ☒ Yes No☐ ; ___

16. Instructions govern the taking of physical inventories ☒ Yes No☐ and are under the control of *controller*

17. The issue of count cards is controlled ☒ Yes No☐

18. The original count is verified by *different inventory crew*

19. The year-end inventory count is supervised by *single individual* and pricing by *same*

20. Percentage adjustment of book inventory to agree with physical inventory was (show + or - before %): year *1950* *+1%*; year *1951* *+1%*; year *1952* *-2%*; year _____.

21. Detail of work-in-process is adjusted to physical count ☒Yes No☐

22. Consignments from others are omitted from inventory totals ☐ Yes No☐ ; _____ *none*

23. Consignments to others are included in inventory totals ☐ Yes No☐ ; _____ *none*

24. Warehouse stocks are controlled by _____ *none*

25. Shipments charged to customers are omitted from physical inventories ☒ Yes No☐ because *of well-established cutoff procedure which we review each year*

26. Scrap of materials is authorized by *George Shuffle, plant mgr.* _____ and is accounted for by *scrap tickets numbered serially*

PF-28

VII. FIXED ASSETS

1. A plant ledger is maintained ☒ Yes No ☐

2. The acquisition or construction of new plant and equipment is authorized by *a committee appointed by Board consisting of president, controller, and plant manager; a requisition or work order is signed by the president.*

3. The existence of items shown in the plant records is verified ☒ Yes No ☐ with a frequency of *several years. In 1952 detailed comparison was made except for patterns and furniture + fixtures.*

4. Excess equipment consists of *none, 1950, 1951, 1952*

5. Title of all plant items is in company's name ☒ Yes No ☐ ; _____

6. Propriety of balances of reserves for depreciation is tested by the client as follows: *Each year experience reviewed on different class of fixed assets; see J-2 in each year's papers.*

VIII. PAYABLES

1. Procedure followed monthly and at year end by client in making sure that obligations to trade creditors are complete: *cutoff procedure is reasonably complete — see F-6 in 1950 papers*

2. Methods for insuring that all accruals have been made are: *a check list is maintained by controller which is reviewed each month by him.*

PF-29

IX. LONG-TERM DEBT

1. Provisions in indenture or other loan agreement requiring annual review (i.e., limitation on use of funds, on other borrowings, or on dividends; working-capital requirements) are: *"working capital, as the term is generally used in accounting, shall be maintained in an amount not less than $500,000". This requirement has always been met. No other requirement in indenture.*

2. Procedure governing redemption: *to be made by S.F. trustee at rate of $20,000 per annum and by open-market purchases; see PF-88-89. See also S-1 to S-4 (1952).*

3. Method of paying interest: *a check is issued semiannually (Jan. 2 and July 1) to Liberty National Bank, trustee*

X. NET WORTH

1. Method of control over stock outstanding (where no registrar): *registrar does this (Harris Trust & Savings Bank)*

2. Surplus limitations imposed by agreements with stockholders: *none*

3. Controls over payments of dividends: *preferred dividend, cumulative and preferred in liquidation, limited to 5% per annum*

4. Authority for and purpose of nonvaluation reserves: *only such item is pension reserve — see PF-82-83.*

PF-30

C.R.S.
3-14-46

The company's costing methods have been simple, and, although there has been considerable discussion of changing over to a full-fledged system of standard costs, little has been accomplished in developing the idea. Shop orders are issued for each factory "run"; material and direct-labor costs (the latter from payroll distributions) are posted to shop-order forms promptly; average unit costs are worked out at the conclusion of the run and these are kept in a "unit-cost book" maintained by the controller; but no attempt is made to tie the total costs shown on the completed shop orders to general-ledger accounts. As we pointed out in our 1943 and 1944 reports to the company, this could be done without much extra work. We have also recommended the adoption of a standard-cost system, accompanied by a care-fully worked-out plan for the monthly review of variances. The unit costs now obtained--which serve as a basis for determining costs of sales on monthly worksheets--are sub-ject to the qualification that they are average unit costs, not modified by any fifo concept except at the end of the year when the physical inventory is priced. At each year end the amounts on hand are priced according to the aver-ages derived from the latest completed work orders on a true fifo basis.

Because overhead constitutes less than 25% (1941-1945) of total factory costs--since so large a part of factory operations is assembly--we have not regarded the rate of overhead as a serious problem. In computing unit costs, overhead has been figured in consistently as 50% of direct-labor cost, and, in total each year, this relationship has been close. Our recommendation that service-center-cost accounts (see p. 8 of draft of report to management) be established is the first step in getting at the possible modification of the 50% overhead rate in accordance with the varied amounts of work performed on shop orders by these centers. In our conversations with Mr. Johnson, the cost clerk, a likely range, overall, of 40-65% would be estab-lished. An increase or decrease of 10% in the ratio to direct labor would have the average effect of 5% on total product cost, but since total cost of overhead will prob-ably remain at its present level in relation to total dir-ect labor, the effect on the year-end inventory would be small. However, our argument has been that the main reason for refining the overhead rate is to get at more accurate unit costs, especially now that competition must again be reckoned with.

jr

PF-31

Additional notes on costs (1952). Since the preceding
was written two trends have developed that have curbed further experimentation with standard costs: more parts formerly
manufactured by the company are now being purchased from outsiders, further simplifying operations and reducing the ratio
of overhead to direct-labor costs (in 1945 around 50%; in
1952 less than 40%), and the growing disparity between the
ratios of prime cost to selling price among the several types
of factory output. The management has tended to think in
this connection in terms of (a) <u>direct</u> cost--i.e., cost
that could be dispensed with if a product or operation were
discontinued, and (b) contributions--determined as a top-
management policy rather than as a cost allocation--that
products should make (however unequally) to the recovery
of fixed factory costs and selling & general overhead. In
TB-4 of the 1952 working papers appears for the first time
a segregation of factory costs between fixed and variable
as the management has viewed it; for comparative purposes
1951 costs were rearranged in the new form. There are, of
course, a number of arbitrary features in this segregation:
e.g., the rough 50-50 split of supervision and factory ex-
pense--the latter a catchall that should be broken down by
the costs of the operating units of which it is composed.
In 1953 we have a promise that so far as possible an operat-
ing-center or activity concept will be experimented with
whereby the responsibility for each direct cost will be
charged in the first instance to the center or activity unit
at which the cost is incurred. There will probably be 20
or more of these units each headed by some person at a
supervisory level and for 1954 a goal of performance and
limitations on the character and amount of each class of
cost each such person will be permitted to incur will be
established by a team consisting of the factory manager,
controller, and the unit head himself, the "team" thus varying with each unit. In each case the "goal" will include
some attainable standard of performance including a number
of elements--wherever possible of quality, quantity, and
unit-cost objectives. The budget will be "personalized"--
i.e., for the factory, broken down primarily in terms of the
units and unit heads where and upon whom responsibility
for costs is to devolve, and secondarily by objects of expenditure for each unit--with certain latitudes to be extended to the unit head as an incentive to good management.
During 1953 we are to be called upon to review the proposed
features of the plan as they are developed. The general objective has been stated to be: to spread variable costs--
more or less as they are now constituted--in such a manner
that they will be kept to a minimum and contribute measur-
able performances to the production objectives of the plant
as a whole.

jr

PF-32

p. 1 of 2

Original entry

Cash-receipts book   Payroll record
Check register   General journal
Accounts-payable register   Booking sheets (bkpg machine)

Final entry

General ledger: Contains real and nominal accounts required
for overall statement purposes; supported by subsidiary ledgers

Investment ledger: Separate sheet for each type of security showing –
    Carrying value (cost or amortized cost)
    Dividends or interest, in latter case less purchased interest
    Accrued interest receivable – year end only.
    Sales
    Gain or loss on sales

Notes-receivable register: Separate sheet for each note showing
dates and amounts of individual maturities opposite each of
which collections of principal and interest are posted, the
latter serving as partial support for a/c 782, other interest earned.
Accrued interest recorded only at year end.

Accounts-receivable ledger: Three trays of ledger sheets maintained
on bookkeeping machine; proof sheets of individual postings
accumulated for each class of item and for each tray, are
posted monthly (in total) to tray-control cards and general ledger.
Balances of accounts in each tray balanced monthly against
tray-control card, and total of three cards against general-
ledger control account. Accounts with employees including
advances for expenses, advance payments by customers
appear as a matter of convenience in this ledger but are reclassified when financial statements are prepared. Posting mediums:
    Ditto copy of sales order   Journal vouchers for
    " " " credit memo   Writeoff
    Remittance advice   Transfer of past-due note
    Carbon copy of check covering   Approved travel expenditure
    refund or travel advance

PF-36

Supplies-inventory record: Separate card for each item of supplies showing stock number, description, bin number, minimum and maximum quantities, quantities (with dollar amounts) ordered, received, issued, on hand, and ordered but not received. Receipts posted from receiving ticket, withdrawals from requisitions priced, extended and footed by stock-records clerk; cost clerk tests clerical accuracy and maintains requisitions journal. Dollar balances taped monthly and compared with general-ledger control.

Property ledger: Nine subdivisions to correspond with general-ledger accounts. Sheet or card for each unit of property showing description, source, manufacturer's serial number, and location in plant. Costs taped about once quarterly and balanced against general-ledger controls.

Three expense ledgers (factory, selling, general): Postings from accounts-payable vouchers and journal vouchers; taped monthly and balanced against general-ledger controls.

Employees earnings record: Payroll check, payroll record and earnings record produced or posted in one operation. This record supplies detail and total on quarterly and annual reports including state unemployment, FICA returns & contributions, W-2's covering tax withheld.

Accounts payable: Voucher register – usual form and chronological entries; open items taped monthly and balanced against general ledger.

Employees bond-payment record: Individual accounts for each employee purchasing U.S. Savings Bonds on payroll-deduction plan. Payroll deductions are posted from payroll recap via bookkeeping machine. Charges against individual accounts for twice-monthly deliveries of bonds. General-ledger control supported by total of individual accounts less bonds purchased but not yet delivered to employees.

Income:
1. On sales to the Cleveland subsidiary the 10% profit additive is recognized as earned by the parent only when realized as a sale by the subsidiary; the balance remaining appears in the reserve for intercompany profit which on the parent company's balance sheet is a reduction of the amount due from the subsidiary. The adjustment because of the subsidiary's sales is made at the year end.
2. Cash sales are processed in the same manner as charge sales, except that the invoice mailed to the customer is marked paid.
3. Dittoed copies of approved sales orders serve as
   Invoice
   Posting medium
   Packing slip
   Shipping ticket (or receipt)
   Basis for sales statistics
4. Checks accompanied by invoice are received through mail for scrap sales.

Costs and expenses:
1. Costs of product design and product development are expensed currently.
2. Fixed overhead is expensed as a period cost (commencing in 1952).

General:
Accounts are maintained on the accrual basis except as noted in paragraphs below.

Assets--
  Cash:
1. Weekly transfers are made of round amounts approximating the net cash payroll from the general bank account (01-1) to the payroll back account (01-2).
2. Receipts are deposited daily.
3. The petty-cash fund is reimbursed at irregular intervals.
  Investments:
1. Premiums on U. S. Government securities are amortized to the earliest optional maturity date; discounts on such securities are amortized to the maturity date.
2. Investments in stocks are carried at original cost; a reserve is employed, when necessary, to reduce the cost of stocks and the amortized cost of bonds to a lower market value.
3. Investment in subsidiary is carried at original cost; income on parent company's books recognized upon receipt of cash dividends.
4. Cost of securities sold is determined by use of fifo.
5. Dividends on minority holdings are recorded as income in the year received.
  Receivables:
1. Customers are billed as goods are shipped.
2. Terms of sales on account are 2% 30 days, net 60, except on government contracts which are billed net. No installment or conditional sales. No trade or volume discounts.
3. Extended-payment sales are made net and are represented by notes which are unsecured or secured by chattel mortgage.
4. All shipments made FOB shipping point via public carrier or customer's conveyance.
5. Past-due notes are transferred to accounts receivable.
6. Accounts-receivable ledger includes accounts with customers, officers and employees, and others. Advance collections on sales contracts are carried as credits in this ledger awaiting offsetting charges for shipments.
7. Accounts with individual employees are charged with travel advances and credited through the general journal for audited expenditures.

PF - 38

-150-

8. Uncollectible notes and accounts are charged against the reserve for bad debts and recoveries are credited to this account. The year-end balance is based on graduated percentages applied to account-receivable balances classified by age, plus estimated losses on individual notes receivable. No reserve is now provided on officers, employee and sundry receivables.
9. Accruals of interest on notes and investment are adjusted once annually at the year end.
10. Sales invoices are analyzed monthly by sales department to show quantity and amount of sales of each item in each line. Small-equipment sales shown in dollars only. Incomplete analysis made of returns and allowances.
11. Sales discounts recognized as expense in period of collection of customer's account.

Inventories:
1. Inventories of raw material, purchased parts, work in process, finished goods and merchandise purchased are determined by annual physical count at end of fiscal year. These are priced at cost on the first-in-first-out basis or market if lower. Work in process and finished stock are priced at direct cost consisting of material, labor and variable overhead, the latter applied on the basis of a percentage of direct-labor cost.
2. In classifying overhead into variable and fixed categories, arbitrary divisions of one-half each are made for supervision and shop expense.
3. Supplies are under perpetual-inventory control. Individual stock cards show units and amounts. Amounts proved monthly with general-ledger control. Withdrawals priced on fifo basis. Quantity balances counted during year and corrected immediately. Obsolete items written off during year following counts and other studies of individual items. Balances on stock cards taped to support amounts listed on year-end-inventory summary.
4. Markdowns of work in process and of finished goods to expected realization are reflected on inventory-reduction sheets included with physical inventory; no reserves provided.
5. Basis of inventory pricing for slow-moving purchased parts:
   2/3 of original cost--for items 1 year old
   1/3 of original cost--for items 2 years old
   0 of original cost--for items 3 years old (listed but not extended)
6. Unit inventory prices are invoice prices unadjusted for freight and cash discount.

Fixed assets:
1. Fixed assets are recorded at cost. Acquisitions from predecessor corporation were made at cost to predecessor less recorded accrued depreciation.
2. Cost of facilities constructed by the company includes no overhead.
3. Additions, betterments and improvements are capitalized.
4. Repairs and maintenance costs including costs offsetting accrued depreciation are charged to expense.
5. Asset accounts are relieved of retirements at original cost as shown on plant-ledger sheet or card.
6. Capitalizable items of less than $25 are expensed.
7. Construction-in-progress account serves to control work orders covering constructed facilities and retirements.

Reserves for depreciation:
1. Fixed assets are depreciated on a straight-line basis at the following rates:

	Annual rate
Buildings--	
Foundry	3%
Factory	2%
Office	2%
Machinery and equipment--	
Foundry	4%
Factory	5%
Patterns and flasks	10%
Furniture and fixtures	5%
Trucks and automobiles	20-33 1/3%

PF - 39

2. Buildings, and machinery and equipment are depreciated at composite rates applied to balances at the beginning of the year. Upon retirement of individual items no gain or loss is recognized. Reserve account for each asset is charged with original cost of items sold or retired and credited with salvage less cost of removal. Engineering studies are made periodically to determine reasonableness of composite rates.

3. Lapsing schedule maintained for furniture and fixtures to permit depreciation of annual additions at 5% per annum. The reserve is relieved of accrued depreciation on items sold or retired and the gain or loss is carried to office expense (a/c 278-4).

4. Units of trucks and automobiles are depreciated at individual rates ranging from 20% to 33 1/3% applied to original cost less estimated salvage. Gain or loss on disposition of trucks is carried to shop expense (a/c 2443) and on disposition of automobiles to automobile (selling) expense (a/c 2724).

5. Depreciation recorded in accounts agrees with that deducted on Federal income-tax returns.

Liabilities--

1. Liability for raw materials and other tangibles are recorded in the period received. No attempt is made to record liability for items in transit.

2. All major accruals are recorded monthly. Liabilities for items such as water, light, power, telephone and a few others are recorded in the period billed. Interest accrued on notes payable is adjusted at the year end. Liability for Federal income tax is recorded at year end. Estimated amounts appear on monthly financial statements.

3. Trade accounts are recorded at their gross amount, cash discount being recognized as income on date of payment.

4. Liability for bond-purchase payroll deductions at any one time is partially offset by purchased bonds on hand not yet delivered to employees. These are limited to $25-50-100 denominations.

5. Pension-fund obligation consists of original $50,000 contribution by company plus voluntary contributions by employees based on tables and equal contributions by the company less postretirement pay to pensioners. Tests will be made from time to time of adequacy of remaining balance.

BB:jr
3-23-53

PF - 40

Problems and Questions

1. After careful study of the twenty accounting principles of the American Accounting Association, name and discuss briefly the five most important ones that you would like to see adopted by business enterprise generally.

2. A number of the principles referred to in the preceding question are often grouped under a single head and referred to as "the cost principle." Define "the cost principle" as best you can in a brief paragraph, without repeating any of the phrases of the statement of principles.

3. The general manager of a manufacturing plant tells you that he has general, staff, and departmental assistants. Contrast their probable functions.

4. Professional accountants often say that the strongest link in a system of internal controls is a good controller. What are the principal administrative abilities they are likely to hope to find in him?

5. The New York Stock Exchange recommends that the controller be appointed by and report to the board of directors. What possible conflict with the general manager may this direct relationship cause?

. 6. The controller of a large manufacturing enterprise explains to you that each of five fully owned subsidiary companies has a controller who is "functionally" responsible to him and "administratively" responsible to the individual company head. Describe the meaning of this relationship.

7. What elements do you think a controller's internal reporting and external reporting should have in common?

8. Has a controller who reports to the president been given "responsibility without authority" where the salary scale of his assistants is established by a personnel division whose head reports to the vice-president and general manager?

9. Sometimes the professional auditor will find accounting policies being established by committees within the accounting division of large organizations. What do you imagine are the advantages and disadvantages of this procedure, as compared with policy-forming by the controller alone or in consultation with other top-management officials?

10. What are the principal responsibilities that you would like to see given to an internal auditor?

11. Systems of cash controls often provide for bank reconciliations by employees having no other responsibility for cash. Would you regard this as a proper function for the internal auditor?

12. How may the professional accountant cooperate with the work being done by the internal auditor on his client's staff?

13. Why are good internal controls of primary importance to the auditor?

14. Outline the elements of internal control you would regard as essential to the effective operation of the receiving division of a factory.

15. Distinguish between "principle" and "policy" as applied to the accounting practices of a business enterprise.

16. Why does it often happen that the auditor finds operating policies in conflict with management policies?

17. Contrast the meaning of "internal control" and "internal check" and secure, where possible, an independent definition for each term from other texts or from some outside source.

18. What do you understand by the following expressions:

   (a)   Stock control by proxies

   (b)   Minority-stockholder interest

   (c)   A conflict of interests in a board of directors dominated by management

   (d)   A rubber-stamp board of directors

19. Name a number of accounting policies that, in your opinion, might well be adopted by the top management of a business and with which it should be familiar at all times.

20. "Jurisdictional problems" are frequent recurrences in almost every top-management organization. What are their nature and origin?

21. Expand on the meaning of the statement, ". . . conflicts with . . . the beliefs or habits of individuals may operate to decrease, modify, or even destroy the original intent [of business policies and controls]."

CHAPTER V

Operations

A review of the management characteristics of an organization, such as that described in the preceding chapter, prepares the auditor for probing more deeply and understandingly into what has taken place on the operational level and to recognize and interpret—as he must—the main events, both ordinary and extraordinary, for the audit period. Thus far only the formal pattern of the organization has been under consideration: the combination of individuals and resources that makes possible the orderly consummation of transactions. Policies and their origins, along with the institution and maintenance of the controls necessary to their enforcement, have been reviewed.

By "operations" is meant the activities of the organization reflected in the income statement: revenues from all sources, and costs (expenses and losses) of carrying on the business that are judged not to be recoverable from future revenues. Costs of assets purchased and of plant-construction activities (also occasionally classified as "operation") are covered in subsequent chapters.

Certain revenues and costs are omitted from present consideration because of their close association with various assets and liabilities. Thus, maintenance and depreciation are discussed in Chapter X (Fixed Assets), material costs in Chapter VIII (Inventories), sales (in part) and bad debts in Chapter VII (Receivables), and expense accruals in Chapter XII (Liabilities). For the same reason, in practical audit procedures operating costs are not taken up in the order of their appearance in the income statement, nor are they studied all at one time. They are considered as the opportunity presents itself, frequently in conjunction with examinations of related balance-sheet items. In fact, rare is the balance-sheet item that does not somehow involve operations.

The auditor's objective in his review of the income statement
is to determine the "fairness" of the presentation of the operating
results for the period. This he does by testing the accuracy of
recorded revenues and expenses, by appraising them in terms of
goals established for the year and in comparison with performances of other years, and by reviewing operating details with
officials and employees.

Principles and Practices

Revenues. Revenues are amounts received and receivable from
any source as the result of marketing goods or rendering services
to *outsiders.* By "outsider" is meant one who bears an arm's-
length relationship to the business and whose payment for the
goods or service comes from a source independent of the business.
Revenue to the organization as an economic unit does not arise
from the attachment of a market price to a departmental output
nor from an increase in the possible disposal price or replacement
cost of an investment or other asset. Amounts representing
market prices of departmental outputs as yet unsold should be
reduced to cost when financial statements are prepared.

"Sales" means revenues from the disposal of goods normally
dealt in by the business. It may also include revenues from
services rendered, although it is somewhat more common to
designate such amounts as "operating revenues" (as do transportation companies and power and other utilities). A sale is
recognized and recorded when title passes and goods change
hands. There are some exceptions. For example, revenue from
a construction contract is usually held to arise at agreed points
(that is, monthly or at certain stages of completion) at which
time partial-completion payments become due. Another example
is found in installment accounts where the buyer does not
ordinarily acquire title until his payments have been completed:
revenue is often recognized prorata as individual payments are
received. In some instances, as in casual sales of property, an
account with the purchaser may be of unknown collectibility,
thus warranting the adoption of the "cost-recovery" basis, all
receipts being credited against book value until the latter has
been absorbed, receipts thereafter constituting revenue.

"Other revenue" (or "other income") is the general designation of revenue from minor activities of the business; as, interest
on customers' notes and installment accounts: dividends and

interest from temporary or incidental investments; gains from the disposal of assets other than inventory. Interest is accrued, or recognized as revenue when actually received: either method being acceptable to the auditor as long as the amount is small in proportion to net income from all sources. Dividends may be recognized as income when declared or, like interest, not be recorded by the recipient until reduced to cash. Where material in amount, interest should be accrued and dividends accounted for as declared. Further principles relating to these items appear in subsequent chapters.

Cost of sales. Conceptually, cost of sales consists of direct labor, material, and assigned overhead pertaining to the acquisition and processing of the items appearing under sales. In a merchandising organization, this will consist of invoice cost less discounts, returns, and other cost reductions, plus freight and sometimes storage costs; in a manufacturing establishment, in addition to the material and labor costs going into finished product, factory overhead may be allocated between goods sold and those still on hand on any of numerous bases.

There has been in many instances a tendency to combine on the income statement costs of sales and all operating costs, on the theory that as commonly determined cost of sales has little meaning. For example, the allocation of factory overhead is often incomplete, certain items such as depreciation expense and other "fixed" costs being shown in the income statement as separate items and thus as period costs. Occasionally the entire amount of factory overhead is treated as a period charge. The effect on income may be minor if the overhead applicable to inventory at the beginning of the year has the effect of offsetting a similar allocation to product on hand at the end of the year. Again, the amount of a reduction by which the cost of a closing inventory is reduced to market is held by some accountants to be in the nature of a financial expense that should be separately disclosed in the income statement. Similarly, where during a period of rising prices the lifo method has been applied in costing sales, the cost-of-sales item in the income statement is burdened with an excess of cost (lifo cost less fifo cost), which many accountants hold should be separately reported. Another example may be found in the disposition of development expense—costs of experimental work leading to new methods, components, or products, or costs of opening up mineral properties and timber lands, drilling oil wells, and the like. Such expenses may be capitalized and written off at a fixed rate per unit of product or over a limited initial period of operations, or they may be written off as incurred. In recent years the tendency has been to write off such costs immediately in view of the indefinite and intangible character of any amount that might be carried forward, and high taxes have stimulated this movement. Other examples may be found in costs of maintenance when separately displayed—as in income statements of utilities— and in property and other taxes where these items are featured in the income statement.

Cost of sales does have statistical value, however, if computed consistently from year to year in accordance with established procedures, and many accountants follow the practice of footnoting the items included therein that might be separately displayed. Thus if operating expenses appear on an income statement in a half-dozen or more functional divisions of cost, depreciation expense may be present in each of them, and a footnote bringing out the total of such expense becomes a useful device.

Operating cost (or expense). Broadly, the term "operating cost" is applied to all outlays appearing in the income statement excepting, perhaps, income deductions as described below. In particular instances it has been observed as a caption that excludes cost of sales, income taxes, and income deductions; as thus employed it consists of selling and administrative expense, and depreciation and other items separated out from cost of sales. Selling expense includes salesmen's salaries, commissions, travel, and entertainment costs, general sales overhead, and advertising. Administrative expense is made up of such items as the compensation and expenses of top management, the accounting department, the treasurer's office, and legal and auditing fees.

Income deductions (or adjustments). Income deductions are expenses and losses recognized as belonging to the current year but of a character that warrants their exclusion from operating costs. Like other expenses they are outlays necessarily incurred in the current conduct of the business and are thus regarded as necessary charges in arriving at net income. But they are more in the nature of costs imposed from without rather than costs subject to the controls exercised through everyday operating procedures. They are made up of such items as interest, amortized debt discount, income taxes, losses from sales or closings of plants and branches and from other major property disposals, carrying charges on inactive property, prior-year adjustments as for additional income taxes, charges to contingency reserves, bonus and profit distributions to officers and employees, writeoffs of intangibles, major changes in accounting procedures as in inventory-valuation methods, casualty losses, and losses on foreign exchange. If any such item is both material and non-recurring and its inclusion in the income statement would "seriously distort earning power" the Committee on Accounting Procedure of the American Institute of Accountants (Bulletin 32 [1947]) would permit a direct charge to earned surplus, thereby increasing current net income. The practice supported in the 1946 Statement of Principles of the American Accounting Association (with which the author is in agreement), is to include these items in the income statement—but in a specially designated final section—thereby leaving a "clean" earned-surplus account.

Income taxes. For most business corporations, the figure of income tax in its income statement is the amount of Federal income and profits taxes shown on its tax return for the current year, along with adjustments arising during the year in connection with prior-year returns. Although this represents what appears to be the better practice as well as the practice generally followed,considerable impetus has been given in recent years to the allocation of that portion of the tax accrual pertaining to each material difference existing between book net income before tax and taxable income. There are six types of items making up such a difference, each affecting the current year's tax accrual: (1) charges and (2) credits to surplus; deferrals on the books of (3) revenue or (4) expense, where any of these items must be included in the computation of taxable income; and (5) income or (6) expense appearing in the income statement but taxable or deductible for income-tax purposes in some preceding or subsequent period. For example, assuming a flat tax rate of 40%, net income per books of $100,000, and a credit of $10,000 to earned surplus that must be included in computing net taxable income, an allocation to earned surplus of $4,000 would be made of the tax payable, thus:

Income-tax expense	$40,000	
Earned surplus	4,000	
Taxes payable		$44,000
Accrual of income tax at 40% on net income of $100,000 and credit to surplus of $10,000		

Again, assuming the same tax rate, net income per books of $100,000, a deferral for balance-sheet purposes of certain overhaul costs of $10,000 which may be immediately deducted for tax purposes, the deferral would be decreased $4,000 as the result of the following accrual:

Income-tax expense	$40,000	
Deferred overhaul costs		$ 4,000
Taxes payable		36,000

Accrual of income tax at 40% on
net income of $100,000 decreased
by deductible deferral of $10,000

Although all six adjustments were approved in *Accounting Research Bulletin No. 23 (1944)* of the Committee on Accounting Procedure of the American Institute of Accountants, the U. S. Securities and Exchange Commission in its *Accounting Series Release No. 53 (1945)* has opposed them, a position with which the statement of principles of the American Accounting Association (1946)(as well as the author) is in agreement.

Internal Controls

Internal controls over operations are numerous, and the auditor's interest in them, it will be remembered, derives from the need of understanding the origin and meaning of transactions— to the summation of which, in the form of financial statements, he is to attach his report. He cannot, of course, examine every transaction; he must rely on analysis, testing, scanning, and inquiry. The worth of his examination is enhanced by an intimate working knowledge of the internal controls that have given rise to the transactions and at the same time have shaped their character and amount. Conformity to the internal-control pattern does not in itself give complete assurance of transaction and account propriety; it does carry the responsibility back from those who incur expenses to those who originate and enforce policy, thus establishing a basis for dual accountability. The propriety and effectiveness of the internal controls are also objects of the auditor's examination; he must study, appraise, and report on them in the light of what he conceives suitable internal-control standards to be. With respect to the principal classes of items appearing in the income statement, the desirable standards for an average-size manufacturing enterprise—to which it is likely that most auditors would agree—are summarized in the paragraphs that follow.

Sales. Mediums of control over cash sales include prenumbered sales slips, cash registers, receipts from independent cashiers, inspection of goods at points of packaging or delivery, and the preaudit process of bringing together for comparison some or all of the preceding steps. There are many ways of combining these elements into a well-coordinated system, but it usually happens that a point is rather quickly reached at which transactions are slowed down by paperwork, customers are inconvenienced, and the cost of supervising and maintaining the controls exceeds the risk of loss.

A credit sale involves a number of additional, independent steps: acceptance of the order, approval of the customer's credit, removal of goods from stock, dispatch of goods to shipping room, shipping record, invoice preparation, coordination of these actions, entry on the customer's account, and finally collection. Most systems provide for the duplication of the customer's order on a multicopy form and the use of designated copies at each of the indicated steps in such a way that the task of coordination is principally a matter of assembling proof that the several steps have been satisfactorily completed.

Purchases. A qualified purchasing agent should be responsible for *all* acquisitions of materials and equipment, and he should report directly to the chief executive officer. He should act only on written authorizations from individuals the extent and character of whose authority to incur obligations have been clearly established. He must rely on and in the end conform to specifications of others, although he may challenge those he believes too restricted and suggest substitutions that would have the effect of concentrating purchases, accelerating delivery, increasing quality, decreasing price, and in other ways bringing the transaction under more desirable purchashing standards. He should make such suggestions a matter of record, and where their importance warrants, refer individual cases to the chief executive officer before final approval. His functions should *not* extend to the keeping of quantity stock records, the control of warehouse stocks or of the stockroom or storekeepers' operations, the receipt and inspection of goods, or the approval of invoices. He should be sent a copy of receiving and inspection reports and he must be prepared to act promptly on adjustments required by rejections and imperfections. He must have a workable system of unfilled-order controls by means of which he follows up with dispatch on delayed deliveries. He should send copies of each purchase contract or purchase order to the receiving and voucher-audit divisions, together with such collateral data as may be helpful in passing on invoices subsequently to be rendered by the supplier. He must give ample evidence of following the best purchasing practices and securing the lowest prices, and of not having "most favored" suppliers—as the result of his own volition or as the result of adherence to unnecessarily narrow specifications. Finally, he should not be the recipient of gratuities or other favors from suppliers; on this point the auditor has as a rule no means of investigation and must rely on whatever facts the internal auditor is able to pass along to him.

Receipt of purchases. The receiving division is best placed under the storekeeper in most circumstances, with responsibilities for both quantity and quality, the latter, where necessary, aided by but not subordinated to members of the engineering staff or other persons having special qualifications. Copies of purchase orders sent to the receiving division should have specifications but no quantities indicated on them, and one copy, with quantities filled in as the result of the actual count by the receiving clerk following quality inspection, should be dispatched promptly to the voucher-audit division.

Voucher audit. With carefully maintained controls preceding the audit of invoices for materials received, the work of the voucher-audit division is limited to a review of the propriety of terms, prices, discounts, extensions, footings, receiving and inspection reports, and transportation costs—all of which should be completed on the same day or within twenty-four hours after receipt of the receiving report. Typical filing practice is by discount date for unpaid invoices, and alphabetical sequence for paid vouchers, the latter with receiving and inspection reports and purchase-order copy attached. Vouchers covering partial deliveries (except the last) should be referenced to final-delivery voucher (and vice versa) where but one purchase-order copy is available. Cash discounts should be taken full advantage of wherever possible, if necessary by advance payments of invoices on which receipts have not yet been acknowledged. Petty-cash or working-fund reimbursements may be examined and cleared through regular voucher-audit procedures.

Voucher distribution. The "coding" operation, or indication of the number or name of the ledger account to be charged and the explanation, if any, of the transaction, which is also to appear in the account, should be placed on the voucher by some person other than the posting clerk. This may be done as part of the work of the voucher-audit division. Most expenditures, often as many as 95 per cent, are routine in character and the coding and posting operation is just as routine. The remaining 5 per cent should be tentatively coded by the coding clerk and reviewed finally by his superior before the posting operation takes place. The careful formulation of explanations in the coding operation is a worth-while element of internal controls, since the analysis that must precede their composition may lead to a more accurate identification of the expenditure.

An objective of every scheme of expense distribution should be to avoid redistributions by every possible effort, except possibly for service-department costs. The more vouchers that can be posted direct to their final resting place in the accounts, the more intelligible and useful the accounts are likely to be.

Accounts payable. With adequate working capital there need be no lag between completion of the voucher audit and the preparation of the check, thus eliminating accounts payable except for the small group of items in process at the end of the period. Voucher number and check number may be the same and the check prepared for signature in the voucher-audit division. Expenditure accounts may be posted direct from vouchers, and, if bookkeeping machines are used, the backing or proof sheet may serve as the record of checks drawn. The auditor should regard systems involving a voucher record or accounts payable as intermediate steps that may be removed under adequate control conditions, and he should regard internal controls as having been improved, at least potentially, by removing such intermediate steps and reducing the operation to its simplest terms.

Payrolls. An ideal payroll division is one that critically reviews independently determined payroll data and from them prepares the payroll and payroll checks. These data may include master employment cards bearing approvals of original employment and of pay rates and rate changes, time reports bearing the signatures of foremen, reports from piece-work inspectors, clock cards or other attendance reports, and authorizations for payroll deductions. It is sometimes possible to institute controls over payroll totals whereby changes from one payroll to another are effected by individual change authorizations; predetermined payroll totals may thus be arrived at before the payroll is prepared. Payroll machines have been devised that greatly speed payroll work and add materially to internal controls. Checks are always to be preferred over cash distributions, and the checks should be distributed to the individual recipients by an independent official who may be designated "paymaster." He should have authority to hold undistributed checks for a limited period, thereafter to forward such checks to some higher official such as the controller or his assistant. Where a satisfactory system of control cannot be effected along these or similar lines, it may be desirable to have a fairly complete internal audit of the payroll before cash or checks are distributed.

Checks issued. Many accountants recommend two signatures on each check, one indicating that the necessary accounting and preaudit steps have been taken, the other that the proper bank account is being drawn on and that the total of the check or checks corresponds in amount to the supporting document. One of the signers should be responsible for seeing to it that the voucher and its attachments are canceled (preferably by perforation, as are checks returned each month by banks), so that they cannot be again presented in support of a proposed payment. Further comments on disbursements will be found in the following chapter.

Monthly reviews of accounts. An always effective method of internal control over expenditures is the employment of responsibility- or activity-accounting procedures throughout the organization whereby the content of operating accounts is reviewed monthly by the organizational heads incurring the expenditure. This review is readily assumed, provided only that the content of any one account is confined to expenditures within the jurisdiction of the reviewer. The reviewer's task is to examine each item making up the monthly total. He may call for supporting vouchers or distribution details on unfamiliar items; he may challenge any service charge or periodic fixed cost and appeal to the controller for its modification or elimination—or failing therein, carry his appeal to the chief executive officer of the company. Wherever such a plan is instituted the accounting classification must be carefully redrawn so that every expense is related to some organizational unit, with subdivisions for such activities as may be defined by the organization head with the assistance of the controller. Activities should be agreed upon that lend themselves to unit-cost analyses, or, where comparative unit costs within or without the business are unavailable or have no significance, to monthly or other periodic comparisons. Each organization head selected for the task thus becomes an important link in the fabric of internal control; he may be a top executive or the supervisor of a comparatively minor operation, but it is always desirable to select the person as far down the line as the responsibility goes. Once he has made a number of monthly reviews the task ceases to be onerous. He is given the accounts pertaining to his activities, say, on the second of each month, reports not later than the fifth to the controller on any disagreement as to content, thereafter automatically keeps informed on his portion of operating costs, and at the proper time each year is prepared without extended research to submit budgetary estimates for which he can intelligently assume personal responsibility. Other advantages that develop almost immediately are the following:

1. Organization heads become much more accounting- and cost-conscious; their unit costs and periodic cost comparisons can be interpreted by top management as indexes of their operating efficiencies and supervisory talents.

2. Not only are more intelligible budgetary estimates made possible, as already mentioned, but the enforcement of the budget becomes the ever-present, personal problem of organizational-unit heads. The budget is thus converted into a much more active agent of expense control.

3. New and valuable ideas are contributed to the problem of distributing joint or common costs, with the result that top management is soon participating in policies leading to decisions on cost spreads—a situation welcomed by every controller and public accountant as a much-needed extension of cost controls and management interests therein.

4. Crosschecks are secured for service activities, which auditors often find have gotten out of hand, especially where service charges have been spread to product lines, production departments, or other activities that make up costs of sales. Where, in the interest of simplicity, service costs are not prorated and carried to other accounts, independent judgment should be periodically secured on the necessity of the service and the justification of its costs.

5. A new unity is given the enterprise as a whole. It can be more clearly discerned as an organism of clearly defined parts, held together—in part at least—by a common interest in cost controls and by the common language of accounting.

Where these methods are employed, it is usually necessary to make up fresh expense-ledger sheets each month. Bookkeeping machines with typewriter attachments are preferable, since they permit detailed transaction explanations to be written in, at least for more unusual items. Abbreviations and "object" codes may also be employed, and explanations may vary in character in accordance with the wishes or needs of different organizational heads.

Cost methods. In the ordinary annual audit, the auditor does not devote any considerable amount of his time to the details of the cost system in use. He must understand the cost basis and the general operating practices in recording and spreading costs, for he must appraise the methods of inventory valuation. In this book, valuation methods and their relation to the cost system are discussed in Chapter VIII (Inventories). The auditor is usually inclined to regard the item of cost of sales in the income statement as a residuum—a conglomerate of costs obscured by opening and closing inventory *values* and, as already observed, often combined in a single figure with selling and administrative expenses. Occasionally he attempts to compare it with similar amounts of previous years and account roughly for variations.

But just as the balance-sheet item of retained income has emerged as a figure with a history behind it and is no longer the excess of assets over liabilities and capital, so cost of sales is now coming to be looked upon as the resultant of the logical combination of specific costs—an item that contains or should contain the elements essential to its critical examination.

In addition to the general cost controls given consideration in preceding paragraphs, the auditor may profitably inquire into such conditions as the following—which were observed in a particular manufacturing establishment—and where pertinent suggest more carefully worked-out controls over them:

1. Lack of careful planning in the spread of work over the year resulted in lost machine hours and idle-labor costs. The auditor found some evidence of planning, but frequent shifts in production schedules, occasioned by attempts to utilize facilities more fully, gave rise to costly setup time and a loss of productive hours.

2. Wide ranges in the quantities of various materials and parts on hand at different times during the past year pointed to the desirability of a more careful coordination of purchasing and stores with production.

3. Rising unit labor costs indicated the need for the institution or revision of incentive plans.

4. Cost reports and their preparation were reviewed for their timeliness, content, and arrangement, with the thought that every effort should be put forth to make sure that they supply management with a maximum of data useful as a basis of information and action.

5. The volume of rejects arising during the year suggested that studies to remedy the causes were not being instituted quickly enough and that quality-control methods ought to be modified and extended.

6. Changes in designs and specifications had been put through

without recognition of their effect on materials, parts, and in-process work.

Operating budget. A budget is an indispensable device in the institution of management controls. To assure its operability the budget plan should possess such elements as the following:

1. A budget officer or budget committee should be appointed, charged with the responsibility for fixing the annual budget before the beginning of the period to be covered, which should be the full fiscal year, and for budget supervision once it has been adopted. In many instances, the budget officer is the controller.

2. In its initial stages the budget should be prepared at the lowest possible level of operating responsibility so that by the time it reaches the budget officer or committee for preliminary review it will have been subjected to criticisms and adjustments by organizational supervisors.

3. Whatever adjustments are made during the course of the top-management review of the budget, assurance should be obtained of their feasibility at the operating level.

4. The budget items should follow the same classification of revenue and expense as that appearing in the account classification, and should be broken down by months.

5. Monthly reporting should be required, comparing the budgetary apportionment for each component with actual revenue and expense or other predetermined standard of measurement.

6. Procedures for modifying budgetary allotments during the budget period may be provided, but it is usually best to retain originally determined budgetary allotments for comparison purposes. The adjustment resulting from reallotment then becomes a partial explanation and approval of variances.

Explanations of differences between budgetary and actual figures furnish valuable clues to the auditor, and they supply him with a good basis for discussing with officials the effect of recent changes in revenues and costs.

Income-Statement Standards

1. Sales and manufacturing cost or merchandise cost of sales should appear in every income statement. Sales are preferably shown net, after deducting discounts, rebates, returns, freight, and other allowances. Sales statistics such as departmental break-downs may be on a partly net basis because of the difficulty of spreading cash discounts. Commission expense may be more in the nature of discount than expense; if so, it too should be deducted in determining net sales. Bad debts or provisions therefor are rarely shown as a sales deduction but are classified as an

administrative or selling expense. There is some tendency to regard bad debts as being on a par with discounts—a portion of the sales figure that will never be realized—and thus a deduction, along with discounts, from gross sales. "Cash discounts" are still found frequently among expense accounts, and this item might even appear as a "financial" expense; however, with the prompt payment of invoices that takes place in ordinary times, it has now become fairly well recognized as a sales deduction.

2. Items deducted from gross sales in arriving at net sales are usually omitted from the income statement unless they possess more than ordinary significance.

3. Where an important trend would be indicated by a breakdown of sales and cost of sales as by departments or product lines, such a breakdown should appear in the income statement or the trend that would be thus revealed should be covered in a footnote.

4. The nature and amount of any material writedown of inventory as from cost to market or fifo to lifo should be indicated on the income statement.

5. Substantial differences between net income before taxes and net income subject to Federal income tax should be explained in a footnote.

6. Dividends on treasury stock should be credited against dividends paid and never shown as income.

7. Income earned by a sinking-fund trustee (excluding interest and dividends earned on the company's own securities) should be included in the income statement along with the trustee's expenses; additions to the sinking fund by way of interest and dividends on the company's own securities should be reflected in a credit to interest expense and dividends paid; gain or loss from acquisition or resale by the trustee of the company's own securities should be accounted for as though they were the company's own transactions.

8. Occasionally attempts are made, particularly during a period of rising prices, to give credence to the notion that the income statement ought to reflect earning power. Accounting principles 15, 16, and 17 on pages 129–130, the comment on page 16 relating to an objective basis of accounting, and the surplus standard described at the bottom of page 501 should be examined. It has been asserted that earning power may be given expression by omitting from among the elements of net income such irregular items as those listed on page 489. The accountant who pursues this aim fails to reckon with the fact that much of what remains as "recurring" income and expense may actually be

*non*recurring in character. An auditor who has been painstaking in his operational inquiries will almost certainly have discovered many items within ordinary income and expense accounts that reflect purely adventitious events and conditions and that have had a surprisingly substantial effect on operations: an effect never disclosed, if indeed its existence is known, by the "earning-power" advocate. To cast out only a portion of the nonrecurring constituents of net income and to ignore the remainder is to exhibit a lack of realism. It is doubtful, however, that anyone can develop the omniscience required to segregate the elements that contribute to earning power from those that do not; hence the author regards the principles enunciated on the preceding page as inescapable.

Representative Audit Program

1. Review comparative profit-and-loss items on working trial balance and make note of and ascertain reasons for principal variations; review client's monthly income statements and note important item variations between months.

2. Make sure, during review of profit-and-loss accounts, that no unearned income has been included, particularly where the customer has made payment, in whole or in part, before delivery.

3. Obtain as detailed a product breakdown as possible of sales and cost of sales for several years and note trends.

4. Analyze income from rents, interest, scrap, and miscellaneous sources; review for completeness and variation from prior year; ascertain whether any new sources of income have arisen during current period.

5. Scan any income account not analyzed.

6. Follow through selected sales transactions for principal products sold, from original order to collection of account, noting whether internal-control procedures are being observed.

7. Test selected discount, return, and allowance transactions relating to principal classes of customers.

8. Test a number of transactions involving different classes of purchases, from requisition to payment, observing procedures and adequacy of controls.

9. Review operating budget; investigate method of preparation, attention paid to it by operators, proffered explanations of variations, and action taken when unfavorable variations are

discovered. Compare with next forward budget and make note of anticipated major variations.

10. Scan factory-expense accounts for variations as between months, trends, extraordinary items, and changes in classification.

11. Analyze accounts reflecting executives' compensation and allowances, legal fees, interest, taxes, major miscellaneous expense, nonoperating items, and unusual losses.

12. Scan other selling and general and administrative expense accounts and any minor, unclassified expense accounts, compare with similar accounts for past year, and note material differences; develop readily available background of extraordinary items.

13. Review and prepare brief summary of basis of computation followed in preparation of current year's Federal income-tax return and in accrual of year-end Federal income-tax liability.

14. Where the auditor is to prepare the Federal income-tax return, the following items (other data may be required by changes in the tax law) should be listed on a worksheet and referenced to schedules following the worksheet, or to other sections of the working papers if the information has already been secured in connection with the audit:

Account analyses, for the year, of
    Fixed assets
    Depreciation and amortization reserves and reconciliation with related expense accounts
    Other valuation reserves
    Capital stock: dates and amounts of changes
    Cost of sales: opening and closing inventories and purchases, or materials used; labor and details of overhead
    Officers' salaries and distribution; addresses, titles, time devoted to business, percentage of stock owned
    Donations: name and amount
    Dividends received
    Interest on government bonds; par value and class; when issued
    Interest expense
    Tax expense
    Capital gains and losses: description of property sold, date acquired, cost, depreciation accrued and allowed, selling price
    Extraordinary losses, detailed
    Income or expense attributable to other years
Tie-in of reserves with expense accounts
Agents' reports: borrow copies for tax-department review
Tax-savings possibilities

15. Review and discuss with principal any revenue agents' reports received during year by client.

16. Discuss with appropriate executives causes of variations,

unusual items, and trends as noted in 1, 3, 9, 12 above and else-where, following generally the scope of inquiry noted below.

Audit Procedures

Whatever the item being considered, the auditor's work calls for the appraisal of internal controls, the analysis, testing, and scanning of accounts, and the securing of qualitative information from department heads and other employees directly concerned. However, the emphasis in an examination of revenue and expense activities, although involving these elements, is necessarily differ-ent from that present in the examination of balance-sheet ac-counts. In a repeating audit the auditor looks at a revenue or expense item as embodying either or both (a) a continuum—a flow of transactions similar in character and amount from period to period—and (b) variants—transactions influenced by condi-tions peculiar to the period under review. The former he tends to accept with limited testing once its propriety has been established in a preceding period; the latter are objects for a more intensive examination provided their character, volume, or amount is found by testing to be of importance.

Basic data for review. In acquainting himself with the methods by which revenue and expense data are collected, preaudited, and classified, the auditor will find it helpful to have at hand for preliminary study and constant reference the following reports and schedules:

1. The controller's worksheet or equivalent from which the in-come statement has been prepared and which ties in income-statement items with the books. If the income statement has not yet been prepared or the worksheet is not available the auditor's own trial-balance copies will answer the purpose. They should include both general-ledger and expense-ledger trial balances.

2. A breakdown of revenues and expenses by component months or other subdivisions of the audit period. This may be available in reports issued by the controller's office or may be obtained di-rectly from the books. A much more extensive breakdown than that appearing in the income statement is the objective.

3. Comparative income statements for the past several years. In repeating audits these will be found in the permanent file.

4. A comparison of budgeted revenue and expense approved before the beginning of the period (a) with similar figures as finally revised during the period and (b) with the actual results of the period.

5. Analyses or recapitulations, often prepared for the auditor by the controller's staff, of such operating accounts as sales (by

months, product, character [e.g., credit, cash, conditional], sales offices, salesmen—whatever breakdowns are available); cost of sales (similarly classified); dividends, interest, rents, and royalties received; gain or loss on the disposal of noninventory assets; depreciation, amortization, insurance, rents, royalties, officers' salaries, donations, legal expense, taxes, and possibly other expenses, especially those appearing for the first time and those in which major variations have occurred during the year. The requirements for each analysis should be outlined in advance by the auditor before the work commences; in fact, in many instances, the auditor may find it to his advantage to head up worksheets and prepare brief memorandums indicating the character and extent of the analyses desired so that there will be no wasted effort by the client's staff. The nature of the analysis will vary from account to account. In general, the purpose is to have at hand information that may be compared with similar data pertaining to preceding years.

Before analyses and other data supplied by the client's staff can be used, they must of course be reviewed and tested by the auditor. This he does by obtaining from the author of each worksheet an oral account of the procedure he has followed, the extent to which original data (vouchers, reports, and so forth) have been consulted, information as to persons believed responsible for the transactions making up the account, and opinions of the character of the work done and of the meaning and significance attributable to the account. The auditor then retraces a sufficient number of the steps taken in building up the worksheet to satisfy himself of the accuracy of the analysis or compilation and of the opinions expressed.

Explanations from executives. At no other point in his examination is qualitative information more necessary to the auditor than in his review of operations. There are, however, practical limitations on the scope of his inquiry: he may not be able at the time of his examination to speak with those persons who could furnish him with the best answers; much of the information supplied may contribute little to the auditor's objectives; and the auditor himself may not have acquired a sufficient background of the industry to elicit more pointed responses from the individuals he talks to. On occasion the auditor's principal undertakes the job, especially in larger engagements where executives hesitate to reply fully to questions from persons with whom they have not been long and well acquainted.

In addition to schedules and notes on operating accounts narratives should be prepared by the auditor during the period of his field work indicating briefly the results of his operating inquiries. Names of persons should appear; sometimes the dates of conversations may be of importance. The auditor regards these comments from individuals not as conclusive evidence upon which he is bound to rely, but as useful, interpretative information that will constitute a helpful supplement to his survey of revenue and expense accounts: information that will often change the character of the attention he gives to these accounts.

Consequences of inquiries on operational activities that may be anticipated may include some or all of the following:

1. A better understanding of operating methods and accounts is acquired, thereby adding to the background essential to an intelligent audit.

2. It may be found that certain related balance-sheet items require a more thorough examination than they would normally receive at his hands.

3. The reasons for and significance of changes during the year in accounting and other policies and procedures may be more readily grasped.

4. The need for reclassifications and adjustments may be made apparent.

The auditor's inquiries on the operating accounts may precede or follow his review of the accounts themselves. As a rule, some preliminary acquaintance with each major account is desirable.

The paragraphs that follow suggest points the auditor will likely consider in examining revenue and expense accounts and in conferring with operating personnel.

Sales activities. Sales and cost-of-sales breakdowns are often available for internal use, though, as previously noted, their totals may not tie in precisely with net sales appearing in the income statement. It is usually unnecessary for the auditor to ask for analyses other than those readily available at the time of his examination. His purpose in examining sales or operating revenues and cost of sales is to form an opinion of their meaning and reliability as the first item in the operating statement. He may be aided in forming his opinion by ascertaining the interpretations of those for whom the analyses have been prepared.

From comparative breakdowns of sales and cost of sales by product lines, departments, sales territories, or classes of customers, trends in the business may be disclosed: the relative profitability of different products, causes of changes in gross profit, future sales and gross-profit prospects. Demands for the company's products or services may have been increased by various stimuli applied during the year or perhaps in a preceding year: an intensive sales campaign, a new radio program, change in advertising media, or other "educational" or promotional effort reflected in various sales-expense accounts; a change in distributors or sales representatives; a new foreign-trade outlet; a decline in competition; lowered sales prices—generally, or for a limited period; rebates or special allowances to customers. A decrease in sales for one or more products may be attributable to the gradual elimination of less profitable items; an increase in competition from direct competitors or competitors offering substitutes; a failure or inability to lower prices to meet changed demands; the marketing of a faulty product followed by a material volume of returns; preparation for the marketing of a new product—accompanied by a diminishing sales volume during the setup or readying period; a cutting down of sales-promotion expense because of top-management pressure to reduce costs—with consequent loss of volume. These examples by no means exhaust the possibilities. They are cited here to illustrate the infinite variety of circumstances that affect over-all volume.

Thus the auditor's first step in his examination of the sales account is to acquire a well-rounded picture of the meaning of *total* sales. Sometimes quantities, unit prices, and breakdowns by principal products and styles are available or are readily obtainable; as a consequence the sales account or its principal subdivisions can be approximated by computation. Another test may be afforded by comparing breakdowns of the current year's weekly or monthly sales and sales reductions (returns, allowances, discounts, and so forth) with similar breakdowns for the past year and by obtaining reasonable explanations for any important variations. In connection with such tests as these, which often appear to the uninitiated as inexact and hence repugnant to the ideas of accuracy and precision ordinarily associated with accounting, the objective on the part of the auditor is to arrive at an *opinion of "fairness"* with respect to the account he is examining. This does not mean that exactness has been sacrificed, because a skilled auditor will not accept any account of major importance until the precision, accuracy, authorized sources, intended content, and other characteristics typical of such an account have been satisfactorily tested. The auditor's emphasis today is on "fairness" or propriety—terms that imply the presence to a satisfactory degree of *all* the characteristics that should attach to an account, not simply a portion of them.

Other over-all considerations given by the auditor to the sales account may be found in the chapters on receivables and inventories.

Instruction 6 in the representative audit program calls for tracing a group of sales transactions from the receipt of the sales order to the final collection of the account. This permits a testing of the various details of internal controls governing sales. It also provides an introduction to the procedures surrounding receivables. For this test the auditor may select all recorded sales for a week or other limited period (far enough removed from the end of the year to allow for normal collection), sales of certain types of items subject in the past to irregularities, sales of a specified amount or greater, sales of a given branch of the business (other branches being selected in other years), or sales of *any* kind selected at random.

Wherever a limited number of sales transactions have been selected for examination the auditor is likely to pursue the following procedures:

Verify the source of the transaction, noting correspondence of customer, date, quantity, quality, and price

Examine evidence of removal from stock and shipment or other delivery in the quantity billed

Look for entry in journal or for inclusion in total posted to receivables (or cash) and sales

If a chronological group of sales items are being examined—
Verify the footing of the salesbook or the sales recap for the period
Trace individual postings to accounts receivable
Trace debit and credit postings of period total
Observe sequence of invoice numbers and account for missing or odd numbers
Verify stated terms, prices, extensions, and footings appearing on invoice copies

Sales reductions. Where orderly processes have been followed in the authorization of discounts, allowances, returns, and other sales reductions the auditor's examination is generally limited to the testing of representative items in each account. This will consist of such steps as these:

Verify authority for reduction. A cash discount is a routine allowance automatically approved if timely payment is made and the discount ratio conforms to regular terms or has been individually specified at the time of sale. Other reductions however generally require item-by-item approval. In his review of internal controls the auditor will have noted the procedure expected to be followed and will test the selected items for their conformance.

Where merchandise has been returned, look for required four-way adjustment recording re-entry into stock, credit to customer's account and reduction of both sales and cost of sales.

In addition, working "in the other direction," the auditor

should trace all credits (other than cash) in a selected group of accounts receivable to the authorizations therefor.

Purchasing activities. A first step in reviewing purchases is to prepare a breakdown of the purchases account or accounts into whatever summary detail may be available along with similar breakdowns for one or more preceding periods. The detail may be by classes of raw material or parts, departments, locations, or even principal items; it will indicate the relative importance of different classes or groupings and suggest to the auditor the points at which he should lay first emphasis.

In his contacts with the purchasing division the auditor will probably first discuss any major change in purchasing policy or in the character of items purchased. He will inquire about reports from warehouses and stockrooms and the practical operation and general effectiveness of minimum-and-maximum quantity controls: whether the lead time between purchase requisitions and the expected applications of various items to production is adequate. If not he may expect to find fewer requests for bids, smaller quantities acquired, higher prices paid, and even stoppages in production. He will ask about scarcity, rationing, or sharing of certain supplies within the industry, the existence of any of these conditions leading to somewhat similar results. He will discuss relations with suppliers: whether the purchasing division has been restricted in any way by having to confine its relations to one or a limited number of suppliers in the procurement of one or more items; whether for any of various reasons relations with suppliers have improved or declined during the year; whether suppliers have maintained delivery schedules; and whether in holding suppliers to close tolerances or other standards in furnishing parts the field of supply has been limited or prices have been affected. He may ask next about counts and inspections upon receipt of goods: whether they are made promptly and accurately, the reactions of suppliers to reported differences in quantity or quality, and any trend in returns to and allowances from suppliers. He will discuss prices: trends generally, methods devised for obtaining lower prices, the effect of price-maintenance legislation, the relation of prices paid to market quotations (as in trade journals) or to prices paid by others, FOB customs within the trade (that is, who pays the transportation costs), how quantity and cash discounts and other terms of payment are determined, whether suppliers have been paid promptly and full cash discounts have been taken, and whether purchases of "distress" merchandise or spot purchases have been made.

Production activities. Factory operations can be very generally understood and reviewed by the auditor without his becoming involved in engineering and management problems. As an observer and questioner he is interested in learning the significance of what he has noted in the factory expense accounts. His experience elsewhere has taught him that there are common factors in production everywhere that give rise to financial and accounting problems affecting revenues and expense. The following are characteristic:

Actual output may be less than plant capacity, resulting in larger charges for overhead (and sometimes labor) per unit produced.

Production planning should be related to budgetary estimates of factory operations; the method of tying the one into the other would be of aid in understanding explanations of the divergence of either or both to actual.

Changes in production methods should explain at least some of the variations in departmental and unit costs. Such changes may also account for retirements of certain fixed assets during the period and may lead to questions concerning other assets not yet retired and to commitments on new assets not yet recorded.

Discontinuance of a product line during the period gives rise to questions concerning the valuation of certain items of inventory on hand at the close of the period.

One or more accounts may reflect activities in the design of new equipment or new products or in carrying on experimental and developmental work; inquiry should reveal the character of the work done during the year, its relation to the work of past years, and the effect if any on existing production methods, assets, and future plant utilization.

Present plant facilities may not be wholly suited to estimates of the future volume of production, assuming no change, or minor changes only, in product lines. Shortage or overage of current capacities suggest that a factor of obsolescence should be included in depreciation rates.

Shutdowns during the period may have been occasioned by labor difficulties, plant overhaul, vacation period, inventory count, and other causes; effects may be noted in output volume, idle time, overtime allowances, labor distribution rates, and other costs.

A study of transfers to scrap accounts or of changes in the volume of scrap sales may lead to a discussion of production deficiencies that have given rise to higher costs or may suggest allowances for imperfections in the closing inventory.

Methods by which service departments are controlled and service-department costs are reviewed and charged out to other departments or to operations are almost always subject to some degree of criticism by the auditor. Disputes on service charges may suggest inefficiencies and the alternative of an equivalent service purchased from the outside. Failure to review and evaluate periodically the propriety of unit service costs is regarded by some auditors as a reliable indication of management's general lack of cost-consciousness.

A discussion of the plant's relations with other divisions may bring out an absence of coordination with the sales division: the forcing of production to meet market demands or promises of delivery, the acceptance of returns with minor defects that could have been remedied in the field, promises of factory service for which the factory was unprepared, failure to allow the factory sufficient time for orderly scheduling and delivery, continued production of an unprofitable item, and many other causes.

Relations with the purchasing division may be less than perfect because of leniency on the part of the purchasing officer in dealing with suppliers, permitting delays in delivery, less-than-standard requirements, substitute materials or qualities, favoring of particular suppliers, high prices and poor terms. From the purchasing division a much different account of such troubles will be given to the auditor who from such a melange must be prepared to point out to management any weaknesses in internal controls and his suggestions for improvements.

Methods of costing provide a fertile field of inquiry and discussion. Whatever the method, it should provide costs not only thought to be useful, but actually put to use. The auditor bears in mind the feedback principle: that internal reports are worth continuing only if they lead to acceptance or corrective action. He notes their timeliness, determines for himself whether suggestions for improving the form would be in order, and directs his attention particularly to the character and completeness of the narrative accompanying and explaining the report figures.

Where a standard-cost system is in effect the auditor is concerned with the reliability of the standards used: the basis of estimate (ideal or other standard, or expected actual cost), when the last revision of standards was made and the reasons therefor, management analysis and study of variances, conclusions reached, and actions taken following such study, the method of distributing or otherwise disposing of variances, the dependability of present standard costs as a basis of inventory valuation.

In analyzing or scanning accounts there will always be items picked out by the auditor for further inquiry: the purchase of materials, supplies, merchandise, or services—items that may be found in varying proportions in any expense account. The purpose of his inquiry may be merely identification: a description of the item not available, say, in a ledger posting. This will require the "pulling" and brief examination of a voucher, requisition, or payroll without more than passing notice of supporting detail. But if the auditor's intention is to study the item thoroughly he will follow all or the applicable portion of the voucher- or payroll-examination procedure appearing in Chapter XIV.

Illustrative Audit

The eight worksheets making up this section are divided into two parts: Sales and Cost of Sales (A 1-5), prepared by the auditor; and Expense Comparisons (A 6-8). A fairly comprehensive review of the accounts making up the income statements is reflected on these worksheets. This review is for the most part concerned with an attempt to develop an intelligent understanding of the meaning of the nominal accounts, and contains only minor formal account analyses, aside from those made in connection with the review of assets and liabilities. (References to the latter appear on TB 3, 4, and 5).

The first half of A 1 is a summary of sales and cost of sales, obtained from different sources. The sales analysis is derived from the sales record (here, a sheet added to monthly by the billing unit, the additions representing recaps of invoices booked during that month); the cost of sales by basic or objective accounts is obtained from the general ledger (see TB 3); and the product or department costs are abstracted from cost estimates by products that go into the monthly operating statements, modified by variations at the year end (after the introduction of the physical inventory in the records and after new average unit costs by products have been computed by the controller).

In the present instance, the auditor's main point of attack is to make comparisons of sales and costs of sales with the same items in the preceding year. By studying and synthesizing the analyses already made by company employees, and by following these by conversations with management concerning this year's variants and a scanning of income and expense accounts, the auditor arrives at conclusions of propriety and accuracy that in most instances will be found to be much more comprehensive (and hence of greater value to the client and affording fuller protection to the auditor himself) than conclusions based primarily on account analysis.

Worksheet A 3 summarizes the auditor's work on sales. He scans the sales account for the year, reviews internal controls, confers with the invoice clerk on actual procedures, observes the scope of internal audit during the year, and makes notes of observations on the more important items coming to his attention. From A 2 the auditor may determine what happened to prices during the year; on A 4 he figures out cost variations and the reasons therefor. On A 5 and on A 6-8, he discusses changes in specific items of costs, going into cost of sales and into selling and general expenses. Several "rough" account analyses may be noted as the result of his scanning of the expense accounts.

A word should be said regarding the arrangement of the working papers. Here, the auditor's principal, when he reviews the papers, will have to examine the following worksheets in order to gain a full view of income and expense:

If repetition is to be avoided (and on this all are agreed), the worksheet on which the item appears may be introduced into the current sheaf of papers at any one of a number of points, with cross references at the remaining points where it might have been

F 1-12	*General content*
H 1	Review of current income and expense
PF 31-2	Notes on cost system, made in part this year
	Inventory review
A 1-8	Trial balance of income and expense accounts, and
TB 3-5	certain notes
Worksheets	Comment on repairs

What constitutes the best arrangement and sequence of working papers is always a matter for argument in every public-accounting office. Any one item investigated and noted in the papers may be more or less directly related to a half-dozen other subjects. included. In most situations, the point of inclusion is of only slight importance. Working papers are reviewed (and at a later date may be re-reviewed) rather quickly, and the emphasis of the reviewer (and hence the preferred point of inclusion) may be different from that of the auditor or subsequent reviewer. Careful cross-referencing, however, nearly always forestalls potential criticism of working-paper classification.

Martin Manufacturing Company
Sales and Cost of Sales
Year ended December 31, 1952

F. L.
2-6-53

ol, etc.

	Budget 1953	Budget 1952	Actual 1952	Actual 1951	Increase (+) Decrease (-)
Sales, net					
A Heavy machines	3500000 00	4500000 0	3683333 62	3549875 55	+ 133046 07
F Light machines	4550000 00	4300000 00	4570006 58	4841267 88	- 271261 30
H Appliances	1800000 00	2000000 00	2089626 64	1904639 32	+ 184987 32
R Merchandise	800000 0	750000 0	732921 48	662331 05	+ 70590 43
Totals, as adjusted	7500000 00	7500000 00	7760888 32	7763225 80	- 2337 48
Cost of Sales, by object (from general ledger)					
Purchased		3000000 00	3145362 73	3133030 98	+ 12319 75
Direct labor		2550000 00	2686247 88	2540900 93	+ 145346 95
Factory overhead (entire)		900000 00	958547 85	970486 45	- 11938 60
% to direct labor		35.3%	35.6%	38.2%	-2.6%
Inventory variations -					
Finished stock			- 14543 81	- 3418 01	- 11125 80
Work in process		See X-4	- 112317 25	- 74884 3	-104828 82
Raw materials			+ 438558 4	- 216438 0	+ 654996 4
Shipments to affiliate at cost		100000 00	- 982832 8	814263 8	- 16856 90
Realized additive on affiliate's sales			- 78092 7	110256 0	+ 32163 3 (a
Installation and service		100000 00	+ 1131590 9	1001547 4	+ 130043 5 (b
Totals, as adjusted			6712500 78	6617843 88	+ 94656 90
Cost of Sales, by product lines (standard costs; 1951 adjusted, note c below)					
A Heavy machines	2600000 00	2800000 00	2708015 9	2658164 7	+ 49851 2
F Light machines	3560000 00	3660000 00	3814274 27	4104419 38	- 290145 11
H Appliances	1590000 00	1650000 00	1939855 53	1640770 94	+ 299084 59
R Merchandise	510000 00	330000 00	327000 47	246166 86	+ 73833 61
Unabsorbed factory costs	320000 00	320000 00	367568 92	360670 23	+ 6898 69
Totals as above			6712500 78	6617843 88	+ 94656 90

Reconciliation of cost of sales with books and monthly statements -

Total of a/cs 221-261 before our adjustments		6630250 74	
Overabsorbed recorded costs, net -			
Finished goods	+ 44168 4		
Work in process	+ 63149 1		
Raw material	- 40002 0	+ 67315 5	
Total on December report (F-9)		6636982 29	
Unrecorded purchases (AJE 16)	+ 23850 1		
Our inventory corrections (F-1 & AJE 18)	- 291100 0		
Factory-expense adjustments (TB-4)	+ 36252 1		
Reductions for above overabsorptions	- 67315 5		
Items a & b above (a/cs 264 and 266)	+ 1053498 2	+ 755184 9	
Total, as above		6712500 78	

✓ = agrees with T/B

Notes:

(a) & (b) - items excluded on A-4

(c) 1951 cost of sales put on 1952 basis with respect to overhead by Mr. Johnson; inventory variation, being minor in amount, was not adjusted.

A-1

Martin Manufacturing Company
Sales data
Year ended December 31, 1952

Following is a divisional analysis of sales from report of H.C. Prodder for executive staff meeting of Feb. 6, 1953:

Type	1952 Number	1952 Amount (thousands)	1951 Number	1951 Amount (thousands)
Heavy machinery –				
AX240	23	156.4	4	28.4
AX241	55	124.3	56	126.0
FS2203	5	57.5	7	95.9
FS2205	1	11.0	6	84.0
G20	1	5.5	3	17.4
Other Models	2	12.9	1	5.2
Totals		367.6 ^		356.9 ^
Light machines –				
CNX1 series	2525	4191.5	2681	4557.7
DX line	201	335.9	204	244.8
5881	1	12.0	2	20.6
Special orders	4	22.9	2	25.8
Totals		4562.3 ^		4848.9 ^
Appliances –				
Washers	9110	1093.2	8460	972.9
Dryers	1860	446.4	2230	557.5
Freezers	1750	577.5	820	213.2
Small equipment	–	109.3	–	333.7
Totals		2226.4 ^		2077.3 ^

The above is a recapitulation of invoices by the sales department, returns being deducted but not all adjustments. Principal differences between years appear to be these:

1. 1952 sales, although differing little in total from 1951's showed some variation as between divisions and models (budget figures on A-1).

2. An order for 30 AX240 machines was received in 1952, and six each were delivered before the year end.

3. The decrease in the sales of clothes dryers indicates that high costs have reduced the company's ability to compete with newcomers on the market.

4. Sales of deep freezers more than doubled last year's, being 70% greater in $ than budgeted in December, 1951.

5. Losses from sales of small equipment (no or negative gross margin) now eliminated because of abandonment of this line of product. Small inventory on hand at 12-31-52 will be sold out by April, '53 (Mr. Avery).

More accurate tie-in with books planned for 1953 (see A-3).

A-2

Sales procedures:

    Sales orders, upon approval by sales and credit departments and after check with stockroom, are dittoed, copies serving as invoice, posting medium, packing slip, shipping ticket (or receipt), and as basis for sales statistics. Cash sales are few in number and are not distinguished from other sales, customer's invoice being marked paid and mailed to customer on the same day as the sale.

    Each month's invoice copies are bound together, recapped, and the total posted to customers' control and sales. Commencing with November credits, a summary is made for credits to receivables and charges to returns, allowances, and discounts, with a recap for product lines. This will make possible a more accurate summary of net sales than is now available (e.g. on A-2). At present, although information is available, no attempt is made to tie in sales analyses with the net sales per books.

Sales activity (thousands of dollars):

Mo.	52	51	Mo.	52	51
J	770	570	J	820	600
F	430	510	A	850	850
M	380	490	S	770	1010
A	400	450	O	670	920
M	510	410	N	720	760
J	660	440	D	830	750

    Unfilled orders: $862,500, including Ordnance order for $84,000, covering 12 AX240 machines for delivery from April to August 1953.
    No records of more than minor returns and cancellations from Jan. 1 – Mar. 2, 1953.

    Audit work: Traced 30 sales transactions from original order taken by salesman to final payment (in 2 cases to account receivable). Procedure above indicated had been followed. In one instance (inv. #2-121) no record of approval by credit man but account already paid. In another (inv. #5-48) error in arithmetic of freight allowance; corrected by credit memo (11-2) under new method, requiring approval of sales division and controller. Examined reports of internal auditor who appears to have postaudited nearly one-half of year's invoices.

A-3

Martin Manufacturing Company
Comparison of Production Costs (1951-2)
Year ended December 31, 1952
B.B.
2-14-
xxl, etc.
(analysis furnished by J. Johnson)

1952	Material	Labor	Overhead % Variable	% Fixed	Total
Adjusted costs	3143623.73	2686267.88	595361.14	363186.71	6788439.46
Opening inventories—					
Finished stock	195978.04	224558.47 ²⁴	53894.04 ¹⁴	31438.18	505868.73
Work in process	56214.03	90576.62 ²⁴	21738.38 ¹⁴	12680.73	181209.76
Raw materials	496208.59	—	—	—	496208.59
Closing inventories—					
Finished stock ⁵¹ ⁵²	-87113.20 -168258.98	-69058.33 ²⁴ -139108.91 ²²	-16543.99 ¹⁴ -30603.96	-9668.17 —	} -520412.54
Work in process	-156960.35	-111939.88 ²²	-24626.78	—	-293527.01
Raw materials	-452352.75	—	—	—	-452352.75
Shipments to affiliates	-45823.27	-43000.01 ²²	-9460.00	—	-98283.28
Cost of sales—1952	2981488.84 ᵃ	2638295.84 ᵃ	587.12883 ᵃ	397637.45 ᵃ	6607150.96 ᵃ
Closing inventory B.M. ⁵¹ ⁵²	28424.14 60207.88	11260.00 ²⁴ 21892.41 ²²	27024.06 ¹⁴ 48163.2	15756.40 —	} 130879.55

1951					
Adjusted costs	3130303.98	2540900.93	619655.44	350831.01	6642691.36
Opening inventories—					
Finished stock	195585.62	219189.36 ²⁴	52605.44 ¹⁶	35070.30	502450.72
Work in process	54077.50	85459.88 ²⁴	20510.37 ¹⁶	13673.58	173721.33
Raw materials	474564.79	—	—	—	474564.79
Closing inv. (see above)	-748400.66	-315135.09	-75632.42 ¹⁴	-44118.91	-1183287.08
Shipments to affiliates	-52549.15	-20925.53 ²⁴	-5022.13 ¹⁴	-2929.57	-81426.38
Cost of sales—1951	3054582.08 ᵃ	2509489.55 ᵃ	612116.70 ᵃ	352526.41 ᵃ	6528714.74 ᵃ
Closing inventory B.M.	727399.34	273018.9 ²⁴	65524.15	40952.8	1106889.6

If the 1951 basis had been followed in 1952 an additional 13.6%
(35.6%-22%) of direct labor would have been added to the closing
consolidated inventory and to consolidated net income; i.e., 13.6%
of (139,108.91 + 111,939.88 + 21,892.41) = 37,120.00 (see footnote, RS 2&3).

If an adjustment of $48,214.19 (=31,438.18 + 12,680.73 + 4,095.28) of the
consolidated earned surplus had been made as at 1-1-52 for
fixed overhead included in the opening inventory, cost of sales for
1952 would have been relieved of that amount less $11,244.57
(=9,668.17 + 1,576.40) included in the consolidated closing inventory,
a net of 36,969.62, and 1952 consolidated net income would have been
increased by a like amount.

ᵃ See note, A-1.

A-4

Martin Manufacturing Company
Raw Materials and Parts Used in Production and Sales
Year ended December 31, 1952

	1952	1951
Purchases of raw materials, parts to be consumed in production, and merchandise (a/c 221)	3 125 056 16	3 097 279 35
Freight in (a/c 222)	33 528 94	52 828 13
Discount on purchases (a/c 224)	− 14 961 37	− 18 803 50
Totals x-4	3 143 623 73 ⌐	3 131 303 98 ⌐
Opening inventory	496 208 59	474 564 79
Closing inventory including AJE #18 in 1952 } a/c 251 {	− 452 352 75	− 496 208 59
Consumed during year	3 187 479 57 ⌐	3 109 660 18 ⌐

Disposition of raw materials, etc. consumed (from an analysis prepared by
J. Johnson, to which we have added AJE's #16 + 18) —

		1952	1951
Parts entering production	x	2 468 110 72	2 434 582 21
Raw materials entering production	x	399 368 38	430 129 08
Merchandise sold (see F-9)		320 000 47	244 948 89
As above		3 187 479 57 ⌐	3 109 660 18 ⌐

Reconciliation with monthly statements —

		1952
Total cumulated on monthly statements } from {		2 877 807 62
Costs underabsorbed } F-9 {		+ 4 000 20
AJE #18 (from F-1)		− 16 713 73
AJE #16 (from A-1)		+ 2 385 01
Total, 2 items above	x	2 867 479 10 ⌐

But one account (#221) is employed for the 3 types of purchases indicated above. No breakdown into the 3 types is made for additions, but the cost clerk keeps a memorandum record of withdrawals from which the above "disposition" summary was derived. The "disposition" is reflected in the monthly statements which have been put together for the 12 months and shown in some detail on F-9. The memorandum record is a compilation of material requisitions (for raw materials and parts) and sales orders (for merchandise). Fifteen items in the memorandum record were traced to their origin; no errors found. No further examination was made of item sources or of the accuracy of the classification as between raw materials, parts, and merchandise.

100 items traced from requisitions to purchase orders to delivery tickets to stores; total of these items, $247,948.35; no exceptions.

A-5

Martin Manufacturing Company
Expense Comparisons
F.L.
r31-2451
Year ended December 31, 1952
2-26-5

All expense accounts were scanned for the purpose of observing classification, unusual items, reasonableness of total, reasons for variations from 1951 rates of expenditure, and any irregularity in month-to-month accruals.

231- Direct labor - Charged with weekly factory payrolls and adjusted at beginning and end of year by accruals. Rates of pay are approved as payroll is audited by personnel director, Mr. Calsp. The audit, made quarterly, is limited to the identification and rate of pay of each employee. Other figures in payrolls are gone into every other month by internal auditor; these include comparisons of clock cards with time reported by foremen, extensions, footings, and comparison of canceled checks against payroll items.

Data from IA's reports:	Average Compensation		Average number on payroll	Total factory payroll	Year paid
	Hourly	Annual			
	1.45	362	702	2540.9	1951
	1.53	384	701	2686.3	1952

Number of employees on 12/26/52 payroll: 695; 12/28/51 payroll, 688. Pay increases up to 10% were granted during year according to Mr. Calsp. Only minor layoffs during 1952 and range of factory employees' pay (through foremen) has been $1020 - $7,400 on annual basis.

2411- Supervision - Consists of shop superintendent, assistant, and 10 foremen; no salary increases. One foreman added on March 15. Total supervision split ½ each as between fixed and variable costs. This arbitrary basis rests on assumption that with greatly reduced operations at least ½ supervision will still be required.

2431- Insurance - Small rate increases; addition of $1,250,000 business interruption coverage.

2441- Depreciation - No increase in rates; substantial asset additions.

2443- Shop expense - Increase of 5% in labor rates caused 15.3 increase in account; also increased cost of some supplies, and small savings in services supplied. Arbitrary split as in 2411.

2451- Repairs - Savings of 4.6 caused principally by dropping of most contract repair work which in 1951 was 18.0 and 13.2 in 1952 (Mr. Hanson)

Martin Manufacturing Company
Expense Comparisons
Year ended December 31, 1952

F. L.
2-26-53

2452 - 2731
(continued)

2452 - Pattern expense - Done increased activity relating to new
appliance models; three pattern-makers; two last year.

2481 - Equipment rental - Same basis as in 1951; see A-6a, 1951 papers.

2484 - Changes in design - Reduction of 14.1, nearly all in labor transferred to other divisions. No major projects during year; 1951
redesigning of several appliances now in tooling stage.

2485 - Product development - Consists of costs of appliances installed
in homes under test conditions, salaries and expenses of engineers
who make periodic checkups and adjustments, and repair
supplies. Installations are not reclaimed. Activity cut in half
during current year.

2491 - Spoilage - During past 10 years charges to this account have fluctuated
from 2.0 (1950) to 53.4 (1946). Causes arise mainly from parts and
product scrapped because of imperfect settings of machines, poor
inspection at early stages, and occasionally too-exacting tolerance
standards. Part of current-year costs are ascribed by Mr. Shuffle
to the institution of rigid quality-control over stamping machines,
and the employment of more highly trained inspectors.

2464 - Installation and service - Analysis by Carl Hibbs:

	Labor	542,494 + 178,955	721,479*	
	Material (supplies)	27,829.01	27,829.01	
	Travel	863,817 + 295,172	1,158,989*	
	Communication	161,540	161,540	
see D-3	Burton-Makin charges	208,272.7 - 208,272.7*		- thru 12-28
	Total	1,131,590.9*	1,131,590.9*	

Above analysis tested; no exception.
During 1953, according to Mr. Hanson, service policy and servicing
will be mainly responsibility of dealers who will be reimbursed
on basis not in excess of 1% of the dealer price of the equipment.
Service personnel will be trained at factory, at dealer's expense.

2731 - Advertising - With switch in agency representation (in 1952,
Prince & Paul, Inc.) 1952 appliance advertising changed from
direct placements (48.3 in 1951) to dealer allowances (45.7 in 1952).
Volume of advertising due to double in 1953 and budget has been
adjusted therefor according to Mr. Parry.

A-7

2761-2791

(continued)

Martin Manufacturing Company
Expense Comparisons
Year ended December 31, 1952

F.L.
2-26-53

2761 - Officers salaries -

Name	Post	1952	1951
Ernest Holdover	chairman	1 000	1 000
Edw. Stebbins	president	48 000	47 800 (from 1-15-51)
B.G. Hanson	vice-president	20 000	20 000
Earle C. Peyton	secretary	12 500	12 500
JB Huddle	treasurer	8 250	8 250
A.P. Collins	controller	15 000	15 000
Totals (see PF-3)		104 750 ~	104 550 ~

2784 - Office expense - Contains contributions of $5,000 each to Democratic and Republican National Committees. Also noted fines of $576.92 for violation of municipal trucking code. See PF-86.

2785 - Legal & accounting -

		1952	1951	
Boggs Boggs & Boggs - retainer	(a)	19 540 00	16 000 00	(a) Includes
H.P. & Co		6 200 00	6 000 00	invoice of
A.H. Barside, special counsel				Dec. 30 for
in Ditto case			15 000 00	$9,500; see
Collection fees to attorney				P-3.
(L.M. Oatis)		435 00	448 75	
Totals		26 175 00 ~	37 448 75 ~	

2788 - Recreation - Included in assessment of $6,000 by Ridgway Recreational Association (Mr. Stebbins is a director) for company's agreed contribution to neighborhood (i.e. near plant) fieldhouse. Employees will have privileges there. Board approved on Dec. 15; per X-3.

2791 - Donations - Contains welfare payments to employees' families, supplementing payments from other sources, and relates to illnesses, accidents outside the plant, and other emergency situations. Board approval given retroactively on December 15 (X-3). Also contains contribution of $2,000 to Associated Colleges of Illinois, Inc. which was approved by Board on March 15 (X-D2)

A-8

Problems and Questions

1. During your examination of the records of the S Corporation as of December 31, you established the following facts:

During the greater part of the year, the company had conducted its business in a building which it had leased for a term of ten years. The rental contract was dated February 1 of the year under audit. Prior to that date and in anticipation of occupancy at that time, it had arranged to have installed in the building certain partitions and other permanent equipment, including new lighting fixtures. The costs of these alterations, you determined, had been charged to "Office Improvements," a fixed-asset account.

The lighting fixtures, which had cost $720.00 installed, proved to be inefficient, and on October 31 they were replaced by new fixtures at a cost of $932.40. The new fixtures had also been charged to "Office Improvements."

There were two credit entries in the account: one for $515.40 had been made on November 1, the second, for $337.40 on December 31. The first credit entry represented the proceeds from the sale of the replaced fixtures; the second, one-fifteenth of the balance in the account on that date, the company's engineers having approved a physical life of fifteen years for the improvements.

Draw up a worksheet analyzing the account "Office Improvements" and prepare journal entries correcting the conditions described.

2. From PF 73 prepare a schedule of automotive equipment still in service, showing for each item cost, estimated and remaining years of life, accrued depreciation, and undepreciated cost.

3. Following a study of the causes of increased operating expenses of a manufacturer during the past year, an auditor discusses the following points with the management: (a) product guarantees; (b) trend of raw-material prices; (c) changes in product lines; (d) changes in production methods; and (e) methods of controlling stores. Where would you look for the effects produced by each of these factors?

4. What points do you think should be covered by the voucher-audit branch of a controller's office? Your answer should take the form of a step-by-step procedure in the processing of an invoice received.

5. What procedure do you think an auditor should follow in reviewing the distribution during the year of factory overhead to the several product lines, where a system of standard costs has been in use for a number of years?

6. You find during the course of an annual audit that the president's salary account has been credited with a "bonus" of $5,000 for "extra service," in addition to the usual salary paid him. What steps should be taken to insure the correctness of this item?

7. What of value would you expect to find, in your study of operations, in the minutes of the meetings of directors and stockholders?

8. In making up a profit-and-loss statement at the end of a fiscal year, are you stating a fact or opinion?

9. The president of a manufacturing company is suspected of inflating the profits of the company, his compensation being a fixed percentage of net income. Indicate a number of methods by which inflation might be effected, and the steps you would take to determine their existence.

10. In examining sales expenses you find that the salaries of several salesmen and the sales manager have been materially increased during the year. The cashier informs you that the sales manager has jurisdiction over the salaries in his department, and you are shown notations signed by the sales manager, authorizing the increases in question. Would these notations constitute a satisfactory verification of sales salaries?

11. A firm whose accounts have been audited annually for a number of years loses, through a fire, all its expense vouchers for the past year; its other records were saved. You are requested to make your regular annual audit. How would you proceed in connection with the missing vouchers?

12. A certain industrial company with several widely scattered factories has a staff officer whose title is "vice-president in charge of purchases." He is a man with extensive practical experience as a purchasing agent and he informs you that he maintains functional controls over the activities of the purchasing agent at each plant. Outline the specific controls he would be expected to exercise.

13. Why do many accountants look with disfavor on the maintenance of accounting controls on warehouse stocks by a purchasing agent?

14. Accountants occasionally disagree with the general rule that quantities should not appear on copies of purchase orders going to the receiving room. If quantities *do* appear, what safeguards would you suggest to insure that the results of actual counts rather than purchase-order amounts are put on receiving tickets?

15. Purchasers of raw material and parts sometimes pay invoices in advance before the receipt of the goods in order to avail themselves of cash discounts. What internal-control devices does this practice make desirable?

16. Suggest a followup method for a purchaser of supplies where back orders are the rule rather than the exception.

17. Outline at least five controls suitable for safeguarding an active petty-cash fund.

18. What value do you attach to explanations accompanying postings to an expense ledger?

19. In a certain business an average of 1200 invoices pass daily through the hands of the voucher-distribution unit. The unit consists of a clerk and six assistants. The clerk reports to the chief bookkeeper who reports to the assistant controller. Frequent complaints are registered to the effect that the distribution coding of fixed-asset purchases is inaccurate and requires many adjusting journal entries. List a number of possible causes for this continued inaccuracy and indicate briefly what you would recommend in each case to improve the situation.

20. The inventory-valuation methods of a manufacturing company

have changed in two respects during the past year: (a) Work in process
and finished goods at the beginning of the year were priced at factory
cost, including factory overhead; at the end of the year these classes
of inventory were priced at prime cost. (b) Raw materials at the beginning of the year were priced on the first-in-first-out basis and at the
end on the moving-average-cost basis. What effect would these changes
of procedure have on operating results? Are they likely to be important
enough to warrant disclosure on the balance sheet?

CHAPTER VI

Cash

Appearing as a single item of current assets on most balance sheets, cash consists of unrestricted bank balances, currency (paper money and coin) and checks and money orders on hand awaiting deposit, currency and checks in transit, and petty-cash and working funds. Occasionally items of cash having restricted uses may appear under fixed assets, sinking fund, and elsewhere, as the restriction may require.

In his review of cash and cash records, the auditor's objectives are to (a) determine whether the item of cash that is to appear on the balance sheet was in fact the correct amount of cash available on the balance-sheet date, and (b) test the adequacy and effectiveness of the methods of internal control surrounding cash receipts and cash disbursements. Certain individual cash items and groups of cash items may be examined in connection with other balance-sheet or operating accounts; an example may be observed in cash receipts from customers to which the auditor may direct his attention when he is reviewing accounts receivable and the internal controls relating to receivables. On the other hand it is possible in some cases that time may be saved and a second handling of records and documents may be avoided where the cash elements of receivables and other items are reviewed when cash is under audit. The choice of methods is usually left to the auditor.

Cash is the most mobile and at the same time the most appropriable and easily manipulated asset, and the volume of cash transactions is usually more than double the number and amount of those pertaining to any other asset. An examination of cash becomes relatively detailed and many-sided where tests reveal that internal controls have not been thorough and continuously effective. Carefully devised and fully operating internal controls materially simplify the auditor's work.

Principles and Practices

Cash in bank. Cash in bank, appearing on the books as the balance on deposit, is ordinarily an amount freely available for application by the management to any business purpose. It differs from the amount reported by the bank mostly because of the natural lag in the bank's recording of a depositor's transactions. Following are characteristic differences:

Checks outstanding: that is, checks (and drafts, if any), issued and recorded by the depositor or any branch or agent of the depositor, but not yet presented to the bank for payment. In the average situation it will be found that the bulk of checks issued will clear within a period of a week or ten days.

Deposits in transit: checks and other receipts dispatched to but not received by the bank, or received by the bank after its daily closing and recorded on the next business day.

An item in a deposit received by the bank but not credited to the depositor's account pending its collection, such as a large check from a customer in a distant city whose ability to make good on the check is unknown or doubtful. Most banks, however, give immediate credit for all items deposited, or have a standard practice of withholding credit for a fixed number of days (depending on the location of the paying bank) until final clearance may be assumed.

Certain types of transactions may be first recorded by the bank, notification of the transaction not having reached the depositor before the end of the period. The following are examples:

A deposit made directly with the bank by a branch office or collection agent (including the bank itself).

A draft, accepted by the bank under a letter of credit or other arrangement with or instruction from the depositor, such as one drawn by a creditor, branch, or foreign representative.

A debit memorandum issued by the bank, as for an NSF check or other faulty paper included in a deposit on an earlier date; a mistake by the depositor, for example, in transcription or addition on a deposit slip, unnoted at the time of the deposit; an interest charge on a loan; a service charge for a collection; a protest fee.

A credit memorandum issued by the bank, as for a collection made at the request of the depositor; interest collected on loan collateral; an understated total on a deposit slip.

Adjustments are customarily made retroactively on the depositor's books for bank charges and credits; the entry of minor service costs, however, is sometimes deferred, usually without protest, by the auditor until the period following. An outstanding check may not be regarded by the depositor as cash in bank without evidence that it has been lost, destroyed, will not be presented for payment, or had not been mailed by the depositor until after the balance-sheet date; putting a check into the mail is assumed to initiate a train of negotiation that is beyond the control of the depositor unless at his request the bank has issued a stop-payment order against it.

Foreign deposits. Cash balances abroad, in foreign currencies, may be free or blocked. In either case their equivalent in dollars is commonly determined by employing the rate of exchange in effect at the date of the statement. Sometimes there are several rates in effect and a choice must be made between them. For almost every country since World War II there has been an official rate, sometimes a commercial (unofficial or free-market) rate, and often a black-market rate: the first established by government fiat and remaining unchanged perhaps for many years; the second, a rate found quoted within and outside the foreign country for the settlement of certain types of business transactions, usually lower (much lower in a period of inflation) than the official rate (that is, less dollars per foreign unit) and varying somewhat from day to day; the third, a rate still lower than the official or free-market rate, established by persons engaged in illegal trade, and subject to substantial daily fluctuations. The usual translation is made at the official rate, although the commercial or other rate may be applied if settlements are habitually made on that basis.

Some foreign countries in an effort to retain investments from dollar sources restrict the amount of a local-currency balance that may be converted into dollars. The restriction may apply to the amount that may be withdrawn during a given period or may limit the withdrawal to a stated percentage of the profits from the foreign operation.

Cash on hand. Cash on hand is found in a variety of forms: checks and currency awaiting deposit, change funds, petty-cash and working funds, cash held for the accommodation of others. Standard practice calls for the deposit of cash receipts intact and the making of disbursements by check save for small items more conveniently paid for in cash through the medium of a petty-cash fund.

Cash arising from receipts and on hand at the end of an accounting period is ordinarily represented by the balance appearing in a cashbook on that date or by a deposit made on the bankable day next following. Change funds are always to be found in the form of actual cash—the ledger amount of the funds, occasionally plus or minus "overs" or "shorts." Petty-cash and working funds are in the form of bank accounts or currency—and sometimes IOU's and paid vouchers.

Cash records. Methods of receiving, disbursing, and recording cash are many and varied. To permit a wide degree of flexibility and control and to reduce unnecessary recordkeeping only daily totals may find their way into the cashbook, remittance advices or other forms serving as the basis for crediting receipts to customers' ledgers, and copies of checks as the basis for debiting payments to the voucher register. Variations or omissions of more usual procedures should, however, be accompanied by protective measures of internal control.

Internal Controls

Many sorts of controls have been devised for safeguarding cash receipts and disbursements, and no single pattern of procedure is to be preferred over all others. Much depends on the character of the business, relations with customers and creditors, the point at which the original record is made, the type of employee on whom the responsibility for custody or documentation must rest, the relative efficiency and cost of the operation, and the nature and extent of internal audit. The separation of receipts from disbursements and the use of the imprest system for minor disbursements is generally conceived to be the minimum standard; it provides for a natural division of labor and function.

Cash receipts. Receipts of cash are satisfactorily safeguarded in most cases by independent controls over (1) incoming mail, (2) collectors, (3) cash sales, and (4) bank deposits. Incoming mail should be opened by a bonded employee other than the cashier or accounts-receivable bookkeeper, the same person preparing a list of the checks and cash received both the detail and total of which are later compared by a different employee with entries in the cash-receipts book and, after a deposit has been made, with the items and total of the bank-deposit slip. Collectors receiving cash directly from customers may give only temporary receipts; customers are informed that official receipts will be sent to them when the money has reached the collector's office. Cash sales wherever possible should be registered mechanically in the presence of the customer or recorded in sales books with a duplicate to the customer, and totaled and compared daily with the cashier's deposits. Receipts from cash sales, both checks and cash, deposited intact, should not be merged with mail receipts. As in the case of mail receipts the duplicate deposit slip, stamped by the bank, and covering no more than one day's receipts, should be compared with the details and totals of the receipts record, and the deposit should be made by an employee or officer independent of the cashier or the receivables bookkeeper.

Cash disbursements. Disbursements should be made by pre-numbered check, each check accompanied by a supporting voucher that has been examined for authorized approvals by the signer of the check. Those authorized to sign checks should not be bookkeepers or cashiers. Checks should never be signed in advance. Such a practice by one of two authorized signers, sometimes observed, always warrants the auditor's criticism. One or more petty-cash funds, maintained for small disbursements, are reimbursed upon presentation of signed receipts or vouchers. Other protective measures are helpful in maintaining internal controls over disbursements. The use of a check protector that effectively prevents the alteration of the amount of a check has become very nearly universal. The perforation of each voucher along with its attachments as the voucher is paid, by use of the device employed by banks in canceling checks, prevents the voucher and attached documents from again being presented for payment. The perforation may be made, for example, in the office of one of the signers of checks. If a check-signing machine is employed, its operation at any time should be under the strict control of the person whose name is inscribed on the signature plate then in use. The establishing of a payroll bank account to which periodic additions are made representing exact payroll totals aids in keeping under prescribed limits both payroll checks issued and payroll checks outstanding.

Cash balances. Monthly bank reconciliations are often made by a person responsible to the treasurer or controller and having no custody of or other connection with cash or receivables; monthly statements and canceled checks may be sent directly to him by the bank. Sometimes the internal auditor does this, but, as noted in Chapter IV, his function is best performed when he is free of repetitive administrative burdens. Like the external auditor, he should be available for testing the performances of others.

The reconciliation should include comparisons of amounts shown by the bank as having been deposited with corresponding cashbook totals, an item-by-item comparison of canceled checks with check-register entries, noting the correspondence of number, date, payee, and amount, and noting also the authenticity of the signature and the endorsements.

A check outstanding more than six months should be eliminated from the reconciliation, the amount of the check being transferred to a liability account or to income if investigation shows that an obligation no longer exists; at the same time the bank should be instructed to issue a stop-payment order against it. The disposition of payroll and dividend checks unclaimed or uncashed may be dependent, however, on the requirements of state laws.

Closing date. Occasionally internal policy concerning the cash cutoff at the end of the period is found not to conform to standard practices. As a result, the auditor may encounter such irregularities as the holding open of the cashbook for receipts after the closing date, or the entry of checks not transmitted to payees until after that date. The effect of the former is to improve the cash position of the business, although the amount of working capital and the working-capital ratio may be changed but little, if at all, since receipts may represent only the liquidation of accounts receivable already appearing in current assets. The reason cited by the company's representatives may be quite different, however: the assertion may be made that these postclosing receipts are simply in-transit items, already in the mail on their way from the customer by the closing date. The reason given for the second of these irregularities is likely to be that the money was actually available for the purpose of liquidating the debts, or that payment was delayed through oversight; the real reason may lie in an attempt to improve the working-capital condition, not by changing the amount of the working capital but by increasing the working-capital ratio, since the reduction of both dividend and divisor by a like quantity creates a larger quotient. Needless to say, the auditor should be firmly opposed to these deviations from normal procedure. In a single instance, the effect might be small; but once the practice is tolerated it would be difficult to overcome at a later date when the effect on financial position might be substantial. If the client should refuse to change the practice at such a time, the auditor would be justified in qualifying his report.

Bonding employees. Every employee who has access to cash, negotiable paper, or other personal property that may be appropriated to his own use, should be bonded. Ability to furnish bond should be a condition precedent to employment. Premiums should, of course, be paid by the employer. Blanket coverage is the rule in many concerns.

Financial-Statement Standards

As already noted, the one item "Cash" may appear on the balance sheet; it will be understood to cover bank balances, cash on hand, and petty-cash and working funds.

Bank balances should be free and unrestricted and subject to check for the full amount. Some banks require minimum balances or balances having a minimum percentage relationship to outstanding bank loans; these minimums are not to be considered restrictions because the bank will ordinarily honor checks drawn upon them. The formal letter from the bank to the auditor will reveal any real restriction on availability. A bona-fide restriction is usually material enough to be noted on the balance sheet.

A question is often raised as to the practice of offsetting bank overdrafts against other cash balances, with the net amount appearing on the balance sheet. If this procedure is adopted, the primary purpose of a balance sheet is defeated, and an actual liability will have been set off against an asset. Of course, no business enterprise will have a bank overdraft if its funds have been carefully controlled.

Cash from the proceeds of a bond issue or cash set aside by board action and available only for construction or other noncurrent purpose should appear "below the line" as a noncurrent asset.

Cash and other assets held for application to a particular liability are sometimes deducted on the face of the balance sheet directly from the liability. This procedure is proper only if the cash has passed beyond the legal control of the depositor. Thus cash deposited with or invested by a sinking-fund trustee, or tax-anticipation warrants purchased from a municipality, may be applicable only to the settlement of an outstanding obligation; in such event they may be deducted on the balance sheet from the liability they will ultimately cancel. Treasury notes held for payment of a Federal income-tax liability are not in the same category, however, since the proceeds upon maturity may be used for any purpose.

Representative Audit Program

Where the internal controls surrounding cash are unusually complete, the auditor's examination may be relatively simple. He may omit the count of cash on hand at the balance-sheet date or at the time of his audit, relying on the verification of undeposited cash at the year end through the bank deposit of the day following, and on the verification of petty-cash and other funds by the internal auditor whose count he will review. He may omit an extended examination of bank accounts, relying on careful reconciliations by employees of the business having no other responsibilities for cash, and on a comparatively brief examination of checks outstanding at the year end that are sent directly to him, with a cutoff statement, by the bank. A typical minimum procedure meeting these specifications follows.

1. Prepare standard letter to bank, for client's signature, with copy to auditor, requesting that year-end balance be confirmed to auditor and that as at named later date (preferably within two weeks after year end—the cutoff period) bank statement with related canceled checks be sent direct to auditor. Request also duplicate deposit slips if procedure 11, below, is to be followed.

2. Obtain copy of client's bank reconciliation at year end, including tape or other list of outstanding checks, prove footings, investigate each detail of reconciliation, compare totals with book balance and bank confirmation, and make inquiry concerning unusual items.

3. Arrange, in numerical order, canceled checks returned with cutoff statement, and:

(a) Compare them with year-end outstanding-check list, noting the date of cancellation, and trace open items remaining on such list to cashbook;

(b) Examine for their propriety large or unusual items and those representing payments to employees (excluding ordinary payroll checks), banks, the company itself, related offices or companies, and petty cash. Record and investigate any apparent irregularity in date of issue, name, signature, endorsement, or date of cancellation.

4. Trace, to cutoff statement, year-end cash on hand awaiting deposit, in-transit deposits, bank transfers, and other items appearing in the year-end reconciliation.

5. Determine whether any checks, shown as issued on or before year end, were on hand on that date.

6. Compare totals of receipts and deposits for period of five days or more before year end and for cutoff period, in order to note whether they correspond and whether deposit has promptly followed receipt; if not, ascertain reasons.

7. List and trace recorded bank transfers for same periods

as in procedure 6, look for possible lag in deposit, and determine why such transfers were made and with whose authority.

8. Scan general-cash, petty-cash, and working-fund counts or reconciliations at year end for independence of counts; review accompanying reimbursements, advances, holdovers, NSF checks, and general method of operating such funds. Scan one month's transactions involving each fund.

9. Determine restrictions, if any, limiting use of any cash balance.

Many auditors take the position that only in the largest enterprises will it be possible so to abbreviate the examination of cash, and, even then, merely in those instances where internal controls are in all respects unimpeachable. They contend further that a greater coverage of cash transactions is indispensable to the annual review of the methods of internal control, is dictated by long-established custom, and has a strong inhibitory effect on employees who handle cash. The following additional procedures may, therefore, be regarded as typical of those adopted for the purpose of satisfying the demand for greater coverage in all situations or simply in those situations where internal controls are not as strong as they could be.

10. Count general cash, petty cash, and other funds on hand, at year end or at cutoff date, in presence of client's representative, and:

(a) Secure cashier's receipt or signature on working-paper record of count;

(b) Reconcile count with books, and trace deposits, other than those already covered in procedure 4, into next regular bank statement;

(c) Investigate noncash items, and secure approval of higher official on such items, if significant;

(d) Scan transactions during period, if any, between year end and count.

11. Extend procedure 6 by obtaining certified duplicate deposit slips for same periods and for undeposited cash on cutoff date; trace items thereon, where possible, to cash-receipts record, and trace totals to recorded deposits.

12. Complete reconciliation of bank balance at cutoff date, following the form suggested on page 204, and independently determine items to be included therein.

13. Foot cash-disbursements record for final month, trace totals to general ledger, and prepare tape of debits and credits on final month's bank statement.

14. Examine, as in procedure 2, above, canceled checks returned with year-end bank statement, trace them to cash-disbursements record for final month or to preceding month's bank reconciliation and account for missing serial numbers in connection with checks issued during month.

15. Verify total of recorded receipts during last month of fiscal year and trace to recorded deposits, general ledger, and bank statement, thus extending procedure 6, above, back a full month.

16. Obtain copy, prove footings, and examine details of client's bank reconciliation at end of next-to-last month preceding year end.

17. Carry out procedures 13-16, inclusive, at the conclusion of some other month within the audit period.

18. Scan and foot cash-receipts and -disbursements records for one or more months earlier in period, and investigate unusual items.

Audit Procedures

Where the auditor has elected to follow a simpler cash-audit program such as that outlined in items 1-9 above he relies on a testing of internal controls, an observation of procedures, a scanning of transactions, and the examination of certain details of a bank cutoff statement to assure him of the propriety of the amount of cash that is to be reflected in the balance sheet. His skills in these several directions, as well as the adequacy of the protective devices surrounding cash transactions and their summarization, are equally important factors in such an election. Also essential is the consent and understanding of the client. Many businessmen would regard the omission of a cash count by the auditor as a serious break in the chain of desirable periodic tests. Year-end counts and reviews by the internal auditor, however, usually convince the client of the propriety of the omission in those situations where a well-ordered and well-directed program of internal control has been carried out.

Preliminary survey. A preliminary survey of procedures and the controls surrounding them enables the auditor to firm up that portion of his program relating to cash. In certain instances he may wish to proceed with one or more of items 8, 9, 10, 17, and 18 of the above program before the close of the audit period, thereby lightening his workload after the year end, and taking whatever steps seem to him necessary for calling the client's attention to procedural weaknesses that appear to have developed since the last examination.

A listing of depositories, locations of cashiers or other custodians, and the names and purposes of the various cash funds should be procured. A comparison with a similar list relating to the preceding year may lead to modifications of the audit program or in the emphasis on certain features of the program. Consultation with the internal auditor will aid in evaluating the importance and practical effect of any changes during the year in operating procedures affecting cash.

If a cash count is to be made at the close of the last business day of the audit period or at any other agreed time, arrangements for it are best completed several weeks in advance. These will include the determination of the locations of the count; provision for temporary cessation of activity in and temporary control by the auditor over cash funds, securities, notes, and other convertibles during the period of count and reconciliation; the clearing out of noncash items; the reduction of handling time by the advance packaging of coins and paper currency; agreement on when and how the day's receipts are to be deposited in the bank; a decision as to the persons to be present; and the disposition of other details relevant to the client's business and the nature of the count. If a surprise count is to be made, details of the conditions to be met between the time of the auditor's announcement of the place and character of the count and the beginning of the count should be agreed to between the auditor and the client's controller or treasurer.

Cash in bank. There are a number of satisfactory ways of verifying the item of cash in bank. Some auditors emphasize the need for at least one reconciliation by the auditor himself, independent of the reconciliation, if any, already made by the client. In minimum procedures 1-9 an independent reconciliation is not made by the auditor, but the client's year-end reconciliation is carefully examined and the "open" items are traced into the cutoff statement received directly from the bank by the auditor: a procedure often deemed to be the equivalent of an independent reconciliation. Alternative procedures include the following:

1. An independent reconciliation is made by the auditor as at the end of the audit period, following or immediately preceding a similar reconciliation by an employee of the client. The two reconciliations are then compared. Where the auditor's reconciliation precedes, the envelope containing the bank statement with its complement of canceled checks is usually presented to him unopened. Because bank statements may be altered, canceled checks withdrawn, or the contents of the envelope otherwise

tampered with, the envelope then being resealed, the auditor may find it desirable to compare the statement with the duplicate in the hands of the bank or with a triplicate statement that the client has requested be sent to him directly from the bank. The items composing the reconciliation with the bank balance, including in-transit deposits and issued checks, are traced to the next following monthly bank statement or, where adjustments of the books have been required, to adjusting entries.

2. Reconciliations as regularly prepared by the client's employees are reviewed in detail by the auditor for the year end, the month preceding, and the month following. Deposits are compared with the record of cash receipts over the two-month period; canceled checks are examined for their dates of issue and cancellation, those issued in one month and canceled in the next being held out for comparison with the list of outstanding items accompanying the reconciliations; other reconciling items are examined for their propriety, and their proper disposal is traced.

3. An independent reconciliation is made by the auditor as at a date preceding the close of the audit period—which may be the end of the month preceding or some day within a week or two of the year end. Open items are subsequently traced to the year-end reconciliation, which is carefully reviewed by the auditor following its preparation by employees of the client.

In reconciling bank accounts, the auditor commences with the balance appearing in the bank statement at the balance-sheet date and adds and subtracts the details necessary to arrive at the balance on the books. The details may be classified thus: adjustments of bank balance, in-transit deposits (including transfers), outstanding checks, balance per books unadjusted, charges and credits originating with the bank and placed on the books after the close of the period, and, finally, the balance per books as adjusted.

Where the auditor has decided to make an independent reconciliation of a bank balance, perhaps the most satisfactory one will be a reconciliation as at the cutoff date, assuming that a cutoff statement is to be procured as outlined in the first item of the representative program. If that date is not far removed from the year end the assembling of the necessary materials of the reconciliation will not be onerous in the average situation, since much of the preliminary work necessary will already have been completed if representative-program items 2, 3, 4, 6, and 7 or their equivalents have been carried out fully. Each item of the reconciliation is carefully reviewed or determined independently by the auditor and put into a schedule form such as the following:

Particulars	Balance December 31, 19–1	Cutoff Period Deposits	Cutoff Period Withdrawals	Balance January 10, 19–2
Bank statement	$30,475.11	$465,896.52	$423,165.68	$73,205.95
In-transit deposits—				
Beginning	+1,522.43	− 1,522.43	—	—
End	—	+ 647.88	—	+ 647.88
Outstanding checks—				
Beginning	−2,583.15	—	− 2,583.15	—
End	—	—	+ 3,365.61	−3,365.61
Reconciling items—				
Service charge	+ 12.00	− 12.00	—	—
Collection fee	—	—	− 4.00	+ 4.00
NSF check	—	—	− 40.50	+ 40.50
Books	$29,426.39	$465,009.97	$423,903.64	$70,532.72
Adjustments—				
Auditor's (December)	− 12.00	+ 12.00	—	—
Cashier's (January)	—	− 44.50	—	− 44.50
Books after adjustment	$29,414.39	$464.977.47	$423,903.64	$70,488.22

The sources of the items inserted by the auditor in the above illustration may be presumed to have been as follows:

First money column: from the client's (or the auditor's) reconciliation at the year end.

Bank deposits: the total deposits (taped) shown by the cutoff statement from the bank.

Bank withdrawals: the total of returned and canceled checks (taped) appearing on the bank cutoff statement.

Bank balance: the balance appearing at the end of the bank cutoff statement.

In-transit deposits: (beginning) any deposit made by the cashier on December 31 or before, received by the bank after the close of business and recorded by the bank on January 2 or thereafter; (end) a like situation on January 10, the duplicate deposit slip for $647.88 in the possession of the cashier bearing the bank stamp of January 11 or some subsequent date.

Outstanding checks: (beginning) the total of the outstanding checks appearing on the client's reconciliation, a tape showing this amount having been run by the auditor; (end) the taped total of outstanding checks at January 10 prepared by the auditor from open items remaining after comparing checks returned by the bank (serially arranged by the auditor) with the list of outstanding checks at December 31 and with the January check register. December (or prior) checks unreturned by the bank at January 10 are of course in both totals.

Reconciling items: a bank service charge for December appearing on the December bank statement as a withdrawal, and traced by the auditor into the client's cash-receipts book where it appeared as a red figure in the deposits column on January 2; two January charges on the cutoff statement recorded in the cash-receipts book after January 10 (see below).

Books before adjustment: the total deposits equal the total appearing in the deposit column of the January cash-receipts book; the total withdrawals equal the total of checks drawn reflected in the January check register.

Adjustments: (auditor's) correction of December 31 bank balance for December service charge and at the conclusion of the audit put on the books as a correction of December 31 balances; (cashier's) charges reported by the bank on the cutoff statement and recorded by the cashier on January 11 (again through the cash-receipts book) when his attention was directed to them.

Books after adjustment: the balance at December 31 is now in agreement with the general ledger as adjusted and with the auditor's reconciliation shown elsewhere in his working papers, and total deposits and withdrawals are in agreement with January totals to date; the client's January cashbook totals will not be posted to the general ledger until the end of the month and hence the book balance on January 10 does not agree with any total appearing on the books.

A bank balance is verified by a letter from the bank written at the request of the client and sent directly to the auditor, following some such form as that illustrated below:

A. L. JONES & Co.
Chicago, Ill.

January 5, 19–2

First National Bank
Chicago, Ill.

Dear Sirs:

Enclosed is a form, partially filled out, that we request you to complete and transmit to our auditors, Messrs. Hyatt, Paterson & Co., 960 Hudson Bldg., Chicago. We also request that you send send them direct, following the close of business on January 10, 19–2, statement of our account from the beginning of the year through that date, including therewith canceled checks and any other usual memoranda in support thereof.

Very truly yours,

A. L. JONES & COMPANY
J. P. Stebbins
President

An example follows of such a form, used by auditors to make sure that the information they desire, including data on bank loans and other items, if any, will be furnished by the bank.[1] A number of the larger banks have their own forms for this purpose that provide essentially the same information. Items accompanied by asterisks are filled in by the client before the form is sent to the bank. The same information is requested from each

---

[1] See also AIA form, page 220.

bank with which the client has done business during the period or which has been authorized as a depository by the board, whether or not a balance remains at the end of the period.

Bank balances are also reported in monthly statements, but since bank statements may easily be altered the figures appearing on them cannot be relied upon except as prima-facie evidence. In instances now rare, the passbook may be ruled off by the bank once a year or oftener to show closing balances. The same limitation applies to the passbook as evidence, however, and it is disregarded by most auditors.

Hyatt, Paterson & Co.   Date_____
Certified Public Accountants
Chicago 4, Ill.

Dear Sirs:

Following are the credit balances, subject to withdrawal on demand, of accounts appearing on our books in the name or for the account of
_____

Title of account	Balances at close of business	
	_____19—	*_____19—*

The above balances are subject to restrictions as follows:

Accompanying this letter are duplicates of deposit slips relating to the above accounts for *_____*

On *_____* the above-named depositor was not obligated to this bank directly or indirectly except on the following items:

Maker	Kind of obligation	Direct or indirect	Date of obligation	Date due	Rate of interest	Date interest paid to	Amount

Collateral or other security on the above obligations _____

On *_____* we were holding as trustee or agent or holding in safekeeping for this depositor the following items

Very truly yours,
_____

By_____

Amounts of outstanding checks at the year end, dates of issue, and payees, as they appear on the check register or other disbursement record, should be compared (1) with the vouchers against which the checks were issued, in order that their authenticity may be assured, and (2) with the checks returned with the cutoff bank statement. The dates of cancellation on the checks should follow within a week of the date of issue for most creditors. Each check that has been outstanding for more than sixty days should be the subject of inquiry; an item in dispute may suggest the existence of a contingent or additional liability not yet recorded. Internal controls over checks long outstanding should be reviewed, and the disposition after the previous audit of each check outstanding should be noted in the working papers. Outstanding checks at the year end should consist only of checks drawn within or prior to the period under review. The practice of holding the books open after the end of the period and adding to disbursements checks written (or cash paid out) in the succeeding period has the effect of decreasing both cash and accounts payable, and hence inflates the working-capital ratio on the balance-sheet date. Wherever this situation is found, an adjusting entry, adding such amounts back to cash and accounts payable, will be required.

Deposits at the year end are carefully reviewed. One practice is to secure copies of deposit slips for several days—perhaps the last two or three days at the end of the fiscal period and the same number at the beginning of the month following. Details on the slips are compared with the cash-receipts record, and each slip is refooted. Where the receipts are in the form of checks representing individual sales or payments on account, the comparison usually offers no difficulty. With a large number of items, items of the same amount, or a quantity of currency in the deposit, the auditor may be able to compare totals only. But the details on the slip may help him identify the dates of the various receipts that are being deposited, and he will follow up carefully any items that were not deposited within twenty-four hours after their receipt. The main object in obtaining the duplicate deposit slips is to discover irregularities, if any, in prescribed procedures and unusual items that are put into the bank or omitted from deposits just before and after the end of the period. Deposits credited within the period must not include the receipts on any day of the following month; where this practice exists the auditor is compelled to reduce the cash balance and charge receivables or other accounts in the amount of the cash overstatement. If the auditor is present at the end of the period, asking for duplicate deposit slips is obviated, and he is in a position to review individual deposits just before they are made.

Transfers between bank accounts are reviewed for several days or even a month before and after the end of the period, and the reasons for each transfer should be ascertained, with particular attention directed to the possible "kiting" of checks. Each transfer in transit at the balance-sheet date should be examined closely. Was the check drawn and recorded shortly before the end of the period, at a time when a cash balance in the drawee bank was available? Was it deposited without delay in another bank account?

Service and other incidental bank charges and credits may appear for the first time in a debit memorandum accompanying the monthly statement from the bank. Even though small in amount, these items are best recorded in the period to which they relate, since they are usually known or can be made available by the first or second of the month, at which time the general books are almost always still open.

Cash not deposited intact. Some small business enterprises—now fortunately, few in number—make no attempt to deposit cash receipts intact and make disbursements from them. This means that the cash balance is constantly changing and that the amount on hand on the day of the auditor's count will be different from that at the close of the audit year. In such a case it is customary to reconcile the bank balance at the later date, scan the cash transactions between the two dates, trace deposits where possible from the cashbook into the bank, examine the returned canceled checks listed as outstanding at the earlier date, and prepare a reconciliation statement along the lines of the illustration following:

	Books	Bank	Cash transactions
Balances March 5, 19–1, as determined by auditor—			
Books and bank certificate	$20,116.70	$25,261.83	
Outstanding checks		5,145.13*	
Cash on hand, per count	909.01		$ 909.01
Cashbook transactions, January 1, 19–1 to March 5, 19–1—			
Disbursements, testchecked against paid vouchers, and against such checks as were issued for paid vouchers—			
January	10,433.25	9,009.43	1,423.82
February	8,242.16	7,838.65	403.51
March	2,306.91	2,000.00	306.91

	Books	Bank	Cash transactions
Receipts, testchecked to customers' accounts or general-ledger accounts and traced to bank statements—			
January	8,113.45*	6,540.80*	1,572.65*
February	14,677.32*	14,211.55*	465.77*
March	863.80*	725.00*	138.80*
Balances December 31, 19–0	$18,353.46	$17,487.43	$ 866.03
Bank certificate		$21,835.54	
Outstanding checks		4,348.11*	

* Deduction.

The totals of receipts and disbursements entered in the above statement were prepared by the auditor from the cashbook. He should note any large or unusual receipts and disbursements and satisfy himself of their propriety. On remaining items he should scan the explanations or vouchers supporting them and testcheck the postings of a number of items, particularly those at the beginning and end of each month. The items making up the outstanding checks on March 5 were prepared by the auditor and represent the total of the checks shown by the cashbook to be outstanding after noting therein the canceled checks returned by the bank with the March 5 cutoff statement. The list of outstanding checks at December 31 was prepared by the cashier and independently footed by the auditor; the items making up the list were found to be among the canceled checks returned by the bank in 19–1, all of which were noted by him to have been issued in connection with ordinary business transactions. These procedures and the results secured from them give the auditor reasonable assurance of the essential propriety of the balance in bank and on hand at December 31.

Cash on hand. If cash on hand is to be counted, a surprise examination is always preferable, though seldom possible. The date of the auditor's visit is usually made known some time in advance to members of the client's staff so that they may be prepared for him. Some auditors make a practice of counting cash on the last day of the fiscal period, thus automatically eliminating the surprise element; but they generally supplement the last-day count by another, perhaps a week or a month later. Both the surprise and last-day count are difficult, often impossible to arrange and the auditor must rely on other tests.

In addition to cash that will be deposited in the bank, the auditor may find change funds, and one or more petty-cash or working funds, all of which should appear in their full amount on the balance-sheet date. If more than one cash fund exists, it is preferable to count all of them at the same time in order to prevent the substitution of the funds of one account for those of another; in some cases (see Chapter IX), it may be necessary to count securities at the same time. The count of cash should always be made in the presence of the cashier, and the cashier should give the auditor a receipt for its return in the form of an "ok" and a signature at the bottom of the working paper.

As a first step in counting cash on hand, checks and other paper are listed. Here, as elsewhere, the auditor may accept an adding-machine tape from a client's employee, but it will be necessary for him to rerun the tape or verify the addition mentally, since a careless or dishonest machine operator can always produce incorrect totals without leaving on the tape any indication of the amount added or omitted. Moreover, in this instance, the maker of each check should be noted on the worksheet so that each item may subsequently be traced to the deposit slip and into the account that receives the credit. Items received after the end of the fiscal period must be excluded, but if the count is being made on the last day of the period, the auditor should make sure that he has included the receipts that have come in after the last deposit on that day.

General cash and petty-cash funds at the balance-sheet date may consist in part of such noncash items as (1) paid vouchers, (2) checks held for redeposit, having been returned by the bank marked "NSF" or having improper endorsement or other fault, (3) debit memoranda from the bank and other vouchers that have been paid in cash, (4) IOU's, and (5) counterfeit or damaged currency that cannot be passed on. The auditor should always emphasize the desirability of disposing promptly of items of this character, and he should review a detailed list of them with a responsible official. Even though their total is not material, the presence of questionable items often signifies a laxity in internal controls, which, for the sake of the organization, should be corrected promptly, since they may reappear at a later date in a more harmful form. An adjusting entry is usually required, therefore, despite the lack of materiality; the entry is normally reversed at the beginning of the following period, and the auditor should follow the subsequent history of the items of adjustment, making sure they are finally disposed of.

A certain degree of manual facility should be acquired by the auditor in the handling of currency—the counting of a pile of

loose coins or a sheaf of bills—and he should know the contents
of the common packages of money. These are:

Unit	Number in Package	Value of Package
Cent	50	$0.50
Nickel	40	$2
Dime	50	$5
Quarter	40	$10
Half-dollar	20	$10
Dollar (silver)	20	$20
Dollar bill	25, 50, or 100	$25, $50, or $100
Two-dollar bill	50, or 100	$100, or $200
Five-dollar bill	20, 40, or 100	$100, $200, or $500
Ten-dollar bill	20, or 50	$200, or $500
Twenty-dollar bill	25	$500

It is generally not necessary to count the contents of coin packages, but if for any reason a coin package is opened, the coins
should be returned to the cashier for repackaging. On the auditor's worksheet the kinds of currency should be listed in detail.

Cash counts should include an examination of the entire contents of the cash drawer, safe, or other office repository for cash.
The auditor may find small sums of money, even marketable
securities, on hand in safekeeping for employees, checks to be
cashed for employees, sometimes "overs" from previous cash
counts, and unclaimed payroll envelopes. Where there are change
funds or an office petty-cash fund in which the transactions are
numerous, "overs and shorts" will be of frequent occurrence; the
best practice is to account for them daily through an "over-and-
short" account, thus avoiding a temporary holdout in the case of
an "over" and a temptation to "lap" in the case of a shortage.
Use of the cashier's office facilities is sometimes a necessary convenience for employees; more often it should be discouraged in
order that the opportunities of manipulating cash may be mini-
mized. The cashier's functions should be as direct and uninvolved
as possible. Unclaimed wages should be noted by the disbursing
clerk on the payroll and after a week or two returned to general
cash with a credit to a special liability account, under some carefully considered form of internal control; where this is not done
the auditor may find it difficult to verify the unclaimed wages
that should be on hand.

Branch-office cash counts are sometimes waived by the auditor,
especially where the cash is limited to a small petty-cash fund.
If the business is large enough to maintain an internal-audit staff,
a recent examination by a member of the staff—on the balance-

sheet date if a bank account of any size is involved—may be accepted, provided the usual precautions have been observed, the staff member is queried, and his working papers are reviewed. If no internal-audit data are available, the auditor may accept the certifications made to him by the custodians of small funds or seek the help of a local public accountant if the amounts are material. Cash advanced to salesmen and other employees as a rule can be verified only by a letter direct from the employee to the accountant; in most cases the letter constitutes satisfactory evidence of the existence of the fund.

Where cash is not deposited intact, the auditor's presence on the last day of the audit period is highly desirable, in order that he may make an independent cash count; if that is impossible he will have to depend on a cash reconciliation at a later date and a working back to the last day of the audit period as demonstrated in the preceding section.

Cash frauds. The term "fraud" is usually associated with cash losses, but merchandise and other assets, as well as cash, may be appropriated, even under well-operated systems of internal controls, and the auditor must always bear this possibility in mind, although as previously stated the detection of fraud is no longer a major purpose of an audit as it once was. The possibilities of fraud are numerous, and the time ordinarily spent on an annual examination could easily be multiplied several times without covering them all. Reliance must be had by the client on effective internal controls designed to prevent them; his dependence on the auditor in this respect should consist of having the auditor once a year, and where warranted, more often, review the methods of internal control including internal audit and give his recommendations concerning the handling of appropriable assets. Features of internal control often cited as deterrents of fraud include the bonding of employees having contact with removable cash, securities, storeroom items, and other assets; the participation in every transaction by at least two operating units dealing at arm's length with each other, the one automatically and routinely verifying the work of the other; the rotation of cashiers, accounts-receivable bookkeepers, storeroom employees, and voucher clerks; annual vacations; a careful tracing of differences disclosed in cash counts, receivable balancing, and inventory reconciliations; the planning of transaction handling or insistence on the strict observance of carefully conceived handling plans; and unannounced examinations by internal auditors.

In inspecting cash records an awareness of how various cash

frauds have been committed will assist the auditor in recognizing such causes as the following:

1. Not recording a cash sale
2. Recording a sale or a remittance from a customer in an amount less than that received
3. "Padding" or otherwise overstating a payroll
4. Raising a check, after it has been returned by the bank, to agree with an overstated entry in the cash-disbursements record
5. Forging a signature on a check
6. Forging a paid bill
7. Presenting a bill twice for payment
8. Making out a false cash voucher
9. Understating a cash discount or allowance on a purchase
10. Overstating a cash discount or allowance on a sale
11. Entering a bank transfer in one period and recording its receipt in another
12. Forcing a footing to make a cash record balance
13. Kiting
14. Lapping

Kiting is the act of drawing and cashing an unrecorded check on one bank, followed shortly by drawing an unrecorded check on another bank that will act as a deposit to cover it; the second check, in turn, is covered by a check drawn on a third bank, and the process may go on indefinitely among several banks. The time taken for checks to clear through banks is thus taken advantage of in order to cover an unauthorized "borrowing" or theft of money. A necessary part of the kiting process is to overstate the cash account by having entered as a deposit in the year under audit a check drawn as a disbursement of the succeeding year. Occasionally a rough comparison of cash deposited with total credits to accounts receivable may indicate that kiting has been going on.

Lapping is not an unusual procedure for a defaulting cashier to follow, since it affords a comparatively easy way of obtaining cash for temporary use and then replacing it later, provided the perpetrator does not get in too deep. Under this system the cash received, say, from a customer, is withheld, but on some later date the amount is entered as a credit in the cash-receipts book. On or before this date other remittances are withheld, and the cash therefrom is deposited in lieu of that retained the first day. Thus, except for the first day on which the fraud is committed, the total amount of receipts is actually deposited unless, of course, the process is repeated. Where deposit slips are prepared by a person other than the cashier, the detection of such a fraud can usually be ascertained by comparing the detail on such slips with entries in the cash-receipts book. In making this comparison the auditor must be positive that the slips are copies of those actually used in making the deposit; this can be verified at the bank since most banks file deposit slips by days. Their officials have become accustomed to such requests by auditors, and the auditor need not be afraid of imposing on any bank's goodwill by asking permission to inspect a reasonable number of deposit slips or requesting certified copies of them.

Illustrative Audit

There are five worksheets and three letters or letter copies relating to cash. The first sheet is a summary of what the auditor did and what he found. At the top of the sheet are the amounts of the three general-ledger cash accounts—one general bank account, one payroll bank account, and a petty-cash-on-hand account. No object is served by this small dollar schedule, since the method of group segregation followed on TB 1 yields the same total for cash. Worksheet totals on C 2, 3, and 4 each tie in with corresponding items on the working trial balance.

The eight items listed under "Work done" (C 1) epitomizing the program followed by the auditor and his assistant in their review of "cash" consist of positive statements of audit procedures, precautions taken, and findings. Since no exceptions are cited it may be concluded that the adjusted total of the three ledger acounts, or $399,654.35, is a proper balance-sheet item. An auditor's skill is often rated by his superiors in accordance with his ability to put into his working papers an intelligible summary of his performance in the field and the conclusions to be drawn from it.

For both bank accounts, the method of verifying the year-end balance is the same. Four summary figures (on the first line of the worksheet), representing totals obtained from the cutoff bank statement sent directly to the auditor, must be worked back to the books because of the time lag between mutual recordings. If the auditor has established satisfactory proof of the reconciling items (for example, items a, b, and c on C 2), he has made an objective verification of the year-end cash-in-bank balance. The only items for which additional proof may exist are checks or other items outstanding, both at the year end and on the cutoff date. On C 2 checks 86012, 88775, and 88785 were outstanding on the two dates, but the last two were returned with the bank statement of January 31. Check 86012 may have been lost; a followup is to be made by the internal auditor (see footnote on worksheet C 2).

The bank letters follow a more or less standard form. Some banks will reply with a printed form with filled-in blanks. In other instances, the auditor uses printed forms that are to be signed and sent to the bank by his client, and filled out and returned to the auditor by the bank. In any case, the auditor initiates the correspondence by preparing the letter or form to be sent to the bank and having it signed and sent out by the company's president or other officer.

Adding-machine tapes may be pasted to worksheets, as on C 3, or to separate following sheets. Items on the tapes are best accompanied by check number, page number, or other identification that will facilitate the location of their source, should the occasion ever require. The broken lines on tapes *a* and *b* on C 3 indicate the omission of detail simply for purposes of this illustration; obviously, in actual practice, no such omission would be permitted and the whole tape would be required.

Items appearing on C 5 are intended to illustrate types of notes made by auditors in a detailed audit of cash. Sometimes notes such as these will lead to adjustments to which, of course, the notes should be indexed, whether or not the reference is to book entries made before the trial balance is extracted or to an AJE prepared by the auditor himself.

The adjustment of petty cash is minor and could have been passed by the auditor. Sometimes the auditor makes small adjustments as a reminder to the client's staff not to overlook future reviews of certain areas where adjustments could conceivably be much more important.

Martin Manufacturing Company
Cash Summary
December 31, 1952

F.L.
2-12-53

	a/c	W/P	Per books	As adjusted
Cash in banks—				
Jackson National Bank — general	01-1	C-2	385209 67	383 238 39
Howard National Bank — payroll	01-2	C-3	16 185 57	16 185 57
Petty cash	01-9	C-4	500 00	230 39
Books before adjustment			401 895 24	
AJE #12 – NSF check taken up in January 1953			– 1971 28	
AJE #27 – Petty-cash vouchers reimbursed in January			– 269 61	
As adjusted			399 654 35	399 654 35
				TB

Work done—

1. Cash-receipts book and check register were scanned for unusual items (none found) and were footed for May and October 1952 (no errors noted).

2. Entries in Jackson National Bank account were traced to footings appearing in cash-receipts book and check register for last three months of year (no errors discovered).

3. Cutoff statements were received unopened directly from each of above banks.
   a) Checks received with cutoff statements were compared with outstanding checks at 12/31/52 and January 1953 check register.
   b) Deposits in transit recorded as receipts on 12/31/52 and 1/10/53.

4. Checks drawn on or before Dec. 31, 1952, appeared to have been mailed before yearend; cutoff in cash receipts appears also to have been proper.

5. Deposits 12/26/52 to 12/31/52 were traced to cash receipts recorded during that period; a similar verification was made of deposits from Jan. 2 to 1953.

6. Checks outstanding and not examined on previous audit were all returned with Feb.–April 1952 bank statements; see C-2 and C-3 in 1951 papers.

7. Bank reconciliations are prepared by Andrew R. Fisher, cashier, and are reviewed monthly by Carl Hibbs, internal auditor, and at yearend by Arthur P. Collins, controller. Reconciliations at 5/31 and 10/31 were reviewed and both details and totals were traced to original records and to bank statements. This review was performed in connection with the examination of the cash transactions for the months of May and Oct. 1952. The results of this examination are summarized on C-5. The cashier is bonded for $25,000.

8. Controller approves petty-cash reimbursements and reviews supporting vouchers prepared by Mrs. Sarah Jopplin, petty cashier. These vouchers for Oct., Nov. and Dec. were examined and traced to reimbursement distribution. Reimbursement was made on Dec. 23 and the next following reimbursement (Jan. 18, 1953) included two 1952 items (AJE

C-1

Martin Manufacturing Company
Cash - Jackson National Bank
December 31, 1952 & January 10, 1953

Items		Balance 12-31-52	Cutoff period Deposits	(withdrawals)	Balance 1-10-53
Bank statement 1-10-53	(C-2a)	42891486	20866164	29013747	34743903
Deposits in transit -					
12-31-52	(a)	+ 3367481	- 3367481		
1-10-53	(c)		+ 4986195		+ 4986195
Checks outstanding -					
12-31-52	(b)	- 7935128		- 7935128	
1-10-53	(c)			+ 11885822	- 11885822
Chargeback on NSF check	(d)	+ 197128		+ 197128	
Per books		38520967	22484878	33161569	27844276
AJE 12	(d)	- 197128			- 197128
Balance as adjusted		38323839			27647148

TB

a) Deposits 12-31-52 to 1-10-53

c/R book	Bank	Amount		
12-31	1-2	3367481		
1-2	1-5	1997257		
1-3	1-5	2637852		
1-5	1-7	2974175	20866164	
1-7	1-8	2421892	22484878	
1-8	1-9	3590617		
1-9	1-10	3876890		
1-10	1-12	4986195		

c) Checks outstanding 1-10-53

#	Amount	Returned
86012	26378	(e)
88775	97125	1-31
88785	309175	1-31
Total	432678	
88893	7562987	1-31
5	1592177	✓
6	75248	✓
7	126708	✓
8	5742	✓
88901	920601	
2	50909	1-31
3	1118772	✓
Total	11885822	

b) Checks outstanding 12-31-52

#	Amount	Returned
86012	26378	(e)
88768	319754	1-10
75	97125	1-31
8	1570468	1-10
9	52673	✓
80	167821	✓
1	2592878	✓
2	1247659	✓
3	718947	✓
4	70638	✓
5	309175	1-31
6	8762	1-10
7	195272	✓
8	87578	✓
Total	7935128	

d) Gates Mfg Co. #324 redeposited on 1/21/53 and cleared; originally deposited on 12-29-52.

e) Check drawn to Arthur Rohrer, voucher 10-483 in order and apparently not in dispute. CH is to follow this up.

C-2

G/L
01-2

Martin Manufacturing Company
Factory Payroll Cash — Howard National Bank
December 31, 1952 & January 10, 1953

H.R.
2-3-53

Items		Balance 12-31-52	Cutoff Period Deposits	Withdrawals	Balance 1-10-53
Bank statement 1-10-53 (C-3a)		3679408	1200000 00	8448006	7x31402
Deposits per bank and C/R book –					
1-3-53	6000000				
1-10-53	6000000				
Weekly payrolls –					
1-2-53	6168728				
1-9-53	6058225				
Checks outstanding –					
12-31-52	a) -2060851*		-2060851		
1-10-53	b)			+5637468 -	5637468
Per books		1618557*	1200000 00	12024623*	1593934*

a) Outstanding checks 12-31-52 –   TB   b) Outstanding checks 1-10-53 –

38475	117.90 *		39050	156.30 *
6	47.50		41112	131.45
38502	322.48		8	342.00
3	49.76		41242	56.10
10	87.95		5	108.45
26	267.92		53	93.76
31	288.62		5	62.99
39050	156.30		7	110.23
1	122.34		72	91.56
5	65.25		9	63.08
9	124.88		81	100.01
	20,608.51*			56,374.68*

Notes:
Payroll week and work week end on Friday
Checks are dated Friday but are passed out on Monday
Covering deposits are made Saturday
Office payroll is semimonthly and is paid out of general account in
Jackson National Bank.

C-3

(copy for auditors)

MARTIN MANUFACTURING COMPANY
1688 S. Federal St.
Chicago 16, Ill.

December 15, 1952

Jackson National Bank
Chicago 2, Illinois

Dear Sirs:

Please furnish our auditors, Hyatt, Paterson & Company,
960 Hudson Bldg., Chicago 4, with the following information and statements:

1. The amounts of any balances of
   checking or other accounts in
   our name at December 31, 1952

2. Statements, together with canceled checks and other customary
   enclosures, covering the period
   from January 1 through January 10,
   1953

3. The names of persons whose signatures you honor on our checks

4. Details of amounts for which we
   were liable to you, directly or
   indirectly, on December 31, 1952

                    Very truly yours,

                    Martin Manufacturing Company

              by Edw. Stebbins
                        President

[A similar letter was
 sent to Howard National
 Bank.]

                    c - 2a

DUPLICATE
To be mailed to accountant

January 12 19 53

Dear Sirs:

Your completion of the following report will be sincerely appreciated. If the answer to any item is "none", please so state. Kindly mail it in the enclosed stamped, addressed envelope direct to the accountant named below.

Report from

Yours truly,

Martin Manufacturing Company

By _____
Authorized Signature

(Bank) **Jackson National Bank**

Chicago 2, Illinois

Bank customer should check here if confirmation of bank balances only (item 1) is desired. ☐

Name of accountant

**Hyatt, Paterson & Company
960 Hudson Building
Chicago 4, Illinois**

Bank should check whichever is applicable: This report covers all accounts
1. with this office ☐ or
2. with this office and all other domestic offices ☒

Dear Sirs:

(a) December 31, 1952

1. We hereby report that at the close of business on (b) January 10 1953 _____ our records showed the following balance(s) to the credit of **Martin Manufacturing Company**

AMOUNT	DESIGNATION OF ACCOUNT	IS BALANCE SUBJECT TO WITHDRAWAL BY CHECK?	DOES ACCOUNT BEAR INTEREST? GIVE RATE
(a) $428,914.86 (b) $347,439.03	General checking account	Yes	No

REMARKS

2. We further report that the above mentioned depositor was directly liable to us in respect of loans, acceptances, etc., at the close of business on that date in the total amount of $ none _____, as follows:

AMOUNT	DATE OF LOAN OR DISCOUNT	DUE DATE	INTEREST RATE	PAID TO	DESCRIPTION OF LIABILITY, COLLATERAL, LIENS, ENDORSERS, ETC.
$					

3. Said depositor was contingently liable as endorser of notes discounted and/or as guarantor at the close of business on that date in the total amount of $ 25,611.00 _____, as below:

AMOUNT	NAME OF MAKER	DATE OF NOTE	DUE DATE	REMARKS
$10,500.00	Banks Toddman & Co	11-15-52	5-15-53	Discounted note
$15,111.00	Whiteman & Co	10-30-52	120 days	" "

4. Other direct or contingent liabilities, open letters of credit, and relative collateral, were

We honor checks bearing the signature of Andrew R. Fisher, cashier, or Frank Markham, assistant cashier, and the countersignature of J. B. Huddle, treasurer, or John Sutherland, assistant treasurer

Yours truly,

(Bank) **Jackson National Bank**

By _____
Authorized Signature
Cashier

Date **January 12,** 19 53

If the space provided is inadequate, please enter totals hereon and attach a statement giving full details as called for by the above column headings.

January 13, 1953

Hyatt, Paterson & Company
960 Hudson Building
Chicago 4, Ill.

Gentlemen:

At the request of Mr. Edward Stebbins of Martin
Manufacturing Company of Chicago, we are mailing you
under separate cover a statement of the company's payroll checking account relating to the first ten days
of this month, together with the canceled checks for
the same period. On December 31, 1952 the balance in
this account was $36,794.08 and at the close of busi-
ness on January 10, 1953 the balance was $72,314.02,
according to our records. Our records show only one
deposit account with this company.

In accordance with instructions in our files from
the company's board of directors checks may be drawn
on the above account only when signed by Sidney Shell
or Jack Johnson, and countersigned by John Sutherland
or Andrew R. Fisher.

As at December 31, 1952 the Martin Manufacturing
Company was indebted to us on two notes: the first
dated November 19, 1952 and due February 17, 1953
amounting to $450,000 and bearing interest of 2 1/4%;
the second on note dated December 16, 1952 and due
March 20, 1953 in the amount of $100,000 also bearing
interest at 2 1/4%. In both cases the interest is
payable at the maturity of the note.

Very truly yours,

Howard National Bank

by _Gordon Hassell_
Gordon Hassell
Vice-President

C-3

N-1

c - 3a

Martin Manufacturing Company
Petty-Cash Count
December 31, 1952

G/L
01-9

F.L.
2-4-53

	Quantity	Denomination		Amount	
Currency:	7	$ 20		140	00
	3	10		30	00
	9	5		45	00
	30	1		30	00
Coin:	10	50		5	00
	15	25		3	75
	20	10		2	00
	18	05			90
	59	01			59

1. Temporary loan —
   1/10/53 — Jacob Kline — approved by
   Arthur P. Collins; originally $160;
   payable $10 per week; balance — 130 00

2. Disbursements from January 19, 1953 —
   Checks —
   1/19/53 — Arthur P. Collins (payable to cash) — 50 00
   Vouchers —
   1/22/53 — Horders - office supplies — 3 89
   1/23/53 — postage — 30 00
   1/24/53 — cab fare — 2 90
   1/29/53 — supper money (6 employees) — 9 00
   1/30/53 — Race Mfg. Co. — COD shipment repair parts — 16 29 — 112 08

3. Cash shortage — 68
   Total per a/c 01-9 — 500 00

The cash and other items listed above were returned to me.
              (Mrs.) Sarah Jopplin, Petty Cashier 2/4/53

1. The petty cashier stated that the above check would be cashed at
   the bank in the near future. The practice is not to cash checks of
   employees. This was an emergency according to Mrs. Jopplin.

2. Cash shortage will be included in next reimbursement voucher.
   The one reimbursement voucher since Dec. covers the period Dec. 23-
   Jan. 18, inclusive. Examination disclosed the following:
   Disbursements pertaining to period 12/23 - 12/31 —

AJE 27 { 12/29 Emergency repair work on office roof — 233 86
       { 12/24 Christmas gifts to postman and truckers — 35 75
   Other vouchers — all 1953 items — 69 11
              Check 89003 4/18/53 — 338 72

C-4

Martin Manufacturing Company
Examination of cash transactions for months of May and October 1952

Cash receipts:

To determine the promptness of deposit of daily receipts, a comparison was made of the total daily entries in the cash-receipts book with deposits in the Jackson National Bank as shown by the monthly bank statements.

a) No undue lag occurred in the deposit of collections.

b) The following differences were found between the amount of the deposits and the total of daily entries in the cash-receipts book:

Jackson National Bank:

Date of deposit	Amounts per Books	Amounts per Bank statement	C.R. book exceeds deposit	Explanation
5-8-52	18 901 67	16 772 56	2 129 11	Check from Orange Mfg. Co. record-
5-14-52	27 674 89	29 804 00	- 2 129 11	ed in C.R. book on 7/8/52 was returned to company for signature and was redeposited 5/14/52
10-24-52	- -	5 267 59	- 5 267 59	N.S.F. check from Brooks & Wolff redeposited on 19/24; no entry made when returned by bank on 19/16/52

Howard National Bank — None

Cash disbursements:

Checks returned by banks were compared with entries in the cash-disbursements book and with payroll records. The following differences were found:

CK No	Date	Payee	Amount	Explanation
		Jackson National Bank		(Entered as $1900.75; corrected
81 675	5-7-52	Mason Mfg. Co.	1960 75	by journal entry in June 1952
82 009	5-16-52	Arts & Crafts Co.	736 01	No countersignature
82 176	5-21-52	Boyce & Reed Co.	36 89	No endorsement
87 298	10-27-52	Bangs & Bangs, Inc.	6 879 92	No endorsement
		Howard National Bank		
P 6981	5-10-52	Bruce Bacon	87 59	No endorsement
P 13758	10-25-52	Joseph Kowal	58 62	No countersignature

The above irregularities were reviewed with Mr. Collins, controller on 2-7-53. No adjustments were required. F.L.

C-5

Problems and Questions

1. In the course of your examination of the records of the Pickering Packing Company as of December 31, you have verified the following items relating to the company's account with the Tenth National Bank and Trust Company, its depositary:

(a)	Bank balance, per books	$120,251.50
(b)	Receipts charged to bank on books 12/31; credited by bank 1/2	9,423.68
(c)	Checks outstanding 12/31	21,300.49
(d)	Bank's service charges for December; not recorded on company's books	5.88
(e)	Proceeds of customer's 90-day non-interest bearing note for $8,400, discounted at bank 12/29; omitted from books	8,295.00
(f)	Deposit of 12/18 credited by bank in error to Packard Pickling Company	10,786.45
(g)	Error by bookkeeper in recording check from customer— Correct amount .... $274.16 As entered 247.16	27.00
(h)	Debit memo mailed by bank 12/30 and charged to company's account for payment of creditor's draft; company paid draft with check #1782 same day	15,000.00
(i)	Deposit made to special sinking fund was credited by bank in error to unrestricted checking account	9,660.74
(j)	Balance on deposit, per bank statement and certificate ..	124,318.72

Prepare a reconciliation of the bank account of the Pickering Packing Company as of December 31, and an adjusting journal entry for the correction of the company's books.

2. While examining the books of the Paragon Rendering Company, the following bank reconciliations were submitted to you by the company's cashier:

	November	December
Cash on deposit (per bank's statement)	$54,271.82	$29,137.42
Deposits in transit	6,005.18	7,144.10
Checks outstanding	−16,312.41	−10,948.06
Cash on deposit (per books)	$43,964.59	$25,333.46

Your assistant, to whom you had assigned the work of auditing the cash accounts, reported that both schedules were in order. He noted on his worksheet that (a) he had compared balances shown in the schedules with those in the ledger account and on the bank's statements, (b) he had inspected each of the returned checks for authority and endorsements, (c) all checks returned with the December statement had been compared with the entries in the check register, which, in turn, had been traced through the voucher register to the vouchers involved, (d) the checks outstanding had been properly recorded in the reconciliation, (e) all such checks had been returned with the bank's interim or cutoff statement of January 20, (f) he had traced the December postings to the cash account from the check register ($287,288.35) and from the cash-receipts journal ($268,657.22), (g) he had noted in detail the correspondence of receipts with the items of duplicate deposit slips, (h) cash shown in the reconciliation as "in transit" had been properly reflected on the cutoff statement, and (i) the cashier had been very cooperative and had assisted him in the preparation of his schedules.

In answer to your questions, he reported that the bank's statement for December showed deposits of $269,518.30 and that although all deposits had been made up by the cashier, each duplicate deposit slip had checked in detail with the record of receipts prepared daily by another employee who opened the mail.

Draw up a schedule to demonstrate to your assistant the incompleteness of his work. Point out to him at least two possible reasons for the discrepancy revealed by your schedule.

3. Upon arrival at the offices of the Safety Match Company where you had been assigned to audit the company's records for the preceding calendar year, you were handed the tentative balance sheet of the company, which had been prepared by the bookkeeper as of December 31. The first asset on the balance sheet was

Cash and Cash Resources...........$51,921.88

Later analysis revealed that this figure was supported by the following elements, each of which was eventually verified:

(a)	On deposit—M & M Bank & Trust Co.	$33,102.13
(b)	Savings deposit (established by action of board of directors for purchase of equipment now unavailable)	7,000.00
(c)	Cash on hand—in counter registers	3,521.68
(d)	Petty cash (including an uncashed check for $90.50, which had been written on 12/31 to reimburse the fund for various expense vouchers	100.00
(e)	U. S. Government (Series F) bonds	3,500.00
(f)	Cash surrender value of life insurance	3,180.00
(g)	NSF check, returned by bank 12/31, redeemed by customer 1/2	218.07
(h)	Funds held by salesmen to cover traveling expenses	950.00
(i)	Officer's demand note	100.00
(j)	Deposits with utilities	250.00
	Total	$51,921.88

Can the foregoing classification be justified? If so, give your reasons for each item. If you prefer other dispositions for some of the items, explain your position.

4. The Quillagua Corporation maintains a petty-cash fund but not on an imprest basis. A check is drawn for the amount of the estimated currency requirements for the next ten days and this amount is charged to the fund. Three times each month, on the 10th, the 20th, and on the last day of the period, the petty-cash slips are assembled, journalized, and reviewed by the cashier's superior, the proper expense accounts being charged and the fund account credited. Another check is then drawn to cover the needs of the next ten days less the amount remaining in the fund. You, the auditor, are informed that this system was adopted because of the wide variation in the amount of funds required from time to time.

What arguments, if any, would you advance to convince the management that the imprest system should be substituted? Discuss.

5. On page 204 is an illustration of a dual-bank-reconciliation schedule as at December 31 and January 10, with component details. Prepare a similar schedule for the same bank account covering the month of December, working back to what the bank totals for that month should be by taking into account the following December totals on the books of the depositor: deposits, $1,275,465.44, not including $2,563.84 in transit to the bank on December 1, but including the amount in transit at the end of the month; checks issued, $1,438,662.01; checks outstanding on November 30, $36,468.38; bank charges on the November bank statement recorded on the depositor's books (in the same manner as the entry of January 2) on December 16, $15.75. Included in the above figures for December deposits and November outstandings is a check for $1,500.00 issued by the depositor and returned in November by the payee because of an imperfect signature; immediately upon its receipt the check was destroyed and replaced by another of equal amount, which was also recorded on the books during November, the entry for the first check remaining unadjusted until December 12, at which time the destroyed check was treated as a "deposit" in the cash-receipts book and a credit was made to the overstated expense account. Also in December, in the deposit column of the cash-receipts book was noted a red figure of $10.05, the same figure appearing among the withdrawals on the bank statement and representing a charge by the bank for credit ratings supplied by the bank to the depositor's credit department.

6. In the reconciliation schedule referred to in the preceding question how would you have shown the following items on the December schedule?

(a) A customer's NSF check deposited and returned in December and redeposited in January.

(b) A direct deposit made by a branch and recorded by the bank in December, but not reported by the branch nor recorded on the depositor's books until January.

(c) A canceled check, not the depositor's, appearing on the December bank statement, and corrected by the bank in January.

7. The cashier of a company concealed for several years a defalcation by the following process: on December 31 of each year he deposited in C Bank a check, equal to the amount of the defalcation, drawn on D Bank. He would charge C Bank on that date but credit D Bank several days later. How would the auditor have detected the fraud in an examination as at December 31?

8. State the purpose of the following items in an audit program:

(a) Foot the cashbook for July and September.

(b) Reconcile bank deposits in total with cashbook receipts.

(c) Examine paid checks for December by comparing date, check number, payee, and amount with corresponding data in cashbook.

(d) Prove agreement between total paid checks and total bank withdrawals.

(e) Account by check numbers for all checks issued during a period selected for testing.

9. What purpose is served by obtaining bank statements and paid checks as of a date later than the close of an accounting period? State how such statements and paid checks are utilized by the auditor.

10. On its balance-sheet date a company under audit has always had a large amount of undeposited cash and checks received on the last day of the period What is the possible significance of this fact and what procedure would you follow in auditing these amounts?

11. What procedures may be added to an audit program upon discovering that cash had not been deposited intact?

12. Give brief directions for the disposal of the following items brought to your attention during the audit of cash:

(a) checks, shown as issued at year end, actually on hand on that date;

(b) cash in transit from main office to branch at year end;

(c) noncash items in petty-cash count;

(d) canceled check, cleared through bank, not countersigned;

(e) check, of substantial amount, to important supplier, outstanding four months.

13. May the accuracy of a depositor's statement received by him each month from the bank be assumed by the auditor?

14. You are assigning an assistant to examine canceled checks returned with a bank statement. There are certain types of checks with respect to which you urge him to be particularly alert and inquisitive. Indicate what some of these types may be.

15. Many auditors make a regular practice of asking for duplicate deposit slips from banks covering the last few days of the fiscal year and the first few days of the following year.

(a) If the bank's receiving tellers, as so often happens, pay attention only to the totals on slips and do not verify the detail listings, is the auditor's purpose defeated?

(b) If the auditor should discover check names and amounts on a deposit slip that are not reflected in the cash-receipts book, what should he do?

(c) Many depositors no longer make use of their passbooks but retain a receipted copy of the deposit slip stamped and initialed by the receiving teller. May the auditor rely on such receipted copies, and thus save the bank the trouble of reproducing its copies?

16. What internal control is aided by the rotation of collectors for dealers who sell on the installment plan?

17. Where on a balance sheet would you show bank balances representing undisbursed proceeds from the sale of a bond issue if—

(a) No restriction has been placed on the use of the funds,

(b) The proceeds may be used only for the purchase of new tank cars,

(c) The proceeds may be used only for the retirement of other long-term obligations as they mature, or

(d) The proceeds, although not restricted by agreement with bond-holders, are to be applied to the reduction of current obligations so that full advantage can be taken of cash discounts, in accordance with a resolution of the board of directors.

18. The assistant treasurer of a corporation refuses to sign checks (as one of two consigners) unless the vouchers sent by the accounting department to him along with the checks have been stamped paid. Comment.

19. In the interest of expediting the handling of customers' returned merchandise, the clerk at the "adjustment" counter of a department store is permitted to examine the merchandise and make immediate cash refunds while the customer waits. Suggest several points of internal control that might well be observed as safeguards.

20. Upon examining a series of bank statements relating to the reconciliation of a payroll account you observe that the book balance of the "Payroll-Cash Deposit" account at the end of each month is zero but that on the bank statement over a considerable period a gradually increasing balance of several thousand dollars has been accumulated. Explain the most probable cause and what you would do about it should adjustments be called for.

CHAPTER VII

Receivables

Receivables are amounts owing from customers, advances to officers and employees, and other types of "intangibles" that may be looked upon as being in the process of liquidation and as being held only for that purpose. Receivables take many forms: open accounts, notes, acceptances, claims, and installment paper having their origins in oral or written agreements, purchase orders, and contracts; cash sales in transit (COD's); loans; returns of material to or overcharges by suppliers; and so on. In each case there is an expectancy of the eventual receipt of cash or money's worth equal in amount to the receivable less, in many sales transactions, a possible discount for prompt payment; often there are possibilities of other allowances. The term may be modified by "gross" or "net," the latter meaning the result obtained by subtracting from the former prospective losses or allowances against which one or more reserves have been provided. "Long-term" is often applied to receivables that will not be liquidated in less than twelve months.

In an annual audit the objectives of the examination of receivables are to—

1. Determine the origin, character, and classification of amounts reported as receivable.

2. Determine whether any receivables have been discounted, pledged, or sold.

3. Form an opinion of the collectibility of receivables and of the adequacy of any allowances for uncollectible items, returns, discounts, and other possible credits.

4. Look for and report on weaknesses in internal controls governing credit practices, sales, receivables, collections, and methods of granting allowances and determining bad debts.

Principles and Practices

When does a receivable arise? Transactions with customers that result in receivables are supported by centuries of custom and law. The most common event giving rise to a sale *and* a concomitant receivable is the *delivery* of goods to a customer who has ordered the goods or to a carrier or other agent for delivery to the customer: the point at which title passes. Trade customs vary somewhat, and there may be deviations from this very nearly universal standard, but a deviation is not regarded as important where the practice is general within the industry, is consequently understood by both seller and buyer, and is consistently followed from year to year. A COD sale and a sale on a FOB-destination basis are examples of such deviations: the sale is recorded as the shipment is made, although title does not pass until arrival. In certain types of transactions, particularly those involving long periods of time or sales of services, the agreement between buyer and seller or trade custom may specify the conditions under which partial billings are made. An architect, for example, may bill a portion of his fee when the plans are accepted, another portion when the construction contract is let, and the balance when the structure has been completed: the contract with his client will so provide. This should not be confused with understandings between buyer and seller as to the method or time of payment. The architect's full fee is dependent upon events that may never occur, and he records no income from services until the anticipated event has taken place. But an agreement permitting merchandise to be paid for two months after its transfer from seller to buyer does not defer recognition of the sale; the whole of the transaction is customarily recorded as a sale when the transfer is effected.

A shipment against which an arrival (sight) draft has been issued does not give rise to a transfer of title from the shipper until the draft has been accepted or paid by the customer, yet a common practice is to record the sale on the date the goods are delivered by the shipper to the carrier. A receivable account may thus be represented by accepted drafts and drafts awaiting acceptance or payment. Or, a draft that must be paid before shipping documents are delivered to the buyer, often regarded as the equivalent of a COD awaiting collection, may be classified as a "draft receivable."

The appearance of a receivable as delivery is made to the customer may precede both the recording of the sale and the passage of title. In an installment sale, discussed in a subsequent paragraph, credits may be recorded as payments of successive fractions of the selling price are received, gross profit not yet recognized being reflected in a deferred-income account.

A sale to the supplier of goods or services is a purchase to the buyer, the tests being identical. Under ideal conditions the sale and purchase are recorded at the same time. At the end of every fiscal period, however, there will be goods in transit that will have been recorded as sales but not as purchases. End-of-the-year sales may have an important effect on the seller's net income, and customary rules are likely to be rigorously applied; but since recording purchases in transit has no effect on the buyer's profit (aside from certain instances of lifo inventory valuation) but does decrease his working-capital ratio, counterpart entries on his books may lag. The generally recommended practice for the buyer is to record goods in transit as inventory, in-transit items being reflected in invoices or shipping notices indicating that the date of shipment coincided with that of the balance-sheet or preceded it.

In recent years instances have not been infrequent where manufacturers have recorded sales to customers but have held the goods pending orders for delivery. In such cases the auditor must make certain that title has passed and that the seller is in effect warehousing the goods for the customer. To accept transactions of this character as receivables the auditor may require that there be a specific agreement with the customer covering the arrangement, that the practice is common in that line of business (for example, where the customer characteristically has little storage space of his own), has been followed for a number of years and is satisfactorily verified by sampling correspondence, and that the available evidence indicates that the goods will be delivered and the account paid within a few months.

Certain receivables arise from the periodic accrual of income such as interest and rent pertaining to periods or partial periods of time already elapsed. In the average commercial enterprise they are minor in amount, and their establishment at the balance-sheet date is often neglected. The accounting procedure concerning them is guided by their relative size and consistency of treatment from year to year. Although the effect on the income statement might be nil if accrued rentals receivable were omitted both at the beginning and the end of the income period, the current financial position of a building corporation would be seriously understated if accrued rentals receivable were neglected, and the auditor should insist on their inclusion. On the other hand, accrued rental of $50, as an item of unpaid miscellaneous income of a manufacturing company having a net profit of a million dollars, is in itself a wholly unimportant item; the auditor's only interest in it would be to ascertain whether the sum total of all unrecorded miscellaneous-income items is likely to have a material bearing on the company's income statement or financial position at the close of any reporting period, and to make sure that the omission is not a breakdown of internal controls governing miscellaneous receipts.

Goods shipped on consignment are sometimes treated as ordinary sales. However, they are a part of the shipper's inventory and should be so classified.

Amounts of claims covering losses and damages arising from shipments and other sources are often placed on the books when the claims are filed. This procedure affords a book control over a troublesome type of transaction and insures a future followup, but the usual practice is to provide an ample reserve, based on past experience, to absorb claims that may not be allowed.

Installment accounts. In most installment sales, title passes to the customer when the last payment has been made; sometimes it passes at the time of initial payment or when a specified portion of the total price has been paid, a chattel mortgage or other form of lien being taken for the unpaid balance. Because the customer immediately takes possession and has full use of the asset, the sale is recorded at that time. For both accounting and income-tax purposes the profit derived from installment sales may be spread over the period of collection, and the accounts should reflect such procedure. At present, the installment method of accounting is much less commonly employed than formerly. The advantage of the method, from the income-tax point of view, arises only from the deferment of profit from large, isolated deferred-payment sales. Where installment sales occur in approximately the same volume year after year the net income subject to tax tends to remain the same regardless of the method of accounting, provided the method is followed consistently.

If the practice of deferring gross profit from installment sales is followed in the accounts the usual procedure is initially to credit the gross profit to a deferred-income account, and thereafter to regard as income earned the amount obtained by applying the gross-profit ratio to collections. Because gross-profit ratios differ greatly it is common to find an average ratio in actual use. The average may have been derived from the sales of certain product types, or from the total of installment sales of the month or year with which collections are identified. Or, disregarding the month or year or origin, a moving gross-profit average may be applied to all collections: a simplified procedure of general application except where gross-profit ratios on new sales differ materially from month to month or from preceding ratios.

An equipment transfer under a lease-purchase agreement is generally regarded as a sale, notwithstanding that title does not immediately pass and that a legal claim may not yet exist for the full amount of the recorded unpaid balance. The test of its validity as a receivable rests on the probable continuance of installment collections until the account is fully paid; past experience should reveal that comparatively few repossessions have resulted from such sales, and there should be no present indication that similar results are not to be expected from sales currently being made.

Long-term production. Billings may be required from time to time on construction work or on orders for equipment the manufacture of which involves a substantial investment and extends over a period of time. To justify the entry of such billings in books of account the method and amount of the billing should conform to trade custom and accord with the terms of the contract with the purchaser. On a construction project, particularly where the contractor is being paid by a trustee out of the proceeds of an issue of securities, a procedure for interim billings is often provided in the contract whereby the amount of the billing is dependent on the percentage or stage of completion as certified to by an independent engineer. If the total profit from the work can be estimated with what appears to be a reasonable degree of accuracy a proportionate part of the billing may be regarded as income; if the total profit is estimated as nil or is in doubt, the amount of the billing is credited against the cost of the work in progress.

In other instances, a deposit in the form of earnest money (or perhaps no deposit at all) may be required at the outset of a contract for the construction of a building or manufacture of a machine, the balance of the contract price being paid upon completion, or upon delivery of the finished product. It has become a well-established practice in many concerns that where the work requires more than a year for completion a portion of the expected profit may be accrued as a receivable, notwithstanding that it will not be collected until the work has been fully completed. The usual practice is to credit the initial payment, if any, against costs incurred, to add the profit accrued to such costs, and to designate the total on the balance sheet as construction in progress, with the included profit parenthetically disclosed.

Officers' and employees' accounts. Amounts owing from officers and employees should be studied for the purpose of determining their sources and the meaning of the balances unpaid. In some states loans by a corporation to officers are forbidden. In any case, large accounts and the basis therefor should bear the approval of the board of directors and collections should be made in conformity with the board authorization. Expense advances to employees should be authorized and, from time to time, reviewed by an officer of the company. If variations in this group of receivables just before the year end are followed by similar variations in the other direction immediately thereafter, the character and propriety of the change may well be questioned. It is always important, therefore, to scan the transactions in these accounts at the beginning of the following year for such possibilities.

Notes. In the average situation, notes receivable are regarded as a somewhat more tangible and, at the same time, a more liquid form of obligation. Yet an unsecured note is often observed to be little more than a converted account receivable: an acknowledged debt the collection of which has been difficult. With improvements in trade relationships and in the availability and reliability of credit information, the practice of requiring a note as the evidence of a debt has declined in recent years. It persists in the settlement of equipment sales and other transactions involving substantial amounts and deferred payments where the seller deems it necessary to protect his investment by formal measures for which notes are regarded as more suitable than secured or unsecured accounts.

Protested or dishonored notes are, as a rule, regarded as accounts receivable together with the amount of any protest fees and other collection costs. An overdue note may be as good an asset as an account remaining unpaid after the agreed credit period, both being subject to practical judgments as to their eventual collectibility.

Discounted and pledged items. Both accounts and notes may be sold, or pledged or hypothecated: a procedure sometimes followed in order to increase working-capital cash or to avoid expenses of collection. When sold, a discount covering interest (and risk also if the sale is without recourse) is deducted by the buyer, and the customer may be notified of the sale, in which case the buyer collects. Such sales are mostly with recourse, which means that the buyer may collect the full amount from the seller if the customer does not pay when the account or note falls due. The pledging of accounts or notes receivable against loans or accounts payable is evidenced by an agreement and a list of pledged receivables. The list is modified periodically as the receivables are paid, and the proceeds may be deposited in a special bank account or paid directly to the bank or creditor in the gradual reduction of the indebtedness. When notes are pledged, the creditor usually takes physical possession. "Hypothecation" is a term sometimes used in place of "pledging" where the receivable (note or account) remains in the hands of the debtor but the ledger account or other record is stamped with a reminder that collections thereon are to be applied to the account of a designated creditor.

Proceeds from sales of discounted accounts and notes are generally credited direct to the receivable along with the discount; the latter may be regarded as a deferred expense to be written off over the normal holding period of the account or note or, preferably, as an immediate expense, since it closely resembles a cash discount. Where an account or note is sold with recourse, a contingent liability is created that exists until the debt has been paid; better practice dictates that the proceeds be carried in a separate account until that event has taken place.

Trade acceptances are a variety of notes receivable. They are taken in payment of specific shipments of merchandise and are as a rule readily negotiable. Should they be sold, the same contingent liability attaches as in the case of other forms of commercial paper disposed of.

Records of receivables. Records of customers' accounts vary greatly. They may in some cases be found in old-fashioned, hand-posted, bound ledgers; elsewhere the ledgers may be machine posted; in other instances, retained copies of invoices may serve as the ledger, and a typed list of the invoices remaining unpaid at the year end may be the "trial balance" supporting the balance-sheet item of receivables.

Internal Controls

Internal controls over receivables commence with sales. The objective should be to insure that sales and receivables accounts are neither over- nor understated and that classifications have been accurately made. Safeguards over receivables merge at a number of points with those that apply to cash.

Original sales orders. Sales orders when received should be reviewed in the sales department for price, delivery date, guarantees, and special features not within the discretion of the sales agent or branch to approve. Where the supply of the product is limited, the sales office maintains constant contact with the storeroom and specifies the sequence in which the orders are to be filled. The sales office also periodically reviews billings to make sure that approved orders have been accurately priced, invoiced, and shipped. The internal-audit interest in the procedures indicated is to determine whether the work of the sales department ties in with the daily routine of order taking and order filling, thereby assuring a crosscheck on the legitimacy of orders received, the conditions under which orders are filled, and the approval of the quality, quantity, and pricing of shipments actually made.

Credit approvals and terms. The credit office in the organizational pattern may be subordinated to the controller, treasurer, or office manager; it is preferably not a part of the sales organization, and its operations should be mantained at arm's length with the organizational unit responsible for records of receivables. The credit manager, in approving new accounts or in increasing credit limits of old accounts, should operate with a great deal of freedom, and the auditor in reviewing his procedures should make sure of that fact. If he does not, the risk of collection may be greater than anticipated in normal cases, and the bad-debt experience as reflected in the chargeoffs during the year may be unfavorable. On the other hand, the credit manager may not share his responsibility with his immediate superior as often as he should. Ordinarily, pressure from the sales division affords an adequate counterbalance for the conservatism of the credit granter. Occasionally the auditor will find that the credit office has subordinated its own opinions to those of others and that the result leaves something to be desired. Where this condition exists, the auditor should review the problem with the credit-manager's superior. The auditor should also ascertain, in his review of credit-office procedures, whether both commercial standards and company polices are being followed in extending credit and in making collections; any apparent conflict discovered by the auditor should be discussed with both the credit manager and his superior in order to make sure that the policy actually followed, generally and in specific cases, has been given official endorsement.

Invoices and statements. The billing function may be a part of the controller's activities or it may be attached to the sales office. It should always be completely separated from accounts-receivable ledgerkeeping, and its activities should include shipping-office contacts that make certain that shipments have been made and that the necessary shipping data are accurately set forth on invoices. The billing unit usually accumulates monthly dollar totals for receivables-controlling-account entries, and the auditor should carefully investigate any adjustment that has been made in regularly compiled totals at any time during the period under review. The billing unit may also prepare sales analyses, and quantity summaries needed in maintaining inventory controls: an operation that should be scanned by the auditor for the purpose of determining the objectivity and accuracy of the results produced.

Many business concerns no longer issue formal monthly statements to customers but rely on payment being made from individual invoices. The omission of periodic statements requires the adoption and careful observance of followup procedures designed to remind customers of unpaid invoices. In effect these follow-ups amount to statements of account but the work is spread fairly evenly over each month instead of requiring periodic concentration and interruption of normal work. In organizations with many customers the followup work is best performed by persons independent of the billing operation; their function tends to combine the work of receivables bookkeepers and collection specialists. The internal audit of their work should include tests of their procedures: whether prescribed methods are being closely observed; if so, whether the measures are adequate in holding down the amounts uncollected to planned levels. In ogranizations such as department stores, payments by debtors are made *only* from monthly statements; in such cases, it is desirable to have third persons (an assistant to the controller, for example) compare the statements with the receivables trial balance and mail them.

Bookkeeping. Accounts-receivable bookkeeping should be an independent unit wherever possible, with separate sources for the various classes of entries made in customers' accounts; for example, invoice copies from the billing division; cash-receipt slips from the cashier; credit memos, credits for returns, and bad-debt-authorization writeoffs from the treasurer's office; journal entries covering miscellaneous transactions from the controller; control totals from the general-ledger bookkeeper. In a public utility having many thousands of customers' accounts, a common practice is to rotate accounts-receivable bookkeepers to prevent possible collusion with customers. As in the case of cashiers, annual vacations may be insisted on. In any case comparisons of the totals of customers ledgers (or unpaid invoices) and controlling accounts should be made at least once monthly.

Notes. In many instances notes, as already observed, may be no more than formalized accounts receivable. The possibility of their negotiation, however, coupled with the necessity of returning them to their makers when paid require all notes to be kept under careful control. Notes and acceptances are of prime importance where they are being received regularly as evidences of indebtedness, as in the case of a dealer who sells on the installment plan or a producer of heavy equipment who sells to small manufacturers. In such cases the custodian of the notes (and any collateral supporting the note such as a chattel mortgage) should be wholly independent of those responsible for the general records or for the handling of cash or cash records. He should be under bond. His note records should be balanced once monthly with the general-ledger control account, entries in the latter coming in total from sources independent of the custodian, and he should maintain a card or other record for the note or group of notes received in connection with each transaction that will reflect such information as date, number (or other identification), name of maker or acceptor, endorsers, nature of transaction, amount, payments of principal and interest, character and amount of collateral, if any, and current location of both note and collateral. Collections of note principal should always be endorsed on the back of the note. The notation of location is of importance since notes may be pledged on a bank loan, may have been discounted or sold, or may be in the hands of attorneys for collection. The records of the note custodian, including notes paid, should be subjected to internal audit several times yearly.

Cash controls. Controls over cash receipts have been described in the preceding chapter. An essential feature of controls over cash receipts from cash and credit sales is to have at the source a procedural device directly under the jurisdiction of the controller that will act automatically as a safeguard against incorrect amounts of cash turned over to the cashier or banked by the cashier. Such a device is illustrated by an independent listing of mail receipts, a cash register in which the amount of the receipt is recorded on a tape to which the cashier does not have access; a control over and accounting for numbered sales slips; a ticket-taker who mutilates tickets in the presence of the purchaser so that they may not be resold; charges of merchandise at retail to branches, so that a total amount must be accounted for in the form of cash or merchandise on hand. Those who in any way participate in a cash transaction or have access to cash should have no access to the control device, or to any reading or record made up from it.

Returns and allowances. Credits for customers' returns and allowances (as for defective shipments) should be the responsibility of a major officer of the business such as the treasurer or sales manager—that is, one who has no direct contact with cash (the treasurer himself usually has no such contact). Returns and the consequent credits to customers' accounts should be authorized for entry only after a receiving report has been made a part of the record.

Bad debts. Bad-debt writeoffs may also be authorized by the treasurer or other designated person having no direct contacts with customers, sales, receivables, or cash, but they should always be finally approved by the president or other major officer acting under specific delegation of authority from the board of directors, or by the board itself.

Confirmations. Many business organizations provide for test confirmations of receivables, both accounts and notes, throughout the year as an important element of internal control. The confirmation procedure resembles that followed by the external auditor and is usually of the positive type (see page 251); it may be the responsibility of the internal auditor to pass on the results secured from the tests. Where no monthly statements are sent to customers those responsible for invoice followups may for limited periods be made functionally responsible to the internal auditor for the preparation of informal statements of account covering various sectors of the unpaid invoices. A careful record of the results secured, including the correspondence, should be kept for the inspection of the external auditor, since the thoroughness and independence of the tests may be important factors in determining the scope of the confirmations the latter individual finds it necessary to secure.

Internal audit. An important element in the institution and maintenance of effective internal controls over receivables, as has already been observed, is constant testing and general watchfulness on the part of the internal auditor, or, where no such post has been established, the person delegated by the controller to re-examine from time to time the actual operation of existing controls such as those just described. These tests include personal observation of how entries for the different types of sales are initiated; how cash sales are handled; how cash refunds, credits, allowances, and returns are safeguarded and their propriety assured; how errors are disposed of: in each case determining whether the individuals responsible for the controls over both cash and credit sales have the necessary competence for and interest in their work, and whether the arm's-length relations so necessary for the continued existence of these controls are being adequately maintained and are being operated smoothly.

Financial-Statement Standards

The single item "Receivables" often observed on a balance sheet is properly interpreted as consisting primarily (for example, 95 per cent or more) of ordinary trade accounts or notes. However, the following items should be separately disclosed on the balance sheet whenever they are material in amount:

Installment accounts (shown separately with noncurrent portion indicated in sidehead or displayed below current assets)

Officers and employees (unless of minor amount and arising from ordinary merchandise transactions)

Noncurrent items (appearing beneath current assets unless trade practice justifies their inclusion with ordinary customers' accounts, in which case the balance-sheet sidehead should show the amount thereof)

Affiliated organizations (the classification as between current and noncurrent will depend on the customary method of settlement)

Credit balances (to be shown as current liability, unless they are to be applied against future orders and the total amount is small: for example, under one per cent of the receivables group to which they refer)

Reserves for bad debts, discounts, and so on, should be deducted on the face of the balance sheet from the related receivables or, if the receivables are shown net, the reserve amounts should be disclosed in the receivables sidehead.

Notes and accounts receivable discounted (with recourse) and not yet collected are contingent liabilities and should be disclosed under that balance-sheet caption or in a footnote; when overdue, they are current liabilities.

The amount of accounts pledged as security for a loan should be brought out both in the receivables sidehead and in the sidehead that refers to the obligation.

Representative Audit Program

1. Review representative sales transactions for sales methods, controls over sales, guarantees, normal delivery lags, timing of billing, shipping practices, credit terms, collection methods, servicing of product.

2. Compare recorded sales invoices with shipping and other pertinent records for the last two weeks of the audit period and the two weeks immediately following to make sure that the necessary cutoff has been made between receivables and finished-stock inventory, that invoices recorded as sales have not been predated or postdated, that billings have been made to recipients of shipments, and that returns and allowances recorded after the year end are bona fide and should not have been recorded at an earlier date.

3. Procure list or tapes of accounts receivable; refoot tapes; procure list of notes receivable showing maker, date, maturity, interest rate, amount unpaid, past-due installments, accrued interest, nature and location of collateral. Test accuracy of totals and compare totals with ledger controls.

4. Where the information is readily available, classify receivables into such groups as ordinary customers, customers having extended credit, accounts with government agencies, installment customers, conditional sales, and consignments. Ascertain credit terms for each class and unusual credit terms allowed individual customers. Compare groupings for relative size with similar groupings of preceding year, noting any trend and judging its effect, if any, on the accounts.

5. Post, where practicable, collections and any major noncash credits since year end to receivable lists as an aid in determining collectibility of accounts.

6. Scan control accounts for year and follow through on nonregular transactions from their origins. Compare periodic postings in accounts with totals appearing in books of original entry. Foot the accounts. Test the origins and propriety of new (or renewed) notes received and notes paid during the last month of the fiscal year.

7. Establish "negative" confirmation program for customers'

accounts that reflect regularity of purchases and prompt payments, samples being selected at random. Circularize "positively" customers whose balances are 5 per cent or more of outstanding balances of any class, or whose balances include transactions substantially greater than customary in past months or transactions unliquidated over a relatively long period. Circularize "positively" officers' and employees' accounts other than those arising from ordinary transactions, and other nonrecurrent accounts of material character. Compare circularization letters with list of receivables, indicate on list the items circularized, make certain that transmittal envelope bears return address of auditor's firm (which may be postoffice box number), and that stamped, self-addressed envelope is enclosed, and be responsible for mailing.

8. Compare notes by sampling against list; circularize another sampling; trace notes paid off since year end to bank, and trace disposition of collateral; obtain confirmations of notes in hands of outsiders.

9. Obtain particulars of any existing discount agreement, confirm notes discounted, and determine contingent liability thereon.

10. Note on lists replies from circularization received by auditor and action taken, if any.

11. Review interest received on notes during periods covered by cash audit and trace to cash-receipts book; test interest accrued; test total interest received for over-all accuracy in method of computation and for proper amount.

12. Obtain client's aging of accounts and most recent report of credit manager; test for accuracy; review credit policy, age-groups, and representative individual accounts with credit manager, noting any trend or change in policy since last examination; compare credit manager's opinion of collectibility a year ago with actual collections.

13. Determine meaning of credit balances; if total is significant, classify as current liability.

14. Review client's estimate of reserve requirements; compare last year's estimate against experience; look for major modifications in condition of market, nature of product, rate of returns, and character of customers.

15. Examine in detail noncustomer or other miscellaneous receivables, trace the character and source of transactions that have given rise to them, confirm major and doubtful items, and discuss propriety and collectibility at top-policy level.

Audit Procedures

Sales. The auditor must be thoroughly familiar with the methods followed in securing and recording sales; in fact, his examination of this main source of gross revenue preferably precedes his audit of receivables. In connection with his review of procedures and internal controls over sales, he has already acquired a working knowledge of the significance of the sales account and the conditions under which sales are made.

As already stated, passage of title accompanied by the creation of a legal claim against the buyer is the usual test of the occurrence of a sale. Comment has been made that neither may exist in the case of installment sales, lease-purchase agreements, and similar transactions where the seller protects his interest by retaining title. In testing the proper timing of an entry for a sale, the auditor must be guided by past experience, probable future experience, practice within the industry, and consistency as between years.

In the case of construction work in process the contract, as already noted, may provide for periodic billings, and the auditor under such circumstances must make sure that the conditions precedent to the recognition of billings unpaid on the balance-sheet date have been met. Other construction in process may appear as a separate receivable (or inventory) on the balance sheet, or as an amount not yet billed but including, where past practice appears to justify, a portion of the profit expected on completion. The auditor must make sure that the profit included has been adjusted for contingencies, guarantees, and other possible losses, and that its ratio to total profit does not exceed the ratio of costs already incurred to total costs. A review of the client's experience on similar types of construction, now completed and paid for, is likely to be a helpful guide.

Notes. If notes receivable are examined after the balance-sheet date, some notes will have been paid and returned to their makers; others may have been sold or sent to banks and attorneys for collection or as collateral on loans. In lieu of a physical inspection of the notes not on hand, entries for cash receipts may have to suffice for those paid, and correspondence with banks and attorneys examined for notes still unpaid and not in the client's possession. However, the only certain way of establishing the validity of notes, paid or unpaid at the date of audit, is by communication with makers. A notes-receivable register is always a valuable reference for the auditor; information may often be found therein that does not appear on the notes themselves.

Many auditors have found that a comprehensive review of notes before the end of the period supplies the best basis for an opinion of the propriety of this type of receivable, leaving for a later, briefer examination a followup on uncompleted points and a general scanning of transactions between the earlier examination and the year end.

Confirmations should as a rule be secured from persons other than the custodian holding notes appearing as unpaid. The reply should contain information comparable with that described in the preceding paragraph and should indicate the purpose of the holding, any action taken or to be taken, disposition of collateral, and an opinion, if any, of collectibility.

Collateral held as security on a note may have a bearing on the adequacy of the reserve for bad debts. Depending on audit arrangements, the auditor may in some cases examine it in detail; in others, he may test it or examine internal reports covering its existence and review.

Miscellaneous receivables. Accounts with officers, stockholders, and employees, and with noncustomers generally, demand a careful examination by the auditor and a review in detail with a noninvolved officer at the top-policy level. Small amounts representing minor purchases conceivably applying to individual consumption by an officer or employee may as a rule be safely passed, and even classified with ordinary receivables; such accounts should, however, be in accord with established general policy as to prices, frequency, and amounts, and they should be settled promptly—as by an immediate payroll deduction. Accounts with officers or stockholders in which a balance has remained unpaid for more than a nominal period of time should bear the original authorization by (or subsequent approval of) the board of directors, and the auditor may find it desirable to obtain opinion of counsel as to the legality of any such account under state law. Confirmation from the debtor of any major amount outstanding is always desirable, and the request therefor should be accompanied by an analysis in which the sources of the outstanding balance are clearly indicated.

Control accounts. Each controlling account for receivables should be scanned for the entire period under review, the purpose being to note the principal sources of the items in the account, unusual debits and credits, and variations in totals carried into the account. Postings from less common sources should be traced to original records and documents. For one or two months debits representing sales should be compared with the sales summaries or sales accounts for those months, credits representing cash received should be compared with cash-receipts-book totals, credits for returns with the sales-return journal or similar record of original entry.

Reserve for bad debts and deductions. The possibility of bad debts among accounts and notes receivable is always present. Occasionally, the auditor finds the risk of collection slight where the number of debtors is not large and each has a recognized credit standing. Whether the risk exists and whether it is material are matters of judgment that the auditor as an independent examiner must establish in each case. His conclusions are based on the past experience of the business, a review of outstanding balances, and credit conditions generally. Past experience may be epitomized by comparisons for several years of actual bad debts with sales, provided their years of origin can be identified, and with year-end balances unpaid. Where such an analysis has not been made by the client, the auditor may find it desirable to encourage not only the identification of past bad debts with years of origin but also the maintenance of a running analysis of each future bad debt. The review of outstanding balances covers both individual accounts and the age groups into which they fall. General credit conditions refer to periods of prosperity or depression for industry as a whole and for individual industries and types of business enterprise.

An illustration of a study of a bad-debt risk is given on the next page. The first of the three sections of the worksheet contains a summary of bad debts (actual prior to December 31, 19–5 and estimated for balances unpaid on that date) over a period of five years, broken down by years of origin. In the second worksheet section, which has been derived from the first, ratios are computed showing the relation of the portions of uncollectible sales and remaining receivables to the total of collectible and uncollectible. The third section contains a comparative aging of outstanding receivables at the beginning and end of the year and what appears to be an arbitrary selection of ratios used in the determination of the uncollectibility of the several age groups. However, the first ratio, .0015 (.15 per cent), reflects the average relationship, for at least the past two years, between estimated

GEORGE BARNES & CO.
Bad-debt Analysis
December 31, 19–5

| Year of sale | Year bad debt discovered and charged off (net) | | | | | Estimate 12–31—5 (from below) |
	19–1	19–2	19–3	19–4	19–5	
19–0 and prior	1,445.06	743.92	46.21	5.20	—	—
19–1	687.45	787.95	760.22	32.18	75.43	50.00
19–2		1,547.33	881.49	683.91	122.00	175.24
19–3			1,496.85	624.53	342.11	454.10
19–4				1,021.03	777.40	1,836.25
19–5					1,186.29	2,635.02
Total	2,132.51	3,079.20	3,184.77	2,366.85	2,503.23	5,150.61

Year of sale	Total uncollected and estimated uncollectible at 12–31—5	Net sales (000's omitted)	Rates of uncollectibles to net sales	Uncollectible at end of year of sale	Outstanding accounts at end of year (000's omitted)	Ratio of uncollectibles to outstanding accounts
19–0 and prior	2,240.39	1,843	.12%	2,240.39	156	1.45%
19–1	2,393.23	1,827	.13	2,501.11	132	1.89
19–2	3,409.97	1,932	.18	2,831.88	150	1.89
19–3	2,917.59	2,108	.14	2,564.70	161	1.59
19–4	3,634.68	2,110	.17	3,832.53	225	1.70
19–5	3,821.31	2,275	.17	5,150.61	303	1.70
Totals	18,417.17	12,095	.15%*	3,186.87*	188*	1.70%*

Age	Number of a/cs	Amount Last year	Amount This year	Uncollectible Per-centage	Uncollectible Amount	Collections 1–1—6 to 4–25—6
Under 30 days	412	135,687.20	228,916.41	0.15	343.36	212,139.50
30–60 days	130	64,803.02	52,510.00	2.	1,050.20	—
60–180 days	31	17,786.50	9,567.41	5.	478.37	53,004.11
180–360 days	22	5,487.26	7,630.92	10.	7(.09	—
1–2 years	3	806.21	3,672.50	50.	1,836.25	10.00
Over 2 years	5	563.15	679.34	100.	679.34	—
Totals	**520	225,133.34	302,976.58	1.70*	5,150.61	265,153.61

* Averages.

** *Different* customers at December 31, 19–5.

Notes. (1) The company's average experience with bad debts has been quite uniform. The reserve balance of $5,150.61 is the result of the computation shown immediately above, and the two most significant percentages (0.16 per cent and 1.70 per cent) coincide with the averages for the past five years.

(2) Collections to April 25 were obtained by taking a tape from customers' ledgers. Of the total of $37,822.97 uncollected on that date the principal item is $15,244.20, due from J. L. Maxton Machinery Corp. This customer has always been "slow pay"; according to B. L. Borsch, credit manager, a promise to pay one-half of this balance on May 15 and the remainder on June 15 was made during the past week over the phone. He states that past promises of a similar nature have always been kept. The G & A (local credit agency) rating is A2A (good risk but slow).

bad debts (including, in part, actual chargeoffs) and net sales, the derivation of the ratio being shown in the second section of the worksheet. The other percentages are experience percentages; and the over-all average, 1.70 per cent, coincides with the second average ratio appearing in the second section of the worksheet: the relationship, at the end of each of six years, of estimated bad debts (with the obvious advantages of hindsight applied up to the end of 19–5) to outstandings. Thus the bad-debt percentage applied to 60 per cent plus of the receivables and the average over-all percentages are both justified by past experience. With a moderately large number of active customers (520), and with 519 of them having average unpaid balances of something over $550 each, the bulk of the risk seems well spread. This analysis is not intended to be a pattern to be followed in all cases but is simply an illustration of how the adequacy of a bad-debt reserve may be tested by employing certain types of information that are often available; in many instances it may be desirable further to test reserve requirements by a study of the improvement or deterioration of credit conditions within the industry or in business generally.

Estimates of bad-debt-reserve requirements should include the several varities of receivables that will be classified under that head on the balance sheet. Following his own first estimate of what such requirements should be, and with an aging schedule at hand, the auditor should consult with the credit manager, particularly with reference to the larger, older balances, and obtain his estimate of reserve needs. Confirmation tests are valuable primarily as a verification of existence of accounts on the balance-sheet date; they do not as a rule throw light on collectibility. Often, however, they have the effect of speeding collections.

An aging schedule is simply a columnar breakdown of total receivables by dates of origin. A common standard for such a schedule is to show totals of unpaid billings originating in the first, second, and third months prior to the balance-sheet date, and in the period preceding the third month. Another example may be found in the illustration on the preceding page. Individual accounts are divided between age classifications where invoices for more than one month remain unpaid. Cash received during the same period is applied against the charges to which it relates, which normally would be the earlier items. However, the auditor must be on the lookout for old unliquidated balances that have persisted for some time. An aging schedule is a good example of a worksheet that can be prepared by the client's staff, the auditor establishing its form and upon completion testing its accuracy, of course, before making use of it.

In listing the accounts on an aging schedule the details of each account are as a rule spread over the age-analysis columns on the assumption that any credits therein apply to the earliest debits. Thus one of the accounts making up the group summarized on page 246 has been analyzed thus:

19–5	Item	Amount
April	Sale	$ 48.50
July	Sale	6.82
August	Sale	75.47
September	Cash on a/c (August item)	− 40.00
November	Cash (July item)	− 6.82
December	Sale	84.61
	Balance	$168.58

The conventional method of analysis would yield the following:

Under 30 days	$ 84.61
30–60 days	–
60–180 days	82.29
180–360 days	1.68
Total	$168.58

However, since the September and November credits have been identified with the July and August items, something is lost if the indicated rule is followed indiscriminately, notwithstanding that the creditor may have the legal right to apply his customer's remittances (even though earmarked) to the oldest unpaid balances. As the above analysis has been made, only the amount of $1.68 is represented as being more than six months old, whereas the item of $48.50, possibly in dispute or reflecting an unrecorded return, is hidden from the view of those likely to be in a position to take action on it. It is always best, therefore, to match the credits of each account against the items indicated by the customer as those against which they should apply.

A summary of collections of receivables subsequent to the balance-sheet date should be obtained wherever possible, broken down according to the aging classification. Such a summary may be of considerable help in evaluating the bad-debt reserve. Here again the data is usually best prepared by the client's staff, with subsequent tests by the auditor.

In addition to a reserve for bad debts, and notwithstanding the credit position of debtors, other reserves may be necessary for deductions that are customarily allowed, such as discounts, returns (less, of course, amounts that will likely be reclaimed as inventory), freight, and spoilage. Cash discounts may be omitted from the requirement estimate if consistently regarded as an expense of the year within which the discount is actually taken. The need for such additional reserves will depend on the importance of the possible maximum that may be involved. A rule-of-thumb test sometimes applied is that reserves should be provided if the net deductions collectively are likely to exceed 2 per cent of the receivables outstanding. Past experience may be invoked by comparing several years' actual deductions with collections from customers during the same periods. Opinions as to possible changes in these averages should be sought in the auditor's discussions with the credit manager and possibly the sales manager. A summary of the actual experience with deductions after the balance-sheet date and before the audit is completed, if this period is, say, more than a month, may be all that is required to determine how material the deductions are likely to be.

A provision for losses on installment accounts is often neglected on the theory that the downpayment ordinarily required, along with the right of repossession, gives adequate protection to the seller. The auditor should apply several tests before agreeing to such an assumption. The first is to examine the course of events following sample repossessions during the audit period. Perhaps the seller's accounting procedure for repossessions is to transfer the net debit to an inventory account, charge any cost of reconditioning to expense, and absorb the inventory amount in a cost-of-sales account. The auditor should trace through each sample he selects, taking into account all costs and comparing the total with the price realized from the resale, thus establishing a basis for judging outstanding accounts. A second test would be to compare the character of the merchandise sold during the current period with that sold in previous periods; sales of a new product may be followed by larger-than-usual returns. Credit terms should also be compared, smaller downpayments sometimes leading to failures to meet future payments. Again, in times of increasing unemployment more repossessions may be necessary.

The collectibility of foreign accounts is dependent on all the factors affecting the collectibility of domestic accounts, plus the risk of political and economic changes, the latter including fluctuating rates of currency conversion. Provisions for bad debts may thus be justified at a comparatively high rate.

Confirmation. Verifying accounts receivable by written confirmations, or circularization, has long been a feature of many annual audits. Its purpose is to test for the existence of fraudulent accounts. The "positive method" is to request customers to indicate directly to the auditor whether or not the stated balances are correct; the "negative method" is to request customers to reply only if balances are found to be incorrect. In a few cases the whole customer list, including even those whose accounts show no balances at the year end, is circularized, especially where management regards circularization as a collection aid; but sampling methods are usually followed. This involves the selection and listing by the auditor of the largest accounts that collectively will total, say, one-half of the dollar amount outstanding, and the picking at random and listing by him of another 10 per cent or more of the balance, making sure that samples are selected from each customer class in accordance with the testing principle laid down in Chapter II. Regardless of which of the two methods is adopted, a return envelope requiring no postage and addressed to the auditor (at his home office or local post-office box) is enclosed with a monthly statement of the account or a special statement, and mailed, under the auditor's supervision, to the customer.

The confirmation process may be applied by the auditor to receivables within the year under audit rather than at the year end, thus making possible a more leasurely followup and correction of observed defects before the close of the period. This procedure is always accompanied, however, by a careful review of credit and billing practices between the date selected and the year end.

An answer cannot be expected from every request sent out; but if favorable replies are received from at least two-thirds of the number of requests (under the first method), or unfavorable replies from not more than one per cent (under either method), the propriety of the balance may be assumed. It is customary where the positive method has been adopted to follow up the larger amounts comprising the bulk of the outstanding accounts until replies are received; some auditors endeavor to secure confirmations on not less than 90 per cent of the total dollar amount of customers' accounts. On the other hand, where internal-audit procedures include a carefully worked-out program of circularization, tests being made on several unannounced occasions during the year, the auditor in the most favorable situation may find it necessary only to review the method followed and the results secured.

The following form is characteristic of those used in positive confirmations:

(date)

(Name and address of customer)

We enclose a statement of your account with us. If you find it is in agreement with your records, please confirm the balance to our auditors, Messrs. Hyatt, Paterson & Co., 960 Hudson Building, Chicago 4, Illinois, using the form below and the enclosed return envelope for reply. If it is not in agreement with your records, please furnish them with whatever information you may have that will help them in determining the cause of the difference.

This is a request for the confirmation of an account balance, not a request for payment.

(Signature of company official)

— — — — — — — — — — — — — — — — — — — —

(this portion may be made detachable)

Messrs. Hyatt, Paterson & Co.
960 Hudson Building
Chicago 4, Ill.

The statement showing a balance of $*_____*$ agrees with our records at _____ except for the following: _____

_____
_____
_____
_____

_____
(name of customer)
(name of person preparing reply)
_____

* To be filled in by auditor.

If the confirmation is to be a negative one, the first paragraph may be replaced by the following:

We enclose a statement of your account with us. If you find it is NOT in agreement with your records, please furnish our auditors, Messrs. Hyatt, Paterson & Co., 960 Hudson Building, Chicago 4, Illinois, with whatever information you may have that will help them determine the cause of the difference, using the form below and the enclosed return envelope for reply.

Instead of a formal letter a rubber stamp is sometimes impressed on the monthly or special statement, a printed sticker may be attached, or a card enclosed, in each case containing language similar to the above, along with a no-postage-required envelope addressed to the auditor. One firm of public accountants employs a rubber stamp containing an inscription similar to the following:

If the amount shown hereon is incorrect please notify our auditors, Taylor, Lorton, and Lotus, 20 E. Wacker Drive, Chicago 2, Illinois, and supply them, if possible, with details that may be helpful to them in verifying your account with us.

Such a stamp should be under the strict control of the auditor and should be impressed only on statements selected, listed, and mailed by himself or an assistant.

Replies from customers under either method of circularization are noted on the auditor's list of mailings along with any comments that may call for inquiry by the auditor. Occasionally a remittance accompanies the customer's reply; whenever this occurs the auditor turns it over immediately to the client's cashier or other person designated to accept it, secures a written acknowledgment, and records the event in his papers. Some comments from customers call for adjustments; a similarity of complaints may point to a weakness in internal controls that should be corrected, or to a defect in a product that may influence the auditor's judgment as to the worth of the remaining inventory of that product. Whatever the nature of the comments accompanying customers' replies, their significance should be discussed with the client's officials who have the authority to act on them. Subsequently—sometimes during the course of the next following audit —the auditor should determine whether the necessary general or specific corrective action called for has been taken.

Where the replies reveal widespread errors that lead to material adjustments, an increase in the number of confirmation requests may be called for.

Illustrative Audit

Four ledger accounts, including the bad-debt reserve, apply to receivables. The first of these (27-0), after eliminating uncollectibles and adjusting for a NSF check, is split five ways by reclassification entries B and C. It would of course have been impossible to have divided the account into five parts at the time the trial balance was prepared, since the different amounts could not at that time have been obtained. As shown on E 1, the three receivables accounts (27-0, 27-1, and 27-2) are reclassified under nine possible balance-sheet headings.

The receivables control account, in its unadjusted and unreclassified form, is a good example of a mixed account, for it contains assets, liabilities, and expenses. In his postaudit suggestions to the client, the auditor in such cases as this will probably not propose that these very different kinds of items be carried in separate general-ledger accounts, for the slight inconvenience caused him (by the multicolumnar analysis of E 2 and reclassification entries B and C) is much less than the added bookkeeping that would probably be called for in maintaining rigid receivable classifications and making frequent transfers between classifications during the year.

As indicated by the note in the square brackets on E 2, the listing and aging of receivables in the audit from which these papers have been taken required seven pages. Where the client's staff prepares worksheets such as this, the auditor or his assistant must trace the detail back to its source and make sure by tests that there has been a correct interpretation of classification and aging. The worksheets are headed up, and the definitions of what is to be done are carefully explained by the auditor to the staff member assigned to the work by the controller; and the auditor keeps himself available for answering questions during the process so that the job may be completed without interruption. The auditor's assistant, in this case, made the notes and summaries on the right margin and at the bottom of worksheet E 2. The latter section of the worksheet should be studied carefully, as the devices there employed find their counterpart on other worksheets where summaries are necessary, following a detailed analysis. After these worksheets were totaled and the crossfooting of $1,070,238.92 was found to agree with the general-ledger account (27-0), the doubtful accounts were reviewed with the credit manager and treasurer in accordance with the audit program (X 7), and a determination was made that 13 uncollectible balances, including four old accounts with employees (see AJE 2), were to be charged off. A summary of the older balances of customers accounts was then made under the columns headed "October and prior," the bad debts (designated "a") were spread according to the month or period of their origin, and the "recap" was prepared in the extreme right-hand column. Summaries of this sort often appear in management reports; in the present instance, one reappears on E 7 where the reserve for bad debts was adjusted.

Collections from January 1 through February 26 have been noted under comments (E 2). An additional money column could have been provided for this purpose. The auditor might then have recapped the detail of these receipts according to the aging of the accounts to which they apply, but here he ran off a single tape which shows that more than 74 per cent of the monetary amount of the outstanding accounts was collected during the two-month period.

Results of the test confirmation of unpaid balances by correspondence are summarized on E 5 along with notes on the confirmation of trade notes and officers accounts. Here it was not possible to send out the requests with monthly statements, since no monthly statements are issued (see PF 26). Ninety positive or negative confirmation requests were sent to customers, and 28 replies were received of which four may lead to adjustments. One account, the Ordnance Division of the U. S. Army, was not sent a request, because experience has proved to most auditors that agencies of the government are too far behind in their accounting to know within any reasonable time after a given date what they owe. From the note on E 6, the Ordnance receivable was the result of production under a certain contract. The best procedure for reviewing this receivable was determined by the auditor to lie in a discussion with the plant management of progress under the contract, its probable termination, rejections on deliveries, and other matters leading to an opinion of the propriety of the outstanding year-end balance.

Confirmation replies have been omitted from the working papers. They may be expected to be in almost any form and worded in various ways. Where the auditor supplies a blank to be filled in by the customer, he finds them signed and returned by clerks, bookkeepers, occasionally by officers. He has no way of verifying the identity or signatures of these individuals. However, he may rightfully presume, without specific information to the contrary, that the replies are bona fide and can be relied on. Confirmations secured on the two accounts with officers consisted of their signatures on the worksheet (E 4). Obviously, although the informality and directness of the method may be commended, this form of verification is less reliable than written statements dictated by the individuals themselves (see item 5 on worksheet X 7, prepared by the auditor's principal).

A study of the details of E 7 and AJE 2 reveals that the bad-debt reserve at January 1 was $1,206.70 less than the net amount charged off during the year and originating prior to that date, and $2,392.73 less than required if the provision for uncollectible accounts originating in prior years, as determined in AJE 5, is included. However, if the conditions giving rise to the unanticipated loss from prior-year accounts arose during the current year —a situation that may well be true but, as here, remaining undetermined by the auditor—the reserve balance at the beginning of the year might retroactively be justified. In most cases, the answer to the inquiry will have no effect on where the larger-than-expected losses are charged, but may have some influence, should any of the causes continue to exist, on the provision at the end of this year. The auditor finds that this year's percentage allowances made by the company provide for $692.88 more on customers accounts than would have resulted from the application of last year's percentages. A study of the relationship between sales and balances uncollected in past years, provided in PF 61, yields nothing of significance.

p. 1 of 2

	a/c no.	W/P			
Receivables, as adjusted and reclassified —					
Customers notes receivable —					
Due in 1953		E-3	101 767 89		
Due after 12/31/53		E-3	158 167 00	259 934 89	
Customers accounts receivable		E-2		1 104 590 47	
Due from —					
Employees		E-2		5 289 64	
Officers		E-4		13 100 00	
Travel advances		E-2		2 000 00	
Credits —					
Advance payments on contracts		E-2	44 146 72		
Due to employees		E-2	4 127 29		
Customers credit balances		E-2	18 162 31	- 66 436 32	
Total, as adjusted				1 318 478 58	
Reconciliation with books —					
Accounts receivable — customers	27-0		1 070 238 92		
Notes receivable — customers	27-1		259 934 89		
Officers accounts	27-2		13 100 00		
Bad accounts written off (aJE #2)			- 20 221 26		
NSF check reclassified (aJE #12)			1 971 28		
Invoice on which no shipment made (aJE #7)			- 6 545 25		
Total, as above			1 318 478 58		

Comments —

Trial balance and aging of customers accounts (27-0) was prepared
by Myra Lyons (A/R bookkeeper) from subsidiary ledger;
compared with ledger and corrected by H.R.

Trial balance of notes receivable (27-1) was prepared by F.L.
from note register.

There are no installment or conditional sales accounts; credit terms
standard for the industry, are 2% 30 days, net 60. Test checks
of discounts allowed during July indicated that they related
to less than 30-day accounts. Some of the larger customers
are "slow-pay" and make no attempt to deduct discount.
Government contracts are always priced net.

The sales-allowances register for January 1953 was reviewed for
1952 credits; 12 credits applicable to 1952 were found, including
credit of $376.19 to Roswell-Armstrong Supply Co., who dis-
puted balance shown on negative-confirmation (E-5). All

E-1

27-0
27-1
27-2
121-1

Martin Manufacturing Company
Receivables
December 31, 1952

H-h
2-26-53

p. 2 of 2

other items were less than $200 each. Total of such allow-
ances was not significant; no adjustment made.

A summary of the results of the circularization of notes and
accounts receivable appears on E-5. Positive confirmations
(indicated on E-2, 3, and 4 by a *) were obtained for
officers accounts and for customers notes and accounts in
excess of $20,000. Negative confirmations (**) were sought
for 65 other customers accounts selected at random; only
three replies received; no adjustments necessary.

Reserve requirements (E-7) were reviewed with Samuel Mackin,
credit manager, and J. B. Huddle, treasurer; they agreed
to the additional provision of $14,604.96 (aJE*5). Charge-
offs are approved by Mr. Huddle.

Advances to employees are approved by Mr. Collins.

Control accounts were scanned by F.L. on 2/26/53; no comments.

A review of the cash-receipts book for January 1953 revealed
that cash discounts in the amount of $5,802.45 were taken
on unpaid balances at December 31, 1952. No provision in
1952 was made for this item. A similar practice was followed
in 1951. Recommendation to the client is being made that
at 12/31/53 a separate reserve for cash discounts be provided in the accounts. No adjustment was made at 12/31/52
since the amount is not large in relation to the total estimated net profits for the year.

E-1a

Martin Manu
G/L   *Accounts*
27-0   *Decem*

* Positive confirmation sent out ** Negative " " . Customers	advances received	Employees accounts	Travel advances	Credit balances
Abbott & Co.				
Ackerman & Jackson Co.	b)- 10 000 00			
Addington Co.				215 89
Aeolian Mfg. Co.				
Aluminum Products Co.				
Amberg & Amberg Co.				1 210 65
Andrews, Harold		a) 285 00		
Apelian - Gates Co.	c)- 5 000 00			
Arrow-Scott Mfg. Co.				
Ayers, George B.		e)- 1 592 08	100 00	
[Note: This analysis and aging of receivab pared by the receivables bookkeeper, it by the auditor's assistant who made cor				
Thompson, Charles Q.		d) 100 00		
U.S. Army - Ordnance Div.				
Western Products Mfg. Co.				
Whiteman, Edward G.		e) - 116 91	300 00	
George Worthington & Co.				
Wrigley Mfg. Co.				
Yates Tool Mfg. Co.				
Zuckerman & Oglesby Co.				27 58
Debits	1 165 784 96	7 271 16	2 000 00	
Credits	95 546 04	- 73 256 44	- 4 127 29	- 18 162 31
Books unadjusted	1 070 238 92^n			
Adjustments -				
a) Bad debts - a) E #2	- 20 221 26	a) - 198 62		
NSF check - a) E #12	1 971 28			
Unfilled billing a) E #17	- 6 545 25			
Books adjusted	1 045 443 69^n	- 73 256 44	1 162 25	2 000 00	- 18 162 31
Reclassifications -				
b) Receipts applicable to billings	b) 29 109 72			
c) Receipts - no billings R/E B	c) 44 146 72			
d) Due from employees }		- d)- 528 954		
e) Due to employees } R/E C }		e) 4 127 29		
Travel advances }			- 2 000 00	
Credit balances }				18 162 31
Balance after adjustment & reclassification				TB

Basic worksheet
prepared by   H-L
Myra Lyons   2-28-53

	Customers		accounts			
		Debit	balances			
	Total	December	November	October & prior		Comments
**	1895 62	5 276 89	10 709 29	Sept.	2989 44	allowance of $500 claimed on Sept.
*	23 192 37	22 519 24		Oct.	673 13	balance; $10,709.29 received 1/22/53
	4 271 73		4 271 73			
*	73 275 19	56 112 72	16 952 19	Mar.	a) 210 28	allowance not yet recorded on books
	9 146 28	8 915 20	231 08			

les continues for six more pages; pre-
was compared with the subsidiary ledger
rections of occasional errors.

	95 723 47	51 351 72	36 089 16	Oct.	8 282 59	33 809 72 rec'd 2/18/53
	500 72	500 72				
**	3 890 25	3 890 25				
**	12 267 43	12 128 09		May	a) 139 34	Disputed items; w/o per J.B.H.
	1 804 56			June	a) 1 804 56	uncollectible per J.B.H.
						Recap of
	1 156 513 80	821 768 14	256 174 15		78 571 51	Customers accounts
						1951 560 72
						1952 Mar. 2 190 18
						" May 767 22
	-1 823 964				a) -1 823 964	" June 3 908 75
	1 971 28	1 971 28				" July 5 373 49
	- 6 545 25	- 6 545 25				" Aug. 7 509 28
	1 133 700 19ⁿ					" Sept. 10 672 58
						" Oct. 29 349 65
	- 29 109 72	-18 397 62	- 10 712 10			Subtotal 60 331 87ⁿ
						" Nov. 245 462 05
						" Dec. 798 796 55
						Total 1 104 590 47ⁿ
						Collections
						thru 2/26/53 826 576 29
	1 104 590 47ⁿ	798 796 55ⁿ	245 462 05ⁿ		60 331 87ⁿ	
	TB					

E-2

Maker	Date issued	Maturity	Interest Rate	Payable	Due in 1953
The Babylon Company	5-24-51 ^	500 on ¼ / 500 on ¾ ^	5% ^	J-D 1 ^	1 000 00 ^
Canfield Stove Company	9-18-52 ^	9-18-54 ^	4% ^	9-18 ^	−
Davis & Davis Mfg. Co.	10-17-51 ^	10-17-52 ^	5% ^	10-17 ^	800 00 ^
Emory Foundry Co.	2-21-52 ^	2-21-53 ^	5% ^	2-21 ^	3 580 00 ^
					[Note: Additional pa
Zuckerman & Oglesby Co.	9-1-52 ^	5,000 on 9/1 ^	3% ^	9-1 ^ +	5 000 00 ^
				259 934 89	101 767 89 TB

Work done:
1) The above schedule was prepared from Notes-receivable register
2) On 2-11-53 notes on hand were compared with above list (✓)
3) Endorsements on notes of 1952 collections were compared with
     entries in Cash-receipts book.
4) Notes on above list which were returned to makers prior to 2-11-53
     were verified by examination of collection entries in Cash-
     receipts book or of renewal notes on hand.
5) Collectibility of notes was reviewed with credit manager
6) The company follows the practice of charging back to
     customers accounts the amount of past-due notes.
7) Interest on the Davis & Davis Mfg. Co. note is to be waived
     if paid before April 30 (see letter of 11/28/52 from Samuel
     Martin to R. S. Morse of D&D)
8) Notes receivable account is credited at time of discounting
     notes. According to Mr. Huddle notes are discounted only
     with Jackson National Bank. Notes are discounted in
     anticipation of exceptional drains on Cash. Notes of
     companies with better credit ratings are selected for
     discount. Since the probability of nonpayment by the
     maker at maturity is remote, the company follows the
     practice of crediting the proceeds on such discounted
     notes directly to the notes receivable account. We have
     no objection to this practice. For list of notes receivable
     discounted at 12-31-52 see P-4

+ = Positive confirmation sent
− = Negative confirmation sent

E-3

facturing Company
Notes Receivable
1952

HH
2-11-53

Due after 12-31-53	Acc. Rec. from same customer (from E-2)	Collateral	Estimated uncollectible	Interest Collected in 1952		Interest Accrued 12-31-52
5500 00	821 62	Chattel mortgage	–	6-1 / 12-1	18750 / 17500	27 08
– 1000 00		None	–	9-18	40000	136 00
		None	800 00			(note 7)
		Endorsed by Ef Emory	–		–	154 14

[...ge of notes omitted.]

+ 1500 00	27 58	Chattel mortgage	–		–	150 00
158167 00 TB	14467 53		7228 95		8461 79	2156 19 TB
R/E-D						

Origin of estimated uncollectibles:
1950-51 .... 905 67
1952 .... 6323 28

Interest earned (o/c 282):
Collected in 1952 .... 8461 79
Interest allowed by S/F Trustee 163 16
Accrued - 12/31/52 ... 2156 19
12/31/51 ... 1801 17 + 355 02 AJE-3
Interest income - 1952 .... 8979 97 TB

E-3

Martin Manufacturing Company
Officers Accounts Receivable
December 31, 1952

	Amount	Acknowledgment of indebtedness	
B.A. Hanson, vice president	1 350 00	B.A. Hanson	2/25/53

This loan was originally $10,000
and was approved by the Board
of directors (see X-3, 1945 WPs)
It is to be liquidated by
application of assigned dividends
on 25 shares of M. M. Co. common
stock owned by Mr. Hanson.
Dividends of $500 (20% × $2,500) were
so applied in 1952. The account
bears no interest.

	Amount	Acknowledgment of indebtedness	
Earle C Peyton, Secretary	11 750 00	Earle C. Peyton	2/25/53

Outstanding and unchanged since
July 18, 1948. Not formally approved
by Board but shown as a separate
item on internal balance sheet
prepared by Controller and distributed
to all Board members. 100 shares
of M. M. Co. common stock endorsed
in blank, are held as collateral
and Mr Peyton so acknowledged
last year in a letter to us.
Non-interest bearing

Total officers accounts   13 100 00
           TB

ʸ = Examined certificates at 10 AM
on 2/1/53 in presence of Messrs. Huddle
and Collins in safe-deposit box
at Jackson National Bank

E - 4

Results of circularization - Positive

Officers accounts: (E-4)	Amount per books	Reply received and comments
B. G. Hanson	1350 00	2-25-53
Earle C. Peyton	11 750 00	2-25-53

Notes in excess of $20,000 (E-3)
5 inquiries and replies
received - no differences
reported - aggregated ... 138 762 95

Accounts in excess of $20,000 (E-2)
(20 accounts totaling $602,096⁵⁴)

Aluminum Products Co.	73 275 19	Disputed amount of $210²⁸; written off by AJE-2

17 other replies received -
no differences reported -
aggregated ... 475 726 12
Total replies received (91%) 549 001 31

Results of circularization - Negative:
65 inquiries sent out
2/9/53 on accounts and
notes labeled on E-2 & E-3
aggregating $395,676.81
Replies received:

Abbott & Co.	① 18 975 62	Claim an allowance of $500⁰⁰ on unpaid invoice for Sept 1952; expect to settle on basis of a smaller allowance
Courtney Mfg Co.	6 329 18	Disputed charge of $1709.87, amount represented shipment on 12-31-52
Roswell-Armstrong Supply Co.①	1 875 42	Disputed $376.19 representing credit given on 1/5/53 for merchandise received by us on 12/29/52

① No adjustments made; reserve for bad debts believed adequate
to cover amount of this overstatement if allowances claimed are approved.

E-5

Amount due from Ordnance Div., U.S. Army on 12-31-52	95723.47

This account was reviewed in detail with Messrs. Shuffle and Collins since it was deemed impracticable to verify by correspondence any portion of the unpaid balance.

Contract W-151-06-1258, dated 3/8/52, calls for the delivery of 30 AX240 model heavy machines at a specified scale of prices.

No portion of the account appears to be in dispute. Deliveries have been made on schedule; all known complaints or rejections have been adjusted, and no cancellation of this contract is expected.

On 2/18/53 collections were received on billings in October and November amounting to   33809.72

Leaving 1952 billings unpaid on 2/18/53 of   61913.75

Represented by the following invoices:

Date	Number	Amount	Explanation	
10-6-52	10-109	6903.29	①	③
11-18-52	11-332	13737.08	②	③
11-25-52	11-478	6850.00		③
12-17-52	12-310	13775.13		③
12-29-52	12-627	20648.25		③
Total as above		61913.75		

① Billing price of a machine returned in November 1952. Defects were corrected and machine reshipped in Dec. 1952.

② No apparent reason for delay in payment; no portion of this shipment was rejected. Letter will be written to ascertain reason.

③ Shipping documents examined in support of these billings.

Martin Manufacturing Company
Reserve for Bad Debts
December 31, 1952

A/L
29-0
278-1

H.R.
2-14-53

1-1-52 balance					15 875	00
Monthly provisions during 1952 (12 × $2,000)					24 000	00
Bad-Debt recoveries - 1951 customers accounts					3 582	07
Chargeoffs (all pre-1952 accounts):						
Customers			- 12 062	10		
Employees			126	09	- 12 188 19 *	
12-31-52 balance per books					31 268 88 *	
Additional chargeoffs - 1/1/53 to 2/17/53 - all but $8,475.58						
relating to 1952 balances (AJE-2):						
Customers			- 18 239	64		
Employees			1 981	62	- 20 221 26 *	
12-31-52 balance prior to additional						
provision for 1952					11 047	62 *
Reserve requirements, computed as in past years:						
Customers accounts:						

Age	Receivable	This Year %	(Last Year) %	Reserve
1 mo.	798 796 55	1	(1)	7 987 97
2 mos.	245 462 05	2	(2)	4 909 24
3 mos.	29 349 65	4	(3)	1 173 98
4-6 mos.	23 555 35	10	(10)	2 355 54
6-12 mos.	6 866 15	25	(20)	1 716 54
over 12 mos.	560 72	50	(40)	280 36
	1 104 590 47 * (E-2)			18 423 63 *

Customers notes:						
Amount determined by reviewing						
each note with credit manager						
and controller (see details on E-3)				7 228 95		
Total requirement				25 652 58 *		
Balance in reserve, as above				- 11 047 62		
Additional requirement - AJE 5					14 604 96 *	
12-31-52 balance as adjusted					25 652 58 * TB	
Recapitulation:						
1-1-52 balance					15 875 00 *	
Provision for bad debts			24 000 00			
			14 604 96		38 604 96 * TB	
Bad-debt recoveries					3 582 07	
					58 062 03 *	
Chargeoffs			- 12 188	19		
			- 20 221	26	- 32 409 45 *	
12-31-52 balance					25 652 58 *	

E-7

Martin Manufacturing Company
Reserve for Bad Debts

Year	net sales	Provision	Recoveries	Chargeoffs Customers	Chargeoffs Employees	Balance
Balance taken over from Holdover Radiator Co. on Aug. 1, 1941						10 260 44
8-1 to 12-31-41	645 925 92	6 000 00	264 11	3 421 08	10 20	13 093 27
1942	1 681 943 41	7 272 00	5 00	12 436 77	245 00	7 688 50
1943	9 940 010 26	26 858 42	846 95	14 332 57	216 44	20 844 86
1944	5 740 561 10	22 177 34	2 050 12	30 518 55	2 218 67	12 335 10
1945	6 446 129 81	40 680 59	–	27 906 14	1 665 92	23 443 63
1946	6 795 793 57	37 090 52	1 275 08	38 695 02	1 209 57	21 904 64
1947	7 202 578 42	26 701 28	509 70	24 219 75	762 88	24 132 99
1948	6 487 901 76	30 264 90	2 857 63	29 708 63	931 62	26 615 27
1949	8 190 786 09	39 376 42	1 762 48	35 876 67	508 47	31 369 03
1950	8 472 609 75	32 714 68	1 028 75	31 835 52	92 39	33 184 55
1951	7 763 225 80	25 449 95	678 47	43 437 97	–	15 875 00
1952	7 760 888 32	38 604 96	3 582 07	30 301 74	2 107 71	(a) 25 652 58

(a) Commencing with December 31, 1952, no further advances will be made to employees and the reserve balance will be deemed to be applicable only to customers notes and accounts.

PF-61

Problems and Questions

1. While engaged in the audit of a company that, in the normal course of its business, had received a large number of interest-bearing notes from its customers, you delegated to an assistant the task of examining the notes-receivable account. He reported to you as follows:

(a) He had inspected the notes submitted by the treasurer of the company and had obtained from the bank's confirming letter information on two notes that had been discounted.

(b) He had secured information concerning each note: maker, date, due date, unpaid balance, rate of interest, interest accrued to the audit date, and a notation that no collateral had been deposited.

(c) The total of amounts unpaid at the balance-sheet date equaled the control-account total.

(d) He had compared each of the notes with returned confirmations and found that each maker had acknowledged his obligation without comment.

(e) He had traced the entries recording the notes and had determined that each had been properly credited to the account of its maker.

(f) One of the notes held by the bank on the date of the audit had been paid subsequently and the bank's letter to that effect had been cited.

(g) Although no note had been past due on the date of the audit and none was a renewal, he had discussed the credit standing of each maker with the credit manager who had expressed confidence in the collectibility of all notes.

(h) He had prepared a certificate that had been signed by the company's treasurer who represented therein that each note constituted a valid claim against the maker and that each note was believed to be collectible in full.

You informed your assistant that as far as he had gone his work had been well done, but that to complete the assignment at least one more step was essential. What step was this? Outline the work to be done in taking this step.

2. Determine the probable sources of the unpaid balance of the following customer's account at March 31:

Item	Date	Invoice number or source	Debit	Credit	Balance
1	1–1	Balance forwarded	574.84		574.84
2	1–18	2301	244.21		819.05
3	1–19	2387	872.58		1,691.63
4	1–28	Cash		267.84	1,423.79
5	1–30	2862	450.00		1,873.79
6	2–12	Cash		539.33	1,334.46
7	2–13	Discount		4.88	1,329.58
8	2–15	Return		53.50	1,276.08
9	2–20	Cash		500.00	776.08
10	3–4	3945	2,871.40		3,647.48
11	3–5	Allowance on claim		174.52	3,472.96
12	3–8	Cash and discount		198.06	3,274.90
13	3–9	Discount chargeback	3.49		3,278.39

Item	Date	Invoice number or source	Debit	Credit	Balance
14	3–15	Cash		201.75	3,076.64
15	3–16	4624	847.20		3,923.84
16	3–24	Cash		830.26	3,093.58
17	3–25	5766	38.50		3,132.08
18	3–26	Allowance		7.00	3,125.08
19	3–31	Discount		16.94	3,108.14

3. A large retail store maintains a conservative policy on uncollected accounts whereby balances in inactive accounts more than four months old are carried to a "bad-accounts" ledger. There they remain under general-ledger control and each month the reserve for bad debts is brought into agreement with the total of the ledger. After twelve months in the ledger uncollected balances are charged against the reserve. Experience over a number of years has indicated that at any one moment of time approximately one-half of the ledger total will turn out to be collectible. At January 31, 19–0, the closing date of the store fiscal year, the ledger (and reserve) total was $35,263.20; one year earlier it had been $44,891.78. Because of narrow selling margins the store's net income for the fiscal year was $31,200.42: a figure varying little from preceding years. Comment on the practice and indicate the position you think the auditor should take.

4. The information in the paragraphs following, pertaining to two general-ledger accounts—notes receivable from customers at December 31, 19–4 of Henshaw Products, Inc., $117,286.22, and accrued interest receivable of $1,499.20—has been prepared by a clerk from subsidiary-ledger cards and other sources of information known to the clerk:

(a) Henry Adams, original amount, $3,900; now unpaid, $1,200. Dated April 30, 19–0, payable in 13 equal 6-month installments, paid through October 30, 19–4. Interest at 4%, paid to October 30, 19–4; accrued, $8.00.

(b) F. T. Alderson Bros., $3,216.47. Dated December 6, 19–4, payable in 60 days with interest at 5%; interest accrued, $26.80.

(c) George Baum, Inc., original amount, $15,700; now unpaid, $10,990. Dated July 11, 19–4, payable monthly through May 11, 19–5, last payment October 11, 19–4; prior installments paid promptly. Interest at 5%, paid through October 11, 19–4; accrued, $120.58. Although two months in arrears the account is believed by the credit manager to be collectible in full.

(d) N. S. Cassidy Corp., $5,000. Dated December 30, 19–4, payable in 30 days without interest.

(e) Evanson Mfg. Company, $7,239.33. Dated January 15, 19–4, due in 2 years. Interest at 4% payable semiannually and paid through July 15, 19–4; accrued, $13.27.

(f) Francisco Products, Inc., $50,000. Dated January 13, 19–1. This company is a wholly owned subsidiary and the amount of the note—noninterest-bearing and repayable on demand—is an advance for working-capital purposes.

(g) Hawkins Die & Tool Company, $6,400. Dated August 8, 19–3, payable with interest at 3% in equal quarterly installments through

August 8, 19–4. The last and final payment was made on August 8, 19–4.

(h) McDonnell & McHugh, original amount $7,600; now unpaid, $2,850. Dated April 20, 19–1, payable in equal qaarterly installments through April 20, 19–5. Last payment made October 20, 19–4. Interest at 3%, paid through October 20, 19–4; accrued, $16.63.

(i) Pilarski Mills, original amount $2,500; unpaid. Dated April 18, 19–4. Payable in one year; noninterest bearing. See note below.

(j) Quam Radio Co., original amount $8,000; now unpaid, $4,000. Dated September 3, 19–3. Payable in two equal installments. Last payment made September 3, 19–4 with interest at 3% through that date; accrued, $39.00.

(k) Oscar Schultz, Ltd., original amount $5,430; now unpaid, $3,642.63. Dated October 6, 19–4, payable monthly through January 6, 19–5. Date of last payment November 6, 19–4. Interest at 5% deducted from remittance of $1,810 on November 6, 19–4; accrued, $27.32.

(l) Sebolt-Ely Corp., original amount $3,000; unpaid. Dated February 2, 19–0 and due February 2, 19–4. Interest at 3%; accrued to maturity, $360.00. Paid in full on January 10; interest waived from February 2, 19–4.

(m) Toolcraft Corp., original amount $16,246.95; unpaid. Dated March 30, 19–0 and due March 30, 19–5. Interest at 4%, paid through March 30, 19–4; accrued, $847.41.

(n) Vincent Service Stores, original amount and amount now unpaid, $2,100.84. Dated December 15, 19–4 and due in 45 days; noninterest-bearing.

(o) Weaver and James, original amount and amount now unpaid $1,000. Dated January 2, 19–4. Due in one year, without interest.

(p) Wilder Mfg. Co., original amount and amount now unpaid $1,500. Dated June 30, 19–4 and due in six months with interest at 5%; accrued, $37.50. Paid in full January 2, 19–5.

(q) York-Yost Tool Co., original amount $11,600; now unpaid, $2,800. Dated April 23, 19–1, due in equal monthly installments through February 23, 19–6. Date of last payment of principal and interest, December 23, 19–4. Interest at 4½% paid through December 23, 19–4; accrued $2.18.

(1) As a member of the audit staff examining the accounts of Henshaw Products, Inc., you have been called upon to prepare a worksheet on the notes receivable with the following column headings: name, date, when due, date to which principal has been paid, original amount of principal, unpaid balance of principal, rate of interest, date of last interest payment, interest accrued at December 31, 19–4, and (if instructed) interest earned during year.

(2) Interest has been computed on the basis of a 30-day month, a basis that you accept as proper. You are to verify the accrual at the year end, and prepare and put at the bottom of the worksheet an adjusting journal entry for any corrections you may find necessary. Append to the journal entry an explanation of the apparent causes of the errors.

(3) If instructed, compute the amount of interest earned on each

note for the year, which should compare with the general-ledger account for interest income amounting before adjustment to $2,193.78. Except as noted, collections were made on their due dates.

(4) Your examination reveals that only one-half of the amount of the note of Pilarski Mills is believed to be collectible and that a settlement on that basis will shortly be made. An addition to the reserve for bad debts is thus called for, and you should prepare the entry therefor and add it to your worksheet.

(5) Upon positive circularization, satisfactory replies were received from all but Wilder Mfg. Co. whose note was paid in full on January 2, 19–5, and was not circularized.

(6) Prepare also a reclassification entry, bearing in mind that it has been the practice in prior years to include under current assets only amounts due within 12 months after the balance-sheet date.

5. To what extent do you think an auditor may rely on a test circularization of customers' accounts during the year by the client's internal auditor?

6. Describe the positive method of confirming accounts receivable by correspondence with debtors. How would you determine which method to use?

7. What additional auditing procedures may be undertaken in connection with the confirmation of accounts receivable where customers having substantial balances fail to reply after second-request forms have been mailed directly to them?

8. Describe a sales "cutoff" and indicate the auditing steps you would follow in verifying a sales "cutoff."

9. Describe briefly the more important provisions of a system of internal control in connection with allowances to customers.

10. What would be the effect of each of the following conditions on the auditor's certificate? (a) Accounts receivable are relatively large, and the client's treasurer has refused to permit their confirmation by correspondence, no other satisfactory means of establishing their substantial correctness being available. (b) A substantial amount has been advanced to a wholly owned subsidiary. The parent company has expressed its willingness to request the subsidiary to confirm the amount of its indebtedness directly to you but has refused to give you access to the subsidiary's books and records.

11. You are engaged in an examination of detailed trade accounts receivable for the purpose of appraising the adequacy of the reserve for uncollectible accounts. Indicate the lines of inquiry you would pursue in the examining of a past-due account.

12. You are informed by a client that because none of numerous notes from customers is past due, no reserve for bad debts is required. What circumstances might compel you to disagree with him?

13. What procedural modification would you as auditor suggest upon discovering that bad-debt writeoffs and allowances to customers had been authorized and recorded by a cashier-bookkeeper?

14. Your client from time to time sells its accounts receivable to a discount corporation, with recourse, 80 per cent of the account being advanced in cash. What balance-sheet notations does this call for, and how would you determine the unpaid accounts at the balance-sheet date?

15. A manufacturer, having in excess of 1,000 active customers, keeps no formal accounts-receivable ledgers because he finds the universal practice among his customers is to pay from the invoice, several invoices frequently being covered by a single remittance. Suggest a number of internal controls that might make up for this absence of customers' ledgers.

16. An auditor discovers that a client is making secret rebates to a few large customers in the form of advertising allowances, apparently in violation of the Robinson-Patman Act. What do you believe the auditor's responsibility should be under such circumstances?

17. A review by an auditor with a manufacturer's sales manager of the principles followed in granting terms to customers reveals that a number of "sales" during the year have actually been consignments— mostly of heavy farm equipment that country dealers have been unable to pay for until sales to farmers have been made. The farmer usually buys on the installment plan, the installment paper is sold to finance companies, with recourse on the manufacturer and dealer, and from the proceeds the manufacturer is reimbursed. What possible adjustment in the manufacturer's accounts will this practice necessitate, and how will the manufacturer's balance sheet be affected?

18. What is the meaning of "accrued" when applied to receivables and payables?

19. What is the preferred position in the income statement of (a) bad debts and (b) cash discounts on sales?

20. Prepare a narrative on the bad-debt analysis shown on page 246 that will serve to explain to the president of the company the computation of the bad-debt reserve at the year end.

CHAPTER VIII

Inventories

The word "inventory" refers to the physical assets of a business that are held for (a) sale (merchandise purchased for resale, finished [manufactured] goods and replacement parts therefor), (b) fabricating operations that will convert them into merchantable products (partly finished goods, finished parts, subassemblies, and raw or direct materials), and (c) service operations (for example, indirect materials, factory supplies, office stationery). The auditor's task is to make sure that the items making up the inventory had physical existence at the balance-sheet date, and are priced at cost that can be said to be fairly applied to and recoverable in the future. He accomplishes this by studies of procedures, observations of counts, and tests of completeness, prices, and clerical accuracy.

The inventory of an average manufacturing enterprise is second in amount only to fixed assets, its value notwithstanding the recent trend toward lifo pricing having constituted for many years roughly one-half of current assets and one-quarter of all assets. In chain merchandising stores extending credit the fractions are roughly the same; in department stores the corresponding ratios appear to be a little less. In audit importance the inventory ordinarily ranks first among the assets, the auditor's concern with fixed assets in repeating annual engagements normally being confined to changes during the year.

Principles and Practices

What constitutes inventory. Physical existence and prospective consumption within a short period of time are the attributes commonly associated with an item identified as inventory. Exceptions are found in supplies such as stationery, which is option-

272

ally classified as a prepaid expense; construction materials, which are more accurately identified with fixed assets; and materials and parts that may be applied to either construction or maintenance. In the last case the classification is sometimes made dependent on the principal use to which the items are customarily put, or an arbitrary split may be made as between fixed-assets and inventory classifications. The auditor is likely to accede to the employment of either of these alternatives, the amount involved having no effect on total assets and usually only a negligible effect on balance-sheet subtotals; however, the practice should be consistent from year to year.

Relation to receivables. The relation of inventory to receivables has been set forth in the preceding chapter. There it was stated that the usual test for the transformation of an item of inventory into a receivable is the passage of title to a buyer but that there are important exceptions, chiefly with respect to construction work where the contractual relationship between buyer and seller permits progress or other interim billings, or installment sales where the rights and obligations of ownership are acquired by the buyer often substantially in advance of the passage of title.

Relation to payables. The same tests apply to both receivables and payables. On the purchaser's records the entry of an item purchased customarily follows its receipt except that at the end of each fiscal year purchases in transit title to which has passed to the purchaser may be added, thereby complementing the recording of a sale on the books of the seller. Year-end adjustments by the buyer for in-transit items are sometimes neglected, particularly where nominal in amount.

Consistency. At this point the notion of "consistency" deserves a brief examination. By this term accountants mean adherence to the same methods of computation, valuation, and accrual from one year to another. Many, for example, believe it more important for the auditor to make sure that his client, in determining inventory cost, has followed the costing method of the preceding year than to be greatly concerned over the method itself. Applied to an inventory, specific or actual cost may yield substantially different results than fifo, average cost, retail cost, or lifo, but the auditor as a rule will accept any one of these standard bases for the closing inventory if he finds that the same method was also applied to the opening inventory. The reason can be understood from the effect on net income. Thus if opening and closing inventories on a fifo basis are $500,000 and $400,000, respectively, and $300,000 and $220,000 on a lifo basis, a difference of $200,000 and $180,000 in working capital will be observed but only $20,000 in inventory variation. Sometimes auditors condone what appear to be minor irregularities such as lags in recording receipts from suppliers or in billing customers, expensing supply inventories, under- or overvaluing certain minor items, and recording nominal or arbitrary quantities for others. The omission of inventories altogether from financial statements would have no effect on net profit provided—and only provided—the dollar amount thereof remained constant over the years. The same is true of accounts payable for purchases and of expense accruals. But the proviso is all-important. The quantity of the inventory of every business enterprise *does* fluctuate, usually in a substantial way, and often from unpredictable and uncontrollable external causes; so do the dollar amounts of payables and accrued expense. Further, without these items current solvency—revealed by the balance sheet —would not be disclosed. With regard to small items, the failure to record them or to allocate them between accounting periods will affect no one's conclusions as to operating results or financial position, and a strict application of conventional rules to such items is occasionally relaxed. The justification for relaxation can rest only on the assumption of a negligible fluctuation over the years and on the smallness of any one item and of the total of all other excepted items in relation to financial position at any one time. Regardless of the size of the amount involved, however, the observance of correct practices is greatly to be preferred, lest the infection of laxity spread to other more material accounts.

Quantities. Inventory quantities may be expressed as physical units or in terms of weight, volume, or other measure. They may be actual or estimated, or book balances resulting from the continuous recording of the inflow and outflow of raw materials, parts, completed product, or merchandise. Ideally, quantities should be actual counts on the balance-sheet date; but counts on other dates may be practicable and acceptable to the auditor when conforming with the requirements of an adequate system of internal controls. Thus a physical determination of quantities made say a month before the balance-sheet date may be adjusted for subsequent acquisitions and issues by temporary book-inventory methods maintained from that point to the year end. Or permanent book-inventory records from which quantities for balance-sheet purposes are extracted may be systematically tested by actual counts, the book balance of each item at some point during the period being conformed to the correct amount.

Age and condition. Accounting policies of most organizations provide for the recognition of inventory spoilage, damage, or other form of deterioration whatever the cause. This recognition may take a number of forms such as an arbitrary, lump-sum reduction of cost or a writedown to exchange value or to some form of value in use. A reserve or allowance account may be provided for the writedown.

Title. To be classified as inventory, each item (certain exceptions have already been indicated) must be owned. It is because of this general rule that items in transit from suppliers are preferably included in inventory as are also goods that have been sold on approval or that are out on consignment or are in the possession of others as samples or for display.

Valuation. The traditional valuation of an inventory has been and continues to be cost: actual cost or such portions of actual cost as under accepted practices are carried forward for absorption in the next following period or periods. In recent years the "lifo" method of valuation has gained some headway, primarily because of its incorporation in the internal-revenue code as a means of tax reduction for established business enterprises during a period of rising prices; in its present form and as sanctioned for income-tax purposes it is an allocation of cost.

Cost. Inventory items like other assets are priced at original cost or such portion thereof as may be regarded as "reasonably applicable to future operations." However the fungible character of inventory items, the variations in cost-accounting practices, the possibilities of tax savings by the adoption of certain valuation devices, and the individual judgments that of necessity enter into determinations of costs to be carried forward, create widely different cost patterns.

The cost of purchased materials, parts, and merchandise is invoice cost plus transportation, duty, and other direct acquisition costs, less allowances and discounts, the last-named including trade discounts and now usually cash discounts. The current trend is to record costs net of *all* discounts, and to regard the loss of a cash discount as a financial expense. On the other hand there are those who look at a cash discount of 2 per cent as being in the same category as interest received. Discounts received being credits, the likening to interest undoubtedly arises from the notion of *prepayment*—that is, payment before the "net" date. However, terms of "2 per cent 10 days, net 30" mean that if the interest concept is accepted the 2 per cent discount relates to the period lying between the 10th and 30th days, $\frac{1}{18}$ of a year, and thus implies an "interest" rate of 36 per cent a year. Since the current rate of interest is only a small portion of this amount, most accountants regard the whole of any cash discount as a reduction of both the invoiced amount and the unit cost derived therefrom.

The cost price to be applied to units sold or remaining at the end of a fiscal year may not be their individual costs even where the units can be identified beyond a doubt with particular purchase transactions. The fungible or interchangeable nature of most purchased items, particularly those of the average manufacturing enterprise, gives rise to a number of distinct types of cost applications the use of any of which is recognized as valid in inventory valuations.

Actual cost. Determination of the cost of individual inventory items is possible as, for example, where each bears a serial number, cost tag, or other means of identification with the original invoice, or is one of a lot the identity of which is maintained by its location or other device. For example, it might be expected that the inventory of a job-order shop would likely consist of individual jobs in process, each valued at cost: direct materials, direct labor, and a charge for overhead the cost of which has perhaps been spread in proportion to direct-labor cost or direct-labor hours. A dealer in slow-moving, relatively expensive merchandise may take pains to identify each item of his stock with a particular purchase, thus making it possible to say that actual cost attaches to his stock on hand as well as to the items he has sold.

First-in-first-out. On the "first-in-first-out" (fifo) basis, the cost of raw materials entering production or of merchandise sold is identified with the values attached to the same class of items in the "opening" inventory; when these quantities have been "costed out" the identification proceeds with the earliest purchase of the period and follows through each successive purchase, thus leaving the latest purchases to be identified with the closing inventory. Where the formula for determining the cost of sales for the period is the excess of opening inventory plus purchases over closing inventory, as is often the case with smaller concerns, a reverse process is followed: the quantities on hand at the close of the period are "worked back" from the latest invoices leaving cost of sales as identifiable with earlier purchases and the opening inventory. This method, employed for many decades, is still the most frequently observed inventory-cost basis in current use; and it will likely remain so despite the present popularity of lifo, described below. It is probably the most realistic basis, also, since it is good management and good merchandising to dispose of oldest acquisitions first, leaving the most recent acquisitions on hand.

Average cost. There are several types of average cost. The simplest is that of a single product whereby total cost for a year (opening inventory plus purchases and, where applicable, plus manufacturing cost) is spread prorata over units produced, the same unit cost being applied to both units sold and units on hand at the end of the year. Or where costs are subject to material changes a new average may be obtained several times during the year. The moving-average principle may also be employed whereby at the time of each addition to stock differing in cost from the average a new average is computed for each unit of stock remaining. Still another method is to use the average cost of the previous period (month or year) in costing out sales for the current period, the inventory then becoming a residual account to be adjusted at the end of the period when a physical inventory is taken.

Retail cost. The retail method of determining cost of sales and inventory involves the recording of opening inventory and purchases at expected resale prices as well as at cost, obtaining markon percentages that may be applied to sales and closing inventory (priced at retail) in order to arrive at cost of sales and inventory cost. In essence it is another method of averaging cost. Separate percentages are maintained for each class of stock or department.

Joint products and byproducts. Where several grades or types of endproducts are obtained from a common source or single operation the method of allocating costs as between products is wholly arbitrary. The most-used device is to identify as many costs as possible with individual endproducts and spread the joint or common costs in proportion to the expected selling prices of such endproducts. If an endproduct is also classified as a byproduct the usual practice is to credit production costs with its discounted market value—that is, its prospective selling price less an allowance for handling and marketing. Occasionally questions arise as to the difference between a joint product against which production costs are allocated and a byproduct against which no production costs are allocated. The distinction is wholly one for administrative decision; or custom within an industry may determine the practice. Thus in the oil industry in the early '20's gasoline, which had been a byproduct in the refining of kerosene, became generally recognized as a major product; and in more recent years fuel and lubrication oils have been accorded a similar rank.

Standard costs. Standard costs are sometimes used as a basis for inventory valuation. A standard cost may be regarded as a variety of average cost where it represents an estimate expected to be maintained under actual operating conditions during a limited future period of time. So-called ideal standard costs or standard costs that remain unchanged over long periods of time are not well suited as an inventory-valuation basis unless they are carefully adjusted by those elements of variances attributable to normal actual costs: an adjustment in some cases difficult if not impossible to make. But where variances consist principally of abnormal costs that are more in the nature of period charges than regular costs of production standard costs—without adjustment —are well suited as an inventory base, and their employment for that purpose is increasing.

Overhead. Some accountants believe that only direct or variable costs of material, labor, and overhead should be associated with product costs. They would exclude fixed overheads such as rents and depreciation by regarding them as period costs and hence classifiable as a separate addition to cost of sales. Direct costs are commonly regarded as including service costs such as power.

Where standard costs are used as a basis for inventory valuation they may include standard rates for overhead and they are subject to approval or disapproval as are standard rates for material and labor mentioned above.

Occasionally the argument is heard that selling and administrative expense should be added to production costs and thus prorated to inventory. However, a well-established accounting rule requires that such types of overhead be wholly excluded from inventory costs, even though certain elements of these items may be directly associated with the product.

Lifo. The widespread use of the last-in-first-out method has arisen from the claim that it more nearly reflects the operating point of view, whether or not selling prices are affected, since operating people are inclined to think in terms of margins between current market prices—wholesale and retail, or raw material and intermediate or finished product. The effect during a period of rising prices is to keep the cost of the inventory at a "safer" lower level than current replacement cost, thus reducing margins and making it possible to decrease selling prices when the market swings in the other direction, without having to provide for inventory losses. If inventory quantities tend to be constant and inventory costs are kept at the lowest point in a long-range price cycle, the lifo method of costing inventories becomes the "base-stock" method.

The lifo method, once advocated principally within metal and other industries where the ratio of inventory to sales is relatively large, has spread to various forms of enterprise as a tax-saving device. It is not particularly advantageous in any situation where inventory stocks are small or variable, turnover is rapid, or hedging operations protect future sales. It has the effect of creating a secret reserve, and it does not obviate the need in many instances of reducing cost to an amount not exceeding market.

Market. By "market," as the term is usually employed in the phrase "cost or market," is meant that portion of inventory cost that may be justifiably carried forward to future periods when weight is given to the conditions likely to accompany disposal. In practice the unit price may be any one of several valuations, all presumably less than cost: a quoted price on the balance-sheet date, a quoted price less the cost of selling and less a hoped-for profit, or some other cost fraction that experience or custom has indicated as a "safe" base for application against estimated realization.

As a rule there should be no reduction of cost to a market figure for that portion of the inventory that will remain in the business as a minimum quantity to be kept on hand, or in situations where the selling price will probably not react to a reduction in raw-material cost. Raw material that has been purchased in connection with the manufacture of a product for which a firm price exists and on which a normal profit is expected should not be marked down despite a lower market. The purpose of any write-down of cost before a sale is made is to absorb that portion of cost estimated to be nonrecoverable in the period in which it is first recognized as such.

The market price of work in process and finished stock is usually held to be the lower of (a) the cost of replacement or (b) the selling price less the cost to complete less selling expense and less the customary gross margin. Some accountants omit the last item because it does not represent a loss of cost.

A market quotation should reflect the price on the balance-sheet date that would have to be paid in the area in which the purchase would ordinarily be made for a similar item in the quantity usually acquired at one time. Market prices are ordinarily applied to individual items rather than groups or classes, and when once a market price less than cost has been adopted in an inventory valuation it remains as the cost of the item for all future reckoning.

Reductions of costs to amounts equal to market are often collected in an inventory reserve, thus avoiding the alteration of stores or other records. To justify the reserve as a valuation account rather than as a subdivision of retained earnings, details of reductions to market by individual items or groups should be available; and in the succeeding period the reserve should be adjusted as these items are disposed of.

Markdowns of cost because of age or surplus quantities may be regarded as equivalent to market reductions since the purpose is to carry forward only those costs that may fairly be applied against future realizations. These markdowns are often accomplished by adopting a percentage scale whereby the cost of an unsold item is progressively decreased as it is continued in stock until scrap value is reached. In the retail method of determining inventory cost the same purpose is served by reducing the expected selling price by the original markon percentage.

In all these situations cost reductions made in accordance with the principles indicated should be based on past experience or present facts and be fairly applied to the inventory as a whole.

Internal Controls

In Chapter V the functions of the purchasing division of a business enterprise were described as being primarily concerned with procurement standards, prices, followup, and delivery, and not including controls over receipt, inspection, or stores; the receiving function as embracing responsibilities for quantities (counts) and quality (inspection); issues of stores and merchandise as involving a number of steps designed to provide authority to transmit goods from stock to the production line or shipping room.

Controls over inventories, at the center of many of these activities, are usually conceived as including at least the following elements:

1. *Quantitative controls.* In a manufacturing establishment perpetual inventory records are generally regarded as a necessity. They may provide for only quantity controls, but include wherever practicable dollar controls also. In a merchandising concern such controls may be provided for warehouse stocks and store "reserves," but they usually do not extend to the shelf or display stocks. Where factory production requires a steady flow of many

types of raw materials, "balanced" inventories of such materials are required. This means that for uninterrupted, economical operations the quantities on hand must be adequate but no more than adequate. Planned production is essential. Such planning calls for the scheduling of purchasing, the flow of material in and out of the storekeeper's hands, the timing of finished parts and subassemblies, controls over quality maintenance and defective work: all based on realistic sales estimates or contract delivery requirements prepared by the sales department. A production-control executive may be required in larger enterprises.

Wherever possible, the auditor encourages the installation and careful maintenance of book-inventory controls. They should be kept as a rule under the direction of the storekeeper, with a functional line of authority extending from the person who keeps the records to the controller. Internal-audit procedures should call for a verification of the book quantities with the physical at least once yearly, differences being subject to review and disposition by higher authority. Where the size of the business and the number and importance of the items warrant, one or more inventory crews may be employed on a full-time basis. They will not only make the necessary counts and comparisons but the investigations required in order to account for errors discovered.

2. *Quantity ranges.* Minimum and maximum quantities are specified as control devices for storekeepers to whom the responsibility for maintaining balanced quantities has been assigned. The setting of quantity limits should, however, be the task of the planning staff, and changes during the year in the production schedule should be accompanied by the necessary changes of quantity limits.

3. *Issues.* Deliveries from storerooms should be made only upon specified authority, an authority that should emanate from levels having a high degree of responsibility. The authority in some instances may consist of approved bills of material following the adoption of production plans and the issuance of production orders. Deliveries of finished stock or merchandise should be the consequence of approved shipping orders.

4. *Eliminations.* Periodic reviews should be made by qualified persons within the organization for the purpose of discovering and taking action on slow-moving, obsolete, and damaged stock. Because the quantities of certain stocks, such as repair parts that must be kept available for both old and new styles of products in the hands of customers, cannot always be accurately measured very far in advance, it is important that quantities on hand be

regularly appraised for their sufficiency, based on latest available estimates of probable requirements.

5. *Obsolescent stock.* In the event old stocks are retained, formulas or other methods of reflecting conservative decreases in costs should be adopted for the guidance of the storekeeper or others who deal with price.

6. *Safeguards.* Physical housing for inventory items should be provided wherever required as a protection against theft, action of the elements, and inaccuracies in recording receipts and issues. In addition, custodians or storekeepers should be appointed who have the proper qualifications for their role in maintaining prescribed internal procedures surrounding stock controls.

Physical inventories. Physical inventories are a necessary supplement to the accounting processes of every manufacturing and trading organization. Where perpetual records have been instituted they may be taken in sections or by individual items more or less continuously during the year, thus facilitating the tracing of differences and making possible more than one count of critical items. In most organizations an annual physical count is considered indispensable even though quantities have been compared during the year with perpetual records.

The annual physical inventory is a formidable undertaking. It may be taken or completed during a temporary shutdown of the plant at the year end; or it may be completed before the year end and adjusted to the balance at the close of the period by employing an informal stock record.

The most important feature of a physical inventory is a carefully drawn plan under the provisions of which the counting, listing, pricing, and the extensions and footings are made. A well-laid plan, skillfully administered, not only saves work by the auditor but justifies his confidence in the totals finally arrived at. The plan, even in a small enterprise, should be in writing, and if possible the auditor should be given the opportunity of reviewing it while it is still in the draft stage, adding his suggestions wherever necessary. Points included should be similar to the following:

1. *General responsibility:* one individual is named who will carry out the plan and who is given commensurate authority, including the supervision of any special in-and-out count between the inventory date and the year end.

2. *Dates,* including closedown dates, on which the inventory or sections of the inventory are to be taken: these may often be arranged to coincide with the time when the external auditor will

be available—for example, a month or more before the end of the year.

3. *Location of stock:* floor plans may be necessary in many instances showing the location of the various classes of items to be inventoried; subsequently, tags and sheet numbers assigned to each location may be shown on such plans.

4. *Training of employees:* the organization and instruction of crews so that there will be no loss of time when the counting and listing process begins; they must be told precisely what to put on paper, and in some instances it will be necessary to familiarize them with the stock they are to count. It may be preferable to assign counters and checkers to stocks with which they are already familiar.

5. *Forms:* the forms and precise function and use of inventory tags and sheets are described in detail so that their printing, numbering, distribution, filling in, collection, and summarization may be clearly understood by all inventory workers. Once printed and numbered they are kept under strict control, carefully allotted to locations and individuals, and each accounted for when the inventory count has been completed.

6. *Improvements in procedures:* defects in earier physical-inventory procedures should be borne in mind in preparing the current year's procedures in order that whatever mistakes were made last year will not be repeated.

7. *Interim records:* quantity controls, if not already in existence, whereby additions and subtractions will be made between the inventory date and the year end.

8. *Sorting of stock:* the plan for the sorting and rearrangement, in piles or other orderly form, of materials and supplies, especially those items not in the storeroom, wherever the count will thereby be facilitated.

9. *Work in process:* where possible, the plan provides for cleaning up work in process, particularly delayed or abandoned work before the count begins; and, for active in-process items, for developing temporary cost-collection sheets for individual items or lots if job or work orders cannot be readily identified with physical work.

10. *Items of same type:* if the possibility of double counting exists with respect to items of the same type, arrangements may be made to count them all simultaneously.

11. *Two independent counts:* where no stockroom quantity records are maintained, the best procedure is to provide for two separate and unrelated counts. One method is to have tags made

in two sections each bearing the tag number. The tag is attached to the item, bin, or pile by the first counter who fills in the lower, detachable section. Subsequently, the lower section is removed by an employee who makes sure that tags have been attached to all items. The top section of the tag is filled in by a second counter, and collected by another employee who also notes the completeness of the attachments. Other employees match the two sections and trace differences, if any. A *single* count is usually adequate where stockroom records have been kept.

12. *Duplicates:* where counts are transcribed directly to inventory sheets during the calling operation the same degree of control is exercised over their issue as that surrounding tags. In addition, they may be prepared in duplicate, the duplicate to be held by the external auditor until the originals have been priced, extended, footed, and summarized, perhaps several weeks later. By this device the auditor is assured that inventory items and quantities are not modified except as changes are revealed by comparing duplicates with completed originals. With respect to quantities, the external auditor's main job will then be to test the propriety of additions, reductions, or changes made since the joint preparation of both copies.

13. *Condition:* defects, age, and other comments on the condition of inventory items are an essential part of every count and are noted on the tag or sheet as the count is made. A coding may be provided to show condition.

14. *Cutoff on receipts:* on the balance-sheet date a part of the physical inventories may be found in the receiving room and in trucks or freight cars yet to be unloaded. The inventory procedure should provide that these items are to be included in the count on that date, one procedure being to give them distinctive labels. When the date of count precedes the balance-sheet date and additions and subtractions are to be expressed only in dollar amounts rather than in item quantities, it may be necessary to follow the same procedure on the date of count also. To facilitate the count in the shipping room, the instructions may call for closing the shipping room for several hours.

15. *Accounts payable:* a search for and listing of receiving reports, for the period under audit, not yet matched with recorded invoices is called for, and also a search for and identification of items received on which no receiving report has as yet been issued.

16. *In-transit purchases:* a figure is built up for purchases in transit and to avoid duplication a comparison is made of supporting details with items recorded as being on hand. In some cases a

satisfactory solution to this problem is found by comparing the dates appearing on receiving tickets for the first few weeks of the next following fiscal period with the shipment dates appearing on suppliers' invoices. It is always better practice to include in-transit items in the inventory, although some accountants take the position that this is unnecessary where in-transit items (a) are nominal in volume, year after year, and (b) relate to normal amounts of recurrent purchases.

17. *Cutoff on sales:* of no less importance is the cutoff procedure to be established for sales. This usually involves the closing down of the shipping room for the final hours of the last day of the year, everything in the shipping room at that time being regarded as inventory. The date of shipment appearing on the retained copy of the invoice, as well as the date of the invoice itself, will ordinarily give a satisfactory clue, provided an internal control exists safeguarding the accuracy of these dates.

18. *Inventory belonging to others:* provision is made for an internal procedure that will develop an accurate list of materials and finished goods in the hands of others but not sold to them; and in contrast a list of items on hand that are on consignment or on approval from others. It may be that sales to others have been made for which shipment has not yet taken place; agreements with customers will provide for storing them at the convenience of the customer. The first of these three classes of items should be included in the inventory, with due allowance for possible recovery (which may be small if samples or display goods are involved); the second class should be excluded from the inventory, and the third class also, provided the customer has been billed.

Financial-Statement Standards

In the balance sheet a breakdown of the amount of the inventory as between merchandise, finished goods, work in process, raw materials, and supplies is always to be preferred. If the relative investment in these items remains more or less constant from year to year, some accountants do not object to the appearance on the balance sheet of a single monetary amount. In-transit purchases should be combined with raw materials (or merchandise) and where the practice in this respect has been uniform over a period of years no disclosure of such inclusion is necessary. Consignments-out are likewise included without disclosure under finished product.

Supply inventories may appear as a part of prepaid expenses, especially where they are of the type that will ultimately be charged to administrative or selling expense. Factory supplies are usually regarded as inventory since they more nearly resemble raw materials and more directly concern production. Construction materials in minor amounts may be included with raw materials; but if a large supply has been acquired for a future project its classification under fixed assets is to be preferred. Returnable containers are usually placed in the later category as described in Chapter X.

The valuation basis for inventories should always be disclosed. "At cost or market, whichever is lower" describes the valuation basis appearing more often than any other on published financial statements. Other frequently noted designations are "at cost on first-in-first-out basis" or "at cost on last-in-first-out basis," the former being generally regarded as the usual interpretation of cost. In either case where the indicated basis has been adjusted because of lower market prices (replacement or reproduction cost) that fact should be added to the sidehead.

If any portion of the inventory has been pledged as security for a loan, the existence of the pledge should be noted in the sidehead and the related loan appearing among liabilities should be identified with it. It is not considered good practice, however, to deduct the liability from the pledged amount notwithstanding that the proceeds from the sale of the items so pledged must first be applied to the payment of the loan.

Progress payments from customers are regarded as reductions of work in process, the amount of such payments appearing parenthetically in the sidehead.

Where an inventory reserve is a true valuation account, such as one representing a writedown from cost to market, it may be applied for balance-sheet purposes directly in reduction of the asset to which it relates without disclosure of the amount. But if the reserve was created in anticipation of some indefinite future decline in value, that is, a decline reflected neither in current market prices nor physical condition, it is not a current-asset reduction but a species of contingent reserve and should be classified as an appropriation of retained earnings.

In the income statement the amounts of the opening and closing inventories often appear. Where the latter has been written down from cost to market and the writedown is material in amount it should appear as a separate item.

Representative Audit Program

1. Plan inventory examination early in audit year. Review last year's inventory program; recommend to client immediate drafting or redrafting by staff of inventory instructions for year covering perpetual-inventory tests, test counts for items not covered by quantity controls, and the year-end physical inventory. Review draft and make suggestions for improved procedures. Recommend, also, prompt appointment of employee to be made responsible for administering the inventory program.

2. Be present at inventory-taking. Review controls over issue of inventory tags and their recheck after being collected; compare and make note of variations in actual methods followed as revealed by personal observation and through conversations with individuals participating in count. Call immediately to attention of supervising official any infractions of instructions. Select items for test recounts and for reconciliation with controlling records, showing whatever adjustments made in controls and details; determine causes for material differences; compare with differences of prior years. Describe remedies instituted or proposed for reducing future discrepancies.

3. Where physical count has been incomplete or none was made at or near year end for all or substantially all the inventory, and reliance is had on continuous quantity controls, ascertain adequacy of interim counts and prepare memorandum thereon for working papers. Determine possible ranges of error based on past differences between book and physical inventories; select items in each class covered by quantity controls for test-counts to be made under auditor's observation, reconcile with book records, and where possible scan recorded additions and deductions since year end. If test-counts during year were not properly supervised, were not frequently enough repeated, did not cover substantially all items, or disclosed substantial differences with book controls, it may be necessary to qualify inventory item on balance sheet or in report.

4. Become familiar with location of inventory, discover from what sources and how item quantities and descriptions were entered and checked back for accuracy, how prices were determined and inserted, conditions under which extensions and footings were made and subsequently verified, how page totals were classified and summarized, and establish identities of persons responsible. Verify representative extensions and footings and scan

bulk of remaining inventory pages for extensions and footings.

5. Prepare comparative summary of inventory at present and two preceding year ends, somewhat as follows:

Comparative Inventory Summary

| Class of items | Type of count | Unit of count | Location | Pricing method | Amount | | | Remarks |
					This year	1 Year ago	2 Years ago	

List in spaces provided different classes of inventory (for example, raw materials or some subdivision of raw materials), divided, where possible, by types of count (physical, book, bin record, lot record, warehouse receipt or other outside certification), units of count (items, containers, unit of weight or measure), location, and method of pricing.

6. Review cutoff controls applied to purchased materials and parts, finished products sold, and in-transit items; trace selected receiving reports and shipping records during three work days preceding and following year end to recorded obligations and receivables, and for same period trace back samples of recorded purchases and sales to records of receipt and shipment.

7. Select individual items under jurisdiction of as many departments as possible for turnover study; prepare three-year turnover ratios for these items, determine number of months' supply at year end, and reasonableness of each supply and of minimum and maximum controls in effect.

8. Study over-all inventory characteristics and trends within business and market generally, prepare a brief statement on causes of inventory variations between years as revealed by the comparative summary; tie in with analysis of sales trends; compute comparative ratios to sales for each of the three years and for the final quarter and final month of each year.

9. Investigate possibility of inclusion in inventory of materials and parts owned by others, or consigned.

10. Request written confirmation, to be sent directly to auditor, of inventory items consigned to others, showing quantity, condition, and, for warehouse stocks, liens and conditions of withdrawal.

11. Make sure no "deadwood" remains in work in process, and production orders remaining are being or will presently be worked on.

12. Look for maintenance, repair, and other expense orders in work in process, and see to it that they are cleared to expense, regardless of state of completion of order.

13. Analyze inventory (asset) and inventory-reserve (valuation) accounts for year and test elements for their character and propriety.

14. List on inventory summary pricing method followed for each inventory section:

If "invoice" cost indicate elements included;

If work in process, or finished stock, indicate whether book cost has been followed or cost derived from physical survey, and describe basis for including materials, labor, and overhead;

If market show source of quotation and cost;

If obsolete or slow-moving stock compare sample items (quantity and price) with past years' inclusions, and indicate basis of pricing.

15. Test individual prices of each class and each inventory section in such a manner as to cover substantial portion of whole inventory.

16. Investigate outstanding purchase commitments at year end and ascertain possible liability for items exceeding ordinary contractual practices. If no list is available, examine open purchase-order and contract file for such items at audit date and review, very generally, major acquisitions and cancellations since year end.

Audit Procedures

As indicated in the preceding section it is important that the auditor determine the elements of his inventory program as early as possible in the year that is to be covered by his examination. The general character as well as the details of the program will, to a great extent, be dependent on the corresponding tests for the year preceding. If he was not in charge of the preceding year's audit, he should examine the working papers carefully in order to pick up the points that he believes need emphasis during the current year.

Internal controls play a major part here as elsewhere. Such controls relate not only to book inventories and the handling of acquisitions and issues during the year but also the controls relating to the planning and execution of the client's physical-inventory procedures at the year end. The auditor should inquire concerning changes in these controls during the year and at some point in his investigation he should determine that they have been adequately instituted and carried out.

Program inspection. The auditor's preliminary work on inventories can be best accomplished by one or more plant visits while the period under audit is still in progress. He should bear in mind that there are a number of persistent problems that are present in some form on almost every assignment: problems that if not satisfactorily solved could seriously weaken the auditor's examination. These points may be put in the form of questions as follows:

1. Has an inventory supervisor been appointed who is likely to assume the responsibility necessary for such an assignment?

2. If the tag system of inventorying is to be followed, will the tags be ready in sufficient quantity, numbered serially, and kept under proper controls?

3. Is it likely that the instructions governing the issue of tags and their preparation will be strictly adhered to at all points?

4. Have the cutoff procedures been reviewed for their practicality and completeness with receiving- and shipping-room supervisors, the stockkeepers, and the plant superintendent? Are the cutoff instructions sufficiently comprehensive?

5. Have the procedures governing the treatment of obsolete, slow-moving, and damaged items been satisfactorily prepared both as to preliminary surveys and methods of valuation?

6. Is the training program for inventory participants adequate and will it be completed satisfactorily before the inventory period begins?

7. Will the stock be so arranged and where necessary collected at one point as to facilitate inspection and count, and will all items be so identified that those who list them will be able to describe them in such a manner that others may understand their meaning?

8. Will work in process be arranged and will bills of material and other basic data be available so that accumulated costs will be readily determined?

9. Has the procedure for listing ins and outs during the period between the inventory and the close of the year been carefully outlined and is it likely to be understood and observed by employees responsible for following it out?

Finished and partly finished goods. In most situations involving fabricated and semifabricated products the inventory at the end of the year is much less, perhaps only a fraction, of the year's production and the costing of sales and inventory is a joint problem. Where however the ratio of the cost assigned to the inventory to the year's gross margin is large—and this is usually the case—a good deal of importance attaches to the distinctions between normal and exceptional production costs, the natural tendency being to exclude the latter from the inventory and load it, sometimes as an extraordinary item, on operations. Among cost-determination problems of finished and partly finished goods that the auditor must consider are the following:

1. How costs of work-in-process and finished-stock inventories have been computed in past years; how estimates of items sold and on hand have been made during the current year in budgets and monthly statements and for other purposes. These computations may point to excluded costs which may deserve consideration in the present year-end valuation.

2. Tie-in of costs with accounts. The inventory valuation may be a residual cost, rather than a figure representing a control over specific details in a stockroom record. Where a stockroom record exists, there should be frequent tests for the accuracy of the control in the general ledger. Controls over quantities are more common than controls over both quantities and costs.

3. Method of determining costs carried into inventory accounts. The accuracy of these costs, particularly with respect to material and labor content will depend on the method of compiling the details—whether it be done by using standard or other estimated costs, how variances are disposed of, how long present estimates have been in use, and changes made in estimates to reflect new material costs and labor rates.

4. Worth of cost system. The auditor must make a practical appraisal of the cost system in use. This he will have done if he has pursued well his operational inquiries into production activities as outlined in Chapter V.

5. Exceptional or abnormal costs excluded from the inventory-cost base. These will consist of such items as costs of shutdowns not anticipated, costs during a major conversion from one method or line of production to another, inefficiencies that have resulted in rejects or wastage not attributable to normal operations, or other costs which are of the type that are customarily written off as they are incurred.

6. Overhead and its distribution. Factory overhead should be justified against costs included under the same head in previous years, should contain no administrative or selling expense, and should be distributed on some reasonable basis.

Book inventories. The auditor may accept a book inventory, provided periodic tests with physical quantities are regularly made and provided the differences thereby disclosed are not important. In every case, however, the auditor should direct and observe test counts of at least a few of the more important items that past experience indicates are more likely to be in error. He should also ascertain the nature of any internal-audit procedures and reports relating to book inventories during the period covered by the audit and discuss larger and frequently recurring differences or problems with the storekeeper, stores-record clerk, and the controller.

Where perpetual records are competently maintained, the auditor's principal studies, observations, and tests may be made at various times during the audit period rather than following the close of the period. In any event he must decide as early in the year as possible what his audit program for inventories is to cover, and he must review the general scope of his proposed inquiries with his client so that his work may be coordinated closely with operating plans. The auditor must always be vigorous in his espousal of what he deems to be adequate in the way of controls over inventories, and in the institution of physical-inventory tests that conform to a carefully conceived internal program extending throughout the year.

Illustrative Audit

Fourteen worksheets are devoted to the auditor's summaries and comments on inventories. The main elements in the auditor's review are: the assistance given in July 1952, in the drawing up of a plan for the physical inventory to be taken at the end of the following December (F 2); the presence of the auditor and his assistant on December 30–31 and January 1 at the inventory-taking and the observations and checks then made.(F 4–5); an examination of the cutoff procedures at that time (F 6–7); a study of the valuation methods followed (F 8); a comprehensive testcheck of clerical accuracy (F 12); and a brief analysis of the leading features of the three principal inventory classes (F 9, 10, 11).

A plan for the inventory count is always best prepared several months in advance so that those responsible can be trained and familiarized with their part in the counting, listing, pricing, extending, footing, and summarizing process with a minimum of lost time at the year end when these operations take place. The full plan is not stated on F 2–3 but only the changes in 1952 as compared with the previous year. Ordinarily, the inventory plan conforms to a method, repeated year after year, that should be briefed for the permanent file. A detailed analysis for the current file is not required here. Changes and defects in the plan and its operation should, however, be carefully set forth each year.

On F 4 are the auditor's comments on the count. Not all his observations are reproduced here, but those given should illustrate the type of irregularity deserving a note. The irregularities that appeared are mostly minor in character, but they reflect situations that should be forestalled, if possible, in planning next year's count.

An attempt to account for the listed inventory tags appears on F 5. On 334 pages of inventory sheets there are 12,287 entries, and this figure corresponds to the number of tags used according to a summary of used and returned tags. The auditor's interest in an accurate accounting of tag numbers is to make sure that there have been no omissions or duplications.

Cutoff planning (F 6–7) appears to have been well carried out, no exceptions arising during the course of the auditor's examination. The bottom half of F 7 is, in one sense, a story of the in-process cutoff; it could also have been combined with other in-process-inventory data on F 10.

Although in the general representation from the management (X 1) the statement is made that the inventory is valued at the lower of cost or market, the detail on F 8 indicates that causes other than a low market have given rise to less-than-cost valuation. Hence, in presenting the inventory figure in Exhibit I (RS 2), the more accurate phrase "at cost or less" is employed.

A feature of the examination of in-process items was a study of six shop orders in process that made up 84 per cent of the year-end total; not only were the material and labor charges traced to their sources, but the auditor inspected the unfinished stock in the factory and the subassemblies and other items were counted for him. At the bottom of F 10 is the description of a loss that has worked through inventory variation into profit and loss and is nowhere brought out as a separate item or as a part of a labeled group of "loss" items—a typical procedure in many manufacturing enterprises. Had losses such as these been numerous in the current year (no other such losses were apparently found), comparisons of cost-of-sales elements with those of the prior year might have been seriously distorted.

Following the summary on F 11, an attempt is made to explain the difference in raw-material inventories; book inventory and physical determination of the location of the difference within any section of the inventory has been impossible because of the lack of detailed book figures. Even in the case of supplies, where, as explained at the bottom of the sheet, a quantity record has been maintained, an allocation of the difference cannot be made to individual items because of the basis of pricing out withdrawals. A full explanation of these differences would have added to the completeness of the auditor's survey at this point, but its absence has in no way impaired his confidence in the propriety of the closing inventory.

Samples of the details making up the auditor's inventory corrections, and the methods by which these details are recorded, are given in F 12.

Martin Manufacturing Company
Inventory Summary
December 31, 1952

Source	Finished stock 31-3	Work in process 31-2	Raw material and parts 31-1	Supplies 31-4	Total
Physical inventory	1 151 225 18	1 13 777 53	1 43 115 00	1 36 135 41	
subtotals representing	2 286 756 01	2 28 200 73	2 187 084 40	2 21 178 22	
amounts shown on	3 95 393 80	3 23 487 60	3 58 886 52	3 13 104 46	
tapes rerun by H.R.	4 -16 093 03	4 12 154 64	4 68 455 78	4 47 714 04	
on totals of inven-		5 844 90	5 87 643 71	5 7 000 02	
tory sheets before		6 201 510 18	6 - 9 546 39		
adjustments below		7 3 285 74			
Total, put on books	517 281 96	284 261 32	435 639 02	125 132 15	1 362 314 45
Auditor's adjustments (AJE #18) —					
Listing	- 26 45	+ 16 587 45	+ 23 824 49	- 2 731 05	+ 37 418 44
Pricing } F-12	+ 3 393 03	- 7 319 26	- 6 297 50	-	- 10 223 73
Extension	-	- 2 50	- 813 26	+ 15 25	- 800 51
Total adjustments	+ 3 130 58	+ 9 265 69	+ 16 713 73	- 2 715 80	+ 26 394 20
Total, as adjusted	520 412 54	293 527 01	452 352 75	122 416 35	1 388 708 65
	TB	TB	TB	TB	TB

The above subtotals correspond to those made by the company and
are supported by separately bound groupings of 334 inventory sheets kept
in the company's bookkeeping-department vault. To each group a tape is
attached, each item on the tape representing one inventory-sheet total;
31-2-4-5 means sheet 5 of group 4 (the group total being $12,154.64
above) under work in process. 31-3-4 (one sheet) contains a list of
markdowns by items from cost to less. These are minor in character
because of elimination in latter part of 1952 of old stock.

Conclusions as to quantities: Our tests indicate the quantities accurate.

Conclusions as to pricing: Fifo generally. Finished stock and work in
process are based on direct material and labor costs; variable overhead
rather than all overhead included in product costs from January 1 to
December 31.

Conclusions as to clerical accuracy: A few inaccuracies not greatly
different in type and amount from previous years.

Martin Manufacturing Company
Inventory Plan
December 31, 1952

F. L.
7-23-52

p. 1 of 2

On July 22, 1952, I met with Mr. Collins and Mr. Hanson and discussed with them the inventory plan for the year end. Last year's methods and results were reviewed and a few changes were suggested and adopted. The principal points brought out were these:

1. The plant will close on the evening of December 29 and reopen January 2. This will give 2 working days and if necessary New Year's. Last year's count was made in 2 days (January 2 & 3).

2. George Shuffle was agreed on as the inventory supervisor and he was called in for a few moments during our meeting. As heretofore the supervisor's duties will include the training of crews and helpers (taggers, checkers, listers, and clerks), the determination of prices, control over the issue, collection, and check of tags, listing, direction of computing- and adding-machine operators, and final summarization. Separation of pricing function last year was not a success since it was difficult to isolate. Jack Johnson (cost supervisor) will prepare a price book under Mr. Shuffle's supervision.

3. All inventory items will be listed except supplies which are under perpetual-inventory control (units and dollars); separate tapes will be made for each of the 5 locations of supplies and will be made up of balances reflected in storekeeper's books.

4. Finished stock and work in process will be priced on basis of direct cost: that is, actual cost of material and labor, and "variable" overhead, the last-named having been a separable element during past 2 years — in anticipation of this move. Change in basis, urged by Mr. Hanson for several years, now accepted by us with proviso that the differences caused in balance-sheet and income-statement figures by change from FIFO to new basis be disclosed in financial statements this year and for several years to come since this represents a departure from more usual practices. Reduction to market will be followed if market is lower although there will likely be no cases this year unless major recession develops.

5. In-and-out movements of F/S and W/P have been computed by factory-cost unit but not put on books. Factory output in terms of units is relatively small and rough checks on theoretical balances of F/S and W/P are made each month.

6. Raw materials and purchased parts will be priced as heretofore on FIFO basis with markdowns where required for lower market prices, spoilage, overstock, or other cause. On inventory sheets market prices on December 31 will appear in separate column regardless of whether

Martin Manufacturing Company
Inventory Plan
December 31, 1952

F. L.
7-23-52

p. 2 of 2

they are more or less than cost. This will supply us with a more convenient means of testing for market than we had last year. At that time market prices were quoted on inventory sheets only in 20 or 30 cases (out of 320) but we were unable to find any other cases of lower market. This year more price recessions are likely.

7. Factory supplies, on perpetual inventory basis, will be counted during year rather than at end (and corrections made immediately) except for test counts requested by us which will be made in conjunction with Carl Hibbs. CH will run down any differences discovered and report to us on findings. We will also review reports of differences arising during year and causes thereof. FIFO is still supposed to be the basis for outpricing.

Later addition: 10-14-52: (F.L.)

8. Price book will include details of bases for all costs, including makeup of work-in-process items. This will be completed on or before January 10.

9. Work in process will be arranged so as to facilitate inspection. Estimates of stages of completion and accumulated costs will be undertaken by Mr. Conway on basis of cost breakdowns appearing in price book. Mr. Conway has promised that old work in process will be cleared out and returned to stock or scrapped before end of year.

On December 15, 1952, Mr. Shuffle informed me that the above writeup was correct and that he and his crews were ready for the count. I informed him that I and one assistant would be on hand on December 30-31. (F.L.)

Form of tag (about ½ size) —

| Martin Manufacturing Company |
| 1952 Inventory Tag |
| Description |
| Department |
| Location |
| By _____ 52038 |
| Quantity _____ 52038 |
| Unit |
| Condition |
| By |
| Quantity _____ By |
| Unit |
| Condition _____ 52038 |

Hole for string or tack, or removable adhesive on back

Inventory crews were given lists of material names and descriptions covering their portion of inventory. These included sizes, finishes, and other data needed for identification with price book.

Initials of tagger and (subsequent) checker.

2nd count

1st count

F-3

-297-

F. L., H. R., and C. H. were present throughout the physical-inventory period; by prearrangement each covered separate sectors of the plant and inventory locations. From field notes the following comments have been prepared:

1. H. R. found in dept. 16 that a number of tags covering finished product had been removed and destroyed. The foreman explained that he had found the descriptions appearing on them so far wrong that replacement seemed easier than erasure. He had overlooked the instruction that the upper quarter of canceled tags containing the tag number should have been retained for recheck purposes. There were 11 missing numbers on the recheck and this number (approximately) was verified by the employes who had the job of making the replacements.

2. Certain machinery accessories had been tagged that H. R. found should have been associated with machines sold and billed but held for pickup by customer or shipping instructions. These tags were removed and canceled.

3. At one point in dept. 10 a quantity of partly assembled machines was noted bearing the label "do not inventory; work order 2068b". Reference to the work order which was an order to remove and dispose of scrap indicated that the order was dated 12/10/52 and had not been completed at time of inventory.

4. Because of illness of assigned taggers in dept. 3, uninstructed recruits were found tagging items rather than lots of various stacked materials. C. H. corrected their procedures and stayed with them for an hour. At 2 p.m. on the 30th F. L. found everything apparently properly tagged.

5. All tagging had been completed by 4 p.m. on the 30th. Tag checking (observation by foremen or assistants of completeness of tagging and correction where necessary of descriptions and indicated quantity units) had been commenced or completed on same day. Removals of lower tag sections were begun promptly at 8:30 a.m. on 31st in all depts. except shipping. Recounting, completed by 2 p.m. on 31st, was indicated by checkers on upper sections in green to avoid confusion with lower sections which are of same size (this will be corrected next year). Some initial double-counting last year took several days to run down. Upon comparison of green with black (12,300 times 2) sections about 100 differences were noted. These were adjusted by a special crew working on January 1, with H. R. present to observe some recounts; no large differences. Where no differences appeared removal of tags was completed on 31st.

F-4

15,000 tags were printed and 12,287 were used and listed:

Block	Series issued	Used and listed	Used and canceled	Returned	Missing	
A	40,001 - 40,685	530	10	145	-	
B	40,686 - 41,985	940	38	322	-	
C	41,986 - 44,649	2318	67	268	11	See F-4, #1
D	44,650 - 46,060	1304	2	105	-	
E	{54,288-54,387 {46,061-50,720	4656	-	104	-	
F	50,721 - 52,634	1402	87	422	3	(note 2)
G	52,635 - 52,967	125	12	196	-	
H	52,968 - 54,287	1012 (note 1)	59	249	-	
unissued	54,388 - 55,000	-	-	613	-	
Totals	15,000	12,287 ∼	275 ∼	2424 ∼	14 ∼	

(1) attached to trays + bins
(2) Found on 1-26-53; unissued (52,632-4)

The following tags with 2 detached sections each were examined for internal consistency, checks, erasures, traced to listing sheets, and upper portions verified by makers as being in their own handwriting:

Block	Number	Amount	% of total	
A	50	200 000	86	} Finished stock
B	100	250 000		
C	200	100 000		}
D	100	50 000	76	} Raw materials
E	400	100 000		}
F	50	100 000	99	Purchased parts
G	50	280 000	95	Work in process
H	50	40 000	33	Supplies
Totals	1000 ∼	1120000 ∼	80	

Listings were made on 40-line inventory sheets and as an overall check C.H. prepared the following summary:

Number of items on sheet	Number of sheets	Tags listed
40	40	1600
39	105	4095
38	96	3648
37	73	2701
35	5	175
Less than 35	15	68
Totals	334 ∼	12287 ∼

F-5

Purchases cutoff was accomplished as in past years by the following procedure, each item below having been observed or tested by us:

1. Receiving-room records show that last ticket issued on December 29 was R22658. Tickets 22,559 to 22,658 (100 items), extending back to December 20, were examined by H.R. and traced to recorded purchases except for 22,567 which was a return from a customer recorded as a return sale and charged to finished stock in accordance with usual practices.

2. The receiving room remained open on December 30 and 31 but no deliveries were made from receiving room to stores or elsewhere. Any items received during those two days were tagged with a yellow sign "Do not inventory".

3. Before the receiving room was opened on December 30 each item on hand was tagged with the regular inventory tag and on December 31 all these items were located on 28 of the 100 tickets appearing in (1) above. H.R. thereupon examined each item in the receiving room to make certain that each bore a white or yellow tag. See 5 below.

4. The receiving room's copies of the remaining 72 tickets were all signed by the storekeeper (or department representative where the item received bypassed the storeroom). One exception (22,585); this item had been checked into stock by storekeeper but signature on R/R copy had been overlooked.

5. A quantity of steel scrap, sold and awaiting delivery to the buyer was noted by H.R. as being in the receiving room. This was not tagged and was identified by the foreman with a shipping order held in his desk (#365A1) authorizing him to deliver the scrap (1,125#) to one H.S. Silers and Sons. The scrap had been sent to the receiving room rather than the shipping room because of the latter's crowded space. H.R. traced the item to a credit to scrap-sales account (2449).

6. The contents of a freight car at the receiving door (SF101651) was found to have been accounted for on R22654-6.

7. Several items received had not yet been set up as liabilities. See worksheet P-2 and AJE #16.

8. The preceding information is based mostly on notes made on the last two days of December. On January 12 receiving tickets (receiving-room copies) R22659-R22720, covering reported receipts from January 2-10 were scanned. In each case date of receipt and disposal indicate that they pertain to January transactions.

F-6

Sales cutoff was made with invoice C-12586, based on advices from shipping room indicating that this was the number appearing on last delivery (customer's truck) on December 29.

A "runback" was made of 52 numbers preceding C-12586 (to about Dec. 26). All shipments had been made except for C-12581 where it appeared that an advance billing had been made of merchandise at the request of the customer, Arthur Fries & Company, but order was not made up until Jan. 6.

Dec AJC 17:

Upon approval of a sale a shipping order - invoice - packing slip is prepared, all bearing the same number. Six of such orders were made up on December 29-31 but were not delivered to stockroom or shipping room until January 2 because of inventory closing. These orders, totaling $25,647.80, could have been filled and delivered to carrier before December 31; reference to last year's papers indicate that there was but one unfilled order a year ago amounting to $2,387.50. This was discussed with Messrs. Hanson and Collins, our position being that the inventory shutdown had the effect of cutting short the fiscal year and that hence no adjustment for the unrecorded sales would be proper.

Work-in-process cutoff was made on evening of December 29. Material and parts moved out of stores but not yet added to assembly were segregated by shop orders and arranged for convenience in counting. Copies of bills of material were examined. Quantities of materials and parts on floor and quantities already assembled were each listed opposite the amount called for on the bill of materials and in no instance was the controlling amount less. Where no controlling bill of materials was present (i.e. for special orders) materials on floor were tagged and ultimately listed (see F-10). Under Mr. Conway's direction items assembled were twice checked against listing on bill of materials and items tagged were inspected and recounted in usual way. There were 6 orders the total of which was $247,298.36 (see F-10, and 31-2-2 and 31-2-6 and listing adjustment on F-11), these constituting slightly less than 90% of the book inventory of work in process. With Mr. Conway's aid F.L. traced amounts stated as having been assembled and it was discovered that in the case of shop order 16,303 (see F-10) materials and parts had been incorporated in assembly that had been left over from completed order 16,231 and not credited to the earlier order ($16,587.45). Total orders in process were 26 and in only one case was doubt expressed as to whether it would be completed. This was order 16,490 but no adjustment was made because of its small size ($565).

F-7

Overhead charged to work in process during the year was reduced to 22% of the cost of direct labor as compared with a total overhead ratio of 35.6%. Last year's total-overhead ratio of 38% (actual was 38.2%) was allowed to attach to 1951 production still in the 1952 inventory. Had the same method been followed as that in operation in 1951 the 1952 inventory valuation would have been increased $34,742.63 as follows:

Finished goods would have been increased by—
13.6% of $139,108.91 (from details on F-9), or .... 18 918 81) see also
Work in process would have been increased by— ....) computation
13.6% of $111,939.88 (F-10), or .... 15 223 82) on A-4

We have approved the "direct-costing" basis but will disclose the method and the effect of its application in our report or approve the disclosure in a balance-sheet footnote (see A-4). See PF-31.

Finished goods, subject to the above comments, have been priced at direct material and labor costs, which are within 1% of direct actual for 1952 production and on the same basis (including overhead of 38%) for 1951 production still on hand. The former has been reduced by $12,250.64 and the latter by $3,842.39: a markdown from cost to expected realization from sales of certain heavy machinery.

Work in process, all 1952 production, has been priced at direct costs which were within 2% of account balance after transfers to finished goods. No reserve or reductions to "market" as all work orders are active and are covered by firm contracts or purchase orders. Addition of cost to complete to six principal (84%) work orders does not reduce anticipated margin.

Raw materials & parts are priced at cost. No reduction to market as all raw materials & parts prices have risen steadily throughout year. Reduction has been made however for obsolete parts amounting to $9,546.39 and listed as 31-1-6 of F-1.

Supplies are priced at cost. Many smaller obsolete items were written off during year following counts and other studies of individual items. C.H. believes all items listed in inventory are active and that writedown during year (which totaled $4,667.25) were liberal, notwithstanding overstocking. These adjustments should complete the liquidation of the excess of supplies that were acquired in 1943 as the result of large contracts undertaken in that year.

F-8

3/L
31-3

Product class and number of styles produced	Listed items produced in 1951	1952	Materials	Direct Labor	Overhead %	Overhead Amount	Total	1951 Inventory
A 26	10		12 555 36	8 268 52	38	3 142 03	23 965 91	8 758 631
		26	17 923 05	14 489 27	22	3 187 64	35 599 96	
F 115	65		48 382 09	62 825 00	38	23 873 50	135 080 59	30 559 568
		123	94 220 83	98 032 97	22	21 567 25	213 821 05	
H 38		32	44 118 96	34 494 18	22	7 588 72	86 201 86	8 131 690
R 500	51		1 278 40				1 278 40	4 869 698
		334	4 055 780				4 055 780	
Reductions —1951			− 1 033 83	− 2 035 19	38	− 773 37	− 3 842 39	− 1 732 714
✓ —1952			− 2 603 48	− 7 907 51	22	− 1 739 65	− 12 250 64	
Totals, as adjusted			25 539 918	208 167 24		56 846 12	520 412 54 [TB]	505 868 73

Reconciliation with monthly reports

	%c	Per books	Our adjustments	as adjusted Excerpt & through
Raw materials & parts —				
Purchases	221	312 267 1 15 (16)	+2 385 01	} 314 362 373
Freight in	222	+ 3 352 894		
Discount on purchases	224	− 1 496 137		
Transfer to cost of sales (mdse)	(a)	− 3 200 047		
Inventory decrease (496,708.59 − 435,639.02)	251	+ 6 056 957 (18)	− 16 713 73	4 385 584
Unabsorbed		− 4 000 20		
Work in process —				
Transferred from raw material	(a)	2 877 807 62		
Direct labor	231	+26 862 67 88		26 862 67 88
Variable overhead at 22%	241	+ 5 909 78 93		5 909 78 93
Inventory increase (284,261.32 − 181,909.76)	251	− 10 305 156 (18)	− 926 569	− 112 317 25
Overabsorbed		+ 631 491		
Finished goods —				
Transferred from work in process	(a)	60 583 17 78		
Shipments to affiliate	261	− 982 832 8		− 982 832 8
Inventory increase (517,281.96 − 505,868.73)	251	− 1 141 323 (18)	− 3 130 58	− 1 454 381
Overabsorbed		+ 4 416 84		
Cost of sales —				
Transferred from finished goods	(a)	595 303 8 11		
Transferred from purchases (mdse)	(a)	3 200 047		
Underabsorbed variable overhead	241	+ 2 173 73 (x)	+ 2 208 48	438 221
Fixed overhead	241	+ 3 617 698 (x)	+ 14 16 73	363 186 71
Cost of sales, per monthly reports	(a)	663 698 229		
Net overabsorption, as above		− 673 155		
Cost of sales (note b)	221-261	663 025 074	− 23 099 78	660 715 096

a) These 6 items appear on 12-31-52 statement of company prepared 1-20-53
b) Excluding ① realization from subsidiary's sales and ② installation & service costs shown on A-1

F-9

x) Details on TB-4.

Martin Manufacturing Company
Work-in-process Inventory
December 31, 1952

Shop order	Materials & parts	Direct Labor	Overhead at 22%	Total	Estimated to complete Material	Labor
14783	9324 81	7455 88	1640 29	18420 98		5000
15675	37378 83	36424 73	8013 44	81817 00	48000	62000
15676	24104 65	20768 73	4569 12	49442 50		3000
16494	10098 03	9901 86	2178 41	22178 30		10000
16501	15365 94	13701 64	3014 36	32081 94	5000	6000
16503	(a) 23294 42	16445 26	3617 96	43357 64	135000	210000
Subtotal	119566 68	104698 10	23033 58	247298 36	188000	296000
20 others	(b) 37393 67	7241 78	1593 20	46228 65	23000	42000
Totals	156960 35	111939 88	24626 78	293527 01 TB	211000	338000

(a) Includes $16,587.45 materials transferred from 16231.

(b) Includes $565.00 accumulated on 16490 which may be cancelled; some salvage likely; too small to adjust.

The above are all active items. Sixteen old orders were cancelled during the period from October 15 to December 15. These had been on hand awaiting disposition for periods of six months to four years. The total accumulated cost had been $23,278.47 on these 16 orders, and $12,654.07 was realized from their disposal as scrap ($2,318.81, a/c 2449) or as a return to raw-material stock ($10,335.26, a/c 221). The loss of $10,624.40 is to be brought out in our report to management.

F-10

31-1
31-4

Martin Manufacturing Company
Raw Materials & Parts
December 31, 1952

H.H.
2-13-53

Raw materials & parts—

During the year the only item in this account (31-1) was the opening inventory of $496,208.59. On January 8, 1953, but as of December 31, 1952, this amount was reduced by $60,569.57 to agree with the physical inventory at the year end and "inventory variation" (a/c 251) was charged. This was partially offset by our adjustment for $16,713.73 (AJE #18) which brought the amount to $452,352.75. Raw materials consist of steel wire, rods, and sheets in various dimensions and grades, tool steel, copper wire and rods, malleable and forged steel and aluminum castings, and several thousand manufactured "parts" purchased from others and ranging from lockwashers to motors. "Merchandise", included in finished-goods inventory is limited to purchased, packaged items intended for the repair and replacement of parts of equipment already on the market including equipment no longer manufactured because of changes in style or product specifications.

The allowance for obsolete parts, $9,546.39, is broken down in detail on the inventory sheets supporting 31-1-6 (F-1). There are 128 items, each a fraction of original cost. The practice of long standing has been to reduce inventory items ⅓ if they were purchased in the first preceding year and ⅔ if purchased in second preceding year; if more than two years old an item is listed but no value is attached to it. The amount of the allowance does not appear in a separate reserve but is re-estimated each year and is simply an adjustment of original cost that would otherwise appear. In each case we compared the individual allowance with the inventory item listed on another sheet.

number of items	original cost	minimum age	allowance
46	21 813 40	1-2	7 271 13
82	3 412 89	2-3	2 275 26
25	5 678 20	3 or more	cost not extended

Purchases account (221), adjusted by a/cs 222 and 224 (freight and discount) was broken down for internal-statement purposes as between raw materials, parts, and merchandise (see F-9 and A-5). The materials figure (3,143,623.73) in the summary on A-1 is the total of the 3 accounts, 221, 222, and 224, adjusted by AJE #16, as shown on F-9 and TB-3.

F-11

MARTIN MANUFACTURING COMPANY
1688 S. Federal St.
Chicago 16, Ill.

December 19, 1952

Robertson Foundry Company
Chesterton, Indiana

Dear Sirs:

Please furnish our auditors, Hyatt, Paterson & Company, with a statement of the
amount of the castings and any other assets
of ours in your possession on December 31,
1952. Please inform them also of the conditions under which you hold these assets.

An addressed envelope is enclosed for
your convenience in replying.

                    Very truly yours,

                    Martin Manufacturing Company

                        Edw. Stebbins (signed)
                    _____
                              President

        [copy for
         auditors]

                    F - 11a

ROBERTSON FOUNDRY COMPANY
Chesterton, Indiana

January 25, 1953

Hyatt, Paterson & Company
Chicago 4, Illinois

Dear Sirs:

As requested by Mr. Edward Stebbins of
Martin Manufacturing Company, we wish to
inform you that at December 31, 1952 we
were holding for their shipping instructions 284 castings produced by us during
the year 1952. As we have completed our
work we have billed them and have been
fully reimbursed except for two December
invoices totaling $1,782.54. As these
castings are needed, Martin Manufacturing
Company requisitions them from us and
shipment is promptly made to their plant
in Chicago. We make no charge for holding
these castings in our storeroom.

The total invoiced cost of the 284 castings was $18,862.40.

Very truly yours,

Robertson Foundry Company

C.C. Robertson Jr.
Vice-President

F - 11b

31-4

Martin Manufacturing Company
Supplies
Listing and other inventory corrections
December 31, 1952

BB·
2.13-

Supplies-

This account, under continuous inventory control, was made up of opening inventory, $302,539.82; purchases, net, $113,695.14; issues as adjusted by AJE 18, $289,151.36; write-down of $4,667.25 (see F-8); closing inventory at end of year, $122,416.35. The errors of listing were discovered by the internal auditor and testchecked by us. Overstocking (see F-6 in 1951 papers) is now believed to be fully corrected, the closing inventory being limited to active items all of which have been added to during the past 3 years.

Listing errors discovered by us and corrected by AJE 18 totaled $40,149.49 (omitting $2,731.05 correction of supplies by internal auditor):

Omitted parts transferred to S/016503 (see F-7)	1658745
Item on 31-1-4-3 omitted from tape	2142201
Minor items, each OK'd by Mr. Shuffle	214003

Pricing errors, $10,223.73, were more numerous than in prior years. Those applicable to finished goods and work in process were attributable for the most part to changes in bills of material after the price book had been prepared (around Nov. 15). In each case the charge was formally incorporated in the price book, thus being given official approval. The net reduction of $6,297.50 in raw-materials pricing arose through not noting lower prices on most recent arrivals in stock during Dec. 15-31; the largest single item, $1,291.50 (see 31-1-2-18), related to a shipment of steel (36.9 t.) received on December 23 and originally priced at $169.50 per t. when its invoiced cost, net, was $134.50 per t. All OK'd by Mr. Shuffle.

Extension errors were minor and were corrected on inventory sheets and OK'd in each case by Mr. Shuffle. No footing errors were found upon running new tapes covering 100 of the 334 sheets; we scanned the remaining 234 for possible footing errors.

The recapitulation of the inventory sheets, summarized in F-1, was in the form of a worksheet that had been bound up with the inventory forms. The individual-sheet forms were traced into the recapitulation and we reran the totals thereon.

Problems and Questions

1. At the start of an audit of the records of Neath Supply Company as of December 31, the following tentative balance sheet, prepared by the company's bookkeeper, was submitted to you:

ASSETS		LIABILITIES	
Cash	$ 12,000.00	Accounts payable	$ 32,235.00
Accounts receivable	39,500.00	Capital stock	100,000.00
Inventory in warehouse	43,200.00	Earned surplus	42,265.00
Consignments	734.00		
Fixed assets	79,066.00		
	$174,500.00		$174,500.00

An examination of "Consignments" revealed the following information:

	Cost of goods shipped	Freight charges	Drafts drawn when shipped	Proceeds from account sales	Balance in accounts
L Company	$1,435.00	$ 26.00	$500.00	$ 918.00	$ 43.00
M Company	980.00	21.00	350.00	–	651.00
N Company	2,050.00	30.00	750.00	1,290.00	40.00

Reference to the accounts sales rendered by the three consignees covering operations through the end of the year disclosed the following:

	Sales	Fraction of consignment sold	15% commission	Incoming cartage	Balance
L Company	$1,700.00	2/3	$270.00	$12.00	$1,418.00
M Company	200.00	1/8	30.00	7.00	163.00
N Company	2,400.00	3/4	360.00	–	2,040.00

(a) Prepare the adjusting journal entry required.
(b) Redraft the balance sheet.

2. You are engaged in making the audit of the records of the T Manufacturing Company covering its operations for the calendar year. Your representative was present at the time that the physical verification of inventories was made, and he has reported to you that all material received up to and including the 30th of December was included in the physical count and that the results of the count will shortly be recorded in the company's books. The company does not maintain perpetual inventory records.

Your examination of the voucher registers immediately before and after the close of the year under audit revealed the following entries relating to the purchase of materials; none of the invoices had been paid before the end of the year.

	Date of invoice	Shipped FOB	Merchandise received on	Amount	Creditor
	Dec. 26	Destination	Jan. 5	$ 4,500.00	MPF Corp.
DECEMBER	Jan. 2	Shipping point	Dec. 29	6,253.00	TX Iron Co.
REGISTER	Dec. 27	Destination	Dec. 31	11,425.00	LDC Company
	Dec. 28	Shipping point	Jan. 3	1,250.00	RVN Bros. Co.
	Dec. 20	Destination	Dec. 28	4,760.00	ZOD Company
JANUARY	Dec. 26	Destination	Jan. 3	2,111.00	PHD Corp.
REGISTER	Jan. 6	Shipping point	Dec. 31	7,640.00	TG Supply
	Dec. 14	Shipping point	Jan. 6	227.00	CBR Company

(a) Prepare a journal entry that will correct the records, (b) state the accounting principles involved, and (c) indicate the adjustment, if any, necessary to correct the closing inventory.

3. A manufacturer of stove parts, mostly castings, maintains several retail branches in a large city. Part of the goodwill of the company depends on its asserted ability to supply grates, doors, lids, and other frangible parts of any model of "furnace or kitchen stove manufactured during the past eighty years." In producing most parts it has been found by experience that a "run" from ten to twenty identical castings in the foundry costs little more, except for raw material, than a run of, say, a half dozen. Consequently, an auditor's examination of perpetual-inventory records at the end of 19–6 has revealed several thousand items similar to the following:

Part number	Year made	Sales—each 19–3	19–4	19–5	19–6	Original cost each (in dollars)	Last markdown stage	On hand 12–31—2
DS-46 G 008	19–0	0	0	0	0	.494	5	9
DS-46 J 891	19–2	2	0	0	0	.472	3	5
DS-47 K 891	19–3	1	3	0	0	.495	2	8
DS-49 S 453	19–5	–	–	1	0	.648	1	11
DS-46 J 846	19–6	–	–	–	5	.821	–	15

For some years the company's valuation policy on such items has been annually to mark down cost wherever during any of the four preceding years (including the current year) there have been no sales, by applying to the remaining unit cost the next higher markdown-stage percentage as shown in the following table:

Number of "stage"	Age not more than (years)	Carrying cost: expressed as a percentage of cost brought forward	
1	1	100	The balance remaining
2	2	80	when an item has
3	3	70	reached the sixth stage
4	4	60	(5.04%) is deemed to
5	5	50	be not in excess of its
6	over 5	30	worth as scrap

You are required (a) to value and extend the inventoriable cost of the above six items and (b) to set forth your opinion of the propriety of the method.

4. Describe briefly how a storekeeper operates under an established "minimum-maximum" policy.

5. Why should the costs incurred on a maintenance work order, only half completed, be "cleared to expense"?

6. What are the conditions under which a commitment will be regarded as a contingent liability?

7. A mercantile company has consistently valued its inventory on the basis of cost or market, whichever is lower. At the close of the year under examination it changed from the "first-in-first-out" to the "last-in-first-out" method of determining cost. As the result of the change, the net income and Federal income taxes have been substantially reduced. How should the change be disclosed in the auditor's report?

8. What are the features especially to be noted in the auditor's observation of a physical inventory, and what is the purpose of each such procedure?

9. A client asks your advice with respect to the preparation of instructions to his staff concerning your presence as an "observer" of the inventory-taking at the end of the year. What matters would you cover in your reply?

10. What special procedures should an independent auditor adopt in observing an inventory-taking involving large quantities of packaged materials stacked in solid formation?

11. How may an auditor test for raw-material overstock in a manufacturing business where perpetual-inventory records are kept?

12. What valuation of repossessed merchandise would you suggest?

13. Part of the inventory of the E Company at June 30, 19–2, was also on hand at June 30, 19–1. On the latter date the cost of this portion of the inventory was reduced to market but, during the year following, the market price rose to a figure exceeding original cost. The company has restored original cost in the June 30, 19–2, inventory. Give reasons for or against this procedure.

14. In determining a cost base for inventory items manufactured during the past year, you have encountered the following items of cost in the factory accounts; indicate whether or not you would include them in the base, and give a supporting reason in each case: (a) overhead during shutdown caused by factory rehabilitation; (b) award by labor board of increased wages for prior year; (c) employee training; (d) rejects; (e) loss on canceled purchase commitments.

15. Name five desirable internal controls governing perpetual inventories, of particular importance to the independent auditor.

16. How would you dispose of the following problems that have been referred to you in connection with a client's physical inventory of raw materials, the count having been completed two weeks ago, that is, four weeks before the end of the fiscal year?

(a) Temporary quantity controls were set up for keeping track of new acquisitions and issues of raw materials but a portion of these controls has been accidently destroyed.

(b) A possibility of duplication in count is indicated by the addition of a certain raw material to the temporary quantity controls equal in amount and identical in description with an item reported by the receiving room at the time of the physical count.

(c) Not included in the count are amounts of a certain material, payment for which has already been made. You find that the supplier has agreed to make shipment whenever required but has not set aside in his warehouse any specific quantities earmarked for your client.

17. What procedures on the audit of the supplies inventory of Martin Manufacturing Company could be performed before and what ones after December 31, 1953?

18. State the source (book of original entry) and the nature of the entries classified as to debits and credits that you are likely to find recorded in the following accounts:

> Accounts receivable
> Reserve for bad debts
> Supplies
> Fixed assets
> Reserve for depreciation

19. A perpetual-inventory account relating to a certain item of merchandise contains balances of 38,192 in units and 23,679.04 in dollars and corresponding balances at the beginning of the year of 31,461 and 18,247.38. During the year two additions were made of 57,500 units and 34,500.00 dollars, and 48,648 units and 30,160.76 dollars; the withdrawals totaled 99,417 units and 59,236.10 dollars.

In connection with this account you have been asked the following questions:

(a) What basis of valuation appears to have been followed in stating the closing inventory?

(b) What was the turnover for the year?

(c) You, as auditor, are told that in view of the fact that the items are small both in size and weight (less than one-half ounce each) and have been kept under the personal supervision of the storekeeper, no physical inventory has been taken of quantities on hand for several years. Would you be willing to accept this explanation and waive a physical inventory at the year end?

(d) Have you any suggestions for a physical inventory of this item?

20. The following abbreviated and combined details relate to the work-in-process and finished-stock accounts appearing on the books of Schlaue Processors, Inc.:

| | | *(00.00's omitted)* | | |
| | | Factory overhead | | |
Item	Prime cost	Allo-cable	Fixed	Total
Inventory January 1	47.2	11.8	30.7	89.7
Year's operations	225.6	67.7	146.6	439.9
Previous year's operations	224.9	56.2	147.0	428.1
Year's cost of sales	234.4	69.9	152.4	456.7
Inventory December 31	38.4	9.6	24.9	72.9

No further information is available at the moment.

You have been asked to determine as best you can—

(a) Whether the inventory valuation at the year end is consistent with that followed at the close of the preceding year.

(b) Whether any adjustment of the closing inventory appears necessary.

(c) What the effect on the current year's net income would have been had fixed factory overhead been consistently omitted from inventory computations of both years.

CHAPTER IX

Investments; Deferred Charges; Intangibles

Long-term corporate equities—bonds or stocks—and municipal obligations are referred to very generally as securities, or, in the hands of owners, investments. When acquired by another corporation they may be classed as a current or capital asset or they may be given a separate caption between current and capital assets, depending on their marketability and the purpose for which they are held. The auditor's objective in examining investments is to establish their ownership, cost, present worth, reason for acquisition, expected disposition, location, and, if not on hand or in safekeeping, why they are in the possession of another.

Deferred charges, often the title of a balance-sheet grouping, may contain several classes of items, most of them minor in amount. They represent costs that in the judgment of the management and the accountant are fairly allocated to the operations of succeeding periods. The most frequently encountered example of deferred charges is prepaid insurance premiums.

Intangibles are long-term prepaid expenses such as patents, leaseholds, licenses, term franchises, and "short-run" goodwill; or expenditures yielding benefits over an indefinite future period such as perpetual franchises or other rights, goodwill presumed to have perpetual existence, and organization expense. Conceptually they differ from deferred charges in that they usually are larger in amount and have been acquired in an organization or consolidation.

The auditor's purpose in examining items of deferred charges and intangibles is to verify their cost and purpose, and to judge the "fairness" of amounts carried forward against future operations.

Principles and Practices

Valuation of investments. Investments are valued generally at cost, cost being purchase price plus commissions and taxes. Where marketable securities have been acquired as a temporary investment of cash and in the event of conversion their proceeds may be utilized for any corporate purpose, the securities qualify as a current asset and are subject to the valuation basis of other current assets: cost, or an amount less than cost provided some reasonable valuation can be objectively established. This is held to be the closing transaction price of a marketable security listed on an exchange, or the closing bid price of an "over-the-counter" security.

Where the proceeds of an investment in marketable securities may at any time be applied only to certain purposes and the investment cannot be classified as a current asset, the same valuation basis is followed. But if the application is not to be immediate and the market price has declined, the cost of the security may continue without adjustment unless evidence is at hand that the decline is likely to be a permanent one.

If securities have been acquired other than for cash or for assets having a quoted value, entries on the books of the issuer or transferor may be of aid as a measure in establishing "fair market value" on the books of the purchaser or transferee. A practice recommended by many accountants is that a stock dividend— except for a dividend in common stock issued to common stockholders—should be recorded (a) by the issuing corporation as a charge against retained earnings in an amount equal to the *higher* of (1) the equivalent average paid-in capital already attaching to shares of the same class, or (2) the market value of the new shares issued, and (b) by the recipient as a credit to income in the same amount. A dividend of common stock to the holders of common stock needs no cost or "value" recognition on the books of either issuer or receiver since the book equities of the different classes of stockholders have not been altered; recipients simply allocate a reduced amount of cost to each share, the transaction differing from a splitup only in name. Although no official pronouncement has as yet been made regarding the issue, sale, and exercise of stock rights, an analogous treatment would require that they be recorded at their market price by both issuer and receiver—as a charge to earned surplus and a credit to income, respectively. Another illustration may be found in the suggested limitation of cash dividends as income, even where no affiliation exists, in an amount not in excess of surplus earned since the stock was acquired, any "unearned" distribution being regarded as a reduction of investment cost. In any of these cases the method of valuation should be disclosed in the annual statements if, by following any other method in current use, the remaining cost carried forward has been materially altered.

A dividend of shares of one class to holders of another class (for example, preferred shares to common stockholders or vice versa) is generally looked upon for both tax and accounting purposes as income—in an amount equal to the market value of the dividend shares, and such value thereupon becomes their cost. Occasionally the cost of the older stock is transferred in part to the dividend shares—and no dividend is recognized—the reasoning being analogous to that applied to the distribution of common shares to common stockholders. The public accountant in most instances accepts the book method provided it is in harmony with regulations of the U. S. Bureau of Internal Revenue and with opinion of tax counsel. The Bureau's regulations on investment and dividend questions have for the most part conformed closely to practices generally accepted by accountants; and it is on these rulings that counsel's opinion has likely been based.

A similar recognition of cost may be found in the treatment of a parent company's holdings in a subsidiary. However, recent practice has been to reduce over a period of years or in one lump sum any excess of the cost of such holdings over the parent company's underlying equity as reflected on the subsidiary's records. The basic reason for the writeoff is the same as that given for the elimination of goodwill from the books and financial statements: the consolidation excess represents the capitalization of expected profits or other benefits over and above a "normal" return; but if, after several years, "above-normal" profits or benefits are still present they are almost invariably found upon analysis to be attributable to events and conditions that have arisen since acquisition. "Goodwill" from consolidation as thus interpreted becomes a kind of prepaid expense: a cost from which only limited returns may be expected, and a cost therefore allocable to periods of anticipated benefits.

Bonds may be purchased at a premium or discount that is best amortized over their remaining life on a straight-line basis. No objection is raised, however, to an unadjusted basis, unless the amortizable amount is material to the balance sheet or income statement—which is not often the case.

Cost reduced to market or otherwise decreased in recognition of value shrinkage becomes the new cost of the security as in the case of an inventory item, and the old cost is not restored in a later period when the market value has risen.

An auditor always takes the position that he is not an appraiser or valuer. This should not deter him, however, from seeking evidence of value in testing the propriety of continuing to carry at cost securities for which no established market price exists. He may call for recent certified statements of issuers and review their financial position, operating results, and dividend-paying abilities with some member of the client's staff familiar with the situation. He may even examine the books or talk with issuers' officials. A large investment of this type may call for a valuation comment in the form of a balance-sheet footnote if doubt continues to exist in the auditor's mind as to the reasonableness of the cost or cost fraction at which the investment is carried.

Investment income and expense. Dividends, interest, and gains and losses from sales of securities are frequently found in income statements. They arise in the following situations:

1. A dividend is recognized as income when declared; interest when accrued. Until converted into cash the offset is a receivable classed as a current asset.

2. Occasionally dividends are paid in property or in some form other than cash. The rule is that "fair market value" (which thereupon becomes "cost") must be assigned to the asset acquired, with the credit of a like amount to income. If an identifiable portion of the asset received is liquidated in part, a corresponding portion of the assigned cost is expensed.

3. A dividend is current income, notwithstanding that the issuing corporation may have paid it from earnings of a prior year. As indicated above, a possible limitation on its recognition as income arises when it is paid from earnings before acquisition.

4. A dividend stock should be valued as outlined in a preceding paragraph.

5. When sold, the selling price of a security, less its cost, is income that should be reported in the current income statement, although such income may in effect be a realization of stored-up earnings over a period of years. If the security sold came from holdings purchased at different prices, cost may be determined on any one of four bases: (a) actual cost if the security can be identified with a particular lot, (b) earliest cost, or "fifo," (c) average cost, the method usually followed, or (d) "lifo" or other arbitrary cost such as the highest or lowest actual cost. For

Federal income-tax purposes, only (a) or (b) may be employed by the taxpayer. Most accountants reject method (d) without reserve.

6. Following a reorganization or recapitalization, the exchange of old securities for new, plus, in some cases, the receipt of "boot" —cash or other form of property—gives rise to income or expense, depending on the valuation given the new securities. Here again, the usual practice is to follow the Federal income-tax regulations in determining the gain or loss, since the valuation rules they contain are equitable and tend to set a standard known to many individuals.

7. An investment in an affiliated company is best treated like any other investment. Occasionally, the practice of taking up the undistributed earnings of a subsidiary or controlled company is encountered—a practice followed, for example, by E. I. du Pont de Nemours & Company, which owns a 22 per cent interest in the common stock of General Motors Corporation. Although General Motors is undoubtedly controlled by du Pont, notwithstanding the minority holding, the practice is not a good one, for it permits earnings to be included in surplus (in the du Pont case, its interest in General Motors' undistributed earnings is credited directly to a mixed-surplus account): earnings that are reflected neither in the income statement nor in an increment of working capital.

Deferred charges. Four classes of items may be found under deferred charges:

1. Expenses, often captioned prepaid expenses, such as insurance, rent, and office supplies, that have been paid for in advance of benefits shortly to be received.

2. Costs of promotional or developmental work the anticipated benefits from which will extend over a substantial period of time.

3. Expenditures not yet paid, the single example of which is unamortized discount relating to a bank loan or to bonds outstanding.

4. Losses as from casualty that in certain systems of accounts (for example, of the Federal Power Commission) are arbitrarily allocated to future operations.

The primary reason for deferred charges is that certain services must be paid for before they can be received. It has sometimes been said that this is the credit system working in reverse. Aside from insurance and supplies, prepaid expenses are uncommon, and because of the smallness of the amounts involved many concerns charge them off at the time they are incurred.

Prepaid interest on notes payable is a misnomer. Like unamortized bond discount, prepaid interest is a debit valuation account, offsetting in part the par value of a liability on which something less than par was originally realized. It would be better practice if the "prepaid interest" were subtracted from the face of the obligation to which it is related.

Nearly all taxes are in one sense prepayments of the protection and benefits conferred by government. Since these benefits accrue to all citizens and to all business enterprises alike and are of a character so unrelated to the expenses that a person or business voluntarily incurs, it has become preferred practice not to regard taxes as prepaid expenses at all; rather, they are accrued for the coming year as a current liability, representing, as they do, an inevitable diminution of working capital without the direct and tangible services that accompany prepayments. Nevertheless, it has been a long-established practice in many industrial concerns to treat property taxes and certain forms of excise taxes as prepaid expenses. Sometimes the period covered is specifically indicated on the tax schedule filed or the tax bill received. Where the practice is of long standing, the auditor will most likely follow precedent, the amount being small and the use of one method in preference to the other not seriously affecting working capital. If the item is permitted to stand as an asset, the portion carried forward should be consistent with the nature of the tax, the amount and period of deferment, and past practices.

Supplies, as noted in the preceding chapter, may be classified as inventory or as a prepaid expense. If minor in amount the cost may be expensed as incurred: the usual practice in smaller enterprises.

Prepaid royalties covering mineral rights are governed by the contract between the parties. Most royalty contracts call for minimum periodical payments, which may be in excess of actual royalties accrued; but they are usually deductible from the excess of future royalties over minimum requirements. If the excess is not so deductible the royalties are in no sense prepaid.

Some expenditures classified as deferred charges might better be regarded as additions to fixed assets; illustrations are mine-stripping and well-drilling costs, the cost of building access roads, the cost of temporary structures, and property-development costs generally. Development and improvement costs involving product, design, improvement, packaging, and marketing, processing changes to increase output or reduce costs, and the costs of promoting new sales outlets—and carrying them through initial unprofitable years—are examples of less tangible expenditures that are often "capitalized" by regarding them as deferred charges and amortizing them over a limited number of succeeding years during which benefits from them are expected. But if developmental work of this sort is always in progress, it is more common to find each year's outlays expensed. Such costs resemble maintenance costs in that their purpose is to keep up without break a continuously high level of operating effectiveness.

Bond discount and expense. Bonds are nearly always issued at a price that yields less than par to the issuer. The net yield involves the deduction from par of not only a discount to the purchaser but also legal, accounting, appraisal, and engineering fees and other costs necessarily connected with the issue. The simplest method of determining the annual expense is to divide the amount of the discount and expenses by the number of years the bonds will run. In the case of serial bonds it is allotted to the various years in proportion to the bonds outstanding during those years. An aliquot portion of unamortized discount on bonds acquired before maturity should be subtracted from par in determining the gain or loss from a repurchase.

When a bond issue is refunded before its maturity and a new bond issue takes its place, the better procedure is to charge off the unamortized discount on the old issue as an extraordinary expense of the year of refunding. Some accountants prefer to carry forward the unamortized discount as part of the expense of the new issue, thereafter writing it off over the life of the new issue; other accountants would continue to amortize it at the same rate as that established before the refunding or at a somewhat more accelerated pace. However, these secondary methods have as their one purpose the avoidance of full recognition of the loss in the year of its occurrence and the avoidance of what might otherwise be characterized as a "bad showing" for that year; they thus have no more validity than a procedure that has the effect of omitting ordinary expense from the income statement.

Intangibles. Intangibles are sometimes given a fixed-asset classification; their valuation is usually represented as an attempt to reflect an earning power beyond that required for an investment in tangible assets. Intangibles are no longer as common as they once were; most of them have been written off or are carried at nominal amounts. Often the auditor finds that goodwill is no more than an excess of the par or declared value of stock issued over the value attaching to a group of purchased assets, and that it is not the result of any precise calculation. Even where the consideration paid for goodwill has been in the form of cash and represents the formal capitalization of a number of years' excess of profits over a normal return, the accountant has frequently recommended, and with good reason, that it be written off by the purchaser during a similar (or less) number of years following its acquisition. It is now recognized that only in the rarest cases can purchased goodwill survive more than a few years. If, indeed, excess earning ability persists, its causes, more likely than not, cannot be attributed to the peculiarities of the business purchased, but to a situation that has arisen since acquisition from wholly different sources. The excess earnings of almost any year may more justly be attributed to transient factors whose roots point to causes over which the business, certainly a predecessor enterprise, has little or no control.

The gradual extinction of acquired goodwill over a period of ten or fifteen years, by provisions for its amortization charged against income, can thus be readily accepted by the auditor as both desirable and conservative.

Patent costs are now, as a standard practice, charged off as expense when they are incurred. At an earlier date, these costs, which often included experimental expense preceding the patent application, plus attorney's fees and often the expense of subsequent patent litigation, would be carefully capitalized, and then amortized over the patent life of seventeen years or charged off at once if the patent were unobtainable. But the earning power of a patent, except in unusual cases, cannot in most situations be separated from earning power arising from many other factors. In any event, the cost that has been incurred on a patent bears no relation to what it does or should earn; and usually the outlays that can be readily agreed to as the *direct* cost of the patent are wholly nominal in amount.

Internal Controls

Investments. Before his security examination begins, the auditor should become acquainted with the investment policy of his client: why securities of certain types are purchased or otherwise acquired, what is to be purchased and when, how they are to be held or liquidated. Investment policies may be expected to originate with the board of directors. The auditor should discuss with the management any nonobservance of such policies, policy conflicts, and policies that might lead to better controls.

Purchases and sales of securities should be made only under individual authorization or under general delegations of authority; often the signatures of two or more officers are required for each purchase or sale. If the price is not a quoted market price plus brokerage and taxes, a detailed explanation should be prepared at the time of purchase or sale and approved by the board or management representatives. Purchases from or sales to officers or stockholders should be prohibited.

Records reflecting transactions in securities may be made in duplicate, as follows: one in the office of the treasurer or other official primarily responsible as custodian; the other in the controller's office against which occasional tests may be made at the insistence of either the controller or internal auditor. No fewer than two management representatives, no one subordinate to another, should be required to be present when safety-deposit boxes or other security repositories are visited. Income schedules should be prepared at the beginning of each year, with expected receipts and the dates thereof set down in advance; they should be maintained throughout the year in both offices and added to as dividends are declared or other distributions (as in liquidation) are announced. Notations of actual receipts may also be made on them.

Another desirable internal control is an examination of and report on individual investments and the income therefrom toward the end of each year by the Finance Committee of the Board or by a management committee, the purpose being to review and approve investment transactions and year-end valuations, and to verify recorded revenues from sales and from interest and dividends.

Deferred charges and intangibles. No deferred charge or intangible should be created except with top-staff and even board approval. The approval should not only specify the character of the item but the basis of amortization, if any.

Financial-Statement Standards

Investments. The basis of investment valuation should be indicated on the balance sheet, along with the total market value of quoted securities.

On the balance sheet of an investor having but few holdings, the character of the investments should also be stated. Temporary investments of cash available for general purposes are classified as current assets. Long-term investments or investments available only for construction or other noncurrent purposes are given a separate caption following current assets.

On the balance sheet of an investor having diversified holdings securities should be given a separate section or detailed in an attached exhibit, and divided as between the principal classes of stocks and bonds, with industry subclasses where their importance warrants. Investments in affiliated organizations should always be grouped separately on the balance sheet and clearly labeled.

The portion, if any, of securities pledged and the identity of the liability involved, should be shown on the balance sheet.

Income from securities, both gains and losses from sales and income from interest and dividends, should be subdivided on the income statement to correspond with the divisions and subdivisions of securities appearing in the balance sheet or balance-sheet attachment.

Advances to affiliates may be added, on the face of the balance sheet, to the investment in affiliates.

Where a consolidated balance sheet does not accompany the financial statements, financial statements of affiliates (combined statements of two or more affiliates are often practicable) should supplement any presentation of financial position and operating results, provided their importance warrants. Footnotes should call attention to intercompany transactions of material amount and the basis of their valuation.

Deferred charges. Prepaid expenses should always appear as a current asset.

Promotional and developmental work carried forward usually appears between current and fixed assets, with its character indicated in the sidehead.

An item of unamortized discount is properly a reduction of the liability to which it refers, but by custom it has been permitted to appear as a deferred charge rather than being gradually added to the liability account. This comment applies equally well to both the unamortized discount on a short-term loan and that on a bond issue or other long-term obligation. A caption such as "Unamortized bond [or loan] discount" is all that is usually required.

A loss carried forward is actually an earned-surplus valuation account; it may as a rule only be found on the balance sheet of a public utility, and in most instances the item and the rate of its amortization bear the approval of a utility commission. The reason for this treatment is to avoid showing a large reduction in profit or a loss for the current year—so that dividends and interest contingent on the existence of adequate profits may be paid, and also to make it possible to carry the loss gradually against future earnings, in that way providing additional justification for the current rate structure.

Intangibles. In many instances where goodwill appears on a balance sheet no description accompanies it, and the reader has no basis for knowing whether the item is simply a writeup or a part of a group of assets purchased in some prior year from a predecessor company. The auditor should take care to see that every intangible item is given a full and complete description on the balance sheet.

Representative Audit Program

Investments. 1. Obtain list of securities, prepared by client's staff.

2. Obtain certificate on securities pledged or in safekeeping at year end, and detail of transactions between year end and date of proposed count.

3. Count other securities, in presence of client's representative:

 (a) Simultaneously with cash, where cash is counted; or

 (b) At any time, where it is known that there have been no transactions during the year, or safety-deposit company's certificate can be obtained showing that there has been no opening of box since balance-sheet date.

4. Determine the reason why securities, if held in the name of others, have not been transferred to client.

5. Secure, where practicable, receipt on working-paper record of count.

6. Obtain market prices, if available, for onhand items; and obtain and review financial statements relating to other investments.

7. Obtain or prepare analysis of security transactions for year, including income received or accrued therefrom, and:

 (a) Compare opening items with last year's working papers;

 (b) Verify principal changes during year, and dividends (by reference, wherever possible, to investment manuals), interest, and profit or loss from sales, earned or sustained during year, by reference to source documents and related accounts;

(c) Compare details of sales and purchases with authorizations of investment committee, board minutes, or other source of authority; and

(d) Compare closing items with security count.

Deferred charges. 1. Prepare analysis of each deferred charge or prepaid expense for period, showing basis and determining propriety of accumulating and writing off costs; compare opening and closing balances with previous reports and current trial balance, respectively.

2. Establish propriety of deferment and amortization of uncommon deferred charges.

3. Examine insurance-register entries for year, test them against invoices, test accuracy of spreads, and prepare tape of year-end balances unexpired.

4. Scan insurance policies in effect at year end; note who, what, and how much is insured, and the significance of any special clauses; compare items outstanding with register.

5. Confirm by correspondence deposits on mutual policies, and the cash surrender value, if any, of life policies.

6. Compare unamortized and amortized long-term discount and expense in year-end trial balance with permanent-file schedule; verify adjustment for bonds retired during period; analyze any additions arising from new financing and prepare amortization schedule for permanent file.

Intangibles. Determine origin of each intangible and its conformity with accepted principles of accounting. Make certain that board approval has been given to each intangible and that amortization procedures, if any, are likewise in agreement with board policy.

Audit Procedures

Investments. It was noted in Chapter VI that under a well-organized plan of internal control the count of cash may be dispensed with. In effect, the counting is done by the bank. Again, an inventory count may be *observed* by the auditor, and he may direct test recounts. Similar principles may be followed when the auditor satisfies himself as to the existence of investments.

Where investments exist in quantity and change often, the auditor may decide to examine cash at the same time, since the interchangeability of cash and marketable securities creates a situation difficult at times to keep under control. The dual count need not be made on the final day of the period under audit; some auditors prefer that it be without prior notice. As in the case of inventories, the first count may take place a month or two before the end of the period and the transactions thereafter kept under close scrutiny and control until the close of the year, at which time limited tests will suffice.

An initial step by the auditor in a security count is to put all of the securities under his control until the count is completed. They can be brought together at one point and kept under his personal observation while the count is proceeding; if this is impracticable, the auditor secures in advance envelopes or boxes in which he and his assistants seal the securities handed them until they can be counted. The seals may be of wax or lead, and they may bear the auditor's imprint so that they cannot be tampered with without detection.

Lists of securities should always be prepared in advance of the count by the client's staff, the auditor prescribing the form and content. Columns may be provided for issuer, character of security, maturity date, number of shares or bonds, par or other nominal value, cost, market quotation, total market (or other) value, date of next coupon, and income received, with separate sheets or subheads for (a) whatever classes of securities are to be shown on the balance sheet or in supporting schedules, (b) securities having no value, and (c) securities held in safekeeping or as pledges on accounts or notes receivable. Every security found to be on hand must be listed.

Where the securities are numerous, the auditor should have an assistant to whom the details examined may be called. It should always be borne in mind that no securities may be touched by the auditor except in the presence of a responsible official of the client's staff. Arrangements are often made whereby securities are handed only by the client's employees; the periodic examination of securities for internal-audit purposes may be arranged to coincide with the auditor's examination. In that event, the auditor sits beside the employee designated for the job of handling, and duplicate lists are checked off as the count proceeds.

All the details appearing on the list should be verified positively and precisely from observing the security itself. Thus, the "date of next coupon" that has been filled in in advance should be called out by the person handling the bond; at the same time it should be noted whether all future coupons are attached. Other things to be observed are the name of the owner (except for coupon bonds), the corporate seal, and signatures of issuing officers (which are usually in facsimile if the security is listed) and of the registrar and transfer agent, if any, or of the trustee. Security numbers are not usually traced except where internal controls are poor and the auditor has reason for following up on individual transactions. A column is then added to the security-list form, which is filled in before the count, and ultimately the auditor traces the number to purchase-voucher attachments.

The cost of securities in liquidation should be decreased by amounts already received—these being usually indicated by endorsement on the security itself.

Where mortgages appear among the investments, the auditor examines supporting documents such as trust deeds, title policies or abstracts, and insurance policies. The nature of these supporting documents differs in various states; the authenticity of unfamiliar documents should be verified by counsel where their importance warrants.

Confirmations direct to the auditor should be procured for securities held by others, as collateral pledged or in safekeeping; securities loaned; and securities in a sinking fund or on deposit elsewhere for some special purpose. Confirmations should also be sought for balances due on securities in liquidation, long-term notes, or mortgages. In all these cases the possibility exists that payments have been diverted, or that credits have been allowed that have not been recorded.

Unexpired insurance. A schedule of insurance policies in force during the year may be prepared for the auditor by the client's staff; they should be arranged by classes so that the total amount of each kind of insurance in force may be determined. There are many forms of insurance. In the average case, the auditor would expect to find fire, tornado, use and occupancy, plate-glass, boiler, sprinkler, elevator, burglary, holdup, liability and compensation, and fidelity policies.

Important points to be watched in scanning policies are: (1) the indicated ownership, (2) the coverage, whether general or specific, both as to kinds of property and its location, and (3) the coinsurance clause. The coinsurance clause may be found in many policies, and from the auditor's viewpoint it is of significance in that, should a partial loss occur, the insurer stands only the same proportion of the loss as the insurance carried bears to the stated percentage (for instance, 80 or 90 per cent) of the cash value of the property. The cash value is generally defined as replacement cost new, less depreciation. If mutual fire-insurance companies are represented among the policies examined, the amount returnable in the form of a dividend should be estimated, using past experience or other information as a basis; the remainder is prorated, as is the entire premium in other cases.

Insurance policies covering the lives of company officials may possess a cash surrender value, the amount of which may be ascertained by reference to the table contained in the policy, or preferably, by confirmation from the insurer. Occasionally, this value is not carried on the books, the full credit being taken when the policy expires. The better practice is to record the increase in surrender value on the books as a partial allocation of each premium paid and to classify the accumulated total under the noncurrent heading of investments, since it represents a tangible asset ultimately to be liquidated in cash.

Where an insurance register has been carefully maintained, the auditor may forego a list of policies for his working papers and test policies directly against the register. The register will ordinarily contain the policy number, class of insurance, name of the insurer, date and term of the policy, property coverage, amount of insurance, premium paid, and amount of premium expiring each year. The straight-line basis of premium amortization is invariably followed, although cancellation values are always much less. Where circumstances prevent the auditor from inspecting the policies, he may rely upon the information shown in the insurance register, together with a confirmation secured direct from the trustee or other holder.

Premiums for policies listed on the worksheet or in the register should be tested against the insurance account to make certain that they have been paid for. A liability may exist for additional premiums on liability or compensation insurance, premiums on policies of this nature being based on estimates of the insured's payrolls. To determine whether such liability exists, the total payroll from the date of the policy to the close of the fiscal period may be multiplied by the rate shown in the policy; from this result the premiums already paid should be deducted. An overpayment of liability premiums may be carried forward as in the case of the portion of premiums paid to mutual companies that will be offset by dividends.

Officials and employees who have access to cash or other movable property, or who are otherwise in positions of trust, should be bonded in line with the client's policy; if they have not been so bonded, the attention of the responsible official should be directed to the omission.

The sufficiency of insurance carried should be discussed annually with the management.

Other deferments. From his list of notes payable the auditor may verify the amount of "prepaid" interest.

Rent paid in advance may be verified by an examination of the lease contract. Sometimes the lease demands the deposit of a certain amount as a guarantee. This item, however, may be carried among miscellaneous receivables unless deductible from rental payments.

Where the auditor finds organization expense on the books, he should analyze the account and ascertain the amortization policy. Ordinarily organization expense, consisting of legal fees, incorporation fees, and printing of certificates, is comparatively small in amount, and the most conservative plan calls for writing off the entire amount the first year. Some companies, less fortunate in the size of the expenditure or in their early operations, will spread organization expense over a period of years. In those cases the auditor must ascertain expressed company policy and see that it is being accurately followed. Occasionally, the auditor finds that the management desires to capitalize organization expenses permanently. Practical rather than theoretical objections interpose; the auditor will probably not permit the asset, if it be called such, to be merged with any other balance-sheet item, and standing alone it becomes virtually an eyesore to management. No one future period derives any direct benefit or productive use from it, and it is an item that must frequently be explained.

Discount on capital stock should not be classified as a deferred charge. It should be regarded as a valuation account, deductible from the par value of the stock to which it refers; ultimately it may be charged against retained earnings by action of the board, thus resembling a dividend. In some states it may be regarded as an unpaid subscription.

Illustrative Audit

A single account for investments (11–0) is maintained in the general ledger. To obtain a convenient grouping supporting the financial statements in their final form, the account was divided by the auditor on the working trial balance into three sections: U.S. securities (a current asset), minority interests in other companies (a long-term asset), and interest in (full ownership of) the subsidiary, Burton-Makun Company. The summary at the top of D 1 shows how the book balance of account 11–0 was adjusted by the auditor (AJE 24) and shows also the division of the adjusted balance between the three classifications. The bottom half of D 1 summarizes the auditor's activities in examining the items making up the account and their valuation.

Worksheet D 2, except for seven lettered footnotes, was prepared for the auditor by the assistant controller, following the general style of the worksheet in last year's audit papers. Last year's worksheet was given to the assistant controller as a model. The footnotes A to F were added subsequently by the auditor. The amortization adjustment made by the auditor was incorporated by him on this worksheet, and the balance-column detail and total were altered accordingly.

At the bottom of D 2 is an analysis of interest received during the year on the government securities.

An adjustment made by the auditor may be added on the bottom of an account analysis, in which case a separate recapitulation may be necessary where a summary of the account must be attached to an income-tax return or other report; or the adjustment, as in D 2, may be placed in the body of the schedule. The latter procedure has some advantages over the former, a separate recapitulation being unnecessary where the account analysis extends in two directions, provided, of course, that the number of adjustments is not so great as to confuse the analysis or to cause too many corrections of extensions and totals. In planning the worksheet layout, allowance may be made at various points for prospective adjustments, particularly where experience indicates that they may develop.

Financial statements of the subsidiary company appear on D 4 and also on PF 52–3. The duplication involved is not serious. Those on D 4 aid in the preparation of comparative data such as the statement of application of funds and analyses of profit changes. These two worksheets illustrate the vertical and horizontal methods of compilation. Both methods are useful and practicable.

D 3 presents an analysis of the intercompany current account between parent and subsidiary. The two important items that the auditor must review are the installation charges made against the parent company and the 10 per cent additions on merchandise shipped to the subsidiary. The former is found by the auditor to be short in the amount of a charge in transit for December, and the amount, taken up by AJE 22, becomes a part of the installation-cost account (G/L 264). When merchandise is shipped to the subsidiary, the 10 per cent "gross profit" is credited to a real account (28-1), "reserve for intercompany profit." This account shows an unadjusted balance (see TB 1) of $20,897.23, which is found, in the analysis at the bottom of D 3, to be the intercompany profit on the Burton-Makun inventory at the beginning of the year plus the intercompany profit on shipments during the year. To bring this reserve to the proper level at the year end, as reflected in the same analysis, a reduction of $7,809.27 (AJE 23) was found necessary. On TB 3, the credit becomes, in effect, a reduction to actual cost of the subsidiary's reported cost of sales of $85,901.96.

Because the safety-deposit box in which the stocks were kept was not examined by the auditor until February, he secured, as an extra precaution, a certificate from the safety-deposit company to the effect that the last previous opening of the box was on November 28, as stated by the controller (see D 1).

Insurance is carried with old-line companies and a mutual company. The deposit ($35,367.32) at December 31, 1952, with the mutual company represents the major portion of the unexpired insurance at December 31, 1952. This deposit is large in comparison with the amount of Martin Manufacturing Company's share of 1952 losses ($2,741.40). The deposit balance could be carried alternatively as a receivable since the amount, less any losses accrued, would be refundable upon termination of the policy.

On the old-line companies the amount of the unexpired premiums represents a prepaid cost for insurance protection. However, in the case of the workmen's-compensation policy, the amount of the premium earned to December 31, 1952, as computed on G 3, exceeded the amount of the deposit on the policy by $4,756.00. This amount could also have been shown (and somewhat more accurately) as a current liability on the balance sheet rather than as a reduction of prepaid premiums on other policies.

G/L
11-1
11-2 281
11-3 283
     298

F. L.
2-5-53

Martin Manufacturing Company
Investments and Income Therefrom
December 31, 1952

	11-1 U.S. Securities	11-3 Stocks	11-2 Burton-Makins Company
Principal:			
Balance per books at 12-31-51	303618 46	739 000 00	100 000 00
Purchases	149164 00	91 000 00	−
Sales or maturities	− 50 000 00	− 631 000 00	
Profit from sales	−	175 152 10	
Amortization of premium and discount (AJE #24)	− 513 89	−	−
Balance as adjusted at 12-31-52	402268 57 TB	374152 10 TB	100 000 00 TB
Market price	405809 57	474 000 00	
Income:			
Dividends received	−	7376 2 50	10 000 00
Interest—			
Accrued at 1-1-52	− 2243 64		
Coupons cashed or interest sold	5665 98		
Accrued at 12-31-52 (a/c 27-4)	3317 08		
Premiums (less discount) amortized	− 513 89		
Dividends received a/c 283	−	7376 2 50 TB	10 000 00 TB
Interest on investments a/c 281	6225 53 TB	−	−

Work done:
    Schedule D-2 was prepared from subsidiary ledger; adjustment for amortization of premium or discount incorporated in schedule at time of preparation.

× Opening balances compared with 12-31-51 W/P's

+ Cost at 12-31-52 compared with adjusted balance in general-ledger control account

    Physical verification:
ɴ Compared with confirmation from Howard National Bank, which holds U.S. securities in safekeeping (D-2b).
ˣ Compared with stock certificates in safe-deposit box in Jackson National Bank at 10 A.M. on 2-2-53 in presence of Messrs. Huddle and Collins; all certificates were registered in name of M.M.Co.

D-1

Before making the count, a review of the accounting
records and inquiry of Mr. Huddle revealed no
transactions in stock and bond investments during
the period from January 1 to February 2, 1953.
Vault record showed that last access to S/D box was on
November 28, 1952 (D-2c).

Verification of transactions:

✓✗ Examined bank and broker's advices in support of pur-
     chases and sales during year; all such transactions
     authorized by Board.
✓   Traced to cash-receipts book.
✗   Examined dividend notices, annual reports, or copies
     of Form 1099 received from companies.
⊗   Verified computations.

Market prices at December 31, 1952:

1) Treasury bonds, obtained from Wall Street Journal of 1-2-53.
2) Stockholdings, all minority, obtained by telephone from
    security dealers trading in these stocks on an over-the-
    counter basis.
3) Burton-Makun Company, a wholly owned subsidiary, acting
    as sales representative in the Cleveland area, had earn-
    ings in 1952 of $8.22 per share, and the common stock
    had a book value per share at 12-31-52 of $153.25.
    There is no quoted price.

D-1a

D/L 11-1 281
    11-2 283
    11-3 298
      27-4

Martin Manufac
Investments and
Dec

Item	Particulars	Maturity	Interest %	Interest Dates	Number of shares or face amount	Cost 1-1-52
	U.S. Securities –					
1	Treasury bonds"	6-15-62/59	2.25	6-12/15	100 M	101 935 13 x
2	Treasury bonds"	3-15-59/56	2.75	3-9/15	100 M	101 683 33 x
3	Treasury certificates of indebt-edness, Series A-1952 (see X-2)	4-1-52	1 7/8	B	50 M	50 000 00
4	Treasury certificates of indebt-edness, Series A-1953 (see X-2)	2-15-53	1 7/8	B	50 M	
5	Treasury savings notes, Series D-1953" - Dated 8-1-50	8-1-53	C	C	50 M	50 000 00 x
6	Treasury bills": 201-day tax-anticipation series (see X-3)	6-15-53	D	D	100 M	–
	Amount appearing as current asset					303 618 46
		Par value	Dividends			
	Investment in subsidiary company (100%)–					
7	Burton-Makun Company, common, eliminated in consolidation	100 00	10 000 00 x	1 000 00		100 000 00 x
	Investments in stocks of sundry companies (A)					
8	Barkley Corp. common (see X-3)	20 00 $6	60 000 00 x	2 000 00 / 10 000 00		525 000 00 x
9	Rawhide Products, Inc. 4% pfd.	50 00 2	1 000 00 x	500 00		20 000 00 x
10	Vault Importers Co. common (see X-3)	25 00 1	9 200 00 x	7500 00 / 9200 00		194 000 00 x
11	McGrew Mfg Co. common (see X-2) nopar 2		3 000 00 x	2 000 00		–
12	Liberty Products Co. common (see X-3) nopar	1.25	56250 x	750 00		–
	Total dividends received (283)		83 762 50			
	Amount appearing as investments					739 000 00

Interest –

Item	accrued at 1-1-52	Coupons cashed or interest sold	accrued at 12-31-52	Discount or premium amortized and added to principal	Earned, less amortization Nontaxable	Partly taxable	Fully taxable
1	93 75	June 1125 00 ✓ Dec 1125 00 ✓	93 75	–259 46 E			1 990 54
2	802 08	mar 1375 00 ✓ Sept 1375 00 ✓	802 08	–400 00 F	117 50	2 232 50	
3	507 81	3-1-52 665 98 ✓	–				158 17
4	–		781 25				781 25
5	840 00	–	1 640 00				800 00
6	–	–	–	145 57			145 57
	2 243 64	5 665 98	3 317 08	–513 89	117 50	2 232 50	3 875 53
	AJB 25		AJB 25 TB	(AJE #24)		6 225 53 TB	

D-2

-334-

...ing Company
...come Therefrom
...nber 31, 1952

Basic data on this
work sheet prepared   H R
by Mr. Shell   2-5-53

Additions	Date Acq.	Sold	Proceeds	Gain	amortization of premium (+) or discount	Cost	market value
					− 259 46	101 675 67	99.5 99 500 00
					− 400 00	101 283 33	107.0 107 000 00
		3-1-52	− 50 000 00 ✓	−		−	−
50 000 00 ✗	3-1-52		−	−		50 000 00	50 000 00
						50 000 00	50 000 00
99 164 00 ✗	11-26-52				145 57	99 309 57	99 309 57
149 164 00			− 50 000 00	−	− 513 89 (AJE#24)	402 268 57 + TB	405 809 57
						100 000 00 + TB	−
	1945	10-10-52	8000 − 580 000 00 ✓	160 000 00		105 000 00	75.00 150 000 00
	1945					20 000 00	38.00 19 000 00
	1943-5	11-28-52	1700 − 51 000 00 ✓	15 152 10		158 152 10	28.00 210 000 00
76 000 00 ✗	3-22-52					76 000 00	40.00 80 000 00
15 000 00 ✗	8-4-52					15 000 00	20.00 15 000 00
91 000 00			− 631 000 00	175 152 10 TB		374 152 10 + TB	474 000 00

Notes—

A Minority stockholdings in suppliers of raw materials and parts.

B Interest payable with principal at maturity; not acceptable in payment of income taxes.

C Interest accrues monthly at amounts varying from 80¢ per $1,000 per month for the first 6 months of the 3-year term to $1.40 per $1,000 per month during the 12 months preceding maturity; acceptable in payment of income taxes; tax-payment or redemption value of $1,032.80 per $1,000 on the 29th month after date of issue.

D Purchased on a discount basis: 35/201 of discount amortized in 1952; acceptable at par in payment of income taxes due on June 15, 1953, and to the extent not so used redeemable at par.

E Fully taxable

F Interest on $5,000 exempt; balance subject to surtax only.

D-2

(auditor's copy)

Martin Manufacturing Company
1688 S. Federal St.
Chicago 16, Ill.

December 14, 1952

Howard National Bank
Chicago 1, Illinois

Dear Sirs:

Please furnish our auditors, Hyatt,
Paterson & Company, 960 Hudson Bldg, Chicago 4,
Illinois, with the following information as
of December 31, 1952, which you may be holding in safekeeping for our account on that
date:

Name and description
Serial number
Face or par value
Number of shares
Coupons attached

Please state whether any of these securities are pledged or assigned, and furnish the
names of persons authorized to withdraw these
securities.

An addressed envelope is enclosed for
your convenience in replying.

Very truly yours,

Martin Manufacturing Company

by _Edw. Stebbins_
Edw. Stebbins, President

D - 2a

Howard National Bank
Chicago 1, Illinois

January 8, 1953

Messrs. Hyatt, Paterson & Company
960 Hudson Building
Chicago 4, Ill.

Dear Sirs:

At the request of Mr. Edw. Stebbins, president of the
Martin Manufacturing Company, we submit below a list of
the obligations of the United States Treasury held by
us in safekeeping on December 31, 1952, for the company's
account:

Name of issue	Interest rate	Maturity date	Principal amount	Serial number	Coupons attached commencing with
Treasury bonds--					
Series	2.25	6-15-62/59	$ 100,000	7527	6-15-53
Series	2.75	3-15-59/56	100,000	3491	3-15-53
Treasury bills--tax-anticipation series	*	6-15-53	100,000	1509	*
Treasury savings notes Series D - 1953	#	8- 1-53	50,000	31207	#
Treasury certificates of indebtedness--Series A - 1953	1 7/8	2-15-53	50,000	18192	**

D-2

*Purchased on a discount basis; payable at par at maturity
#Interest accrues monthly at varying amounts per $1,000 of principal amount and is payable at maturity or upon presentation for payment at an earlier date
**Interest is payable with principal at maturity

None of these securities is pledged or assigned. The
persons certified to us as authorized to withdraw any of
these securities are J. B. Huddle and Arthur P. Collins,
acting jointly.

Very truly yours,

Howard National Bank

by John Hotchkin
          Cashier

D - 2b

Jackson National Bank
Chicago 2, Illinois

February 2, 1953

Hyatt, Paterson & Company
960 Hudson Building
Chicago 4, Ill.

Dear Sirs:

Mr. Huddle, treasurer of Martin Manufacturing
Company, requested us orally to advise you of the
date of entry prior to the one made at 10 A.M.
today to safe-deposit box number 1862 rented to
Martin Manufacturing Company.

Our records show the last previous entry was
made on November 28, 1952.

Very truly yours,

Jackson National Bank

by *Herbert Franzen*
Vault Manager

D - 2c

G/L
27-9
28-1

Martin Manufacturing Company
Intercompany Accounts — Burton-Makun Company
December 31, 1952

BB
2-14-53

9 Advances to Burton-Makun Company—
  Balance 1-1-52 (debit)   19 816 49
  Merchandise shipped to B-M Co. during 1951—
    18 shipments, at cost + 10% (analysis below)   108 111 61
  Service charges—
    Representing charges against the home office for
      services on sales by the home office; on the
      books of B-M these services are charged
      directly to the interoffice account and are
      not cleared through its operating expense
      accounts; last interoffice memorandum is
      dated 11-30-52 (see below)   -18 695 52
  Cash collections   -71 517 63
  Balance per books at 12-31-52 (debit)   37 712 95
  Less— Additional service charges billed by
   B-M on December 28, 1952, not yet recorded on
   home-office books (see below)   -2 129 75   AJE #22
  Balance, as adjusted at 12-31-52 (debit)   35 583 20   TB
Analysis of invoices sent to Burton-Makun shows the following—

	Amount	account credited
Cost to M.M.Co. of goods shipped to B-M	94 967 19	
Freight charges	3 316 09	
	98 283 28 26-1 Cost of shipments to branch	
Arbitrary addition of 10%	9 828 33 28-1 Reserve for intercompany profit	
Total billings to B-M in 1951 (as above)	108 111 61	

Analysis of service charges (taken from interoffice memos)
  Labor, charged directly to service order from
   payroll distribution   17 875 55
  Travel costs   2 951 72
   Total, 2 items above   18 695 52 }   20 827 27
                 2 129 75 }

1 Intercompany profit on Burton-Makun inventories—

Particulars	Cost on B-M books	Intercompany profit	Cost to M.M.Co.
Balance 12-31-51	121 757 86	11 068 90	110 688 96
Shipments from M.M.Co. to B-M in 1952	108 111 61	9 828 33	98 283 28
Total	229 869 47	20 897 23	208 972 24
Less— Cost of sales AJE #23	85 901 96	7 809 27 TB	78 092 69
Balance 12-31-52	143 967 51	13 087 96	130 879 55
		TB	

D-3

Martin Manufacturing Company
Unexpired Insurance
December 31, 1952

G/L
27-7
2431

BB.
2-18-53

		Per books	Adjustment	Expense as adjusted	
Balance 12-31-51		26 857 72			
Premiums paid, 1952		52 687 02			
Charged to expense:					
Factory (2431)	33 600 00		2 578 12	36 178 12^ TB	
Selling (2749)	2 400 00		184 15	2 584 15^	
Administrative (2784)	2 400 00	-38 400 00^	184 15	2 584 15^	
Balance, unadjusted		41 144 74^			
AJE #19		-2 946 42	-2 946 42		
Balance, as adjusted		38 198 32^ TB		41 346 42^	

Payments of premiums, including additional amounts due on audit of
workmen's compensation and of public-liability policies were charged to
Unexpired Insurance Premium account. No insurance schedule is maintained.

The attached schedule (G-2) was prepared by us. Our 1951 working papers
supplied the list of policies in force at 1-1-52. Those in force at 12-31-5
were compared with data listed from 1951 working papers or were liste
on the attached worksheet. Additions during year were verified
with supporting invoices or with deposit requests (items 2 and 3).
Items 2 and 3 unexpired at 12-31-52 were based on audits of
workmen's compensation and public-liability policies.

At our suggestion, an insurance survey was ordered by the company
from B. C. Decker and Associates. The survey report
showed adequate coverage of fire insurance on buildings,
machinery, and equipment, but an undercoverage of the busi-
ness-interruption risk. Certain other changes will be made when
current policies expire, according to Mr. Huddle. There have
been no discernable changes in the amount of insurable assets or
in the nature of business since date of the survey.

The basis of allocation to expense was considered to be satisfactory.
Unexpired premiums and accrued liability on workmen's compensation were computed by us, and the balance of deposit premium
on mutual policy is covered by letter from insurer. (G-4)

The insurance coverage appears to be adequate and the amount
of unexpired-insurance premiums (net) at December 31, 1952.
is substantially correct.

G-1

Policy	Risk	Insurer	Coverage	Dates Issued or added	Dates Of expiration	Coinsurance
468011	Fire	Chgo. Mutual	3 500 000	4-1-50	4-1-53	-
2-367-449	Pub. Lia.	Travelers Ind	100-300 M	9-1-51	9-1-52	-
2-709-542	"	"	"	9-1-52	9-1-53	-
WC-701-496	Work. comp.	Royal Ind		1-20-51	1-20-52	-
WC-867-542	"	"		1-20-52	1-20-53	-
2-449-508	Trucks & autos	Travelers Ind	100-300,000	12-1-51	12-1-52	-
2-867-002	"	"	✓	12-1-52	12-1-53	-
275-149	Bus. int.	Amer. Ins.	1 000 000	11-6-50	11-6-53	50 %
509-081	"	Phoenix Ins.	1 250 000	5-20-52	5-20-55	50 %
67-109	Boiler exp.	Hartford	100 000	8-7-51	8-7-54	-
356-027	Sprink. leakage	Natl. Union	200 000	8-10-50	8-10-55	10 %
29-702	Fidelity	Amer. Surety	100 000	7-19-51	7-19-54	-

Premiums

	Total premium	Unexpired 1-1-52	Paid in 1952	Unexpired 12-31-52	Expense 1952
	-	22 108 72	16 000 00	35 367 32	2 741 40
(1)	1 050 00	540 00	128 43	-	668 43
(1)	1 500 00	-	1 500 00	989 00	511 00
(1)	24 000 00	-1 354 00	2 958 59	-	1 604 59
(1)	27 000 00	-	27 000 00	-4 756 00	31 756 00
	1 800 00	1 650 00	-	-	1 650 00
	2 100 00	-	2 100 -	1 925 00	175 00
	2 500 00	1 541 00	-	708 00	833 00
	3 000 00	-	3 000 00	2 388 00	612 00
	225 00	195 00	-	120 00	75 00
	1 600 -	1 155 00	-	835 00	320 00
	1 200 00	1 022 00	-	622 00	400 00
Totals - Unexpired		28 211 72	-	42 954 32	-
Accrued		-1 354 00	-	-4 756 00	-
Paid during 1952		-	52 687 02	-	-
1952 expense		-	-	-	41 346 42

Allocation of expense as adjusted:

42431	Insurance (factory)	36 178 12 TB
2749	Misc. selling expense	2 584 15
2784	Office expense	2 584 15
		41 346 42

(1) Deposit on premium liability which is determined at expiration of policy.

G-2

Martin Manufacturing Company
Insurance in Force – Unexpired Premium
December 31, 1952

BB·
2-18-5?

Computation of premium earned on –

Public liability policy:	Amount	Rate (1)	Premium earned	Amount of deposit	Unexpired accrued* at 12-31-52
Public liability – Salaries and wages paid from 9-1-52 to 12-31-52 ($5,200 limit per person)	1 060 000 00	.025	265 00		
Products liability – Net sales from 9-1-52 to 12-31-52	2 458 000 00	.10	246 00		
			511 00	1 500 00	989 00
Workmen's compensation: On salaries and wages paid from 1-20-52 to 12-31-52 ($5,200 limit per person)					
Factory employees	2 600 000 00	1.25	32 500 00		
Salesmen	65 000 00	.20	130 00		
Office employees	210 000 00	.06	126 00		
			32 756 00	28 000 00	4 756 00*

(1) Rate per $100 except for products liability which represents rate per $1,000.

Chicago Mutual Fire Insurance Company
1412 North Michigan Avenue
Chicago 14, Illinois

January 28, 1953

Mr. J. B. Huddle, Treasurer
Martin Manufacturing Company
1688 S. Federal St.
Chicago 16, Ill.

Dear Sir:

The amount of the deposits and of the estimated
unexpended portion thereof at December 31, 1952,
on your mutual fire-insurance policy number
468-011 are as follows:

Particulars	Amount
Original and subsequent deposits	$52,000.00
Estimated unexpended portion at December 31, 1952	35,367.32

According to our records, all calls for premium
deposits on the above policy have been paid.

In conformity with your telephoned request to
the writer, a copy of this letter is being
sent today to Messrs. Hyatt, Paterson & Co.,
960 Hudson Building, Chicago 4, Ill.

Very truly yours,

Chicago Mutual Fire Insurance
Company

by _____
Elmer T. Branch
Assistant Treasurer

Copy to--
Hyatt, Paterson & Co.

G - 4

Martin Manufacturing Company
Amortization of Premium or Discount on U. S. Government Securities

F. L.

	Bonds	notes Series B	notes Series D	Bonds	Bonds	Bills			Totals added to cost upon sale	amortized premium
Date –										
acquired	5-15-41	6-5-44	6-1-45	9-1-48	3-15-50	11-26-52			–	–
Due	9-15-58/61	3-15-45	3-1-46	6-15-62/59	3-15-58/52	6-15-53			–	–
Premium or discount	*7,400.00	600.00	200.00	2,800.00	2,400.00	836.00*			–	–
Amortization –										
Period in months	148	9⅓	9	129½	72	(3)			–	–
Per month	50.00	64.2857	22.2222	21.622	33.3333				–	–
Amortization for										
Year ended 12-31 –										
Prior to 1943	975.00									975.00
1943	600.00									600.00
1944	600.00	439.29								1,039.29
1945	600.00	85.71 (1) 78.00	155.56						75.00	841.27
1946	600.00		44.44							644.44
1947	600.00									600.00
1948	600.00			86.49						686.49
1949	600.00			259.46						859.46
1950	600.00 1,791.67 433.33 (2)			259.46	316.67				1,791.67	1,009.46
1951				259.46	400.00					659.46
1952				259.46	400.00	145.57*				513.89
1953						690.43*				
1954										
1955										
	7,400.00	600.00	200.00			836.00*				

Notes –

(1) Sold 2-10-45.

(2) Sold 9-30-50.

(3) 201-day bills; 35/201 of discount amortized in 1952, balance in 1953.

Martin Manufacturing Company
Financial Statements of Burton-Makun Company

W.S.C.
F.L.

abstracted from audit reports of
Burns, Sutton & Co., CPAs, Cleveland

Year ended Dec. 31	Sales	Cost of sales	Service cost	Sales expense	Federal income tax	Net income or loss (-)
1933	no transactions					
4	3,562.18	2,638.20	520.03	2,873.96		- 2,470.01
	[8 income summaries omitted]					
1943	45,551.15	33,440.07	1,820.50	18,351.13		- 8,060.55
4	55,264.11	30,752.67	2,318.50	19,661.13		2,531.81
5	82,688.01	44,227.83	2,264.45	23,187.34		13,008.39
6	97,127.64	61,559.27	12,476.09	20,352.13	575.43	2,164.72
7	114,692.59	69,703.95	17,009.53	24,035.71	828.11	3,115.29
8	132,327.91	85,541.09	15,957.42	27,155.15	771.59	2,902.66
9	123,709.17	79,062.54	17,428.26	22,646.78	960.03	3,611.56
50	139,343.61	90,007.32	21,598.19	21,987.00	1,322.75	4,428.35
1	190,748.37	121,281.59	38,665.76	23,875.90	1,990.97	4,934.15
2	148,117.49	85,901.96	25,908.49	24,569.80	3,521.17	8,216.07
3						

Dec. 31	Cash	Customers	Reserve for bad debts	Inventories	Furniture	Reserve for depreciation
1933	50,000.00					
4	34,560.37		600.82	17,525.33		
	[8 asset summaries omitted]					
1943	5,322.13	2,819.64	- 200.00	144,504.61	3,460.12	- 1,608.29
4	9,627.18	3,991.00	- 250.00	146,964.22	3,460.12	- 1,964.30
5	8,472.90	15,648.33	- 800.00	153,427.63	3,817.05	- 2,300.31
6	16,859.12	9,542.17	- 800.00	148,328.65	5,068.05	- 2,407.02
7	26,922.86	12,065.33	- 800.00	143,721.18	5,299.55	- 2,913.83
8	12,113.95	10,787.49	- 800.00	161,138.08	6,105.55	- 3,443.79
9	4,699.41	15,290.07	- 800.00	160,376.26	6,810.55	- 3,459.35
50	35,880.40	11,725.08	- 900.00	153,470.43	8,362.95	- 3,976.87
1	43,898.38	13,087.75	- 1,000.00	121,757.86	9,268.74	- 4,478.17
2	34,281.04	16,237.52	- 1,000.00	143,967.51	9,268.74	- 5,405.04
3						

This company was created by Holdover Radiator Company in 1933 to complete and service sales made in eastern Ohio and points east.

Dec 31	Trade creditors	Federal income tax	Due M.M.Co.	Capital stock	Dividends	Earned surplus	Total liabilities (and assets)
1933				50 000 00			
4	325 00		4 831 53	50 000 00		− 2 470 01	52 686 5.
			[8 liability summaries omitted]				
1943	8 222 56		12 735 00	100 000 00		33 340 65	154 298 21
4	12 998 10		12 967 66	100 000 00		35 872 46	161 838 22
5	5 419 22		28 965 53	100 000 00		43 880 85	178 265 60
6	1 907 56	575 43	28 062 41	100 000 00		46 045 57	176 590 97
7	3 126 07	828 11	31 180 05	100 000 00		49 160 86	184 295 09
8	1 559 28	771 59	36 506 89	100 000 00	5 000 00	47 063 52	185 901 28
9	1 608 46	960 03	29 673 37	100 000 00		50 675 08	182 916 94
50	3 906 72	1 322 75	44 229 09	100 000 00		55 103 43	204 561 99
1	5 689 52	1 990 97	19 816 49	100 000 00	5 000 00	55 037 58	182 534 56
2	4 991 75	3 521 17	35 583 20	100 000 00	10 000 00	53 253 65	197 349 77
3							

Dec 31 — Intercompany sales and purchases

Dec 31	Cost	10% loading	Total	Inventory 1-1	Total available	Inventory Dec 31	Cost of sales
1941	9 257 69	925 77	10 183 46	106 609 82	116 793 28x	109 761 08	7 032 20
2	53 911 01	5 391 10	59 302 11^	109 761 08	169 063 19x	131 026 81	38 036 38
3	42 652 61	4 265 26	46 917 87^	131 026 81	177 944 68x	144 504 61	33 440 07
4	30 192 98	3 019 30	33 212 28^	144 504 61	177 716 89x	146 964 22	30 752 67
5	46 082 95	4 608 29	50 691 24^	146 964 22	197 655 46x	153 427 63	44 227 83
6	51 327 54	5 132 75	56 460 29^	153 427 63	209 887 92x	148 328 65	61 559 27
7	59 178 62	5 917 86	65 096 48^	148 328 65	213 425 13x	143 721 18	69 703 95
8	93 598 17	9 359 82	102 957 99^	143 721 18	246 679 17x	161 138 08	85 541 09
9	71 182 47	7 118 25	78 300 72^	161 138 08	239 438 80x	160 376 26	79 062 54
50	75 546 81	7 554 68	83 101 49^	160 376 26	243 477 75x	153 470 43	90 007 32
1	81 426 38	8 142 64	89 569 02^	153 470 43	243 039 45x	121 757 86	121 281 59
2	98 283 28	9 828 33	108 111 61^	121 757 86	229 869 47x	143 967 51	85 901 96
3							

Analysis of intercompany profit on M. M. Co. books

Year	Additions	Adjustment	Balance	Year	Additions	Adjustment	Balance
8-1-41			9 691 80	12-31-47	5 917 86	6 336 72	13 065 56^
12-31-41	925 77	639 29	9 978 28^	8	9 359 82	7 776 46	14 648 92^
2	5 391 10	3 457 85	11 911 53^	9	7 118 25	7 187 51	14 579 66^
3	4 265 26	3 040 01	13 136 78^	50	7 554 68	8 182 48	13 951 86^
4	3 019 30	2 795 70	13 360 38^	1	8 142 64	11 025 60	11 068 90^
5	4 608 29	4 020 70	13 947 97^	2	9 828 33	7 809 27	13 087 96^
6	5 132 75	5 596 30	13 484 42^	3			

PF-53

Problems and Questions

1. A corporation temporarily invested some of its funds in stocks of other companies listed on established exchanges. In the course of your preliminary work you ascertain that all such stocks were acquired through a brokerage firm at various dates during the year under examination, and that the stock certificates are in the name of the corporation (your client) but are being held in safekeeping by the brokerage firm referred to. The corporation does not maintain an investment ledger. You are requested to outline the audit procedure for the examination of the stocks and the income therefrom as reflected in the books of the corporation.

2. How would you spread the cost of an investment under any of the following conditions?

(a) A stock dividend of 50 X-company common shares is received on a holding of 150 X-company common shares.

(b) A stock dividend of 50 X-company preferred shares is received on a holding of 150 X-company common shares.

(c) A dividend of 37.5 Y-company common shares is received on an investment of 150 X-company common shares, following a court order compelling the disposition of the Y-company shares.

(d) In a reorganization, Z-company bonds and common stock are received in exchange for X-company common stock.

3. On the books of a company you are examining you find an investment of $100,000 labeled "Eastwood Chemical Company"—a corporation that went out of existence twenty years ago. You are informed that this investment was made originally for the purpose of acquiring a valuable trade name. How should this item be disposed of?

4. A note payable by a company is secured by 100 shares of stock of another corporation. The debtor fails to pay, and the stock is transferred to the creditor. What should be the basis of valuation on the creditor's books?

5. In determining the propriety of the continued valuation at cost of an investment by your client in 25 per cent of the common capital stock of the Playders Corporation, the suggestion is made that you visit the Playders office and make such inquiries as you may think desirable. Access to the books and other records may be had, if necessary. What would be the nature of your investigation?

6. In prospectuses filed with the SEC, the financial statements of a holding company are required to be included, in addition to consolidated statements. What is the reason for this practice? Do you believe the practice should also be followed by such corporations in their annual reports to stockholders?

7. May an advance to an affiliate be regarded as a current asset on a nonconsolidated balance sheet?

8. The Federal Power Commission permits power companies to defer extraordinary expenses, such as fire losses, and has often approved a company policy of charging such a loss to a "deferred-asset" account and amortizing it over a period of, say, ten years. Its reason for continuing this practice is that it does not wish to burden rate-payers for any one year with a large loss. Is this a valid argument? Discuss.

9. Under what conditions would you be likely to pass without comment a failure on the part of the management of a manufacturing enterprise to set up unexpired insurance as a deferred expense?

10. State briefly the distinctions between prepaid expenses and deferred charges and how they should be classified on the balance sheet.

11. The corporate owner of a certain parcel of land on December 31, 19–1 leased it for twenty years to a mining company that is removing mineral deposits from it. Under the terms of the lease, the lessee paid $10,000 at the date the lease was signed, and has paid thereafter "advance rentals" of $12,000 on the first of January each year. In addition, a royalty of $5.00 accrues for each 1,000 pounds of mineral removed from the property, but this amount may be credited against the "advance rentals" of the year of production and the next proximate year; if the royalties exceed the rentals, the established excess will be paid when the following year's "advance rentals" are paid. During the five calendar years over which the lease has been in effect the lessee has certified to the lessor (your client) the following production in pounds: 2,640,000, 2,630,000, 2,040,000, 2,390,000, and 3,100,000. You are asked (a) to set up a schedule, suitable for your permanent file, in which from year to year the facts relating to the lease can be recorded and that will serve to support the record of cash received from the lease, (b) to fill in the schedule for the five-year period with such figures as you would expect to find recorded on the books under the circumstances described, and (c) to state the amounts relating to the lease that would appear in the income statement of the fifth year and in the balance sheet at the end of that year.

12. A corporation's net worth consists of the following items:

5% preferred stock 10,000 shares, par $10, authorized, issued, and outstanding (2 years' dividends in arrears) $100,000

No-par common stock, 50,000 shares authorized, 12,500 shares issued and outstanding; declared value of $10 per share 125,000

Paid-in surplus from sale of common stock at $14 per share 50,000

Earned surplus 525,000

If the corporation should issue a 100 per cent dividend to common stockholders payable in common stock, how would you suggest that the dividend be recorded? If sold to the public, the additional issue of common stock would yield $11 per share. What would be the book value per common share before and after the dividend?

13. Schlaue Processors, Inc. at the beginning of the current audit year purchased the assets and business of a retail competitor, as shown on the next page.

Receivables, less allowance of $2,000 for uncollectibles	$ 52,100
Merchandise at cost plus 10% (estimated retail selling price, $154,000)	84,700
Fixed assets at replacement cost less accumulated depreciation of 30%	103,600
Goodwill, based on 5 years' purchase of average annual net profit for past ten years of $30,000 before income taxes, less income taxes at current rate of 60%	60,000
Total price	$300,400

Payment was made by Schlaue in cash, $50,400, and 2000 shares of common capital stock having a par value of $100 and a market value of $125 per share.

At the end of the first full year of ownership you find an entry on the books charging "financial expense" $6,000 and crediting "reserve for amortization of goodwill" in the same amount. Discuss the propriety of this writedown.

14. On January 1 of each year Concessionaires Associates, a partnership, pays out to cities, counties, and other public bodies approximately $500,000 for annual licenses covering privileges to operate in certain parks, fairs, and other recreational locations. Several types of business are carried on ranging from individual soft-drink dispensers to cafeterias. The chief accountant of the business prepares weekly operating statements for the management of each constituent concession and has been in the habit of expensing license costs as soon as paid, thus resulting in operating losses for the first month in most departments. He explains that he does not regard recurrent license costs as an asset.

What suggestions would you offer under such circumstances?

15. The proceeds of a certain corporate bond issue may be applied only to the purchase of a specific type of new equipment, and at the end of the fiscal year of the sale less than one-half had been so disbursed. The remainder, it is expected, will be paid out during the year to come. Where should the cash available at the end of the first fiscal year be shown on the balance sheet? Prepare language suitable for a descriptive sidehead covering the balance-sheet presentation of this item.

16. Suggest a plan for amortizing the discount and expense on a bond issue under the following conditions, and indicate the amounts involved:

Face value of issue	$800,000
Date	7-1-19-0
Maturity—	
$500,000	7-1-19-5
$300,000	7-1-19-8
Discount—	
19-5 maturity	$ 12,000
19-8 maturity	3,000
Expense of issue	8,000

Premium on—

19–5 retirement	3%
19–8 retirement	2%

17. Among the prepaid expenses in the balance sheet of a manufacturing company at the end of its fiscal year is an item labeled "deferred maintenance," amounting to $20,681.77. Tracing this sum to its sources you find that it is made up of material, labor, and overhead expended on two factory work orders, one relating to the rebuilding of several machines, the other to the installation of a new roof on a factory building that had been severely damaged late in the year by a windstorm. Neither work order had been completed at the year end and the factory manager informs you that both orders are now nearing completion and will be charged to "repairs" as soon as the final costs have been posted to the orders—which will probably be in April or May of the postaudit year.

(a) What general usage attaches to the term "deferred maintenance"?

(b) Do you regard the amount indicated as a prepaid expense to be included among current assets in the year-end balance sheet? Have you suggestions for its disposition?

18. Your opinion is asked by a client as to the possible disposition of the costs incurred during the current year of the following: (a) overhaul of an old truck, fully depreciated in a preceding year at regular depreciation rates, lying idle, and awaiting sale; now reconditioned and put back into service for what is estimated to be a two-year period; (b) replacement of old tires on another truck with new tires of an improved type; (c) tuckpointing of factory building; (d) removal of unsatisfactory self-constructed installation of smoke-abatement equipment installed a few months earlier in the year; (e) repainting of executive offices, required each third year.

19. Your client has recently purchased a number of patents for cash, a substantial cost attaching to each. The devices and processes covered by them will be employed in the client's plant, and other processors will be licensed at a rate, already announced, that is to be applied to each item produced. Suggest an amortization policy for the patents.

20. Summarize your concept of the distinction that should be drawn between "deferred charge" and "prepaid expense."

CHAPTER X

Fixed Assets

"Fixed Assets," "Property," "Plant and Equipment," "Property, Plant and Equipment," and "Land, Buildings, Machinery and Equipment" are the captions commonly employed in published balance sheets to designate land and other assets that are held, not for sale, but for the services they contribute or are capable of contributing.

The objectives that may be ascribed to an auditor's examination of fixed assets are to determine that—

1. the assets shown by the accounts exist and are the property of the client,

2. the current year's additions and retirements have been given proper expression, and

3. valuation practices have followed a consistent pattern of accepted standards.

Principles and Practices

Fixed assets are acquired for the services they are capable of yielding—services purchased in advance for cash or money equivalent. The bulk of the cost thus incurred is spread over useful life, thereby assigning to operations a matching cost for services consumed; only the investment in land and the residual values of other fixed assets remain undisturbed—because land is presumed to have a useful life of infinite length and because residual values are normally recovered by sale or exchange. Accounting problems associated with fixed assets are numerous and not infrequently complex; basically they relate to the identification of incurred costs with fixed-asset units or groups of units and the disposition of such costs.

Cost alternatives. Periodically the cost basis for valuing fixed assets is assailed as unrealistic, as in times of rising prices. Thus in the 1920's, appraisal values were often substituted for cost in the belief that the financial position of the business would be more accurately portrayed, but the continuance of depreciation based on cost as an operating expense and of cost as a basis for subsequent purchases was common. In the end, the demand for consistency and, in the early 1930's, the fall of prices and profits led to an almost universal reversion of appraisal values to cost. In recent years as the result of inflationary pressures there has been a revival of interest in proposals for giving effect to current values in financial statements. The discussion has not yet reached a stage where any principles or standards have emerged.

Advocates of present values as the basis of fixed-asset accounting assert that—

1. Original costs wherever less than current replacement costs measure neither economic sacrifice nor borrowing power.

2. Depreciation measured in terms of original cost cannot provide for replacement based on current price levels.

3. Ordinary methods of accounting result in the creation of an income statement in which costs and sales are measured in units of unequal purchasing power.

4. Investors, labor, and even management are misled by understated costs into believing that the future profits of a business will compare with past profits.

5. The income-tax burden is too great on business concerns in which costs of past years carried into the present are materially less than current costs.

Proposals for changes in the accounting process growing out of such assertions have generally been advanced by economists and other nonaccountants; whether the arguments supporting them will become a part of the accountant's thinking is by no means certain. At present the accountant's objections to the raising of original costs to replacement or other current values— objections with which the auditor should be fully conversant— are these:

1. The object of a business enterprise is to produce profits on its owners' investment, and accounting procedures are premised on that basic notion. Thus the income statement ends with the net profit of stockholders which is transferred to earned surplus, a subdivision of the stockholders' equity in the business. Cost to the stockholder is what he (or his predecessor as a stockholder)

and his share of the undistributed earnings have contributed to the enterprise, their total representing his "economic sacrifice." A credit from the revaluation of fixed assets that is neither contributed nor earned can have no meaning to him.

2. Borrowing power is rarely influenced by increased amounts reflected in revaluation figures. Established earning capacity and the prospect of its continuation together with conservative financial management are the major factors that attract investors and give security to their investments.

3. A professional appraiser, given the task of finding the current value of plant, labors under a fatal handicap: he must make assumptions that bear no necessary relation to the future conditions under which the business will operate. These assumptions if disclosed in a published financial statement would prove to be more confusing than informative, yet they must be stated in the interest of accuracy. An appraisal that verifies costs or, where records are incomplete, develops original costs is quite another matter. In the installation of a plant ledger or in the determination of insurable values the appraiser also serves a most useful function.

4. Suggested bases for determining current values have included, in addition to the usual cost-of-reproduction basis of the appraiser, statistical ratios such as index numbers. No single business corresponds, however, to the average implicit in such ratios, and the substitution for highly individual asset costs of values obtained by the application of a common multiple to such costs can succeed only in subtracting from the uniqueness and independence ordinarily associated with competitive enterprise.

5. Professional accountants are well aware that even in organizations where fixed assets have been restated and lifo methods of valuing inventory have long been followed, business managements persist in thinking in terms of original cost. They feel that it is their prime responsibility to recover from their manufacturing and selling activities at least historical outlay and as much more as their pricing policies and marketing limitations permit. To management, replacement costs are matters for future, rather than present, consideration.

6. Business income has always involved standards of measuring revenues differing from those applied to operating costs. Net income, the result of many factors, in general reflects the success of management in obtaining as large an excess as possible of revenue over the necessary outlay to acquire it, whatever—and

however varied—the sources of the excess may be. Eliminating the factor of profit attributable to rising prices may have the effect of removing from the income statement of a given period a material source of funds arising from what might easily have constituted a major management activity during that period.

7. In the long run accounting, without changing its fundamental basis, will reflect increased prices—through the realization by the sale of products to which the services of low-cost fixed assets have contributed, and through the purchase at higher costs of new fixed assets replacing old fixed assets. The natural lag thus reflected in the normal accounting process may prove to be most salutary to the wellbeing of the business since any contemporary measure for identifying the portion of a recent price rise that may be attributed to any cause other than an impermanent inflation has not yet been devised, if indeed it is ever capable of being devised.

8. Current values may be as "misleading" as original costs since current values of fixed-asset services may again change before the services have been consumed in production.

9. Accountants have always been careful to point out the dangers of regarding an income statement—whatever the basis of its "costs"—as an index of future earning power. Accounting can measure only past performance—based only on the conditions and events peculiar to the single enterprise. It can never hope to put the measurement of income and expense of all enterprise on a common level. To attempt to do so would have the immediate effect of altering the individual character of the enterprise. A most valuable feature of present-day accounting is its ability to disclose variations in the profit productiveness of otherwise comparable business organizations. Again, the ability of many a business organization to "make money" is dependent on its continued ability to buy its fixed assets as well as its raw material or merchandise at less than the market prices its competitors are paying.

10. Too much of the movement in the direction of current costs has been influenced by temporary expedients—the hope of income-tax savings, the avoidance of a tax on retained profits, the possible quieting effect on labor demands, and the amelioration of clamors by stockholders for dividends. Yet the adoption of a device having as its purpose an increase in the amount of stockholders' equity is unnecessary since without any special device earned surplus may be accumulated for the purpose of meeting higher replacement outlays without fear of taxation. Further-

more it is difficult to believe that diverting earnéd surplus into a revaluation-surplus account will operate to satisfy those who may demand a larger share of corporate earnings.

Some accountants advocate the addition of an informative footnote to financial statements wherever a substantial portion of net income appears to be ascribable to changes in price levels: a subject again referred to in Chapter XV. Another possibility lies in the development of statements of projected income—estimates by management of forward income and expense in which both past experience and estimates of future operating conditions are incorporated. As yet little has been done by accountants to encourage this expansion of the budgeting process.

Writedowns may be as objectionable as writeups. In the mid-depression 1930's reductions in fixed assets became very common and were inspired by the desire to rid the books of costs that had doubtful or no remaining worth. Often the decline could be attributed to plant or equipment disuse brought about by the depression; in some cases book reductions followed appraisals aimed at carrying forward only conceivably "useful" costs. In other instances writedowns were arbitrary and could not be allocated to specific assets, the aim often being to ease depreciation provisions for future years and thus achieve some degree of competitive advantage over business rivals. During the war many plants were completely amortized as war facilities, despite the likelihood of their continued use after the war, because large profits were available and because the operating hazards in their postwar use loomed large. In many medium-size enterprises the lack of stable fixed-asset-valuation policies has occasioned not a little misinterpretation of their financial statements.

Aside from the fact that he must disclose the valuation methods employed, as outlined in a succeeding paragraph, the auditor must always be in a position to offer his advice on what a well-conceived fixed-asset-valuation program should be. His counsel against indiscriminate writedowns should, of course, be constructive but it should also be forthright. Most accountants now take the position that no loss of cost other than through the application of normal, well-established depreciation rates should be expressed on the books except under some such rules and conditions as the following: (a) the complete abandonment of a specific plant or other major fixed asset, evidenced by a plan for its disposition and by the consideration and approval of the plan by the board of directors; (b) the abandonment of a specific minor fixed asset, after a review of alternatives by a management committee reporting to the board; (c) the recognition of a partial loss of value of specific fixed assets arising from construction premiums, excessive prices paid for materials or labor, the excess costs of a type of construction or of unusual capacity or other feature—that is, the extra outlay that can be justified for a particular emergency such as the recent war—provided the determination of the amount follows engineering or other objective, fact-finding studies and provided all such actions are reported to the board, leaving to the board the final determination of the writedown of any major asset or of any large number of minor assets.

Any material modification of practices in the customary record-keeping, depreciation, or disposal of fixed assets is a financial matter of first rank to be decided on, not merely as the result of factual research but from the many-sided points of view of business heads. The consequent discipline imposed by such a policy on management adds measurably to internal controls, to the prestige of management policy-making, to the confidence with which the outside accountant can accept such decisions, and to the protection of investors from arbitrary and ill-considered actions.

Where original cost has not been maintained and a writeup or writedown has been effected, standard practice requires a full disclosure of the basis followed in financial statements; and the dollar amount of the effect of the writeup or writedown on accrued depreciation and depreciation expense for the audit period is disclosed in a footnote.

Basis in reorganization. Traditionally a reorganization in which fixed assets are conveyed from one corporation to another has been presumed to constitute a sufficient justification for revaluing fixed assets.

It has often been suggested that it is wholly within the spirit of such tradition to give expression to appreciated values of fixed assets by a procedure resembling a quasi reorganization—a procedure whereby the credit offsetting additions to fixed-asset and depreciation-reserve accounts is carried to a revaluation-surplus account. At the same time, any balance of earned surplus is transferred to a paid-in surplus account, thereby bringing about what would have been produced had a full-scale reorganization and change of ownership occurred. A number of accountants have, however, recently taken the position that where there has been no substantial change in stock ownership the original-cost basis should be adhered to, even though legally a reorganization has been effected and the assets have been transferred to a new corporation. The weight of present-day accounting opinion appears to favor the latter point of view. A change of corporate name or domicile does not establish a purchase having the objective characteristics essential to accounting recognition.

Public-utility costs. Public utilities under state and Federal law are quite generally required to value a purchase of property already in operation in an amount not exceeding cost to the predecessor owner who first devoted the property to public use. The effect is to focus attention on writeups occuring either from refinancing without change in ownership or from a bona-fide sale by one owner to another. Any excess of the price paid for such property over original cost less accrued depreciation has been designated by regulatory agencies as "acquisition adjustment"—an intangible amount to be amortized over a short term of years: a period generally much less than the remaining life of the acquired tangible assets. The effect. has been to discourage the presence of speculative elements in public-utility financing, thereby stabilizing in a substantial way the market for utility securities.

Acquisitions at less than "arm's length." The acquisition of a fixed asset from an affiliated company, or the performance of services or the doing of construction work for an affiliate raises the question of the propriety of including both overhead and profit as a "cost." "Affiliated company" means here a subsidiary, a parent company, or a company controlled by the same interests —as these terms are commonly employed in commercial practice and by regulatory bodies—including situations where minority stockholders' interests exist in either or both of the two or more companies involved. In commercial and utility enterprises alike, a leading reason for the formation and continuance of affiliated interests is to gain the economic advantages enjoyed by a single business organization. Deals between affiliates are never actually at arm's length; if they are made so artificially the very large economic advantage of low cost may be denied the ultimate recipient of the asset or the service that the asset supplies. In the case of utilities it has often been asserted that the public has the right to demand an accounting on a strict cost basis to the whole economic unit when rates are established. In commercial organizations the competitive advantages inherent in low costs should lead to the exclusion of intercompany profit. Based on such premises the rule may be stated thus: on the sale of fixed assets or services to an affiliate, exclude profit; include overhead only to the extent approved for a single enterprise. The presence of a minority stockholders' interest will not affect the application of the rule; such an interest is rarely on the "selling" side of fixed-asset sales to affiliates, but if it is and the loss of profit is material in amount other financial devices are available whereby the investment of minority stockholders may be protected.

In commercial practice the rule is at times violated, the notion of the economic unit being obscured by the problems of separate corporate managements and the assumed need for a strong semblance of competition and arm's-length relationships between the organizations they represent. In any event, in the published financial statements of single affiliates or of the whole economic unit the basis of valuation must be clearly stated, and should any element of intercompany profit remain in the gross amount of consolidated fixed assets its nature and amount should be disclosed.

Lump-sum purchases. The amount of any lump-sum or "basket" purchase of fixed assets that has not been separated into its elements may lead to difficulties of interpretation. Not only may the item contain an intangible that should be excluded from the fixed-asset category, but the provision for and accumulation of depreciation based on the total amount may be grossly inaccurate. The auditor, in every such case, is usually in a position to recommend to the management that the elements of the item be separated following an analysis of the records of the seller or a special cost study on the part of independent engineers.

General basis of capitalizable costs. A many-faceted problem is the quantity of cost that may be permitted in fixed-asset accounts. Much will depend on the definition of a unit of capital-asset expenditure, and the permissible costs that may attach to each such unit when it is acquired and the costs thereafter added to it in the way of improvements during its useful life. Some accounting textbooks have referred to the problem as involving the drawing of the line between "capital and revenue" expenditures—that is, expenditures to be capitalized and hence carried as an asset as contrasted with those to be charged against operations and absorbed by revenues.

For individual assets purchased, the standard of valuation practice is invoice cost plus freight and installation, less discounts including cash discounts. For assets constructed, the standard is cost, less discounts, of material and parts, plus direct labor and in some instances overhead. Undoubtedly the best practice with respect to overhead is to include only the demonstrable overhead differential—that is, only the increments in the customary amounts of specific overhead accounts that can be positively identified with construction. Salaries and other expenses of an engineering staff that has devoted its time exclusively to construction is of course an addition to construction costs, either as a direct expense or as overhead. But the similar treatment of even a part of the expenses of a maintenance-supervisor's office that in a brief interruption of its maintenance operations has designed a new structure or has helped install a new machine is a questionable practice. The preferred procedure is not to include in construction costs any such overhead except where obvious additional costs have been incurred because of the design or construction—and then only in an amount not exceeding the additional, directly identifiable costs. In any event the total should not exceed the cost that would have been incurred if the construction had been performed under a contract with an outsider.

Land costs. The acquisition cost of land consists of the purchase price plus the cost of acquiring good title. The latter may consist of legal fees, as for drawing up the bill of sale, searching the records for liens or other attachments or restrictions, unpaid claims including special assessments, back taxes, and other levies or fees payable to local and state governments; any payment required to remove such an obligation; a suit to remove a cloud in the title, to defend title, or to establish boundaries; and title insurance.

Accrued property tax at the time land is purchased is a part of cost of land, the corresponding credit being a current liability. Occasionally a property tax is regarded as prepaid, particularly in communities where the local governments are on a pay-as-you-go basis; in such instances the debit amount deemed to be prepaid is removed from the gross price and carried to a prepaid-expense account. Most accountants although favoring the first of the two alternatives will defer to local custom if the second presents itself. The amount involved is small, and the conflict is in business practice rather than in accounting theory.

Railroads and public utilities after acquiring parcels of land and rights of way (which are classified as land) must clear the land or otherwise prepare it for a use differing from its previous employment. A farmer who purchases a woodland tract must also clear it before it can be devoted to the production of crops. In such cases the cost of the clearing operation precedent to the altered utilization is a necessary element of the cost of the land.

Where a purchase of real estate includes a building that is ultimately razed, the cost of demolition less recoveries from scrap is disposed of in either of two ways: (a) if the removal of the improvements at a loss was contemplated at the time of purchase, presumably the prospect of the likely additional cost entered into the judgment leading to the approval of the purchase price, and hence such cost is as much a part of the cost of the land as the purchase price itself; or (b) if the removal was the result of a decision independently made *after* the purchase had been consummated, the loss is an operating cost rather than an addition to the cost of the land, regardless of the fact that the defect in the structure or other cause of the removal was present (but not observed or reckoned with) when the purchase was decided on. Where the building or other improvement is to be put to use, the portion of the purchase price allocable to the improvement is transferred to a separate account. It may be that an appraisal before the purchase was made will supply the necessary basis of the allocation; in the absence of such information a real-estate appraiser may be called upon for such a determination. If the price breakdown is made by the management, the files should contain details leading to the basis employed such as prices of contiguous land, assessed valuations of the land and improvements (often made separately), the opinion of the seller, and information supplied by his records.

Other costs not taken into account at the time of purchase that may be added to the purchase price of land are generally held to be limited to grading, sewer, water, and other service connections; street, sidewalk, and similar improvements; special assessments relating to nearby community betterments. Resurfacing of roads and sidewalk-repair assessments and similar replacement outlays are typical of current operating expenditures that may not be added to land costs but are disposed of as costs of maintenance and upkeep. However, if the land has been purchased for resale in total or in smaller units, as in real-estate development, most accountants would regard it as permissible to add to the cost of the land "carrying charges"—taxes, interest actually paid on a loan secured by the land, and maintenance costs—provided the total cost thus accumulated does not exceed the best available estimate of market value less estimated costs of selling.

If the land is to be subdivided and sold by individual lots, the capitalization of maintenance costs ends when the property is put on sale, and the allocation of total cost to any unit is ordinarily accomplished by the application to total cost of a ratio representing the relation of the unit selling price to the estimated over-all selling price.

Building costs. In the cost of buildings the auditor may expect to find architectual and engineering fees, costs of permits and construction inspections, legal fees, costs of work stoppages, and uninsured damages and other losses, provided these items are outlays both necessary and unavoidable during the construction process. Comment has already been made on overhead chargeable to construction. Also occasionally found among construction costs, particularly in the case of public utilities, are property taxes and interest during construction. Under the regulations of most state and Federal bodies such costs, at the option of the utility, may be capitalized or expensed. Some commissions even permit the capitalization of interest when there are no interest-bearing obligations outstanding, the corresponding credit being made to income. The accepted accounting standard is that taxes applicable to the property and to the period of construction may be capitalized if desired, but that interest should never be capitalized unless it can be identified with a loan the proceeds of which are not only available for—but have been applied directly to—the particular construction.

Machinery and other factory items. In addition to net invoice cost the outlay required for machines and other plant installations may include manufacturers' and sales taxes, delivery and setup costs—the latter beginning with the cost of any special foundations that may be required and perhaps continuing through and including costs of labor and material consumed in experimental runs or other operations preceding a formal dedication to production. Once production has started, similar costs during operation or periods of adjustment or shutdown are regarded as operating or maintenance costs. The point at which production commences should be made a matter of record so that the operating division of the business may be clearly aware of the break in the disposition of charges. Where the machine has been designed within the establishment, any separable and identifiable design costs may be added to the other costs of the machine, but the total cost should not be permitted to exceed a predetermined limit—such a limit being established on the basis of what the cost would have amounted to had the design and production been put into the hands of an outsider.

Tools and dies; patterns and drawings. Tools, dies, patterns, and drawings, even in a large manufacturing establishment, are numerous and almost always offer accounting difficulties. They may be kept on an "inventory" basis with periodic physical counts at cost or, where necessary, estimated cost, to which the books are thereupon adjusted. Accrued depreciation may be estimated at the time the physical inventory is taken, and the book reserve may be modified accordingly. Or, lapsing schedules may be set up on the basis of a composite average life of say five years, with annual reductions of the asset account for items depreciated throughout that period. A third variety of accounting may be to fix the asset amount at a "basic" figure and to charge all additions thereafter to expense. Only in exceptional cases is this class of asset accounted for by perpetual-inventory methods. Occasionally a resemblance to such methods is found in subaccounts, such as models, that are eliminated when the models become obsolete.

Trucks and automobiles. Automotive-equipment costs include delivery charges, manufacturer's tax, sales tax and installed tools and equipment. Replacements such as tires may be added to the equipment cost (and corresponding costs of replaced equipment removed) or they may be regarded as maintenance costs, according to the convictions and practices of the division of the establishment charged with the responsibility of supervising truck operations. Under a carefully guided plan of depreciation, there is little choice between the two plans provided the one selected is consistently followed.

Maintenance and repairs. The relation of maintenance and repairs to fixed assets and to internal controls is of great importance; the details of the account reflecting their costs should be consistent with the policy of capitalizing items that meet the tests of adding productivity, lessening cost, or extending useful life. The details of the account should also compare with similar types of expense in previous years. Fluctuations in dollar amounts as between years may be material, for the account is a variable with wide limits; it may reflect in one year the full-capacity operation of fixed assets and, in another, idle time or a shutdown that has made major overhauls possible. The management of every enterprise knows the meaning of deferred maintenance— the putting off of repairs until a chance opportunity arises—and it can readily furnish the auditor with information on fluctuations not only as between years but as between months of the current year as well.

Maintenance reserves that have as their purpose the equalization of maintenance-and-repair expense as between years are sometimes encountered. Combined *depreciation-and-mainte-nance reserves* also exist. They are subject to the same objection as other equalization reserves held over from one year to another. Where such a reserve is found its amount is almost invariably an arbitrary figure that is not the endproduct of studies of maintenance deferred. A blast-furnace relining reserve, often present in the accounts of steel producers, is usually more of a reserve for depreciation than deferred maintenance, and it is preferably so treated on the balance sheet.

What constitutes an improvement? It is difficult in any business to frame rules that will cover precisely all future work that may be performed on existing fixed assets. The general test for an addition is that it increase dimensions (for example, a new wing on an old building) or productivity, or lower future operating costs (for example, a fitting that will speed up the normal productivity of an old machine, lengthen its useful life, or cut down on maintenance costs). Occasionally, certain types of expenditure, including exceptional maintenance costs, are charged against the reserve for depreciation, but the better practice today is to charge against depreciation reserves only the cost of units replaced or retired, consistently clearing costs affecting fixed assets through asset and expense accounts.

Because of these variations in the disposition of both old and new costs and the need for consistency from year to year, the establishment and maintenance of a well-defined capitalization-and-retirement policy accompanied by carefully observed unit definitions are most desirable practices.

Property units. Reference to additions and improvements raises the question of fixed-asset "units." A "property unit" is a carefully defined (a) size or type of fixed asset or (b) expenditure relating to a fixed asset. An expenditure involving a lesser size or amount does not give rise to an adjustment of the cost of the fixed asset affected; but one involving a greater size or amount leads to an adjustment. There may be units of capitalization, depreciation, replacement, retirement, and accounting. A purchased building or a purchased machine is a unit of capitalization: either is universally recognized as a fixed asset. A machine may be a unit for accounting purposes; or machinery, collectively, may be the unit, where there is no plant ledger. A building may be an accounting unit, and its cost may be carried in the books without diminution until it is torn down or sold; or the cost of the building may be broken down into several replacement and depreciation units, such as foundation, wall, and roof.

Depreciation at varying rates may be provided for these elements, or for depreciation-accounting purposes a composite rate may be applied to the building's total cost. The cost of replacing a roof is an expense if the retirement unit is the building; or an addition to the fixed asset, if the roof is a retirement unit. In the latter case, the cost of the old roof is charged against the reserve for roof depreciation, or against a composite reserve for the building as a whole.

Minimum-dollar units are also common, the idea being to eliminate minor charges to fixed assets; charging small amounts to expense avoids what is often characterized as "double handling" (that is, capitalization and depreciation). Such a unit is commonly set for new assets as well as for additions, replacements, alterations, and improvements. Every hand tool and small machine may be capitalized, or only those above a certain dollar cost. In practice minimum-dollar units vary widely—$10 perhaps in a small enterprise and as much as $500 or $1000 in larger concerns.

Internal Controls

Internal controls over fixed assets are poor in the majority of business enterprises. One reason is that the accounting profession has not interested itself sufficiently in the subject, accounting literature dealing with fixed-asset controls being meager and incomplete. Another reason is that business management has likewise taken little interest; not infrequently the impression is formed that fixed assets, unlike current assets, cannot easily disappear and that depreciation provisions and accumulations are at best good guesses not made more accurate by an elaboration of the records. The auditor is often prevented from making a fully satisfactory examination by reason of the lack of supporting detail and of competent studies by management of depreciation-expense-and-reserve requirements. In a first audit of a long-established concern, the auditor by custom assumes little responsibility for balances carried over from periods preceding his audit.

Internal-control standards for fixed assets have been slowly developing in recent years, however, and the auditor should lose no opportunity for calling attention to these standards wherever he finds information on fixed assets inadequate. In this connection, it is always a good plan to bear in mind that accounting records for fixed assets—and for every other purpose as well—can be justified only to the extent that they will be put to intelligent use. A part of his job, in recommending changes, is to make certain that the client's staff will be instructed in the use of the new records, and that, at the top levels of management, conviction exists that the results sought are necessary to the orderly conduct of the business.

The several basic elements of fixed-asset internal controls are generally held to be the following:

Acquisition controls. In organizations whose financial operations are controlled through budgets, additions to fixed assets are usually planned far in advance of purchase. Planning may take such forms as lump-sum provisions for various departments, established at the beginning of each year, or detailed breakdowns with a description of each asset to be purchased. Regardless of the breakdown or even of the existence of a budget, it is common practice to have major specific fixed-asset purchases (for example, those above $1000) authorized by some management group, such as an equipment committee, which reports to the board of directors or the chief executive officer. Whatever the basic authority, the elements of control are: an independent review of the need for new equipment; the choice of a contractor or manufacturer, by selecting from requested bids or otherwise; a decision as to price, installation and other costs, and the method of financing; an approval for the disposal, physically and in the accounts, of superseded equipment, together with the costs, past and prospective, that will be involved; and a review after its completion of the cost and other details of the construction or purchase. Decisions to contract or purchase are usually accompanied by some form of authorization such as a work order. When larger acquisitions or construction have been completed a cost report is desirable as an aid to the equipment committee's review and approval of the project; such a report, tying in with the books of account as at a certain date, should bring out the division of costs among the accounting units to be recognized, with reasons for variations of detail or totals from original estimates and from similar costs incurred elsewhere. Dispositions of major fixed assets not accompanied by new acquisitions are often considered by the same or a similar group: its records should reflect such details as reasons for the removal, the consideration of alternative methods of disposal, the selection of the highest bidder, the book cost and accumulated depreciation, and the treatment of remaining balances.

Whenever any one of these elements is missing or has been

imperfectly applied, the auditor should recommend in specific terms the procedural improvements necessary to meet standards such as those just outlined.

The most satisfactory form of internal control over small tools, dies, and patterns is a periodic inventory-and-depreciation study, and between inventories the capitalization of items exceeding in amount an established sum accompanied by the accumulation of depreciation based at least in part on past experience. The book figure of cost-less-depreciation for a period of years should be reasonably related to model life, changes in production, and volume of product manufactured, and the management should follow a consistent practice in the application of accounting controls.

Maintenance and repairs. The same care that surrounds equipment purchases should be exercised over maintenance-and-repair operations. The equipment committee or its equivalent often supervises them and issues blanket or open work orders for ordinary repairs and special work orders for extraordinary or emergency repairs. In some instances a separate department is established the head of which is a maintenance engineer who reports to the top executive of the organization; in others, the responsibility resides in the plant superintendent, occasionally with no apparent upper limit on expenditures. Obviously these are widely varying practices. But present in all cases should be an agreed-upon delegation of maintenance-and-repair authority to some individual or organizational unit: work orders or their equivalent; estimates of costs followed by studies of variations with actual costs; and an active interest within the management in maintaining low-cost levels already established or seeking cost levels lower than the present.

Plant ledger. A plant ledger is of value to any enterprise, regardless of size. It may be difficult to install after years have passed without one, but the trouble experienced in getting it started and the small expense of maintaining it thereafter are repaid many times in more accurate costs, wiser planning, and safer internal controls. A practicable plant-ledger standard involves the use of a card or sheet for each accounting unit on which appear such data as location, identification, date of purchase, invoice and other costs, reports of condition, and, after retirement, the cause thereof, and the amount realized from sale or scrap. When, for example, this information is written or punched on Keysort cards, the cards may serve as a detail ledger; after assets have been disposed of, the cards become the basis of retirement studies, invaluable in the setting of depreciation rates.

Unit definitions. When units have been carefully defined a more accurate and consistent treatment of fixed-asset charges is possible. Following are sample definitions applicable to average situations:

(1) Capitalization unit—an expenditure in excess of $100 for a single fixed asset or for an addition thereto that clearly has the effect of increasing physical dimensions or productivity, lengthening future life, or lowering future costs. In doubtful situations, the amount of an expenditure, if it is to be capitalized, must be well under either (a) the capitalized value of the resultant added service to be yielded, or (b) future costs saved.

(2) Accounting, retirement, or replacement unit—a capitalization unit or the sum of two or more such units when they constitute a closely related group; or any replaceable part of a capitalization unit where the cost of the part exceeds, say, $100. An accounting unit usually coincides with a retirement or replacement unit, but it may also consist of several retirement units when it is a single structure; in that event it should be supported by a cost report from which the cost of each such retirement unit may be readily obtained.

(3) Depreciation unit—buildings, factory machinery, small tools, patterns and dies, furniture and fixtures, automotive equipment.

In many cases it may be desirable to adapt the definitions to each class of assets, particularly with respect to the test for capitalization.

Internal reporting. Where the fixed assets of an organization are scattered over a number of plants or locations a method of internal reporting can be readily instituted whereby property-accountability clerks at each location prepare monthly or quarterly reports of existence and condition. These reports serve to verify the details of the plant ledger and to supply information invaluable to those responsible for current depreciation provisions and the accumulated reserves.

Property clerk. A property clerk or staff in the controller's office can perform a number of useful functions—be responsible for the accuracy and general propriety of the general-ledger control accounts for fixed assets and related depreciation reserves; keep detail plant ledgers or functionally supervise the keeping of such records in operating divisions; secure general agreement on unit definitions; establish property accountability at points where property is in use, and receive and act on periodic reports of existence and condition; initiate or approve documentation covering changes in property accounts; determine depreciation

rates with the aid of plant and outside technicians; initiate management studies of adequacy of depreciation reserves. In a
smaller organization these functions may be performed by a
part-time clerk.

Financial-Statement Standards

Cost less accrued depreciation is the accepted balance-sheet
valuation of fixed assets, and where the valuation basis is not
revealed in the balance sheet it may be assumed that this is the
basis followed. The better practice is to indicate the basis, as
in the case of inventories; for example, "Plant & Equipment, at
depreciated cost." If at an earlier date an appraisal was introduced into the accounts the caption might read, "Plant & Equipment, at values determined by Messrs. Blank & Blank, appraisal
engineers, as at November 15, 1928, plus additions since at cost,
less accrued depreciation"; but if only depreciable assets were
appraised on that date the point may already have been reached
where all the revalued assets have been retired, making any
further reference to the appraisal unnecessary.

A minimum breakdown on the balance sheet should be made
for the purpose of showing separately the investment in land and
any other nondepreciable item. It is desirable also to disclose the
amount of assets subject to "tax amortization," the meaning of
which is explained in the next chapter. Construction work in
process when material in amount should also appear as a separate
item since it has not yet been made a part of the depreciation
base. The amount of any material contractual obligation on
future construction should be shown in a footnote, or parenthetically in the sidehead of construction in process.

If fully depreciated assets still in use have by custom been
eliminated from the balance-sheet a footnote should disclose the
amount; the better practice is to leave them on the books and in
the balance sheet until they have been disposed of, thus obviating the need for the footnote.

A further breakdown is required when any considerable portion of the fixed assets (for example, more than 10 per cent of the
total amount) is not in use and is likely to remain in that status
for an indefinite period of time. The accrued depreciation related
to this portion should also appear.

Disclosures of other types, made necessary by oddities of
capitalization, valuation, or depreciation, are usually more satisfactorily conveyed to the reader when in the form of footnotes.

Representative Audit Program

1. Obtain analysis of changes during audit period in fixed-asset accounts and tie in opening totals with previous year's papers and closing totals with current trial balance.

2. Test authorizations for bulk of plant additions during period. Observe whether required procedures relating to advance approvals, budget limitations, and final review have been observed; inquire into exceptions.

3. Examine source documents supporting cost of additions; analyze and summarize main cost elements. Test material and labor costs of client's own construction and note basis for any overhead elements included. Examine cost reports, if any, test accuracy of cost summary, and trace totals into accounts. Secure opinion of company's counsel on title restrictions on use of any land acquired, and nature of liens thereon.

4. Analyze retirements, cost of removal, and resale or scrap credits. Ascertain what events have determined the recognition of retirements and how retirements have been disposed of in the accounts. Investigate possibility that fixed assets, in excess of requirements or obsolete or otherwise out of service, have not yet been recorded as retirements.

5. Review practices governing the capitalization and expensing of tools, dies, patterns, and drawings, and review representative items capitalized and expensed.

6. Scan repair-and-maintenance accounts; summarize nature of charges therein and how they were authorized and approved. Determine practice in disposing of costs of major overhauls, expenditures tending to "offset" depreciation and lengthen the life of an asset, and similar borderline costs.

7. Summarize any activities during the period directed toward an inventorying or verifying of existence or condition of fixed assets.

8. Ascertain whether any fixed asset not owned is on hand or has been in use during the period.

9. Look for restrictions on asset use in equipment-loan or other loan agreements, government contracts, and equipment leases, and determine whether such restrictions have been observed.

10. Examine any unfulfilled contracts for construction, and review with principal the need for disclosing contract balances in financial statements.

11. Review insurance policies on fixed assets for the purpose

of determining extent of coverage and whether policies in force conform to client's desired coverage of risks.

Audit Procedures

Because of the nature of fixed assets and the frequent lack of adequate internal controls over them the auditor's responsibility varies from that which he assumes in the case of current assets. Plant ledgers, periodic physical inventories of fixed assets, and reviews of prospective usefulness by the management are not as common as they should be; in less favorable situations the auditor's work is limited to an examination of the propriety of the additions during the audit period, recorded retirements, and a lapsing schedule maintained for the purpose of removing from the depreciation computation and often from the books assets fully depreciated. Despite notable exceptions business management as a whole does not yet fully recognize the need for rigorous controls over costs projected as fixed assets into future operations, even when they are substantial.

In addition to determining the propriety of the amount of fixed assets and related reserves the auditor always endeavors to encourage improvements in controls and procedures wherever he finds them lacking, thus paving the way for a more satisfactory examination in future periods. This may take the form of discussions of general policy with top management or of the character and extent of the detail covered in reviews of proposals and end results with departmental heads or an equipment committee.

Plant inspection. In his survey of a manufacturer's fixed assets the auditor will have a more intelligent approach once he has acquired a background for the general layout of his client's plant, the character of the fabricating processes going on within the plant, and a working knowledge of the types and adaptations of the machinery in everyday use. If he is able to recognize the principal operations that the machines are performing, a trip through the plant before his annual review of fixed-asset changes and factory operating costs will give him a better insight into the business and what has happened to it since his last review than he would obtain from the most detailed audit. On a first visit to the plant he should be accompanied by the plant superintendent or one of the company officers familiar with the fabricating processes. From such officials he can acquire a general knowledge of plant operations commencing for example with the foundry and continuing with metal forming, cutting, and boring, parts manufacture, and finally the assembling and inspection of the final product. He should ask questions concerning recent installations, machines that are standing idle or are regarded as standby and their likely disposition, prospective changes in the plant such as building extensions or shutdowns, possible new machinery, changes in or modernizations of processes, and studies in progress that have as their object the lowering of costs or the modification of factory output. If the auditor has seen the plant in previous years he will be able to make rough notes of changes, from observation and memory, or by requesting his guide to point them out as they proceed through the plant.

Although no one expects to find developed engineering talents in an auditor, his academic training—or private reading—should introduce him to the more important manufacturing processes. Books are available for this purpose, written for engineering students, shop foremen, and executives who desire to expand their operating horizons. The approach is primarily informative and nonmathematical, and from the text material and illustrations the auditor can readily acquire a good acquaintance with manufacturing phenomena. Particularly useful is a knowledge of foundry practice, die and pattern work, metal casting, heat treatment and welding, production machines and their setup, cutting tools, and guages and other measuring and testing instruments. So equipped, the auditor will find himself better able to discuss and arrive at opinions on fixed-asset additions, retirements, and improvements, maintenance problems, rates and accumulations of depreciation, and even work-in-process inventories.

Historical summary. In a first audit of a going concern that has been in existence many years, the auditor develops for his permanent file a historical summary of each fixed-asset account. A plant ledger with carefully maintained supporting detail will usually supply him with whatever analyses he wishes to make. Occasionally it is possible for him to prepare a breakdown of the balance of each fixed-asset controlling account by years of origin, thus supplying a convenient over-all basis for testing the adequacy of the related depreciation reserve.

Where there is no supporting plant ledger, the problem faced by the auditor in a first examination of a going concern is a difficult one. In the usual situation he may choose from several alternatives. He may accept the findings appearing in regular or special reports of the auditor preceding him; and it may be possible for the client to arrange a review of his predecessor's working papers, a courtesy common among public accountants as has been pointed out in a previous chapter. He may accept an analysis by the client's staff either already in existence or made at his request. Or he may prepare one of his own without reference to work done by others. In relying on schedules not made under his direction he would of course examine the conditions, including the limitations, under which they had been prepared and test the accuracy of individual items. Perhaps the minimum requirement for each major class of fixed assets may be assumed to be an analysis for possibly a 10- or 15-year period containing total additions, total retirements, a summary of the principal items that have entered into each year's changes, a description of each year's audit procedures covering such principal items and the remaining items, a brief history of the internal controls governing additions and retirements, and an outline of the internal controls actually in operation during the current audit period.

A recent appraisal made for insurance purposes or in support of an issue of securities may aid in identifying the principal components of the property accounts and in satisfying the auditor that the cost reflected in the records was not in excess of the cost of reproduction or other basis shown in the report. Older appraisals may also be available that will serve at least to identify the principal items in existence at an earlier date, thus giving some indication of how far back analyses must go if they are to include all major components of existing plant.

Cost reports covering various items or groups of fixed assets and prepared by the client's own engineers or accountants may also be available. These may have been prepared at the conclusion of construction periods, or in connection with depreciation studies or proposals for replacements. Where a building has been put up under contract, interim and final cost reports of independent engineers may be available that will supply reliable information not only on total cost but on the cost of component parts of the structure. Assessed values as a rule cannot be depended on for information useful to the accountant on either cost or present value.

Inquiry will reveal the policy that has been followed on the removal from the accounts of replaced buildings, machinery, and equipment generally. Some information in this respect may be gained from a scanning of past-years' credits in fixed-asset accounts and of related debits in the depreciation reserves, but in many instances, without a comprehensive plan for the removal of replaced items, such entries may prove to be both inaccurate and incomplete.

The ratio to cost of the accumulated depreciation for a given class of assets may give a further clue to the retirement policy that has been followed, as illustrated in the next chapter.

Changes during audit period. Having established in his mind the background of the fixed-asset accounts the auditor is prepared to review current changes. It is always preferable to review them before the close of the audit period, at which time measures can more readily be taken to correct any errors discovered and additions and retirements can more realistically be viewed and discussed. Changes during the remainder of the period can be covered upon the auditor's return after the close of the period.

A first step is to scan the fixed-asset accounts for the purpose of determining the character and volume of the changes. The amounts of additions and retirements supported by work orders or other authorizations should be traced to their sources. The details making up such amounts should be testchecked with original documentation or payroll summaries; in each case the auditor should satisfy himself that the item is properly capitalizable and relates to the structure or equipment to which it has been charged. The meanings of component elements or of work done not at once apparent to the auditor can be clarified by discussing them with engineers, shop foremen, or others whose names appear on supporting documents. Recapitulations of costs should be compared with original authorizations and estimates, and satisfactory explanations should be obtained for major differences. Charges added after installation or construction has been completed should be carefully reviewed; they may turn out to be items of maintenance or upkeep.

Payments on construction work under contract should be compared for character and amount with applicable provisions of the contract. Additional payments under escalator and similar clauses should be testchecked for accuracy.

Work orders may also be prepared for contemplated maintenance and repair activities covering a type of work to be done and a stated period over which the expenditure may occur. Although remaining uncompleted at the end of the audit period they should not be carried forward as work in process or otherwise capitalized but charged off along with closed orders of the same type.

In smaller organizations where no work-order system is in operation and no equipment committee passes on acquisitions and retirements it may be desirable to secure from management a list by principal categories of fixed assets acquired and of fixed assets sold or otherwise retired. The list may then be used as a check against recorded changes.

An acquisition of land will be supported by several or all of the following: a purchase contract, a settlement sheet, a board resolution, a deed, an opinion of counsel on title or liens, a title-insurance policy, the receipt of a tax bill on the property. The auditor in addition may ask his client to request counsel for an opinion of ownership, and a statement as to the amount and character of any foreclosures, judgments, mortgages, tax bills, and other liens standing against the property.

Expenditures for improvements that may be capitalized should meet the customary tests: they should have the effect of prolonging life, increasing productivity, bettering an operation or otherwise decreasing future unit costs. Alterations, moving costs, and rehabilitation costs such as those pertaining to reconditioning after an asset has been devoted to emergency or other special uses, are rarely classifiable as fixed-asset additions or even as deferred charges since their effect is to maintain or restore rather than to improve an originally existing operating effectiveness.

Bottlers, food processors, oil companies, and producers of chemicals and other commodities requiring special protection in handling and shipping may employ any of several common commercial devices for recovering containers. The investment in containers is not infrequently substantial, and a careful accounting for the investment is essential. Perhaps the most common practice is to bill the customer for the container (often in a separate account or memorandum record) and credit the account when the container is returned. If the container is not returned and the custom is not to press the customer for payment, a reserve or allowance for unrecovered retainers will be necessary. In addition, through natural wear and tear a reserve will be required for the depreciation of the containers that are recoverable. Still larger reserves will be necessary where the customer is not billed but is expected to return the container as through a "pickup" service. Where a cash deposit is required or where the billing to the customer includes a figure for the container, the offset to the container charge is usually some form of deferred-income account from which the credit is removed upon the return of the container. If the container charge collected from the customer exceeds the cost of the container a periodic income credit will be made for unrecoverable containers in an amount representing the container charge less such cost.

Illustrative Audit

Worksheet H 1, requiring 14-column paper, summarizes fixed-asset changes during the year by principal classes. The unadjusted book amounts of fixed assets are in the 6th money column, adjustments and reclassifications in the 5th, and adjusted amounts in the 4th. This reversal of the usual sequence of unadjusted and adjusted figures makes possible a showing of adjusted additions and deductions in columns 2 and 3. Worksheets H 2 and H 3 supply details for these two columns. The general-ledger accounts are nine in number; for example, 91–123 is the office-building account. On the working trial balance these accounts have been summarized in one total. Subtotals of the buildings and machinery sections appear at the top of the "as adjusted" detail; on the original worksheet, these subtotals were in green, as were also the figures for land, furniture and fixtures, and trucks, thus aiding the obtaining of schedule totals.

The notes at the foot of H 1 bring out the scope of the audit and the general character of the detail supporting the changes during the year and the balances at the end of the year. Note that no overhead has been included on work done by the company acting as its own general contractor on the extension of the factory building, installation of machinery, and the manufacture of patterns.

Worksheet H 2 details most of the individual additions to plant during the year. This was possible because they were comparatively few in number and the character of the items lent themselves to a physical inspection by the auditor. Inspection is not a feature of most reviews of plant additions but it may be employed in the audit of smaller concerns to make up for any laxity in internal controls. Invoice numbers are occasionally noted by the auditor, as here; in some instances they may serve as a check against presenting the same invoice twice. But with customary internal controls in force and with a supporting plant ledger the possibility is remote.

Worksheet H 2c provides a breakdown for future reference on the assembly plant, showing the principal classes of costs that now constitute the finished product. Presumably a similar breakdown on the foundry-building extension has not yet been completed. Note that work order 1–253 (patterns & flasks) will cost $15,500 to complete. No mention of the additional cost is required on the balance sheet or elsewhere since the total is nominal compared with the whole amount of the asset and no greater than an average amount in process at any one moment.

Retirements of buildings and machinery summarized in H 3 are charged in total, less salvage, to the reserve. On furniture and fixtures, and trucks and automobiles, depreciation has been provided on a lapsing-schedule and individual basis, respectively, and hence gain or loss is recognized on each retirement; the note on TB 5 indicates the accounts affected.

Martin Manufacturing Company
Fixed Assets
Year ended December 31, 1952

Basic data prepared by Mrs. Cowles

	Balance 12-31-51	Additions H-2	Retirements H-3	Balances December 31, 1952 As adjusted	adjustments and restorations	Books unadjusted
Land	25 000 00 x			25 000 00		25 000 00
Buildings:	1			(1 143 746 46)		
Foundry	489 224 34 x	95 768 29	27 519 37	557 473 26		557 473 26 ↑
Factory	464 699 34 x	325 127 89	15 008 73	474 818 50 6)	684 53	474 133 97 ↑
Office	111 454 70 x	–		111 454 70		111 454 70
Machinery				(963 967 84)		
Foundry	146 495 50 x	65 203 74	4 927 86	206 771 38 7)	957 23	205 814 15 ↑
Factory	385 235 43 x	175 609 72	45 912 37	514 932 78 8)	622 80 1 624 36 1 001 33	511 684 29 ↑
Patterns, etc	258 997 03 x	32 092 67	48 826 02	242 263 68 10) A)	677 84 3 088 91	238 497 43 ↑
Furn. + fix.	31 709 81 x	6 110 00	1 562 41	36 257 40		36 257 40 ↑
Trucks + autos	21 021 19 x	7 660 00	3 270 00	25 411 19		25 411 19 ↑
Const. in prog.	–			10) A)	– 880 34 – 3 088 91	3 969 25 ↑
TOTALS	**1 633 837 34** ↑	**707 572 31** ↑	**147 026 76** ↑	**2 194 382 89** ↑	**4 687 25** ↑	**2 189 695 64** ↑

The above changes have been recorded on TB PF 71-72-73.

Work done:

The above summary and H-2 and H-3 were prepared by
   analysis of G/L accounts.
Balances at 12-31-51 were compared with last year's papers. (x)
Requisitions and shop orders were approved by the Equipment
   Committee and signed by the President as chairman.
Exception: 4 items in AJE #8; these were subsequently
approved by Mr. Stebbins. In support of items listed
on H-2 invoices from manufacturers were examined,
or work orders were reviewed with Sidney Skell and Jack
Johnson, the cost clerk who determined the costs of the
manufactured equipment. The costs of the latter
included no overhead. Labor costs were posted from
time tickets on which work-order numbers appeared.
Charges for materials came from requisitions approved
   by George Shuffle showing deliveries to factory.
Retirements are made on individual work orders
   initiated by the plant manager and approved by the
   President as chairman of the Equipment Committee.
Disposal credits are approved by Porter Addon

Work done (Continued):
purchasing director, who obtains bids for retired
equipment and scrap. Proceeds on W/O's 639 & 640 were
net after retirement costs of $188.10 for labor.

Repair and maintenance a/c's, reviewed with Mr. Shuffle,
indicated that the present policy is to charge off
all repairs, even though "offsetting" depreciation.
The items in AJE #9 were erroneously treated as
repairs.

Verification was made during the year for the first
time of the existence and condition of all fixed
assets by comparison of the physical units with a plant
ledger maintained by the cost clerk. This comparison
was made for all fixed assets except patterns and
flasks, and furniture and fixtures for which a
similar comparison will be made in 1953. Approved
journal entries were examined in support of minor
corrections for items on the plant ledger which
were not found to be on hand. These differences
resulted from scrapping equipment in prior accounting periods without observance of the formal accounting
procedures. The detail in the plant ledger has been
proved against the controlling account twice yearly.
The last proof was made on 10-31-52. We made no
independent test of the detail with the control.

There was no construction in process except
patterns on W/O 1-253

91   Martin Manufacturing Company
Additions to Fixed Assets   H-R
Year ended December 31, 1952   2-19-53

p. 1 of 4

	Voucher or W/O number	Purchased or manu-facturing cost 2	Freight	Instal-lation
Foundry buildings:				
Extension on main building	W/o 4-12	84 445 18 (H-2c)		
Replacement of lighting equipment in main bldg.	W/O 8-27	8 062 96		
Other items under $500 (10)	-	3 260 15		
		95 768 29		
Factory buildings:				
New assembly plant on NE corner of plant site	1952 W/O's 1-1 and 3-4			
40 x 250 - 2 floors - contract with Austin Company dated 12-13-51; completion date, March 10, 1952	JV-3-107	298 563 18		
Own materials and costs	JV-3-108 AJE-6	26 564 71		
		325 127 89 (H-2c)		
Foundry equipment:				
* Sand-conditioning and mixing equipment - Johnson and Procter - inv 21985-A, installed in July	Vo.9-3261	26 498 02	1 058 00	-
Installation of above	W/O 8-1138 AJE-7			957 23
* Sand-slinger - Marplon, Inc., inv. BC-49	Vo 8-345	4 222 15	366 72	
Installation of above	W/O 8-88			145 44
* Molding machines (5) - Osborn Mfg. Co., inv. OM-66750	Vo 8-346	22 005 75	2 883 57	
Installation of above	W/O 8-89			574 89
* Additional unit-core ovens Foundry Equipment Co. - inv. 3115405, delivered	Vo 9-3275	6 300 00	-	
Installation	W/O 9-39			191 97
		65 203 74	59 025 92	4 308 29	1 869 53
2 Factory machinery:				
* Hydraulic press - Birmingham Company inv. 2387, 3478 Model AH 68; 8-ton model; installed by mfr.	AJE-8 W/O 4-53 Vo 3-730	62 540 00	-	-

p. 2 of 4

a/c 91-		Voucher or W/o number	Purchased or manufacturing cost	Freight	Installation
132	Factory machinery (cont'd):				
+*	16 lathes and planers — Morrison Mfg. Co. inv. 62-48, 63-8	Vo 3-74	52 412 44	2 751 02	–
	Installation	W/o 1-333} AJE-9}			1 087 00
*	3-way automatic drilling machine, Pratt + Whitney inv. 30 G 72	Vo 8-37	22 175 13	–	–
	Installation cost on above charged to machinery repairs	AJE-7} W/o 8-1138}	–		1 001 33
	Other items (38) consisting principally of small drill presses and shapers	–	30 484 99	2 514 81	643 00
		175 609 72*	167 612 56*	5 265 83*	2 731 33*
134	Patterns and flasks:				
	64 patterns covering 1953 models	** AJE-10} W/o 1-252}	20 161 50	–	–
	36 patterns covering 1953 models	*** R/E-A} W/o 1-253}	3 088 91	–	–
	Patterns replaced	W/o 5-683	8 842 26	–	–
		32 092 67*	32 092 67*	–	–

* Physically inspected; all new equipment
+ Replacements for equal number retired
** Completed October 15
*** Uncompleted; estimated cost to complete: $ 15,500.

H-2a

Martin Manufacturing Company
Additions to Fixed Assets
Year ended December 31, 1952

HH
2-19-53

P 3 of 4

	Voucher or w/o number	Purchased or manufactured cost	Freight	Installation
Furniture and fixtures:				
National payroll machine	Vo 4-78	1482 00		
Burroughs bookkeeping machine	Vo 4-152	723 00		
Mosler safe	Vo 4-276	1150 00		
Additional drawers for safe	Vo 4-571	42 59		
Friden calculator	Vo 4-399	575 00		
Diebold rotary file	Vo 8-98	219 00		
Remington electric typewriter	Vo 8-163	435 00		
SH steel filing cabinets - 4	Vo 8-178	360 00		
Mimeograph machine	Vo 8-217	585 00		
GF steel desks - 2	Vo 8-225	420 00		
GF steel arm chairs - 2	Vo 8-225	65 00		
GF steel chairs - 3	Vo 8-225	53 41		
		6110 00		
Trucks and automobiles:				
3 T G.M.C. truck	Vo 3-668	4680 00		
1952 4 door Oldsmobile	Vo 9-374	2980 00		
		7660 00		

H-2 b

Martin Manufacturing Company
H 2-1
91

Additions to Fixed Assets

p. 4 of 4
Analysis of building work orders over $5,000

Year ended December 31, 1952

	Vo No	Outside services Amount	Other charges Material	Labor	Misc.
W/o 4-12 - Extension of foundry building					
Nels Jensen, Inc. - Bldg. Cont.	5-86	10 000 00	(Sept) 1 829 16	1 251 28	468 62
✓ ✓	6-203	20 000 00	(Oct) 587 49	498 57	327 19
	9-49	34 087 87			
Bates & Yates, Arch.	5-132	5 000 00			
✓ ✓	10-67	5 500 00			
Mound City Htg. & Vent. Co.					
Ventilating system	10-364	4 895 00			
Total cost (H-2) 84 445 18*		79 482 87*	2 416 65*	1 749 85*	795 81*
Appropriation 90 000 00*					
W/o 4-1 - Assembly plant:					
Analysis of invoices of					
Austin Company plus					
own materials orders.					
Basis was cost + fixed					
fee of $30,000 Construction					
started in January;					
first invoice Jan. 31, 1952:					
Foundation		3 746 585	650 00	350 00	
Superstructure	JV-3-107	130 243 42	1 412 02	698 68	3 232 20
Windows & glazing	JV-3-108	26 476 07	-	-	-
Roof		22 822 86	100 50	-	-
Bldg. equipment		81 554 88	18 143 61	1 513 91	463 89
Total cost (H-2) 325 127 89*		298 563 08*	20 306 13*	2 562 59*	3 696 09*
Appropriation 300 000 00*					

* Cost report approved by Board
on June 16; see X-3

H-2c

-382-

p 1 of 2

	Work Order	Year of acqui-sition	Cost	Net proceeds	Charged to accrued deprecia-tion	Gain or -loss	
Foundry buildings:							
Estimated cost of wall removed to permit extension on main building (A)	3-3	8-1-41	(B) 4 000 00	-	4 000 00	-	
Estimated cost of structure razed to make way for extension of foundry bldg.	3-15	8-1-41	22 000 00	-	22 000 00	-	
Other retirements (3)	-	various	1 519 37	-	1 519 37	-	
			27 519 37^	-	27 519 37^	-	
Factory building:							
Storehouse shed torn down on NE corner of property where assembly plant now located	7-8	8-1-41	15 008 73	-	15 008 73		
Foundry machinery:							
Crucible furnace for nonferrous castings	6-37	8-1-41	4 500 00	200 00	4 300 00	-	
Minor items	-	various	427 86	52 00	375 86	-	
			4 927 86	252 00	4 675 86		
Factory machinery:							
Stationary cutter, Morton Mfg. Co.	6-38	12-6-45	3 481 15	500 00	2 981 15	-	
Rockford hydraulic shaper	6-39	8-1-41	6 000 00	250 00	5 750 00		
American engine lathe	6-40	4-22-44	32 750 00	2 615 48	30 134 52		
Other items	-	various	3 681 22	243 02	3 438 20		
			45 912 37^	3 608 50^	42 303 87^		

(A) Costs of removing wall were charged to a/c 245-1 Repairs, buildings and equipment in the amount of $4,863.52.

(B) Cost estimated by Nels Jensen, builder of foundry extension.

H-3

p 2 of 3

a/c 91-	Description	WORK ORDER	Year of acquisition	Cost	Net proceeds	Charged to accrued depreciation	Gain or - loss
134	Patterns + flasks.						
	Patterns on discontinued products	1-2	various	1287849	23450	1264399	-
	Patterns on discontinued products	7-1	various	1511135	10000	1501135	-
	Worn-out patterns and flasks	1-3	various	2083618	16550	2067068	-
				4882602✓	50000✓	4832602✓	-
16	Furniture + fixtures:						
	Estimated cost of old desks, chairs, filing cabinets, and sundry items of office equipment acquired as part of the bulk purchase on 8-1-41	{JV-8-67} {CR-198}	8-1-41	112976	5000	112976	5000
	Multigraph machine (traded in on a Mimeograph)	{Vo 8-217} {JV 8-92}	4-8-42	43265	7500	22354	- 13411
				156241✓	12500✓	135330✓	- 8411✓
17	Trucks and autos.						
	1947 - 4-door Buick (traded in on 1952 4-door Oldsmobile)	{Vo 9-374} {JV 9-38}	6-7-47	327000	75000	277000	25000

H-3a

Problems and Questions

1. During an audit of the Bolen Company, a manufacturing corporation, your examination of the Land, Building, & Equipment account has revealed the following detail. No plant ledger was available.

Item	19–3		
1	4–15	Incorporation fee	$ 52.50
2	5–20	Legal service covering incorporation	200.00
3	6– 1	Purchase of assets of Bolen Bros.	58,794.36
4	6– 8	Payment of liabilities of Bolen Bros.	7,543.13
5	6–30	Sales tax—state of Zenith	1,175.90
6	7– 1	Discount of 10% on sale of stock	24,500.00
7	7– 1	Commission of 3% to stock salesman	6,615.00
8	7– 1	Purchase of 135' x 200' addition to plant site	7,830.00
9	7–15	Legal and other fees on plant-site addition	346.25
10	8– 1	Architectural fees on extension	4,100.00
11	8–31	Part payment on construction contract	32,784.90
12	9– 3	Final payment, Bolen Bros. liabilities	633.04
13	12–15	Final payment on construction contract	18,956.71
14	12–31	Interest during construction	700.00

The following information was also obtained by you:

(a) The Bolen Company was incorporated as at April 18, 19–3, and immediately took over the fixed assets of Bolen Brothers. The owners of Bolen Brothers were also the incorporators of the new company, and the ownership and management thus remained unchanged. The purpose of incorporation was to make possible the securing of outside capital for expansion.

(b) Payment for acquired fixed assets was made on June 1 in capital stock of the new company, 500 shares of a par value of $100 each having been transferred to the partnership. The amount appearing in item 3 was the net amount of the fixed assets (cost less accrued depreciation) on the books of Bolen Bros.; the transaction as recorded on the books of the new company included a credit of $8,794.36 to "Capital Surplus." It was explained that the purpose of the capital surplus was to absorb any liabilities of the old firm paid by the new company.

(c) On July 1 as the result of arrangements with security brokers 2,450 shares of the company's capital stock were sold to the public at 90 less a 3 per cent commission to the brokers on the amount of the sale. On the same date, the partnership, having distributed its remaining assets to the partners, was dissolved and from that day on business was done under the name of the new company.

(d) During the next six months a plant addition was under construction. The completion date was December 31. Because of the interference of the construction activity with normal operations, the president of the company directed the bookkeeper to charge interest at 4 per cent on construction outlays up to the completion date. Item 14 was the result. Net income for the year had been slightly more than the $40,000 originally budgeted.

(e) An appraisal by Old Reliable Engineering Company was made as at the date the assets were taken over by the new company. The following four-column summary appeared in the appraisal report, each item representing a total supported by details of individual assets in the body of the report:

Class	(a) Cost	(b) Cost of repro- duction	Accrued depreciation On (a)	On (b)
Land	$ 5,000.00	$ 15,000.00	$ –	$ –
Buildings	45,275.89	53,475.00	13,752.19	5,347.50
Machinery	35,897.13	43,222.87	20,411.51	8,644.57
Tools	19,014.27	28,730.74	12,229.23	1,436.54
Totals	$105,187.29	$140,428.61	$46,392.93	$15,428.61

Your recommendations concerning the fixed-asset account have been solicited by the president of the company who has expressed a desire to conform the company's records with preferred accounting practices. He is particularly concerned with the propriety of placing on the books the net cost of reproduction reflected in the appraisal report.

Outline your recommendations briefly, appending the adjusting journal entries required to put them into effect.

2. You are called upon to prepare a worksheet embodying the information that follows. You are to include in your worksheet whatever explanations and adjustments of the existing accounts you regard as necessary:

(a) On January 2, 19–9, the Ajax Company sold the building housing its plant to the Lifeguard Insurance Company for a cash consideration of $400,000. The building had been constructed in 19–0 at a cost of $250,000 and depreciation of $57,143 had been accumulated over the eight years preceding the date of sale.

(b) Coincident with the preceding transaction Ajax contracted to lease the building from Lifeguard at an annual cash rental of $46,892 payable at the end of each year for a period of ten years. Taxes and all other expenses of the building were to be borne by the lessee. You are told that this fixed annual rental will be sufficient to return to the insurance company over the ten-year period the purchase price of the building plus interest at 3 per cent and that the profit to the insurance company will consist only of such interest.

(c) At the end of the ten-year period Ajax is obligated under the terms of the lease to repurchase the building for $10,000.

(d) On the books of Ajax the capital gain of $207,143 was credited to earned surplus and the resultant accrued Federal capital-gains tax of $53,857 (the amount of which you may assume to be correct) was charged to buildings.

(e) At the end of 19–9 upon auditing the Ajax books you find entries that may be condensed thus:

```
Rent ........................................ $54,078
     Cash paid out ..........................        $46,892
     Reserve for depreciation—buildings ......          4,698
     Interest income .........................          1,616
     Accrued liability for building ..........            872
```

You are informed by the bookkeeper that the above items were recommended to her by the representative of the insurance company and that the corresponding transactions for the following year may be summarized thus:

Rent	$54,078	
Interest expense	26	
Cash paid out		$46,892
Reserve for depreciation—buildings		4,839
Interest income		1,475
Accrued liability for buildings		898

By consulting interest tables you ascertain that (a) the item of interest expense ($26) is 3 per cent of the accrued liability for the preceding year, (b) the last-named is the periodic "deposit" required at 3 per cent to amount to $10,000 at the end of ten years, (c) the item of interest income of $1,616 is 3 per cent of $53,857, and (d) the sum of such interest and the addition ($4,698) to the depreciation reserve, or $6,314, is the periodic amount at 3 per cent required to amortize the capital-gains tax over the ten-year period.

It is admitted by the management that the accounts as described have not followed accounting principles but that if they are now recast they should be in accord with the best practices.

3. Holfax Stores, Inc., the parent company of several general-merchandise retail stores, purchased a lease on a corner lot for the purpose of erecting a building for office use. The lease when purchased had been running twenty-two years and had twenty-five more to go. The following is a summary of your analysis of the company's "real-estate clearing" account:

Item	19–4		
1	July 1	Purchase of leasehold from Geo. Barber (leasehold expires 25 years after this date) less accrued real-estate taxes of $234.74 for 19–4	$ 26,265.26
2	Aug. 6	Cost of demolishing old structure	2,387.42 _Land_
3	15	Sale of equipment removed from demolished building, brick and other scrap	3,938.87
4	15	Payment of old mechanics liens against demolished buildings	350.00
5	Nov. 16	Real-estate tax for 19–4, covering both halves of calendar year	469.48 _out_
	19–5		
6	Mar. 8	Baker and Jones, contractors, less 2% allowed for prepayment (contracted due date was June 1, 19–5 and building was formally occupied on March 15), representing the full cost of the new building—which has an estimated useful life of 40 years	149,940.00
7	May 16	Prepayment of one-half estimated 19–5 real-estate tax	258.21
8	June 30	Share of administrative expenses for fiscal year ended on this date representing incidental employee time spent on plans, layout, etc., new building	2,374.90

9   June 30   Additional payment to Baker and Jones to compensate them for their net loss on the construction contract; authorized by Board   8,736.54

Total $186,842.94

The leasehold agreement provides for a reimbursement to the lessee of the fair cash value of any useful leasehold improvements remaining at the expiration of the lease. At present the cash value of the building twenty-five years hence cannot be determined with accuracy but a nominal amount of $50,000 as its then value has been generally agreed to.

Your comments have been requested on the propriety of the capitalization of each of the nine items above, and you are to prepare any adjusting journal entries necessary, including (a) the separation of the costs between a leasehold account and a building account, and (b) amortization and depreciation.

4. The following item has been extracted from a fixed-asset schedule accompanying the balance sheet of the Dorbel Company, a small manufacturing concern. You are asked to give your views and suggest whatever modifications that may appear to be necessary:

Building valued at $50,000 and lot at $8,000, first occupied by company two years ago; total price paid and to be paid, $58,000, payable over ten-year period in equal annual principal installments at end of each period; building estimated to last 30 years; two installments already paid with interest at 4½ per cent; amount included in balance-sheet total of fixed assets, $16,559, less accrued depreciation of $832.30, or $15,726.70 net.

5. During your audit of the Euclid Manufacturing Company you find that in accordance with a practice established within the company before World War II no fixed asset or addition to a fixed asset is capitalized if its cost is less than $200. In a study made recently under the direction of the controller it was determined that there were carried to expense during each of the past six years 240, 150, 220, 265, 178, and 203 property units having a cost ranging between $5 and $200, and an average cost of $30, $50, $40, $50, $60, and $70, respectively. Had these items been capitalized their cost would have been spread in equal amounts over five years commencing with the year of purchase.

(a) What has been the effect of this practice on the annual net income of the past year as compared with the year preceding, assuming that the alternative had been the full capitalization of these smaller items?

(b) From the point of view of developing better controls over fixed assets do you believe that in a situation of this kind it would be safer to reduce the capitalization minimum from $200 to, say, $5?

6. In adding a wing to a factory building, a wall of the old building is torn down. What entry, if any, would you recommend to record the demolition?

7. The management of a company has followed a rigid policy of capitalizing all tools and maintaining a control or inventory card for each item. The difficulty of keeping a separate card on which cost and location appear for each hand tool and similar inexpensive item has proven to be out of proportion to any possible savings or accuracy that may have arisen from the process. As the company's auditor, your advice is sought as to whether good accounting demands that whatever method of control is adopted for small tools be linked to the accounting records by quantity or dollar amount or both, with the same degree of precision, say, as that with which records of raw materials are maintained. What would be your answer?

8. By what different methods may maintenance expenses be differentiated from plant additions?

9. Audit procedure 10 refers to the possible disclosure of construction "contract balances in financial statements." When in your opinion is such disclosure necessary? Draft a disclosure of this type and indicate where it should appear.

10. Examine five recent financial statements appearing in corporate reports to stockholders and set forth for each answers to the following questions concerning fixed assets:

(a) How many classes of fixed assets were listed?

(b) Was accrued depreciation disclosed; if so, was it subdivided by classes of assets? What was the ratio of accrued depreciation to the total of fixed assets?

(c) What basis of valuation was indicated?

(d) Were additions and retirements disclosed anywhere in the report?

Select from these reports the least commendable statement of fixed assets and give your recommendations for its improvement.

11. In the annual report of the Hayes Manufacturing Corporation is the following balance-sheet footnote: "The amount at which property, plant, and equipment is carried does not purport to represent realizable value or replacement cost." What is the purpose of this footnote? Do you regard it as a necessary feature of a balance sheet?

12. Following is a note extracted from the balance sheet of a listed corporation: "Note: A building sold by the corporation [to an insurance company] in 1953 for $600,000 was leased back for an initial term of twenty-two years at an annual rental of $42,150 with options to extend the lease thereafter to the year 2025 at a reduced rental. Taxes, insurance, and maintenance costs are to be borne by the corporation." Assuming (a) that the sale price of $600,000 is depreciated cost and does not include any cost of land, (b) that the corporation has an option to repurchase the building in 1975 at $346,760, (c) that the rental after 1975 will be $22,000, and (d) that the building will be abandoned in 2025 with no scrap value remaining, what would you estimate the insurance company's approximate percentage return on its investment for the seventy-two year period?

13. Under what conditions would you approve additions to fixed assets in the form of overhead charges on construction work undertaken by the company whose accounts you are examining?

14. For what points would you look in scanning a maintenance-and-repair account?

15. Under what circumstances, if any, may capital expenditures be charged against revenue expenditures?

16. What are the factors to be considered in determining a lower-than-cost policy for standby machinery? If it should be decided that such equipment is to be written down would you recommend that a credit be made to the asset account or to the related reserve for depreciation?

17. The net assets of a going corporation are sold for cash, without interruption of business, to a new corporation, the consideration amounting to 150 per cent of the net worth of the old company. To the cost thus incurred the new company has added the face amount of payables assumed and from the total has deducted what appear to be accurate amounts for cash, receivables, and inventories; the balance remaining is charged to "Plant" account. You are called in to advise with the president and controller of the new company on depreciation policy. Indicate the lines along which you would proceed, and the likely policy you would recommend.

18. A municipal power department recently completed a new generating plant the cost of which has been approximately $4,800,000. Immediately before work on the plant began, an issue of $7,500,000 3 per cent income bonds was floated at par, the purpose being an addition to working capital as well as the construction of the plant. The city controller has authorized an addition to the plant cost of $450,000 representing interest on the bond issue during the two-year construction period; but before transfering the interest paid to plant cost he has decided to obtain your advice on the propriety of the transfer. It may be assumed that expenditures of $200,000 from the bond proceeds were made at the end of each month of the construction period. What would be your response?

19. In a manufacturing establishment you find references to "property units" in connection with the accounting and servicing of a group of automatic screw machines. These machines have replaceable parts and require periodic overhauls by subgroups. The individual machines in each subgroup have been purchased at different times at different prices and have differing life-spans. Under such conditions what kinds of property units might you expect to find in such references?

20. Why are minimum-dollar units so often established for fixed-asset capitalizations?

CHAPTER XI

Depreciation

Depreciation is lost usefulness: the reduction of the service potential of a fixed asset or fixed-asset group that cannot or will not be restored by repairs or by replacements of parts. Attributable mainly to use, it is often augmented by obsolescence, inadequacy, unfavorable maintenance policies, and other factors that reduce economic, rather than physical, life. In accounting, accruing depreciation is looked upon as giving rise to an operating expense: a cost, in most instances determined by the annual or other periodic application of a fraction or *rate* to the asset cost. As depreciation is given recognition as an expense it is credited to and accumulated in a *reserve* or *allowance* account—a valuation account deductible on the balance sheet from the asset amount to which it relates.

In everyday business and accounting usage the term "depreciation" refers not only to lost usefulness but also to its translation into periodic and cumulative dollar costs. It is always best, therefore, to couple the word with another in order to make the intended application clear; thus, "depreciation rate," "depreciation expense," "reserve [or allowance] for depreciation."

Depletion is a special form of depreciation: the removal of a natural deposit from land, reflected in the accounts by the addition, to expense, of an amount equal to a proportionate part of the cost of the land or lease, the credit being made to a reserve or allowance for depletion or occasionally to the asset account itself. As distinguished from other forms of depreciation, depletion involves a physical shrinkage. The comments in this chapter for the most part apply equally well to provisions and allowances for depletion.

Intangibles are often depreciated, for various causes, the dimi-

391

nution of their cost or other basis of valuation being referred to as *amortization*.

In examining the problems of depreciation peculiar to a single enterprise, the auditor's objectives are to

1. Test the adequacy of the provisions for the current year and the accumulation reflected in the depreciation reserves against industry averages and against any internal reviews.

2. Make sure that policies of accrual, retirement, and adjustment are consistent with those of past years and that changes therein during the current year are satisfactorily supported.

3. Review comments on depreciation by internal-revenue agents and appraise significance of any criticisms of rates or totals.

4. Encourage internal studies of useful lives, rates, bases, and salvage estimates and their practical application to expense and reserve accounts.

Principles and Practices

Depreciation elements. Depreciation, both the current provision and the accumulated reserve, is an estimate—but nevertheless one that can attain a satisfactory degree of accuracy provided expression is given to the several factors that tend to reduce useful life. Among the more common of these factors—applicable, for example, to a machine—are the following:

1. Use ("ordinary wear & tear"): A machine wears out as it is operated from day to day, and it can be expected to wear out much faster when used sixteen hours a day rather than eight.

2. Disuse: An idle machine becomes potentially less and less useful as time goes on; in fact certain machines, for example, farm implements standing in the open, may age even more speedily from disuse than from use.

3. Maintenance: A high standard of maintenance prolongs the life of an asset; from lack of maintenance or for want of skilled maintenance or operation a machine deteriorates rapidly.

4. Change in production: If the manufacturing process in which the machine is used is altered—for example, in the interest of increased over-all efficiency or because of a modification in a product line—the machine may not be adaptable to the change and its future productivity *to its owner* may be greatly lessened.

5. Restriction of production: When the source of supply of a raw material on which a machine operates becomes less or ceases

altogether (as from a natural cause or governmental order) the machine may have fewer employable service units to yield in succeeding periods.

6. Decrease in demand: The falling off in consumer use of products to which the machine contributes or the emergence of increased competition may also curtail its future employability.

7. Progress of the arts: When new devices are perfected and another machine has become available that will perform the same operation more simply, more quickly, or more cheaply, a machine's future usefulness to its owner may be seriously limited or cease altogether.

Obsolescence is loss of usefulness occasioned by progress of the arts or by such other external causes as changes in consumer demand and legislation or regulation leading to the reduction of future production (items 5, 6, and 7 above). *Inadequacy* is loss of usefulness brought about by business change; a building or machine may have to be replaced because it cannot be adjusted to a modified character or rate of output (item 4 above). Since obsolescence and inadequacy and the other factors above mentioned relate to conditions common to all business enterprise, they are normally regarded as determinants of periodic estimates of expired usefulness. To some extent they are always at work in any given collection of buildings, machines, and other limited-life fixed assets, and are closely interrelated and inseparable. Where the advent of any of these factors is sudden and cannot reasonably be anticipated, the obsolescence, inadequacy, or other cause is referred to as "extraordinary" and may be of such material amount as to require special treatment in the accounts and separate disclosure in the income statement.

Because the result produced by any one of these factors is virtually impossible to isolate and because all of them in varying degrees diminish the future usefulness of an asset or asset group, the combination is looked upon by accountants as *linear* in its effect. This means that, whatever the causes, depreciation has come to be almost universally regarded as a function of time. As a consequence, prevailing practice sanctions the spread of the cost of the depreciating asset (less any estimated salvage) over its likely useful life on any of several averaging (straight-line) bases.

There are other influences that have led accountants to the employment of linear methods in determining lost usefulness. One is that, although there has always been a general recognition of the superiority of basing depreciation expense on units of service yielded, it has been impossible to determine a usable service-unit cost because the quantity of potential service units residing in practically every fixed asset is subject to widely varying estimates.

Further, the experience gained from observing the history of fixed-asset usefulness has traditionally been expressed in terms of fixed-asset groups. What will happen to a group can be foretold with greater accuracy than what will happen to an individual asset. Accountants have tended to advocate the determination of depreciation expense by the application of average rates to asset groups. Statistical averages are thus commonly applied to the cost of an asset group in determining the portion of cost that is to be expensed for any year.

Depreciation formulas. It may be said, therefore, that depreciation-expense computations are based on the assumption that a fixed asset or fixed-asset group has a reasonably determinable life over which the cost or other basis may be distributed. In the past numerous proposals have been made for allocating asset costs over the expense accounts of successive periods. Some of these involve heavier charges in earlier years, others heavier charges in later years; "straight-line" methods attempt to equalize the spread on the assumption that in most situations the yield or loss of services tends to be the same, year after year.

1. *Straight-line formulas.* Straight-line methods attempt to spread over service life in amounts as nearly equal as possible the cost of an asset or asset group less whatever can be anticipated in the way of salvage. The following formula expresses the general basis:

$$d = \frac{q}{Q} (c - s), \tag{1}$$

where d is the depreciation expense; q the actual quantity of services given off during the period; Q the estimated quantity of service units that may be expected during the whole life of the asset; c the original cost; and s the portion of original cost estimated to be recoverable from salvage, that is, resale or scrap. Only in rare instances, however, as already noted. can the quantity of service units obtainable from the ordinary fixed asset or fixed-asset group of a manufacturing enterprise be measured. For most fixed assets there is no recognized unit of service, to say nothing of any estimate quantity of units that can be yielded during useful life.

Formula (1) is, however, basic for such wasting assets as coal, timber, and other natural products, in which case d becomes *depletion* expense, q the number of units currently extracted, and Q the estimate of total tons, square feet, or barrels available (including q). But since Q changes as new "proven" areas are developed under or on the land or lease of which c is the cost, a new rate may have to be established for the current year; and the formula becomes

$$d = \frac{q}{Q_1} (c - s - r), \tag{2}$$

Q_1 being the estimate of quantities removed in the current year and to be removed in future years, and r the balance of the reserve for depletion accumulated in and carried over from prior years. When rates (the fractions shown above) change because of subsequent re-estimates of available quantities, it is customary (a) to include all of the year of the change in the new computation and (b) not to alter accumulations of previous years: a procedure also applicable to depreciation computations.

In ordinary depreciation accounting, the simplest practice in determining annual depreciation expense is to apply a percentage rate to the cost of an asset group like "machinery," the formula being

$$d = \frac{1}{y} c, \tag{3}$$

where y is the estimated average number of years the group of assets is expected to be in use. The ratio $1/y$, expressed as a percentage, is a composite rate—one that may have application to many items of the same kind and even to many enterprises. Thus a common depreciation percentage that may be found in all sorts of business enterprise is the furniture-and-fixture annual rate of 10 per cent. As a composite rate it has evolved from general experience with large groups of fixed assets; applied to a particular enterprise, it may prove more conventional than accurate since it is not uncommon to find the cost of an asset group like furniture and fixtures completely written off, notwithstanding that the assets are still in use. Similarly, conventional rates may be applied to other classes of assets; these, too, may be found to be inaccurate when applied to individual enterprises, even though they may represent a reasonable average for an industry.

The above three formulas are so-called "straight-line" formulas, as are also the following two variants:

$$d = \frac{1}{y}\,(c - s) \qquad \text{and} \qquad (4)$$

$$d = \frac{1}{y_1}\,(c - s - r), \qquad (5)$$

where y is the number of years of useful life estimated from the time a new asset or asset group is acquired, y_1 the estimated number of years of remaining life *including the current year*, and r the balance of the reserve for depreciation brought forward from prior years. Each of these variants has its advocates, but in most instances when consistently followed they yield substantially the same results, notwithstanding theoretical distinctions. Of the five formulas, the last tends to be the most satisfactory, provided its application is accompanied from time to time by remaining-life studies leading to the correction of y_1.

2. The *sinking-fund formula* requires the periodic provision of a constant amount plus compound interest i on the accumulating reserve:

$$d = (c - s)\,\frac{i}{(1 + i)^n - 1}. \qquad (6)$$

The common objection to this and other compound-interest formulas is that interest is not recognized in accounting unless paid on borrowed money. For a machine expected to last ten years and having no scrap value the sinking-fund formula (with interest at 3 per cent) would call for a depreciation rate of 8.72 per cent in the first year and 11.38 per cent in the 10th; or, as some would have it, a depreciation rate of 8.72 per cent throughout the period and an "interest expense" increasing to 2.66 per cent in the last year of that period.

3. A variation of the preceding, the *annuity formula* (or compound-interest method) involves a constant amount (d) and two rates of interest—the interest return the asset is expected to yield on its unrecovered cost (i_2) during its estimated useful life of n years, and the interest (usually at a lower rate) the con-

stantly increasing reserve for depreciation is expected to earn (i_1):

$$d = (c - s) \left(i_2 + \frac{i_1}{(1 + i_1)^n - 1} \right) \qquad (7)$$

Thus if a machine is estimated to have a useful life of ten years and at the end of that time to have no salvage value, and during its life is expected to earn 6 per cent on its undepreciated cost (with 3 per cent on the amount accumulating as depreciation) the annual rate will be 14.72 per cent.

Though often referred to in the works of economists, engineers, and some accountants, and thus occasionally coming to the attention of the professional accountant, this and other interest methods have probably never been found in actual use.

4. Under the *reducing-balance method* a constant percentage is applied each period to the balance of the asset account at the end of the preceding period. A formula often cited as the basis of this method is

$$d = c \left(1 - \sqrt[n]{\frac{s}{c}} \right). \qquad (8)$$

If salvage of 10 per cent is assumed, the rate is found to be 20.5672 per cent; salvage of 1 per cent yields a rate of 36.9043 per cent, whereas salvage of $\frac{1}{10}$ per cent gives a rate of 49.8813 per cent. These fantastic variations in rate point to the absence of any relation between the formula and the fact of depreciation.

5. The *replacement method* of depreciation involves the charging of replacements at cost to expense as they are acquired, there being no depreciation reserve. This practice not infrequently meets with the approval of the auditor in connection with small tools and other fixed-asset groups made up of a large number of low-cost items.

6. The *retirement method* of depreciation provides only for the replacement cost of units expected to be retired during the next year or two. This method, at one time in vogue among public utilities, has now been abandoned.

Group depreciation. Group or composite depreciation methods have become standard for American business concerns. In typical instances these methods involve a number of coordinated practices such as the following:

1. An initial annual rate is selected for each fixed-asset class

from some standard guide, such as Bulletin F published by the Bureau of Internal Revenue of the U.S. Treasury. The general propriety of the rates of this pamphlet has been tested by years of experience in many lines of enterprise.

2. The rate is applied on a monthly basis to the total of the asset account at the beginning of the year or month, with half-rates applied to the net additions during the year to date or month. The amount thus determined is charged to current costs and credited to a reserve (allowance) for depreciation.

3. As the experience of the individual business grows, the rates are reviewed and where necessary modified for the current and succeeding years. Often recommendations for rate reductions are made by internal-revenue agents. External auditors may also provide tests for over- or underaccumulations.

4. Upon retirement the cost of an asset sold or scrapped, decreased by its net selling price or salvage, is removed from the asset account and charged to the reserve.

As noted above, depreciation can be measured with less error by a composite rate applied to a whole class of assets because the collective experience from which estimates of future usefulness necessarily derive has a more accurate application to a group than to an individual item.

Unit depreciation. Less common is the application of a depreciation formula to an individual asset. Such a method may be suggested by the detail commonly associated with a plant-ledger card; but a clear indication of the month and year the asset was first made available for productive use will in most cases supply all essential information if a determination of individual accrued depreciation is ever undertaken. Occasionally the depreciation of individual units is necessary—as where the unit represents a single large investment and its nature or behavior is such as to exclude it from any grouping with other assets.

Where a plant-ledger card is employed as the detail supporting depreciation provisions, the sum of the accumulated provisions on all cards may be made to agree with a general-ledger depreciation-reserve account. Some accountants believe this to be a desirable refinement of the methods previously described, provided formula (5) is applied to each item; statistically it offers no advantage over the results produced by the periodic application of formula (5) to an entire asset group.

Lapsing schedule. A further variant arises from the use of a lapsing schedule, a practice commonly followed by Federal internal-revenue agents; it is essentially the application of

formula (3) to each year's acquisitions, a separate schedule being
prepared for each principal class of fixed assets.

Fractional periods. Depreciation is often computed for fractional years on additions and retirements, an average of one-half
year being assumed, or it may be computed down to the month
or half-month. No objection can be raised to this procedure, but
no greater statistical accuracy is added by fractional-year depreciation adjustments for any one period unless there have been
major one-sided changes in fixed-asset accounts during such
period; even then the effect on the balance sheet and income
statement may be negligible.

Retirements. Where depreciation reserves have been built up
by the application of composite rates to asset groups, retirements
are best charged in full against the reserve, exceptions being made
only in the case of individual major assets that have been in use
substantially less than the average life of that class as reflected
in the depreciation rate. A "major" asset might be regarded for
this purpose as one whose cost is greater than 20 per cent of the
depreciation reserve applicable to that class of assets; a "substantially less" life might be one that does not exceed half of the
average for that class. These are not meant as general standards
but as useful sample tests that an auditor might employ in discussing with his client the effects of varying procedures. A more
common but statistically less desirable practice is to regard as
current expense or income any variation between the original
cost of an asset retired, less scrap value, and the proportional
depreciation accrued during the years an asset has been in use.
Thus, a machine, acquired at a cost of $1,000 and scrapped seven
years later, belongs to a class against which, it may be assumed,
an annual depreciation rate of 10 per cent has been applied. If a
half-year basis is followed for additions and retirements, or if
the balance at the beginning of each calendar year is the basis
for applying the depreciation rate, seven years' depreciation will
have been accumulated. With a scrap-value allowance in each
year's computation equal to 5 per cent of cost and with, say, a
presently expected realization of $100 from the sale of the ma-
chine, the problem of classifying the "unrecovered" cost of $235
remains. Is this a charge against the reserve for depreciation on
machinery, additional depreciation for the year, or a loss on the
disposal of fixed assets? Preference is given to the first alternative because a composite rate of depreciation will often result
in apparent overprovision in the case of assets in use for periods
longer than the average, and the remaining cost of $235 will ordi-

narily be absorbed where such averages are in use. The second method can be justified statistically if it can be demonstrated that the average rate of 10 per cent is too low for the class of assets as a whole, but usually such a demonstration is impossible unless a relatively large number of premature retirements have been experienced. The effect of the second method is to modify the annual provision for depreciation by the amount of the net excess of the "underprovision" or "overprovision," respectively. The third method, although often found in practice, should be confined to situations involving a material amount where a sale is made of an asset that, if not sold, would continue to yield useful services to the business. Classification in the second or third category often arises because of the failure to recognize the principle of averages involved in depreciation rates and reserves.

Where depreciation records are on a unit basis, the first of the above three alternatives is automatically ruled out because the reserve or allowance for depreciation is a controlling account and any of the items of which it is composed can be identified with but one item of property. Any adjustment, therefore, upon retirement is regarded as a gain or loss either affecting the amount of depreciation currently reported as an expense or appearing as a separate item on the income statement, the former having some preference.

Occasionally adjustments growing out of the disposal of items of depreciable fixed assets are treated as capital gains or losses and are credited or charged direct to earned surplus. However, the adjustment would not have been required if depreciation had been more exactly computed during the years the assets were in use; it seems inescapable, therefore, that the adjustment is simply the consequence of past years' over- or underprovisions for accruing depreciation. As with other adjustments arising from imperfect accruals it is satisfactorily disposed of by combining it with the current year's provisions.

Many accountants accept the practice of removing from the accounts the costs of fixed assets shown by lapsing schedules to be wholly depreciated. This practice may be modified in instances where larger retirements are individually recorded, but the practice is recognized as a much less desirable alternative to the reporting and recording of a retired asset only as the retirement takes place.

Tests for adequacy. To test the propriety of an annual provision for depreciation an engineering survey may be made by examining each asset covered by the reserve and estimating its remaining years of useful life. A "book value" for each asset, consisting of original cost less accumulated depreciation at rates in force since its acquisition, is then determined and divided by the estimated years of remaining useful life. The sum of the quotients thus obtained, divided by the total original cost of the same asset group, indicates the theoretical rate that should apply. The same basic data will also serve in a test for reserve adequacy.

Depletion. Depletion, like depreciation, involves the recognition as an operating cost of a portion of a fixed-asset outlay. The determination of the fraction to be expensed, however, requires an estimate of total available quantity: a figure concerning which no estimate may be readily available. The practice exists in some companies not to account for depletion, the theory being that to provide a base upon which a depletion computation might be made would mislead investors. The base in the case of certain nonferrous mineral deposits is said to be unknown or to be of such a shifting character that a computation based on information available in one year would mean nothing in the next. Sometimes it is claimed for an oil-producing company or for the owner of timber tracts that exhaustion each year is exceeded by new discoveries or growth. The corporation laws of a number of mining states permit the payment of dividends from income before provision for depletion.

Notwithstanding difficulties of estimation, the preferred practice is to provide for depletion even though frequent redeterminations of the base are required.

Internal Controls

The most satisfactory standard of depreciation practice is to determine through careful study a composite annual rate for each of the main fixed-asset groups or an individual rate for items that cannot be grouped; to apply each rate consistently until study at a subsequent date indicates that a change is in order— a change to be applied, however, only to the current period and future periods; to absorb in the reserve or allowance account the full cost, less salvage, of each asset retired; and to provide periodic tests of reserve adequacy.

Determining rates. Within every organization some one person or group should be charged with the responsibility for devising and maintaining proper rates of depreciation. Commencing with those common to similar types of enterprises, the rates adopted should in the course of years acquire an individuality peculiar to the particular business; and the experience reflected by such rates should be capable of standing up well under whatever tests the auditor may see fit to apply.

Modifying rates. During a war period, several causes contribute to greatly accelerated accumulations of depreciation in corporate enterprise. High prices, established or tolerated by government procurement agencies because of their presumed effect in stimulating the production of materials of war, lead to substantial profits and the incentive to show increased costs as the justification therefor. Accelerated depreciation, called *amortization* in both world wars, has been permitted under the Federal income-tax laws, likewise as a stimulant to war production. The future utility of new plants, or of old plants adapted to war production, is always problematical. At the end of World War II, a review by the author of the balance sheets of one hundred leading industrial corporations indicated that the ratio of depreciation reserves to fixed assets varied between 28 per cent and 86 per cent, with an average somewhat in excess of 50 per cent. These ratios decreased as war plants were sold or abandoned, then increased again with the resumption of the defense effort. Suggestions that these ratios be revised downward by the transfer of "excess" depreciation to earned surplus were, however, hardly attuned to corporate responsibility to the public. A better plan has been to follow the prefered standard practice, already referred to in a preceding paragraph, for revising future depreciation charges; it may be restated thus:

> Where studies indicate that the recorded accrued depreciation of an asset or asset group is over- or under-stated, the current rate of depreciation should be so adjusted as to spread equitably any unrecovered cost over remaining useful life.

An exception might be made where, because of a management decision or other anticipated cause, obsolescence must be recognized in a substantial amount; in that event the resultant sudden increase in the depreciation reserve, or the writedown of remaining cost, may be important enough to be shown as a separate item in the income statement of the current period. Accountants should take a firm stand against the restoration of depreciated costs. Cost, once recovered, should be forgotten. To seek to recover the same cost twice would not only be poor accounting, but where the excessive depreciation was accumulated during the war or defense period it would conflict squarely with the public policy that gave rise to the higher prices or lower taxes that the owner of the assets enjoyed.

The auditor should always seek to keep management policy controlling depreciation on an objective level, and to encourage periodic engineering studies and internal reviews of depreciation rates and reserve adequacy as a major feature of information and control.

Financial-Statement Standards

In the income statement the amount of depreciation expense is shown on the face of the statement or in a footnote. The amount of any amortization provided under permissive tax laws or of any other form of extraordinary depreciation or obsolescence also appears as a separate item.

In financial statements the current provision for depreciation appears in either of two ways. If it has been regarded as a period charge, it will be found as an item in the income statement. If it has been treated as an item of plant overhead, it lies "buried" partly in the closing inventory and partly in the cost of sales, a footnote to the income statement revealing the total amount. Either treatment meets with the auditor's approval, although some preference to look at depreciation expense as a period charge has been noted.

Where depreciation or depletion expense for income-tax purposes differs from that appearing in the income statement by an amount greater than, say, 10 per cent of the latter or 5 per cent of the net income for the period, a footnote to the income statement may be employed to reveal the amount and the reason therefor.

Depreciation reserves on the balance sheet are now as a general rule subtracted from the assets to which they relate. The principal exception may be found in public utilities a few of which are still not on a full "depreciation basis"—that is, their reserves cover only fairly immediate replacements and are classed with other reserves on the liability side of the statement; but the better practice, reflected in the requirements of regulatory bodies, is to subtract the reserves from the assets even though they may not have reached their proper level, since they are still valuation accounts notwithstanding their insufficiency. A reserve for amortization (the 20-per-cent-per-annum reserves permitted under the Federal income-tax law) may appear as a separate item along with depreciation reserves, or the amount thereof may be disclosed in the depreciation-reserve sidehead. A practice of several companies is to subtract the provision for amortization directly from the assets concerned and show only the net figure on the balance sheet; but since amortization is simply rapid obsolescence and therefore a form of depreciation, there seems to be no good reason for this exceptional treatment.

Summary details of annual changes in fixed assets and depreciation reserves in schedule form accompany a few published financial statements. The practice is an excellent one and deserves a larger following. Such a schedule follows:

M COMPANY
Statement of Changes in Fixed-Asset
Costs & Reserves for Depreciation
Year ended December 31, 19–1
(thousands of dollars)

Asset group	Balance Jan. 1, 19–1	Retirements	Additions	Balance Dec. 31, 19–1
Land	15.2		2.6	17.8
Buildings	396.1	32.6	53.8	417.3
Machinery	584.5	87.0	116.2	613.7
Office equipment	78.3	3.9	9.4	83.8
Totals	1,074.1	123.5	182.0	1,132.6

Depreciation reserves	Balance Jan. 1, 19–1	Retirements	Realized on disposal	Provisions for year	Dec. 31, 19–1
Buildings	134.5	32.6	3.8	8.2	113.9
Machinery	264.1	87.0	25.1	47.9	250.1
Office equipment	22.0	3.9	.4	8.1	26.6
Totals	420.6	123.5	29.3	64.2	390.6

Representative Audit Program

1. Obtain or prepare analysis of changes during the audit period in each depreciation reserve; compare opening totals with previous year's papers, depreciation provisions with related expense accounts, charges to the reserves with the corresponding credits in the analysis of fixed-asset changes, and the closing balance with the current trial balance.

2. Review any engineering or statistical studies of depreciation rates made during the period.

3. Review method of computing depreciation and verify provisions for year. Ascertain reasons for any variation of rates or method of computation as compared with previous year or with "standard" rates.

4. Examine most recent report of Federal internal-revenue agent on depreciation, and if it is not in agreement with books, ascertain whether differences have been studied and note the results of any conferences with BIR representatives.

5. Where sales or other disposal credits appear in the reserve analysis, trace representative transactions from authorization to realization. Follow the same procedure for sales of fixed assets accounted for through profit and loss where the whole cost of the retirement has not been deducted from the reserve.

6. Compute percentage relationship of reserve balances with corresponding assets and, in adding summary data to permanent file, note percentage trends for past ten years. Discuss generally these trends and the depreciation problem with management charged with depreciation responsibility.

Audit Procedures

An audit of changes in reserves for depreciation necessarily includes an examination of depreciation expense as well, and the working papers should be prepared accordingly. A first step is an analysis of each reserve or allowance account that will bring out the depreciation expense for the period, sales and other retirements, adjustments, and opening and closing balances. The bulk of such analyses are advantageously prepared during the preliminary audit so that general policy and any changes therein or in procedures can be reviewed and approved or corrected before the books are formally closed. The schedules are then completed after the close of the period. While preparing the schedules the auditor usually notes any major modification of method as compared with the preceding year—changes in rates or bases or in the distribution of the cost; sources and character of adjustments; the recognition of retirements and the sources of information thereon.

The examination of depreciation and fixed-asset accounts should be made at the same time. The auditor should make sure that adjustments found in depreciation accounts are fully reflected in the property accounts and that adjustments of the latter, including retirements, are recognized in their proper amount in the depreciation accounts.

Changes in rates or methods of accrual should be discussed with those responsible for instituting them. Whatever the method of recording depreciation, provision should be made for the prompt correction of existing rates and such changes if approved by the auditor should not be regarded as a violation of the principle of consistency. Disclosure in financial statements of rate changes are not ordinarily required. An exception lies where a rate is arbitrarily changed to one that is out of line with previous rates and in conflict with the judgment of the auditor. The following language appeared in a recent certificate of a public accountant:

> During the year the annual rate of depreciation on machinery was changed from $7\frac{1}{2}\%$—a rate which, based on the past experience of the company, we consider to be a proper one—to $2\frac{1}{2}\%$, the effect being a reduction in machinery-depreciation expense from $17,892.56 to $5,964.19 and a reduction in the net loss from operations. Had the higher figure prevailed the net loss of $334.82 for the year would have been increased to $12,263.19. . . .

The qualification of the net-income figure implicit in the above language leads the reader to conclude that the change of rate was an attempt by management to improve the showing of the results from operations. Had the rate reduction been based on engineering studies of machinery life, decreased usage (not reflecting obsolescence or inadequacy), and other factors, the auditor would doubtless have concluded that no qualification of his opinion of the propriety of the financial statements would have been necessary.

A careful review should be made of any recent depreciation analysis by an internal-revenue agent. This may appear in a regular or special report and may bring to light past transactions, agreements with the taxpayer on method, comparisons with the experience of enterprises similarly situated, and other information that may influence the auditor's conclusions. Any new agreement or acceptance of findings within the last year should be carefully reviewed with the client's officials.

Illustrative Audit

The form of J 1 is somewhat different from that of H 1 because of the desire to display subtotals of charges to three expense accounts. The explanations at the bottom bring out the method by which depreciation was computed, the details of computation being supplied by PF 71, 72, and 73. It will be observed from a study of H 3 and the three permanent-file schedules that the accounting-and-retirement units are the principal building components, the individual machines, items of furniture and fixtures, and individual trucks and automobiles. The depreciation units are the class balances at the beginning of each year except for furniture and fixtures where the depreciation unit is each year's acquisitions, and trucks and automobiles where the depreciation unit is the individual asset.

Auditing depreciation is not a matter of examining vouchers and proving physical existence but involves rather a determination of policy, the translation of policy into periodic provisions, and a frequent, objective judgment of the adequacy of provisions and reserves. Running comparisons such as those appearing in the three permanent-file schedules provide the auditor with quick comparisons of rates, amounts, and balances and aid him materially in drawing conclusions. Tests of adequacy such as that afforded by J 2 also supply him—as well as management—with a solid basis for an opinion of the effectiveness of the depreciation rates and methods that have been employed over a series of years.

The original cost of retirements of fixed assets during the year was $147,026.76, as shown in column 3 of worksheet H 1. The portion of the depreciation reserve allocable to these retirements was $146,317.65, the difference of $709.11 being attributable to the insufficiency of the reserve identified with the retirements of furniture and fixtures ($209.11) and trucks and automobiles ($500.00). The last two amounts are the differences resulting from comparisons of the amounts pertaining to these classes reflected in columns 1 and 3 of worksheet H 3a. A reconciliation of the two retirement totals aids in the preparation of income-tax schedules, reports to the SEC and other agencies, and statements of application of funds.

Worksheet J 2 is an example of a test of adequacy described on p. 400. Such a study is most effective where the results can be presented in such a way that they can be reviewed by several persons familiar with the nature of the operations but having varied points of view and interests. The careful preparation and review of tests of this character, whether covering an entire plant or representative samples (in larger organizations), have the effect of raising the provision for depreciation from the status of a permissible deduction or "good guess" to a statistical judgment in the formation of which engineering determinations and top-management policy play an essential part.

Martin Manufacturing Company
Reserves for Depreciation
Year ended December 31, 1952

F.L.
2-7-53

Item	Balance 12-31-51	Provisions 1952 %	Amount	Retirements	Balances December 31, 1952 as adjusted	Adjustments	Books unadjusted
FACTORY							
Buildings—							
Foundry	250 879 73 *3		14 676 73	27 519 37	238 037 09	13) + 568 77	237 468 32
Factory	74 896 22 *2		3 293 99	15 008 73	63 181 48	13) + 125 97	63 055 51
Machinery—							
Foundry	56 921 06 *4		5 859 82	−252 00 / 4 927 86	58 105 02	13) + 317 96	57 787 06
Factory	228 062 76 *5		19 261 77	−3 608 50 / 45 912 37	205 020 66	13) + 379 76	204 640 90
Patterns, etc.	212 579 91 *10		25 899 70	−500 00 / 48 826 02	190 153 59	13) + 746 63	189 406 96
Trucks	7 648 59 *-		2 228 87	−	9 877 46	14) + 28 87	9 848 59
Subtotal (A/c 2441)			71 220 88 × TB				
SELLING							
Autos	5 182 71 *-		1 287 50	−500 00 / 3 270 00	3 700 21	14) − 12 50	3 712 71
ADMINISTRATION							
Office bldg.	53 423 68 *2		2 229 09	−	55 652 77		55 652 77
Furn. + fixt.	11 526 78 *5		1 562 99	−209 11 / 1 562 41	11 736 47	14) − 187 01	11 923 48
Subtotal			3 792 08 ×				
Totals	901 121 44 ×		76 300 46 ×	−5 069 61× / 147 026 76×	835 464 75 ×	+ 1 968 45×	833 496 30× TB

Work done—

The above summary was prepared from an analysis of G/L accounts. Balances at 12/31/51 were compared with last year's papers. (×)

No changes in depreciation policy or rates were made during the year. Composite rates have been applied to balances at the beginning of the year for buildings, machinery, and equipment. For these assets, reserves are charged with original cost of retirements, and credited with recoveries; depreciation during the year was erroneously computed on the basis of opening balances at 1/1/51 instead of 1/1/52; see AJE #13. A rate of 5% is being applied to each year's additions to furniture and fixtures and a lapsing schedule is maintained for this account. Individual rates ranging from 20% to 33⅓% are applied to individual units of trucks and automobiles after deduction of estimated salvage. On retirements of furniture + fixtures and trucks + automobiles a gain or loss is recognized on individual items and carried to shop expense (trucks) and automobile expense, selling (autos). During the year depreciation was computed on an estimated basis for these two classes of assets; see AJE #14.

In Dec. 1952 Mr. Shuffle and Carl Hibbs tested the composite rate on foundry machinery and equipment (see J-2). No adjustment required.

Present rates, ok'd by the BIR in 1945, applied since 1941.

See PF-71, 72, 73 for summary of depreciation provisions and reserves.

J-1

Martin Manufacturing Company
Foundry machinery
Test of Depreciation Expense and Depreciation-Reserve Adequacy
Year ended December 31, 1952

qr

Particulars	Property Card No.	Year Acquired	y	r	yr	1-yr	Y	$\frac{1-yr}{Y}$	C	P	R
Retired in 1952-											
Crucible furnace	F-41	1929	22	.04	.88	.12	1	.12	4300 00	516 00	4113 00
Bin	F-12	1922	29	✓	1.16	-.16	1	-.16	270 00	- 43 20	261 00
Small items									105 86	57 93	58 00
Items over $10,000 in use -											
Osborn molder	F-1303	1951	0	✓	.0	1	25	.04	10 286 33	411 45	0
High pressure die caster	F-473	1943	8	✓	.32	.68	10	.068	25 106 98	1 707 27	11 159 00
Open-hearth furnace	F-87	1933	18	✓	.72	.28	14	.02	35 590 30	711 81	20 020 00
[6 other items omitted here]											
Items under $10,000 in use -											
Core blower	F-1301	1951	0	✓	0	1	25	.04	3 513 25	140 53	0
Molding machine	F-1237	1950	1	✓	.04	.96	30	.032	3 220 00	103 04	104 00
[68 other items omitted here]											
Totals									- 14 649 55↑ / 146 495 50↑	6 034 39↑	58 369 00
Provision at 4% for 1952 and actual reserve balance at December 31, 1951										5 859 82	56 921 00
Apparent underprovision - too small for adjustment										174 57↑	1 448 00

Explanation of symbols:

y = years of use (to 1-1-52)

r = composite rate in use during y

yr = fraction of cost depreciated prior to 1952

$1-yr$ = fraction of cost to be depreciated in 1952 and succeeding years

Y = estimated remaining years in use - 1952 and thereafter

$\dfrac{1-yr}{Y}$ = necessary current and future annual rate to recover cost

$\dfrac{y}{y+Y}$ = theoretical balance of reserve at beginning of 1952

Explanation of symbols (Cont'd):

C = cost, plus freight and installation; less estimated scrap of 10% representing the average recovery on more than 250 retirements since 1933

P = apparent requirement for 1952 provision =

$$Cost \times \frac{1-yr}{Y}$$

R = apparent requirement for reserve balance at December 31, 1951 =

$$Cost \times \frac{y}{y+Y}$$

Conclusions:

Tests similar to the above have been made over a series of years, the effort being to compare composite with individual-item depreciation. Because of rounded-out estimates of remaining life, the book figures are deemed to be sufficiently close as to require no adjustment.

J-2a

Particulars / Account no.	Land Cost 91-11	Foundry Cost 91-121	Building Reserve 92-121	Factory Cost 91-122	Buildings Reserve 92-122
August 1, 1941	25 000 00	192 842 16	174 811 90	75 477 42	53 306 55
Additions	-	-	3 2 410 53	-	2 628 98
Retirements	-	-	-	-	-
December 31, 1941	25 000 00	192 842 16	177 222 43	75 477 42	53 935 53
Additions	-	224 247 26	3 5785 26	-	2 1 509 55
Retirements	-	-8 105 55	146 50 / -8 103 55	-	-
December 31, 1942	25 000 00	408 983 87	175 048 64	75 477 42	55 445 08
Additions	-	2 342 18	3 1226 9 52	-	2 1 509 55
Retirements	-	- 500 00	10 50 / -500 00	-	-
December 31, 1943	25 000 00	410 826 05	186 828 66	75 477 42	56 954 63
Additions	-	16 466 80	3 1232 4 78	-	2 1 509 55
Retirements	-	-2 028 04	-202 804	-	-
December 31, 1944	25 000 00	425 264 81	197 125 40	75 477 42	58 464 18
Additions	-	5 050 81	3 1275 7 94	35 028 90	2 1 509 55
Retirements	-	-10 252 25	150 02 / -10 252 25	-2 213 33	132 02 / -2 213 33
December 31, 1945	25 000 00	420 063 37	199 781 19	108 292 99	57 892 42
Additions	-	52 176 52	3 1260 1 90	-	2 2 165 86
Retirements	-	-657 0 20	-6570 20	-	-
December 31, 1946	25 000 00	465 669 69	205 812 89	108 292 99	60 058 28
Additions	-	-	3 13970 09	50 108 20	2 2 165 86
Retirements	-	-10 980 00	-10 980 00	-	-
December 31, 1947	25 000 00	454 689 69	208 802 98	158 401 19	62 224 14
Additions	-	-	3 13640 69	-	2 3 168 02
Retirements	-	-	-	-	-
December 31, 1948	25 000 00	454 689 69	222 443 67	158 401 19	65 392 16
Additions	-	15 575 50	3 13640 69	-	2 3 168 02
Retirements	-	-	-	-	-
December 31, 1949	25 000 00	470 265 19	236 084 36	158 401 19	68 560 18
Additions	-	-	3 14 107 96	-	2 3 168 02
Retirements	-	-	-	-	-
December 31, 1950	25 000 00	470 265 19	250 192 32	158 401 19	71 728 20
Additions	-	3 258 90	3 14 107 96	6 298 15	2 3 168 02
Retirements	-	-13 621 75	201 20 / -13 621 75	-	-
December 31, 1951	25 000 00	489 224 34	250 879 73	164 699 34	74 896 22
Additions	-	95 768 29	3 14 676 73	325 127 89	2 3 293 99
Retirements	-	-27 519 37	-27 519 37	-15 008 73	-15 008 73
December 31, 1952	25 000 00	557 473 26	238 037 09	474 818 50	63 181 48

Bases: Additions: cost. Depreciation: composite, except on F&F and T&A; F&F based on lapsing schedule; T&A based on individual items

Office Building Cost 91-123	Office Building Reserve 92-123	Foundry Machinery Cost 91-131	Foundry Machinery Reserve 92-131	Factory Machinery Cost 91-132	Factory Machinery Reserve 92-132	Patterns & Cost 91-134
–	–	46 815 92	34 571 19	184 682 11	148 972 14	126 872 42
Ⓐ 105 422 13	– 31 253 43	30 500 00 4	780 27	26 843 42 5	3 847 54	4 624 18
					4 650 00	
–	–	–	–	–32 867 20	–32 867 20	–847 60
105 422 13	31 253 43	77 315 92	35 351 46	178 658 33	124 602 48	130 649 00
6 032 57 2	2 108 44	16 812 03 4	3 092 64	47 204 18 5	8 932 92	12 018 81
			640 12		22 465 10	
–	–	–920 03	–920 03	–24 139 12	–24 139 12	–10 277 15
111 454 70	33 361 87	93 207 92	38 164 19	201 723 39	131 861 38	132 390 66
– 2	2 229 09	42 944 57 4	3 728 32	2 463 01 5	10 086 17	18 617 25
			1 250 00		10 22	
–	–	–2 500 00	–2 500 00	–1 250 00	–1 250 00	–4 250 04
111 454 70	35 590 96	133 652 49	40 642 51	202 936 40	140 707 77	146 757 87
– 2	2 229 09	46 00 4	5 346 10	5 389 63 5	10 146 82	15 979 43
			48 449 92		2 55 00	
–	–	–57 216 18	–57 216 18	–3 764 79	–3 764 79	–15 421 00
111 454 70	37 820 05	76 897 31	37 222 35	204 561 24	147 344 80	147 316 30
– 2	2 229 09	26 640 79 4	3 075 89	132 419 11 5	10 228 06	107 052 61
					2 820 50	
–	–	–	–	–19 977 51	–19 977 51	–9 011 15
111 454 70	40 049 14	103 538 10	40 298 24	317 002 84	140 415 85	245 357 76
– 2	2 229 09	30 908 50 4	4 141 52	2 781 09 5	15 850 14	21 181 20
–	–	–	–	–	–	–35 740 80
111 454 70	42 278 23	134 446 60	44 439 76	319 783 93	156 265 99	230 798 16
– 2	2 229 09	– 4	5 377 86	58 950 95 5	15 989 20	12 328 75
			250 00		1 901 70	
–	–	–3 450 00	–3 450 00	–15 705 62	–15 705 62	–5 160 52
111 454 70	44 507 32	130 996 60	46 617 62	363 029 26	158 451 27	237 966 39
– 2	2 229 09	– 4	5 239 86	5 109 90 5	18 151 46	8 909 54
–	–	–	–	–	–	–12 167 63
111 454 70	46 736 41	130 996 60	51 857 48	368 139 16	176 602 73	234 708 30
– 2	2 229 09	7 550 00 4	5 239 86	2 420 07 5	1 840 6 96	18 606 01
–	–	–	–	–	–	–6 892 82
111 454 70	48 965 50	138 546 60	57 097 34	370 559 23	195 009 69	246 421 49
– 2	2 229 09	–	5 541 86	7 080 90 5	1 852 7 96	7 718 54
–	–	–	–	–	–	–2 609 37
111 454 70	51 194 59	138 546 60	62 639 20	377 640 13	213 537 65	251 530 66
– 2	2 229 09	20 108 90 4	5 541 86	12 704 20 5	18 882 01	10 675 72
			900 00			
–	–	–12 160 00	–12 160 00	–5 108 90	–5 108 90	–3 209 35
111 454 70	53 423 68	146 495 50	56 921 06	385 235 43	228 062 76	258 997 03
– 2	2 229 09	65 203 74 4	5 859 82	175 609 72 5	19 261 77	32 092 67
			252 00		3 608 50	
–	–	–4 927 86	–4 927 86	–45 912 37	–45 912 37	–48 826 02
111 454 70	55 652 77	206 771 38	58 105 02	514 932 78	205 020 66	242 263 68

(continued)

	Flasks Reserve 92-134	Furniture + Fixtures Cost 91-16	Reserve 92-16	Trucks v Automobiles Cost 91-17	Reserve 92-17	Total Cost -	Reserve -
	108 112 01	15 990 50	12 562 25	4 784 24	2 249 21	672 464 77	534 585 25
10	5 286 35	- 5	333 14	4 646 00 25	498 36	172 035 73 Ⓑ	45 038 60
					300 00		4 950 00
	-847 60	-	-	-1 020 00	-1 020 00	-34 734 80	-34 734 80
	112 550 76	15 990 50	12 895 39	8 410 24	2 027 57	809 765 70	549 839 05
10	13 064 90	8 211 29 5	799 53	- 25	2 102 56	314 526 14	37 395 80
	17 50		250 00				23 519 22
	-10 277 15	-6 656 69	-6 656 69	-	-	-50 098 54	-50 098 54
	115 356 01	17 545 10	7 288 23	8 410 24	4 130 13	1 074 193 30	560 655 53
10	13 239 07	- 5	877 26	- 25	2 102 56	66 367 01	46 041 54
	20 50						1 291 22
	-4 250 04	-	-	-	-	-8 500 04	-8 500 04
	124 365 54	17 545 10	8 165 49	8 410 24	6 232 69	1 132 060 27	599 488 25
10	14 675 79	4 500 00 5	877 26	8 151 31 25	2 102 56	50 948 17	49 211 95
	1 667 31				500 00		50 872 23
	-15 421 00	-	-	-6 134 05	-6 134 05	-84 564 06	-84 564 06
	125 287 64	22 045 10	9 042 75	10 427 50	2 701 20	1 098 444 38	615 008 37
10	14 731 63	3 109 79 5	1 102 26	1 200 00 25	2 606 88	310 502 01	48 241 30
	404 13		160 64		350 00		40 017 39
	-9 011 15	-856 95	-856 95	-1 610 00	-1 610 00	-43 921 19	-43 921 19
	131 412 25	24 297 94	9 448 70	10 017 50	4 048 08	1 365 025 20	623 345 87
10	24 535 78	1 501 75 Ⓓ	1 631 19	5 010 00 Ⓒ	1 189 12	113 559 06	64 344 60
	1 208 60						1 208 60
	-35 740 80	-1 10 68	-1 10 68	-1 756 00	-791 00	-45 176 68	-44 211 68
	121 415 83	24 690 01	9 970 21	13 271 50	4 446 20	1 433 407 58	644 687 39
10	23 079 82	-	866 14	7 420 00	2 890 94	128 807 90	66 569 00
	102 67						2 254 37
	-5 160 52	-208 75	-208 75	-4 142 31	-2 717 38	-39 647 20	-38 222 27
	139 437 80	24 481 26	10 627 60	16 549 19	4 619 76	1 522 568 28	675 288 49
10	23 796 64	2 408 66	925 99	3 580 00	3 576 38	20 008 10	70 728 13
	475 15						475 15
	-12 167 63	-705 98	-200 03	-2 253 00	-1 500 56	-15 126 61	-13 873 22
	151 541 96	26 183 94	11 353 56	17 876 19	6 690 58	1 527 449 77	732 618 55
10	23 470 83	7 508 17	1 050 36	2 280 00	3 436 66	53 939 75	70 642 47
	307 80						307 80
	-6 892 82	-3 491 71	-3 491 71	-2 050 00	-1 134 38	-12 434 53	-11 518 91
	168 427 77	30 200 40	8 912 21	18 106 19	8 992 86	1 568 954 99	792 049 91
10	24 642 15	-	1 319 39	3 150 00	3 470 63	17 949 44	73 007 06
	75 62						75 62
	-2 609 37	-292 19	-68 18	-2 960 00	-2 101 25	-5 861 56	-4 778 80
	190 536 17	29 908 21	10 163 42	18 296 19	10 362 24	1 581 042 87	860 353 79
10	25 153 07	1 801 60	1 363 36	3 925 00	3 469 06	88 094 47	73 914 43
	100 02						1 953 22
	-3 209 35	-	-	-1 200 00	-1 000 00	-35 300 00	-35 100 00
	212 579 91	31 709 81	11 526 78	21 021 19	12 831 30	1 633 837 34	901 121 44
10	25 899 70	6 110 00	1 562 99	7 660 00	3 516 37	707 572 31	76 300 46
	500 00						4 360 50
	-48 826 02	-1 562 41	-1 353 30	-3 270 00	-2 770 00	-147 026 76	-146 317 65
	190 153 59	36 257 40	11 736 47	25 411 19	13 577 67	2 194 382 89	835 464 75

Notes—

Ⓐ Purchased from B Mfg. Co., fully owned subsidiary to whom rent of $15,000 per annum had been previously paid; recorded, as shown here, at cost to B. less accrued depreciation shown on B's books.

Ⓑ Includes accrued depreciation of $31,253.43, at date of purchase of building.

Ⓒ As of 1/1/46, depreciation on a unit basis was instituted retroactive to 8/1/41; the difference of $997.17 between accrued depreciation at 12/31/45 on the composite basis ($4,048.08) and on the unit basis ($3,050.91) was deducted from the depreciation provision for 1946 of $2,186.29 leaving a net expense for 1946 of $1,189.12.

Ⓓ As of 1/1/46, depreciation on furniture and fixtures was determined by use of a lapsing schedule for the entire history of the account commencing on 8/1/41; the $808.85 represents the amount necessary to bring the 12/31/45 balance of accrued depreciation to the amount shown by the lapsing schedule is included in the amount of depreciation for 1946.

PF-71c

a/c 91-16
a/c 92-16

Rate 5%

Date of Acquisition	Disposal	Cost Total	Detail	Accumulated balance	1941	1942 (D)
8- 1- 41		15 990 50	15 990 50	(a) 12 562 25	333 14	799 53
4- 8- 42			3 198 41	—	—	106 61
7- 21- 42			5 012 88	—	—	104 44
8- 1- 41	7- 31- 42	17 545 10	-6 656 69	—	—	-138 70
9- 15- 44		22 045 10	4 500 00	—	—	—
1- 19- 45			821 16	—	—	—
8- 1- 41	5- 4- 45		-856 95	—	—	—
10- 21- 45		24 297 94	2 288 63	—	—	—
7- 8- 46			1 501 75	—	—	—
8- 1- 41	7- 10- 46	24 690 01	-1 109 68	—	—	—
8- 1- 41	11- 2- 47	24 481 26	-208 75	—	—	—
3- 16- 48			1 927 92	—	—	—
7- 21- 42	3- 16- 48		-705 98	—	—	—
5- 9- 48		26 183 94	480 74	—	—	—
8- 21- 49			1 253 81	—	—	—
9- 18- 49			6 254 36	—	—	—
8- 1- 41	10- 3- 49	30 200 40	-3 491 71	—	—	—
10- 21- 45	6- 8- 50	29 908 21	-292 19	—	—	—
2- 10- 51			659 95	—	—	—
7- 6- 51		31 709 81	1 141 65	—	—	—
4- 18- 52			3 972 59	—	—	—
8- 6- 52			2 137 41	—	—	—
8- 1- 41	8- 8- 52		-1 129 76	—	—	—
4- 8- 42	8- 8- 52	36 257 40	-432 65	—	—	—

(a) Ratio of reserve to cost on 8-1-41 is 78.5%.

Yearly total				12 562 25	333 14	871 88
Accrued at retirement				—	—	-555 833
Balance in reserve at 12-31				12 562 25	12 895 39"	8 208 94"

PF- 72

-416-

...facturing Company   Procedure: (1) Depreciation base — balance at beginning of month.
...nd Fixtures   (1a) End of depreciation period — end of month of retirement.
for Depreciation   (2) Recognition of retirement — end of month of retirement.
    (3) Reporting method — loss or gain recognized on removal.

e	p	r	e	c	i	a
1943	1944	1945	1946	1947	1948	1949
799 53	799 53	696 52	—	—	—	—
159 92	159 92	159 92	159 92	159 92	159 92	159 92
250 64	250 64	250 64	250 64	250 64	250 64	250 64
-332 83	-332 83	-294 00	—	—	—	—
—	56 25	225 00	225 00	225 00	225 00	225 00
—	—	37 64	41 06	41 06	41 06	41 06
—	—	-20 00				
—	—	19 07	114 43	114 43	114 43	114 43
—	—	—	31 29	75 09	75 09	75 09
—	—	—	—	—	—	—
—	—	—	—	—	—	—
—	—	—	—	—	72 30	96 40
—	—	—	—	—	-26 47	-35 30
—	—	—	—	—	14 02	24 04
—	—	—	—	—	—	20 90
—	—	—	—	—	—	78 18
—	—	—	—	—	—	—
—	—	—	—	—	—	—
—	—	—	—	—	—	—
—	—	—	—	—	—	—
—	—	—	—	—	—	—
—	—	—	—	—	—	—
877 26	933 51	1 074 79	822 34	866 14	925 99	1 050 36
—	—	-836 95	-1 109 68	-208 75	-200 03	-349 71
-9 086 20	10 019 71	10 257 55	9 970 21	10 627 60	11 353 56	8 912 21

Martin Manufacturing Company
Furniture and Fixtures
Reserve for Depreciation

(continued)

	1950	1951	1952	1953	1954	1955	Total to be carried forward
	-	-	-	-	-	-	1599 50
	159 92	159 92	159 92	159 92	159 92	159 92	2185 57
	250 64	250 64	250 64	250 64	250 64	250 64	3362 76
	-	-	-	-	-	-	-1098 36
	225 00	225 00	225 00	225 00	225 00	225 00	2531 25
	41 06	41 06	41 06	41 06	41 06	41 06	448 24
	-	-	-	-	-	-	-20 00
	114 43	114 43	114 43	114 43	114 43	114 43	1163 37
	75 09	75 09	75 09	75 09	75 09	75 09	707 10
	-	-	-	-	-	-	-
	-	-	-	-	-	-	-
	96 40	96 40	96 40	96 40	96 40	96 40	747 10
	-35 30	-35 30	-35 30	-35 30	-35 30	-35 30	-273 57
	24 04	24 04	24 04	24 04	24 04	24 04	182 30
	62 69	62 69	62 69	62 69	62 69	62 69	390 04
	312 72	312 72	312 72	312 72	312 72	312 72	1954 50
	-	-	-	-	-	-	-
	-7 30	-14 61	-14 61	-14 61	-14 61	-14 61	-80 35
	-	27 50	33 00	33 00	33 00	33 00	159 50
	-	23 78	57 08	57 08	57 08	57 08	252 10
	-	-	132 42	198 63	198 63	198 63	728 31
	-	-	35 62	106 87	106 87	106 87	356 23
	-	-	-	-	-	-	-
	-	-	-7 21	-21 63	-21 63	-21 63	-72 10
	1319 39	1363 36	1562 99				
	-68 18	-	-1353 30				
	10 163 42	11 526 78	11 736 47				

PF-72b

Date of Purchase	Date of Retirement	Truck or car no.	Make and style	Original cost	Cost Estimated salvage
			Trucks		
8-1-41	4-30-45	108	Buick light truck (1939)	1610 00	210 00
9-6-41	9-18-44	110	GMC 2½ T. panel	2318 81	400 00
12-12-41		111	Trailer	666 19	—
9-18-44	10-16-47	112	GMC 3 T.	2875 31	500 00
11-10-44	2-9-48	113	Dodge	2253 00	400 00
1-18-45	5-29-51	114	Chevrolet light truck	1200 00	200 00
10-16-47		115	GMC 3 T.	4150 00	600 00
2-9-48		116	Dodge	3580 00	500 00
5-29-51		117	Ford	2975 00	400 00
8-16-51		115	GMC 3 T. — overhaul	950 00	—
3-4-52		118	GMC 3 T.	4680 00	600 00
			Annual depreciation — trucks		
			Autos		
8-1-41	10-28-41	212	1938 Chevrolet - 4 door	1020 00	250 00
8-1-41	6-5-44	214	1939 Ford - 4 door	1050 14	300 00
8-1-41	9-14-44	215	1941 Ford - 2 door	1104 10	300 00
10-28-41	12-29-44	216	1941 Buick - 2 door	1661 00	400 00
6-5-44	10-11-46	217	1941 DeSoto - 2 door	1756 00	400 00
9-14-44	6-7-47	218	1941 Ford - 2 door	1267 00	300 00
7-20-46	4-19-49	219	1946 Pontiac - 2 door	2050 00	400 00
10-11-46	3-9-50	220	1946 Buick - 2 door	2960 00	500 00
6-7-47	9-8-52	221	1947 Buick - 4 door	3270 00	500 00
4-19-49		222	1949 Pontiac - 2 door	2280 00	400 00
3-9-50		223	1950 Buick - 2 door	3150 00	500 00
9-8-52		224	1952 Oldsmobile - 4 door	2980 00	500 00

Annual depreciation — autos
Annual depreciation — trucks and autos
Amount of depreciation accrued at date of retirement of truck
Balance in reserve at 8-1-41 and at 12-31-41, 12-31-42, etc.

PF-13

...uring Company   Procedure : (1) Depreciation base – balance at beginning of month.
...utomobiles   (1a) End of depreciation period – end of month of retirement.
Depreciation   (2) Recognition of retirement – end of month of retirement.
      (3) Reporting method – loss or gain recognized on removal.

Depreciable cost	Estimated life in years	Balance 8-1-41	D 1941	E 1942	P 1943	R 1944
1400 00	5	583 33	116 67	280 00	280 00	140 00
1918 81	4	-	119 93	479 70	479 70	359 78
666 19	4	-	-	166 55	166 55	166 55
2375 31	4	-	-	-	-	148 46
1853 00	4	-	-	-	-	38 60
1000 00	4	-	-	-	-	-
3550 00	4	-	-	-	-	-
3080 00	4	-	-	-	-	-
2575 00	4	-	-	-	-	-
950 00	2*	-	-	-	-	-
4080 00	5	-	-.	-	-	-
	* from 1-1-51					
		583 33	236 60~	926 25~	926 25~	853 39~
770 00	3	770 00	-	-	-	-
750 14	3	625 13	104 19	20 82	-	-
804 10	3	270 75	111 68	268 03	153 64	-
1261 00	4	-	52 54	315 25	315 25	315 25
1356 00	4	-	-	-	-	169 50
967 00	3	-	-	-	-	80 58
1650 00	4	-	-	-	-	-
2460 00	4	-	-	-	-	-
2770 00	4	-	-	-	-	-
1880 00	4	-	-	-	-	-
2650 00	4	-	-	-	-	-
2480 00	4	-	-	-	-	-
		1665 88~	268 41~	604 10~	468 89~	565 33~
		2249 21~	505 01~	1530 35~	1395 14~	1418 72~
and autos		-	-770 00	-	-	-3991 64
		2249 21	1984 22~	3514 57~	4909 71~	2336 79~

PF-73a

(continued)

E	C	I	A	T	I	O
1945	1946	1947	1948	1949	1950	1951
-	-	-	-	-	-	-
-	-	-	-	-	-	-
166 54	-	-	-	-	-	-
593 83	593 83	494 86	-	-	-	-
463 25	463 25	463 25	77 21	-	-	-
229 17	250 00	250 00	250 00	20 83	-	-
-	-	147 92	887 50	887 50	887 50	369 79
-	-	-	641 67	770 00	770 00	770 00
-	-	-	-	-	-	375 52
-	-	-	-	-	-	475 00
-	-	-	-	-	-	-
1 452 79n	1 307 08n	1 356 03n	1 856 38n	1 678 33n	1 657 50n	1 990 31n
-	-	-	-	-	-	-
-	-	-	-	-	-	-
-	-	-	-	-	-	-
-	-	-	-	-	-	-
339 00	282 50	-				
322 33	322 33	161 16				
-	171 88	412 50	412 50	137 50	-	
-	102 50	615 00	615 00	615 00	153 75	-
-	-	346 25	692 50	692 50	692 50	346 25
-	-	-	-	313 33	470 00	470 00
-	-	-	-	-	496 88	662 50
-	-	-	-	-	-	-
661 33n	879 21n	1 534 91n	1 720 00n	1 758 33n	1 813 13n	1 478 75n
2 114 12n	2 186 29n	2 890 94n	3 576 38n	3 436 66n	3 470 63n	3 469 06n
-1 400 00	-791 00	-2 717 38	-1 505 56	-1 134 38	-2 101 25	-1 000 00
3 050 91n	4 446 20n	4 619 76n	6 690 58n	8 992 86n	10 362 24n	12 831 30n

PF-73b

turing Company
Automobiles
Depreciation

N			Units retired		Units in service (to be erased)	
1952	1953					
-	-		1 400 00			
-	-		1 439 11			
-	-				666 19	
-	-		1 830 98			
-	-		1 505 56			
-	-		1 000 00			
369 79					3 550 -	
128 33					3 080 -	
643 75					1019 27	
475 00					950 -	
612 00					612 -	
2 228 87					9877 46	
-	-		770 00			
-	-		750 14			
-	-		804 10			
-	-		998 29			
-	-		791 00			
-	-		886 40			
-	-		1 134 38			
-	-		2 101 25			
-	-		2 770 00			
470 00			-		1723 33	
662 50			-		1821 88	
155 00			-		155 -	
1 287 50					3700 21	
3 516 37						
- 2 770 00						
13 577 67					1 357767	

PF-73c

-423-

Problems and Questions

1. Prepare a schedule showing dates of acquisition, the original cost, the remaining life, and any undepreciated cost at 12-31-52 of the furniture-and-fixtures account of the Martin Manufacturing Company, and reconcile the total of the undepreciated cost with the adjusted book figures.

2. How would you satisfy yourself as to the adequacy of a reserve for depreciation on motors where the (straight-line) rate of depreciation has been 5 per cent and the ratio of the accumulated reserve to the cost of the motors is 22 per cent? The motors, approximately 2,000 in number, are attached to and run individual machines in a large machine shop and are replaced at the rate of about 100 per year at about 10 per cent of their cost.

3. Following are the yearly changes in a "special-machinery" account opened six years ago:

(a) Additions: $10,000, $15,000, $12,000, $46,000, $14,000, $0.

(b) Physical retirements at original cost: $0; $2,000 (purchased first year); $600 (purchased first year); $4,000 (half purchased first year, half second year); $12,000 ($2,000 purchased first year, $9,000 second year, $1,000 third year); $1,000 (purchased first year).

(c) Recoveries from resale or scrap: $0; $200; $500; $800 ($600 on first-year purchases, $200 on those of second year); $5,000 ($1,000 on first-year purchases, $4,000 on those of second year, none on those of third year); $0.

(d) Estimate of average useful life, remaining unchanged during five-year period: 4 years.

You have been asked to prepare a lapsing-schedule summary for the six-year period following these conventions: (a) depreciation base: balance at beginning of year, adjusted by one-half the cost of additions and one-half the cost of lapses or retirements (the latter, of course, excluding retirements that precede lapses) during year, (b) removal from asset and depreciation-reserve accounts only when physically retired, (c) gain or loss on retirement subtracted or added to each year's depreciation expense. Your schedule should bring out the annual depreciation charges, and the balances of the asset and reserve accounts at the end of the six-year period.

4. The Sunclop Manufacturing Company has maintained a machinery account and an associated reserve for many years. Five years ago the asset and reserve accounts were adjusted to a basis approved by Federal revenue agents and by the firm of public-accountants at that time employed by the company. A summary of the accounts since then follows:

Machinery

Year	Debits		Credits	
19–1	Beginning balance	$138,210		
1	Additions	68,379	Retirements at cost	$ 5,012
2	"	64,364	" " "	25,976
3	"	17,955	" " "	10,085
4	"	725	" " "	16,324
5	"	2,368	" " "	1,926
			Balance	232,678

Allowance for depreciation—Machinerry

19–1	Retirements at cost	$ 5,012	Beginning balance	$ 48,512
			Provision	8,620
			Recoveries	345
2	" " "	25,976	Provision	11,688
			Recoveries	2,746
3	" " "	10,085	Provision	12,447
			Recoveries	1,366
4	" " "	16,324	Provision	12,428
			Recoveries	1,570
5	" " "	1,926	Provision	11,671
			Recoveries	8,553
Balance		60,623		

Because the reserve balance at the end of 19–5 amounted to less than 15% of the asset account, a study was instituted by the management in an endeavor to determine the sufficiency of the allowance account. An analysis of the beginning balance was made by equal-age groups as follows:

Group A			Group B			Group C			Group D
Num-ber	Age thru 19–0	Cost	Num-ber	Age thru 19–0	Cost	Num-ber	Age thru 19–0	Cost	Cost
2	12	$27,436	1	20	$6,573	1	6	$ 1,044	$14,100
1	10	10,664	1	14	888	1	4	882	
1	5	9,717	1	10	1,084	2	2	736	
1	4	6,301	1	8	2,492	3	1	2,601	
1	3	7,602	1	6	2,408	1	1	1,137	
			1	5	5,385				
			1	4	3,252				
			2	2	18,850				
			2	1	15,058				

The allowance account at the beginning of 19–1 was based on an average twenty-year life:

Group	Accrued depreciation
A	$26,623
B	14,089
C	750
D	7,050

Additions and retirements since the beginning date have been:

	A		B		C		D
Additions	Number	Amount	Number	Amount	Number	Amount	Amount
19–1	2	26,592	4	40,325	1	483	979
19–2	–	–	5	60,350	1	1,892	2,122
19–3	1	14,161	–	–	1	2,580	1,214
19–4	–	–	–	–	–	–	725
19–5	–	–	–	–	2	2,368	–

Retirements at cost (identifiable with items on preceding schedule)—

19–1	–	–	2	4,900	–	–	112
19–2	2	18,266	1	6,573	1	1,137	–
19–3	1	9,717	–	–	–	–	368
19–4	–	–	2	1,972	–	–	14,352*
19–5	–	–	–	–	2	1,926	–

* Includes $732 of 19–1 additions.

Changes in estimates of economic life and in processing methods have led to the conclusion that the accrued depreciation applicable to the different age groups should be recomputed from the beginning of 19–1 based on estimated useful lives from the date of purchase as follows:

Group	Years
A	16
B	20
C	12
D	15

Since the number of items is small the following procedure is to be followed:

(a) The accrued depreciation on the books at the beginning of 19–1 ($48,512), divided as then computed for the four groups and for each asset within each group, is not to be adjusted.

(b) Beginning with 19–1, depreciation is to be recomputed and restated for each year by applying the rate determined by you to the unrecovered balance at the beginning of the year without addition for acquisitions or adjustment for retirements during the year, in such a manner that undepreciated costs at the beginning of 19–1 will be spread over remaining useful lives as now estimated. For convenience in subsequent analyses the four groups are to be carried in separate general-ledger accounts. However, a single allowance (reserve) account will be continued.

(c) Gain or loss is to be recognized for the total of each year's retirements and such gain or loss will appear in the company's income statement for that year as a separate item.

Prepare (a) worksheets reflecting the necessary recomputations, and (b) adjusting journal entries necessary to correct and restate the general-ledger accounts; (c) append also summary adjusted schedules for the five-year period (which need not be detailed by years) for the asset and reserve accounts broken down for the four groups.

5. You are examining annual financial statements that are to be published for the information of the company's stockholders. You find that depreciation charged against income exceeds materially the depreciation deduction in the Federal income-tax returns. What would you do about it?

6. For what purpose and in what manner does the auditor study depreciation accounts?

7. State how you would satisfy yourself as to the propriety of a provision for depreciation, during the past year, on factory machinery.

8. What is meant by amortization of defense plant for Federal income-tax purposes? Should it be entered on the books of account?

9. You find that on the books of a certain oil-producing company recoveries from the sale of old equipment are credited against current provisions for depletion. What are your objections, if any, to this procedure?

10. While examining the accounts of a manufacturing establishment you discover that the useful life of a group of machines has now been extended by the improvement of production methods that for several years previous were looked upon as obsolescent. When the machines were first purchased their estimated life was twenty years, and a depreciation rate of 5% of their purchase price was then established. This rate continued for six years until it was increased to 8⅓% because of the prospective abandonment of the operations to which the machines had been contributing. Now, after three years at the higher rate, the machines are estimated to have an average remaining life of fourteen years with a salvage value thereafter of 5% of their original cost. What revisions of the reserve or rate would you recommend? How does your rate for the remaining years of useful life compare with the rate that would have obtained had all these factors been known when the assets were purchased?

11. A depreciation committee with broad powers has been established in the Bandex Company consisting of the controller as chairman, with members representing engineering, maintenance, and operations. Formal minutes have been kept for several years. Prepare a list of the kind of activities and decisions you might find reflected in these minutes.

12. With what different meanings is the word "depreciation" employed?

13. Why do many accountants regard policy as to depreciation accounting as a matter for top-management consideration?

14. You have been told that during the audit year it has been necessary to give expression to the factor of inadequacy. What does inadequacy mean and how does it affect the accounts?

15. The developmental cost of an oilwell has been $68,350.81. During the first three years of its operation the estimate of total available production was 110,000 barrels and actual production was 10,000, 11,000, and 12,000 barrels. During the fourth year production was 15,000 barrels, and it was estimated that as at the beginning of that year total available production would be as much as 132,000 barrels. Straight-line-depletion methods have been followed. What depletion charge would you expect to find for the fourth year?

16. A truck having a cost of $10,500 has been depreciated at the rate of $2,000 a year, its estimated useful life being five years. In the middle of the fourth year before any depreciation was recorded for the year it was traded in on a new truck having an equal capacity and a price of $12,000, the cash consideration being $9,300. In the form of a journal entry indicate your recommendation concerning the recording of this transaction.

17. You are told that a certain furniture-and-fixtures account is being depreciated at the rate of 10% a year on the reducing-balance method, no allowance being made for salvage. A question is raised:

how much of the original cost of $1,200 would remain after seven years?

(a) Derive a formula that could be applied to such situations regardless of the percentage employed or the years elapsed since purchase.

(b) By means of the formula determine the residual amount in the furniture-and-fixtures account above described.

18. From information revealed by a lapsing schedule covering a machinery account, the portion of the account total becoming fully depreciated each year is credited to the account and charged to the depreciation-reserve account. This practice was initiated several years ago upon the recommendation of a Federal internal-revenue agent. Discuss the propriety of this procedure.

19. In the annual report of a corporation to its stockholders appears a statement resembling that appearing on page 404. However, under "depreciation reserve," although the crossfooting is correct, the third money column has been omitted, and the total of the second money column differs from that of the second money column under "asset group." Explain the most likely cause of the difference.

20. From an inspection of a half-dozen recently published reports of corporations to their stockholders calculate (a) the ratio of the allowance or reserve for depreciation to the gross amount of depreciable assets and (b) the ratio of depreciation expense to the same base. Also note and discuss any comment appearing in the reports on the significance of these ratios.

CHAPTER XII

Liabilities

No one term has been universally agreed upon as a caption for the right half of the balance sheet. "Equities" has been suggested but has proved unacceptable since its common, nontechnical usage implies an active ownership. "Liabilities and Net Worth" or "Liabilities and Capital" are frequently used but lack the force of a single word. "Liabilities" alone is often employed and deserves a wider acceptance; its derivation from a root meaning to "tie" or "bind" suggests that it may accurately indicate *any* financial linkage with others, and a legal or moral obligation as well. In this chapter amounts owing to outsiders is implied.

Some auditors claim that they pay little attention to liabilities directly, their position being that if assets and expenses have been given the care they deserve, the correctness of liabilities follows as a matter of course. They may, for example, point to procedures surrounding the inventory cutoff—on the purchases side—as illustrating how an important section of current obligations has been derived, almost as a byproduct, from the study of the inventory. However, an analysis of such a claim indicates that the question is one primarily of emphasis and timing, rather than coverage. What these auditors mean is that their examination of suppliers' accounts payable accompanies and is made a part of their examination of an asset. Yet the point is well worth mentioning, for it brings out two of the important developments during recent years in auditing techniques—that the annual audit often involves cutting across conventional classifications and considering several items simultaneously, and that it is tending in the direction of a review of business procedures. In the illustration cited, the study begins, not with inventories, but with management policies, thence proceeds to the conduct of operations, purchases paid for and unpaid, the cost of materials used, and inventories. The sequence in the study is unimportant, because several parts of these problems must be considered by the auditor together. Their individual meanings, and the meanings of the accounts in which they are reflected, become clearer when they are studied as parts of a larger whole. They are simply different aspects of the problem of material and service flows, brought into being by the artificial cleavage in that flow caused by the ending of a conventional period of time. From this point of view, the examination of either inventories or accounts payable to suppliers is integral with other elements in the over-all picture that the auditor endeavors to draw.

The general purpose behind the auditor's examination of liabilities is to make sure (a) that all liabilities at the balance-sheet date, including accruals, have been given expression, (b) that no liability such as an accrual of tax or other expense is overstated, (c) that any lien on or pledge of assets to secure a liability is determined and disclosed on the balance sheet, (d) that the general character and due dates of noncurrent liabilities also appear on the balance sheet, and (e) that agreements with creditors having a material effect on operations or financial condition be described in the financial statements or in footnotes to financial statements.

Principles and Practices

All liabilities recognized in accounting have two characteristics in common: the events giving rise to them belong to a past period; and they are expressed in the amount at which they are eventually to be liquidated—by the payment of cash or less frequently in goods or services. The basic events are of several kinds, the principal ones being: completed transactions in goods or services where title or an unrestricted right of use has been acquired, borrowed money, the receipt of money before the delivery of goods or services, deposits by customers, collections for others, and accruals.

Current liabilities are by general agreement existing obligations payable within a year following the balance-sheet date. Long-term liabilities are those payable more than a year after the balance-sheet date. Contingent liabilities are obligations, relating to past transactions or other events, that may arise in consequence of possible but not yet probable future events (if probable an actual, usually current, liability exists).

Bank loans. Loans from banks to business concerns are known generally as commercial loans, more particularly as demand loans, time loans, or discounts, depending on the agreed maturity and method of paying for interest. The demand loan has a fixed rate of interest but no maturity and at any time repayment may be made by the borrower or demanded by the bank; the instrument calls for the payment of interest at periodic intervals such as a month, or at maturity. A time loan, as for sixty or ninety days or a specified number of months, bears a fixed rate of interest also payable periodically or at maturity. A discount is generally regarded as a form of time loan but it may be prepaid at the option of the borrower; interest thereon for the term of the note is deducted at the time the loan is made. This means that if the interest rate on a three-month discount note is 4 per cent, the initial proceeds on a loan of $10,000 will be $9,900.00 unless the "true-discount" rate is applied in which case the proceeds will be $10,000 ÷ 101, or $9,900.99. Term loans from banks are described below. Where collateral is required by the bank, a separate collateral agreement is usually executed specifying the purpose of the collateral deposited and the conditions under which it may be converted or released.

Commercial paper is a variety of bank loan that is now seldom encountered. It is issued by banks or by professional note brokers to banks in such denominations as $2,500, $5,000, and $10,000, matures in six months or less, bears a comparatively low rate of interest payable at maturity, and is accepted as a temporary investment by banks as a rule only if the credit standing of the issuer is both substantial and nationally known.

Other notes payable. Occasionally the auditor encounters notes payable to equipment manufacturers, notes given to merchandise and other creditors, and even notes representing loans from stockholders or other persons. The conditions under which they are issued are numerous and varied.

Accounts payable. Accounts payable (or trade creditors) consist of obligations for goods or services on open account, excluding notes, advance payments, deferred credits, and accruals. The details are found in an accounts-payable ledger, a voucher record, or simply a list of vouchers payable.

Advances from customers. Advances from customers are of two kinds: refundable deposits, as on containers, and deferred credits —amounts that will ultimately be credited to sales. Some income is usually earned from container deposits, since not all containers are returned, but the adjustment therefor should be made only as the result of proven experience; in a few cases the credit is transferred to sales but only as the result of a subsequent, unrelated transaction.

Deferred credits. Deferred credits, also known as deferred income or profit, are items as yet unearned; charges for goods or services that offset them have been realized in cash or may still exist in the form of a liquidating receivable, and the goods are yet to be delivered or the services rendered or the accounts collected. They are illustrated by unearned gross profits on installment sales, and by advance deposits on long-term contracts required as evidence of good faith (earnest money) or to supply the working capital needed for the job. In a department store under a "lay-away" plan of sales, customers may make periodic payments against merchandise to be delivered to them in the future. Other examples are: rent and interest received in advance, unearned dues (of a club), and unearned subscriptions (of a magazine publisher). These items offer little accounting or other operating difficulty. If they are numerous, like subscriptions, simple schemes are set up whereby their spread over future periods is automatically provided for.

Deferred credits are normally classified as current liabilities, not because they are ultimately to be paid in cash as are other current liabilities, but because (1) they resemble current-asset valuation accounts although they cannot usually be identified with particular assets (as where the cash realized has become merged with other cash); and (2) at least a moral obligation remains that they be regarded as subject to refund until delivery of the goods or services has been completed or the accounts have been collected. Their gradual release as gross income should, of course, accompany an equivalent flow of goods or services, or the collection of related receivables.

Accrued expenses. Accrued expenses differ from accounts payable in that (a) invoices, in the ordinary sense, are not on hand for them, (b) they are incurred more or less in proportion to elapsed time, (c) they are not necessarily due, and (d) the benefits from them accrue *before* they are paid. In one sense they contrast with *prepaid* expenses where benefits continue to flow after payment has been made. Yet the classification is not a rigid one for minor items of rent, light, heat, gas, and water costs: such items are for the most part settled for on a monthly basis, and they may be recorded at the end of each month on an estimated or actual basis as accounts payable, leaving as major items of accrued expenses payrolls, commissions, traveling expenses, bonuses, taxes, interest, royalties, service guarantees, and similar items.

Long-term indebtedness. "Funded," "bonded," "long-term," and "fixed" liabilities have very nearly the same meanings in commercial practice. They usually refer to the formal type of indebtedness represented by bonds or notes of either the coupon or registered type, originally sold through an investment dealer or banker to the public; they have standard face values, bear a fixed rate of interest, are readily transferable from one owner to another, and mature serially or at a single, specified date. A trustee, as mortgagee, stands ready to act for security holders in case of default or other emergency.

In recent years term loans from banks and insurance companies have gained in popularity. Term loans are generally in the form of five- or ten-year serial notes, the proceeds often being applied to the purchase of equipment. The loan agreement usually does not call for a mortgage or other lien on any portion of the borrower's assets, but provides such safeguards as restrictions on additional secured or unsecured loans, the maintenance of a specified working-capital ratio and amount, and limitations on management compensation and dividends.

When the proceeds of a bond issue are less than the total par value of the issue, a deferred charge (unamortized bond discount) is set up for the difference; when greater than par value, a deferred-income account (unamortized bond premium) is created. In either case the amount is amortized over the life of the bonds, usually in proportion to interest paid. If the bonds are to be retired at a premium, the premium must be built up over the life of the bonds—also in proportion to interest paid.

Bonds reacquired before maturity should be carried at par, notwithstanding that they may be resalable. The difference between the repurchase price and "book value" (par value plus unamortized premium or less unamortized discount) should be regarded as gain or loss for the period in which the purchase is made. It is sometimes advocated that if a reacquired bond can be resold by the issuer it may be carried at cost. The better practice appears to be to regard the resale as unrelated to the repurchase and hence to be accounted for independently—as though being recorded in the first instance.

Contingent liabilities. Contingent liabilities differ from *real* liabilities, not with respect to the definiteness of their amount (either may be computed exactly or estimated), but in the definiteness of their incidence. A *real* liability must be paid by a specific person or organization whose identity is certain and whose obligation to pay has already been established; a *contingent* liability becomes a real liability only upon the occurrence of an event that creates an obligation and determines the obligor.

Certain contingencies represent possible uncompensated losses, and others, losses that may possibly be recovered from others—that is, a contingent liability may or may not be matched by a contingent asset. Both types, however, require similar disclosure, since the chances of recovery on contingent assets is often remote.

The principal types of contingent liabilities and their characteristics appear later in this chapter.

Internal Controls

Controls over expenditures generally, especially as they relate to operations, have been described in Chapter V. Other controls advocated by accountants include the following:

Restriction on issue of notes. Frauds are occasionally found where an official will issue a note in the name of the company, possibly paying interest from his own pocket or even from the company's funds for some time thereafter. In such cases the payee must accept some measure of blame since he has not taken the trouble to ascertain whether or not he is dealing with the company or with an individual. A prospective note creditor should ask for, and expect to receive from the company's secretary, a sworn copy of minutes of the directors authorizing certain individuals to borrow money or issue notes in payment of goods or services. Without such assurance, the creditor has not acted with the prudence customary in business transactions, and in most jurisdictions he would be unable to hold the company liable. Every board of directors should, therefore, issue an authorization of the character indicated, even though no note issue is in prospect. It is usual in such a resolution to require the signature of two top officials, to limit the character of the transaction for which notes may be given, and to specify by name or class the banks or persons to whom notes may be issued.

Note register. A note register should be required as an accounting record, in which the details of every note issued are formally entered.

Interest approvals. Interest vouchers should require the approval of both the treasurer and controller.

Expense authorizations. Routines should be firmly established whereby responsible officials undertake to approve commitments for the various classes of expenditures, within the limitations imposed by operating policies and the budget. In general, each expenditure should require two approvals at the commitment stage: the first from the person whose organizational unit demands the goods or service, his approval being an indication of (a) the *need,* (b) the conformity of the *use* to operating policies, and (c) the sufficiency of the *budget* allotted to his organizational unit; the second from the person (purchasing agent or, for services, some other official) who must choose or approve the *source* of the goods or service and arrange for and follow up on timely delivery or performance. Under a clearly defined policy of this type, it is not difficult for operators, even those who take pride in independence of action and in "getting things done," to subordinate their spending habits to a procedure that benefits the business as a whole.

Other controls should cover the preaudit of invoices before payment to insure correspondence with authorization, a certification of the actual receipt of the goods or services by someone other than the person who authorized the purchase, and payment with maximum discount deducted. In addition there should be frequent tests of individual invoices and reviews of procedures by the internal auditor to make certain that routine safeguards are adequate and have not been relaxed at any point.

Accruals. Procedures are needed in every business, regardless of its size, that will act both as an aid and a check on the setup of accrued expenses at the close of each month and at the year end. Such procedures may take the form of "precast" journal entries, or a single journal entry that includes a list of the needed adjustments and provides for their computation, approval, and distribution as far in advance of the end of the period as possible. They will focus attention within the period to questions then requiring investigation and action that, if left until after the period has ended, may be difficult to answer and will interfere with other matters then demanding attention.

Bonds. Controls over bonds, following their authorization by the board of directors and the stockholders, are automatically provided with the appointment of a registrar and transfer agent. The same bank may serve in both capacities and may in addition act as trustee for the issue and paying agent for interest.

Where these functions are performed by the borrower, controls begin with the printing of the bonds. The bonds should be numbered serially by the printer, who should be bonded, and they should be in the custody of the corporate treasurer. Validation of a bond at the time of its issue should be possible only by the securing of two signatures; none should be signed in advance. A register should be maintained showing the conditions under which each bond was issued and there should be a separate record for registered bonds; space should be provided for recording reacquisitions and their disposition. A register should also be opened for each interest-coupon series, so devised that the internal auditor may from time to time verify the amounts paid and outstanding; one form provides for the pasting of coupons on numbered blanks as they are paid.

Contingent liabilities. Records should be maintained for notes and other forms of receivables that have been discounted, sold, or otherwise assigned with recourse until they have matured and have been paid. Where collections are made direct by holders the record should be held open for several days after the due date until the possibility of adverse notice has passed.

Accommodation endorsements, guaranties, possible additional income taxes, and contractual obligations that may lead to future losses are examples of types of contingent liabilities that are usually not found in formal records of any kind. Their discovery and the determination of their amount by the auditor does not follow any routine procedure.

Financial-Statement Standards

In displaying liabilities in a balance sheet, the following three characteristics must appear or be implicit in their position or title: the general nature, security, and due date of each item. Convention supplies most of these. Thus it is not customary to show the due date of a bank loan because it appears under "current liabilities" and current liabilities are accepted as being payable within a year. Again, unless certain current payables are secured by pledged assets no mention of security need be made because current liabilities are usually not secured. However, the three characteristics should be clearly indicated in setting forth long-term liabilities, since the conditions under which they arise vary greatly; in addition, the interest rate should appear, in view of the fact that interest paid to long-term investors is of importance to many persons.

Any portion of a long-term liability that becomes due within the next twelve months must appear under the heading of "current"; this includes payments that are to be made to a sinking-fund trustee.

Current liabilities should be divided, as a rule, into the following classes, where they exist:

Short-term loans from:
    Banks (demand loans should appear separately)
    Others (the source class should be given)
Current maturities of bonds, term loans, and other long-term liabilities
Trade notes (acceptances should appear separately)
Notes to or advances from (specify which):
    Officers and employees
    Stockholders
Trade creditors
Federal income and profits taxes
Accrued interest
Dividend payable

Individual liabilities should be displayed where they are material and are likely to have importance to persons who customarily rely upon balance-sheet information. This requirement may be defined roughly as involving any item that exceeds 5 per cent of the total of current liabilities.

Both pledged assets and the liability secured should be identified on the face of the balance sheet, so that the effect of a possible future setoff may be apparent to the reader.

As noted in Chapter IX, unamortized bond discount and expense is a proper, though uncommon, deduction from bonds outstanding, along with "treasury" or reacquired bonds, and bonds and assets held by a sinking-fund trustee. In most cases unamortized bond discount and expense is carried as a deferred charge.

Contingent liabilities may be shown "in short" between liabilities and net worth or in a balance-sheet footnote. The latter of these alternatives has some advantages in that the description may be less formal and more detailed than a sidehead. The existence of contingencies revealed by the presence of a surplus reserve, or a so-called "liability" reserve, does not need to be repeated under the contingent-liability caption.

Representative Audit Program

1. Prepare or obtain schedule of notes payable, showing date of origin, renewal date, due date, payee, nature of original transaction, amount, payments, endorser, collateral given, rate of interest, and interest paid and accrued.

2. Confirm by correspondence all notes payable, and any assets held as collateral.

3. Compare record of notes canceled during year, as shown on the books, with year's additions to canceled notes on hand.

4. Note changes in notes payable since year end and ascertain reasons therefor.

5. Obtain list of accounts payable at year end; compare details with voucher register or payable ledgers, and total with controlling account; verify total of list.

6. Review effectiveness of cutoff controls, for items other than materials-and-parts purchases already covered in inventory examination.

7. Trace selected items from each class of transaction from authorization through to payment, noting returns, discounts, or other reductions and their possible effect on the amount outstanding at year end.

8. Examine items payable at year end that are also unpaid at time of audit and ascertain why payment has been delayed.

9. Examine file of open-purchase orders and contracts dated prior to year end, make note of unusual items, and discuss them with management.

10. Scan voucher register subsequent to year end and invoices not vouchered at time of audit (after year end) for items in transit or actually received during period under audit.

11. Test creditors' regular monthly statements against recorded liability at year end.

12. Request from selected creditors list of unpaid invoices at year end, where cutoff controls are weak and detailed statements are not at hand.

13. List separately amounts owing officers and employees, deposits and advance payments from customers, and deferred income, and other items requiring separate disclosure; determine whether any of these items is in effect a trust, requiring a corresponding segregation of cash.

14. Prepare schedule of accrued liabilities outstanding and how computed or verified.

15. Determine whether adequate accruals have been made for such items as the following:

Income and excess-profits tax
Sales tax
Franchise tax
Real-estate tax
Personal-property tax
Excise tax
Capital-stock tax
Social-security taxes
Payrolls

Pension-fund contributions
Bonuses
Salesmen's and others' commissions
Rentals
Interest on notes payable
Interest on funded debt
Dividends declared but unpaid

16. Make sure that property-tax accruals have been made for the taxing jurisdictions in which the company's property is located.

17. Refer to (auditor's) tax staff for determination of liability that should be reflected on balance sheet against any item of deferred income.

18. Look for and determine the significance of contingent liabilities relating to such items as accounts and notes discounted, claims for damages, guarantees of product or of performance by others, endorsements, patents, threatened or active litigation, compliance with orders of governmental agencies, purchase orders on a falling market or involving unusual quantities, or inability to deliver under contract.

19. Secure representation from client's independent legal counsel on any such items with which he is conversant.

20. Confirm amount of long-term debt outstanding by correspondence with trustee, mortgagee, creditor, or bank; if indenture or other loan agreement has been modified, obtain certified copy of change.

21. Determine whether bond-indenture provisions affecting current year have been met.

22. Examine reacquired bonds or cremation certificate evidencing their destruction, or secure from holder statement of their existence, and reason for their being so held; review bond transactions during year and bring permanent file on bonds up to date.

23. Verify interest paid during audit period and accrued at end of period, and verify changes in bond-discount or bond-premium account.

Audit Procedures

Notes payable. In the typical request for information from banks, illustrated on page 206, space is provided for a listing by the bank of direct and indirect obligations, and the form is sent to every bank with which the board of directors has authorized the management to do business. From the information called for by the form and supplied by the bank the auditor will be able to verify the date of each bank loan, the net proceeds, the interest paid, and the accrued interest at the year end.

Occasionally, the auditor will find that a note has been given in settlement of an obligation, although the obligation continues to appear as an account payable. This possibility should be borne in mind when scanning the detail of outstanding accounts payable.

Because of the importance of notes payable, and because in ordinary situations they are few in number, the auditor should prepare (or have prepared for him by the client's staff) a schedule of notes that have been outstanding at any time during the year. It will commence with those reflected in last year's balance sheet and will show such details as date made, renewal date, due date, payee, nature of original transaction, amount, date and amount of payments, name of indorser, collateral held and dates given and returned, and dates and amounts of interest paid or accrued. From this schedule interest expense and accrued interest should be verified.

Confirmation by correspondence is a standard procedure for notes payable. Besides letters to the banks, letters should be addressed to every payee shown on the note schedule even though the records show that some or all of the notes have been paid. Information as to the amount outstanding and the collateral held at the year end should be called for. The letter may take the form appearing on the following page. Confirmation of commercial paper may be had through the note broker who contracted for the issue in the first instance.

Accounts payable. Cutoff procedures relating to purchases have already been described (Chapter VIII, page 284). Determination of purchases in transit should be followed by adjustments, adding to both inventories and payables.

The auditor should procure from his client a trial balance of accounts payable, consisting of a formal list of voucher numbers, payees, and amounts, or, perhaps, an adding-machine tape showing amounts only. This he should compare with the voucher or disbursement record to make sure of its accuracy. Procedures followed at the year end for the purpose of bringing into the accounts all expenses as well as purchases unpaid should be reviewed and tested. A reclassification entry will then be necessary (for the working trial balance) in which accrued items and other obligations required to be separately stated on the balance sheet will be removed, leaving in the account "trade" accounts payable, creditors for merchandise, supplies, equipment, outside services, and expenses generally.

A debit balance among accounts payable may mean any one or more of several things: a return of merchandise, an overpayment, failure to record a purchase, a lost discount, or an error in posting. If, after adjustment or reclassification, the debit balances remaining amount to as much, say, as one per cent of the credit balances of accounts payable, they should be reclassified as "miscellaneous" receivables.

(Letterhead of client)

Staple Products Company
15 North LaSalle St.
Chicago, Ill.

Gentlemen:

Please send to our auditors, Hyatt, Paterson & Co., 960 Hudson Bldg., Chicago 3, a statement on the bottom half of this letter of notes and other obligations, direct or contingent, owing by us to you at December 31, 19–5, and the nature and amount of any collateral that you were holding on that date.

An addressed envelope is enclosed for your convenience in replying.

Very truly yours,
Austin Mfg. Company

by J. P. Stebbins

Date made	Date due	Nature of obligation	Amount	Rate of interest	Interest paid to	Collateral

The above statement is correct.

Date_____   By_____

A confirmation of the amounts owing to creditors may be desirable where payments have not been made on the basis of individual invoices or groups of invoices, or where the cutoff procedure at the year end has been none too rigorous. Samples selected for the test should include smaller creditors as well as larger.

An indication on the list of accounts payable of items outstanding for more than the "cleanup" period of thirty or sixty days may bring to light unrecorded returns or disputes that may lead to adjustments downward or further accruals.

If it should develop during the course of the audit that merchandise has been received on consignment, the records in connection therewith should be obtained and the status of each consigner ascertained. Where the handling of goods on consignment is the exception rather than the rule, the auditor must make sure that sales, less agreed commissions and expenses, have been set up as a liability and that no merchandise still held in the name of the consigner has been included in the inventory.

Dividends payable. In his examination of the minutes of the board of directors, the auditor will have noted any dividend declared but not payable before the end of the year. Such a dividend is, of course, a current liability, which can be easily verified by multiplying the rate appearing in the declaration by the number of shares outstanding in the hands of the public. The auditor should remember that no dividend should be accrued on treasury stock or stock held in funds owned or controlled by the company. However, the prevailing practice is to accrue dividends on intercompany-held stocks as though they were held by outside interests.

Unclaimed dividends occasionally appear. Where they are minor in amount they may be included with dividends payable or with accounts payable; and they should continue to be carried as a payable as long as the shares of stock to which they relate are outstanding.

Federal income taxes. At the end of Chapter V, audit procedures 13, 14, and 15 relate to the review of the Federal income-tax liability for the current year. The information called for is suggestive only because the basic law changes to some extent each year and auditors must examine accruals of income taxes in the light of these changes. The instructions indicate some of the points the auditor should not overlook in the development of his working papers—points that will probably be considered in the computation of taxes for at least some years to come. Most public-accounting firms have tax departments or individuals to whom the tax problems of clients are referred. The specialization now necessary for an adequate review of the year's tax expense of a business organization having problems beyond those of the simplest type cannot be acquired by the average auditor within the time at his disposal.

Where, as a part of the audit engagement, the income-tax return is to be prepared, it is preferable to have the firm's tax specialist perform the work in the field while the annual audit is in progress.

Property and other taxes. State and local taxes are generally levied on persons who are owners of property on a specified date in each year. A property tax is the result obtained by multiplying the assessed value of the property—often a variable—against the rate established for the year. The auditor's function can be no more than to examine the bill for its authenticity, or to offer no objection to accruals based on last year's bill plus or minus estimated or known changes in assessments or rates. Assessed valuations usually have no relation to cost or depreciated cost and are often a fraction, established by law, regulation, or custom, of the assessor's determination of "full" value. The preferable accounting for property taxes is to accrue them (as an expense and current liability) during the twelve-month period immediately preceding the earliest payment date. Sometimes property taxes are regarded as prepaid since they often are used to pay governmental expenditures of the period following. To this, the auditor does not seriously object, since no accounting principle has been developed that prefers one method over any other, and the amount is not usually important from the point of view of its effect on the balance sheet (points already noted in connection with deferred charges).

Royalties. On machinery not owned, a royalty or a straight monthly rental may be paid. Or, royalties may accrue because of patents owned by another company or person, the business under audit being merely the licensee and paying an agreed amount per unit of production or sale. The quantity of production or sale to the date of the balance sheet should be ascertained through the operating records and an examination made to see if full adequate credits have been accumulated.

Commissions. Salesmen for manufacturing concerns and wholesale houses are nearly always employed on some sort of commission basis, and the various arrangements that may exist should be ascertained by examination of employment contracts. Sometimes the commission remains unpaid until the customer has settled his account in which case it is necessary for purposes of internal control to separate commissions deferred and commissions earned and payable.

Salaries and wages. Officers and executives are as a rule paid on a monthly basis, whereas the shop and office forces are paid weekly or semimonthly. The liability for each class is nearly always separately determined. From the shop payroll, for example, for the week containing the last day of the fiscal year, can be obtained usually satisfactory proof of the accrued liability by applying to the gross amount of the payroll a ratio equal to the number of hours pertaining to the fiscal year divided by the total hours included in the payroll.

Long-term obligations. External controls over security issues make the auditor's examination of long-term indebtedness a comparatively light task. When the issue is sold, or on the occasion of a first examination, the auditor makes a detailed study of the transaction—the trust deed or indenture, the marketing agreement, qualification details prepared for state security commissions or the Securities and Exchange Commission, the prospectus, opinions of counsel, minutes of stockholders and of the board of directors. He examines vouchers or other support for expenses attending the sale and reviews transactions since the original sale. He compares the recorded proceeds from the sale with the marketing agreement and examines the trustee's reports of bonds issued. He makes a list of the financial requirements imposed by the indenture, such as the method of paying interest and principal, the method of computing the trustee's annual fee, restrictions on the use of proceeds or profits, minimum working-capital ratio or amount, and periodic reports. Indentures do not make easy reading and the auditor may wish to review his interpretations of them with his client's counsel. From this initial study he prepares a point list or synopsis for his permanent file that will serve as the basis for the annual review thereafter. He also prepares an analysis of the original sales transaction for the permanent file with provisions thereon for future transactions. As a rule, no current papers need be prepared during succeeding audits —transactions may be summarized, with whatever comments may be necessary, on the permanent-file worksheet.

A bond-discount schedule is necessary for the permanent file and, where maturities are fixed and are likely to be met, the amortization expense may be computed several years in advance or for the entire period of the issue. The bond discount and expense is nearly always spread in proportion to the amount of interest scheduled to be paid each year (or in accordance with each year's outstanding principal—which is the same basis), and compliance of book entries with the schedule should be noted on the permanent-file worksheet each year. Prepayments of maturities call for an immediate amortization of the portion of the remaining deferred charge pertaining to the retirement.

Periodic deposits with a sinking-fund trustee may be required by the indenture. Confirmation should be procured from the trustee as to the makeup of the sinking fund at the balance-sheet date, including bonds repurchased. Occasionally it will be found that the trustee is permitted to purchase bonds as a fund investment and hold them alive until their maturity. However whenever a repurchase is made by the trustee, regardless of the reason for the repurchase or of the fact that the bond may be held alive in the fund, a corresponding entry should be reflected on the books of the corporation by means of which the bond repurchased is recorded at par, any premium or discount adjusted by the portion of the unamortized discount on the company's books pertaining to the repurchased bond being carried to current income or expense. This procedure permits the sinking-fund balance, which excludes the bonds held by the sinking-fund trustee, to be deducted on the face of the balance sheet from the bond obligation outstanding. Interest paid on bonds so held—the amount of which reduces the future liability—should not, of course, be charged to expense but as an additional payment to the trustee.

In addition to payments to the trustee the indenture may require the creation of a sinking-fund reserve—in reality a simple reservation of earned surplus. The auditor should see that the balance thereof conforms to indenture requirements. These may provide, for example, that it be maintained at a level equal to the payments made to the sinking-fund trustee, to the cash and bonds held in the sinking fund, or to some other figure. But in any case the preferable classification of the reserve on the balance sheet is as a subdivision of earned surplus.

Unissued or reacquired bonds should be fully accounted for by examination as at each audit date or, where they are in the possession of others, by written confirmation. If they have been pledged, balance-sheet disclosure must be provided for.

Interest accrued and paid during the audit period may be verified as long-term obligations are being reviewed. A simple interest check excluding interest on unissued or "treasury" bonds is usually deposited with a paying agent (who is often the trustee) and the obligor's liability therefor is then fully discharged; in this case it is not customary to regard the assets and liabilities of the paying agent relating to interest on the obligation as those of the obligor. But where the paying agent functions in a true agency capacity cash on hand at the balance-sheet date and a current liability of the same amount for coupons not cashed must be taken up in the financial statements of the obligor. In either case the semiannual interest check must be in the paying agent's hands on the date specified in the indenture; otherwise a default will probably have occurred. Paid coupons should be canceled by the paying agent through the use of a perforating stamp and returned to the obligor as evidence of payment; or they may ultimately be cremated, in which case a certificate of cremation should be secured for the obligor's files.

A confirmation request from the client, similar to that shown below, should be addressed to the trustee.

(Name and address of trustee)

Dear Sirs:

Please confirm to our auditors, Messrs. Hyatt, Paterson & Co., 960 Hudson Bldg., Chicago 3, the following items, as at December 31, 19–2, relating to our issue of First Mortgage Bonds for which you are acting as trustee:

1. Name of issue.
2. Date of indenture (or mortgage).
3. Principal certified and outstanding.
4. Principal amount reacquired by you:
    (a) Held alive in sinking fund.
    (b) Retired and canceled.
5. Date to which funds for the payment of interest have been deposited with you.
6. Amount of interest funds on deposit with you.
7. Makeup of sinking fund in your hands.
8. Other funds on deposit with you.
9. Collateral or other securities on deposit with you.
10. Any direct or contingent liability on our part, not mentioned in your answers to the above, owing to you.

An addressed envelope is enclosed for your reply.

Very truly yours,

by _____

Discounted receivables. Notes and acceptances discounted are probably the most common form of contingent liability. Provision is made in the bank-confirmation letter (page 206) for a listing by the bank of contingent obligations—including not only discounted receivables but also accommodation endorsements or guaranties of which the bank has direct knowledge. The auditor's review of the notes-receivable register will usually reveal the items discounted. If the discounting has taken place with persons other than the client's regular depositories, confirmations as to any notes still outstanding should be secured by the auditor. For purposes of internal control it is good practice to maintain a notes-receivable-discounted account, which is relieved of its credit entries when makers of notes have paid them.

Endorsements and guarantees of performance. As an accommodation to customers, suppliers, and affiliated interests, business enterprises may be called upon to endorse commercial paper that is the primary obligation of others, or to guarantee performance under a contract to deliver a product or to perform services. The endorsement of specific notes involves a definite risk that requires disclosure on financial statements; guarantees of performance may, however, give rise to such remote risks or risks offset by recoveries of such value as to make their disclosure unnecessary. The auditor must judge each case on its merits.

Judgments, damages, suits. Examination of legal bills and inquiry as to the services attorneys have rendered often reveals the existence of litigation that involves a contingent obligation; a minimum-settlement estimate by the client's attorney may warrant the accrual of an actual liability. Confirmation as to estimated contingent and actual liabilities should be obtained directly from attorneys. The average corporation lawyer is well acquainted with the auditor's requirements in this connection. Damage claims may be covered, wholly or partly, by insurance, and consideration should be given to this possibility when determining the amount of the contingency.

Additional income taxes. Additional income taxes may have to be paid covering years still open to audit by the Bureau of Internal Revenue. Revenue agents' reports may actually be on hand, indicating additional liability—reports that the controller or tax officer may believe can be overcome by argument or by the presentation of additional facts. The auditor's conclusions will be affected in part by the amounts of additional taxes paid in the past few years because of the same or similar points on which the latest reports are based. Whether additional or contingent liabilities should be recognized, in case the auditor finds his opinions in conflict with the client's representatives, is a matter the auditor should review with his principal.

Product guarantees. During his inquiries on sales activities and as a result of his scanning of returns and allowances the auditor will have determined whether an adequate provision has been made for returns and losses in the form of a valuation reserve that has been based on past experience or other probabilities; he also will have determined what further contingencies exist because of guarantees attaching to new products, the risks on which, the future may show, have not been fully provided for, or attaching to individual sales of a class not usually guaranteed. The auditor must always distinguish between risks that past experience and present practical judgments can evaluate, and risks for which these determinants do not exist. The latter class may run into material amounts and thus require mention, even though the risk cannot be stated in dollars; on the other hand it may be too small or imaginary to justify inclusion among disclosed contingencies.

Where the sales contract or recognized customer policy calls for the rendering of a replacement, repair, or adjustment service over a period of more than a year, the deferral of a portion of the selling price as unearned income may be called for, the deferral plan involving the periodic amortization of the unearned amount over a specific number of periods.

Contracts. In his talks with the sales group and other management representatives, the auditor should seek information as to the existence of any contracts under the operation of which losses or other uncompensated-for risks are likely to be encountered. Occasionally the auditor finds an alternative contingency: damages that would follow nonperformance of an unprofitable contract.

Sell-and-lease agreements. Improved real estate occupied by the business may be sold to an insurance company or other investor and a long-term lease taken back on the property. Or the investor may finance the acquisition of new assets, which are immediately leased to the business. Numerous varieties of such financing have been entered into in recent years for the purpose of avoiding the time and expense involved in a public sale of securities. These arrangements and the documents supporting them require a careful reading by the auditor to make sure that the full amount of any direct liability thereunder has been recorded. Balance-sheet disclosure is made of the number and character of such leases, the amount and nature of the minimum and conditional rental obligation, the years effective, the options enjoyed by the lessee, and the obligation of the lessee upon the expiration of the leases.

Purchase commitments. The existence of commitments for future purchases at a cost in excess of the present or a likely future market price may affect materially the financial position of a business, unless there are offsetting sales contracts or continuing sales prices against which the commitments have been made. The possible loss may be measured by the amount (usually less than the contract-market differential) for which the supplier is willing to settle if the commitment be canceled, or by the potential loss of gross profit. But since the actual purchase will bring about a loss only if prevailing sales prices decline (a possibility on which reasonable opinions can only rarely be secured), the prospect of loss is too uncertain to justify full recognition as an accrual on the books. In his list of contingent liabilities the auditor will probably value it at the price differential, with the understanding that the figure shown is in the nature of a maximum. Occasionally, situations are found where commitments greatly in excess of normal volume have been entered into to cover orders or contracts that have since been canceled or sales that are no longer made. If the quantities are too large to be stored by the client or ultimately absorbed in production, a possible loss may develop that should be included among the contingent obligations.

Another type of obligation needs to be disclosed on the balance sheet: commitments covering construction or new equipment—provided the dollar amount substantially exceeds normal yearly replacement requirements. Such items are not contingent liabilities in the ordinary sense, but they must be revealed because of their effect on financial position.

Infractions of law. Penalties may arise from violations of laws or regulations administered by governmental agencies. Occasionally, the liability will be substantial and the possibility that it has already reached the "actual" stage should be discussed with the person responsible for maintaining relationships with the agency.

Liability remaining from property sold. A vendor of real estate may have a contingent liability with respect to a mortgage that he has passed along to the new owner, unless he has secured a release from the mortgagee or has received a bond from responsible third persons guaranteeing him against any future liability. Opinion of counsel should be obtained in such cases.

Illustrative Audit

Liabilities other than those arising from current purchases of materials, outside services, and accruals, are ordinarily verified by correspondence with creditors. Thus the outstanding bank loans and trade notes are found to be in agreement with acknowledgments by creditors (C 3a and N 1a).

Part of the auditor's examination of accounts payable (worksheet P 1) consists of running a tape on the open items in the voucher record for November and December, the open items being those bearing a payment date or check number belonging to 1953. As the auditor scans the register, he follows through on the payment by comparison with the January and February (to the 12th) check register.

A number of unrecorded obligations are discoverd by the auditor when he reviews the January and February voucher record (worksheet P 2). Most of the items are too small for adjustment.

No 1952 receiving ticket remains unaccounted for. The contingencies reported by the attorneys are negligible (P 3).

Customers' credit balances come from deposits on contracts as well as from other sources. As deliveries are made, these amounts are transferred to sales. Each balance was examined for its conformance with a confirmation reply from the customer. The timing and completeness of the sales account was found to accord with accounting standards (see A 3).

Details of accrued payroll and accrued taxes appear on worksheets Q 1 and Q 2. Because payments and accruals of six kinds of taxes were kept in account 132, the assistant controller prepared worksheet Q 2 for the auditor, using as a basis a running analysis that he had maintained on this account throughout the year. This method made it possible to split the account according to the tax source when TB 3 was being prepared. For purposes of the report rendered at the conclusion of the audit, nothing is gained by the split on the worksheet; its purpose is to facilitate the annual analysis. In years past, a more detailed summarization of taxes was reported, which would indicate that the present practice is, in some measure, simply a survival. The rates of tax and other data appearing on schedules such as Q 2 and Q 3, should always be complete enough to make it possible to verify from the working-paper summary each accrual against the payroll or other tax basis.

Income-tax laws and regulations have been changed so extensively from year to year that most auditors find it extremely difficult to be sure that their review of clients' computations is adequate. The practice in many public-accounting offices is to maintain a tax "staff" or "department" capable of reviewing or preparing returns and of assisting in the disposal of differences with tax authorities. The adjustments of income and expense noted on worksheet PF 86 indicate the differences between taxable income and income per books.

4/2
111-0
135-1
291

H-A

2-5-53
2-21-53

Basic data prepared by Myra Lyons

Payee	Rate %	Dates			Notes Payable		Comments
		Issued	Due	Paid	Issued	Unpaid 12-31-52	
Bank loans:							
Howard Natl. Bank	2½	11-15-51	2-13-52	2-13-52	(a) 300 000 00	–	For major
Howard Natl. Bank	2½	2-13-52	5-14-52	5-14-52	(a) 200 000 00	–	material
Howard Natl. Bank	2¼	5-14-52	7-14-52	7-14-52	(a) 100 000 00	–	purchases
Howard Natl. Bank	2¼	11-19-52	2-17-53	(b)	(a) 450 000 00	(c) 450 000 00	For spring
Howard Natl. Bank	2¼	12-16-52	3-20-53		100 000 00	(c) 100 000 00	production
Trade notes:							
Lamson Products Co.	3	4-16-52	5-16-52	5-16-52	(a) 7 500 00	–	
✓	3	✓	7-16-52	7-16-52	(a) 7 500 00	–	For
✓	3	✓	9-16-52	9-17-52	(a) 7 500 00	–	equipment
✓	3	✓	11-16-52	11-17-52	(a) 7 500 00	–	purchased
✓	3	✓	1-16-53		(a) 7 500 00	(d) 7 500 00	(N-1a)
✓	3	✓	2-16-53		7 500 00	(d) 7 500 00	
Total notes unpaid at 12-31-52 (a/c 111-0)						565 000 00	
						TB	

Interest

	Expense for 1952	Accrued 12-31-51	Paid in 1952	Accrued 12-31-52
1		958 33	1 875 00	–
2		–	1 250 00	–
3		–	375 00	–
4		–	–	1 181 25
5		–	–	93 75
6		–	18 75	–
7		–	56 25	–
8		–	93 75	–
9		–	131 25	–
10		–	–	159 38
11		–	–	159 37
Interest on Notes Payable	4 435 42	958 33	3 800 00 ←	1 593 75
	(a/c 291) TB			(a/c 135-1) TB

Source of data: Notes Payable register

Notes:
(a) Paid notes on file agree with above detail
(b) Paid 2-17-53; $300,000 renewed
(c) Agrees with certificate from Howard Natl. Bank (C-3a)
(d) Checks with attached letter (N-1a)

N-1

-451-

LAMSON PRODUCTS COMPANY
General office: Empire Building, New York 3, N. Y.
Plants at: Canajoharie, N. Y.
Skaneateles, N. Y.

February 10, 1953

Hyatt, Paterson & Company
960 Hudson Building
Chicago 4, Ill.

Gentlemen:

At the request of Mr. J. B. Huddle we
wish to report that we hold the following
notes of Martin Manufacturing Company in
connection with the sale of machinery:

Dated	Due	Interest rate	Amount
4-16-52	1-16-53	3%	$7,500
4-16-52	2-16-53	3%	7,500

N-1

Interest on each note is payable at maturity.

Very truly yours,

Lamson Products Company

Samuel Bertrand
Treasurer

N - 1a

-452-

Martin Manufacturing Company
Accounts Payable
December 31, 1952

A/L
115-0

F.L.
2-21-53

Tape of unpaid vouchers at 12-31-52:

	1,527.53 *		70,955.40S
	23,985.46	X	1,966.25-
	12,519.38		596.32
U 12-34	154.96		2,588.74
	35.76		38.96
	52.49	U 12-410	721.36
	758.26		5,896.58
	109.84		19.45
	8,609.87		2.39
	10,996.08		126.32
	4,226.80		66.35
	2,584.67		54.78
	16.59		11,125.64
	75.00		[Several columns of detail omitted.]
U 12-68	6.94		
	2.38		816.54
U 12-173	569.63		3,157.89
	2,236.75		12.57
	129.50		
	88.56		177,393.81 *
	458.63		
	297.56		
	826.54		
	79.99		
	606.23		
	70,955.40S		

U = unpaid on 2-12-53

[A trial balance such as this may be made directly on working paper from the adding machine usually found in any bookkeeping office; for a narrow carriage the paper may be folded down the middle. A good practice in the case of a carryover is to repeat the subtotal, as illustrated.]

Total as above, per controlling A/c	177393 81
Unrecorded liabilities:	
AJE-16 - Raw material and parts	2385 01
-20 - Fuel and freight	2976 83
Total as adjusted	- 182755 65^ TB
X = Jasper Mfg Co.- Vo 12-309- credit items	
for defective parts returned	+ 1966 25 (R/E-E)
Balance after reclassification	184721 90^

Work done

Ran tape of client's list of unpaid vouchers at 12-31-52;
total agreed with balance in A/c 115-0.

P-1

Martin Manufacturing Company
Accounts Payable
December 31, 1952

115-0

7.7

2-21-

Work done - Cont'd:

Using client's list showing voucher numbers, compared individual vouchers over $100 with amounts recorded in voucher register. These vouchers were examined for completeness of supporting documents:

Invoices - for evidence of verification of quantities, qualities, prices, extensions, and footings.
— for observance of discount terms.

Receiving and inspection reports - for authorized signatures evidencing receipt and inspection of goods.

Purchase orders - for authorized signatures and for conformity to quantities and qualities and items in receiving reports and invoices.

Vouchers - for approvals by authorized personnel.

Only minor defects found, mostly absences of authorized approvals. These were discussed with Mr. Collins who will follow up to avoid recurrence.

All vouchers represented liabilities for merchandise, supplies, services, expense vouchers for officers and salesmen all of which were applicable to period under audit and appeared to be usual and recurring expenditures.

Notation of payment on vouchers over $500 were compared with entries in check register; items unpaid at 7-12-53 are identified on our list by "O"; inquiry revealed various reasons for delay in payment, primarily differences in billed unit prices and quality of material, none of the reasons indicated the presence of additional liabilities.

Balances shown by creditors' statements on hand were found covered by vouchers recorded in 1952, with the exception of unrecorded invoices listed on P-2. Statements are now received from relatively few creditors. System of internal control was found to give assurance that no significant liabilities were unrecorded at 12-31-52; therefore circularization of trade creditors was considered to be unnecessary.

P-1a

-454-

Martin Manufacturing Company
Search for Unrecorded Liabilities
December 31, 1952

Scanning of general journal:

1-20-53   On basis of a resolution of
Board of directors dated 7/5/52, each
salesman was to be paid a bonus
of 5% on his 1952 sales over $400,000;
liability recorded in general journal
on 1-20-53   6117 43   AJE-4
Work sheets supporting entry were
tested and reviewed. entry approved by
Mr. Huddle   approved by Board 1/7/26

Castings in hands of suppliers, included in
inventory, but not recorded as liability:
Robertson Foundry Co., represented by 2
December invoices - See F-11B (see Vo 1-392)   1 782 54   AJE-16

Receiving reports from December 20 to 31, 1952, were
found to have been accounted for in vouchers payable
and included in 12/31/52 inventory except for:
    R 22601   Anderson Bros. Co. - Raw material (Vo 1-216)   347 80   AJE-16
    R 22608   M. S. Larks Co. - Parts   (Vo 1-196)   254 67   AJE-16

Examination of 1953 voucher register of items for
more than $500 revealed 1952 liabilities as follows:
   Vo 1- 67   Pocohantas Fuel Co. - Coal   850 28 ⎫
      1- 82   C. M. N. Railroad Co. - Freight on shipments   158 67 ⎬ AJE-20
      1-103   Inter Mountain Express Co. Freight on shipments   545 58 ⎭
No suppliers' invoices on hand on January 12
showed 1952 deliveries except invoice 26 4371 from
Hoskins Mfg. Co. (vouchered on Jan. 12) for parts, $25.32; passed

Petty cash - first reimbursement voucher (1-28) in 1953
included the following December 1952 items:
    Repair of office roof   233 86 ⎫ AJE-27
    Christmas gifts to postman and truckers   35 75 ⎭

Scanning of expense accounts - No adjustments; see A-6, 7, 8

Open purchase orders examined for December 20-31, delivery notations -
Were checked to voucher register; no exceptions

P-2

Joseph C. Beggs
Arthur Baggs II
Justin Boggs

BEGGS, BAGGS, & BOGGS
Attorneys and Counselors at Law
111 W. Washington Street
Chicago 6, Illinois

February 4, 1953

Messrs. Hyatt, Paterson & Co.
960 Hudson Building
Chicago 4, Illinois

Dear Sirs:

P-4

At the oral request of Mr. Edw. Stebbins, president
of the Martin Manufacturing Company for whom we act as
general counsel, we wish to inform you that aside from
minor litigation involving a maximum liability not in
excess of $5,000 we know of no pending action against
the company involving any financial obligation on its
part. The actual liability arising from these suits
will in our opinion not exceed $400.

Our fees for services, covering the latter half of
the year 1952, amounted to $9,500 and were billed to
the company under date of December 30, 1952.

We shall be glad to supply any other data in our possession which you may desire in connection with your
audit for the year ended December 31, 1952.

Sincerely yours,

BEGGS, BAGGS, & BOGGS

Justin Boggs
Justin Boggs

P - 3

Martin Manufacturing Company
Contingent Liabilities
December 31, 1952

J.L.
2-27-53

Notes receivable discounted at Jackson National Bank: (C-2a)

Maker	Int rate	Dated	Due	Amount	Accrued interest
Banks Toddman Co.	3½%	11-15-52	5-15-53	10,500 00	46 00
Whiteman Co.	—	10-30-52	120 da.	15,111 00	
				C-2b	

Pending suits, as per company's attorneys $5,000 00   P-3

10-year lease dated 3-1-50 on premises
occupied by Burton-Makun Company,
subsidiary of M.M.Co., executed by M.M.C.
annual rental of $4,800 being paid by B.M.C.

Federal income tax returns for the years 1950, 1951
and 1952 have not been examined by the BIR.
These returns were reviewed by our Tax Department,
as were returns for earlier years. Returns
for several years prior to 1950 were reviewed by
the BIR and were accepted without adjustment.
It is believed that no substantial adjustments
will be made on the returns which are still
open. (PF-85)

P-4

Martin Manufacturing Company
Employees Bond Payments
December 31, 1952

40.00 *
1.25
18.75
8.75
62.50
50.00
35.00
10.00
3.75
6.25
31.25
55.00
62.50
11.25
60.00
16.25
6.25
[242 items omitted]
25.00
2.50
6.25
10.00
70.00
3.75
15.00
8.75
375.00 -
6,300.00 *
T̄O

Work done:

1. At our request Carl Stibbs, internal auditor, on Jan. 2, 1953 ran a tape for us of the balances in the Employees Bond Payments ledger. total agreed with balance in control.

2. Because of the smallness of the individual balances, our verification of the list of account balances was limited to a test comparison with the subsidiary ledger of the individual balances (without proving total of tape).

3. The debit balance of $375 represents bonds purchased weekly to be available for prompt issue to employees.

4. Count of Series E - U.S. Savings Bonds on 1-2-53

1 -	$100 denomination		75 00
3 -	50	✓	112 50
10 -	25	✓	187 50
	Total cost		375 00

Bonds were returned after count in my presence.   (Sinc.) Elsa Ray
1/2/53

Martin Manufacturing Company
Accrued Payroll
December 31, 1952

Office employees paid through 12-31-52
Factory employees paid through 12-26-52

Accrual for period from December 27 through 31:

The fraction $3/5$ (Dec. 29-31) was applied to the factory payroll for the week ended on 1-2-53:

Detail	Payroll 1-2-53	Accrual (3/5)	a/c.	Ref.
Checks issued	61687 28	39 239 86	131-1	TB-2
Bond purchase deductions	3 712 50			
F.I.C.A.	1 109 58	665 76	132	Q-2
Withholding tax	7 601 58	4 560 95	132	Q-2
Totals, already on books	74 110 94	44 466 57		
Add. Employer's taxes on accrued wages of $44,466.57:				
Unemployment				
State 2.7%		1200 60	132	Q-2
Federal .3%		133 40	132	Q-2
F.I.C.A. 1.5%		667 00	132	Q-2
Total		46 467 57		

Q-1

-459-

g/L

132-1	2421
132-2	2422
132-3	277-1
132-4	277-2
132-5	

				132-2	132-1	132-3	
					R.E. &	Unemployment	
				Franchise	P.P.	State (2.7%)	Federal (.3%)
Balance Jan. 1, 1952:							
Prepaid				− 2805 −			
Accrued				−	4 210 75	18 898 59	7 962 17
739 08						739 08	82 12
Accruals:							
1-1-52 reversal of 12-31-51 accrual						− 739 08	− 82 12
January						8 563 14	951 46
February						7 048 71	783 19
March						6 585 57	731 73
April						6 229 27	692 14
May						7 717 86	857 54
June						5 886 10	654 01
July						5 597 02	621 89
August						7 159 15	795 46
September						5 415 49	601 72
October						6 888 24	765 36
November						5 316 05	590 67
December				7305 00	21 821 90	5 113 75	568 19
December 29-31, 1952 accrual (Q-1)				−	−	1 200 60	133 40
Total − charged to expense				7305 00	21 821 90	77 981 87	8 664 64
− prepaid (AJE-1)				− 2250 00			
− collected from employees							
Payments - verified:							
3/31 Personal property -1952-½					8 219 76		
9/30 ✓ -1952-½					8 219 75		
3/31 Real estate -1951-½					2 096 57		
9/30 ✓ -1951-½					2 096 57		
10/31 For year ended 6-30-53				4 500 00			
1/31 4th quarter -1951						18 898 59	7 962 17
4/30 1st quarter -1952						22 197 42	
7/31 2nd quarter -1952						19 833 23	
10/31 3rd quarter -1952						18 171 66	
				4 500 00	20 632 65	79 100 90	7 962 17
Balance - Dec. 31, 1952							
Prepaid (Q-3)				− 2250 00			
Accrued (Q-3)					5 400 00	18 518 64	8 746 76
				TB	TB	TB	TB

Q-2

turing Company   Basic worksheet
Taxes   prepared by Mr. Shell   F.L.
December 31, 1952   2-21-53

132-4 F.I.C.A.		132-5 Federal		Reconciliation of taxes accrued with
Employer (1.5%)	Employee (1.5%)	withholding	Total	charges to Expense
			− 2 805 00	
410 60	409 65	2 757 42	} 73 496 08	
9 208 15	9 207 82	19 609 73		
− 410 60	− 409 65	− 2 757 42		Manufacturing ⁰/c
4 766 58	4 766 30	25 763 58		Real estate 2421	3 091 61 TB-4
3 916 41	3 915 95	21 408 13		Social security 2422	111 850 38 TB-4
3 677 02	3 676 65	20 915 07		
3 470 11	3 469 70	19 571 26		Administrative
4 296 58	4 296 70	24 092 75		Personal property 2771	18 730 29 TB-3
3 274 61	3 274 55	20 801 29		General − 2772
3 127 66	3 127 45	21 147 98		SS 18 521 90
3 986 41	3 986 30	26 087 71		Franchise 5 055 00	23 576 90 TB-5
3 053 68	3 053 60	20 662 08		
3 880 86	3 880 80	25 911 26		
3 043 39	3 043 35	21 088 67		
2 976 06	2 975 95	20 608 89		
667 00	665 76	456 95		
43 725 77	−	−	} 157 249 18	157 249 18
	43 723 41	270 186 20	313 909 61	

Note:
Taxes applicable to accrued wages at the end of each month are credited to this account and are reversed in the following month. This schedule shows only the accrual recorded at 12-31-52 and the reversal of the 12-31-51 accrual on 1-1-52

9 208 15	9 208 15 (Dec.)	19 609 73		
12 360 01	12 360 02	68 086 78		
11 041 30	11 041 30	64 465 30		
10 167 75	10 167 76	68 221 77		
42 777 21	42 777 23	220 383 58	418 133 74	
			− 2 250 00	
10 567 31	10 563 65	72 169 77	125 966 13	
TB	TB	TB		

Q-2

Martin Manufacturing Company
Analysis of balances of accrued general taxes
December 31, 1952

F.L.
2-21-53

a/c 132-2 - Franchise tax:

New York franchise tax paid per return filed
on 7/1/52 for year ended 6/30/53 (return prepared by H.P.&Co.) 4,500 00

Less - 6/12 of tax - for 6 months ended 12/31/52 .... 2,250 00

Prepaid tax - 12/31/52 (½ of amount paid)   AJE-1 .... 2,250 00*

a/c 132-1 Real-estate and personal-property tax:

Personal-property tax by custom accrued on
January 1. no liability at 12-31-52

Real-estate tax - 1952

Valuation for 1952 per assessor's records,
$300,000 @ 1951 rate of $18.00 per M 5,400 00

a/c 132-3 Unemployment insurance:	Total	State	Federal
Payment made in Jan 1953 - per returns filed		17,318 04	8,613 36
Amount applicable to payroll accrued at 12-31-52: (Q-1)			
$444,466 57 @ 2.7%		1,200 60	
444,466 57 @ .3%			133 40
	27,265 40	18,518 64	8,746 76*

a/c 132-4 Federal withholding and F.I.C.A.:	Total	F.I.C.A.	Withholding
Amount due per return for quarter ended 12-31-52, filed in Jan. 1953	87,409 47	19,800 65	67,608 82
Amount applicable to payroll accrued at 12-31-52 (Q-1)	5,893 71	1,332 76	4,560 95
	93,303 18*(A)	21,133 41*	72,169 77*
Less - Deposits made (Q-4):			
Receipt #178972 - Oct.	33,673 00		
#219767 - Nov.	27,175 46	60,848 46*	13,848 53	46,999 93
Balances - 12-31-52	32,454 72*	7,284 88*	25,169 84*

(A) No adjustment made for the $2.45 understatement
of the liability at 12-31-52.

Q-3

Martin Manufacturing Company
G/L
Deposits on Federal Withholding
B.B.
27-8
and F.I.C.A. Taxes
2-20-53

December 31, 1952

Date of receipt	No. of receipt	For month of			Amount	FICA	Withholding
11-10-52	178972	October			33673 00 x	7761 74	25911 26
12-9-52	219767	November			27175 46 x	6086 79	21088 67
					60848 46*	13848 53^	46999 93^
					TB		

x: Compared with depositary receipts listed
on back of copy of report of Federal
withholding and F.I.C.A. taxes for
quarter ended 12-31-52

Note:
On January 1, 1952, the company commenced charging
to this account the monthly payment to the Federal
Reserve Bank of Federal withholding taxes collected and
F.I.C.A. taxes due. At the time of filing with the Collector
of Internal Revenue the quarterly report of Federal
withholding taxes collected and F.I.C.A. taxes due,
accompanied by the depositary receipts from the Federal
Reserve Bank for the monthly payments, an entry
is made crediting the above account for the
amount of the depositary receipts surrendered and
debiting A/c 133-5 Accrued Federal withholding tax
and A/c 133-4 Accrued F.I.C.A. taxes. Thus the accounting
records recognize the existence of the depositary
receipts and the extinction of the liability only
upon the surrender of formal receipts from the
Federal Reserve Bank.

Q-4

Martin Manufacturing Company
Accrued Royalties
December 31, 1952

Month	Conrad Steel Supply Company				Cleveland Grid Company		
	Accrued on shipments		Payments	Balance	Accrued on shipments	Payments	Balance
12-31-51				600 00			620 24
Jan		-	600 00		1120 48	620 24	
Feb	1	300 00	-		1661 66	1120 48	
March	3	900 00	300 00		1400 34	1661 66	
April	-	-	900 00		1796 34	1400 34	
May	4	1200 00	-		1120 48	1796 34	
June	-	-	1200 00		1622 08	1120 48	
July	2	600 00	-		1307 15	1622 08	
Aug.	1	300 00	600 00		1436 83	1307 15	
Sept.	1	300 00	300 00		1337 33	1436 83	
Oct	3	900 00	300 00		720 00	1337 33	
Nov.	-		900 00		540 10	720 00	
Dec.	2	600 00	-		880 68	540 10	
Totals	17	5100 00	5100	600 00	(A) 14943 47	14683 03	880 68

Quantities shipped - Cleveland:

Size (inches)	Quantity shipped	Rate	Amount
1/8	59	120.00	7080 00
1/4	7	130.56	913 92
3/8	2	138.00	276 00
7/16	18	140.24	2524 32
1/2	1	200.00	200 00
9/16	9	300.10	2700 90
5/8	2	416.11	832 22
3/4	1	416.11	416 11
	99		(A) 14943 47

Summary =	Conrad	Cleveland	Total	%c	
Royalty expense (1952)	5100 00	14943 47	20043 47	213	TB
Royalty accrued at 12-31-52	600 00	880 68	1480 68	131-3	TB

Provisions of the royalty
agreements are given on PF-81.

Q-5

Martin Manufacturing Company
First Mortgage Bonds
December 31, 1952

F.L.

2-7-53

Particulars	a/c 151-1 Bond principal	a/c 292 Interest at 4%
Balance at 12-31-51	745000 00	29800 00
Less - Bonds retired by S.F. trustee - 6-30-52 (see below)	− 20000 00	− 4000 00
Balance outstanding at 12-31-52	725000 00 ✗	
Less - Bonds repurchased by company and held by Jackson National Bank at 12-31-52, which were delivered on 1-9-53 to the Liberty National Bank, Trustee, for cancellation (see comments below)	− 410000 00 ✗✗	− 5041 50 ✗
Adjusted balance at 12-31-52 (See PF-88)	315000 00 ✗	−
Bond interest expense for 1952 (see PF-89) (per AJE 5)		24358 50 TB
a/c 151-4 - Sinking fund:		
Balance at 12-31-51		2131586
Deposits - $10,000 each on 6/27 and 12/29/52		20000 00
Interest allowed by Trustee - 1% - credited to a/c 282 (Interest on Notes Receivable)		163 16
		41479 02
Bonds retired at 6-30-52 by Trustee, per annual report		− 20000 00
Balance at 12-31-52 (see PF-89) (S-4)		2147902 ✗✗ TB

Work done:

✗ = Liberty National Bank, Trustee, confirmed the amount of bonds outstanding at December 31, 1952, and at January 16, 1953, after cancellation of $410,000 of bonds received from Jackson National Bank (S-4).

✗✗ = Confirmed by Liberty National Bank, Trustee (S-4).

✗ = Charges to "First mortgage bonds repurchased" account (151-5) were verified by comparison of scheduled amounts with weekly statements from bank. Accrued interest on bonds repurchased was recomputed as shown in schedule on S-2; no exceptions.

✗ = Annual interest on bonds repurchased in 1952 (410,00 @ 4%)   16400 00

    Less - Interest paid on bonds repurchased in 1952 -
    7-1-52 coupons, less $1,520 attached to bonds
    repurchased ($8,200 - $1,520)   6680 00

    Interest accrued to date of repurchase
    (including $1,520 of matured coupons)   4678 50   11358 50⁺

    Reduction in 1952 bond interest expense   5041 50⁺

S-1

A/L
151-1

Martin Manufacturing Company
First Mortgage Bonds
December 31, 1952

F.L
12-19-5

Comments:

On 5-21-52 the directors authorized the repurchase of as many of the outstanding bonds as possible since money could be borrowed more cheaply at current rates ($3\frac{1}{2}$% v. 4%.) They accordingly directed the president to advertise the following offer:

"To buy outstanding 4% first-mortgage bonds at par plus accrued interest plus a premium equal to
.5% on 1953 maturities,
1.0% on 1954 maturities,
1.5% on 1955 maturities, plus $\frac{1}{2}$% additional for each succeeding maturity until the premium reaches 10% on the 1972 maturities."

The president was further authorized to "negotiate with the trustee, Liberty National Bank, and Porter, Houseman & Co., security dealers, to solicit repurchases," in return for which the bank and the dealer were to be "paid a 3/4% fee plus any out-of-pocket costs." Advertising was to begin in June and repurchases were to be made "at any time between July 1 and October 31." (see X-3)

Following was the result:

Maturity June 30	Premium per 1M	Outstanding 6-30-52	Repurchases			
			Date	Principal	Premium	Interest
1953	5	20 M	10-15	10 M*	50 00	116 70
5	15	20	7-1 / 10-1	13 / 2 *	195 00 / 30 00	— / 20 00
6	20	20	8-10	20 *	400 00	88 90
7	25	20	7-27	1 *	25 00	3 00
9	35	20	10-1	18 *	630 00	180 00
60	40	20	10-20	10 *	400 00	122 20
2	50	20	8-1	15 *	750 00	50 00
5	65	20	10-31	5 *	325 00	66 70
6	70	20	8-5 / 8-10	1 / 10 *	70 00 / 700 00	3 90 / 44 40
7	75	20	7-4	10 *	750 00	4 40
72	100	345	9-15	295 *	29 500 00	2 458 30
	Totals			410 M	33 825 00	3 158 50

* Compared with cremation certificate (S-2a)

S-2

4/L
151-1

Martin Manufacturing Company
First Mortgage Bonds
December 31, 1952

F.L.
12-19-52

Comments (Cont.):

An initial deposit of $100,000 was made with the Jackson National Bank on June 25. Thereafter, additional amounts were advanced for the amount of disbursements reported by the bank which was to hold the repurchased bonds. After reimbursement for the last bonds purchased in October, 1952, the bank deposited the $100,000 in the general account in the Jackson National Bank.

The general ledger account "First Mortgage Bonds Repurchased" showed at December 31, 1952, a debit balance of $450,593.25. Analysis by the client of the charges to this account showed the following:

Principal amount of bonds (which on the analysis sheet was classified by maturities to permit verification of premium)		410 000 00
Premium payment as authorized by B/D (which amount was proved by multiplying principal amount for each maturity date by authorized premium)	33 825 00	
Repurchase fees, per invoices, in full	3 609 75	37 434 75 ^
Interest purchased	4 678 50 °	
Less: collections on matured coupons dated 7-1-52 —	1 520 00	3 158 50 ^
Total — account 151-5 (see AJE 11)		450 593 25 ^

On January 5, 1953, a credit memo for $8,175 was received from the Jackson National Bank, representing the amount of January 1, 1953, coupons ($8,200) less $25 service charge.

On January 9, 1953, the Jackson National Bank was directed to deliver the bonds for cancellation to the Liberty National Bank, Trustee under the bond indenture. From the Trustee the M.M.Co. received a cremation certificate dated January 16, 1953, listing by maturities bonds totalling $410,000, and stating that all unmatured coupons were attached to the bonds. The list on the cremation certificate was compared with the schedule of bonds repurchased on S2.

S-2a

Martin Manufacturing Company
1688 S. Federal St.
Chicago 16, Ill.

February 3, 1953

Liberty National Bank
Chicago 11, Illinois

Dear Sirs:

Please furnish our auditors, Messrs. Hyatt, Paterson
& Co., 960 Hudson Building, Chicago 4, Illinois,
with the following information on our issue of
first-mortgage-4% bonds for which you are the trustee:

1. Status of sinking fund as of December 31,
   1952, on the above issue:
   a. Amount of cash on deposit
   b. Amount of our own bonds or of
       any other investments carried
       in sinking fund
2. Amount of first-mortgage-4% bonds of this
   company outstanding on
   December 31, 1952
   January 16, 1953
3. Other information regarding this issue of
   bonds which will be of interest to our
   auditors

                    Very truly yours,

                    Martin Manufacturing Company

                    by _J.B.Huddle_____
                                    Treasurer

                    S - 3

-468-

LIBERTY NATIONAL BANK
Chicago 11, Illinois

Trust Department
Harris C. Buhl, V. President

February 6, 1953

Hyatt, Paterson & Co.
960 Hudson Building
Chicago 4, Ill.

Dear Sirs:

At the request of the Martin Manufacturing Company we submit the following information on the first-mortgage-4% bond issue of that company of which we are the trustees:

    a) Status of sinking fund on December 31, 1952
       Amount of cash on deposit $ 21,479.02 ∿ *S-1*
       Amount of Martin Mfg. Co. bonds
       or of any other investments
       carried in the sinking fund   none

    b) Amount of first-mortgage-4% bonds
       of the Martin Mfg. Co. outstand-
       ing on
       December 31, 1952   725,000.00 ∿ *PF-88*
       January 16, 1953 (after cancella-
       tion on this date of $410,000 of
       bonds received from the Jackson
       National Bank)   315,000.00 ∿ *PF-88*

    c) Other information regarding this issue
       On January 2, 1953, check for $14,500
       was received to cover interest coupons
       matured on January 1, 1953
       Cash in the amount of $740 is held for
       payment of outstanding coupons which
       matured on or prior to July 1, 1952

                Very truly yours,

                Liberty National Bank

                by *Harris C. Buhl*
                Vice-President
                Trust Department

Copy to-
   Martin Mfg. Co.

S - 4

-469-

Conrad Steel Supply Company:

Agreement dated 6/10/40, expires 6/10/52, (Ⓐ) (12 years)

Accrual of royalty of $300.00 per unit occurs with every invoice covering sale of a machine employing the "Conrad" transmission; payable monthly - within 30 days after close of month in which sales are made.

Cleveland Grid Company:

Agreement dated Jan. 7, 1942.

Royalty payable once monthly on sales of screw machines sold with slotting attachments made under U.S. patent # 1746 9403; covers the following widths:

1/8"	$ 120 00	1/2"	$ 200 00
1/4"	130 56	9/16"	300 10
3/8"	138 00	Larger	
7/16"	140 24	sizes	416 11

Ⓐ Examined agreement extending expiration date to 8/9/54, the date on which the patent expires.

PF-81

Martin Manufacturing Company
Pension Plan (adopted 10-12-43)   W.S.C.

__Contributions__: Employees' contributions - which are to be matched by company - are based on tables appearing in the plan. The tables cover retirement payments and death benefits. Company agrees to make an initial contribution of $50,000 for the first year (1943).

__Eligibility__: To participate an individual must have been in company's (or predecessor organization's) employ for at least 5 years, as certified by treasurer and personnel director. Certain added requirements where there have been employment breaks (except for war service).

__Payments to fund__: At present made by employees separately rather than as payroll deduction. May be put on a payroll-deduction basis and administration of fund made independent of company after 4 years, depending on certain percentages of participation. Officer-employee committee administers fund (ie authorizes payments); 2 officers, 2 employees, 5th chosen by 4 from either officers or employees. "Officer" defined as person whose employment has been by Board of Directors of company.

__Interest on fund__: Interest at 3% to be allowed in even hundreds, on December 31 of each year, based on average balance during year.

__Benefits__: Amounts of benefits appear in table in pension-plan agreement. Committee to certify rates or amounts of payments to be made from fund by company treasurer.

__Note__: Notwithstanding nature of "committee" to administer fund, this fund remains company property until reconstituted as independent trust. Present basis is not strictly actuarial, since fund can be dissolved, further payments of benefits canceled, and balance refunded to donors - all at pleasure of company. It is the intention of the present set-up to experiment with a fund which on or after Oct. 12, 1947, may be transferred to a separate trust, provided the employees like the idea.

A BIR ruling (1-3-44 in company's files) holds that any net increase in the fund during the year is taxable income, and any net decrease, a deductible expense.

PF-82

-471-

			Year ended			
			1943	1944	1945	1946
Balance at beginning of period			0	61 750 00	81 300 00	100 000 00
Additions:						
Provision charged to P+L			30 000 00	14 000 00	15 000 00	18 000 00
Contributions from employees			11 300 00	14 000 00	15 000 00	18 000 00
Interest at 3% on average balance			450 00	2 100 00	2 700 00	3 600 00
			61 750 00	91 850 00	114 000 00	139 600 00
Deductions:						
Benefits paid (listed below)			0	10 250 00	13 500 00	10 100 00
Refunds to employees			0	300 00	500 00	1 400 00
			0	10 550 00	14 000 00	11 500 00
Balance at end of period			61 750 00	81 300 00	100 000 00	128 100 00
Beneficiaries + payments made:						
a	Sylvia Baker	2-1-44	–	550 00	600 00	600 00
b	Tom F. Carey	6-20-44	–	3300 00	–	–
b	George S. Thomas	7-31-44	–	6400 00	–	–
b	Farley Johnson	5-3-45	–	–	5000 00	–
b	Eugene C. Parker	7-15-45	–	–	4500 00	–
b	Florence James	7-16-45	–	–	2000 00	–
a	Orson Towle	8-1-45	–	–	500 00	1 200 00
a	Howard T. Scanlon	8-15-45	–	–	900 00	2 400 00
b	Charles F. Powell	1-31-46	–	–	–	5 600 00
a	Harry Harrison	9-30-46	–	–	–	300 00
a	Grace Butcher	7-1-47	–	–	–	–
a	Clarence Burkhardt	10-15-47	–	–	–	–
b	Eustic Hammond	6-17-49	–	–	–	–
a	Guy C Jacobs	3-1-50	–	–	–	–
a	Kenneth O. Richards	8-1-51	–	–	–	–
a	Samuel C. Peck	10-1-51	–	–	–	–
b	Oscar Hansen	12-16-51	–	–	–	–
a	Otto Buchen	7-1-52	–	–	–	–
a	Stanley Ostrow	10-1-52	–	–	–	–
Total paid			–	10 250 00	13 500 00	10 100 00

a: Life annuity
b: Death benefit

PF - 83

December 31

1947	1948	1949	1950	1951	1952	1953
128 100 00	163 110 00	200 710 00	229 510 00	260 460 00	293 135 00	336 820 00
19 600 00	20 100 00	20 500 00	20 600 00	21 100 00	23 900 00	
19 600 00	20 100 00	20 500 00	20 600 00	21 100 00	23 900 00	
4 400 00	5 500 00	6 600 00	7 500 00	8 400 00	9 300 00	
171 700 00	208 810 00	248 310 00	278 210 00	311 060 00	350 235 00	
5 790 00	6 600 00	14 000 00	8 550 00	10 425 00	7 515 00	
2 800 00	1 500 00	4 800 00	9 200 00	7 500 00	5 900 00	
8 590 00	8 100 00	18 800 00	17 750 00	17 925 00	13 415 00	
163 110 00	200 710 00	229 510 00	260 460 00	293 135 00	336 820 00	
600 00	600 00	1 500 00	—	—	—	
—	—	—	—	—	—	
—	—	—	—	—	—	
—	—	—	—	—	—	
—	—	—	—	—	—	
—	—	—	—	—	—	
1 200 00	1 200 00	1 200 00	1 200 00	1 200 00	1 200 00	
2 400 00	2 400 00	2 400 00	2 400 00	2 400 00	1 200 00	
—	—	—	—	—	—	
1 200 00	1 200 00	1 200 00	3 000 00	—	—	
240 00	480 00	480 00	480 00	480 00	480 00	
150 00	720 00	720 00	720 00	720 00	720 00	
—	—	6 500 00	—	—	—	
—	—	—	750 00	900 00	900 00	
—	—	—	—	500 00	1 200 00	
—	—	—	—	225 00	900 00	
—	—	—	—	4 000 00	—	
—	—	—	—	—	540 00	
—	—	—	—	—	375 00	
5 790 00	6 600 00	14 000 00	8 550 00	10 425 00	7 515 00	

PF - 83a

Martin Manufacturing Company
Federal Income-Tax Liability

	Payments	Accruals	Balance
Balance 12-31-45 (see 1945 W/P's)			1 158 000 00
1944 and prior years – E.P.T.	a 335 000 00		
1945 tax	b 807 300 88		
1946 accrual less overprovision of $15,699.12 for 1945		144 000 00	15 969 12
1947	b 159 225 93	177 000 00	177 473 19
1948	c 177 432 78	110 000 00	110 040 41
1949	d 109 473 18	131 000 00	131 567 23
1950	e 130 919 80	121 000 00	121 647 43
1951	121 601 92	151 000 00	151 045 51
1952	150 703 88	205 000 00	205 341 63
1953			
1954			

Note: On March 2 1953, Joseph Allen of our tax staff gave us his opinion that permission of the Commissioner of Internal Revenue is unnecessary to change to the direct-cost method of valuing inventories of work in progress and finished goods at 12-31-52, and furthermore that the chargeoff of fixed overhead that would otherwise have gone into the inventory was deductible for tax purposes in 1952.

Comments:
a: Claims for relief under Sec. 722 denied. balance due on Excess profits tax for 1944 and prior years paid on December 6, 1946.

b: Years 1945 and 1946 reviewed by BIR in Feb. 1948; accepted as filed.

c: Year 1947 reviewed by BIR in Oct. 1949; accepted as filed.

d: Year 1948 reviewed by BIR in Dec. 1950; accepted as filed.

e: Year 1949 reviewed by BIR in May 1951. accepted as filed; apparent overpayment of $2.00; see PF-86

Details on 1945 and prior years appear in 1945 working papers

PF-85

Martin Manufacturing Company
Accrued Federal Income Taxes

Year	Net income subject to surtax (a to g) and normal tax (a to h)		Rates of surtax and normal tax	Federal Income Tax Detail	Total
1946	a 263 458 19	e 184 56			
	b 144 000 00	f 28 100 00			
	c -3 125 00	g -10 200 00	420 878 76 14%	58 923 03	
	d -1 538 99	h -2 950 00	417 928 76 24%	100 302 90	159 225 93
1947	a 269 101 85	-			
	b 177 000 00	f 350 100 0			
	c -3 500 00	g -11 475 00	468 365 20 14%	65 571 13	
	d 2 228 35	h -2 275 00	466 090 20 24%	111 861 65	177 432 78
1948	a 157 577 17	e 354 19			
	b 110 000 00	f 37 600 00			
	c -3 000 00	g -15 300 00	289 713 64 14%	40 559 91	
	d 2 482 28	h -2 575 00	287 138 64 24%	68 913 27	109 473 18
1949	a 199 723 57	e 124 86			
	b 131 000 00	f 28 800 00			
	e -2 625 00	g -17 000 00	345 894 19 14%	48 425 19	
	d 4 753 76	h -2 175 00	343 719 19 24%	82 492 61	130 917 80
1950	a 151 727 14	e' 11 309 52			
	b 121 000 00	f 30 950 00			
	c -2 750 00	g -11 900 00	302 152 18 42%(-$4750)	122 153 92	
	d 1 815 52	h -2 300 00	- 2 300 00 24%	- 552 00	121 601 92
1951	a 160 576 80	-			
	b 151 000 00	f 32 675 00			
	c -3 200 00	g -14 875 00	308 867 25 50¾%(-$5500)	151 250 13	
	d -1 730 955	h -1 900 00	- 1 900 00 28¾4%	- 546 25	150 703 88
1952	a 208 371 41	e" 10 516 92			
	b 205 000 00	f 43 685 00			
	c - 1 175 0	g -71 198 12	406 095 29 52%(-$5500)	205 669 55	
	d 9 777 58	h -2 232 50	- 2 232 50 30%	- 669 75	204 999 80

a = net income
b = provision for income tax
c = fully exempt interest
d = net charge in bad-debt reserve
e = loss on sale of capital assets
e' = Contribution to Ridgway Community Hospital in excess of 5% limitation

e" = Contributions of $5,000 each to Republican and Democratic National Committees   10 000 00
fines and court costs for violation of municipal trucking code   576 92
f = net increase in pension reserve
g = 85% of dividends received
h = partially taxable interest

PF-86

Title of issue: First-Mortgage-4% Bonds
Trustee: Liberty National Bank
Date of sale: July 1, 1942 (to Porter, Kane & Holdover, a syndicate)
Amount received: $1,000,000 (par)
Due: $20,000 at par each June 30 after 1943; $440,000 June 30, 1972
Interest: Paid twice annually, January 1 and July 1, through trustee
Sinking fund: not less than $20,000 after Dec. 30, 1945, to be kept
by trustee, with contributions of $10,000 from company each six
months commencing Dec. 31, 1942; required retirements to be made
therefrom; interest of 1% per annum to be allowed by trustee on
unused balance, to be credited annually on Dec. 31.
Open-market purchases may be made by company, or by trustee
(at premium of not more than 5 points), upon direction by
company, at any time.

Date	Transaction			Principal Amount	Discount or premium*	Balance
7-1-42	Original sale			1 000 000 00	—	1 000 000 00
10-15-43	Repurchase by company			a) 15 600 00	600 00*	985 000 00
2-1-44	✓	✓	✓	a) 52 000 00	2 000 00*	935 000 00
6-30-44	✓		trustee	20 000 00	—	915 000 00
6-30-45	✓		✓	20 000 00	—	895 000 00
3-1-45	✓		company	a) 10 700 00	700 00*	885 000 00
10-1-45	✓		trustee	a) 5 250 00	250 00*	880 000 00
6-30-46	✓		✓	20 000 00	—	860 000 00
6-30-47	✓		✓	20 000 00	—	840 000 00
9-1-47	✓		company	a) 10 400 00	400 00*	830 000 00
6-30-48	✓		trustee	20 000 00		810 000 00
6-30-49	✓		✓	20 000 00	—	790 000 00
7-1-49	✓		✓	a) 5 200 00	200 00*	785 000 00
6-30-50	✓		✓	20 000 00	—	765 000 00
6-30-51	✓		✓	20 000 00	—	745 000 00
6-30-52	✓		✓	20 000 00		725 000 00
5-21-52 to 12-31-52	✓		company	b) 443 825 00	33 825 00*	315 000 00

a) Bonds due June 30, 1972
b) Various maturities

Sinking Fund (cash)

Date	Payments to Trustee	Repurchase by trustee	Interest allowed by trustee	Balance
1942	10 000 00			10 000 00
1943	20 000 00		150 00	30 150 00
1944	20 000 00	20 000 00	251 50	30 401 50
10-1-45 (par $5,000)		5 250 00		
1945	20 000 00	20 000 00	240 88	25 392 38
1946	20 000 00	20 000 00	203 92	25 596 30
1947	20 000 00	20 000 00	205 96	25 802 26
1948	20 000 00	20 000 00	208 02	26 010 28
7-1-49 (par $5,000)		5 200 00		
1949	20 000 00	20 000 00	184 10	20 994 38
1950	20 000 00	20 000 00	159 94	21 154 32
1951	20 000 00	20 000 00	161 54	21 315 86
1952	20 000 00	20 000 00	163 16	21 479 02

Annual Amounts of Interest Paid

Year	Explanation	Opening rate	Reduction	Amount paid
1942	½ year — from July 1	20 000 00		20 000 00
1943	15,000 purch. by company on 10-15	40 000 00	125 00	39 875 00
1944	50,000 ″ ″ ″ ″ 2-1	39 400 00	1 833 33	
	20,000 ″ ″ trustee ″ 6-30		400 00	37 166 67
1945	″ ″ ″ ″ ″ ″	36 600 00	400 00	
	10,000 ″ ″ company ″ 3-1		333 33	
	5,000 ″ ″ trustee ″ 10-1		50 00	35 816 67
1946	20,000 ″ ″ ″ ″ 6-30	35 200 00	400 00	34 800 00
1947	″ ″ ″ ″ ″ 6-30	34 400 00	400 00	
	10,000 ″ ″ company ″ 9-1		133 33	33 866 67
1948	20,000 ″ ″ trustee ″ 6-30	33 200 00	400 00	32 800 00
1949	″ ″ ″ ″ ″ 6-30	32 400 00	400 00	
	5,000 ″ ″ ″ ″ 7-1		100 00	31 900 00
1950	20,000 ″ ″ ″ ″ 6-30	31 400 00	400 00	31 000 00
1951	″ ″ ″ ″ ″ 6-30	30 600 00	400 00	30 200 00
1952	″ ″ ″ ″ ″ 6-30	29 800 00	400 00	
	410,000 ″ ″ company ″ 12-31		5 041 50	24 358 50
1953		12 600 00		

PF-89

Problems and Questions

1. During the examination of a notes-payable register you find a line devoted to a $50,000 5% demand note stated to be owing to the Second National Bank. However, an employee informs you that this note, now nine months old, is an "accommodation" note, the real borrower being the treasurer of the company, that this is known to the bank and other company officials, that the amount of the note has not been extended in the record and hence is not included among the company's liabilities because the treasurer will eventually repay it, that interest has been paid at the end of each quarter by the company and deducted from the treasurer's compensation, and that the note is fully covered by a deposit of Government bonds that have been produced for your inspection. You examine the bonds and ascertain that their market value is $70,000. Under the conditions described would you agree that the obligation has been properly omitted from the records? What steps would you take in investigating this item?

2. Following is an abstract of the notes-payable register mentioned in the preceding question, omitting the memorandum item therein described:

Date made	Date paid	Number	Term	Rate of Interest	Amount	Remarks
19–2	19–3					
Dec 1	Jan 30	1405	60 d	5 %	$45,000.00	Bank loan (discount)
19–3						
Mar 18		1406	5 y	3	25,000.00	A. B. Jackson, V.P.
Apr 2	July 1	1408	90 d	4½	8,058.00	Trade note
Apr 30	July 1	1409	60 d	4½	5,000.00	Trade note
July 6	Oct 5	1410	90 d	5	30,000.00	Bank loan (discount)
July 25		1411	30 d	4	16,800.00	Trade note, extended 6 months at 4½%
Sept 1	Oct 1	1412	30 d	4	23,814.00	Trade note
Oct 19		1413	3 m	5	3,744.00	Trade note
Dec 8		1414	60 d	5	60,000.00	Bank loan (discount)
Dec 13		1415	6 m	3	10,000.00	A. B. Jackson, V.P.
Dec 22		1416	30 d	4	6,000.00	Trade note

Interest on these notes, per books, was $1,082.53, including the whole of the discount on the bank loan of December 8 but excluding "prepaid" interest carried forward from the preceding year.

You have been asked to prepare (a) a schedule of the notes and interest expense (accrual basis) on the notes, (b) a recapitulation (at the bottom of the schedule) of the outstanding notes by preferred balance-sheet groupings, and (c) an adjusting journal entry correcting interest expense.

3. A manufacturer of a household device guarantees its product to operate satisfactorily for one year after the date of sale (through independent local dealers) to the consumer. The consumer is required to mail back a postcard direct to the manufacturer as soon as his equipment is satisfactorily installed. What tests would you apply to the controller's accrual of the estimated liability? Would you insist on an accrual for each unit (a) produced, (b) sold to a dealer, or (c) sold by the dealer to the consumer? Should the unit estimate include full costs (imperfect units are shipped back to the factory by the consumer) or simply the likely cost of parts requiring replacement?

4. To what items would you pay attention in examining reacquired bonds that have been purchased direct from bondholders?

5. Explain how you would establish the propriety of an unamortized bond-premium account on the books of the issuer where a number of bonds have been repurchased and retired during the year.

6. Outline an audit procedure for cash discounts on purchases. Where would the auditor expect to find cash discounts recorded?

7. How may the auditor assure himself that all liabilities pertaining to the items making up a physical inventory have been taken up on the books?

8. What are the usual documents making up or supporting a paid voucher, and what authorizations and proofs would you expect to find on them?

9. How would you verify a "dividends-payable" item appearing among current liabilities?

10. The *B* Corporation having an outstanding bond issue makes periodic payments to the trustee of a sinking fund that has been created for the purpose of ultimately supplying funds for the retirement of the issue. Among the *B* Corporation's balance-sheet assets—under "sinking fund"—are several items among which is "accrued interest on *B* Corporation's bonds purchased and held." What would you expect this item to be? How would you verify it and where would you classify it on the balance sheet?

11. During an audit of a corporation, you discover a material claim against the company that you believe is likely to be paid but the directors do not wish to provide any liability to cover it. What would you do under the circumstances?

12. You find that the contingent assets of a company are in excess of its contingent liabilities. An officer of the company argues that this condition eliminates the necessity of displaying contingent liabilities on the balance sheet as heretofore. Do you agree?

13. Distinguish between current liabilities, long-term obligations, accrued liabilities, and liability reserves.

14. Name several terms and conditions under which short-term (commercial) loans are made by banks to business enterprises.

15. In determining a client's liability on consignments from others, what elements enter into the computation and how would you test or verify the accuracy of these elements?

16. A number of debit balances are discovered in the creditor's ledger of a retail store. You are informed that they have resulted from the payment of invoices before the receipt or inspection of merchandise purchased in order to take advantage of discount privileges, and you are given a file containing the invoices that are "prepaid" at the time of your examination, which is made two months after the close of the

audit period. In reviewing these debit balances, what procedure would you follow?

17. Your client, a distributor, has a number of traveling representatives to whom cash advances are made averaging $500 each. Every month or so each representative files an expense report and is reimbursed promptly for the expenses he has incurred. Often a representative is negligent in the filing of his report and the reimbursement request may amount to several thousand dollars. As at the closing date and during the month thereafter several reports had not been rendered. What action would you take as auditor in order to determine the company's liability to these representatives, and what minimum internal controls should be instituted for this type of expense? On the balance sheet would you show the advances as an asset and the full amount of the estimated or actual payment to be made as a current liability?

18. Shortly before the end of a corporation's fiscal (calendar) year the board of directors declared a dividend in owned government bonds, payable on January 15 to common stockholders. How should the dividend be valued, and if the liability should appear on the balance sheet how should it be displayed?

19. Objection has been raised by a client to your proposal to put the following item on the balance sheet following current liabilities:

"Possible additional income-tax liability arising from disputed deductions in returns of past years, $212,500."

The amount has not been extended since you regard it as a contingent liability. The objection arises from the belief that mention of the money amount is a tacit admission of the liability. The client's appeal in this case is now pending before the Tax Court.

What argument would you advance to sustain your disclosure?

20. A stock dividend was declared before the end of a corporation's fiscal year, but it was to be delivered two months after the balance-sheet date. The argument is advanced that since the dividend stock has a very definite market value exceeding the par value that is ultimately to be transferred from earned surplus to capital stock such "cash" value should be shown as a current liability, just as a cash dividend would appear. What is your opinion?

CHAPTER XIII

Paid-in Capital; Surplus

Net worth, capital stock, paid-in surplus, and earned surplus—terms long in use among accountants—often give way in published financial reports to a variety of descriptive phrases in an endeavor to avoid allegedly misleading inferences and to point more clearly to the meaning of the several components that make up the equity of stockholders. Among the more frequently recurring of these experimental titles have been the following:

Net worth	*Capital stock*	*Paid-in surplus*	*Earned surplus*
Invested	Stockholders'	Capital surplus	Retained
capital	investment	Additional	income
Capital	Contributions	paid-in	Earnings rein-
Stockholders'	by share-	capital	vested
interest	holders	Capital in	Profits em-
Investment	Capital paid in	excess of par	ployed in the
	Paid-in capital	value	business
	stock	Other capital	Accumulated
			profit

The search for new titles. None of the innovations has as yet gained sufficient currency to warrant a recommendation for its general adoption; but regardless of the titles now or eventually appearing in financial statements it is likely that the four captions of the above tabulation will continue to be employed by accountants themselves. It may even turn out that they will again be as freely used on published statements as they were a few years ago—once it is discovered that underlying meanings have not changed, that these meanings are precisely definable and can as readily be associated with the older as well as the newer terms, that readers of financial statements cannot be expected to gain a full understanding of any product of the

481

accountant's art merely from headings or titles, and that equally misleading inferences may as readily derive from any of the more recent phrases. In less unseasoned fields of human endeavor it has long been recognized that even the simpler concepts can only be imperfectly portrayed by the words that custom or invention has attached to them, and there is little reason for believing that the concepts of accounting can acquire either a greater degree of certitude or a more widespread acceptance as the consequence of present endeavors to discover more revealing labels. A concept once established tends to associate itself with a single name the popular understanding of which demands much more in the way of exposition than the few descriptive words that can be compressed into a title. Once the reader of financial statements has gained a working knowledge of underlying concepts, conventions, and practices—a knowledge indispensable to an intelligent under- standing regardless of the terms employed—titles cease to have importance to him.

Capital. "Capital," in textbooks and in general financial usage, has a number of generally recognized meanings: paid-in capital, net worth, and net worth plus long-term borrowings ("economic" capital). Accountants as a rule do not use the word independently but use it in a phrase: for example, capital stock, capital invested, capital contributed by investors.

Capital surplus. "Capital surplus," a term frequently under fire, has in the past covered items arising from so many possible sources that its use has very largely been discontinued even among accountants; "paid-in surplus" and "revaluation surplus" —often the elements of capital surplus—are in good current use in the financial world and are undobutedly more informative to readers of financial statements.

Paid-in capital. Contributions by stockholders to the business, though legally divisible between *par* or *stated* value and paid-in surplus, have in recent years often been displayed as a single item, and the practice is growing. Once accountants had taken the position that paid-in surplus ought to be as inviolable as par or stated value, its use dwindled as a repository for items un- wanted in the income statement, thus promoting the simpler concept that the sum could be more readily understood by readers of financial statements than its two components standing by themselves.

Net worth. "Net worth" is another widely critized term. Its appearance on a balance sheet has given rise to fears that it might signify *too much* since the balance-sheet amount to which the term applies may have little relation to the disposable worth reflected in stock prices or earning power. But the fact remains that "net worth" *does* measure what is perhaps the most important, certainly the most objective, of the possible valuations of the worth of an enterprise: the valuation resulting from the operation of the accounting process. The valuation thus obtaining constitutes the basis of a wide variety of executive determinations, is indispensable to investors in arriving at decisions to buy, hold, or sell, is widely quoted in statistical services as a measure of business size and growth, and constitutes, moreover, one of the most important elements of the periodic financial statements on which professional accountants report.

Revaluation surplus. To the two usual elements of net worth—paid-in capital and earned surplus—is sometimes added a third: revaluation surplus or unrealized depreciation. This term, of frequent occurrence on balance sheets in the 1920's, and representing the excess of the appraised value of fixed assets over their depreciated cost, largely disappeared during the 1930's as the result of gradual realization through provisions for depreciation greater than cost, or as the result of reversals during the depression years in the then widespread effort to rid the operating accounts of all possible cost burdens. Recent proposals again to reflect "current costs" in financial statements have revived interest in this type of account.

In his examination of net-worth accounts the auditor's aim is to (a) determine the history of each component, (b) verify additions and deductions and make sure that top-level authority exists for each change, (c) confirm the existing classification of net-worth elements or develop a proper classification suitable for presentation in the balance sheet.

Principles and Practices

Capital stock. Investments of stockholders in business corporations—paid-in capital—are by custom evidenced by transferable shares registered in the name of the owner and taking the form of *certificates* calling for a stated number of shares. Because of varying risks and capital availability it has often been necessary to extend special privileges to one or more classes of stockholders as compared with other classes; and to any special class of stock the term "preferred" is generally attached, "common" referring to the class having no such privileges. Where but one class of stock has been issued, the term "common stock" is used interchangeably with "capital stock." Occasionally two or more classes of common stock (known as "A," "B," and so on) have been created, the superior class or classes being preferred stock in all but name. Details of the rights and privileges of stockholders are found in corporate bylaws; the same language, sometimes abbreviated and appearing on the face or back of each common or preferred stock certificate, is often referred to as the "agreement with stockholders."

Preferred stock. Among the privileges extended to preferred stockholders that the auditor has an interest in reviewing are the following:

Preference in dividend distributions is an invariable attribute of preferred issues: an obligation imposed by the bylaws on the board of directors to declare "out of profits" (of current or past years or both) a periodic (for example, quarterly or yearly) dividend of a stated amount before any dividend to common stockholders. Usually the dividend is *cumulative,* sometimes for a limited number of years: if undeclared (and unpaid) in one year, and thus "in arrears," it must be made up in some subsequent year before any common dividend is declared; but if the stock is noncumulative a dividend not declared in any given year has no effect on the dividend procedure for the following year unless under the bylaws, state statutes, or court decisions the missed dividend must be made good wherever the profits of the year of nonpayment were sufficient to absorb it. The privilege of dividend participation may by specific agreement also attach to a preferred stock, whereby after a dividend at rate a has been declared on the preferred and a dividend at rate b (often equal to a) on the common, further dividends of rate c on the preferred and rate d (often equal to c) on the common may be declared.

Preference in liquidation is a customary attribute of preferred stock, the usual agreement providing for the repayment of a stated amount per share, plus accrued and unpaid dividends, before any payment is made to common stockholders; here there may also be a participating arrangement under which the preferred stockholders share on a stated basis with common stockholders once distributions at specified rates have been made to each class. Voluntary liquidation may call for somewhat larger payments to preferred stockholders than those required in the event of involuntary liquidation.

Redemption of preferred stock is usually provided for at the issuer's option after the issue has been outstanding for a specified number of years, the price to be paid being par plus a stated premium. Some states require that all preferred issues bear a due date.

A conversion privilege may also be given to preferred stockholders whereby within a given period each preferred share may be exchanged for a specified number of shares of common stock.

The right to vote does not often attach to preferred stock, although in some instances voting is permitted on certain questions (as the sale of the business) or under certain conditions (one or more dividends in arrears, decline in working capital or in some other measure of financial position, and so forth). A few state corporation laws prohibit the denial or limitation of full voting rights to any class of stock.

As in the case of many issues of bonds, various protective devices may appear in agreements with preferred stockholders, such as the requirement of a minimum amount of working capital or the existence of a given working-capital ratio before a dividend on common stock may be declared; or limitations on the issue of new securities having a superior status, on new types of property acquisitions, or on management compensation.

Occasionally the auditor encounters situations in which a corporation has issued two or more kinds of preferred stock. They are distinguished by such titles as "first preferred" and "second preferred," or "class-A preferred" and "class-B preferred," and their dividend rates are likely to be different. Dividends must always be paid on the first or class-A preferred before a distribution can be made to the second or class-B preferred. However, no stockholder of any class may be given preferences that rank him with or superior to unsecured creditors. "Preferred" has meaning only with respect to other classes of stockholders.

Par-value stocks. When an issue of par-value capital stock is sold the proceeds less selling commissions and other costs of the sale are credited to one or more accounts maintained for that issue. If the stock has a par value it has long been the practice to credit the account with the par value of the shares sold and to carry the difference, if any, between the selling price and the par value to another account: a discount (deferred charge) account if the selling price is less and a premium (paid-in-surplus) account if the selling price is greater. The deferred charge, carried on the balance sheet under some such title as "Stock discount and expense," is customarily amortized by periodic charges to earned surplus as quickly as possible after the new enterprise has commenced operations, thereby increasing the "paid-in" equity of stockholders by a process similar to that followed in giving expression to a stock dividend. A premium account, on the other hand, remains indefinitely as paid-in surplus on the books and in financial statements—unless under conditions resembling a recapitalization a stock dividend or an earned-surplus deficit is charged against it as commented on in a subsequent paragraph. The practice of paying dividends other than stock dividends out of paid-in surplus or of charging such surplus with various types of costs or losses that would normally be reflected elsewhere in the income statement has in recent years been forbidden by many state laws and has now largely disappeared. Capital contributed by stockholders, sometimes referred to as a quasi trust fund, constitutes an amount that the corporate management must endeavor to maintain unimpaired.

No-par-value stocks. Proceeds from the sale of no-par-value stock are as a rule carried to a single capital-stock account; but under permissive state laws they may also be divided between a capital-stock account and a paid-in-surplus account, the amount credited to the former being known as stated (or declared) value; stated value may be determined by the stockholders, the board of directors, or even by the management as the stock is sold. The original purpose of creating paid-in surplus out of no-par-stock sales was to provide a legal source for the payment of dividends and absorption of losses without waiting for profits to be earned. In extreme cases a selling price of $100 has been split by crediting $1 to capital stock and $99 to paid-in surplus, the latter immediately available for dividends. The better practice today as in the case of par-value-stock premiums is to credit the entire proceeds from the sale to a capital-stock or paid-in-capital account, there to remain undisturbed as long as the stock remains outstanding.

Issues of stock. As stock is paid for, a certificate is given to the purchaser. Each certificate, calling for a specific number of shares and bearing the name of the owner, serves not only as a receipt, but also as the evidence of ownership that may be transferred by endorsement to another. Since the standard trading unit is 100 shares, larger corporations have separate forms for 100-share certificates and sometimes 500- and 1000-share certificates.

Where a corporation sells additional shares of an outstanding class of stock or shares of a new class, unwaived preemptive rights are recognized by the issue of a transferable warrant to each stockholder permitting him during a limited period to subscribe to his fraction of the prospective issue. No entries in the accounts of the corporation are made for such warrants or for warrants attached to original issues of securities permitting the purchase of another security of the corporation at a stated price and within a stated period. However, upon the exercise of such privileges by payment to the corporation of the subscription price, usual entries accompany the transaction.

An issue of capital stock (a) for services, (b) under an option given to officers, or (c) as a dividend, together with the value to be recorded, requires the prior approval of stockholders. The value to be put on the books is the market value of the stock at the time of issue or if there is no readily determinable market value or if market value is less, the average paid-in value of the stock of that class previously issued. Where the amount paid in upon the exercise of an option given to officers is less than such value, the difference is charged to current expense as compensation for services. Amounts paid in as the result of the exercise of warrants or stock rights given to all stockholders of a certain class are customarily credited to paid-in capital without adjustment, although in some instances the right may have aspects of a stock dividend.

An issue of capital stock for property is recorded in an amount equal to the market value of the stock. If there is no market value the fair market value of the asset governs. Occasionally no market value can be found for the asset acquired, particularly where there is an absence of arm's-length relationship between the corporation and the person contributing the property. The basis of valuation then becomes the depreciated cost in the hands of the contributor or the best estimate of what his depreciated cost should have been. Most regulatory bodies empowered to set the standards for the accounts of public utilities require that operating properties purchased with stock—whether from affiliated or nonaffiliated owners—be valued at depreciated "original cost": cost less depreciation to the owner first devoting it to public use. This valuation problem has already been referred to in Chapter X.

Unpaid subscriptions. Occasionally stock subscriptions are encountered. They may be thus labeled or they may be in the form of ordinary accounts or notes receivable. The general rule is that no certificate may be issued for shares unless the shares have been fully paid for. In most states accounts, notes, or other forms of receivables are not permitted to be recognized as constituting payment for shares. A "call" on unpaid subscriptions is a notification to subscribers that a portion or all of any amounts unpaid is to fall due on or before a certain date.

Reacquired stock. The cost of stock reacquired (whether designated as "held in the treasury" or retired) is best charged at once against the capital-stock account of the same class up to the average par or stated value per share in that account. Any balance of the cost may be offset against the amount of any paid-in surplus account pertaining to that class of stock, up to the average amount per share in that account, and any remaining excess of cost may then be regarded as an effective distribution of earned surplus. If the stock is resold the proceeds would be disposed of in the same manner as the proceeds from an original issue. An alternative but less desirable practice is to carry treasury stock at cost and on the balance sheet to deduct the cost from the sum of the capital-stock and surplus accounts, on the theory that until sold or retired the disposition of its component elements cannot be determined; subsequently, if sold at a profit, to credit the profit to paid-in surplus; or, if sold at a loss, to charge the loss on each share to paid-in surplus in an amount not in excess of the average paid-in surplus per share, any loss not thus absorbed being carried to earned surplus.

A few well-known corporations have always regarded reacquired stock as an asset, particularly where the stock is listed and has been purchased for resale or other disposition to officers or employees. This practice is, however, no longer sanctioned by the great majority of accountants.

Earned surplus. Earned surplus is the accumulated excess of net income over dividends paid. Operating results for each year and charges for dividends are the only entries ordinarily found in an earned-surplus account. Other earned-surplus charges and credits as described below occasionally appear and are approved by some accountants, but the author believes that an auditor should convince his client wherever possible that a "clean" surplus account will stand the organization in better stead than any attempt to make the income statement conform to the necessarily subjective concept of what management or the accountant thinks income should be. Adjusting net income to reflect either present or future earning power, so often the asserted objective of surplus charges and credits, may succeed only in misinforming readers of operating results and their financial consequences. It has been the experience of the author that an income statement yields the maximum of information to all persons when it is regarded simply as a historical summary of recognized events and conditions which the business has enjoyed or from which it has suffered during the statement period. If the accountant accompanies the statement with sufficiently descriptive sideheads or footnotes covering unusual items, the reader is free to make his own choice, if he wishes to do so, of items for adjustment or elimination.

Surplus charges and credits. There are thus two viewpoints among accountants concerning the propriety of surplus charges and credits other than for dividends and periodic net income. The first is that the income statement should be *all-inclusive* in its coverage; the second, that the income statement should be the measure of *current operating performance* or earning power. The former was advocated by the executive committee of the American Accounting Association in its statements of principles in 1936, 1941, and 1948; the latter by the Committee on Accounting Procedure of the American Institute of Accountants in Accounting Research Bulletins 32 (1947), 35 (1948), and 41 (1951). The principal items of difference, listed below, would appear in the all-inclusive statement covering the period during which they are recognized and recorded; they would be excluded in the statement of current operating performance for the same period unless they (a) are minor in amount, (b) have no distorting effect, or (c) are recurrent or likely to be recurrent:

1. The reduction or elimination of a valuation account created in one or more previous periods by charges to expense accounts of those periods.

2. An expense or loss charged directly to a reserve created by a transfer from earned surplus or other nonincome source.

3. Additional income tax for a past period.

4. A provision for a pension plan applicable to services rendered in a past period.

5. Any other adjustment of a past period.

6. Gain or loss from the sale of a good or service other than the regular product of the business.

7. Loss from a risk not normally insured.

8. Amortization of an intangible.

9. Elimination of amortized discount upon the premature retirement or refunding of a bond issue.

10. Loss from the devaluation of foreign exchange.

The leading reasons supporting the "operating-performance" income statement and hence the exclusion therefrom of the above items have been these:

1. The income statement should reflect only *"usual* or *typical*

business operations under the conditions existing during the year" [italics added].

2. Business managements, aided by professional accountants "are in a stronger position than outsiders to determine whether there are unusual and extraordinary items which if included in the determination of net income may give rise to misleading inferences with respect to current operating performance."

3. The "net income for the year should show as clearly as possible what happened in that year under that year's conditions, in order that sound comparisons can be made with prior years and with the performance in other companies."

Those who argue for the all-inclusive statement reason thus:

1. The viewpoint of accounting is primarily historical, and the accountant must therefore report whatever gain-or-loss events have taken place during the period without discriminating between usual and unusual items.

2. An income statement is a report of decisions of management and other events that have led to increases and decreases in net worth. An incomplete report of them with unusual items omitted could readily lead to the presentation of grossly distorted results and would actually invite manipulation since it is most unlikely that standards of materiality, nondistortion, and nonrecurrence can be put on any consistent, objective basis to which management, public accountants, and readers of financial statements could even partially agree.

3. The supposition that the management or the auditors of a business enterprise, or both working together, are in a "stronger position than outsiders" in deciding what items should be omitted from an income statement carries with it the assumption that the investor or other "outsider" reading the statement cannot be relied upon to discover for himself its unusual elements. Such an assumption, it is argued, is hardly fair to the intelligence of the investor; moreover it suggests an esoteric quality in accounting: an involved, complex determination at management and audit levels that the facts themselves fail to justify, since the items most often considered for exclusion are uncomplex in nature, explainable in simple terms, and readily understood by the layman.

4. Whether any item is sufficiently material, distorting, and nonrecurrent to be omitted from an income statement is a question that in practice may be resolved in numerous ways, much depending on the training and experience of corporate officers,

professional accountants, investors, and the lay public. Thus a decision of management to exclude an unusual expense might not be in harmony with the public interest or with the viewpoint of investors, and what constitutes the public interest or the investors' viewpoint will be found to vary markedly as between auditors. An auditor cannot afford to risk his reputation for objectivity by selecting what is the best, safest, or even the least misleading information to give to investors and the public. He would remain in a much more defensible area of responsibility to others by continuing to report in "one package" all the events and conditions recognized during the audit period and leaving to report readers the interpretation and whatever qualification is to be made of operating profit.

5. What is unusual in the current year may prove to be not so unusual in future years. It may be necessary in a subsequent period to restore items omitted in earlier statements in order to make such statements comparable with more recent operating results in which similar items have been included as "ordinary," thus creating confusion in the minds of those who read financial statements as to whether they may be relied on and whether any stated net income is final.

6. Experience has frequently demonstrated that the unusual expenses and losses omitted from the income statement of one year have been paralleled in other years by dissimilar but equally unusual items even though of a wholly different origin, character, and consequence. Thus in attempting fairly to display earning power by casting out costs likely never to be duplicated in the same form the endproduct may prove to be a serious overstatement.

7. Those who favor an "operating-performance" income statement do not give enough credence to accounting as a well-developed, self-contained discipline capable of "standing on its own feet" and possessing its own peculiar brand of logic. A departure from the established practice of reporting all of a period's gains and losses in the income statement is an action resembling in some measure the introduction of lifo as a basis of inventory valuation and the advocacy of index numbers as a means of translating the cost of fixed assets into current values. The results are the same: the imposition on accounting—on the pretext of making it "more useful"—of concepts that can only have the effect of weakening its objectivity.

It is the author's view, already intimated, that a full account of all gains and losses in a single statement provides the most objective basis for reporting annual operating results. Exceptional items such as those above listed are segregated in an all-inclusive statement in a final section following operating income, as explained and illustrated in Chapter XV.

Reserves. The term "reserve" has been frequently applied to any of the following:

1. A liability representing the accrual of an expense that at the time of the accrual can only be approximated, a frequent example being the provision for Federal income taxes covering a period just ended. Such an obligation, classified as current or long-term according to the probable time of its liquidation, is sometimes referred to as a *liability reserve.* A pension reserve representing an accrual of payments to be made in future years covering services rendered in past years is an example of a "reserve" that is actually a long-term liability.

2. An allowance created by monthly or other periodic charges to expense and relating to operating costs yet to be incurred, the purpose being to spread such costs over a limited period of time. Known as an *equalization reserve,* the device is commonly employed within a fiscal year so that maintenance and other "bunched" costs may be apportioned in amounts as nearly equal as possible to each of the twelve months. Any balance at the end of the year, debit or credit, is eliminated by prorata adjustments of the previously recorded charges. Occasionally such a balance is carried into the next year as a current liability (credit) or prepaid expense (debit), but the practice is disapproved by most accountants.

3. A *valuation* account, created by charges to expense representing expirations of costs previously incurred. Examples may be found in a reserve or allowance for depreciation, a reserve for amortization, and a reserve for bad debts. On the balance sheet such a reserve appears as a reduction of the asset to which it relates.

4. *Appropriated surplus,* created by one or more transfers from earned surplus and preferably remaining intact except for further transfers of the same kind or a return to earned surplus; for example, a sinking-fund reserve; a reserve for contingencies, for working capital, or for the retirement of preferred stock. A reserve of this type is classified on the balance sheet as a subdivision of earned surplus, and has been referred to by some accountants as the only form of *true reserve.*

5. A *mixed reserve*—which is any combination of the above. Examples are discussed below. Where the purpose or effect is or is likely to be a smoothing out of operating results as between years, a mixed reserve serves the same purpose as an equalization reserve, and is subject to the same objections. On published balance sheets mixed reserves usually appear between liabilities and net worth.

6. A *secret* reserve is not a specific account but rather an understatement of financial position brought about by any of a number of irregular and at times improper devices; as, the expensing of new construction; the provision of excessive amounts for depreciation; the overstatement of liabilities. One of the objects of an audit is to determine whether the current conventions of accounting have been followed in the building up of inventory, fixed-asset, and other asset valuations and, in the reporting of liabilities, to make sure that any important deviation from such standards has been given quantitative disclosure.

Reserves created by charges appearing in the income statement, with balances at the end of the year, should represent liabilities or valuation accounts and be so classified on the balance sheet. However, during World War II it became a common practice for management to follow the same procedure in establishing or adding to reserves for contingencies, postwar adjustments, and similar remote, indeterminate, possibly never-to-be-incurred liabilities, and accountants failed to recognize any impropriety in such provisions. Moreover, no uniform standards were established by accountants whereby future charges against such reserves, if any were to be permitted, might be determined. In a few years these reserves (a few still survive) turned out to be interyear equalization reserves, which most accountants, at least on paper, had long condemned, although such an outcome could not have necessarily been predicted at the time of their creation. The ultimate effect—which can only be viewed in retrospect—had been to transfer a portion of the profits of prosperous war years to subsequent periods when profits were likely to be cut by reductions in governmental spending and by a return to competition. As viewed today, the same financial purpose could have been carried out with fewer misunderstandings by means of appropriations or other earmarkings of earned surplus, or more simply still, by permitting earned surplus to be built up, undisturbed.

A distinction has occasionally been drawn between a *general* contingency reserve and a *special* contingency reserve, the implication being that the former is a reservation of earned surplus whereas the latter, possibly a quasi liability created by a charge to expense, is available for the absorption of charges that for one reason or another are deemed not to apply to the operating expense of any one year. Typical of the latter category are inventory reserves created to offset a *possible* future decline of prices below the current market. Provisions for such reserves can be no more objective than provisions for general contingency reserves, and to admit their propriety is to open the door to the artificial smoothing of profits as between years. The better practice is to recognize *all* reserves for contingencies as subdivisions of earned surplus and to conform them to the principle described in (4) above. A true valuation reserve for inventories, however, as explained in Chapter VIII, is a universally approved device.

An insurance reserve in a commercial enterprise is a current liability if created by a charge to expense representing actual or estimated costs of replacement or damages payable covering events that have already occurred. But an insurance reserve created by charges to expense that are the equivalents of premiums otherwise payable to an outside insurer is in part, at least, an equalization reserve the balance of which, under more conservative accounting methods, would be divided between reasonably determinable accrued obligations and an earned-surplus subdivision or unappropriated earned surplus. In practice, however, insurance reserves are often classified with other heterogeneous reservations of net income between liabilities and net worth.

Retirement and similar reserves, augmented each year by amounts charged to income and representing actuarial or other reasonable estimates of the current period's contribution to future payments are as a rule long-term obligations; but the portion estimated to be payable during the year following should appear as a current liability—as has long been the custom with maturing bonds.

Where, notwithstanding prevailing practice to the contrary, items of income and expense appear in appropriated-surplus and mixed reserves, the auditor should endeavor to see that they are transferred to the income statement; in a few instances, however, he may feel that he is justified in accepting the present position of these items provided a full explanation of reserve changes is given a prominence equal to that of the income statement in published financial statements.

Dividends. A dividend is generally understood to be a distribution of cash arising from the net income of the current year, or of preceding years where the current year's income is insufficient. Most dividends are of this type. Occasionally the auditor encounters a stock dividend, and on rare occasions a property dividend. Less frequently he finds that a dividend has been charged to some account other than earned surplus.

Many dividends are paid on a quarterly basis at a rate that is rarely changed, although, where profits warrant, an "extra," "special," or supplementary dividend may be included with the last quarterly dividend at the end of the year. No dividend may legally be paid unless previously "declared" by the board of directors. For larger corporations declaration involves the adoption by the board of a formal resolution setting forth the nature and source of the dividend (for example, a cash distribution of earnings), the rate per share (in terms of per cent of par value or dollars per share), the record date (the date on which the stock records will be closed, and stockholders and the number of shares owned by each will be scheduled), and the date of payment. For smaller companies where changes in share ownership are infrequent, reference to the record date is often omitted (the declaration date then becomes the record date), but the other elements should always be present.

A stock dividend is a prorata distribution to stockholders in the form of a specified number of shares of any class of the corporation's stock. It may be charged to earned surplus, paid-in surplus, or even appreciation surplus. If charged to earned surplus, it is regarded as a capitalization of the earliest available past earnings, in contrast with the assumption that a cash or property dividend is the distribution of most recent earnings. A distribution of the shares of another corporation's stock (for example, that of a subsidiary) is a special form of a property dividend as noted in a subsequent paragraph. The general rule for the amount of earned surplus to be capitalized for each share when a dividend in common stock is paid to common stockholders is the average paid-in capital per share at the date of declaration; if the dividend share has a market value on the same date higher than this average, then such market value governs. The distribution of shares to stockholders of the same class charged to paid-in or revaluation surplus is often termed a *splitup*. In its more usual form, however, a splitup involves merely the issue of additional shares to existing stockholders or the exchange of their shares for a larger number of shares without formal entry on the books of account. It should be noted that the income-tax variety of splitup is the transfer by a corporation of a portion of its net assets to a newly formed, wholly owned subsidiary in exchange for the subsidiary's capital stock.

A property dividend involves the question of valuation if at the time of declaration or payment the property has a market value in excess of book value. Some accountants hold that the transfer of property to stockholders is tantamount to realization and that a profit results. Others, believing that no profit can be recognized in transactions with stockholders, hold that the entry called for is a charge to earned surplus in the amount of the book value. The author agrees with the latter point of view. Sometimes classed as a property dividend is the distribution to stockholders of corporate obligations such as bonds or scrip—scrip in this sense being short-term corporate obligations, perhaps bearing interest. Such a transaction is, however, extremely rare.

In income-tax parlance a *spinoff* is a distribution to stockholders of the capital stock of a newly established subsidiary to which the parent has transferred assets; a *splitoff* is such a distribution accompanied by the prorata surrender to the parent by its stockholders of a portion of their holdings in the parent. In the first action the book value of the net assets is transferred to an investment account and as the stock is distributed the investment account is charged to earned surplus. In the second the book value is set off against the portion of paid-in capital pertaining to the surrendered shares, any balance not thus absorbed being charged to earned surplus.

A liquidating dividend is a distribution to stockholders of cash or property in the windup of the affairs of a corporation; in the event that earned surplus exists, the general rule is that the earned surplus is first distributed—then other net-worth accounts after earned surplus has been exhausted. The term is also applied, as already noted, to a distribution charged to a depreciation or depletion reserve or other non-earned-surplus account; or to a surplus account consisting of income before provision for depletion or depreciation.

Noncorporate net worth. In noncorporate business establishments net-worth accounts are usually simple in form and content. For partnerships and proprietorships drawing and capital accounts are in common use, the former for recording periodic net income, salaries, other credits, withdrawals, personal rather than business expenditures, and other debits; the latter is restricted to investment changes and balances of drawing accounts as they are closed out at the end of a fiscal period.

A nonprofit membership organization, often incorporated, may be expected to have one or more accounts representing contributions by members. Where the contributions have been made for the purpose of providing capital for the enterprise, the account to which they have been credited should be regarded as paid-in capital and maintained intact until members have formally agreed upon another disposition of the amount. An earned-surplus or undistributed-income account is provided for the periodic results from operations. Contributions clearly understood to have been made for the purpose of taking care of operating costs (for example, membership dues) constitute income. Donations for special capital projects or special operating programs require separate accounts and statements and often give rise to separate funds within a single organization with its own self-balancing asset, liability, income, and expense accounts.

Government agencies may maintain several types of accounts having as their purpose the prevention of indebtedness in excess of appropriation limitations. Many of these have been classed as net-worth or "proprietary" accounts. In recent years, with increased emphasis on management controls comparable to those common to business enterprise, net-worth accounts have taken on somewhat the same characteristics as those of corporate and noncorporate organizations as described in preceding paragraphs. This involves an appropriation account reflecting a budgeted figure approved by the legislative body (offset initially by taxes levied or amounts to be received from the central treasury), and a surplus (or deficit) account to which the excess of the appropriated amount (less uncollectible taxes) over expenditures (or of expenditures over the net appropriated amount) is periodically carried. In addition there may be an account for contributed capital separated from the appropriations of one or more years, or specially provided, for fixed and working-capital purposes.

Internal Controls

Issuance of stock certificates. Most of the larger corporations appoint *transfer agents* who prepare stock certificates, maintain the stockholders ledger, approve title to original certificates and subsequent transfers, and issue new certificates following their examination by a *registrar*. A few corporations having listed securities act as their own transfer agents, maintaining offices for that purpose in the financial districts where trading takes place. The stock exchanges usually require an independent registrar who records each new and canceled certificate and makes certain that there is no overissue of the security.

When a corporation acts as its own transfer agent and registrar, stock issues and stock records are customarily under the control of the corporate secretary or treasurer. Protective devices safeguarding issues may include the following:

1. Unissued stock certificates are numbered serially, each attached to a separable stub bearing the same number, and are bound together in one or more books and kept in a secure place. Certificates are usually engraved to prevent duplication. The rights and privileges of stockholders are inscribed on the front or back of the certificate. Space on the back is provided for the endorsement of the owner or agent upon the surrender of the certificate or its transfer to another.

2. Authority and responsibility for the custody, signing, and issuance of stock certificates are assigned by the board of directors to specified officers—usually the secretary and one other.

3. As each certificate is issued, the blanks on the certificate and its stub are filled in showing the date of issue, the number of shares represented by the certificate—in both spelled-out and numerical form—the name of the owner or his authorized agent, and the signatures of the officers to whom has been delegated the responsibility of authorizing and safeguarding the issue and exchange of certificates.

4. Examinations of details of sales, exchange, and reacquisition transactions are made by each such officer or under his direction. His signature on the certificate, which should never be affixed in advance, signifies that he has reviewed and approved both the propriety and the details of the transaction.

5. Replacements of lost or stolen certificates are made only after careful investigation, following the filing of an indemnity bond by the stockholder.

6. The filled-in stub serves as a serial record of outstanding shares. Canceled certificates are pasted to their corresponding stubs.

7. A stockholders' journal and ledger for both shares and capital paid in are maintained in which original issues, transfers, repurchases, and redemptions are recorded and posted. Journal-reference postings are also carried to stock-certificate stubs. Such

records should be the responsibility of a person other than one having authority over certificate issues. Periodic comparisons of the detail with general-ledger controlling accounts should be made by means of a trial balance best prepared by a still different person.

8. Internal audits of issues and records procedures and of individual transactions are made at irregular intervals.

Other net-worth accounts. In general, the control of net-worth accounts is the special function of top management and the board of directors. Each class of entry therein and the total amounts of such entries during each fiscal year should be known to and, where feasible, specifically approved by the board.

Financial-Statement Standards

For each class of capital stock the reader of a balance sheet should be able to determine the number of authorized shares, shares issued, treasury shares, and shares outstanding; the average amount paid in per share; and the total amount paid in.

Paid-in surplus, if received in connection with more than one class of stock, should be shown separately for each such class.

In addition, for each class of preferred capital stock there should appear, wherever these features exist, the amount to which the stockholders are entitled in the event of involuntary liquidation (a policy approved by many accountants is to value the stock on that basis, adding to the amount paid in, where necessary, a transfer, authorized by stockholders, from earned surplus), the price at which the stock may be called (if non-callable, that fact should be stated), preferences as to dividends including participation in added distributions, dividends in arrears, the nature of option or conversion rights outstanding including rate, price, amounts and periods effective, and sinking-fund requirements.

Stock subscriptions should be deducted from "stock subscribed" under net worth and only the amount actually paid in should be extended.

Alternatives have been described in a preceding paragraph for the treatment of treasury stock. Best practice dictates that treasury stock should not appear as an asset.

Changes in earned surplus (retained income) during the audit period may be shown on the face of the balance sheet or in a separate schedule. These will normally be limited to net income and dividends and, with capital stock, may be displayed as follows:

Capital Stock & Surplus:

Common capital stock: 10,000 shares, $50 par value, authorized, issued, and outstanding			$500,000.00
Paid-in surplus, arising from original contributions of stockholders			101,245.00
Total paid in			$601,245.00
Retained income:			
Balance January 1, 19–0		$114,963.12	
Added during year—			
Net income	$297,488.38		
Less dividends of $10 per share	100,000.00	197,488.38	312,451.50
Total at December 31, 19–0			$913,696.50

Objections are sometimes raised to this procedure because the analysis of surplus is the only historical summary on the face of the statement and is therefore an exception compared with the treatment accorded other balance-sheet items. Since the balance sheet is ordinarily conceived to be a statement of "balances" why therefore should not analyses of other items appear? The special justification of the surplus analysis is that it indicates the relationship between the two principal statements in an accountant's report or in a corporate report to stockholders, provides a connecting link with previously issued statements, and does away with the need for a third statement, thereby simplifying the presentation. On the mechanical side, there is often enough space on the liability half of the balance sheet for the analysis, assets ordinarily requiring more space than liabilities. However, if the analysis involves more than a few items, a separate earned-surplus exhibit is usually held to be in order.

The elimination of an accumulated deficit (that is, negative earned surplus) by a "quasi reorganization," having the effect of offsetting it against paid-in surplus or other form of paid-in capital, should always bear the approval of the stockholders. Lacking such approval the full amount of the deficit should appear in the balance sheet. Where, however, the absorption of the deficit has been approved by the stockholders, earned surplus in subsequent financial statements should be "dated" from the time of the offset (by adding to the earned-surplus sidehead "from" followed by the effective date), and for a limited term of years (three is suggested by the U. S. Securities and Exchange Commission) the amount of the absorbed deficit should be shown.

A change in the name, state of incorporation, or characteristics of its capital stock will usually have no effect on the continuity of the earned surplus of a corporation. But a transfer of the business to a new company or the formation of a single new company by combining two or more companies results in the elimination of existing earned-surplus accounts for the reason that a new corporation cannot start operations with distributable surplus: the old surplus, added to the paid-in-capital accounts, has been contributed for new stock issued and has thus become a part of the new company's paid-in capital.

A restriction on the use of earned surplus for dividends should be disclosed in a balance-sheet sidehead or footnote, as in the following situations:

(a) Any voluntary or contractual appropriation of earned surplus reduces free earned surplus and the amount so appropriated should not be regarded as available for dividends until it has been returned to earned surplus through formal action by the proper authority (usually the creating authority). Examples may be found in a reserve for contingencies (a voluntary reservation authorized by the board of directors), or a reserve, required by a bond indenture, of earned surplus of a specified amount or of a total that must be accumulated by a specified date.

(b) A bond indenture may also provide that no dividend be paid that has the effect of reducing working capital below a given ratio or below a specified money amount, the purpose being to establish an adequate measure of safety for bondholders.

(c) A restriction is usually held to exist in the amount by which preferred stockholders' rights in involuntary liquidation exceed the paid-in capital already assigned to that stock. Agreements with preferred stockholders may also call for the annual reservation of a specified quantity of earned surplus (in a sinking-fund reserve) in order to insure the retirement of the preferred stock by a certain date.

(d) Preferred-stock dividends in arrears are sometimes regarded as a contingent liability; but in view of the necessity that dividends be formally declared by the board of directors before *any* liability for dividends can be said to exist, a more frequent practice is to insert after the sidehead of earned surplus some such qualification as "restricted by preferred-stock dividends in arrears in the amount of $2 per share; in total, $40,000."

As previously noted, it is best not to charge any expense or loss to any form of surplus or surplus reserve. Whatever its character or source every expense or loss should be regarded as belonging to the income statement of the year of its recognition, and, if substantial in amount and a clearly extraordinary or nonrecurring item, it should appear in a final section of the income statement.

Revaluation surplus should be (a) eliminated where practicable, with a valuation notation, if desired, in the asset sidehead, (b) deducted, undiminished, on the face of the balance sheet, like a valuation reserve, from its related asset, or (c) where the accounting procedure is of long standing, carried between paid-in and earned surplus. If (c) is followed, consistency requires that depreciation on the full value be included in depreciation expense.

Representative Audit Program

Capital stock. 1. Procure from the transfer agent or registrar or both a statement of the number of shares outstanding.

2. If there be no transfer agent or registrar, run a tape of the stockholders ledger, or where there are relatively few stockholders, compare the stock-ledger accounts with the list of stockholders maintained in the permanent file, and bring the list down to date. Compare changes recorded in the general ledger with the stock-certificate book; make sure that there has been no overissue of any class of shares, that certificates representing stock repurchased and retired have been canceled, that the stubs of new certificates are properly filled in and have been accounted for, and that there is a correspondence of dates. Examine or test the propriety of the value of Federal documentary stamps attached in the case of stock transfers and new issues.

3. Review with the responsible official treasury-stock transactions during the period and prepare an analysis and summary of these transactions.

4. Details of each new issue of capital stock and the recorded amounts should be carefully studied. The consideration received on any issues during the audit period should be traced into the cashbook, or, if property was paid in, the inventory and disposition of the property should be reviewed; the method of valuation, if not cost or depreciated cost, should preferably bear the approval of stockholders.

5. Review preferred-stock agreements and ascertain whether the requirements under these agreements have been fulfilled.

6. Where there has been a reduction of "legal" capital, make

sure that the necessary corporate action has been taken and that the state authorities have been notified as required by law.

Earned surplus. 1. A "clean" earned surplus requires only the examination of dividends. No earned-surplus details need appear in the current working papers. Summarize transactions for the year and add to the analysis maintained in the permanent file.

2. Refer earned-surplus charges and credits, if any, to principal for action to be taken on them. Develop supporting details for each item.

3. Abstracts of minutes of the board of directors will indicate dates and other details pertaining to each dividend declared during the period. Compare with the actual transactions.

4. Review each dividend in the light of the restrictions attaching to the authority for payment, to working capital, and to the use of earned surplus.

5. Obtain opinion of counsel as to the propriety of any dividend, cash or stock, charged to paid-in surplus, depletion or depreciation reserves, or revaluation surplus.

6. Test details of dividend payments by comparison with certified lists of stockholders or with stock ledger.

Reserves. 1. Analyze each reserve account for the entire audit period, and add a synopsis of the analysis, or the analysis itself, to the permanent file.

2. Make sure that every charge against an appropriated-surplus or mixed reserve conforms closely to the purposes of the reserve so that it is not an ordinary or recurring expense chargeable to operations.

3. Note whether additions and deductions are of the same nature as in preceding audits; discuss unsettled points (from previous years) with principal and review analyses with him.

4. Accounting policies and general business policies are inextricably intermingled in setting up and operating appropriated-surplus and mixed reserves. It is always important, therefore, that proposed policies (governing both the creation and subsequent use of the reserve) be clearly formulated when each reserve is established and that the board of directors gives its approval to such policies.

5. The auditor should always counsel against the creation of mixed reserves because of the resulting confusion and uncertainty in the interpretation of the income statement, both during the years in which the reserves are being added to and in the years during which expenses and losses are being charged off to the

reserves. The auditor, well within the limits of professional propriety, should recommend against the establishing of any appropriated-surplus or mixed reserve unless required by contract or by regulatory authority.

Revaluation surplus. 1. A full explanation and analysis of the revaluation excess should appear in the permanent file. This will include a summary of the appraisal report or other source from which the item originated, the initial adjustment placed on the books and the authority therefor, and any subsequent adjustments.

2. "Realized appreciation" is sometimes recognized in an annual transfer from revaluation surplus to depreciation expense (or to earned surplus where the revaluation credit appears under net worth). The amount of this transfer is ordinarily the result of applying a percentage (equal to the current provision for depreciation—based on the original appraisal figure—divided by the original appraisal figure) to the original revaluation excess. The method followed should succeed in amortizing the revaluation excess over the life of the assets included in the appraisal.

Noncorporate net worth. 1. Analyze each proprietorship account or partner's account, bearing in mind the possibilities above mentioned.

2. Discuss each analysis with the proprietor or partner concerned and secure from him a written representation that (a) indicates the correctness of the balances of his capital account and any other account relating to him, his family, or his interests, and (b) states that all transactions affecting the business of which he has knowledge have been properly recorded on the books during the audit period.

Audit Procedures

In a first audit or in the audit next following the sale of a new issue of capital stock the circumstances surrounding the various classes of stock or the new issue should be reviewed in considerable detail with the president or other principal official of the corporation. Documents examined will include the corporate charter or articles of incorporation, state laws relating to the class of stock sold, agreements with underwriters, bankers, brokers, sales agents, or purchasers, the prospectus used in promoting sales, and registration and other statements filed with the U. S. Securities and Exchange Commission and state authorities, together with related correspondence. Copies of the principal documents should be obtained.

Working papers relating to capital stock may in most instances be confined to the permanent file where they may be reviewed from time to time when questions arise concerning reacquisitions, resales, maturities, retirements, and compliance with laws, regulations, and stockholder agreements. A point list covering any matters for annual review should be prepared; changes therein may be required in subsequent periods as new laws, regulations, or conditions within the corporation make their appearance.

A list of stockholders is often maintained by the auditor where the number of stockholders is small and changes in stockholdings are likely to have important effects on corporate policy. For the same reason in the case of larger corporations the auditor may keep a list of principal (for example, the top twenty) stockholdings, modified each year by changes therein reflected on the most recent dividend list or other stockholder record. His audit does not include without specific reference an examination of the transactions between old and new stockholders or the transactions of a voting trust or other continuing agreement between stockholders. He does not inspect the records of the transfer agent or registrar except by special arrangement since the records of such persons may, without evidence to the contrary, be assumed to be accurate and reliable.

Unpaid stock subscriptions should be verified individually, and the auditor should make sure that each item is bona fide, that it is in the process of being collected, that no stock certificate has been issued against it, and that the terms of the subscription agreement have been observed.

On a first audit a full analysis of each item of net worth is desirable. This will include an analysis of each of the various kinds of surplus from the beginning of the corporation and some evaluation of whatever charges and credits may appear therein, so that the net income for each year preceding the audit year may be approximated for present and future reference.

Every charge or credit during the audit year in any net-worth account should be carefully reviewed not only for accuracy but for the authorization and approval of the board of directors and, where required, the stockholders. The explanations secured should be such as to permit a full disclosure of the item in the auditor's report.

In noncorporate enterprise the net-worth accounts include proprietors' or partners' accounts to which both the net profit for the year and withdrawals are carried. The accounts should be analyzed for the full audit period and the auditor should question any item that has the appearance of belonging to the business rather than to the individual. Because the boundaries of noncorporate enterprise are much less distinct than those of corporations, there is some chance that the expenses of the business include personal items, and, on the other hand, it may be that there have been personal transactions that should have been recorded on the books of the business. This is more likely to occur in smaller enterprises where many of the internal controls, such as they are, are in the hands of the proprietors themselves. The auditor should, therefore, be on the alert for these possibilities; if strong business controls, rigidly enforced, are wanting, he may find it necessary to qualify his report. Some auditors in examining partnership accounts obtain a statement from each partner indicating (a) that he has reviewed and approved his personal account and (b) that to the best of his knowledge all business transactions have been recorded, and all recorded transactions (except those appearing in his personal account) are transactions properly pertaining to the business.

Illustrative Audit

From PF 11 and PF 12 it will be observed that—

(a) Martin Manufacturing Company was established as a New York corporation on August 1, 1941.

(b) Two classes of capital stock were authorized: 10,000 shares of cumulative preferred stock of $100 par value ($1,000,000) and 10,000 shares of common stock of $100 par value ($1,000,000).

(c) The three incorporators, Messrs. Holdover, Stebbins, and Huddle, subscribed to 5 preferred shares each and 1 common share each, these subscriptions constituting qualifying shares, and calling for payment in cash totaling $1,800.

(d) Of the subscriptions $500 was immediately paid in by Mr. Holdover on his 5 preferred shares (shown in opening entry), and the remaining $1,300 was subsequently paid in (as at the same date).

(e) The new company acquired the outstanding capital stock of the Holdover Radiator Company on that date, consisting of 3,680 shares ($50 per value) of common stock outstanding (net of 320 treasury shares).

(f) In payment for these shares Martin issued 460 (1 for 8)

preferred shares and 920 (1 for 4) common shares, a total par value of $138,000.

(g) The book value of Holdover net assets was $245,742.10, an amount $107,742.10 in excess of the Martin capital stock issued against it; these figures were placed on the Martin books, the latter amount being credited to paid-in surplus.

(h) In addition to the stock issued for the Holdover assets and the qualifying shares, the brokers, Souse, Maus & Co., who promoted the new corporation, paid in $5,000 in cash on the opening date for which they received 25 preferred shares and 77 common shares, a total par value of $10,200. The resulting discount (or "commission") of $5,200 was charged against the paid-in surplus of the preceding paragraph, reducing it to $102,542.10, its present amount.

(i) On July 1, 1942, a $1,000,000 issue of first-mortgage bonds was marketed by the company (or its president). The expense of $2,022.87 in connection with the issue was immediately charged off.

(j) A year later 4,500 shares of preferred and 4,000 shares of common were sold through brokers and listed on a stock exchange (no discount or expense), thus raising the outstanding shares of the two issues to $500,000 each.

These facts constitute the financial history of the company, and it should be a function of the working papers to supply them accurately and succinctly.

No working papers appear in the current-audit file on net-worth items; PF 11, 12, 91, 92, and 93 constitute the necessary backing for such items, and the only entry made on them at the time of the 1952 audit is contained in the last three lines of PF 93 where the 1952 changes in earned surplus have been summarized.

A letter from the registrar confirms the number of shares outstanding.

HARRIS TRUST AND SAVINGS BANK
Chicago 1, Illinois

February 24, 1953

Messrs. Hyatt, Paterson & Co.
960 Hudson Building
Chicago 4, Illinois

Dear Sirs:

In compliance with the request of Mr. Edward
Stebbins, President of Martin Manufacturing
Company, we wish to inform you that the
issued and outstanding shares of capital stock
of the Martin Manufacturing Company at December 31, 1952 were as follows:

Preferred stock 5000 shares
Common stock   5000 shares

Very truly yours,

John J. Kelly
Assistant Cashier

X - 12

PREFERRED:

Authorized: 10,000 shares, $100 par value, $5 cumulative dividend per annum, preferred as to dividends and assets.

Date	Description		Shares	Amount		Total
8-1-41	Sold on Aug. 1, 1941—					
	E. Holdover		5	500 00		
	E. Stebbins		5	500 00		
	J. B. Huddle		5	500 00		
	Stockholders of Holdover Radiator Co. (1.25 for 1)					
	E. Holdover	(In exchange	100	10 000 00		
	E. Stebbins	for assets;	5	500 00		
	J. B. Huddle	see His-	12½	1 250 00		
	Other stockholders	tory, pp. 1-2)	342½	34 250 00		
	Souse, Maus + Co.		25	2 500 00	500	50 000 00
7-1-43	Sold on July 1, 1943—					
	Barchard, Bankup + Co.		4,500	450 000 00	5000	500 000 00

COMMON:

Authorized: 10,000 shares, $100 par value

Date	Description	Shares	Amount		Total
8-1-41	Sold on Aug. 1, 1941—				
	E. Holdover	1	100 00		
	E. Stebbins	1	100 00		
	J. B. Huddle	1	100 00		
	Stockholders of Holdover Radiator Co. (.25 for 1)				
	E. Holdover	200	20 000 00		
	E. Stebbins	10	1 000 00		
	J. B. Huddle	25	2 500 00		
	Other stockholders	685	68 500 00		
	Souse, Maus + Co.	77	7 700 00	1000	100 000 00
7-1-43	Sold on July 1, 1943—				
	Barchard, Bankup + Co.	4000	400 000 00	5000	500 000 00

On August 1, 1941, the assets of Holdover Radiator Company were acquired by A Company by giving 1/8 share of preferred and 1/4 share of common for each share of Holdover.

Net worth of Holdover Radiator Company (from our audit report)—		
Common capital stock — 3680 shares at $50.		184 000 00
Earned surplus		61 742 10
Total net worth — old company		245 742 10
Less stock of new company issued therefor —		
Preferred — 1 new share for each 8 old shares	46 000 00	
Common — 1 new share for each 4 old shares	92 000 00	
	138 000 00	
Discount on sale of 25 pfd. shares and 77 common shares to Souse, Maus + Co. who handled Holdover deal; par value, $10,200, less cash paid in by Souse, Maus.	5 200 00	143 200 00
Paid-in surplus — August 1, 1941		102 542 10

The predecessor company's balance sheet contained no appreciation and the same bases of asset valuation have been continued by the new company. No adjustments affecting the period prior to August 1, 1941, have been made and none likely will be necessary. Accrued depreciation on that date was 56+% and Federal income-tax returns for the old company were formally closed on that basis.

In a letter dated May 18, 1947, Messrs. Barton and Weeks, attorneys, advised the company that the above earned surplus was applicable to the common stock and that none applied to the outstanding preferred stock.

Martin Manufacturing Company
Earned Surplus

	Net profit	Dividends	Balance
Net profit Aug. 1 — Dec. 31, 1941	123 107 80		123 107 80
1942 — net profit	41 212 04		
Pfd. dividends [1½ yrs. x $5 × 500]		3 541 68	
Common ″ [6% × $100,000]		6 000 00	154 778 16
1943 — net profit	1 384 982 63		
Pfd. dividends [$5 × 500]		2 500 00	
″ ″ [$2½ × 4500]		11 250 00	
Common ″ (June 10) [10% × 100,000]		10 000 00	1 516 010 79
1944 — net profit	281 620 30		
Pfd. dividends [$5 × 5000]		25 000 00	
Common ″ [20%]		100 000 00	1 672 631 09
1945 — net profit	514 647 67		
Pfd. dividends		25 000 00	
Common ″ [5%]		25 000 00	2 137 278 76
1946 — net profit	263 458 19		
Pfd. dividends [$5 × 5000]		25 000 00	
Common ″ [37½%]		175 000 00	2 200 736 95
1947 — net profit	269 101 85		
Pfd. dividends [$5 × 5000]		25 000 00	
Common ″ [25%]		125 000 00	2 319 838 80
1948 — net profit	157 577 17		
Pfd. dividends [$5 × 5000]		25 000 00	
Common ″ [20%]		100 000 00	2 352 415 97
1949 — net profit	199 723 57		
Pfd. dividends [$5 × 5000]		25 000 00	
Common ″ [20%]		100 000 00	2 427 139 54
1950 — net profit	151 727 14		
Pfd. dividends [$5 × 5000]		25 000 00	
Common ″ [20%]		100 000 00	2 453 866 68
1951 — net profit	160 576 80		
Pfd. dividends [$5 × 5000]		25 000 00	
Common ″ [20%]		100 000 00	2 489 443 48
1952 net profit	208 371 41		
Pfd. dividends [$5 × 5000] (x-2)		25 000 00	
Common ″ [20%] (x-2)		100 000 00	2 572 814 89

PF-93

Problems and Questions

1. The following items appear in the unaudited surplus account of Axton, Inc.:

Year	Description	Debit	Credit
19–0	Sale price of capital stock in excess of stated value of $100,000		$25,000.00
19–0	Net loss—19–0	$ 200.01	
19–1	Dividend and net profit, 19–1	2,000.00	6,247.10
19–2	Excess of depreciated replacement value disclosed in appraisal of fixed assets by plant manager over depreciated cost recorded when assets of going concern were purchased in 19–0		8,685.53
19–2	Correction of 19–1 depreciation expense (5% of $8,685.53)	434.28	
19–2	Dividend and net profit, 19–2	4,000.00	4,679.45
19–3	Liability of predecessor partnership, previously undisclosed, settled for 50 cents on the dollar	622.81	
19–3	Expense of 19–2 overlooked	3.57	
19–3	Dividend and net profit	10,000.00	15,880.03

You have been asked to comment on the propriety of the balance in the account, $43,231.44. This may be in the form of proposed adjusting entries.

2. State the factors to be determined by an auditor as a basis for satisfying himself as to the correctness of the earned surplus shown in the financial statements of a company. His examination has been recurrent over the past several years.

3. On July 31, 19–1, a certain partnership enterprise was incorporated. You have regularly made the examination of the financial statements as of December 31 of each year and are requested again to examine them for the calendar year 19–1. Outline briefly any new features that would be added to your examination.

4. How would you verify treasury stock as shown by the client's records?

5. You are employed by a stockholder to investigate an assertion that the management of the corporation has created large secret reserves with the view of buying up the stock of the minority holders. You are given free access to the books. Indicate the nature of the approach you would make to determine the truth or falsity of this assertion.

6. Ascertain the restriction on the use of the term "quasi reorganization" by the Securities and Exchange Commission.

7. By means of a reduction during the year in the stated value of its nopar common stock, a company has absorbed a large deficit existing at the beginning of the year. A net profit results from the year's

operations. How would you state these facts on your balance sheet at the close of the year?

8. Name four types of restrictions on the declaration of cash dividends.

9. What is the preferred treatment in financial statements of the following matters relating to a contingency reserve: (a) the provision creating the reserve; (b) the position of the reserve on the balance sheet; and (c) expenditures relating to the contingent liability against which the reserve was created?

10. A corporation owns nearly all of a block of land. The remaining portion is purchased subject to an existing lease. The corporation sets aside out of earned surplus an amount believed to be sufficient to extend the plant over the entire block at the expiration of the lease. What ledger title should be given to the amount set aside, and how should the amount be shown on the balance sheet?

11. What is a stock dividend? From what sources may it arise? Does the declaration of such a dividend imply that the previous surplus of the corporation has been unreasonably large and not necessary to the business?

12. You are making an annual audit of a partnership. To what extent, if any, will you examine the withdrawal accounts of the partners?

13. During the current year, an officer of a corporation was given as part compensation for services an option to purchase at any time during the next five years 14,000 shares of the company's no-par-value common stock at $15 per share, the option being granted at a time when the current market price of the stock on a national exchange was $25 and the book value of the stock was $18. A few months later the officer exercised a part of the option by purchasing 3,000 shares for cash, the market value at that time being $21, and at the same time surrendered his right to purchase the remaining 11,000 shares. How should these transactions be recorded on the corporation's books?

14. If preferred methods of accounting are to be followed, what will charges against paid-in surplus be limited to?

15. On a certain date the net worth of a corporation was as follows:

Preferred stock: 10,000 shares, par $100		$1,000,000.00
Common stock: 100,000 shares, stated value $1		100,000.00
Paid-in surplus on—		
Preferred stock	$150,000.00	
Common stock	400,000.00	550,000.00
Earned surplus		752,861.12
Total net worth		$2,402,861.12

On the same date 1,000 shares of preferred stock were purchased at $125 per share (accrued dividends were previously paid to date), and 1,000 shares of common stock were purchased at $3.50 per share; both reacquired lots were carried as treasury stock. Restate net worth by giving expression to these transactions. What would be the effect on net worth if the alternative method mentioned in this chapter were followed?

16. What is the objection on the part of accountants to the showing of unpaid subscriptions as an account receivable?

17. Explain the meaning of "legal" capital.

18. Under what conditions may the identity of an earned-surplus account be continued from one corporation to another?

19. Restate the principal arguments against the creation and use of mixed reserves. In ascertaining the book value per share of common stock would you include mixed reserves?

20. Several methods in current use for determining the percentage of "return on the investment" differ from each other because of varying theories of what constitutes "investment." All of them start with the par or stated value of capital stock, and from time to time various adjustments are suggested such as the following:

Additions	*Reductions*
(a) Paid-in surplus	(f) One-half the dividends paid during year
(b) Valuation surplus	
(c) Earned surplus at beginning of year	(g) Valuation in excess of original cost
(d) One-half the current year's profits	(h) Goodwill
(e) Earned surplus at end of year	

What is your opinion on each of these items?

CHAPTER XIV

The Detailed Audit

A detailed audit today is an extension of an ordinary annual audit, required in those cases where, for any reason, procedures are to be thoroughly examined. Its purpose is to review original transactions for their authenticity, clerical accuracy, and completeness, with such attention to their ultimate classification as the occasion demands. A detailed audit limited to particular items may also be required where a defalcation has occurred or irregularities have been noted in order to determine the extent of the loss or error and the procedural corrections necessary to reduce the likelihood of recurrence. Many auditors include in their annual examinations a detailed audit of certain types of transactions or of all transactions over a portion of the audit period for such varied reasons as these: (a) where an internal control is believed to be faulty, a more extensive inquiry into the transactions possibly affected is required; (b) even where no special weakness is discovered, the practical operations of internal controls may thus be more fully tested; (c) by no other means is the auditor able to ascertain whether operating procedures not covered by prescribed policies or controls measure up to the usual standards of business conduct; (d) it is important to have the client's employees recognize that outsiders, at least annually, are going to examine critically the details of individual transactions, thereby providing them with an added incentive for a high standard of performance in their daily work; (e) the client has requested at least some examination of transactions more intensified than testing or sampling. Once it has been established as a recurring feature of an annual audit, the detailed examination is usually limited to one or two months' transactions; it may cover, primarily, sales, purchases, payrolls, and general-journal

515

entries, with some added examination of cash transactions beyond that accompanying the usual audit procedure.

In contrast with the audit methods described in preceding chapters, where the emphasis is on the testing of accounts and the internal controls under which they are built up, the procedures followed in a detailed audit have as their major objective the determination of whether (a) the monetary amounts of transactions appearing on the books are accurate, (b) all transactions have been recorded in full, and (c) a correct classification has been followed. The detailed audit is sometimes referred to as the "acid test" for policies, principles, and practices that are supposed to be in existence at operating levels. In the sampling process, which constitutes the work done in the greater portion of the annual audit, the auditor's labors vary inversely as the excellence of the internal controls; in a detailed audit the auditor's procedures, once the operating sector of the business and the months to be covered have been decided upon, is more likely to vary as between engagements mostly in accordance with the worth of the original records—a situation conditioned to a great extent by the initiative and competence the auditor finds at operating levels.

A detailed audit originating from special causes may be performed at any time; a detailed audit that supplements an annual audit is almost always performed during the audit year, less often after the period has closed.

The program of a recurrent audit engagement may, for example, call for a detailed audit covering two months of the audit year. If November or December is picked, assuming that the latter is the concluding month of the fiscal year, a portion of the "busy period" will probably have to be devoted to detailed-audit work—work better suited to other portions of the year. Yet a November or December coverage will occasionally be necessary if the primary purpose of the detailed audit is to stimulate good work by employees throughout the year. Some auditors as a regular practice make a detailed examination for December and one other month, December being looked upon as the period more likely than any other to affect the content and meaning of year-end financial statements. Other auditors are satisfied merely to scan the transactions of the final month of the audit period, looking for unusual items, the absence of usual items, and variations in transaction volume and in transaction routines. Or a close examination may be given to certain kinds of transactions—such as cash, sales, purchases, and sales and purchase returns—recorded during the last week of the audit year and the first week of the year following.

A program involving detailed-audit work should be accompanied by an understanding between the auditor and his principal on such points as (1) the procedure to be followed, with emphasis on matters needing investigation and noted in the preceding audit or in conversations or correspondence with the client during the year, (2) working papers to be prepared in support of work done, (3) types of problems to be discussed directly with the controller or other official, (4) types of problems to be referred to the principal for review with the client's representatives, and (5) nature of written or oral report, if any, to client on detailed-audit findings.

An audit of a joint venture, syndicate, trust, or small business enterprise, although nominally a "balance-sheet" examination, may prove to be a detailed audit because of the limited number of transactions.

Examining Revenues

In previous chapters the auditor's interest in sales and other revenues has been tied in with his reviews of the income statement and of receivables arising out of sales transactions. In these reviews he has been in a large measure testing internal controls; inquiring into sales policies and observing their effects on operations; noting trends in sales and sales returns, the emergence of new products, and relations with distributors and consumers; comparing the cost of obtaining sales with similar costs for previous years. He has circularized customers from whom sums were owing at the end of the period and has studied their replies. He has evaluated the sufficiency of the reserve for bad debts as a buffer against accounts probably uncollectible. Moreover he has inquired carefully into the marketability of unsold product included in the inventory and compared its costs with the prices the product will bring on the market in an effort to determine whether carrying forward the full cost can be justified as a charge against future sales. From these investigations and probings he has been sitting more or less continuously in judgment on the adequacy and propriety of internal controls governing sales and in most instances requires no further investigation to satisfy himself of the "fairness" of the sales figure for the period. Whatever additional time he devotes to sales will likely be at the transaction level: a testing of weak points that could be present in almost any situation.

Tests may be made of the completeness of records of (a) original sales orders, (b) the filling and recording of orders, (c) withdrawals from stock, (d) the handling of back orders, (e) the invoicing operation, (f) the supervision of decision-making on allowances, (g) the recording of returns including their re-entry on stock records, and the followup and collection efforts applied to unpaid receivables. Although much will depend upon the character of the records and on the thoroughness of internal controls, including internal audit, the most satisfactory procedure will probably be to trace a number of successive transactions from the earliest record of the sales order to the final collection from the customer—a procedure resembling, in reverse, the detailed examination of purchases. Where the detailed audit is to be limited to a month's transactions, and the location of the bookkeeping records permits, it is best to select the orders received during a given month and to follow them through to their liquidation in cash, although billing and collection may occur in later months; by this procedure the auditor can more easily observe (a) the attention given to the order at different points (sometimes revealing unnecessary protective steps and duplication of effort), and (b) the continuity of accompanying detail (for example, nature of items ordered, shipping instructions, terms, delivery date, invoicing, and settlement). If he cannot thus follow through on each transaction, he should, for the reason cited, perform the consecutive steps as quickly as possible. Where original orders are numbered, he should obtain satisfactory explanations for missing numbers; if an order has been altered, the authority therefor should be sought.

In some instances, item quantities can be built up from sales orders that may be reconciled, without too much difficulty, with finished-inventory quantity controls. Occasionally, commissions paid salesmen can be translated into sales dollars. Or, where cash sales are involved, cash-register tapes may be available for the building up of a dollar sales figure. Whatever the procedure, the attempt should be made to set up a total "order" figure that can be accounted for in subsequent steps, thus avoiding questions of completeness for such steps. If the total cannot be evolved, or, if obtainable, cannot by any practicable device be traced through to the sales account on the one hand, and cash or adjustments on the other, the auditor will have to depend upon the examination and tracing of individual orders.

Cutoff procedures at the year end are generally regarded as an object of inquiry belonging to a balance-sheet audit (see Chapter VIII), and are thus not a matter to be considered in a detailed audit.

Because of the possibility of loss through poorly controlled noncash credits to customers, it is usual to find a careful routine through which they must go before they can be recorded. Hence, the task of the auditor in examining each such item is (a) to determine whether the routine was accurately observed, and, in at least partial proof thereof, (b) to scan correspondence with, or advice from, the customer, indicating that the credit has been claimed.

Examining Expenditure Vouchers

The word "voucher," as used by accountants, is usually limited in application to the documentation prepared in connection with the recording of an expenditure (and its payment) or journal entry; the typical voucher consists of a folder or top summary memorandum with several supporting papers.

From the auditor's point of view, the ideal voucher covering a cash disbursement is one that, with its attachments, at the time of its preparation or years later, completely and convincingly justifies the expenditure to any third person such as himself. The auditor always lends his unqualified moral support to a "tough" voucher-audit (that is, administrative-audit or pre-audit) activity within the business—not an activity limited to making sure that authorizing documents bear specified signatures, but one that extends to frequent reviews of the methods being followed at the encumbrance, purchasing, receiving, inspection, adjustment, and approval levels. Whether the whole activity is carried on by the voucher-audit head or is divided (as is more common) among several individuals—the internal auditor, the controller, and a representative of general management—is immaterial, provided only that the endproduct is an unvarying stream of vouchers that will stand up under any audit test.

Following are the points on which the auditor in examining a voucher should satisfy himself:

1. *That the obligation was authorized.* A requisition or other formal request for the purchase should be among the attachments, bearing the signature of the person who has been authorized to incur the particular type of expenditure involved; if it does not, the files of the purchasing division must be consulted.

A list of authorizing signatures should be at hand for comparison.

2. *That the goods or services were ordered.* The purchase should have been made in accordance with existing policies as to the solicitation of bids, or as to other general or special limiting conditions that have been imposed on the purchasing division by higher authority. The order should have been subjected to other routines within the purchasing division that would insure the most favorable deal available in the way of quantity, quality, date of delivery, discounts (both trade and cash), conditions of rejection, and payment. If the auditor finds orders being placed regularly with certain suppliers, without periodic tests of prices and delivery service, he should so report. Many purchasing short-cuts are found in practice. Blanket orders or price orders for a year's requirements or for unspecified requirements of raw materials and other items are of frequent occurrence; for the mutual protection of both the business as a whole and its purchasing division, these should always be placed under rules approved by the general management. If no such rules exist, a recommendation may be made that long-term purchase orders be individually reviewed and approved by some member of the top staff superior to the head of the purchasing division—or even by the board, where the auditor has observed that higher prices are being paid or full-scale competition among suppliers has not been secured.

3. *That the purchase accords with existing policy.* In examining individual purchases there should be no evidence indicating that the purchase created an excess supply, had application to a discontinued line, had been ordered from a supplier with whom no further business was to be carried on, is a duplicate of another order, or was otherwise at variance with customary purchasing policies.

4. *That the goods or services were supplied.* Evidence should be attached showing receipt, inspection, and acceptance or rejection, in the form of either joint or separate receiving and inspection reports, and, where material or merchandise is involved, an acknowledgment that the items received and inspected have been accepted by the storekeeper. Quantities approved should, as a rule, be the result of an actual count by both the receiving division and the storekeeper. Receipt of services is usually indicated directly on a copy of the creditor's work order or invoice or in a separate memorandum from an official authorized to approve the service. Deductions should appear for shortages, rejections, or other indicated adjustments noted on the receiving and inspection reports.

5. *That prices paid were the lowest available.* Tests to indicate the propriety of prices paid are usually possible for a large portion of the purchases of materials and supplies. Purchasing agents, as a rule, have some form of record (sometimes a copy of the purchase order, filed by name of material or supply) in which quoted prices for particular items are recorded, along with names of suppliers and other details, for future reference. Prices appearing on invoices should be compared with this record and with market quotations obtained from independent sources; these sources will be trade journals or financial newspapers for the more common raw materials. Correspondence with suppliers other than the client's is sometimes resorted to.

6. *That quantities, prices, and amounts are clerically accurate.* Quantities and prices on the voucher summary and the several supporting documents should be compared. The auditor should make certain that the number of units received is multiplied against the agreed price for the same type of unit, that extensions and footings are correct, and that deductions for returns, allowances, and discounts have been accurately made.

7. *That payment has been made.* Use of the voucher number as the check number, insertion of the check number on the voucher, or the presence of some other cross-referencing device, will enable the auditor to trace the obligation represented by the voucher through to its payment (or to accounts payable). As a rule, comparison of a group of vouchers with canceled checks will take place as a separate operation, and the checks may, at the same time, be subjected to other tests. An alternative is to compare the voucher with the entry therefor in the voucher record, compare the voucher-record entry with its corresponding entry in the check register, and, finally, compare the check-register entry with the check itself.

8. *That the obligation has not been paid before.* If the approval or payment date has not been perforated through the voucher and its attachments, a comparison of various dates will indicate whether the sequence of events supports this conclusion. Any seeming irregularity should be explained by the voucher-audit clerk. If the existing system permits papers to be removed, the auditor may find it desirable to affix a rubber-stamp impression or distinctive checkmark on each voucher and supporting document, so that it may not be presented to him a second time without detection.

9. *That the expenditure has been correctly accounted for.* Accounts to be charged with the expenditure will appear in the

voucher-summary form. It is not enough to be satisfied with the internal controls surrounding the original "coding" operation; the auditor must be satisfied that the accounts to be charged are the ones he would have charged had the determination been his, and he must examine the accounts indicated, to make certain that they, and not others, were the ones debited in the posting operation. Where the coding operation includes the preparation of the explanation to be posted along with the monetary amount, the auditor should make sure that the explanation is accurate, adequate, and unlikely to mislead.

As this brief summary has indicated, it is always best, when making a detailed audit of expenditures, to commence whenever possible at the beginning—that is, the point where the need for the expenditure originates—and to carry individual transactions through to their payment and final disposition. Only in this way can the significance of operating procedures and the protective devices surrounding the disbursement of funds be fully tested.

Purchase Adjustments

Separate accounts are customarily provided for purchase returns, purchase discounts, and other debits affecting amounts otherwise payable to creditors. Aside from scanning these accounts and tracing down the larger amounts, the auditor's main problem will be to ascertain whether all adjustments have been made that should have been made. He must study the sources of the recorded adjustments, scan the records at these points, and discuss the methods followed and the possibility of open items with each person responsible for initiating adjustments.

Examining Payrolls

If a detailed audit of one month's payrolls is to be made, and during the month two payrolls, say, have been prepared, much time can usually be saved if they are examined together. Following the procedure accorded disbursements generally, the auditor commences with the authorization for employment and traces through intervening steps to the canceled payroll check.

So many variations enter into payroll procedures of different organizations that all that can be assayed here will be an outline of the leading points to be covered in *any* payroll examination, together with their application to a single assumed situation—a manufacturing enterprise having, say, 500 factory and 100 office employees, both paid twice monthly, with a separate payroll for each group. The illustration should also prove helpful in indicating the type of information the securing of which is a condition precedent to an intelligent detailed examination of other items.

1. *Employment authorization.* In the practical situation mentioned, payroll forms are prepared in advance for each payroll, one day following the close of the payroll period and two days before payment. Each employee's name, department, rate of pay (hourly rate for factory employees and semimonthly rate for office employees), and the date on which the present rate of pay was made effective appear on an addressograph plate kept in a locked file in the personnel-records office under the supervision of the personnel officer and his assistant. He is present whenever the payroll forms (an original and two carbon copies) are made up from these plates. Neither the payroll clerk nor any other factory employee has access to the file. When a new employee appears for the first time on a payroll, the personnel officer or his assistant initials the item and inserts the effective date and hour; a similar procedure is followed when a name appears on the payroll for the last time. Plates for former employees are kept in a separate file, and the last day of employment is noted in a space provided on the back of the plate along with the initials of the personnel officer. Since, in this case, the plates are filed alphabetically and are printed in the order of their appearance, the auditor's task is simply to see that the plates and impressions therefrom correspond, and that no new names have been inserted.

2. *Hours worked or work performed.* Continuing the illustration, factory employees punch a clock in and out daily, and one card serves for each two-week period. In addition, a time ticket is prepared daily by each employee and approved by his foreman, showing the job on which he worked, the classification of the work performed, and the hours devoted to each job and type of work. Both the clock cards and time tickets are kept by the payroll clerk; having obtained total hours by the aid of a comptometer, he inserts the total (showing overtime hours separately) on the payroll. The auditor, working from the payroll, checks back to the time tickets, mentally footing the total hours shown by the tickets; this he can do in even hours, without the necessity of an elaborate refooting of the tickets. Subsequently he compares the clock-card totals with the payroll totals. Hours worked by office employees are based on and are compared with the daily record maintained by an attendance clerk.

Where labor is paid on a piece-work basis, the auditor must seek in the underlying wage agreement the method of determining quantities and rates and compare totals indicated by the payroll with operating reports. Most incentive plans providing for bonuses require a detailed review of production records supporting the differentials on which the stated quantities of work performed are based.

3. *Rate of pay*. Continuing this illustration, the rates of pay printed from the addressograph plate have originated with the personnel division and the auditor's work will include the comparison of rates appearing on the payroll with those shown on the addressograph plates, to make sure no alterations or misreadings have taken place.

4. *Gross pay*. Audit of gross pay is simply the product of quantity times rate, or, in the case of office employees in the illustration cited, the gross pay is the rate that has been printed by the plate.

5. *Deductions*. The principal deductions, in the assumed illustration, are for government savings bonds, social-security tax, withholding tax, and advances. A miscellaneous column is also provided on the payroll form for other deductions. When the payroll (in triplicate) is typed by the payroll clerk, an earnings record (a separate sheet for each employee) receives the first impression, and deductions are the same as on the previous payroll, or deduction changes are obtained from notations at the top of each earnings-record sheet in spaces provided for them. Where the employee is given the supporting information that results in the amount shown on his check (and this should always be given him), it is usually sufficient to examine the deductions in total rather than for individual employees. In the illustration, the second carbon copy of the payroll has horizontal perforations that make it possible to give each employee a slip containing the necessary detail making up his portion of the payroll.

Deductions that involve payments to the Federal Treasury should be traced in total to a controlling account the balance of which is a liability subject to separate review.

6. *Net pay*. The amount shown on the payroll to have been paid by check to the individual employee should be compared with the corresponding entry in the check register. Maintenance of a separate payroll cash account simplifies materially the review of both details and totals. Cash payments obviously cannot be verified except in total. Where payment is in cash, the best proce-

dure on the part of the auditor will be to make a surprise visit to the payroll office during the period covered by the audit, thus examining payroll items as the payroll is being made up. He observes the methods of computing payroll details and keeping them under control, examines authorizations for changes in rates and deductions, watches the "envelope stuffing," and accompanies the paymaster (or his equivalent) as he identifies the employee and gives him his envelope.

7. *Distribution.* In an organization employing 500 wage earners, the auditor would expect to find the payroll totals carried to controlling or clearing accounts, details of gross pay having already been spread, on a daily, weekly, or monthly basis, to departmental, job-cost, construction, or other expenditure accounts. He would ascertain the basis for the spread and prove its accuracy and that of the resultant postings.

Petty Cash

Reviewing petty-cash transactions involves the same basic procedure as that required for the examination of vouchers. The principal difference is in the nature of the transactions and in the lack of cross relationships when funds are disbursed. The transactions are those that are customarily paid in cash and for which crude receipts, rather than formal invoices, are received in exchange. Carefare, postage, express charges, repairs of office equipment, emergency supplies and services—these and similar small outlays make up the bulk of petty-cash vouchers. The auditor should be familiar with the review given such vouchers when reimbursements of the fund are made; he will often find the reviewing responsibility assigned to a person who has no other disbursement-control function and who regards the job as a purely perfunctory one. Despite the inevitable informality of the expenditures, the auditor can, as a rule, very quickly reach a conclusion as to the propriety of petty-cash disbursements—by inquiring into repeating items, establishing the identity of persons to whom funds are frequently given, looking for similarity in the signatures of presumably different individuals, and ascertaining reasons for gradual or sudden increases, should they appear. Where he finds weaknesses, he should do his part in insisting, for the future, at least, that supporting tickets, cash-register slips, and other original evidence be rigorously sought for and preserved.

Expense Reports

An often-neglected area of expenditure may be found in travel and other individual-expense vouchers. Although the auditor, as a rule, can do little more than make sure that items of past travel and other personal expense do not violate existing regulations that the company or any of its divisions have promulgated in an endeavor to set top limits, he can frequently regard his detailed audit of these vouchers as furnishing ample cause for advocating needed improvements in expense-allowance standards. Among desirable standards for most organizations are stated per-diem allowances for room and meals, graduated, where necessary, as between employee groups or types of locations, tabulation of characteristic business expenses for which reimbursement may be claimed and personal expenses that the traveler must himself bear, nature of permissible Pullman accommodations, limitations on entertainment expense, and other items, peculiar to the business, on which adjustments have been difficult in the past. Without a reasonably strict code for such expenses, they may easily get out of sensible bounds and be the cause of much embarrassment between top executives whose judgments as to the need for frugality or openhandedness may differ widely.

Journal Entries

The bulk of journal entries, including year-end adjustments, will already have been examined in connection with balance-sheet and operating items. Month-end adjusting entries need to be scanned only for the purpose of discovering (a) changes in amortization or accrual procedures that might influence judgments of comparative monthly operating results, and (b) changes in accounting method. Transfer entries may be passed if they are corrections of classification or postings; if they represent reclassifications, their possible influence on comparative analyses should be weighed and noted. Other entries not answering these descriptions will be few in number; the auditor should investigate them in detail to whatever extent may be necessary in order to assure himself of their propriety and he should trace them into the accounts. It is always good practice for the controller to approve each general-journal entry, at least the nonroutine variety; if his approval does not appear the auditor should discuss the more important entries with him.

Cash Transactions

Although the main *sources* of cash receipts and the main *objects* of cash disbursements may be given adequate examination, it is still necessary, in detailed-audit procedure, to give consideration to the cash items not covered in such examination and to such matters concerning the handling of cash as have not been recognized elsewhere.

The auditor will find in the average case that the categories of cash receipts and disbursements remaining over from the examination described in previous chapters and in the first part of this chapter will be, for any one month, few in number. The items of which these categories are composed should be reviewed at length: their sources, correspondence or other data, originating from without, attesting their nature and amount and their disposition. When expenses or other items that normally make their initial appearance in other records are cleared through the cashbook in the first instance, the auditor's examination, in addition to that prescribed elsewhere, would include an inquiry into the occasion for bypassing regular procedures.

Remaining requirements for the detailed audit of cash transactions will usually be satisfactorily covered if all of the audit procedures, including the "additional" procedures suggested at the end of Chapter VI, are carried out.

Footings and Postings

The extent to which footings and postings are verified is a problem common to all the items already considered in this chapter. Generally, in a detailed audit, books of original and final entry should be footed and the correctness of postings to controlling and other accounts should be proved. But the auditor should not perform these operations blindly; in fact, he should avoid them wherever they would constitute useless duplication. And even if they are considered necessary, he should adopt such short-cuts as are practicable, his object being to save time and avoid getting mired in clerical detail.

Time is often saved by making a spread sheet or analysis of ledger postings by sources. A worksheet is prepared with account names in the first vertical column; successive columns are given headings for posting sources, and a recapitulation of the postings in each account for the period of the detailed audit is spread through these columns. When the analysis has been completed and the columns have been footed, differences between these footings and those appearing in the books of original entry for the same period should lead readily to the detection of such errors as the following: (a) incorrect footings of journals or ledger accounts, (b) the posting of incorrect amounts, (c) errors corrected in one record but not in the other, (d) unjournalized transfers or postings, and (e) offsetting errors. Postings to wrong accounts will not always be detected by this process, except in obvious cases; but it may be sufficient, where a cursory inspection of the accounts does not give assurance of correct postings, to make mental subtotals (for example, in thousands only) of the different classes of items in each book of original entry and compare them with the subtotals appearing in the ledger-analysis columns.

Another form of spread sheet preferred by some auditors commences as does the preceding analysis with a vertical column listing the general-ledger accounts. But the "spread" columns are headed with the same account titles, the final product being a general-ledger analysis displaying subtotals of the debits of each account (vertical money columns) that offset the subtotals of related credits (horizontal money columns) of other general-ledger accounts. This type of analysis is usually much more difficult to compile since it may require a breakdown and recapitulation of totals of one or more books of original entry; but where it is obtainable it supplies the auditor with totals of similar transactions against which independent measures of accuracy may often be applied. Moreover it furnishes a revealing over-all picture of the business useful in the preparation of a statement of application of funds.

Mental additions (again, in thousands or more) are usually adequate substitutes for the formal "taping" of books of original entry or ledger accounts, provided periodic refootings have already been made as a feature of internal-audit procedures.

Where individual postings are being traced from one record to another, distinctive checkmarks should be placed after (or before) the individual items in both records; when the tracing has been completed, a search for original posting references in the second record, not accompanied by checkmarks after them, should reveal any items that have not actually originated from the first record, although they have been so tagged.

The reader must again be reminded that an adding-machine tape not prepared by the auditor or his assistant should never be accepted as proving the correctness of a total. A new tape, prepared by the auditor, is always required.

Illustrative Audit

From the data on X 4–5 it appears that the company's budget was not an instrument of control. It provided no machinery for limiting expenditures or gaging them in relation to sales. Sales in total being larger than the estimate, material purchases and labor costs were allowed to increase but by no predetermined standards. Nevertheless the estimate compared with the actual affords a measure of comparison and supplies a better basis for the development of future budgetary techniques.

Also included at this point is the "agenda" sheet (X 10) kept by the auditor and his assistants. On this worksheet are listed items for investigation at a later point in the audit. Thus the auditor's assistant, while preparing worksheet H 3a, raises a question regarding the gain or loss on the sale of certain items of furniture and fixtures and an automobile. Subsequently the journal entry or other source for the transaction appearing in the fixed-asset account was examined and the results were noted on TB 5.

The 1952 budget was adopted in line with past practice — before the beginning of the calendar year. It was prepared from information obtained for the most part in November, 1951, reviewed by the top staff during the first week of December, and approved without change by the Board of Directors on December 16. Under prevailing custom the controller is responsible both for the its preparation and for its execution. In practice the budget has been a funds-statement estimate that provides no more than an aim and guide in the exercise of financial controls. The actual results of operations are ultimately explained to the Board in terms of the budgetary projection, this being management's method of meeting and reporting on its accountability. In recent years some attempt has been made to prepare and follow a plan of flexible budgeting but this idea has not yet been fully developed.

A separate budget is now provided for the Cleveland branch.

Item		1952 Projected (books omitted)	Actual	1953 Projected (books omitted)
Sources of funds –				
Sales, net, to outsiders	P-1	$ 7500	7760888 32	7500
Sales to subsidiary	D-3	100	1060 92 55	100
Interest	TB-3 (con)	15	15 20550	15
Dividends	D-2	50	8376 250	30
Sale of investment in stocks	D-2	500	6310000	0
Sales of fixed assets	H-3 (Net Reversal)	5	523550	5
Employees' contributions to pension fund	PF 83-a	25	2390000	25
Decrease in working capital, less inventories		930	75838096 (a)	25
Total funds available		9125 ⁿ	938446533 ⁿ	7700 ⁿ
Disposition of funds –				
Raw-material & parts purchases	TB-3	3000	314362373	3000
Direct labor	TB-3	2550	268626788	2600
Variable overhead	TB-4	600	595361 14	600
Fixed overhead (less depreciation $71,220.88)	TB-4	300	29196983	300
Installation & service	TB-3 (BA)	100	11315909	50
Selling (less depreciation $1,287.50)	TB-5 & 51	320	32635791	370
Administration (less depreciation $3,797.08)	TB-5	500	47843596	500
Interest	TB-3(cm)	25	2879392	25
Discount & expense of retiring bonds	TB-3 (cm)	50	3743475	0

X-4

(continued)

Income tax	(TB3 BA)	130	20500000	100
Dividends to stockholders	PF 93	125	12500000	125
Purchase of additional stock	D-2	100	9100000	0
Increase in long-term receivables	TB1	50	9716700	-25
Increase in investment in subsidiary	?	10	1374765	0
Purchase of fixed assets	H-1	750	7075231	20
Payments to pensioners	PF 83a	15	1341500	15
Reduction of bonds outstanding	PF-89 / S-1	500	4301631⁶	20
Total funds applied		9125⁻	93844653³⁺	1100⁻

Breakdown of budgeted sales is on A-1. This shows that sales of heavy
machinery did not meet expectations, principally because
additional order for another 200 of these models was not received
from Ordnance. Had this order been received when originally
anticipated it is estimated that a dozen more could have been
manufactured and shipped before the end of the year, thus
accounting for the excess of the budget estimate over actual (i.e.,
$450.0 - 368.3 = 81.7; 81.7 ÷ 6.8 = 12+$). The last of model AX-241 was
shipped in November, 1952, 55 having been sold in that year; a few
more assemblies are included in finished stock. When existing orders
have been worked out (sales of $350.0 estimated for 1953) production of
heavy machinery (all models) is expected to cease.

Light-machinery demand did not fall down as much as expected
(8% v. 11% in dollars; 6% v. 11% in number of CNX1 units sold
because of 2% markdown in price to meet competition.

Variations in appliance sales commented on in A-2.

Merchandise sales have ranged between 650.0 and 800.0 during
last 5 years and are expected to stay within that range indefinitely
in future. Gross profit ratio varies widely.

Comments on expenses on A-6, 7, 8.

Note: (a) Includes variation in supplies inventory only.

X-5

Martin Manufacturing Company
Agenda Sheet
December 31, 1952

F.L.
B.B.
H.R.

" Depreciation of addition to foundry: should 1953 rate be adjusted for improvement which will have remaining life from Dec. 31, 1951, of 489.2 − 250.9 = 16+ years; hence depreciation rate of 6+% rather than 3. $\frac{14.7}$ This will be topic of discussion in 1953 (Mr. Collins).

" Reserve for cash discounts on receivables? Possibly next year (Mr. Collins)

" Separate subcontrol %cs for trucks and for autos (and for 2 reserves) might make compilation job easier. Would help (Mrs. Cowles).

" Look up correspondence on Davis & Davis Mfg. Co. note on waiver of interest. OK

" Re-examine tax status of interest on government bonds. Done; see D-2.

" Should we ask for receipt for return of securities after count? No; we do not handle them.

" Should we ask bank to inform us of interest rates appearing on notes discounted No; of minor importance only.

" Equipment Committee minutes? None (Mr. Collins)

" Follow up on minute book now at lawyers' offices. Returned 1/6

" Trace gain or loss on disposition of F. & F. (−84.11) and auto (250.00). Scante, TB-5.

" Amount of $11,750 owing from E.C. Peyton not a current asset? Not a major item; no adjustment

" Six sales orders totaling $25,647.80 could have been filled in 1952; corresponding amount last year: $2,387.50. Should sales be adjusted (suggested by Mr. Sorry). Reason found to be that processing operation for sales orders cumbersome; no adjustment proper.

" Disclosure of valuation basis of inventory as balance-sheet footnote. Mr. Stebbins agrees. See balance-sheet draft

" Should adjustment be made for S/o 16,490 ($565)? Too small; follow up next year.

X-10

Problems and Questions

1. The first five items under "sources of funds" on worksheet X 4 and the first ten items under "disposition of funds" on worksheets X 4 and X 5 are related to the income statement. Ascertain their totals and reconcile their difference with the net income reflected in worksheet TB 3.

2. On worksheet X 5 is an item "Increase in investment in subsidiary" amounting to $13,747.65, yet from TB 1 (account 27–9) and D 4 the increase in the intercompany current account during the year appears to be $15,766.71. How do you explain the difference? Outline the procedure followed on the books of the parent company in the recognition of profits derived from its subsidiary.

3. The employees of a company are paid in cash once a week on a fixed-wage basis, no overtime being allowed. The volume of work has been steady and the labor turnover low. The company has 100 employees, all of whom work at one plant; 50 of these employees are on a night shift. They are paid on Friday (on Saturday morning with respect to the night crew) for the week ended on the preceding Tuesday. One employee, the payroll clerk, prepares the payroll from time sheets signed by foremen; he also checks time cards against these payroll sheets, secures a check from the cashier in the amount of the payroll, cashes the check at the bank, stuffs the pay envelopes, and hands them out to employees. Prepare an audit program for such a payroll, assuming an annual audit is in progress.

4. In a detailed audit, you are examining an expenditure voucher covering the purchase of supplies; how would you determine whether the purchase was authorized, the goods were ordered, and the goods were received?

5. In the course of an annual audit, the examination of detailed transactions for one month, as agreed upon, has brought to light many clerical errors of importance. What steps should you now take?

6. A certain public accountant who at one time insisted on the necessity of annually examining at close range all the transactions of his clients for one or two months has now substituted an intensive review of internal controls. He states that (a) his auditors are thus encouraged to do a more workmanlike job and (b) each year, instead of indiscriminately covering arbitrarily selected periods, they make detailed examinations at points that need audit. Discuss this point of view.

7. It is often claimed that a detailed audit makes it possible "to ascertain whether prescribed operating procedures are being followed." Contrast, and evaluate in general terms, the auditor's methods of carrying out a "procedural review" as described in Chapter IV and the methods of performing a detailed audit as described in this chapter.

8. One auditor claims that his clue for whatever detailed audit he makes for a client is secured from a comparison of trial-balance items over a period of years. What does he mean by this statement and what weakness is inherent in this type of "spot" audit?

9. Every business enterprise employs some form of internal voucher "audit" before bills are paid. This may be accomplished by a "voucher clerk" who collates voucher information and formally prepares the voucher document, or by an audit clerk or unit that examines the completed voucher, after supporting papers have been attached by a voucher clerk. Your advice is sought by a client as to the position in the office organization in which this audit function should be located. What would your answer be?

10. What internal controls should prevent the payment of the same invoice twice?

11. The purchases division of a parts-supply company, because of a shortage of specialists in certain fields, has delegated authority for the purchase of a certain line of merchandise to the head of the division responsible for the selling of the same merchandise. If the practice is to go on, what internal controls should be established in order to insure the continued propriety of this arrangement?

12. Suggest the procedure you would adopt in connection with your discovery of the following facts having to do with a client's payroll:

(a) The factory superintendent hires employees, determines their compensation, and delivers biweekly payroll checks to them in person.

(b) Unclaimed checks are returned by the superintendent to the payroll clerk who keeps them until they are called for; he has on hand checks two and three years old.

(c) Weekly attendance summaries are prepared by foremen and initialed by the superintendent, and, because of these approvals, the payroll clerk makes no comparison of the summaries with clock cards.

(d) In some instances the superintendent has informed the payroll clerk orally as to changes in rates of pay.

(e) "Informal" leave is frequently granted by the superintendent, without notations thereof on the attendance summaries or other payroll record.

13. Certain deductions made from the pay of approximately two-thirds of the 100 employees of a company apply against purchases of United States Savings Bonds. Devise a simple procedure for recording these deductions and for providing an adequate bookkeeping support for the balance-sheet liability account called "Deductions from Payrolls for U. S. Bonds."

14. A petty-cash fund of $2,500 is maintained by one of your clients out of which only expense advances are supposed to be made. You find that in addition to making expense advances the petty cashier has cashed personal checks as an accommodation and that on the day of your examination there are two such checks (one issued by an officer) amounting to $1,200, both postdated, making up a part of the fund. What action on your part does this situation demand, assuming that the practice has been going on for several years?

15. Tests applied to a cash-disbursements book reveal errors of footings on two pages, one being overstated by $100, and the other understated by $180. The general ledger, however, appears to be in balance. Prepare a program for whatever detailed audit you think the situation warrants.

16. In examining the sales account of a truck-repair contractor you discover that a block of exactly 100 customer-invoice copies is missing and in this block you have reason to believe that irregularities in the way of arbitrary overcharges (offsetting peculations of the cashier) may be found. No sales journal is maintained, postings to customers accounts being made directly from the invoice copies and to sales from totals of 100-invoice blocks, respectively. Explain how you would proceed to investigate this situation.

17. In examining a group of invoices covering materials purchases you note that one of them dated November 5 was paid on November 14 although the receiving record indicates that the materials were received on November 20. Do you regard this as an irregularity; if so, how would you proceed to investigate the item?

18. You find that a number of checks have been issued by a client's cashier (who is authorized to sign checks), have cleared through the bank, and have been filed with other canceled checks, although they are unnumbered and have not been entered in the cash-disbursements book or check record. The cashier explains that these were issued at the request of employees and that receipts from employees in equal amounts have been deposited by him in the bank, likewise without a record thereof in the books of account. What would your attitude be as auditor and what action, if any, would you take?

19. In auditing the accounts of one of your clients you note that invoices when received from creditors are transmitted by the bookkeeper to persons believed to be responsible for ordering the supplies or services. No record is made of the transmittals. When an "OK" is affixed to an invoice by any such person it is paid without further investigation by the bookkeeper. Comment on this procedure.

20. What is your understanding of a "routine" transaction?

CHAPTER XV

Closing the Audit; Financial Statements

Having ended his formal program the auditor reviews what he has done, disposes of any matters as yet unsettled or incomplete, prepares (or, if already prepared by the client's staff, edits) the financial statements, discusses them with management and procures management's representation thereon; and thereafter drafts his report. During these operations, most of which are carried on in the client's office, the auditor will be working closely with his principal and the principal will be making a general review of the auditor's working papers and procedures. The sequence and place of these events will depend on the nature of the engagement, distance from the auditor's home office, availability of the principal, authority enjoyed by the auditor, and other factors.

Completing the Working Papers

Shortly before concluding his fieldwork the auditor makes sure that his working papers and the permanent file have been fully completed and are in good order.

Where a number of worksheets relate to a single section of the audit (for example, cash or receivables) they are assembled and put in some logical sequence; on the top sheet of each section a summary and index should appear. In larger engagements these sections are bound separately. During the process of assembly the auditor reviews each sheet and makes certain that the details are legible and understandable to others, and that no open points remain. Each page of his papers if not the continuation of a preceding page should tie in with the summary or some other sheet, and cross references should appear on both; likewise any relationship worth noting of items anywhere in the section with items in other sections should be indicated. Totals both unadjusted and adjusted appearing on the top sheet should be cross-referenced to the working trial balance. The purpose of this seemingly elaborate tie-in is twofold: others are aided when they review the papers, and the auditor's principal is assured, subject doubtless to the principal's own testing of the auditor's dependability in this respect, that every figure directly or indirectly fits into the working trial balance. The scheme of cross-referencing followed in the Illustrative Audit may be studied in this connection. Separation should be made of papers belonging to the client; an entry on the auditor's agenda may be provided as a reminder for their return.

Next, the nature and content of explanatory narratives of work done should be carefully restudied; in view of the fact that they were prepared as each section of the audit was completed, perhaps several days or weeks previously, the auditor at the conclusion of the engagement has the opportunity of looking at them with a fair degree of objectivity and can revise them in the interest of greater clarity or add to them information gleaned subsequently from other sources. At the same time he assures himself that they are as complete as he can make them. The auditor strives to improve his narratives so that they may be as terse, realistic, informative, and factual as possible.

During his examination the auditor has probably added material to the permanent file, especially in the case of funded debt, capital stock, surplus, and similar continuing items where no current working papers have been prepared. He should now make the necessary additions to fixed-asset and other schedules and summaries in the permanent file and prepare from his current papers any new schedules or notes that would be helpful in future audits or reviews.

Review with Client

Proposed adjustments and reclassifications of ledger accounts may be reviewed by the auditor's principal before they are presented to the client. Each must have a practical justification—either because it is material in amount or because of the existence of practices of which it serves as a formal reminder. The precise procedure for securing their adoption by the client is likely to be different in each engagement, and it will normally be determined by the auditor's principal before the audit begins. In some cases the principal will review them and discuss them with the client; in others the task will be left to the auditor, at least for certain types of adjustments, or the adjustments may be passed on informally to the client's accounting officer while the fieldwork is in progress.

During the past few years the principle has been well established that the financial statements to which the public accountant subscribes are not his but his client's. He persuades but has no way of compelling his client to adopt preferred accounting procedures and to accept adjustments and reclassifications when they are necessary. As a rule the professional accountant dictates the form and content of financial statements; yet if his audit be considered as a whole this action is no more than a polishing-off process: a job not unlike that of the editor who stands between the author and his public. The transactions that underlie every financial statement are the client's, but the method by which summarized transactions in the form of financial statements are presented to outsiders is traditionally the job of the public accountant. If the client refuses to permit the expression of adjustments, or language, or a form considered by the public accountant as necessary to a fair showing of position or operating results, the accountant may qualify his report or even refuse to issue it.

Explanations accompanying journal entries should be sufficiently detailed so that the client's staff will be directed to sources of information. If for the sake of his own record the auditor wishes in addition to refer to his papers, that portion of the explanation should be bracketed so that it will not be reproduced when the adjustments are given to a typist for copying.

Having secured agreement on the adjustments the auditor should be assured that the books have been conformed to the figures that will be reproduced in his report. He may compare ledger balances after adjustment with the final columns of his working trial balance, or where the books have not been held open he may trace the adjustments into the accounts. In lieu of a personal inspection he may accept a statement from the controller or a statement incorporated in the representation from management (see below) indicating that the adjustments have been made.

The client's approval of the form, content, and footnoting of the financial statements that the auditor proposes to put in his report may take the form of the controller's signature on the final draft of the statements. This may be secured at the time the adjustments are reviewed, sometimes at a later date. The auditor and his principal may also discuss the report draft with the client, although responsibility for the report rests solely with the public accountant: a fact universally respected in business circles and fully recognized and supported by such governmental bodies as the U.S. Securities and Exchange Commission.

Scanning of Books After Year End

A practice followed by many public accountants is a scanning of the client's books of account between the end of the period audited and the date of the audit report. For example, if on March 20 the auditor completes the field work of an audit covering the preceding calendar year, he will by custom put that date on his report. Because the report must be typed and referenced in the auditor's own office a week or two may elapse before the finished document is put into the client's hands; and as to what transpires in the business after March 20 the auditor cannot be expected to be informed. There is a tendency at present to hold him accountable, along very broad lines, for noting any obvious major events that have been recorded on the books of his client during the interval between December 31 and the date of his report: transactions that relate to items appearing in the auditor's report or certificate and accompanying the financial statements and that might conceivably have an important influence on readers' opinions of the financial position at December 31 or the operating results for the period then ended. Following are types of post-audit-period events disclosed in footnotes accompanying financial statements or cited by public accountants in their reports:

Discontinuance of important product lines
Sale of plant
Purchase of plant
Settlement of important price dispute with government agency
Results of profit renegotiation
Settlement of income-tax liability for prior years
Suit for patent infringement against company
Judgment awarded to company against licensee
Refinancing or retirement of securities
Stock splitup
Stock dividend

In general the events requiring such disclosure are always relatively large, of importance in the life of the company, and notable in their effect on financial position, restatements of principal assets or liabilities, or past or future earning power.

The scanning process in this instance has as its sole object the search for out-of-the-ordinary changes in both real and nominal accounts. If in the example just cited the auditor devotes March 20 to the task, he may examine the controller's monthly statements for January and February; compare them with previous monthly statements, including those for the corresponding months of the audit year; review the worksheets supporting the statements, making sure that they have been prepared from the books and that any month-end journal entries follow the usual pattern of adjustments; review the books of original entry for the 20 days of March and discuss with the controller the possibility of any important transactions not yet recorded. If monthly statements have not been prepared, the auditor must scan the general-ledger accounts or if the accounts have not been posted, the books of original entry.

As illustrated below the representation from management may feature a reference to post-balance-sheet events and conditions.

Financial Statements

Standards relating to the items and groupings making up financial statements have been discussed in preceding chapters. In Chapter IV a brief review was had of statement principles and policies. Attention will now be given to over-all considerations of statement form and content.

In recent years financial statements have become fairly well standardized, and for a single organization the same set of statements more often than not serves all purposes. Annual corporate reports to stockholders—where the public accountant's report is chiefly displayed—contain such statements as the following:

1. Balance sheet, usually at the year end but frequently in comparative form (beginning and end of year).

2. Income statement covering the year's operations, also frequently in comparative form (current and preceding years).

3. Statement of Retained Income (Earned Surplus), sometimes incorporated in the balance sheet or appended to the income statement.

4. Statement of Application of Funds, rarely covered by the auditor's report but tying in with comparative balance sheets.

5. Comparative balance sheets and income statements cover-

ing an extended period, not embraced in auditor's report but not inconsistent therewith.

6. Simplified presentations (for example, "highlights") of financial position and operating results: usually a part of management's report.

7. Various analyses, as of property and reserve accounts, summarizing the year's transactions.

It rarely happens that the public accountant is called upon to refer in his report to more than the first three statments, although there is no reason why any or all of the others could not be included if some special circumstance should require. Many public accountants make a practice of reviewing the draft of management's report to stockholders to make sure that the exhibits it contains are in agreement with the statements to which they have certified, and that the facts and figures cited in the narrative harmonize with them.

Special-purpose balance sheets and income statements on which the public accountant may be called upon to report are now generally regarded as the all-purpose variety plus whatever additional features are required. Thus statements filed with the U.S. Securities and Exchange Commission usually comprise more detail than is deemed necessary for the annual statements destined for stockholders; but they should provide no *less* information, the all-purpose models being generally regarded as containing the desirable minimum information for the average reader. Proforma statements may also be looked upon as all-purpose variants—that is, regular statements plus additional, superimposed transactions, the reasons for and the details and effects of which should be made an integral part of the statements. Reconstructed income statements of past years from which "nonrecurring" or "extraordinary" items have been omitted, although frequently prepared and certified to by public accountants, are usually indefensible from attack because while they omit the effect of transactions not likely to be duplicated in kind in future years they provide no substitute: that is, losses arising from new sources will doubtless be incurred for which no provision appears. No management asserts infallibility, and an income statement thus reconstructed may be justly criticized as incomplete because it contains no allowance for the probability of error that accompanies any economic endeavor. It is much safer for both accountant and investor to rely on a historical segregation of income and expense by the years during which they were recognized and reported as such, and to bring to the attention of the reader particular items of an exceptional character.

Occasionally a public accountant is asked to report on a special statement of profit required in rate cases or in various determinations under profit-sharing and pension plans. For the information of those who view the statement, and for his own protection as well, the accountant should supply details that will enable readers to reconcile the statements with published reports. These details may appear in the body of the statement or in an attachment to which the statement is referenced.

Experiments are made from time to time on the structure of financial statements; current liabilities are deducted from current assets, new sideheads are invented, or an objective classification is developed for expenses. The purpose is laudable: to make the statements less "technical" and hence more understandable by the laity. Usually these experiements are concerned more with exposition and less with content; a striking example of this came out some years ago when the "descriptive" balance sheet became popular for a limited period. Attempts to simplify complex concepts may actually give misleading results through omission of essential or customary information. The reader of the balance sheet must have some financial background and he has learned to read it in its customary form. It is doubtful whether any financial statement can be devised for the novice. In the opinion of the author, in lieu of the search for new terminology and new forms a more rewarding effort would be to supply *more* information to the reader, thus widening, rather than curtailing, his horizon.

In the standard short-form audit report (page 582) the public accountant declares that the statements reflect "generally accepted accounting principles" and that these principles have been "applied on a basis consistent with that of the preceding year." Should the statements not conform in either or both these respects the accountant is expected to disclose the character and approximate amount of the divergence or variance; and in the case of a change of principle during the year he is expected to express his agreement or disagreement.

The disclosure of a change in principle or absence of consistency may take any of three forms: inclusion in the body of the financial statement by amplifying a sidehead; a footnote following the financial statement; or mention in the auditor's report. Occasionally a combination of these methods is followed. A material deviation from accounting principles may be footnoted, thus indicating management's awareness of the violation, and it may also appear in the auditor's report, thereby bringing out his approval or disapproval of the practice. A footnote disclosure may be required when the subject matter is too bulky for a sidehead.

Attributes of Financial Statements

General attributes that investors and the public generally expect to find embodied in financial statements are truthfulness, clarity, conciseness, and consistency—truthfulness, so that essential information available to insiders is made more fully available to outsiders; clarity, so that a common, wider understanding may be gained; conciseness, so that points leading to important conclusions may better stand out; and consistency, so that statements of one period may be more aptly compared with those of other periods and organizations. These are more than idealized virtues; they are the commonplace working objectives of which every public accountant is fully conscious when he reviews the financial statements to which he is about to attach his name. Although they demand of him his best skills and an ever-mounting degree of social responsibility, they are like other human virtues in that their pursuit entails the making of value judgments. They are not absolutes subject to rigorous definition and full realization but qualities of whose dimensions even the most able practitioner can never be wholly satisfied; moreover they are likely to vary with time and place. Judgments born of experience are the tools through the application of which these objectives are related to practical situations. What is right in a particular instance may be a matter of opinion over which individuals may differ; whether a proposed disclosure for example should be made may be resolvable in more than one way.

In the Federal Security Act of 1933 and in the regulations of the U.S. Securities and Exchange Commission these objectives are referred to in oblique terms. For example, in statements filed with the Commission there must be "no omission to state a material fact . . . necessary to make the statements . . . not misleading," a material fact being defined as any matter on which "an average prudent investor ought reasonably to be informed." By this language, attention is drawn to the fact that an accountant should not fail to disclose vital information: for if he does fail he may be responsible for a species of untruthfulness that may arise not of necessity from any moral obloquy on his part but rather from an inability to recognize the basis on which an investor's decision to buy or sell may rest. It is thus important for the public acocuntant to realize that the four virtues he is expected rigorously to practice are not only imposed on him from without but may in some instances be subject to interpretation by outside authority. At the same time he bears in mind that what leads an investor—particularly the conjectural "average" investor—to make a "decision" has never been defined. The accountant as best he can must imagine what the investor's needs may be.

Another accounting attribute often associated with financial statements is conservatism. This has been illustrated in the observation that, although accountants follow the practice of anticipating losses (for example, by reducing inventory cost to market when market is lower), they are opposed to anticipating profit (as by advancing inventory cost to market when market is higher). Also as a class accountants have thus far opposed the use of index numbers or replacement prices as a standard for fixed-asset valuation. A third example may be found in the tendency of many accountants to favor immediate recognition as an operating cost of such outlays as extraordinary repairs: costs that may have the effect of extending useful life. Other accountants are at present promoting the idea of "fixed" factory overhead as a period cost rather than something that should be spread over goods and services produced. All of these practices have the effect of reducing both assets and profits; some of them now described as conservative would at one time have been characterized as creating secret reserves. The author sees no objection to this label of conservatism. However, it should be pointed out that accounting—dealing as it does with transaction summaries—has thus far in its history given recognition only to costs growing out of past transactions and excludes from recognition as assets the possible costs that would be involved if the transactions had been consummated at a later date. Services yielded by all economic goods except land are transitory, and the accountant uses a lower market price as well as actual consumption as his measuring stick for estimating the residual service potential.

The Balance Sheet

A balance sheet is a momentary cross section of the complex of forces constantly in play in any organization. It is the function of double-entry bookkeeping to measure for the organization the effects of these forces (transactions) in monetary terms and to maintain a state of equality between their origins and dispositions (debits and credit). The development in modern business of an elaborate system of savings, investment, credits, and organization, made possible by the adaptability and flexibility of double-entry bookkeeping, lies at the root of every corporate-balance-sheet item.

In auditing terms a balance sheet consists on the one hand of cash, investments convertible within a short period into cash, and prepayments of future benefits; on the other, of claims against present and future cash, and residual claims. The measuring stick of investments and prepayments is cash outlay (cost); and as benefits are transferred to others or consumed, or for any reason the likelihood of future benefits decreases, an aliquot portion of such cash outlays is marked down (cost is consumed), and residual claims are correspondingly reduced (expenses are incurred). In a business concern the yield from benefits transferred to outsiders (sales) replenishes cash; and so the cycle of action and reaction goes on and on, year after year.

Balance-sheet elements vary from day to day; some changes, as in cash, are measured and recorded at once. Other changes, involving counts (as in inventories) or estimates (as in the consumption or depreciation of fixed assets), involve judgments as to future usefulness that cannot be arrived at except after careful survey and study; their measure and entry is not therefore accomplished from day to day but only monthly or annually.

In the drafting of a balance sheet the following standards are usually observed:

1. The account or report form may be followed. The traditional balance sheet is in the account form—with assets on the left and liabilities on the right. In recent years a number of American enterprises have adopted the report form. The aims and advantages of the latter, as indicated above, are still a matter of debate among accountants. The same information can be put into either form.

2. In the account form current assets and current liabilities are the first items on their respective sides. In the report form current liabilities are subtracted from the current-asset total, the difference being described as "net current assets" or "working capital." At one time it was common practice to have fixed assets precede current assets because of emphasis on the ownership of property to which the investment of stockholders had been

primarily devoted. With the growing importance of operational problems this practice in America has very nearly disappeared, although it is still followed as a standard in Britain.

3. Five major divisions of current assets are recognized: cash, temporary investments, receivables, inventories, and prepaid expenses. Current assets are often described as including only cash and items that are likely to be converted into cash within the year following the balance-sheet date or within the normal cycle of the business which may exceed one year. The general standard for securities is that they may appear as current assets only if they (a) are not obligations or capital stock of the company or any affiliated organization, (b) have a clearly demonstrable, readily realizable market value, and (c) are held as a temporary investment. The cash-surrender value of life-insurance policies, deposits with mutual-insurance companies, and other items readily convertible into cash, but in the ordinary course of events not expected to be so converted, should be excluded from current assets.

4. Current assets are set forth in the order of their relative liquidity commencing with cash; current liabilities have no strictly logical order but are frequently displayed in the following sequence: bank loans, other loans including matured portions of long-term obligations, accounts payable, deferred income, and accrued expenses.

5. Cash when shown as a current asset may be presumed to be available for general use within the business. Where its withdrawal or application is restricted it is generally excluded from current assets, and the character of the restriction is disclosed in the sidehead or in a footnote.

6. A long-term receivable is given a classification following current assets unless it is of the installment variety that under customary trade practices is included with current assets; the same is true of a claim for a tax refund the ultimate receipt of which seems assured but the time of collection uncertain.

7. Reductions in the form of writedowns or valuation accounts are necessary for current assets whose convertibility is doubtful.

8. Investments in and advances to affiliated companies that appear on unconsolidated balance sheets and on consolidated balance sheets with respect to unconsolidated affiliates are usually accorded a place between current and fixed assets.

9. A frequent breakdown of fixed assets is land, buildings, and machinery and equipment.

10. A separate caption for deferred charges is usually avoided, the portion relating to prepaid expenses now being restored to

their old position under current assets; factory and office supplies are regarded as an item of inventory or as a prepaid expense.

11. The basis of valuation should be indicated in balance-sheet sideheads for all assets except cash, receivables, and deferred charges.

12. Bad-debt, depreciation, and amortization reserves, security and inventory reserves covering the shrinkage of cost to market, and other valuation accounts reflecting expirations of cost or value should appear on the balance sheet as deductions from the assets to which they relate.

The Income Statement

A number of writers on accounting subjects have spoken in recent years about the "growing importance of the income statement." To the author this emphasis is an idle one. The income statement and the balance sheet are interrelated statements; one cannot be produced nor fully understood without the other. They are both necessary to almost any variety of financial analysis and they should both be made as complete and as informative as the auditor's skill permits. What some writers mean by "growing importance" is that they would like to see the income statement develop as fully and as consistently as has the balance sheet on such matters as disclosure and detail; still others would like to see the income statement reflect earning power. But as noted elsewhere in this book the income statement cannot be expected to forecast; it must by its own terms be confined to recognized revenues, expenses, gains, and losses for a period already concluded. Attempts to make of the income statement any more than a historical summary cannot be expected to be successful. But in many instances the income statement can be improved, as by noting trends revealed in comparisons with results of preceding periods.

In Chapter V a number of standards appear that relate primarily to the content of the income statement. Two forms of income statement are in common use: (a) the report form, and (b) the single-step form. The following is typical of the former:

Net Sales	$1,000,000.00
Cost of Sales, including depreciation of $85,000.00	700,000.00
Gross Profit	$ 300,000.00
Other Revenue	50,000.00
Total Gross Profit and Other Revenue	$ 350,000.00

Other Expense

Selling and Advertising	$100,000.00	
Administrative and General	80,000.00	180,000.00

Operating Profit		$ 170,000.00

Income Deductions

Interest Expense		45,000.00

Net Income Before Federal Income Tax		$ 125,000.00
Federal Income Tax		72,000.00

Net Income		$ 53,000.00

In a single-step form the above items would be regrouped thus:

Sales and Other Revenue

Net Sales	$1,000,000.00	
Other Revenue	50,000.00	$1,050,000.00

Operating Costs

Cost of Sales	$ 700,000.00	
Selling and Advertising	100,000.00	
General and Administrative	80,000.00	
Interest Expense	45,000.00	
Federal Income Tax	72,000.00	997,000.00

Net Income		$ 53,000.00

At present many accountants continue to favor the report form for the reason that the intermediate figures, omitted in the single-step statement, have been found to be of considerable interest to various types of readers including investors and credit analysts.

Sideheads in Financial Statements

Sideheads play an important part in giving intelligibility to financial statements. In reviewing the samples of balance-sheet sideheads that follow, the reader should distinguish between those (or portions of them) that convey information indicating that a standard of practice has been followed, and those that indicate exceptions to more common practices. These illustrations have been excerpted from recent reports of industrial corporations to their stockholders.

Cash. Although on the majority of published statements "cash" is probably designated without elaboration, many accountants follow the practice of indicating that the balance-sheet amount is a combination of balances in banks and on hand. No useful information is conveyed, however, by the additional words since in every enterprise small or large such a combination is almost certain to be present, cash on hand including petty cash and change funds as well as amounts awaiting deposit. An overly meticulous critic might even assert that such a title as that indicated in the sixth example below is misleading in two respects: "on hand," appearing before "on deposit," may infer that the amount of cash in the company's offices is the principal constituent, whereas "on deposit" or "at banks" is not actually the amount shown by the bank's records but because of outstanding checks the balance-sheet amount is very probably substantially less. Here as elsewhere in financial-statement terminology the reader is cautioned against a too literal reading. He must bear in mind, as do many professional accountants, that where seemingly no misinterpretation has arisen in the past from the use of an older term there is a natural tendency on the part of both the accountant and the business executive to fear that a misunderstanding might occur from the employment of another term, especially a simpler one. Terminology changes proceed slowly, as perhaps they should.

1	Cash	*United States Steel*
2	Cash on Hand and at Banks	*Continental Can*
3	Cash in bank and on hand	*American Safety Razor*
4	Bank balances and cash funds	*Anchor Hocking Glass*
5	Cash on hand and demand deposits	*Revere Copper and Bross*
6	Cash on hand and on deposit	*Studebaker*

Special-purpose cash, unless relating to working capital, appears below current assets as in the following example:

7	Cash earmarked to acquire capital stock of the Company
	Less—Liability for shares purchased, not paid for *Paramount Pictures*

Marketable securities. A showing of securities as current assets usually includes the basis of valuation. In times of rising prices, this valuation is indicated as cost. If the investment represents bonds purchased at a discount, cost may include that portion of the discount that is sometimes amortized over the period from acquisition to resale or redemption. Where market values are less than cost the valuation of securities, like inventories, may be reduced to the lesser amount; but if the market price is only slightly less and reflects what the accountant has reason to believe is a temporary recession, the lower market price may be inserted parenthetically without adjustment or comment. The title may be "securities," "marketable securities," or in the event that the one class of securities is owned, as illustrated in the examples below, the general class of the investment commonly appears.

1 U. S. Government Securities, at Cost   *Continental Can*
2 Marketable securities, at cost (approximate market)   *Diamond Match*
3 United States and Canadian Government securities—at
   approximate cost and quoted market value, plus ac-
   crued interest   *Elgin National Watch*
4 U. S. Government and other marketable securities (at
   lower of cost, less amortization of premium, or market)   *Westinghouse*

Receivables. Although the single word "receivables" is in common use among accountants as a balance-sheet caption, it is often expanded into "accounts and notes receivable" or "accounts receivable, customers." The fact that some of the items making up the total are in the form of notes is of no interest to the average reader of the balance sheet, however. Use of "customers" is unnecessary since it is a reasonable presumption that readers will assume the receivables to be from customers unless they are otherwise described. Installment accounts if material in amount are displayed separately although they are regarded as a current asset if they are to be paid within the natural operating cycle of the business. Consequently a casual sale of property amounting to a material sum would be classified by accountants as a non-current asset. But the sale of furniture by a dealer who regularly sells on the installment plan would be classified as a current asset. It is always a good plan to describe the character of any such receivables and to indicate the average period over which they are to be collected. Advances to employees, notes receivable from officers, and similar items are shown separately from regular receivables unless they represent minor transactions that are in the regular process of collection, or are amounts that are to be deducted from the next payroll. Accountants are not agreed on the necessity of showing the amount of a reserve for bad debts, although in most instances where a reserve has been provided the title "receivables, less reserves"—or its equivalent—is in common use. Usually the reader has no way of judging the adequacy of a reserve and gains little by its disclosure.

1 Accounts and notes receivable, trade, less estimated
   doubtful balances of $........   *Youngstown Sheet & Tube*
2 Notes and accounts receivable—less allowance for
   doubtful accounts of $........   *Gillette*
3 Receivables, less estimated bad debts   *United States Steel*

4 Accounts receivable—Net of reserves   *Macfadden Publications*

5 Accounts receivable (including $........ current accounts
   of affiliated companies), less reserve   *Florsheim Shoe*

6 Receivables—after reserves:
   Customers
   Nonconsolidated affiliates
   Others   *General Electric*

7 Notes and accounts receivable—
   Customers, less allowance of $........ for doubtful
      accounts
   Foreign subsidiary companies
   Others   *Bausch & Lomb*

8 Accounts receivable, customers—
   Regular accounts
   Instalment accounts, a portion of which is due after
      one year—
         Equity in $........ of accounts sold
         Accounts not sold
            Total
   Less—Estimated doubtful amounts
         Net receivables from customers   *R. H. Macy*

9 Accounts and notes receivable—
   Trade
   U. S. Government
   Employees and miscellaneous
   Less—Reserve for doubtful accounts and discounts *Elgin National Watch*

10 Receivables (including unbilled charges):
    United States Government departments or agencies
    Other   *Bendix Aviation*

Inventories. The section of the balance sheet containing merchandise, finished stock, work in process, and raw materials is nearly always headed "inventories." Whatever is added to the title is intended to furnish some idea of the nature of the component elements and a statement of the valuation basis. For a manufacturing enterprise, a breakdown of the total by principal components is generally preferred. The value of the breakdown comes not from a consideration of a single balance sheet, but from a comparison of successive balance sheets. As a rule, in-transit items are not shown separately as in the third example below but are merged with raw materials. The basis of valuation is of importance and should always appear. Where lifo has been employed in valuing cost of sales, the residual cost remaining in inventory is often compared with replacement cost (eleventh illustration below) or with the valuation that would have resulted had the fifo basis been followed (see under footnotes below).

1   Inventories—paper, cable and work in process on the
basis of cost (first-in, first-out method) or market,
whichever lower   *TelAutograph*

2   Crude and refined oil products and merchandise, at cost
determined on the first-in, first-out method, which in
the aggregate was lower than market   *Texas Company*

3   Inventories—at standard costs which are generally the
lower of cost or market:
   Finished products
   Work in process
   Raw materials
   In transit   *Black & Decker*

4   Inventories—
   Finished cement and process stocks, at average
      cost which is lower than market
   Packages (including those estimated to be in hands
      of customers), fuel, spare machinery parts and
      general supplies, at or below average cost   *Lone Star Cement*

5   Inventories, at the lower of cost (first-in first-out basis)
or replacement market   *Colorado Fuel and Iron*

6   Inventories at cost—
   Paper
   Manuscripts, art, and photos
   Books and supplies
   Production and shipping costs of future issues
      (Less amounts applicable to issues billed in
      advance—see contra)   *Macfadden Publications*

7   Inventories: Materials, work in progress, and finished
goods (at cost on LIFO basis) and reimbursable costs
on U. S. Government subcontract, less progress pay-
ments   *Brown & Sharpe*

8   Inventories—certain products valued at cost on basis of
"last-in, first-out," balance of products and supplies
at the lower of cost or market except as to products
where cost was not ascertainable, which products
were valued at market less allowance for selling
expense.
   Products
   Supplies   *Armour*

9   Merchandise inventories, at the lower of LIFO (last-
in, first-out) cost or market   *Butler Brothers*

10 Inventories, stated on the following bases:
   Pork products and live hogs, at cost on basis of
      "last-in, first-out", principally at prices prevail-
      ing November 2, 1940
   Other products on basis of market less allowance
      for distributing and selling expenses
   Raw materials, certain livestock and supplies, at
      cost or market, whichever lower   *John Morrell*

11 Inventories—substantially all stated at cost on "last-in,
    first-out" basis with current replacement cost ap-
    proximately $........ in excess of stated value:
        Raw materials and supplies
        Work in process
        Resale merchandise and finished products   *National Supply*

Deferred charges. As explained in Chapter IX there has been
a growing recognition of the need for distinguishing on the balance
sheet between prepaid expenses and other types of deferred
charges, the former being classified as a current asset, the latter
as a noncurrent asset immediately following or at the bottom
of the asset side of the balance sheet. Because the amounts involved are characteristically small in relation to other balance-
sheet items breakdowns are uncommon. Frequently mentioned
in descriptive sideheads are unexpired insurance and inventories
of supplies. The first two classes of items in the third illustration
below and the items of the first group in the ninth illustration
are usually classified elsewhere.

As a current asset—

1 Prepaid insurance, supply inventories, etc.   *Marshall Field*
2 Prepaid advertising and other charges   *Sears, Roebuck*
3 Deposits, working funds, prepaid expenses, etc. *Macfadden Publications*

As a noncurrent asset—

4 Prepaid Expenses and Deferred Asset   *Continental Can*
5 Deferred Charges
        Repair and maintenance supplies
        Prepaid insurance, interest, and other expenses
        Unamortized debenture discount and expense   *A. E. Staley*
6 Prepaid Rent, Insurance, Taxes, Etc.   *Walgreen*
7 Insurance premiums and other expenses paid but appli-
        cable to future years   *Baldwin-Lima-Hamilton*
8 Deferred Charges Applicable to Future Periods   *Bethlehem Steel*
9 Deferred Charges:
        Special tools, dies, jigs, and patterns—unamortized
            balance
        Prepaid expenses   *Bendix Aviation*

Fixed assets. A general balance-sheet caption for fixed assets
often observed is "Property, Plant and Equipment"; it is typically followed by the basis of valuation ("—at cost,") and by
mention of depreciation offsetting the basic value ("less accumulated depreciation"). "Amortization" generally relates to defense

plant the cost of which is being spread over a five-year period in accordance with the provisions of the Federal Internal-Revenue Code; occasionally, however, the word may also cover writedowns of leaseholds and certain other items. Occasionally noted is a reference to an adjustment in the asset or depreciation accounts that has had the effect of bringing the books into agreement with the reports of an internal-revenue agent; or there may be a reference to an earlier substitution of an appraisal valuation for cost as in the ninth illustration below. As a rule, several classes of fixed assets appear; these are added together and from the total the accumulated depreciation (and amortization) is subtracted. There is a growing tendency to provide in annual reports a schedule of changes in fixed-asset accounts and accumulated depreciation, following some such form as that appearing on page 404.

1   Plant and Equipment—At Cost Less Depreciation:
    Land
    Buildings
    Machinery and equipment
    Machinery and equipment in process of construction
    Less allowance for depreciation and amortization
                                                American Safety Razor

2   Property, at cost:
    Buildings, machinery, tools, and equipment
    Less portion allocated to operations to date
    Land
         Net Property   *American Steel Foundries*

3   Property, plant and equipment (less reduction for wear
    of facilities—depreciation and amortization, $........)
                                Baldwin-Lima-Hamilton

4   Property, Plant and Equipment—
    Mineral properties, land and water rights, less
      depletion of $........
    Buildings, machinery and equipment, less depreciation and amortization $........
         Property, Plant and Equipment—Net
                              Colorado Fuel and Iron

5   Plant and Equipment—stated at amounts (based in part
    on appraisals) recorded at dates of acquisition of
    properties (including properties acquired for capital
    stock), plus subsequent additions at cost:
    Land
    Buildings
    Machinery, equipment, etc.
    Leasehold and leasehold improvements   *Container Corporation*

6 Fixed Assets:
      Land and land improvements
      Buildings
          Less: Reserve for depreciation
      Machinery and equipment
          Less: Reserve for depreciation
      Unfinished construction   *Crane*

7 Properties:
      Buildings, machinery and equipment
      Less allowances for depreciation
      Construction in progress
      Timberlands and pulp leases, land and logging facil-
          ities, net of depletion and amortization
      Intangibles, principally water power leases and
          licenses, net of amortization   *Crown Zellerbach*

8 Capital Assets—at cost:
      Factory buildings, machinery and equipment
          Accumulated depreciation and amortization
      Emergency facilities
          Accumulated depreciation and amortization
      Land   *Elgin National Watch*

9 Fixed Assets as stated on the books Dec. 31, 1931 after
      applying Special Reserves of $........ created out of
      capital surplus at that date, with subsequent additions
      at cost, less retirements, sales and accumulated depre-
      ciation and obsolescence:
      Land and buildings
      Machinery and equipment
      Less accumulated depreciation and obsolescence   *Gillette*

10 Fixed Assets:
      Land, mineral properties, dwellings, plants, build-
          ings, machinery and equipment
      Less—Depletion, depreciation and amortization
                                              Youngstown Sheet & Tube

11 Property, Plant, and Equipment, at cost:
      Producing and undeveloped oil and gas properties
      Crude oil pipe line systems
      Refineries and natural gasoline plants
      Marketing facilities
      Other fixed assets
      Less—Reserves for depletion and depreciation   *Skelly Oil*

Intangibles. The presence of intangibles on balance sheets is becoming increasingly infrequent. Its appearance generally means that it was acquired with other assets in the purchase of a business; in such cases it has in most instances been written off (or written down to $1) or is in the process of being amortized by charges to earnings or surplus. Showing goodwill and other intangibles at $1 or other nominal amount—a survival from an earlier practice of displaying conservatism—appears to have little meaning in the modern balance sheet.

1 Patents, Patterns, Drawings, and Goodwill (nominal
amount) [$1]   *Allis-Chalmers*

2 Goodwill, Patents and Trade-Marks—
At Cost Less Amount Written Off [$5,000,000]
                                                American Safety Razor

3 Patents and Patent Rights:
At cost, less amortization [$229,632]
At nominal amount [$1]   *Anchor Hocking Glass*

4 Patents and Processes [$1,229,103]   *Armour*

5 Patents and patent applications at $1.00 for items
acquired prior to January 1, 1937, at cost for items
acquired since, less allowance for amortization; 1952,
$........; 1951, $........ [$381,474]   *Crown Cork & Seal*

6 Goodwill, Trademarks and Patents [$3]   *Gillette*

7 Leases, Copyrights, Trade Marks, Goodwill, Etc.—at
cost, less accumulated amortization of $........ and
$........ [$1,964,830 and $2,046,266]   *R. H. Macy*

Current liabilities. The conventional sequence, already commented on, of the items of which current liabilities are usually composed are illustrated in the examples that follow. No due dates appear except occasionally for dividends payable, the presumption intended being that the whole group will be paid within the year following or within the natural cycle of the business if longer. Because of its size a Federal income-tax accrual is separated from other accruals; it may be more or less than the amount shown in the income statement because of prior-year adjustments in process or because of an adjustment during the year to bring the preceding year's accrual into agreement with the amount appearing on that year's tax return. This last adjustment is explained by the fact that corporate reports are often published before March 15—at a time when taxable income has not yet been fully determined. Treasury securities to be used in payment of Federal taxes may be deducted from the liability (preferably on the face of the balance sheet) if by corporate action they may be used only for that purpose.

1 Notes payable
Accounts payable
Wages, commissions and other expenses
United States and Canadian income and excess profits
taxes
Estimated furnace repairs   *Anchor Hocking Glass*

2 Notes payable
   Accounts payable, including payrolls interest, etc.
   Reserve for Federal income taxes:
        For current year
        For possible additional taxes of prior years
   Reserves for general and social security taxes
   Long term debt and subordinated long term debt pay-
        able within one year (less $........ deposited with
        Trustee thereagainst)   *Armour*

3 Notes payable—banks
   Accounts payable and accruals
   Dividend payable on 7% preferred stock
   Reserve for Federal income taxes
   Sundry current liabilities   *American Woolen*

4 Long-term debt maturities due within one year
   Accounts payable
   Accrued interest, taxes and other charges
   Provision for Federal taxes on income, less United States
        Treasury securities and accrued interest $........ in 1952
        and $........ in 1951   *Cities Service*

5 Notes payable to bank
   Accounts payable and accrued liabilities
   Due to unconsolidated subsidiary companies
   Sinking fund installments due within one year
   Provision for federal taxes on income and, at [sic]
        1952, possible refunds under government contracts
   Deposits by customers on uncompleted contracts for
        machinery   *Crown Cork & Seal*

6 Accounts payable
   Dividends payable
   Accrued expenses and taxes—
        Salaries, wages and other expenses
        Personal property, real estate and other taxes
        Federal income taxes
            Less—United States Treasury tax notes   *Butler Brothers*

7 Bank loans of subsidiaries
   Serial notes due within one year
   Accounts payable, etc.
   Dividend payable January 1, 1953
   Accrued liabilities
   Provision for Federal income taxes
        Less—U. S. Treasury tax notes   *Pure Oil*

Long-term obligations. In recent years term loans from banks
and insurance companies have made frequent appearances on
the balance sheets of industrial companies. They are mostly
serial obligations maturing within five or ten years if payable
to banks and up to thirty years if payable to insurance companies. Current maturities are subtracted and included among
current liabilities. The interest rate and some indication of

maturity are the most frequent disclosures; other details may apppear in a footnote giving conditions of redemption and refunding, application of proceeds, nature of lien or other direct security and of working-capital maintenance, restriction on further borrowings, limitations on dividends or use of retained earnings, and other matters affecting financial condition or operations.

1   Bank loans payable not due within one year ....   *Baldwin-Lima-Hamilton*

2   Unsecured $3\frac{1}{2}\%$ notes payable, maturing August 15, 1977 with required prepayments of $........ annually beginning August 15, 1958   *Bucyrus-Erie*

3   Long-Term Debt, $4\frac{1}{4}\%$ notes due $........ annually 1953-1967, less current maturity included above   *Booth Fisheries*

4   Note payable, $3\frac{7}{8}$ per cent, payable $........ semi-annually beginning February 1, 1954, balance due February 1, 1972
    Sinking fund debentures, $3\frac{1}{8}$ per cent, due June 1, 1960, less $........ due within one year included in current liabilities (redeemed in 1952)   *Crown Cork & Seal*

5   3% Notes, instalments due 1953-1968   *Diamond Match*

6   Note payable, $3\frac{1}{4}\%$ due September 1, 1965—
        (Annual prepayments of $........ in 1953 to 1955, $........ in 1956 to 1959, and $........ in 1960 to 1965)
    Notes payable to banks by subsidiary company—
        (Annual payments of $........ in 1953 to 1955)
    Less—Amounts payable within one year included in current liabilities   *Elgin National Watch*

7   Notes payable, bank, due in semi-annual installments of $........ from January 15, 1953 to January 15, 1961
    Less—Current installments, shown above   *Florsheim Shoe*

8   Notes payable to insurance companies
    Notes payable to banks less $........ in current liabilities
    2% Debentures due September 1, 1956   *Allis-Chalmers*

9   Note Payable—$3\frac{1}{2}\%$—payable $........ on September 1, 1957; $........ quarterly from December 1, 1963; and balance, $........, on June 1, 1964   *American Locomotive*

10 Notes Payable to Banks—due November 15, 1956   *Sears, Roebuck*

11 First Mortgage Sinking Fund Bonds:
        Series E—$2\frac{3}{4}\%$ due July 1, 1970; redeemed and retired in August 1952
        Series F—$3\frac{1}{4}\%$ due June 1, 1976; payable $........ annually from June 1, 1957
        Series G—$3\frac{3}{8}\%$ due August 1, 1982; payable $........ annually from August 1, 1958
    Notes payable to banks $2\frac{3}{4}\%$; due December 23, 1957
        Youngstown Sheet & Tube

Minority interests. In a consolidated balance sheet the equity of minority stockholders generally occupies a position preceding net worth. From the point of view of the consolidated position, it is more in the nature of a liability than an equity since the assets to which the controlling company's stockholders lay claim are not those of the minority group. In no published statement that has come to the attention of the author have details of the interest appeared nor has the method of determining the amount of the interest been disclosed. It may be equal to the book value of the interest with or without adjustment for intercompany profit and the portion of the current year's profit pertaining to the minority interest may appear in the income statement among "other [or income] deductions."

As a liability—

1   Minority Interest in subsidiary company   *Anchor Hocking Glass*
2   Minority Interests in Capital Stock and Surplus of
    Subsidiaries   *Pure Oil*

As a part of net worth—

3   Minority stockholders of subsidiaries   *Standard Oil (Ind.)*

Paid-in capital. Sideheads for capital stock as a rule contain more detail than any other balance-sheet item. The minimum for any class is the number of shares authorized, in treasury, and outstanding; the par or stated value; if preferred stock, the annual dividend rate, whether or not cumulative, convertible features, price if called or redeemed, share in voluntary liquidation. In the third example below a summary of the company's stock-option plan appears; usually the details of such a plan are given in a balance-sheet footnote.

1   Preferred stock—7% cumulative, $100 par; callable at
    $115; authorized and issued 200,000 shares less 400
    shares in Treasury—outstanding 199,600 shares
    Common stock—$1 par; authorized and issued 1,783,832
    shares less 4,756 shares in Treasury—outstanding
    1,779,076 shares
    Amount paid the company for capital stock in excess of
    par value (capital surplus)   *American Locomotive*
2   $4 Cumulative Convertible Prior Preference, (conver-
    tible into two common shares; callable at $105; vol-
    untary liquidation value $105) :
       At December 31, 1952, shares authorized 105,812;
       held for retirement 4,761; outstanding 101,051
    7% Cumulative Preferred, par value $100:
       Shares authorized and outstanding 89,852

Common, without par value
   At December 31, 1952, shares authorized 1,180,444;
   reserved for conversion 202,102; outstanding
   978,342
                  Total outstanding stock   *American Woolen*

3 Common Stock—par value $25.00 per share:
   Authorized 20,000,000 shares (400,000 shares reserved for the Stock Option Plan for Salaried
   Officers and Key Employees, of which options for
   209,750 shares are outstanding in two lots at
   prices of $69.35 and $73.51 per share, the average
   being $71.23; these prices representing 95% of
   fair market values on the dates the options were
   granted)
   Issued 8,968,750 shares, of which 266,486 shares are
   in treasury and 8,702,264 shares are outstanding   *Chrysler*

4 Capital stock:
   Preferred and preference stocks—authorized and
   unissued 6,100,000 shares
   Common stock—$10 par value:
      Authorized 5,000,000 shares; issued 3,889,077
      shares, less in treasury 1,977 shares
   Capital surplus   *Cities Service*

5 $2.00 cumulative preferred, without par value, redeem-
   able at $50 per share plus accrued dividends:
      Authorized and outstanding 275,000 shares at
      stated value of $45.00 per share
   Common, $2.50 par value:
      Authorized, 2,000,000 shares at 1952 and 1,300,000
      shares at 1951, outstanding 1,207,790 shares
   Capital surplus   *Crown Cork & Seal*

6 Capital Stock:
   4½% Cumulative Preferred Stock—par value $100
   per share—authorized and issued, 149,600 shares
   —less 1,560 shares in 1952 held for sinking fund
   and not reissuable, which are applicable to sinking fund requirements subsequent to 1957
   Common Stock—par value $10 per share—author-
   ized 2,500,000 shares—issued 1,437,870 shares—
   less 3,409 shares held in treasury
   Capital surplus (increase of $........ since December 31,
   1951, resulted from acquisition, at a discount, of 460
   preferred shares for the sinking fund)   *National Supply*

Retained income (earned surplus). Earned surplus is generally
supported by a supplementary schedule although in a number of
instances changes during the year are given on the face of the
balance sheet. Usually the surplus account is "clean," the

changes being limited to dividends and net income for the year. Other changes noted on recently published corporate reports have included (as credits): refund under section 722 of wartime excess-profits taxes, restorations of inventory, contingency and other earned-surplus reserves no longer needed, profit from sale of real estate during current year, undistributed earnings of nonconsolidated affiliates—a procedure followed by General Electric, excess bad-debt reserve; (as debits): appropriations for earned-surplus reserves, writeoff of goodwill, premium paid on retirement of capital stock.

1 Reinvested earnings *General Electric*

2 Income Retained for Use in the Business *B. F. Goodrich*

3 Earned surplus *Pure Oil*

4 Income Invested in the Business *Firestone*

5 Income reinvested in business *United States Steel*

6 Earnings since April 3, 1934 retained and employed in
   the business *Revere Copper and Brass*

7 Earnings reinvested in the business, per accompanying
   statement—excluding $........ stock dividends trans-
   ferred to capital stock accounts in prior years. Of
   the $........ at August 2, 1952, $........ is not distributable
   to stockholders so long as the Twenty-Five Year
   2⅞% Sinking Fund Debentures are outstanding *R. H. Macy*

8 Earnings retained for requirements of the business
   (earned surplus) ($........ is restricted as to cash divi-
   dend payments on common stock) *Container Corporation*

9 Net Income Retained for Use in the Business ($........
   not available for dividends on Common Shares as long
   as 3¾% Notes are outstanding) *Marshall Field*

10 Earnings Retained in the Business (includes $........
   segregated as reserve for contingencies at December
   31, 1951) *Diamond Match*

Revenues. Income statements in published corporate reports reveal limited information and they are invariably brief, containing on the average no more than a half-dozen items. Revenues consist of net sales, with no breakdowns by products or other details and including undisclosed government sales; dividends from unconsolidated subsidiaries, interest, profits from sales of noninventory assets, gains from foreign exchange, refunds of taxes, royalties, and occasionally cash discounts.

1   Sales and other income:
    Net sales billed
    Discounts, interest, and miscellaneous   *Allis-Chalmers*

2   Gross Sales and Car Rentals, less discounts and allowances
    Other Income:
        Dividends
        Interest
        Royalties
        Cash Discounts
        Miscellaneous   *American Car and Foundry*

3   Net sales
    Income from investments, royalties and sundry non-
        operating income   *American Safety Razor*

4   Sales, including service revenues
    Dividends received from:
        Foreign subsidiaries
        Other investments
    Interest on securities and receivables
    Miscellaneous income   *Armour*

5   Sales
    Operating profit
    Dividends received
    Royalties received
    Interest and discount income
    Non-recurring profit on sale of securities
    Miscellaneous income   *Baldwin-Lima-Hamilton*

6   Income:
    Sales, less returns, allowances and discounts
    Other income, net   *Bausch & Lomb*

7   Net Sales, Royalties, and Other Operating Income (less
    estimated refunds of excess profits on Government
    contracts and subcontracts)
    Other Income:
        Dividends received from non-consolidated sub-
            sidiaries and associated companies
        Interest earned
        Profit on disposal of land, buildings, and equip-
            ment
        Miscellaneous   *Bendix Aviation*

8   Net Sales
    Equity in earnings of subsidiary companies not con-
        solidated (dividends and interest received amounted
        to $........)
    Canadian profits applicable to the years 1940-1950 and
        previously deferred because of exchange restrictions
        (representing amounts retained in Canada for rein-
        vestment)
    Other income less sundry income deductions   *General Motors*

9 Net sales:
      To dealers and users in the United States
      Defense products
      To subsidiary companies
   Dividends received from subsidiary companies (less
      taxes withheld at source)
   Interest earned
   Miscellaneous (net)   *International Harvester*

Deductions from revenue. Operating costs are displayed in a great variety of ways. The present tendency is to condense rather than to amplify, and because of the desired to display depreciation and other costs separately, there has been some decline in the practice of revealing cost of sales and hence gross profit. Items most often shown separately are depreciation, depletion, payments to employees, retirement contributions, interest, and provision for Federal income tax.

1 Cost and expenses:
      Cost of goods sold
      Selling, general, and administrative
      Interest
   Provision for federal income and excess profits taxes   *Allis-Chalmers*
2 Cost of Operations, including Administrative, Selling
      and General Expense, but before Depreciation
   . . .
   Depreciation—Operating Properties
   . . .
   Other Charges:
      Interest and Discount
      Royalties
      Loss on Property Retirements
      Non-Operating Property Expense—Net (Including
         Depreciation of $........)
      Miscellaneous
   Deduct—Provision for Federal Income Taxes—Includ-
      ing $........ Excess Profits Taxes   *American Car & Foundry*
3 Cost of sales, selling, general and administrative ex-
      penses (exclusive of depreciation and amortization)
   Provision for depreciation and amortization
   Provision for United States and foreign taxes on income
      and for renegotiation in 1951:
      Current year
      Less reversal of excess provision of prior year and
         recoverable taxes due to carryback   *American Safety Razor*
4 Cost of products sold and operating expenses:
      Materials and services from others
      Wages, salaries, life, health and unemployment in-
         surance, pension and old age benefits, etc.
      Wear and obsolescence of facilities (depreciation)

Interest and other expense
Provision for federal income and excess profits taxes:
    Income tax
    Excess profits tax   *American Locomotive*

5   Costs:
    Inventories at beginning of year
    Add—Costs incurred during year:
        Materials, supplies, services purchased, etc.
        Wages, salaries, and company contributions for
            group insurance, retirement plans, unem-
            ployment insurance, old age benefits, etc.
        Portion of cost of buildings, machinery, and
            equipment allocated to current operation
        Purchase and sales discount, interest, etc. (net)
        Provision for Federal taxes on income
    Deduct—Inventories at end of year   *American Steel Foundries*

6   Deductions:
    Materials, supplies, labor and sundry costs
    Selling, general, and administrative expenses
    State franchise taxes
    Depreciation

   .   .   .

    Inventory adjustment to lower of cost or market
    Interest and other charges

   .   .   .

    Provision for Federal taxes on income   *American Woolen*

7   *Costs:*
    Cost of products, supplies and service (exclusive
        of items below)
    Selling, advertising, general and administrative
        expenses
    Provision for depreciation
    Taxes (other than income taxes)
    Contributions to employes' pension funds
    Interest expense:
        Current debt
        Long term debt
        Net amortization of debt (premium) discount
            and expense
    Miscellaneous deductions
    Provision for Federal income taxes
    Provision for other income taxes   *Armour*

8   Cost Applied to Billings and Other Services Shown
    Above:
    Employment costs:
        Wages and salaries
        Pensions
        Social security and other employee benefits
    Materials, supplies, freight and other services
    Interest and other charges

Provisions for:
> Depreciation and depletion
> Amortization of emergency facilities
> State, local and miscellaneous taxes
> Federal taxes based on income   *Bethlehem Steel*

9 Cost of goods sold, expenses and other deductions in-
   including depreciation of $........:
> Cost of goods sold
> Advertising, selling, general and administrative
>   expenses
> Pension fund contributions
> Interest expense and miscellaneous charges
> Provision for federal taxes on income   *Elgin National Watch*

10 Deduct:
> Materials and services purchased from others
> Wages, salaries and employee benefit costs
> Provision for depreciation and amortization
> Taxes, other than social security and Federal in-
>   come taxes
> Interest
> Federal income taxes
> Increase or (decrease) in reserve for possible future
>   decline in market value of inventories [decrease]   *Marshall Field*

Footnotes Accompanying Financial Statements

Wherever an item in a financial statement requires for its comprehension more than the few words allotted to the sidehead, a footnote will probably be employed. A footnote may also serve as a vehicle for information that has no accepted place within a statement. Footnotes at the bottom of a financial statement are regarded as a part of the statement. If they appear on a following page they are referred to in the body of the statement.

Among the more important items repeatedly found in published financial-statement footnotes at the time this is written are the following:

Methods of consolidation
Basis of inventory valuation
Earned-surplus limitations
Status of Federal income taxes
Effects of pension plans
Stock-purchase options
Nature of contingent liabilities
Renegotiation status
Fixed-asset valuation
Methods of depreciation and amortization accrual
Financial events following balance-sheet date
Fixed-asset commitments
Meaning of goodwill

The following excerpts, from 1952 annual reports to stockholders, should be regarded as typical of what may be found in current practice; but they do not always illustrate the best practice:

Consolidation policy. During the war period American controlling companies generally omitted from their consolidated financial statements all foreign subsidiaries regardless of location. Since then more stable financial currencies have encouraged the re-entry of many foreign subsidiaries into the consolidated picture. Where the practice is still to omit some or all of such subsidiaries the character of the investment, appearing as an asset, is often told in some detail, and the current year's earnings and dividends remitted are disclosed. In the following example, which reflects an exceptional practice that many accountants would not approve, the accounts of the "consolidated group" have been combined by what appears to be orthodox methods; in addition, the parent company's equity in "nonconsolidated affiliates" has been expressed as an asset following the same basis of inclusions and exclusions as for the "consolidated group," but an increment resulting from the "affiliates" excess of earnings over dividends paid has been included in earned surplus as an extraordinary item.

Basis of Consolidation. These financial statements at December 31, 1952 represent a consolidation of the accounts of the Parent Company—General Electric—and those of the followinng affiliated companies 100% of whose voting stock was owned by the Parent Company: General Electric Realty Corporation; The Mahoning Valley Steel Company; and The Maqua Company. (Hereafter referred to as the Consolidated Group.) . . . Two wholly-owned affiliates included in the consolidation at December 31, 1951 were merged with the Parent Company during 1952. . . . The accounts of other affiliated companies, a majority of whose voting stock was owned, directly or indirectly, by the Parent Company, were not consolidated because their businesses either did not involve manufacturing or were conducted outside the continental United States. (Hereafter referred to as Nonconsolidated Affiliates.) . . . The net earnings of the Consolidated Group reflected (a) the inclusion of amounts received as dividends from, rather than the equity in the net earnings of, the Nonconsolidated Affiliates; (b) the elimination of unrealized intercompany inventory profits; and (c) the application of safety factor discounts to foreign currency asset values. . . . Investments in Nonconsolidated Affiliates consisted of: . . . [here follows an investment-account summary] . . . These carrying values represented the sum of the Consolidated Group's outstanding advances to, and equity in the net worth of, each Nonconsolidated Affiliate as of the close of the year. The net worth of each Nonconsolidated Affiliate was determined on the same accounting basis as was employed by the Consolidated Group, and thus it reflected (a) the elimination of unrealized intercompany profits and (b) the application of safety factor discounts to foreign currency asset values.   *General Electric*

Inventory valuation. Lifo methods more than any other cause lead to balance-sheet footnotes concerning inventories. As noted on page 286, a desirable standard of disclosure has not yet been generally agreed to. Lifo valuations of materials and merchandise entering into cost of sales in many instances have had an extra-ordinary effect in reducing both profits and assets, and the quantitative effect for the year on the income statement as well as the accumulative effect on the balance sheet might well be of interest to investors and analysts. In the illustration that follows the quantitative effect as compared with fifo or average-cost methods is omitted.

Basis of stating inventories. Inventories are stated, with minor exceptions, on the basis of the "last-in, first-out" method of inventory accounting adopted for federal income tax purposes January 1, 1950. This is a generally accepted accounting method designed to allocate incurred costs in such a manner as to relate them to revenues more nearly on the same cost-price level basis than would the "first-in, first-out" method used prior to 1950. The general effect is to exclude from reported profits a major portion of the increases in inventory costs which result from rising cost levels. . . . Accordingly, the quantities of inventories at December 31, 1952, equivalent to the quantities at January 1, 1950, are stated at cost levels prevailing at that earlier date. Quantities at December 31, 1952, in excess of those at January 1, 1950, are stated on the basis of the earliest costs incurred in the year in which the quantities increased.   *Caterpillar Tractor*

Earned-surplus restrictions. Limitations on the distribution of dividends and on other uses of surplus is often required in agreements with preferred stockholders and with bondholders and other creditors, the purpose being to provide a protective cushion in the event of operating losses. The protection is, of course, imperfect where the need for working capital has exceeded the sums made available through profits or other sources, but in most cases it has worked well.

Dividends: Regular dividends were paid on preferred stock during the year. An extra dividend of 75¢ a share on the common stock, amounting to $—, was paid December 8, 1952 to stockholders of record November 12, 1952. This was in addition to the usual annual dividend of $1.00 paid in March. On December 30, 1952, a cash dividend of $1.00 a share on the common stock, amounting to $—, was declared, payable March 2, 1953, to stockholders of record February 2, 1953.   *Pan American Petroleum*

Status of Federal income tax. Because of its substantial effect on retained earnings, unsettled income taxes are of considerable interest to readers of financial statements. Often, however, there is no way of knowing the possible effect, and notes such as the following are quite common:

Federal taxes on income: The Internal Revenue Department has not completed its examination of the tax returns of the Corporation and certain of its subsidiaries for years subsequent to June 30, 1944 nor as to other subsidiaries from various later dates. It is believed that reasonable provision has been made for any additional taxes which may be levied.   *Colorado Fuel and Iron*

Liability under pension or retirement plan. Pension and retirement plans, contributory and noncontributory, involve various obligations on the part of business corporations that have not been funded, annual payments being expensed. Disclosure of a substantial unfunded amount is held by most accountants to be required.

Effective December 1, 1952, pursuant to authorization by the stockholders, the Company established an amended Retirement Plan. The Plan, which is noncontributory, is to be funded by periodic contributions to a Retirement Plan Trust. The Company reserves the right to reduce, suspend, or discontinue its contributions and to amend or terminate the Plan at any time. Funds held by the Retirement Plan Trust must be used for the exclusive benefit of the employees. . . . According to actuarial calculations, the presently estimated cost of providing for current service benefits amounts to about $— a year, and the aggregate unfunded cost for services rendered prior to the effective date of the Plan amounts to approximately $— at December 31, 1952. Payments made to the Retirement Plan Trust for December, 1952, and charged against income were $—, representing $— for current service costs and $— for interest at 3% on the unfunded prior service cost.

Diamond Match

Stock options. Disclosures of stock-option agreements with officers and employees include the date of the agreement, the number of shares made available, the price and its relation to market, and extent of purchases at the balance-sheet date.

Pursuant to a restricted stock option plan dated January 4, 1951 the Company is authorized to grant options to certain employes for the acquisition of 98,844 shares of common stock, and shares were reserved for this purpose. Options were granted May 3, 1951 for 31,900 shares at a price of $38.14 per share, such price being 85% of the quoted market price of the common stock the date the options were granted, in conformity with provisions of Section 130 A of the Internal Revenue Code as amended by the Revenue Act of 1950. During 1952 employes purchased 5,849 shares of common stock under the stock option plan, and as at December 31, 1952 there remained outstanding options for 19,871 shares. The options may be exercised in whole or in part prior to January 31, 1958, and payment for the shares is to be made upon exercise of the options.   *Allis-Chalmers*

Contingent liabilities. Contingent losses exist in every organization but they require disclosure only if they are extraordinary in character or amount or, although nominal at the date of the balance sheet, have customarily been disclosed in past years when they have existed in a material amount. Sometimes leasehold obligations for future years are regarded as contingent liabilities, as in the following example:

Contingent liabilities: (a) Customers' accounts discounted $—; and guarantee of bank loans of distributors, lessors of leased property and of miscellaneous obligations $—. . . . (b) Rental obligations under long-term leases expiring after 1955 aggregating approximately $— per annum, substantially all of which expire within ten years thereafter. . . . (c) Miscellaneous claims and litigation pending—amount indeterminate.   *Cities Service*

Renegotiation status. The net income of business concerns having defense contracts of a substantial character may be subject to renegotiation proceedings under the law, and these proceedings may not have been concluded at the balance-sheet date. Since the possible adjustments may be large, it is customary to append a note, referenced to the income statement, giving some indication of what may be expected.

Approximately half of the Company's sales in 1952 consisted of defense products which are subject to price redetermination and renegotiation and for which final billing prices have not yet been determined. It is believed that adequate provision has been made in the accounts for such adjustments as may result from final settlement of these matters.   *American Locomotive*

Fixed-asset valuation. Cost being the universal basis of valuing fixed assets, exceptions call for the disclosure of the basis actually in use. The footnote illustrated below shows that an appraisal was recognized in 1934 but that cost has been followed since; it would possibly be improved by revealing the portion of the appraisal figure that remains to be depreciated.

The gross amount of property, plant and equipment represents the appraised cost of reproduction—new, with minor exceptions, as determined by The American Appraisal Company as at October

31, 1934, plus subsequent additions at cost. With minor exceptions, the reserves for depreciation and amortization are as determined by The American Appraisal Company as at October 31, 1934, plus subsequent provision for depreciation and amortization at rates recommended by The American Appraisal Company.

McKesson & Robbins

Depreciation policy. Public utilities for the most part have followed the straight-line-depreciation method only in recent years. The procedure generally has been to spread unrecovered cost at the time of adopting the new method over remaining useful life and to set forth in their annual reports the change in procedure.

Effective January 1, 1950 the Company adopted the straight-line method for determining its depreciation accrual and applied for this purpose a composite rate of 1.75%; this composite rate was applied to the years 1950 and 1951. The straight-line method and the adopted composite rate of 1.75% for the years 1950 and 1951 superseded a 40-year term sinking fund method, including a modifying adjustment, which was used in 1949 and several years preceding. The Company during 1951 retained independent engineers to review the depreciation problem with particular reference to the development of a composite rate applicable to the straight-line method of depreciation accrual. The engineers presented their study and on the basis of their report a composite rate of 2.25% was used commencing January 1, 1952, to continue thereafter subject to periodic review. For Federal Income Tax purposes the Company used a rate of 3%. *Hartford Electric*

Subsequent events. Disclosure is required where events following the balance-sheet date are likely to have a material effect on finanical position.

The Company has entered into contracts to purchase from East Texas Pulp and Paper Company (a corporation formed in December 1952), 50% of its authorized common stock and certain of its subordinated notes. The cash required for this purpose after December 31, 1952 is presently estimated to amount to $— payable during 1953, and $— payable during 1954. In the event that (1) funds required for certain purposes by East Texas Pulp and Paper Company should exceed specified amounts, or (2) the pulp and paper mill to be constructed by that corporation should not be completed by a stipulated date, the Company would be obligated to make payments to either East Texas Pulp and Paper Company or others, as the case may be, for the purchase of additional notes or first mortgage bonds of East Texas Pulp and Paper Company. *Time*

Construction contracts. Contracts involving future obligations are not normally given expression on a balance sheet. But since they may require the transformation of working capital into fixed assets their amount may be sufficiently material to warrant disclosure.

> Contract Advances—Unexpended funds restricted to performance under contracts to design, build and operate U.S. Government-owned plants (principally the Atomic Energy Commission project) and under contract to design and build a nylon plant for Chemstrand Corporation amounted in the aggregate to $— at December 31, 1952, and $— at December 31, 1951. These funds, and the corresponding accountability therefor, are not reflected in the Consolidated Balance Sheet.   *du Pont*

Meaning of goodwill. Where goodwill and other intangibles have been acquired in substantial amount, the basis of valuation and amortization, if any, is ordinarily revealed.

> The Corporation's goodwill and patents account includes a nominal amount of $1 for patents. Goodwill is recognized only in connection with the acquisition of a going business, in which case it represents the difference between the purchase price and the value ascribed to the net tangible assets acquired. The Corporation does not amortize items carried in this account.   *General Motors*

Representations from Client

After the financial statements have been prepared, reviewed, and agreed to, it is customary to procure from the client a series of representations concerning financial condition and operating results. These are best incorporated in a single letter, but they may have to be divided where separate signatures are required for different sections.

In securing representations from a client, the auditor has as his purpose three objectives: a confirmation of business practices that he has already tested; an acknowledgment from management of its responsibility for the institution and operation of over-all financial policies; and an opportunity to review with executives basic procedures with which they may not be wholly familiar, thereby paving the way for better top controls over such procedures in the future.

A suggestive sample letter of representation follows. It is brief, almost nontechnical, contains no dollar amounts, and is confined to matters that ought to be well known to informed top officials. Amounts may be omitted in ordinary cases: most executives are too far removed from the general ledger and cannot affirm dollar amounts of their own knowledge; besides, the auditor secures a confirmation of financial-statement figures when the client's controller approves the final statements. Exceptions may be noted by adding at the end of any sentence "except for" or "except that" followed by a summary description of the exception; or, a negative statement (as on contingent liabilities) may be turned into a positive one, the exception being thus more clearly stated. Additional signatures may be called for where important financial and operating controls reside in such officials as the treasurer and general manager, or as previously indicated a separate letter may be provided. The author prefers wherever practicable the single letter, with "subrepresentations" similar to those illustrated below.

Details should be avoided, especially where the subject matter lies outside the normal field of activity of top management. However, independent representations of subordinates should also be avoided, for reasons already cited.

(Letterhead of client)

Hyatt, Paterson & Co.
960 Hudson Building
Chicago 3, Illinois

Dear Sirs:

You have asked that we make certain representations to you in connection with your annual audit of our accounts for the year ended December 31, 19–1.

Receivables represent uncollected sales to customers, or sums owing to the company from others, due within the coming year; the reserve for bad debts is a fair estimate of uncollectible receivables.

Inventories at the year end were based on physical count, weight, or measure at November 30, 19–1, plus and minus changes during December; usable material and salable finished product were priced at the lower of cost or market and not in excess of net realizable value, and obsolete, unusable, or unsalable items at nominal or scrap values; the inventories were clerically accurate; the company's books were adjusted to reflect the physical inventories; and unencumbered title to the inventories was held by the company.

Plant-and-equipment charges during the year, valued at cost, were actual additions to property; property disposed of or abandoned was removed from the accounts; balances at the year end represent all the plant and equipment owned by the company, and on such plant and equipment the company holds satisfactory title and no mortgage or lien is outstanding.

Provisions representing fair allowances for accruing depreciation and obsolescence were added during the year to the reserves for depreciation, and the balances remaining at the year end did not exceed depreciation and obsolescence requirements at that date.

Liabilities recorded on the books of account as at the year end were the company's actual and complete obligations on that date.

No material event or condition pertaining to the year has been omitted from the records and none has arisen since the year end that would affect the interpretation of operating results of the year or financial condition at the year end.

No extraordinary items of income or expense appear in the income statement for the year.

No contingent liabilities existing at the year end.

The twelve adjusting journal entries transmitted in your memorandum of February 19 have been given expression on our records as at December 31, 19–1.

During the year the company's books of account were kept in accordance with accounting principles consistent with those followed in the preceding year.

Very truly yours,

Illustrative Audit

Section X of the working papers consists of 12 pages of data that cannot be readily classified under any other head or that are not extensive enough to warrant separate headings of their own. The first of these is the general "representation" from the management, a letter to the auditor's firm from the principal officers of the company, with the additional signatures of the individuals who assumed responsibility for the propriety of the inventory and plant records. This type of document has only recently come into general use, its purposes being those outlined in this chapter. Some accountants make an elaborate instrument of it and fill it with figures; others divide it into several sections, often with different signatures or different combinations of signatures on each section. As a rule the best plan is to make the document as simple as possible, avoiding the use of dollar amounts unless exceptions are made to general statements. In the accompanying representation (X 1), there are three such exceptions, their identification being briefly but positively established by the dollar amounts. The auditor who drafts a letter of representation should endeavor to see to it that the signers of the letter are familiar with and take an active responsibility for its contents and do not affix their signatures simply because the auditor has asked them to do so or because someone from below has told them that the letter is "all right."

On X 11 the auditor's principal has jotted down a number of points during his review of the auditor's work and the conference with the client on March 13. These points will be incorporated in the 1953 program that the principal will shortly prepare.

The financial statements (RS 2–3) follow conventional forms. A note is appended to each, calling attention to the effect produced by the change in accounting method. Some accountants would look upon the results of the change as immaterial notwithstanding that the year's net income would have been approximately 8 per cent larger than that reported if the change had not been made. In this instance both the auditor and his principal were convinced that materiality was present not merely from the effect on the current year but the effect it might have on the operating results of future years where the inventory variation could be substantial.

MARTIN MANUFACTURING COMPANY
1688 S. Federal St.
Chicago 16, Ill.

March 11, 1953

Hyatt, Paterson & Company
960 Hudson Building
Chicago 4, Illinois

Dear Sirs:

You requested representations from us in connection with your annual audit of our accounts for the year ended December 31, 1952.

Receivables at the year end represented uncollected sales to customers, or sums owing to the company from others, due during 1953 except for notes, or portions thereof, amounting to $158,167.00 and maturing thereafter. The reserve for bad debts was a fair estimate of uncollectible receivables.

Inventories were based on physical count, weight, or measure as at December 31, 1952, except for supplies of $122,416.35--an amount we believe to be accurate-- which were subject to physical count at various times during the year. Usable material and salable finished goods were priced at the lower of cost or market, and obsolete, unusable, or unsalable items at nominal or scrap values. The inventories were clerically accurate, the company's books were adjusted to reflect the physical inventory, and title to the inventory was held by the company. No commitments for materials or parts existed beyond 60-day requirements.

Plant-and-equipment charges during the year, valued at cost, represented actual additions to property; items disposed of or abandoned were removed from the accounts at their original cost; balances at the year end represent all the plant and equipment owned by the company, and on such plant and equipment the company holds satisfactory title. The obligation on first-mortgage bonds is secured by a lien on plant and equipment.

Provisions representing fair allowances for accruing depreciation and obsolescence were added during the year to the reserves for depreciation, and the reserve balances at the year end did not exceed depreciation and obsolescence requirements on that date.

No material contingent liabilities existed at the year end except for notes receivable discounted amounting to $25,611.00.

No extraordinary item of income or expense has occurred during the year, and, throughout the year, the books of account were kept in accordance with generally accepted accounting principles consistent with those followed in the preceding year.

Very truly yours,

Martin Manufacturing Company

Ed. Stebins _____ President

Arthur P. Collins _____ Controller

Other representations:

On inventory amounts, prices,
and clerical accuracy

Geo. Shuffle _____
Plant Manager

On property accounts and reserves for depreciation

Sidney Skell _____
Assistant Controller

X - 1

1. Perform additional audit work prior to year end —
   a. Circularize receivables
   b. Review of adequacy of bad-debt reserve
   c. Analyze changes in fixed-asset accounts and related reserves

2. P-2 — Accrued general taxes —
   a. Eliminate listing monthly accrual
   b. Test annual provision for FICA and unemployment insurance by use of gross annual payroll amounts adjusted for exempt payroll

3. Points for study during preliminary work on our 1953 audit — these points were raised during conference with client at time of delivering our 1952 report —
   a. Development of activity or responsibility accounting to factory operations (see PF-32).
   b. Retirement of all or a portion of the preferred stock by (1) reduction in investment in U.S. Government securities, and (2) greater reliance on bank credit
   c. Method for providing accurate data (quantity and amount) of sales by individual items in each product line (heavy machines, light machines, household appliances) (see A-1,2)
   d. Cost comparison of rented equipment vs. purchased equipment. Equipment rental in 1952 amounted to $46,369.15 (TB-4)
   e. Factory equipment maintenance and repair — compare company with industry trends — obtain from Mr. Collins copy of industry study made by trade association last year.
   f. Further consideration of overall breakdown of cost of sales by objects (see TB-4 & A-4)

X-11

draft
3-10-53
FL:jr

Martin Manufacturing Company
Consolidated Balance Sheet
December 31, 1952

ASSETS

Current assets--			
Cash		$ 433,935.39	
U. S. securities, at cost (market value, $405,809.57)		402,268.57	
Receivables--			
Customers, less allowance of $26,652.58 for uncollectible accounts	$1,195,943.30		
Officers & employees	20,389.54		
Other	7,439.52	1,223,772.36	
Inventories of finished goods, work in process, raw materials, and supplies, at cost or less		1,519,588.20	
Prepaid insurance and taxes		40,448.32	$3,620,012.84
Customers notes due after 1953			158,167.00
Minority interests in common stocks of suppliers of raw materials & parts, at cost which is less than market price			374,152.10
Land, buildings, machinery & equipment, at cost		$2,203,651.63	
Less accumulated depreciation		840,869.79	1,362,781.84
Total assets			$5,515,113.78

LIABILITIES

Current liabilities--			
Bank loans		$ 550,000.00	
Suppliers		204,713.65	
Employees accounts		10,427.29	
Advances from customers		62,309.03	
Federal income tax		208,862.80	
Other accruals		119,849.39	$1,156,162.16
Reserve for pensions under a voluntary plan, including contributions of employees			336,820.00
First-mortgage bonds, less reacquisitions of $430,000 during 1952		$ 315,000.00	
Less cash in hands of sinking-fund trustee		21,479.02	293,520.98
Net worth--			
5% cumulative preferred stock--authorized, issued, & outstanding: 5,000 shares, par value $100		$ 500,000.00	
Common stock--authorized, issued & outstanding: 5,000 shares, par value $100		500,000.00	
Paid-in surplus from original issue in 1941 of common stock		102,542.10	
Earned surplus--			
Balance December 31, 1951	$2,544,481.06		
Net income, 1952	206,587.48		
Dividends on preferred and common stocks	- 125,000.00	2,626,068.54	3,728,610.64
Total liabilities			$5,515,113.78

Note: Because of the adoption during the year of a direct-costing basis for the valuation of goods produced and in process the amount of the inventories shown above, $1,519,588.20, is less by $37,120.00 than it would have been had the costing basis of the preceding year been followed.

RS - 2

Martin Manufacturing Company
Comparative Consolidated Income Statements
Years ended December 31, 1952 and 1951

	1952	1951	Year ended December 31 1952	1951
Net sales			$7,909,005.81	$7,953,974.17
Less cost of sales			6,824,311.23	6,777,791.23
Gross profit from sales			$1,084,694.58	$1,176,182.94
Less--				
Selling expense	$351,965.21	$352,291.10		
Administrative & general expense	482,312.15	470,712.65	834,277.36	823,003.75
Net operating income			$ 250,417.22	$ 353,179.19
Other income--				
Interest	$ 15,205.50	$ 11,644.73		
Dividends	73,762.50	12,500.00		
Profit from sale of stocks	175,152.10		264,120.10	24,144.73
Other expense--				
Interest	$ 28,793.92	$ 34,322.00		
Bond-repurchase costs, including premiums	37,434.75			
Provision for pension reserve	33,200.00	29,500.00	- 99,428.67	- 63,822.00
Net income before Federal income tax			$ 415,108.65	$ 313,501.92
Provision for Federal income tax			208,521.17	152,990.97
Net income			$ 206,587.48	$ 160,510.95

Note: The change during 1952 in the basis of inventory valuation (see footnote accompanying the balance sheet) has had the effect of reducing the gross profit from sales by $37,120.00; net income, after allowance for Federal income tax, has been reduced by approximately one-half that amount.

RS - 3

Problems and Questions

1. What do you understand by the term "management's representation"? What is its purpose?

2. On the basis of an examination completed in accordance with the audit program described hereinafter, would the auditor be warranted in giving a certificate covering the fairness of the statement of the income account for the period? Explain. The audit program provides for the following but no more: (a) a detailed examination of all the profit-and-loss accounts by reference to vouchers in support of substantially all transactions appearing in the respective accounts in the general ledger; (b) proof of the clerical accuracy of all the books of original entry and accounts in the general ledger; and (c) a comprehensive examination of cash for the period under review.

3. Briefly describe the audit procedure that suggests itself in the examination of (a) tuition income of private schools; (b) rental income of office buildings; (c) annual dues of golf clubs; (d) donations received by charity organizations; and (e) plate collections at church services.

4. Completing today an audit for the past year, you are scanning briefly your client's books of account since the year end. Name six events that might have occurred during that period which would warrant disclosure in the financial statements.

5. Devise sideheads or footnotes that will provide adequate disclosure on a balance-sheet of the following inventory items:

(a) Raw materials under perpetual inventory were last physically inventoried two years ago, additions and deductions since that time having been made on a cost basis—that is, purchases at invoice cost and issues at a "moving-average" cost. No allowance has been made for shortages, obsolescence, or deterioration.

(b) In-process inventory is valued at cost, as revealed by cost sheets showing material charged thereto, and labor, but no overhead.

(c) Finished goods have been priced at standard cost. Material, which constitutes roughly two-thirds of prime cost, is underpriced one-fourth; labor, one-tenth; and overhead, which for standard-cost purposes has been computed as 100% of direct-labor standard cost, one-half.

6. Prepare adjusting journal entries, in a form suitable for inclusion in working papers covering a calendar-year audit, to give effect to the following unrecorded items:

(a) No inventory of office supplies had been taken for some years and, at the suggestion of the auditor, the office manager prepared and priced a physical list of stationery and similar items on hand on March 31 (three months after the close of the audit year), the total as thus determined being $12,483.35. Errors discovered by the auditor in extensions and footings reduced this figure by $347.50; pricing errors caused additional reductions of $162.18. Since the beginning of the year purchases have been $3,672.27, and estimated issues $1,500.00.

(b) In the process of verifying working-fund advances to employees at distant points, the auditor finds that the following expenses, paid for from these advances, had not been given expression on the home-office books: traveling expenses (sales), $410.28; traveling expenses (engineering and research), $388.25; salary of engineering assistant, $275.00.

(c) A factory machine, having an original cost of $2,289.40, was scrapped. The machine, in an asset account with several hundred others, had been purchased exactly seven years ago; and the freight and installation, amounting to $120.50, was at that time expensed. The asset account was the basis for composite depreciation of 10% until two years ago; for the past two years the composite rate has been 8%.

(d) A dividend of $1.25 on common stock was declared by the board of directors on December 31, payable on February 15 to stockholders of record on January 20, the resolution indicating a total of $12,500. However, on December 31, 350 shares out of 10,000 outstanding a year prior was being held by the company as treasury stock. Of these 350 shares, 140 shares were sold on January 14 (two weeks later) at the then listed market price of $15 per share plus the dividend.

(e) Interest of $1,468.75 had been received by the trustee of a "voluntary" pension fund. The fund is shown on the company's balance sheet as an asset and is offset by a "pension-fund reserve" of equal amount, carried as appropriated earned surplus.

7. On January 31, one month following the close of its fiscal year but several weeks before the completion of an annual audit, a company enters into an agreement with the Federal Bureau of Internal Revenue whereby an additional income-tax assessment of $12,525.00 becomes the final amount due on a tax return filed two years prior. No liability has been set up for this amount. Is it the auditor's duty to adjust for the additional assessment or to indicate the amount, as a contingency, in a footnote?

8. Your client has purchased a "war plant" at approximately "15 cents on the dollar," or $60,000. This plant is well suited to your client's manufacturing requirements, and adaptation costs are not expected to exceed $10,000. Your advice is sought on revaluation. Cost now under reasonable postwar conditions of a similar plant would be around $250,000, and a suggestion has been made by the president that $200,000 would be a conservative figure after deducting "observed" depreciation. What is your reaction to this proposal?

9. Your principal has suggested to a client that in next year's report it might be well to include a statement of application of funds. The client now asks you to describe to him briefly the meaning of this statement. How would you reply?

10. A certain public accountant follows the practice of reviewing financial statements with management while they are still in draft form. What benefits might result from this practice?

CHAPTER XVI

Reports

Upon the completion of his field work the public accountant submits to his client a report on his findings. There are several varieties of reports. The first of these is the highly standardized "short-form" report. Another is the "long-form" report, the style and content of which ties in only very generally with common standards. A third type containing "system comments" often supplements a short-form report but may be consolidated with other findings in a long-form report. Finally there are many varieties of reports covering such special studies as tax inquiries, system examinations, reviews of internal controls, and credit investigations. In this chapter the short-form and long-form reports are given particular attention.

Short-Form Report

For larger engagements the short-form report or certificate is the general rule. A standard form is followed by most accounting firms. This form was initiated and has been modified from time to time by committees of the American Institute of Accountants. The four principal varieties employed during the past two decades are reproduced on pages 582-583. The first was recommended in 1934 as the result of a joint study of the New York Stock Exchange and the American Institute of Accountants; the second in 1941 after the U.S. Securities and Exchange Commission had drawn up proposals for certificate standards; the third in 1944; and the fourth in 1947 by the Institute's Committee on Auditing Procedure. The first three are no longer found in current practice. All four forms, however, despite language changes, are identical in intent and meaning. Each successive form has reflected improvements in style and wording; and further improvements—

Standard report: scope paragraph

1934	1941	1944	1947
We have examined the balance sheet of the X Company as of December 31, 19—, and the statement of income and surplus for the year then ended.	We have examined the balance sheet of the X Company as of December 31, 19—, and the statements of income and surplus for the year then ended,	We have examined the balance sheet of the X Company as of December 31, 19—, and the statements of income and surplus for the year then ended.	We have examined the balance sheet of X Company as of December 31, 19— and the statement(s) of income and surplus for the year then ended.
In connection therewith, we	have reviewed the system of internal control and accounting procedures of the company and, without making a detailed audit of the transactions, have		
examined or tested accounting records of the company and other supporting evidence	examined or tested accounting records of the company and other supporting evidence	[equivalent language below]	
and obtained information and explanations from officers and employees of the company; we also made a general review of the accounting methods and of the operating and income accounts for the year but we did not make a detailed audit of the transactions.	by methods and to the extent we deemed appropriate.		
	Our examination was made in accordance with generally accepted auditing standards	Our examination was made in accordance with generally accepted auditing standards	Our examination was made in accordance with generally accepted auditing standards
	applicable in the circumstances and it	applicable in the circumstances and it	and accordingly
	included	included	included
		such tests of the accounting records and other supporting evidence	such tests of the accounting records
		and such other	and such other
			auditing
	all procedures which	procedures as	procedures as

1934	1941	1944	1947
	we considered necessary.	we considered necessary.	we considered necessary
			in the circumstances.

Standard report: opinion paragraph

1934	1941	1944	1947
In our opinion,	In our opinion,	In our opinion,	In our opinion,
based on such examination,			
the accompanying balance sheet and	the accompanying balance sheet and	the accompanying balance sheet and	the accompanying balance sheet and
related	related	related	
statements of income and surplus	statements of income and surplus	statements of income and surplus	statement(s) of income and surplus
fairly present,	present fairly the	present fairly the	present fairly the
in accordance with accepted principles of accounting consistently maintained by the company during the year under review, its			
position	position	position	financial position
	of the X Company	of X Company	of X Company
at December 31, 19—, and the results of its operations for the year.	at December 31, 19—, and the results of its operations for the year,	at December 31, 19—, and the results of its operations for the year,	at December 31, 19—, and the results of its operations for the year
			then ended,
	in conformity with generally accepted accounting principles applied on a basis consistent with that of the preceding year.	in conformity with generally accepted accounting principles applied on a basis consistent with that of the preceding year.	in conformity with generally accepted accounting principles applied on a basis consistent with that of the preceding year.

even the elimination of the certificate—may be expected as the public's knowledge of the meaning of auditing increases.

The accountant's report is addressed to the board of directors or the stockholders or both, according to the terms of the employment, and it is signed and dated by the accountant, following usually the style appearing in the Illustrative Audit.

Each of the standard forms contains a "scope" paragraph (or sentence) and an "opinion" paragraph (or sentence). By scope is meant the nature of the examination that preceded the report; in his description of scope the accountant has the opportunity, by modifying or adding to the standard language, of explaining the omission and reason therefor of any standard procedure. In his opinion the auditor may call attention to points on which he finds it necessary to express some qualification. One or two paragraphs more fully explaining any of these matters are sometimes inserted between the scope and opinion paragraphs.

The major propositions appearing in the present version of the short-form report are these: (a) an audit was a condition precedent to the report, (b) customary audit *standards* were observed, (c) the *procedures* of the audit were those deemed necessary by the auditor, (d) the audit was on a "test" basis, (e) the accountant's conclusion as to the propriety of the financial statements is an "opinion," (f) the statements "fairly present" financial position and operating results, (g) the statements are based on "accepted principles of accounting," and (h) the same principles were also reflected in last year's statements. Exceptions to these propositions are incorporated in the report; examples are given on a subsequent page. Changes between the first and last certificate forms may be summarized thus:

1. As the reader is by now well aware an annual audit requires a many-sided approach to the client's affairs, and it would be impossible to put every important aspect of the audit into a single paragraph. The questions facing the professional accountant are: how much information on scope is it practicable to furnish and how necessary is it? It will be noticed that as compared with the 1934 certificate later versions omit the following propositions: (a) information was obtained from officers and employees (that is, as distinguished from information obtained from the records), (b) accounting methods were reviewed, (c) "operating and income" accounts were examined, (d) the auditor's opinion was based on his examination, (e) no detailed audit was made. These items came to be regarded as inevitable and obvious details of the usual type of audit and supplied the reader with nothing he should not already know. As to the desirability of including mention of a detailed audit, the profession until recently was divided; some believed that further education of the average reader of financial statements on this point was neces-

sary. However, the expression "included . . . tests" appears now to be a sufficient disclosure of the omission of a detailed audit from customary procedures.

2. Instead of the reference to the consistent use during the year of accepted principles, there now appears the statement that the accepted principles followed during the year were consistent with those of the preceding year. This statement says as much as its predecessor and more: the addition being that this year's financial statements are said to be comparable with last year's; wherever this is true, consistency must have prevailed throughout the current year.

3. Included in the 1941 certificate but omitted from the 1944 and 1947 variations are references to the review of (a) internal controls, (b) accounting procedures, and (c) the possible limitations attaching to the testing process by use of the expression "by methods and to the extent we deemed appropriate." Here again, it has been regarded as unnecessary to refer to the review of internal controls and accounting porcedures, since it is presumed that the reader should know that such a review is a prime requisite to even the most limited examination. Further, an implication of conflict between the limitation described in (c) and the reference in the next following sentence of the report (see [4] below) to the observance of auditing standards (which would have to be observed notwithstanding the auditor's possible conviction of their inappropriateness) was judged important enough to warrant the elimination of the former.

4. Appearing in the 1941, 1944, and 1947 versions at the end of the "scope" paragraph is a sentence that states that the accountant has observed "generally accepted" *auditing* standards plus such other procedures as were deemed "necessary" by him. In the 1944 and 1947 versions the reference to "testing" appears at this point.

5. The 1947 version differs from its predecessor in only minor respects: (a) "In the circumstances" was moved from an association with standards to an association with procedures, the phrase now indicating that the auditor selects his procedures for each situation according to his best judgment of what the situation demands. He cannot do this with standards since standards reflect what is customary among auditors generally or what has been established by fiat within the profession; that is, standards —which often admit of many procedures—apply to every situation, regardless of the procedures chosen. It is the author's opinion, however, that the phrase might as well be omitted because most people are well aware that procedures must vary from one

engagement to another. "Procedures . . . considered necessary" is a direct indication that free selection tempered only by the auditor's judgment has been employed. (b) "Auditing" now prefacing "procedures" has the effect of clarifying the notion that what the auditor does and the freedom within which he acts are dictated by his judgment of audit—and not, for example, legal—requirements. (c) "Accordingly" was also added as a clarification: to indicate that the auditor's "testing" and "other . . . procedures" grow out of the demands put upon him by the auditing standards he feels obliged to follow. (d) "And other supporting evidence," being tautological, was dropped; the term "accounting records" means not only the books of account but vouchers, files, and all the other details that might be implied by "other supporting evidence."

6. With the immediate origins of the current form in mind, its meaning may be summarized thus: the "scope" paragraph states that relevant auditing standards were observed in the examination which included tests and other necessary procedures; the "opinion" paragraph states that the public acountant believes that the financial statements are a fair presentation consistent with the previous year's. By omitting references to internal controls and the other matters described above the public accountant does not thus deny their importance; rather, he omits what is common knowledge to all who read and depend on financial statements.

Nonstandard forms of the short-form report are often encountered, most of them simplified versions of those illustrated; thus several firms of accountants now employ the following version of the fourth form in which the first sentence is omitted and the order of the remaining two sentences is reversed:

> In our opinion, the accompanying balance sheet and income statement [together with the notes thereto] present fairly the financial position of X Company at December 31, 19—, and the results of its operations for the year then ended, in conformity with generally accepted accounting principles [which have been] applied on a basis consistent with that of the preceding year. Our examination of such statements [or: This opinion is based on an examination of the statements which] was made in accordance with generally accepted auditing standards and [accordingly] included such tests of the accounting records and such other auditing procedures as we considered necessary in the circumstances.

The certificate standards of the U.S. Securities and Exchange Commission previously referred to may be found in Rule 2.02 of Regulations S–X, which provides that the certificate must state

(a) that "the audit was made in accordance with generally accepted auditing standards," (b) that no "normal" or "necessary" audit procedure has been omitted, and (c) that where any procedure deemed necessary by the accountant has been omitted a statement to that effect should appear and it should include the reasons for the omission. As to the second half of the certificate the Commission requires that it contain the accountant's opinion of (a) the financial statements, (b) the accounting "principles and practices" underlying the statements, (c) any material change in principles and practices or methods of applying them, (d) any material adjustment and its effects on past income statements and on the comparability of the statements, and (e) any material differences between principles and practices before and after audit adjustments. These requirements appear to be fully met by the present report form. An exception and its effects on the financial statement must be clearly set forth and identified with the relevant item or items in the statement.

The trend toward report simplification and the gradual acceptance of the assumption that the reader no longer needs to be informed of details of audit scope lead naturally to the question "Cannot the certificate be simplified further?" The answer is that it undoubtedly will undergo further simplification and ultimately may be eliminated altogether. If the auditor's opinion *must* appear, a simple statement such as the following would eventually fullfil the requirements:

> In our opinion the accompanying balance sheet and income statement present the position of the X Company at December 31, 19—, and the results of its operations for the year then ended.

No scope, adherence to auditing standards, or reliance on tests is indicated, and no reference is made to the continuance of last year's accounting principles; only a simple statement of opinion appears which is probably all that the reader of financial statements pays attention to, anyway. If members of the profession can be relied on to report in footnotes or their equivalent major deviations from auditing standards and departures from accounting principles wherever they are present, the need for the short-form report would largely disappear.

Certificate Additions

Following are examples of recent additions to short-form reports that express qualifications or disclosures believed necessary for the information of the reader or for the protection of the accountant. They have been extracted from the scope or opinion paragraph or they appear as an added paragraph between the two.

Receivables

1. It was not practicable to confirm the amounts due from the United States Government as at December 31, 1951, as to which we have satisfied ourselves by means of other auditing procedures.

Mullins Manufacturing

Inventories

2. . . . as we considered necessary in the circumstances, except that, the company not having taken a physical inventory at November 30, 1951, our examination in respect of inventories was restricted accordingly. . . . In our opinion, subject to the exception in respect of inventories, the accompanying balance sheet and statement of income and retained earnings, together with notes thereto, fairly present . . . .

Elastic Stop Nut

3. . . . in conformity with generally accepted accounting principles which, except for the change referred to in the following paragraph, were applied on a basis consistent . . . . As at November 1, 1950 the company changed its method of valuing its inventories from "average cost or market, whichever lower" to cost determined on the basis of "last-in, first-out." This change, which we approve, reduced the inventories at October 31, 1951 by approximately $— and the net income for the fiscal year then ended by approximately $—. *J. I. Case*

Valuation of fixed assets

4. No attempt is made in the balance sheet to reflect actual present value of fixed assets, publication titles, copyrights, subscription lists and goodwill. *McGraw-Hill Publishing*

5. . . . in conformity with generally accepted accounting principles applied (except for the change referred to in Note D with which we concur) on a basis consistent with that of the preceding year.
[Note D read as follows:]

Property, Plant and Equipment: The amounts by which the 1936 and 1937 appraised values of certain of these assets varied from cost has [sic] been largely covered by subsequent depreciation charges. Property, Plant and Equipment—Net substantially represents depreciated cost. . . . Expenditures for mine development and stripping in the amount of approximately $— have been written off for tax purposes as permitted by the Revenue Act of 1951; and the same treatment has been adopted for book purposes in lieu of the amortization method heretofore used. The effect of this change was to reduce consolidated net income after taxes for the year by approximately $—. . . . Under its bond indenture, the Corporation has undertaken to complete a specified "Proposed Plant Expansion Program" as promptly as possible. The remaining cost thereof is estimated to be approximately $— in excess of cash in the Plant Expansion Reserve Account.

Colorado Fuel and Iron

Depreciation policy

6. . . . prepared in conformity with generally accepted accounting principles which, except for the change, which we approve, in treatment of intangible development costs as explained in Note 1 to the consolidated financial statements, were maintained by the companies on a basis consistent with that of the preceding year.

[Note 1 read as follows:]

Intangible development costs—Since 1934, the Company has capitalized the costs of drilling productive wells and has amortized such costs by charges to the income account on a straight line basis, except in Illinois, Indiana and Kentucky, where the costs are fully amortized as incurred. For Federal income tax purposes, however, the Company continued to deduct all intangible drilling costs in the year incurred. As a result, there is an immediate tax deduction for drilling costs capitalized in the current year which costs will be amortized by charges to income in future years. This affects the income account in a way which becomes more significant in periods like the present one in which there are heavy drilling activities and very high taxes. . . . In recognition of this situation, the Company, beginning in 1951, has adopted the policy of providing an additional reserve for amortization of intangible development costs equivalent to the reduction in taxes applicable to the excess of current drilling costs incurred over regular amortization charges. In 1951, such additional amortization amounted to $—.

Texas Company

7. . . . applied on a basis consistent with that of the preceding year except as to the change, which we approve, in the provision for depreciation and obsolescence as explained in Note 1 to the financial statements.

[Note 1 read as follows:]

The Company adopted a policy, beginning in 1951, of making provision for accelerated depreciation and obsolescence on the cost of its machinery and equipment, arising from intensive use under present conditions and the anticipated need for replacements resulting from improved design and processes in advance of the end of the heretofore estimated useful lives of existing facilities. The total provision for depreciation and obsolescence of plant property, included above in costs of goods sold, amounted to $— including $— for such accelerated depreciation and obsolescence of machinery and equipment. The provision for accelerated depreciation and obsolescence has not been deducted in computing the provision for Federal and State taxes on income.

Cannon Mills

Income-tax liability

8. In view of the circumstances stated in Note G of the notes to accounts, we are unable to express an opinion on the federal and state income tax liabilities of a subsidiary company for certain years prior to 1948. . . . In our opinion, which is reserved with respect to the liabilities refered to . . .

[Note G read as follows:]

Federal income taxes of Follansbee Steel Corporation have been settled through the year 1949, and the unrequired balances accrued therefor were restored to income. The provisions for 1950 are believed adequate to provide for the income and excess profits taxes for that year. . . . Federal income tax returns of Federal Enameling & Stamping Company have been settled to and including the year 1941. The income tax returns for the years 1942 to 1944, inclusive, have been examined, and additional liabilities have been asserted. A portion of the additional liabilities asserted has been paid. Pending action on a protest filed in which the full liability is not admitted, provision has been made in the accounts for the major portion of the disputed balance and interest. Concurrently, the estimated portion recoverable under the Indemnification Agreement (obtained upon the acquisition of seventy (70%) percent of common stock of Federal by Follansbee in 1948) has been recorded as a claim against the escrow agent. The escrow fund is substantially in excess of this claim. The years subsequent to 1944 have not yet been subjected to a field examination by the Bureau of Internal Revenue.   *Follansbee Steel*

Pension reserves

9. . . . applied on a basis consistent with that of the preceding year except for the change (which we approve) in the basis of providing insurance and pension reserves and making charges thereto, as explained in Note 4 of the accompanying notes to financial statements.
[Note 4 read as follows:]
Effective January 1, 1951, a change has been made in accounting method with respect to insurance and pension reserves. Heretofore, the amounts set aside in these reserves have been based on estimated future payments, without allowance for tax credits which will accrue to the company when such future payments are made. Under this method, net income is adversely affected when the set-aside is made, and correspondingly benefited when future payments are charged to the reserve and tax credits accrue. To avoid this distortion, it was decided to make the reserve set-asides and charges on the basis of the net cost to the company after taxes estimated at an average rate of 50%. The effect of this change in 1951 was to increase net income by $—.
                                    Hercules Powder

Contingent liabilities

10. In our opinion, subject to refunds, if any, which may be necessary under the Renegotiation Acts (see Note G) and losses which may be sustained in the disposition of idle mill properties (see Note B), the accompanying consolidated . . .
[Note G read as follows:]
Approximately 25% of the Company's sales during the year ended October 31, 1951 are subject to the Renegotiation Acts. No provision has been made in the accompanying financial statements for possible refunds, because no basis presently exists for the determination of the Company's liability, if any.
[Note B read as follows:]
During the year ended October 31, 1951, the Company discontinued substantially all operations at three of its New England mills. The sale of one of the mill properties was consummated during November 1951 and resulted in a loss of approximately $—, provision for which has been made as a special item in the accompanying consoli-

dated statement of income. The other two mill properties, including machinery and equipment, are carried in the accounts at about $—, after deducting accumulated depreciation. The Company expects to transfer a substantial portion of the machinery and equipment at these two mills to other locations and to dispose of the remaining assets. No provision has been made for losses which may be incurred in the sale of these mill properties, because a final determination has not been made of the machinery and equipment which will be transferred and because it is not practicable at this time to estimate the realizable proceeds from the sale of the remaining assets.   *J. P. Stevens*

Stock options

11. In our opinion, subject to the effect which an adverse decision in the matter referred to in Note B to the financial statements would have on such statements, . . .

[Note B read as follows:]

Ten year options to purchase in ten annual, but cumulative, installments an aggregate of 64,800 shares of authorized but unissued common stock of the Company at prices ranging from $24.00 to $54.25 a share, are held by certain of the Company's directors, officers, and employees. . . . During the past fiscal year the staff of the Securities and Exchange Commission took issue with the Company's method of accounting for stock options contending that additional compensation to optionees, equivalent to the excess of the market price of the option shares over the option price, should be recorded as each portion of an option became exercisable regardless of whether the option was exercised or not. The Company believes that no additional compensation is attributable to the options since they were issued at the market price of the stock on the date of issue. The Company on January 6, 1953 appealed to the Commission to review the matter but at the date of this report the appeal had not been heard. . . . If the Company were to reflect additional compensation in accordance with the Securities and Exchange Commission's contention, net earnings for the year would be decreased by $— of which $— would be attributable to prior years, and $— to the past fiscal year. The effect on the balance sheet would be to decrease "earnings retained for use in the business" by $— and to increase "additional capital paid in" by the same amount.

Brown Shoe

Income realization

12. . . . on a basis consistent with that of the preceding year except for the change in the basis of accounting for certain royalties as outlined in Note F, which change we approve.

[Note F read as follows:]

Prior to the current year, royalties were taken into income as received. A recent Federal court decision, however, requires that royalties receivable under agreements calling for a fixed aggregate amount, although contractually due and payable in future annual installments, must be taken into taxable income in the year in which the contract becomes effective. The Corporation has changed its accounting procedure to conform with this decision, and this had the effect of increas-

ing the income for the year 1951 in the gross amout of $—, and the
net amount of $— after deducting Federal income taxes, over what
would have been shown on the former basis of accounting.   *Pullman*

Consolidation policy

13. ... We were furnished with financial statements and reports on
certain domestic and Canadian subsidiaries and divisions by other
firms of certified public or chartered accountants.   *Sperry*

14. ... on a basis consistent with that of the preceding year except
for the exclusion in consolidation of a subsidiary as set forth in Note 2,
in which change we concur.

[Note 2 read as follows:]

During the year 1951 the Company discontinued consolidation of
the subsidiary operating abroad and will take into income only cash
income when received in United States currency. Neither the difference
between the investment and the Company's equity nor the subsidiary's
earnings for 1951 are significant in relation to the consolidated net
assets and current earnings.   *Mengel*

15. ... in conformity with generally accepted accounting principles
applied on a basis consistent with that of the preceding year, except
for the change (with which we concur) in practice of consolidation
mentioned in the note "Principles of Consolidation."

[The note "Principles of Consolidation" read as follows:]

In prior years it has been the practice of the Company to exclude
from its consolidated financial statements the accounts of certain
wholly owned subsidiaries. For the year 1951 the excluded subsidiaries
were Printing Developments, Inc., Michigan Square Building Corporation (merged into Printing Developments, Inc. as of December 31,
1952), and Evadale Manufacturing Company. For the year 1952, the
consolidated financial statements reflect the accounts of all wholly
owned domestic and foreign subsidiaries, including those of a Canadian
subsidiary organized during 1952. Such change in practice of consolidation had no significant effect on the accompanying financial
statements for 1952. For 1951, net profit of Michigan Square Building
Corporation was $—; net loss of Printing Developments, Inc. was $—;
Evadale Manufacturing Company carried on no operations. The net
assets identified with transactions conducted by the domestic companies
and the Canadian subsidiary outside the United States and Canada,
and net assets of other foreign subsidiaries, as well as the results of related foreign operations for 1952, were not a significant part of the
consolidated totals.   *Time*

Reliance upon other accountants

16. We accepted, after review, the financial statements of the Canadian subsidiary as certified to by independent auditors, which are included in the accompanying consolidated statements at parity of exchange.   *Woolworth*

17. The accounts of foreign subsidiaries were examined or tested
by Independent Public Accountants in the respective foreign countries
as of August 31, 1951 in accordance with program which we prepared.
We have reviewed their reports relating to such examinations, have no
exceptions to take to the adequacy and sufficiency of the examinations

and tests made by such other accountants, have accepted such work in the same manner as if it had been done by us, and have accepted such reports as a proper basis for consolidating the accounts of foreign subsidiaries with the accounts of the domestic companies as of August 31, 1951. Current asset and current liability accounts of foreign subsidiaries and other current accounts in foreign moneys have been included at prevailing exchange rates, at rates lower than nominally quoted, or at rates of current remittances. *Loew's*

18. Examinations of similar scope have been made by us of the balance sheets as of December 31, 1952 and of the statements of income and retained earnings for the year 1952 of the principal nonconsolidated subsidiaries of American Telephone and Telegraph Company, except Western Electric Company, Incorporated, and its subsidiaries, and we have reviewed accounting reports for the year 1952 rendered to American Telephone and Telegraph Company by all other nonconsolidated subsidiaries. The consolidated balance sheet of Western Electric Company, Incorporated, and consolidated subsidiaries as of December 31, 1952 and the related statement of consolidated income of these companies for the year 1952, with certificate of examination thereof by other independent accountants, have been furnished to us.

American Telephone and Telegraph

Definition of scope

19. The cash was confirmed by certificates obtained from the depositaries and custodians or by count. Tests were made of the validity of receivables by communication with the debtors, except that it was not practicable to so confirm receivables from U. S. Government departments and agencies, as to which we satisfied ourselves by means of other auditing procedures. We made test checks of prices and computations of inventories and confirmed by actual inspection the quantities of the principal inventories at locations selected by us; in addition, we made test checks of the grades of grain inspected by obtaining independent confirmation of the grades of samples taken by us. . . . Expenditures charged to the land, buildings and equipment accounts during the year, in our opinion, were properly capitalized as representing additions or improvements. The provision for depreciation for the year appears to be adequate based on the original cost of the properties. . . . All ascertained liabilities have been included in the accounts.

General Mills

From these samples the reader will observe that:

(a) It is not always clear whether the accountant means to give additional information to the reader, warn him of what may turn out to be a serious situation, or merely indicate the limitations of his audit. Thus in illustrations 2 and 3 the phrases quoted seem to have as their purpose the giving of information, possibly with respect to matters observed by the accountant for the first time. But the effect on the reader especially in the former illustration might well be to give him an impression that the examination of the inventories was limited and therefore defective. If for some reason the accountant finds it necessary to mention a procedure in his certificate, his opinion of its adequacy should also appear. In the present instance it might have been better if the item had been omitted entirely.

(b) Even where it is clear that the accountant means to question the rightness or wrongness of a principle or procedure, the quantitative effect on the financial statements may be overlooked. Thus in illustration 8 the inference is that the company may have underprovided for income and excess-profits taxes, but the amount of the contingency does not appear and the reader is left in doubt as to the real significance of the accountant's comment. The accountant appears to have no opinion of the amount involved. Putting the reader on notice should ordinarily include giving him the likely financial effect, if worst comes to worst. Occasionally, the accountant claims that mention of the amount of a contingent tax liability may serve as a signal for an additional assessment from the authorities. It has been the author's experience that there is no merit in this point of view although it is often encountered in management as well as in professional circles.

(c) In the opinion paragraph, "except for" (for example, illustration 6) seems to have fairly well replaced "subject to" (for example, illustration 2) where it is the intention to qualify the opinion. The latter phrase has often been criticized as not adequately indicating the accountant's intention since it is never clear to what word the adjective "subject" was intended to relate. "Except," a preposition, seems to lend a little more clarity to the picture in that it definitely indicates a limitation of the accountant's opinion.

(d) Possibly the reader has already noticed the limited character of the language employed in certificates. The style, patterned after a few set forms, is often crabbed, and, in striving for economy and accuracy of words and for euphony as well the accountant occasionally succeeds in being only technical and vague. The accountant must always endeavor to avoid strictly professional language, for his certificate must be understandable to nonaccountants if it is to succeed in its purpose. In phrasing his exceptions he should put himself in the position of the persons who will interpret them. For example, in both forms of the certificate in current use are twice-repeated modifiers, "generally accepted"; these words tend to puzzle the average reader, for the meaning of "auditing standards" and "accounting principles" would be the same without them.

(e) The material appearing in illustration 19 was taken from a 1952 audit report; it followed a "scope" paragraph and preceded an "opinion" paragraph. Only balance-sheet items are referred to and the apparent intent is to provide the reader with additional information. However, though the language employed neither states nor implies that the auditor is taking exception at any point, the suggestion of some hidden balance-sheet impropriety is raised simply because similar comments do not appear in other current reports of public accountants.

No-Opinion Report

In the examples cited above none of the described nonconforming methods of accounting and auditing were sufficiently important to compel the auditor to deny his opinion of the "fairness" of the financial statements referred to in his report. In most of the instances the auditor is content to reveal merely the unusual items—in the text of his report, in footnotes to the statements, or in both. Sometimes (see excerpts 8, 10, 11, and 15) the auditor's opinion is *qualified* because the propriety of the summary position and operating results to which he is subscribing *may* not have been fully established. What does the auditor do where the disclosed deviations from customary principles, standards, and procedures are such as to prevent him from expressing an opinion or are such as to make his opinion (should he venture to express one) meaningless for practical purposes?

Several courses are open to the auditor. He may (a) withdraw from the engagement, (b) append to the financial statements the phrase "without audit" in lieu of his report, or (c) modify the usual form of the report in such a manner as to indicate that he is expressing no opinion.

There are various conditions that give rise to such situations, among them being the following:

1. Statements may be called for at some point within the period normally covered by an audit. A bank, before making a short-term loan, may ask for figures more up to date than those supplied by the most recent audit, and indicate that it would be satisfied with statements "per books." The auditor may thus be called upon to prepare such statements in the form deesired, and to attach thereto whatever remarks the circumstances may require. Or, quarterly reports may be transmitted to stockholders where the auditor is expected to assemble the financial statements from the data revealed by the books alone.

2. The work of the auditor may, for any of various reasons, be too limited. He may be called in by a new client some time after the end of the period to be audited, thus making impossible any observation of the inventory taking or a timely circularization of receivables. Of course in some cases these shortcomings may not be of sufficient importance to deter the auditor from expressing an unqualified opinion. Or, the audit may have been restricted with respect to certain items because of the client's wishes, as where management indicates that it desires only a "cash" audit. In the case of a close corporation, both creditors and owners may be satisfied with something less than a full audit, and are willing to accept a "no-opinion" report.

3. Accepted accounting principles may have been violated to such a degree as to lead to a serious distortion of financial position or operating results—or both, and the client may be unwilling to adopt principles other than those he currently employs.

4. The client's operations may be too small to permit the institution of safeguards that would insure the propriety of the accounts or that would make possible the conduct of the customary form of audit. Internal controls, for example, may be almost nonexistent where the work of employees who originate transactions is subject to neither supervision nor review during the normal course of operations. Thus, upon observing the conduct of a "one-man" shop the auditor may conclude that there is no way of determining whether all cash sales have been reported.

In certain of these and similar situations experience indicates that some accountants might issue a qualified opinion, whereas others would deny the possibility of an opinion altogether. No dividing line can be clearly drawn, for the number of possible situations is very large. A value judgment is required in each case, and value judgments of course vary with the skill, experience, and ethics of accounting practitioners. The following examples will serve to indicate what some of these judgments have been in practical situations and how the auditor's report has been modified in each case.

1. *Restricted audit.* "We have examined . . .[1] in the circumstances except as noted below. In accordance with the request of the management we did not follow generally accepted auditing

---

[1] In this and the example following the ellipses signify the omission of standard report language. In the remaining two examples the auditor's report appears in full.

procedures in our examination of both receivables and inventories. We did not confirm by correspondence any portion of the receivables and we did not observe the taking of any of the physical inventory of merchandise. Because of these restrictions we have been unable to reach any opinion of the over-all propriety of the accompanying financial statements."

2. *Improper accounting practices.* "We have examined . . . in the circumstances. However, the valuation of the company's fixed assets, heretofore appearing at depreciated historical cost, was increased as at the beginning of the year to a valuation as determined by the company's engineers, the accumulated depreciation was also increased proportionately, and the net excess was credited to capital surplus. Moreover, as a consequence of this revaluation, depreciation expense for the year was raised in an amount $78,500 greater than what would normally have been provided had the cost basis of the previous year been followed. We are thus unable to express an opinion of the fairness of the representations contained in the attached financial statements."

3. *Interim statements.* "In accordance with our regular practice, we have made a limited quarterly examination with the object of preparing from the records a balance sheet as at September 30, 19–3, and an income statement for the nine months ended on that date. Annually at the close of the fiscal year (December 31) we complete our examination of the accounts in such detail as will permit us to prepare an opinion of the financial statements based thereon. Because of the incompleteness of the current examination we express no opinion of the attached statements."

4. *Internal controls.* "We express no opinion of the propriety of the accompanying financial statements. The size of the business and the limited number of its employees has made it impracticable for the partners to institute a system of internal controls that would permit us to make an audit in the usual meaning of that term. Our examination did not, however, disclose any impropriety in these statements."

The Committee on Auditing Procedure of the American Institute of Accountants has taken the position that the profession should no longer permit its name to appear in connection with financial statements unless accompanied by (a) the auditor's opinion in conventional form, qualified where required, (b) his denial (disclaimer) of an opinion as illustrated above, or (c) a statement that no audit has been made ("prepared from the

books without audit"). Moreover, where no opinion is to be
expressed, the accounting principle or auditing standard violated
or the audit procedure omitted should appear in explanation.[2]

Long-Form Report

Occasionally, the published reports of accountants contain
various types of information, more extended than that appearing
in the earlier pages of this chapter, sandwiched between the
two standard paragraphs above described. A more common type
of long-form report may be found in the Illustrative Audit. It is
often issued in lieu of a short-form report. A principal function
is that it serves to put into brief compass the outstanding events
of the year so that they may be referred to and quickly interpreted
in future periods. Although the forms of the balance sheet and
income statement are the same as those appearing in the short-
form report, the number of financial statements may be considerably expanded by including schedules such as analyses of
sales and cost of sales, summaries of changes in fixed assets and
reserves, and details of other accounts. Quite frequently the long-
form report is reproduced and given a limited circulation outside
the business—among financial analysts and others who raise questions of detail that such a report can answer. Or a similar report
may be prepared by the controller and reviewed by the public
accountant; it will not contain the certificate paragraphs but
will consist primarily of schedules supporting balance-sheet and
income-statement items and, in the case of consolidated statements, a consolidating worksheet and summaries of eliminations
and other details that are helpful in understanding the method
of preparing the statements.

The long-form report issued for internal and limited external
use is of frequent occurrence in connection with small or medium-
size concerns where the accounting talent available may lack the
ability, confidence, or time to do the job itself. Like the financial
statements it is preferably prepared and reviewed in the client's
offices where additional information can be readily procured and
where statistical details that are not obtained as the result of
ordinary audit procedures are available or can readily be verified.
The following outline is often observed:

Narrative:

   Introduction, including index to financial statements
   Results from operations

---
[2] *CPA Handbook,* Chapter 19, page 9.

Balance sheet
Changes in financial position
Internal controls
Special comments

Financial statements and analyses:
Balance sheet
Analysis of changes in property and depreciation-reserve
    accounts
Analyses of other balance-sheet accounts
Income statement
Detailed cost of sales, departmentalized or by products, quantities,
    and unit costs
Selling, general and administrative expenses
Operating statistics

The scope and detail will vary with the indicated desire of the client. Where a long-form report has been issued for a number of years, the accountant will have had numerous opportunities of studying the interests of those who make use of it; he will endeavor always to meet those interests and to direct attention to new events and trends that should be of significance to report readers. In most cases the auditor will be instructed by his principal as to report content, but the auditor will usually be allowed a good deal of freedom in modifying the content and emphasis as he sees fit. Accounting principals always endeavor to stimulate and encourage the originality of staff members who show competence in writing reports.

Introduction. A long-form report is preferably addressed to the stockholders or board of directors; or it may be addressed to the president or other officer with an indication in the address of his title. The report should, like the short-form report, bear the date that signalizes the point to which the post-audit-period scanning was carried. The introductory paragraph may be a reproduction of the "scope" paragraph of the short-form report. Sometimes a more descriptive indication of the audit is given but this is usually considered unnecessary. An index should appear at this point; or it may occupy the whole of a preceding page—a preferable procedure where the report is extensive and covers many items.

If limitations of any kind have been imposed on the audit by instructions from the client or by limitation of available data, they are preferably described rather fully in the introductory section.

Operations. At the beginning of the operations section, it is usual to present a brief comparative summary of the income statement—this year's and last year's—perhaps more than one prior year's—with columns for increases and decreases and for percentage relationships to sales. This is the sort of statement that, at least in tentative form, the auditor should have well in mind at the time of his inquiries on operations. By the time he is ready to write his report, he should know the causes of fluctuations as between months and years and be able to summarize the current trends, at least as they seem to be reflected in the accounts. Major changes in selling prices, unit material, labor, and overhead costs should be carefully and accurately explained.

A few accountants, although rigorously avoiding adverse criticisms of management's conduct of operations, are in the habit of complimenting the management where the operating results or finanical conditions within the business have improved during the year. This attitude deserves unqualified condemnation. Personalities have no place in an accountant's report. This does not mean, however, that the accountant should avoid adverse criticisms of management and accounting practices. The accountant's general experience in these matters makes his comments worthy of record in annual reports at all times; but they can always be forcefully couched in factual, impersonal language.

Some accountants have become specialists in certain fields and their reports on operations may be much more than ordinary audit reports. Whatever comparable data the accountant has available on other similar enterprises that he has acquired as the result of professional relationships must of course be kept confidential, unless as it often happens some or all of these have been made matters of public record and have therefore lost their confidential status. In some cases clients will permit their operating statistics to be employed elsewhere provided those standing to benefit thereby reciprocate. But whether or not the auditor is able to make use of outside information, his knowledge of cause and effect within the industry will stand him in good stead in analyzing the affairs of any one representative of the industry.

Balance sheet. Neither the operating nor balance-sheet section of the report need define the details of the audit scope unless the accountant has found the management interested in such a matter. In the average situation what seems to be of primary interest to management is the underlying significance of the accounts. The accountant has the opportunity in the balance-sheet section to present compact but revealing summaries of account content and their meaning to the enterprise. Following are typical points covered in this section:

Cash: activity in bank accounts, relative costs (service charges), transfers during year, safeguards over use.

Receivables: separation by notes and accounts if but one figure appears on the balance sheet; sources, aging, characteristics of employee loans, officers' accounts, expense advances, etc.; adequacy of bad-debt reserve; rate of turnover.

Inventories: summary by principal classes, locations, methods of count; periodic (internal) verification; turnover of different classes; excess stock; high-cost stock; adequacy of repair parts; nature of inventory out on consignment.

Fixed assets: analysis of changes during year, summary of principal new items purchased and old items retired, questions of capitalization, repair ratios for various years, reserve ratios, rates of depreciation—their adequacy, changes during year, comparison with last revenue-agent's report, nature of studies now needed of reserve adequacy—nature and extent of standby equipment, comments on future retirement program and probable investment required for replacement needs, propriety of present work-order procedure.

Liabilities: cause of change during year in working-capital ratio, discounts missed, large unpaid items, changes in credit terms, compliance with bond-indenture requirements, advances from others on contracts or for other reasons, detail of bank loans outstanding, analysis of deferred credits, transactions charged and credited to liability reserves.

Financial position. Changes in financial position, in most instances best portrayed in a statement of (application of) funds, are always of interest to management. It may be preceded by condensed comparative balance sheets at the beginning and end of the year, with comments on the leading differences.

Internal controls. A summary of the auditor's review of internal controls—the subject matter of Chapter IV—can be set forth at this point. Sometimes the auditor's comments on internal controls are separated from the rest of the report and put into a special letter, because interest in such comments is usually confined to a much smaller group within the organization, and because of the likelihood of a misunderstanding of their significance on the part of persons not actively engaged in making internal controls more effective. However, these are not ordinarily strong reasons and most long-form reports contain internal-control comments.

A letter on internal controls may also be written where there is no long-form report, this being standard practice on many larger engagements.

Emphasis by the auditor should be put on policies and other matters that he believes should be of major concern to top man-

agement—new management policies instituted during the year
and how they were carried out, old policies not well enough
enforced and suggestions for strengthening them, old policies
formally dropped, imperfect delegations of authority, comments
on stockholder and board policies or on matters that might be
made stockholder or board policies, comments on changes in
general controls exercised by top management, criticisms of
present accounting and financial policies with suggestions for
changes, comments on the internal-audit function and its relation
to the work performed by the public accountant.

Special comments. Under the heading of special comments
would come observations, if any, as the result of the auditor's
detailed audit for limited periods during the year. These may
be of sufficient importance to make them a matter of record in
the report; otherwise, they should be disposed of informally by
discussions with persons directly concerned, and that general fact
recorded at this point.

A summary of the insurance in force may be presented here.

Conclusion. The traditional concluding paragraph is an expression of "appreciation of cooperation" on the part of the
client's staff.

Practical Suggestions in Writing Reports

The following suggestions have been of value to accountants
who have experienced difficulty in expressing themselves in
reports:

Place yourself in the client's position. Study the person or
persons for whom the report is primarily intended and try to form
some idea of the kind of report that will appeal to them. Some
relish details; others do not.

Use unambiguous, concise English. An ability to express ideas
clearly and in good form is indeed a fortunate possession. Long
sentences should be avoided; on the other hand short sentences
may be hard to follow. Avoid beginning sentences with "the."
Good paragraphing is a distinct aid to the reader and the use of
captions for each section of the text likewise facilitates comprehension of the facts presented. Avoid redundant expressions.

Do not be sterotyped. Many accountants fall into the habit
of making sterotyped comments on the various items in the
balance sheet. The same comments repeated year after year are

certain to kill the client's interest in the report; they indicate a dull and unimaginative accountant as well.

An auditor cannot escape discussing facts. They must be presented regardless of whom they hurt. But diplomatic language may be employed in imparting information.

Omit unimportant detail. Small differences may exist between the trial balance of a subsidiary ledger and its controlling account and this is known to be a clerical error; or the petty-cash fund may be short 13 cents. These are matters too trivial for a serious report. Nevertheless if they *must* be mentioned let the narrative be as brief as possible.

Make the text interesting and readable. Businessmen may often be concerned with particular financial or operating problems. Cover them thoroughly if their importance warrants. The use of ratios, statistics, and charts may help the accountant materially in getting his ideas across. Facts that point to likely future trends should be emphasized but there must be no trace of forecasting. Let the reader draw his own conclusions.

Write the text promptly. The text of a report should wherever practicable be written on the job, possibily in sections as previously mentioned while the audit is still in progress. Deferment of the drafting until the auditor has been given a new assignment means that many a point that would have added both interest and value to the report will have been forgotten.

Give reasons. If a comparison of balance sheets or operating results is being made, mere statements that certain increases or decreases have taken place are insufficient unless reasons accompany them. Many an accountant has made an excellent analysis in schedule form, only to forget to set forth in the text the reason for their preparation. Explanations and conclusions must be presented in connection with each summary; otherwise there will be no justification for its inclusion in the report.

Be certain of your spelling. Names of persons, towns, and technical terms had best be printed by the auditor in the draft of his report to prevent typing errors. The handwriting of many persons, including not a few auditors, can be read at a later date by themselves and others only when the context is known.

Report Typing and Referencing

Typists who specialize in reports and financial statements will unless otherwise directed follow a uniform pattern established for their office in setting up headings, sideheads, dollar signs, single and double underscores, margins, and other mechanical details essential to the makeup and appearance of every finished page. Deficiencies in the drafting are often detected and remedied by the typist supervisor. However younger auditors should always avail themselves of opportunities of studying the forms and drafting devices of more experienced members of the staff in an effort to make their own output superior in every respect and to help the typists in their work of adaptation. When a difficult form is to be reproduced, the auditor should learn how to count typewriter spaces, horizontally and vertically, and indicate them on his draft, so that he may conform his copy to page limitations. "Close" rather than "open"typing is always to be preferred in schedule work whether in the body of the text or in separate exhibits, with but one or two spaces between money columns and between sideheads and money columns, even though wide margins result. In larger schedules, each fifth or sixth horizontal line may be left blank in order to aid the eye in following across the page. Column headings and their hyphenation should be studied carefully so that there may be a good "fit" in a limited space. The auditor should never be above experimenting occasionally on the typewriter himself with the setup of a difficult exhibit. He should always bear in mind that schedules can almost always be improved in style, thereby making them more attractive and readable to the person for whom they are intended. A little extra attention paid this year to a schedule the form of which will be repeated next year is always worth the effort.

Larger public-accounting firms maintain a "referencing" staff skilled in verifying, from the working papers, figures, statements of fact, spelling, dates, places, and other matters going into reports and financial statements. Smaller firms assign senior accountants temporarily to such work. The referencing is done usually by a team of two immediately after the typing operation is completed. A referencing sheet is prepared on which proposed changes are noted by the referencers; the changes are subsequently reviewed by the auditor and his principal and approved, modified, or eliminated, after which the material is returned to the typist for correction or rerun; a second inspection is thereupon made by the referencers and cleared through the principal. Usually a final inspection is made of the report text and exhibits after all corrections have been made; the report is then bound and signed, ready for delivery to the client.

Delivery of Report

Circumstances permitting, delivery of the report should be made in person by the principal, with the auditor present also, so that the main points of the report may be again discussed with the client's representatives—and amplified where necessary. Such discussion may lead to immediate action on the accountant's recommendations, and pave the way for discussing the audit scope of next year's examination and for agreement upon the approximate date of preliminary work. It may be that another visit by the principal to the client's office will be warranted at a later date to ascertain whether the recommendations suggested in his report—or their equivalents—have been put into effect. It is at this time, following the delivery of the report, that an audit program for the coming year may advantageously be prepared by the principal, with the help of the auditor.

Limitations on the circulation of the accountant's long-form report should never be suggested by the accountant. He should always be able to back up what he has said regardless of the connection with the management of the person who reads his report. The client's officials may wish to give it only limited circulation within the organization but this should be discouraged whenever practicable since subordinates interested in over-all management and accounting policies who might otherwise not be given the opportunity of studying the accountant's criticisms are often able to devise ways and means of instituting needed changes with the maximum of effectiveness and a minimum of shock to the organization.

Illustrative Audit

A single short-form or long-form report may follow the auditor's examination or he may submit both. In this instance both were prepared.

Financial statements (RS 2–3) with a supporting certificate (RS 1) here make up the auditor's short-form report to stockholders.

Audit reports of the long-form variety follow many styles, and it is well that they do so. The auditor has so many things of importance that he can pass along to management, and management has such varied interests, that both form and content of audit reports can vary markedly. In some cases the report consists only of suggestions on internal controls, in other cases there are detailed analyses of balance-sheet and profit-and-loss accounts or many details of audit scope. In the present instance, the audit report is brief and is divided into the following sections:

Audit scope
Summary and analyses of operating results
Changes in financial position
Comments on financial position
Procedural suggestions

The report follows the customary form of a letter and in this case is not accompanied by financial statements since they would merely be duplicates of those submitted with the short-form report.

The two reports, bearing the same date (March 11), were submitted simultaneously (March 13) to the management. At this time, the auditor also approved drafts by the controller of: (1) Form 10–K, the annual report to the SEC required of corporations having listed securities, and (2) the annual report to the Midwest Stock Exchange where the company's common stock is listed. The management then proceeded to arrange for the printing of the short-form report so that it could be mailed to the stockholders before their meeting on the last Tuesday in April.

draft
3-10-53
FL:jr

HYATT, PATERSON & COMPANY
960 Hudson Building
Chicago 4, Ill.

March 11, 1953

To the Stockholders of
Martin Manufacturing Company

In our opinion, the accompanying consolidated
financial statements present fairly the position
of Martin Manufacturing Company and its wholly
owned subsidiary, Burton-Makun Company, at December 31, 1952, and the results of their operations
for the year then ended, in conformity with generally accepted accounting principles applied on a
basis consistent in all material respects with that
of the preceding year. Our opinion is based on an
examination of the statements which was made in
accordance with generally accepted auditing standards and included such tests of the accounting
records and such other auditing procedures as we
considered necessary. The examination of the
statements of Burton-Makun Company was made by
Messrs. Burns, Sutton & Company, Cleveland, Ohio.

HYATT, PATERSON & COMPANY

RS - 1

draft
3-10-53
FL:jr

Letter dated
March 11, 1953

Martin Manufacturing Company
and subsidiary

————————

Letter to Mr. Edw. Stebbins, President,
commenting on operating results for the
year ended December 31, 1952, financial
changes during the year, and financial
position at the year end.

Hyatt, Paterson & Company
Certified Public Accountants
Chicago 4, Illinois

LP - 0

March 11, 1953

Mr. Edw. Stebbins
Martin Manufacturing Company
Chicago 16, Ill.

Dear Mr. Stebbins:

Following our examination of the financial statements of Martin Manufacturing Company for the year ended December 31, 1952, we have prepared and submitted a report thereon bearing the above date. This letter supplements our report.

Our audit consisted primarily of a review and study of the accounts and other data supporting the balance sheet at the year end and the income statement for the year, and of the internal controls governing the recording of the company's transactions. We also consulted with officers and employees, and through your aid we secured statements from various outsiders who furnished independent proof of the accuracy and propriety of a number of accounts. We made numerous comparisons of this year's accounts with last year's and obtained explanations of variations as between the two years' operations. The cooperation and assistance of your staff materially aided our examination.

The accounts of the Burton-Makun Company, your company's Cleveland subsidiary, were audited by Messrs. Burns, Sutton & Co., certified public accountants of that city, and we have embodied these accounts in our findings.

Operating Results

A summary of the consolidated operating results for the years 1951 and 1952 follows:

| | | Year ended December 31 | | | |
| | | 1952 | | 1951 | |
Item	Notes	Amount	% to sales	Amount	% to sales
Net sales--					
Heavy machines		$ 368,333.62	4.6^	$ 354,987.55	4.5^
Light machines		4,570,006.58	57.8^	4,841,267.88	60.9^
Household appliances		2,237,744.13	28.3^	2,095,387.69	26.3^
Merchandise		732,921.48	9.3^	662,331.05	8.3^
Net sales		$7,909,005.81^	100.0^	$7,953,974.17^	100.0^
Cost of sales--	a				
Heavy machines	b	$ 270,801.59	73.5^	$ 265,816.47	74.9^
Light machines	b	3,814,274.27	83.5^	4,104,419.38	84.8^
Household appliances	b	1,912,598.40	85.5^	1,661,897.79	79.3^
Merchandise	b	320,000.47	43.6^	246,166.86	37.2^
Balance of direct overhead	c	4,382.21	.1	9,839.22	.1
Unabsorbed fixed overhead	c	363,186.71	4.6	350,831.01	4.4
Installation costs	c	139,067.58	1.8	138,820.50	1.7
Cost of sales		$6,824,311.23^	86.3^	$6,777,791.23^	85.2^
Gross profit from sales		$1,084,694.58^	13.7^	$1,176,182.94^	14.8^
Income from interest & dividends		88,968.00	1.1	24,144.73	.3
Profit from the sale of stocks		175,152.10	2.2	-	-
Total income		$1,348,814.68^	17.0^	$1,200,327.67^	15.1^

LP - 1

Expense other than factory costs--

Selling	$ 351,965.21	4.4	$ 352,291.10	4.4
Administrative	482,312.15	6.1	470,712.65	5.9
Interest on bonds & bank loans	28,793.92	.4	34,322.00	.4
Cost of reacquiring bonds	37,434.75	.5	-	-
Provisions for pension reserve	33,200.00	.4	29,500.00	.4
Provision for Federal income tax	208,521.17	2.6	152,990.97	2.0
Total other expense	$1,142,227.20	14.4	$1,039,816.72	13.1
Net income	$ 206,587.48	2.6	$ 160,510.95	2.0

a For comparability with the items making up cost of sales for 1952, the individual
  details of the cost of sales for 1951 have here been restated without, however,
  changing their total. This has been possible because of the comparatively
  minor difference between the beginning and ending inventories of that year,
  regardless of whether a full allotment (or only the variable portion) of manufacturing overhead is assigned to these inventories.
b Ratios relate to net sales of these items.
c Ratios relate to total net sales.

From the following summary it will be observed that as compared with the
preceding year the slight decrease in sales and increase in costs were
accompanied by changes in quantities, prices, and costs of individual
lines that had varying effects on operations:

	1952			1951			Relative cost of production	
Department and line	Units sold	Unit price	Approx-imate yield	Units sold	Unit price	Approx-imate yield	1952	1951
	(t h o u s a n d s			o f	d o l l a r s)		(% of sales)	
Heavy machines--								
AX240	23	6.8	156.4	4	7.1	28.4}	73.5	74.9
Other models	64	3.3	211.2	73	4.5	328.5}		
Light machines--								
CNX1 series	2525	1.66	4,191.5	2681	1.7	4,557.7}	83.5	84.8
Other models	206	1.8	370.8	208	1.4	291.2}		
Appliances--								
Washers	9110	.12	1,093.2	8460	.115	972.9}		
Dryers	1860	.24	446.4	2230	.25	557.5}	85.5	79.3
Freezers	1750	.33	577.5	820	.26	213.2}		
Small equipment	-		109.3	-		333.7}		
Merchandise	-		732.9	-		662.3	43.6	37.2
Discounts, allowances and other adjustments not allocated, net			19.8			8.5		
Totals			7,909.0			7,953.9	86.3	85.2

Further analysis of the above items leads to these observations (sales and
cost figures quoted represent thousands of dollars):

    1. Price decreases in heavy machines were accompanied by a larger
sales volume, the latter attributable to the delivery to Army Ordnance--
during the last three months of the year--of 18 (out of an order of 30)
AX240 models. The increase in the amount of gross profit from 89.2 in 1951
to 97.5 in 1952 cannot be expected to be more than temporary since the manufacture of this model is to be discontinued once the Ordnance order has been
completed.

LP - 2

2. Continued sales of the CNX1 series of mechanical controls has featured the company's activity in this field during the past five years although the volume of demand for other models has remained almost unchanged from year to year throughout the same period. We were informed that although orders for CNX1 controls dropped off in the latter part of 1952, back orders on hand (March 1953) for spring deliveries now amount to more than 800 as compared with only 150 at this time last year. Cost savings in the production of these controls account for the increased margin on their sale, notwithstanding a drop in quantities sold of nearly 6%. Nearly 70% of the gross profit from manufacturing operations came from the sale of light machinery in 1952 as compared with something less than 63% in 1951.

3. Although the company's appliance volume continues its growth and numerous price increases have been effected, production costs have risen at a more rapid rate than prices with the result that the gross margin has steadily declined since 1949--when a peak of 28.3% was reached--to slightly more than half that ratio (14.5%) in 1952. Comparison of the cost records for the last two years indicates that while the margin on washers has remained at approximately 32%, the margin on dryers and freezers has declined from 12% to 6% during the same period. The more than doubling of freezer sales is attributable in part to the continued low price attaching to this line compared with competitive products--this notwithstanding a 25% price increase during the year.

4. Production of small appliances--which for the past two years have been sold at approximately their factory cost--has now been discontinued and sales yet to be made will be from existing stock which at the end of the year was less than 10.0.

5. The margin ratio in the sales of merchandise that the company buys and sells has decreased in recent years (6.4% in 1952) but a corresponding increase in volume has produced almost the same quantity of gross profit.

6. Cost ratios are relatively less and margin ratios relatively greater than the corresponding ratios appearing in our reports of preceding years because of the omission of fixed factory costs from production costs and inventory valuation. To the extent that product prices are influenced by costs it must henceforth be borne in mind that gross margins must contribute to the recovery not only of installation, selling, administrative, and financial costs but to the recovery of these unabsorbed factory costs as well. On the new basis the sales dollar may be divided as follows:

	1952	1951
Factory and merchandise cost	.798	.790
Installation costs	.047	.045
Unabsorbed overhead	.018	.017
	-----	-----
Cost of sales	.863	.852
Other income	-.033	-.003
Selling & administration	.105	.103
Financial & other expense	.013	.008
Federal income tax	.026	.020
Net income	.026	.020
	=====	=====

7. During the year 16 inactive work-in-process orders in the amount of 23.3 were canceled and the materials which they represented were scrapped (salvage 2.3) or returned to stock (10.3), resulting in a loss of 10.6. In addition, as in previous years, valuation writedowns were made of old stock as follows:

Finished stock	12.3
Raw materials	9.5
Supplies	4.7

LP - 3

These losses, totaling 37.1, do not appear unusual as compared with similar losses of prior years (40.3 in 1951 and 36.8 in 1950).

8. Aside from an increase of 13.2 in provisions for bad debts there were few variations in selling and administrative expenses in 1952 as compared with those of 1951. The increase in bad debts is attributable in a large measure to the business failures of appliance dealers with whom the company deals directly rather than through distributors.

9. Most of the net income for the year 1952 may be said to have arisen from the receipt of a substantial dividend (60.0) from the Barkley Corporation and of a profit (160.0) from the sale of 8,000 of the 10,000-share investment in that company. The change of valuation method applied to the closing inventory resulted in a reduction of gross profit of 36.9 and of net profit (after Federal income tax) of approximately half that sum.

37.

Financial Position

Following is a comparison of the financial position of the company and its subsidiary at the end of 1952 and 1951:

Assets	December 31 1952	December 31 1951	Increase (+) decrease (−)
Current assets--			
Cash	$ 433,935.39	$ 418,189.63	$+ 15,745.76
U. S. securities	402,268.57	303,618.46	+ 98,650.11
Receivables, net	1,223,772.36	1,518,349.33	−294,576.97
Inventories	1,519,588.20	1,596,515.86	− 76,927.66
Prepayments	40,448.32	29,662.72	+ 10,785.60
Total current assets	$3,620,012.84	$3,866,336.00	$−246,323.16
Current liabilities--			
Bank loans	$ 550,000.00	$ 300,000.00	$+250,000.00
Federal income taxes	208,862.80	153,036.48	+ 55,826.32
Other	397,299.36	286,963.69	+110,335.67
Total current liabilities	$1,156,162.16	$ 740,000.17	$+416,161.99
Working capital	$2,463,850.68	$3,126,335.83	$−662,485.15
Customers long-term notes	158,167.00	61,000.00	+ 97,167.00
Investments in suppliers	374,152.10	739,000.00	−364,847.90
Fixed assets, net	1,362,781.84	737,506.47	+625,275.37
Total assets available for long-term obligations and stockholders	$4,358,951.62	$4,663,842.30	$−304,890.68
Represented by--			
Pension reserve	$ 336,820.00	$ 293,135.00	$+ 43,685.00
First-mortgage bonds	293,520.98	723,684.14	−430,163.16
Equity of stockholders	3,728,610.64	3,647,023.16	+ 81,587.48
Total as above	$4,358,951.62	$4,663,842.30	$−304,890.68

Principal changes in financial position were the liquidation of the Barkley Corporation stock, increases in bank loans and other current liabilities, the building of a new assembly plant and an addition to the foundry, the purchase of substantial quantities of new machinery and equipment, and the retirement of nearly 60% of the first-mortgage bonds outstanding at the beginning of the year. These facts are brought out in the following statement of application of funds:

LP - 4

draft
3-10-53
FL:jr

Funds were provided from--
  Operations--
    Profit from the sale of investment
      in stocks $175,152.10
    Other income, net   31,435.38

       Net income, per income statement $206,587.48^
    Add back provisions for--
      Pension fund, including allow-
        ance of $9,300 for in-
        terest $33,200.00
      Depreciation   77,227.33 110,427.33^ $ 317,014.81^

Liquidation of investment in stocks (in
  addition to profit shown above)   455,847.90
Contributions of employees to pension fund   23,900.00
Disposal of fixed assets   5,069.61
Decrease in working capital, as above   662,485.15^

    Total funds provided $1,464,317.47^

Funds were invested in--
  Fixed assets purchased $ 707,572.31
  Retirement of First-Mortgage Bonds, not
    including premiums of $33,825.00 and ex-
    penses of $3,609.75 charged as current
    expense   430,000.00^
  Customers long-term notes   97,167.00^
  Additional investments in suppliers   91,000.00^
  Interest on sinking-fund deposit   163.16^
  Payments from pension fund   13,415.00
  Dividend to stockholders   125,000.00

    Total as above $1,464,317.47^

Although a larger decrease in working capital (930.0) had been anticipated
in the 1952 budget as compared with the actual decrease of 662.4 shown above,
sales were higher than the original estimate, thus necessitating a larger
investment in receivables and inventory. Also the realization from the
sale of stocks (631.0) was substantially greater than the amount budgeted
therefor (500.0). Furthermore, the appropriations for the purchase of fixed
assets and the repurchase of bonds collectively (1,300.0) exceeded requirements by nearly 125.0.

Comments on Financial Position

At December 31, 1952, the principal features of the financial position of
the company may be summarized thus:

    Cash and marketable securities are maintained at levels greater than
actual requirements, as we have pointed out in previous reports. During
1952 the lowest balance in banks noted by us was 214.0 at May 31. Present
policy requires that large bank loans be maintained, thus resulting in a
lower working-capital ratio than would normally be the case.

    Securities owned consist of U. S. Treasury bonds, notes, and bills car-
ried as current assets, minority stockholdings in domestic corporations supplying raw materials and parts, and the issued and outstanding capital stock
of Burton-Makun Company, a subsidiary. In each case the investment is carried at cost which is less than its market or quoted price except for the investment in the subsidiary on which no quoted price is available. A portion
of the U. S. obligations, we were informed, is to be applied against the
income-tax liability falling due on March 15.

LP - 5

During the year sales of stocks owned were made in the amount of 631.0; these consisted of 8,000 shares of Barkley Corporation common stock at $72.50 a share, and 1,700 shares of Vault Importers Company common stock at $30 a share. Remaining stocks include continued holdings in these corporations and three others.

Receivables from customers shown as a current asset consist of both accounts and notes due within a year from the balance-sheet date. The notes represent time sales of light machines, most of them accompanied by a chattel mortgage on the object of the sale. Bad debts were larger by 13.2 than in the preceding year, the bulk of 1952 bad debts arising from business failures on the part of appliance dealers.

Inventories, priced at cost or less, consisted of finished stock, work in process, raw material, and factory and repair supplies. As noted in preceding paragraphs overhead has been recognized in the cost-pricing basis only in the amount of its variable elements, thus excluding approximately 37.1 that under procedures followed at the end of 1951 would have been included in the balance-sheet asset of inventories. If the same method had been applied to inventories at the end of 1951 a reduction of 37.0 in the balance-sheet amount at that time would have been effected.

Long-term notes of customers increased from 61.0 to 158.2 because of an increasing demand for time payments on sales of light machinery.

Fixed assets acquired during the year amounted to 707.6: 95.8 representing the cost of an extension of the main foundry building and a replacement of the lighting equipment throughout the building; 325.1, the new assembly plant completed by the Austin Company on March 10; 65.2, new sand-conditioning, molding, and other machines for the foundry; 175.6, a hydraulic press, 16 lathes, an automatic drilling machine, and other equipment for the factory; 32.1, new patterns and models covering 1953 production; 6.1, office furniture and fixtures; and 7.7, two new items of automotive equipment. Retirements included the razing of structures occupying the site of the new foundry building, an American lathe, minor equipment, and a quantity of discarded flasks and patterns relating to discontinued products.

Depreciation was continued on the basis of rates followed in preceding years; because retirements during the year exceeded the current provision for depreciation the total accumulated decreased from 905.5 to 840.9 and by reason of the substantial additions to plant its ratio to asset costs decreased from approximately 55% to 38%.

The pension reserve, 336.8, has been maintained on a basis comparable with previous years. The original plan established in 1943 remains unchanged. The plan is a voluntary one to which employees make contributions matched dollar for dollar by contributions from the company; however, the account maintained for the pension plan is a reserve and no specific assets are earmarked as offsetting the reserve. We understand that within the next year or two a new plan is anticipated whereby an independent trust will be created, with funds segregated from the business under independent control.

First-mortgage bonds were reduced 20.0 by repurchase by the sinking-fund trustee and by 410.0 the latter representing repurchases effected during the period from July 1 to October 31 through Messrs. Porter, Houseman & Co. and the Liberty National Bank, the repurchase rate being face value plus the contractual premiums of 33.8.

LP - 6

Procedural Suggestions

Several possible procedural changes occurred to us during our examination:

1. Checks drawn on the general account are now numbered as used; payroll checks are prenumbered and are adequately controlled. We believe a similar system of prenumbered checks for the general account would minimize any possibility of their misuse.

2. Remittances from customers received by mail are delivered to the cashier without a preliminary listing. We suggest that the mail room prepare twice daily in triplicate a list of remittances showing the gross bill paid, the discount, and the net bill or cash received. The original supported by the checks and cash would be sent to the cashier, the duplicate with remittance advices attached to the accounts-receivable bookkeeper, and the triplicate to the internal auditor.

3. At present, postings to customers accounts of cash collections are made from the cash-receipts book. We suggest that the remittance advices referred to in the preceding paragraph serve as the posting media.

4. Bank reconciliations are now made by the cashier. A better practice would result if the controller should assign this function to an employee who has no duties relating to the recording of cash, receivables, and payables.

5. Checks for unclaimed wages are at present turned over to the assistant controller and held indefinitely. We suggest their cancellation after, say, two months and the carrying of the obligation thereafter as a liability for the period of a year.

6. Copies of purchase orders sent to the receiving clerk now show quantities. Omission of this information would eliminate any tendency to report on the receiving ticket purchase-order quantities rather than actual counts, and would eliminate also tests for actual counts now being made by the assistant controller.

7. The storekeeper now authorizes adjustments to physical counts of book quantities of supplies; a better control would result if such adjustments were made only after review and approval in each case by the plant manager.

8. Purchases (a/c 221) are made up of raw materials, parts and merchandise. At present an analysis showing withdrawals of each of these three classes is maintained on working paper. A simpler procedure would be to establish separate accounts for each of these three classes of purchases, and to and that purchases be recorded net of discounts. Costs of freight in should be charged to the proper purchase account. This would have the effect of eliminating the accounts now maintained for discount on purchases (a/c 224) and freight in (a/c 222).

9. Before December 31, 1953, consideration should again be given to the desirability of providing a reserve for cash discounts.

10. Frequent tests should be made by the internal auditor to make sure that the spread by product lines of sales returns and allowances, inaugurated on November 1, is complete and accurate.

11. We believe that the cost clerk could prepare a monthly analysis of cost of sales by objects (materials, labor, and variable overhead). We made a breakdown of this character in connection with our current examination of the operating accounts.

We shall be glad to discuss these suggestions with you at further length.

Very truly yours,

HYATT, PATERSON & COMPANY

LP - 7

Problems and Questions

1. The accountant's short-form report contains the words "supporting evidence." State three different types of such evidence and give examples of each type.

2. The vice-president in charge of the credit department of a bank, having been given a copy of a customer's annual report you have just completed, asks you to confer with him on certain questions that he feels that you, with your knowledge of the business, can easily answer for him. In view of the confidential relationship between the professional accountant and his client, would you feel free to answer the banker's questions?

3. You have certified to the financial statements of a manufacturing concern and have been asked by a stockholder why you have certified as to their correctness when some of the assets are known by the stockholder to be stated at figures in excess of their realizable (that is, present sales) value. What reply would you make?

4. Should an auditor attempt to eliminate unauthorized uses of his reports and certificates?

5. Name several operating and financial ratios that may be of interest to readers of a long-form audit report, indicating in each case the significance of the ratio.

6. The following excerpt was taken from a long-form report: "The petty-cash fund of $200 was counted and found to be short $1.23." Would you have mentioned the shortage?

7. Why do many accountants include in a long-form report a statement of the insurance in force? Should the auditor also present his conclusions as to whether the company is adequately protected?

8. In preparing a certificate, an auditor is confronted with the following items which he has recognized as possible causes of certificate changes in the case of a corporation having total assets of $1,000,000. Give your opinion on each, suggest the language to be used if the certificate is to be modified, and indicate the place of such language in the certificate:

(a) A subsidiary company in Italy lost most of its assets in the war. In the interest of conservatism, the parent company had previously written down its investment in the subsidiary to a nominal sum of $10; since the war it has made a single advance to the subsidiary of $40,000, which it carries without diminution on its books. A financial statement, translated into dollars at the current exchange rate, was prepared at the parent's balance-sheet date by Italian accountants; it shows net current assets of $24,600, net fixed assets of $3,100, and a liability to the parent company made up of net assets remaining after the war, $2,558, advances since the war from the parent, $40,000, and an operating deficit since October 1, 1945 (when it started up its post-war business) of $14,858, which included an operating loss for the past year of $4,705. No contingent liability of the parent company appears to exist because of the subsidiary's operation.

(b) A physical inventory of finished goods totaling $12,500 was

taken but the auditor was not present. However, he has determined
that as a rule the amount of finished goods on hand is negligible since
a long line of customers has been awaiting the company's product for
several years.

(c) A bond indenture provides that the working-capital ratio shall
be maintained at not less than 3 to 1, and the ratio has fallen to something less than 2 to 1. Although failure to live up to this rule can be
regarded as a technical default, an officer of the trustee bank informs
the auditor that the remedy provided in the indenture is somewhat
obscure, and that, under the circumstances, with the company making
a profit and fully operating, and with no other specific default, no
action will be taken by the trustee.

9. In referencing a report in a public-accounting office, would you
rely primarily on the fact that the typed matter agrees with the working trial balance or would you refer to specific working papers?

10. A statement of application of funds often features a long-form
report The form is flexible, and that appearing in the report draft of
the Illustrative Audit (LP 5) could have been considerably expanded.
Redraft the form in such a manner as to add the following elements:
(a) sales and other gross income, (b) cost of sales by objects and other
principal classes of expense, and (c) principal items of working capital.
Make sure that these added elements tie in or are reconciled with the
financial statements.

Index